Essentials of
Children's Literature

A Story Is a Doorway

A story is a doorway
That opens on a wider place.
A story is a mirror
To reflect the reader's face.

A story is a question
You hadn't thought to ponder,
A story is a pathway,
Inviting you to wander.

A story is a window,
A story is a key,
A story is a lighthouse,
Beaming out to sea.

A story's a beginning,
A story is an end,
And in the story's middle,
You just might find a friend

—Richard Peck

Essentials of
Children's Literature

Sixth Edition

Carol Lynch-Brown
Florida State University

Carl M. Tomlinson
Northern Illinois University

Boston   New York   San Francisco
Mexico City   Montreal   Toronto   London   Madrid   Munich   Paris
Hong Kong   Singapore   Tokyo   Cape Town   Sydney

Executive Editor: Aurora Martínez Ramos
Editorial Assistant: Lynda Giles
Executive Marketing Manager: Krista Clark
Editorial-Production Service: Omegatype Typography, Inc.
Production Supervisor: Joe Sweeney
Manufacturing Buyer: Linda Morris
Composition and Prepress Buyer: Linda Cox
Cover Administrator: Linda Knowles
Electronic Composition: Omegatype Typography, Inc.

For related titles and support materials, visit our online catalog at www.ablongman.com.

Between the time Website information is gathered and then published, it is not unusual for some sites to have closed. Also, the transcription of URLs can result in typographical errors. The publisher would appreciate notification where these errors occur so that they may be corrected in subsequent editions.

ISBN-13: 978-0-205-52032-9
ISBN-10: 0-205-52032-4

Library of Congress Cataloging-in-Publication Data

Lynch-Brown, Carol.
    Essentials of children's literature / Carol Lynch-Brown, Carl M. Tomlinson. — 6th ed.
            p.   cm.
    Includes bibliographical references and index.
    ISBN 13: 978-0-205-52032-9 (pbk.)
    ISBN 10: 0-205-52032-4 (pbk.)
    1. Children's literature—Study and teaching (Higher)   2. Children's literature—History and criticism.   3. Children's literature—Bibliography.   I. Tomlinson, Carl M.   II. Title.
    PN1009. A1L96 2008
    372.64'044—dc22

                                                                                            2007010977

Printed in the United States of America

10   9   8   7   6   5   4   3   2   1   12   11   10   09   08   07

Credits appear on pages 407–408, which constitute an extension of the copyright page.

Contents

part II Categories of Literature   53

4 Poetry and Plays   55

6   Traditional Literature   118

7   Modern Fantasy   133

8 Realistic Fiction   150

9 Historical Fiction   168

10 Nonfiction: Biography and Informational Books   187

part III   Literature in the School   241

12   Planning the Curriculum   243

Features

Notable Authors and Illustrators

Figures and Tables

Figures

Tables

Preface

Essentials of Children's Literature is a brief, affordable, comprehensive textbook with rich resources— a true compendium of information about children's literature. It is tailored to a survey course in children's literature, but by virtue of its brevity and affordability, is also suitable as a companion text in an integrated language arts course.

The primary focus of a survey course in children's literature should be reading children's trade books, not reading an exhaustive textbook about children's books. Students need direct experience with these trade books—reading them, reading them aloud to others, discussing them, writing about them, comparing them, criticizing them, evaluating them, applying them to their own lives, and thinking about sharing them with children.

One of our goals is to awaken or reawaken college-level students to the joy of reading. This reawakening can happen only if they experience the pleasure and excitement of reading excellent trade books. At the same time, the body of knowledge about literature and about teaching literature to children can be conveyed most efficiently through a textbook. *Essentials of Children's Literature* presents this body of knowledge in a clear, concise, direct narrative using brief lists, examples, figures, and tables in combination with prose, thus freeing class time for involvement with literature.

 ## Notable Features of the Sixth Edition

The most apparent change in this edition of *Essentials of Children's Literature* is the handsome and inviting new interior design. The photo-realistic art not only adds interest, but it also serves to remind readers that the ultimate goal of this book is to bring children and good books together.

This edition also includes references to the companion website for the text. The companion website contains questions to guide one's reading of the text, discussion items, ideas for term papers and portfolios, and suggestions for literature-related activities to do with children during school practicums. Other new features of this edition include the following:

- An expanded color insert of full-color illustrations selected from notable children's picture books with accompanying guides to their use as examples of visual elements, artistic styles, artistic media, and contributions to story
- A chapter, "Literature for a Diverse Society" (Chapter 11), that presents much-needed strategies for culturally responsive instruction and the multicultural and international literature to support this instruction
- A new chapter, "Learning about Reading and Literature" (Chapter 2), that establishes literature's vital role in the reading curriculum with particular emphasis on current national policies and issues, resistant readers, and the reading interests of children

- New sections entitled "Gaining Experience with Literature in School Practicums (Chapter 12) and Audiobooks, Films Based on Children's Books, Character Education, and Social Justice Education" (Chapter 13)
- Inclusion of many links to websites for further information about notable authors and illustrators, professional organizations, and resources such as children's magazines
- A new feature, "Topics for Further Investigation," in each chapter

Chapter-by-Chapter Changes

Chapter 1: Learning about Children and Their Literature

This chapter has been reorganized for greater clarity and some content has been moved to Chapters 2 and 3. The following have been added to the chapter:

- A different opening poem
- Four new tables presenting landmark and current research study findings relating to literature, reading, writing, and literature across the curriculum
- Current titles as examples of books appropriate for children in various stages of development
- More links to related websites

Chapter 2: Learning about Reading and Literature

The entire chapter is new and addresses the following topics:

- The reading process
- Literature in the reading curriculum
- The National Reading Panel report
- Accountability and reading
- The Reading at Risk report
- Independent reading and societal changes
- Resistant readers
- Assisting students in book selection
- Research on children's reading interests
- Discovering reading interests of individual students
- Judging the difficulty of reading materials
- Reading incentive programs

Chapter 3: Learning about Literature

- The sections "Approaches to Studying and Interpreting Literature" and "Elements of Fiction" have been revised to include a discussion of genre-eclectic, nonlinear literature with multiple perspectives and plots as well as perspectives on the reader acting as coauthor.
- Most book examples have been replaced with more recent ones.
- A new section, "Changes in Traditional Fictional Forms," addresses *postmodernism.*

- The informational section about the major U.S., British, and Canadian book awards has been revised and placed in this chapter for the first time. Included is a table of these awards, their purposes, and dates of establishment.
- A new section, "Review Journals," provides important information on professional review sources for children's literature trade books.
- Another new section, "Professional Websites," provides important information on websites for information about children's literature.
- The section on categories of literature has been revised and now includes a discussion of a genre organization and its advantages and limitations. Genre boundaries and blended genres are explained. This section includes an overview table of the genres and their subtopics; this table has been revised to reflect the organization of this edition.

Chapter 4: Poetry and Plays

- A new opening poem has been added.
- Three new poems exemplify certain elements/aspects of poetry not previously exemplified.
- New research on poetry preferences has been added.
- Many book examples in the narrative have been replaced with more recent ones.
- In the "Recommended Poetry Books and Plays" lists, substantial numbers of books have been deleted and recent titles added.

Chapter 5: Picture Books

This chapter has been rewritten and expanded to include topics such as visual elements, artistic styles, and artistic media. Additions to the chapter include the following:

- A new opening poem
- An expanded color insert of illustrations from twelve children's books and accompanying "Guide to Illustrations"
- A new section: "Observing the Role of Illustrations in Picture Books"
- A new table: "How Illustrations Contribute to Picture Book Stories"
- Expanded discussion of graphic novels
- Many new titles used as examples of types of picture books
- Updated "Excellent Picture Books to Read Aloud" list
- More links to related websites
- Updated "Notable Authors and Illustrators of Picture Books" feature with webpage of author or illustrator given when available
- Updated list of recommended picture books (approximately half new titles)
- New list of films based on children's picture books: "Related Films, Videos, and DVDs"

Chapter 6: Traditional Literature

This chapter has the following additions:

- New titles used as examples of types of traditional literature
- Updated "Excellent Traditional Literature to Read Aloud" list

- Updated "Notable Retellers and Illustrators of Traditional Literature" list with webpages of illustrators given when available
- Updated list of recommended books (approximately 30 percent new titles)
- New list of films related to children's works of traditional literature: "Related Films, Videos, and DVDs"

Chapter 7: Modern Fantasy

- Many book examples in the narrative have been replaced with more recent ones.
- The "Notable Authors of Modern Fantasy" list has been updated and authors' official web sites have been added.
- In the updated list of recommended books, substantial numbers of books have been deleted and recent titles have been added.
- The new feature "Related Films, Videos, and DVDs" provides a list of films related to children's works of modern fantasy.

Chapter 8: Realistic Fiction

- Many book examples in the narrative have been replaced with more recent ones.
- A new section on communities has been added to the "Types of Realistic Fiction" section. This new type of realistic fiction is explained and exemplified.
- The "Notable Authors of Realistic Fiction" feature has been updated and authors' official web sites have been added.
- In the updated list of recommended books, substantial numbers of books have been deleted and recent titles have been added.
- The new feature "Related Films, Videos, and DVDs" provides a list of films related to children's works of realistic fiction.

Chapter 9: Historical Fiction

- Many book examples in the narrative have been replaced with more recent ones.
- The "Notable Authors of Historical Fiction" feature has been updated and authors' official web sites have been added.
- In the updated list of recommended books, substantial numbers of books have been deleted and recent titles added.
- The new feature "Related Films, Videos, and DVDs" provides a list of films related to children's works of historical fiction.

Chapter 10: Nonfiction: Biography and Informational Books

This chapter has been reorganized for greater clarity and to highlight biography and informational books equally. Changes to the chapter include the following:

- Rewriting of the "Definition and Description" section
- More links to related websites

- Updates to the table on important research studies on reading and nonfiction
- Updates to the "Excellent Nonfiction to Read Aloud" list
- Updates to the "Notable Authors and Illustrators of Nonfiction" feature, includings webpages of authors and illustrators
- Updates to the list of recommended books (approximately 30 percent new titles)
- A list of films related to children's works of biography and nonfiction: "Related Films, Videos, and DVDs"

Chapter 11: Literature for a Diverse Society

This chapter replaces the multicultural and international literature chapter of earlier editions. The chapter is organized into two sections: "Strategies for Culturally Responsive Instruction" and "Multicultural and International Literature." Additions to Chapter 11 include the following:

- Updates to the list of recommended books (approximately 30 percent new titles)
- A list of films related to children's works of multicultural and international literature: "Related Films, Videos, and DVDs"

Chapter 12: Planning the Curriculum

- Sections of the chapter have been rewritten for greater clarity and impact, including "Defining the Literature Curriculum," "Choosing the Approach," "Developing the Literature Curriculum," and "Censorship and the First Amendment."
- A new section entitled "Gaining Experience with Literature in School Practicums" has been added.

Chapter 13: Developing Teaching Strategies

Chapter 13 has the following changes:

- A new opening poem
- Recent books used as examples in the narrative whenever possible
- New sections on the use of audiobooks in the classroom, the use of films in the classroom, character education and the role literature may play in it, and social justice education and the role literature may play in it
- A new table on incorporating literature into the curriculum, with example titles organized by content areas
- A new example of a readers' theatre script

Appendixes

- All book award lists in Appendix A, "Children's Book Awards," have been updated to include award winners and honor books for the years 2005–2007 when available.
- Book award website links have been added to Appendix A.
- Appendix B, "Professional Resources," has been updated to reflect the latest titles and editions.

- Appendix C, "Children's Magazines," has been updated to include current content, target age ranges, and websites for ordering.
- New section, "Recreational Magazines," has been added to Appendix C.
- Appendix D, "Transitional Books," has been updated and expanded.

 ## Acknowledgments

Thank you to the librarians who helped us locate information and books and were always willing to discuss books with us: Pamala Doffek, Goldstein Library of Florida State University; and Gary Crew, Leon County Public Library, Tallahassee, Florida. We also gratefully acknowledge the reviewers of the fifth edition: Sister Louise Auclair, Rivier College; Andrea Bartlett, University of Hawaii at Manoa; Terry Diana Benton, Youngstown State University; Sister Ann Marie Burton, Immaculata University; Patricia A. Crawford, University of Central Florida; Deborah Ann Jensen, Hunter College CUNY; Catherine Kurkjian, Central Connecticut State University; Prisca Martens, Towson University; Virginia McGinnis, Edinboro University of Pennsylvania; and Barbara Smith Chalon, University of Maine at Presque Isle.

We are indebted to David Soman for the wonderful cover for this edition of *Essentials of Children's Literature*. We can hear the happy, interested hum that Mr. Soman's room of readers must generate, and it reminds us of the best moments of our own years as elementary-grade teachers. We hope that it will serve as an inspiration for you, too.

Children and Literature

Part I provides introductory content for a course on children's literature. This material will help teachers and librarians read, select, and evaluate children's books and integrate them into their classrooms and school library media centers.

Chapter 1 defines children's literature, discusses its personal and academic values for children, and provides research evidence supporting its use with children. General guidelines for the types and topics of literature likely to appeal to children as they develop from year to year complete this chapter.

Chapter 2 considers the relationships between reading and literature as they pertain to the reading process, literature in the reading curriculum, independent reading of free-choice material, accountability and reading, children's reading interests, and the difficulty of reading materials.

Approaches to studying and interpreting literature, elements of fiction, changes in traditional fictional forms, and aspects of book format are treated extensively in Chapter 3 and serve as a review for students. An overview of resources for book selection, including review journals, professional websites, and major awards for children's literature, is also discussed in this chapter. The chapter concludes with a discussion of the need for balance and variety in book selection with a table of literary genres and their locations within the book.

Throughout this text, examples of notable books are given as needed, but we include no lengthy plot summaries or book reviews. We believe that more is gained from reading and discussing children's books themselves than reading *about* the books in a lengthy text.

chapter 1

Learning about Children and Their Literature

Reading
. . . We get no good
By being ungenerous even to a book,
And calculating profits . . . so much help
By so much reading. It is rather when
We gloriously forget ourselves and plunge
Soul-forward, headlong, into a book's profound,
Impassioned for its beauty and salt of truth—
'Tis then we get the right good from a book.

—Elizabeth Browning

A child leans forward, head cupped in hands, eyes wide with anticipation, listening to a story: This is an image for all time. Whether that child is seated beside an open fire in the Stone Ages, on a rough bench in a medieval fairground, or in a modern-day classroom, the message of the image is the same: Children love a good story.

Definition of Children's Literature

This book is about literature for children from infancy to adolescence, written for you who will be meeting and working with these children as teachers, librarians, and parents. In these roles, your opportunities to lead children to literature will be unparalleled, if you have the prerequisite knowledge.

Children's literature is good-quality trade books for children from birth to adolescence, covering topics of relevance and interest to children of those ages, through prose and poetry, fiction and nonfiction. This definition contains several key concepts that will be explained in the following sections. Understanding these concepts will help you find your way around the more than 385,000 children's titles currently in print (*Children's Books in Print, 2006*, 2005), the more than 15,000 new children's titles being published annually in the United States (*Bowker Annual: Library and Book Trade Almanac* [Bogart, 2006]), as well as the additional thousands of children's books published worldwide each year in English.

Content

Children's books are about the experiences of childhood, both good and bad. Whether these experiences are set in the past, present, or future, they should still be relevant to the child of today. The content of children's books includes amazingly diverse topics that are of interest to children, such as dinosaurs, Egyptian mummies, world records, and fighter planes.

The manner in which content is treated also helps to define children's books. Childhood stories told in a forthright, humorous, or suspenseful manner are appropriate for young readers; stories *about* childhood told in nostalgic or overly sentimental terms are inappropriate. Likewise, when stories show children as victims of natural and human-made disasters, the stories should emphasize the hope for a better future rather than the hopelessness and utter despair of the moment.

The subject matter of children's literature can be expressed in prose or poetry. If the literary work is prose, it must be presented as fiction (a product of the imagination, an invented story), nonfiction (factual), or a combination of the two.

Teachers and librarians distinguish between the terms *textbook* and *trade book*. A **textbook,** by design and content, is for the purpose of instruction. The basal reader used in many classrooms for reading instruction is an example of a textbook. In contrast, a **trade book,** by design and content, is primarily for the purposes of entertainment and information. Trade books are often referred to as *library books* and *storybooks*. The books that we will be discussing in this text will be trade books, not textbooks.

Quality

Not all trade books aimed at young readers are worth attention. Books ranging in quality from excellent to poor are now readily available to parents, teachers, and children through bookstores and libraries as well as online. Look around and you will see racks of children's books in department stores, drugstores, and even grocery stores. But the question is: Are they *good* children's books?

Quality in writing has to do with originality and importance of ideas, imaginative use of language, and beauty of literary and artistic style that enable a work to remain fresh, interesting, and meaningful for many years. The best children's books offer readers enjoyment as well as memorable characters and situations and valuable insights into the human condition. These books have permanent value.

This is not to say that books of good-but-not-great quality, such as series books, have no value. These works win no literary prizes, but many young readers enjoy them; and because books such as these encourage newly independent readers to read more, they have worth. However, you will probably not want to select books of this calibre to read aloud to your students. Why deprive them of the pleasure of reading such easy and enjoyable books independently?

Many so-called children's books today are nothing more than advertisements for film and television characters and associated products, such as candy, clothing, and toys. These books represent the low end of the quality spectrum.

The Personal Value of Literature to Children

Literature for children leads to personal fulfillment and academic gains. Separating the values into personal and academic is an intellectual distinction, since both types benefit the child and are all proper parts of a child's schooling. The distinction is useful, however, since teachers and librarians must often justify the benefits of literature in the classroom and find the academic benefits the most convincing ones for administrators and parents.

Enjoyment

The most important personal gain that good books offer to children is the most obvious one—enjoyment. Those of you who read widely as children will never forget the stories that were so funny that you laughed out loud, the poem that was so lilting that you never forgot it, or the mystery that was so scary that your heart thumped with apprehension. Such positive early experiences often lead to a lifetime of reading enjoyment.

Imagination and Inspiration

By seeing the world around them in new ways and by considering ways of living other than their own, children increase their ability to think divergently. Stories often map the divergent paths that our ancestors might have taken or that our descendants might someday take. Through the vicarious experience of entering a world different from the present one, children develop their imaginations. In addition, stories about people, both real and imaginary, can inspire children to overcome obstacles, accept different perspectives, and formulate personal goals.

Vicarious Experience

When a story is so convincingly written that readers feel as though they have lived through an experience or have actually been in the place and time where the story is set, the book has given them a *vicarious* experience. Experiences such as these are broadening for children because they, as readers, are taken to places and times that they could never actually visit—and might not want to! A vicarious experience can also be a good mental exercise for children, since they are asked to view situations from perspectives other than their own.

Understanding and Empathy

Literature helps young people gain an appreciation of the universality of human needs across history, which makes it possible for them to understand that all humans are, to some degree, alike. Walking in someone else's shoes often helps children develop a sense of social justice and a greater capacity to empathize with others. All children can benefit from stories that explain what life is like for people who are restricted by disabilities, politics, or circumstance or whose lives are different from theirs because of culture or geography. Likewise, young people can relate on a more personal level with the events and people of history when reading works of historical fiction told from the point of view of a person their own age.

Heritage

Stories that are handed down from one generation to the next connect us to our past, to the roots of our specific cultures, national heritage, and general human condition. Stories are the repositories of culture. Knowing the tales, characters, expressions, and adages that are part of our cultural heritage is part of being culturally literate. In addition, stories based on actual events in the past help young people gain a greater appreciation for what history is and for the people, both ordinary and extraordinary, who made history.

Moral Reasoning

Often, story characters are placed in situations that require them to make moral decisions. Young readers naturally consider what they themselves would do in such a situation. As the story unfolds and the character's decision and the consequences of that choice are disclosed, readers discover whether their own decisions would have had positive outcomes. Regular experience with these types of stories can help young people formulate their own concepts of right and wrong.

Moral reasoning is an integral part of *character education,* a strand in the social studies curricula of many elementary schools today dealing with the principles by which one lives. Character education programs such as "Character Counts" are available for purchase, but reading and discussing well-selected works of literature can serve the same purpose.

Literary and Artistic Preferences

Another valuable result of children interacting with literature is that they quickly come to recognize the literary and artistic styles of many authors and illustrators. Children who read regularly from a wide variety of children's books soon develop their own personal preferences for types of books and select favorite authors and illustrators. Personal preference and interest as expressed through self-selection of reading materials are powerful reading motivators.

The more children know about their world, the more they discover about themselves—who they are, what they value, and what they stand for. These personal insights alone are sufficient to warrant making good books an essential part of any child's home and school experiences. But literature is also valuable for its academic benefits, as will be discussed in the following section.

 ## The Academic Value of Literature to Children

In addition to the personal benefits of literature for young readers, there are several important academic benefits.

Reading

Many of you already may have reached the commonsense deduction that reading ability, like any other skill, improves with practice. Many teachers and librarians believe that regular involvement with excellent and appropriate literature can foster language development in young children and can help them learn to read and value reading. This belief was supported in the landmark study *Becoming a Nation of Readers* (Anderson, Hiebert, Scott, & Wilkinson, 1985), which concludes, "The single most important activity for building the knowledge required for eventual success in reading is reading aloud to children" (p. 23).

In 1997, the *National Reading Panel* (NRP) was formed, at the request of Congress, to assess the status of research-based knowledge about reading, including the effectiveness of various approaches to teaching children to read. The *Report of the National Reading Panel* (National Institutes of Health, 2000) was met with great controversy and skepticism because of its narrow definition of scientific research studies. In this report, the NRP identified the following components of instruction considered to be essential to the teaching of reading: *phonemic awareness* (teaching how to break apart and manipulate the sounds in words); *phonics* (teaching that sounds are represented by letters of the alphabet that blend to form words); and *reading comprehension* (teaching strategies to develop text recall, question generation, and summarizing of information read), including *fluency* (teaching how to read orally with speed, accuracy, and proper expression) and *vocabulary instruction* (teaching the spelling and meaning of new words). Literature-based research studies that support reading aloud to students and independent silent reading by students were not included because they did not meet the NRP's narrow definition of scientific research.

Based on our personal and professional experience with children, we contend that reading aloud to children by parents and caregivers and sharing literature with students in the classroom greatly benefit children's acquisition of reading skills and their attitude toward reading. In addition, we contend that literature-based studies support not only the reading instruction strategies endorsed by the NRP but also the important instructional practices that the NRP report ignores.

As educators, you should be aware of research findings about the worth of literature for children. Research studies summarized in Tables 1.1 and 1.2 show that in teaching children to read,

Table 1.1   Landmark Studies on Literature and Reading

Researcher(s)	Subjects	Findings
Carlsen & Sherrill (1988)	College students who had become committed readers	Conditions that promote a love of reading in childhood include: ■ Freedom of choice in reading material ■ Availability of books and magazines ■ Family members who read aloud ■ Adults and peers who modeled reading ■ Role models who valued reading ■ Sharing and discussing books ■ Owning books ■ Availability of libraries and librarians
Eldredge & Butterfield (1986)	1,149 beginning readers in 50 classrooms	Use of children's literature to teach reading has a much greater positive effect on students' achievement and attitudes toward reading than does use of basal readers with traditional homogeneous grouping.
Fielding, Wilson, & Anderson (1986)	Middle-graders	Students who read a lot at home show larger gains on reading achievement tests.
Leinhardt, Zigmond, & Cooley (1981)	Elementary-grade children	The amount of time children spend reading silently in school is associated with their year-to-year gains in reading achievement. Children improve their reading ability by increasing their reading.
Applebee (1978)	Children ages 2 to 17	Children's sense of story grows as they mature. Hearing and reading literature has a positive effect on children's language development.
Butler (1975)	Cushla, severely disabled, from ages 4 months to 3 years	Reading aloud daily to the subject from children's picture books enabled the child to learn to read.
Durkin (1966)	Children who learned to read before attending school	Children who learned to read before attending school were read to regularly from the age of 3. Early reading and early writing are often linked.

Table 1.2   Important Studies on Literature and Reading, 1990–2004

Researchers(s)	Subjects	Findings
Wilson, Martens, Arya, & Altwerger (2004)	84 urban, low SES second-graders (not special ed. or ESL) taught reading with three different reading programs: Direct Instruction and Open Court, both heavily scripted; phonics-based reading programs; and Guided Reading, a literature-based reading program	No significant difference was found in measures of students' phonics use, regardless of instructional program. Guided Reading students could describe settings and characters, retell stories cohesively, form inferences, and make connections. These findings contradict the National Reading Panel's predictions that phonics-based reading programs would produce better readers.
Worthy, Patterson, Salas, Prater, & Turner (2002)	24 struggling, resistant readers in grades 3 through 5	Most effective factor in increasing these students' motivation to read was a reading instructor who tailored instruction to each student's unique needs, found materials that exactly fit each student's needs and interests, and took time to inspire each student to read.
Ivey & Broaddus (2001)	1,765 sixth-graders in 23 diverse schools in mid-Atlantic and northeastern United States	When asked what made them want to read in the classroom, students ranked as most important: ■ Free reading time and teacher read-alouds of literature as part of instructional time ■ Quality and diversity of reading materials and a choice in selecting these materials Most favored free reading material: ■ Magazines (77%) ■ Adventure books (69%) ■ Mysteries (68%) ■ Scary stories (59%) ■ Joke books (56%) ■ Nonfiction about animals (51%)
Anderson (1996)	Elementary-grade students	Even slight increases (10 minutes a day) in time spent reading independently lead to gains in reading achievement. Amount of free reading in early grades helps determine reading ability in grades 5 and 6.

two procedures seem especially important: reading excellent literature aloud to children and silent independent reading of free-choice material by children, both on a daily basis, if possible. For a more thorough discussion of literature and the teaching of reading, see Chapter 2 and the section titled Literature in the Reading Program in Chapter 12.

Writing

By listening to and reading excellent literature, children are exposed to rich vocabulary and excellent writing styles, which serve as good models for their own speaking and writing voices. The acquisition of a larger vocabulary through reading offers young writers better word choices for their own stories. Devices found in books such as the use of dialect, dialogue, and precise description are often assimilated into students' own writing. Research studies summarized in Table 1.3 show that skill in reading and skill in writing go hand in hand.

Content-Area Subjects

In reading about and discussing children's literature, you will often hear the phrase *literature across the curriculum.* This means using works of literature as teaching materials in the content areas of social studies and history, science, health, and mathematics. Good teachers have always used literature across the curriculum. The logic for this practice is sound. Many trade books contain information that is relevant to the topics studied in school. Moreover, this information is presented through captivating, sometimes beautifully illustrated, narratives. Information thus presented is interesting to students and, therefore, is more comprehensible and memorable. When using literature across the curriculum, teachers and students are not confined to the textbook as the sole resource. Using several sources of information has always been considered prudent both in and out of school, since doing so usually provides fuller factual coverage of topics and leads to wiser, more informed decisions on issues. Using literature across the curriculum is particularly appropriate today, given the abundance of masterfully written, information-relevant children's trade books available to teachers and librarians.

Art Appreciation

Illustration in children's picture books can be appreciated for its ability to help tell the story (cognitive value) and for its value as art (aesthetic value). The cognitive value of illustration in picture books will be dealt with in Chapter 5, but the point to be emphasized here is that if you appreciate art for its own sake, there is much that you can do in your classroom to instill in your students a similar appreciation. For example, call to your students' attention particularly striking and unusual picture book illustrations. By doing so, you show them that you value art. Discuss the artist's style, the medium used (watercolor, oils, pastels, etc.), the palette (range of colors), and how the artist's style compares to the styles of other artists. Suggest using picture book art as a model for applied art lessons. By encouraging your students to use media, techniques, and topics suggested by picture book illustrations in their own artwork, you make good use of a handy, valuable resource and in yet another way show that you value this art.

Table 1.3   Important Studies on Literature and Writing

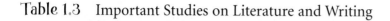

Researcher(s)	Subjects	Findings
Barrs (2000)	18 fourth-grade students in five elementary schools in London whose reading and writing were analyzed over one school year	Children use in their own writing the language and writing styles of books they read. "It seems unlikely that there can be any fundamental writing development without reading development, and vice versa" (p. 59).
Cantrell (1999)	40 third-graders—21 in four classrooms where teachers adhered to recommended literacy practices (both explicit skill instruction and meaning-centered literacy activities) to a high degree and 19 in four classrooms where teachers adhered to these practices to a low degree	In classrooms where teachers frequently used children's literature, integrated reading and writing, and taught reading and writing skills in context, students developed reading and writing skills at higher levels than students in classrooms where teachers provided more isolated skill instruction.
Lancia (1997)	Second-graders	Good books are effective models for children's writing. Students "borrowed" plots, plot elements, characters, stylistic devices, and information from books to use in their own writing.
Dressel (1990)	Fifth-graders	Student writing was directly affected by the characteristics of the stories they heard and discussed, regardless of the students' reading abilities. The better the quality of the read-aloud, the better the quality of the student writing. *Which* stories teachers read aloud is important.

Research studies summarized in Table 1.4 suggest some of the benefits of using literature across the curriculum.

From the foregoing discussion, it should be clear that students are not the only ones in schools who can benefit from children's literature. As a teacher or librarian, you will find that excellent literature is rich in social, historical, and scientific information about the world and its people and that it has great potential for developing the entire elementary and middle-school curriculum.

Table 1.4   Important Studies on Literature across the Curriculum

Researcher(s)	Subjects	Findings
Morrow, Pressley, Smith, & Smith (1997)	Third-graders from diverse backgrounds divided into three groups: 1. Those who received literature-based reading and literature-based science instruction 2. Those who received literature-based reading and textbook-based science instruction 3. Those who received basal reading and textbook-based science instruction	Students who received yearlong literature-based reading and literature-based science instruction scored higher than control groups in reading and total language score on the California Test of Basic Skills and on two measures of science content.
VanSledright & Kelley (1996)	Fifth-grade history students	Students' interest in history and their ability to retain information increased significantly when their history instruction included literature.
Kiefer (1994)	Children in grades 1 through 5	Exposure to picture books can increase children's awareness of art and aesthetics. Children's awareness of stylistic factors in picture books grows developmentally.
Levstik (1986)	Sixth-grade class that used narrative literature to learn history	Children use "human behavior" schemata to make sense of historical information. Personal narrative descriptions of historical fiction have a greater impact on young students than textbooks' depersonalized explanations.

 ## Children's Development and Literature

In this section we will discuss types of books and general topics most likely to be appreciated by children of different age levels. Children's physical, cognitive, language, and moral development are important considerations in book selection, as is their developing concept of story. By

overlaying this general information with the specific interests of any child, you can recognize and make available literature that the children in your care will read with interest and enjoyment.

Ages 0 to 2

Infants can enjoy and benefit from good literature. In choosing books for them, consider the practical aspects of physical development, such as how well infants can see the illustrations and how long they will sit still for a book experience. Most often, these books will be collections of nursery rhymes, which are discussed in Chapter 4, and concept books, board books, and interactive books, which are discussed in Chapter 5. Common features of these book types and formats are relative simplicity of content or story; repetitive text or language patterns; clearly defined, brightly colored illustrations usually placed on a plain background; physical durability; and opportunities for the child to participate or interact with the book.

A classic example of a book appropriate for children aged 0 to 2 is Dorothy Kunhardt's interactive book, *Pat the Bunny* (1962/2001). A more recent example is Harriet Ziefert's (2002) *Who Said Moo,* illustrated by Simms Taback, an interactive board book with lift-the-flaps and language patterns.

The best baby books, whether wordless or with brief text, invite the reader and listener to "talk the book through." In this way the books promote oral language development, which is the child's first step toward literacy.

Ages 2 to 4

Many of the book types enjoyed by babies are also enjoyed by toddlers, but with slight differences in emphasis. Nursery rhymes, for example, can be committed to memory by many toddlers. Concept books can now include letters (ABC books), numbers (counting books), and more complex concepts such as opposites. Word books, another type of concept book, promote vocabulary development.

Picture storybooks featuring simple plots, illustrations that tell part of the story, and characters who exhibit the physical skills (running, whistling, buttoning clothes, tying shoes) that 2- to 4-year-olds take pride in accomplishing are appropriate for this group. Likewise, these children enjoy folktales because of their relative simplicity, repetitive aspects, and two dimensional, easy-to-understand characters. Shirley Hughes's perennial favorite, *Alfie Gets in First* (1982), and the more recent book, *Owen,* by Kevin Henkes (1993), both feature protagonists who overcome problems typical of children aged 2 to 4.

Ages 4 to 7

Increasing independence and enthusiasm for finding out about the world are prominent characteristics of 4- to 7-year-olds. Stories in which children interact with other children, spend time away from home, begin school, and learn interesting facts are popular with this age group. Picture storybooks, folktales, and informational picture books will be at the heart of the literature experience during these years. An old favorite for this group is Bernard Waber's (1972) *Ira Sleeps Over.*

A recent informational book that works well with 4- to 7-year-olds is *What Do You Do with a Tail Like This?* by Steve Jenkins and Robin Page (2003).

From ages 4 to 7 most children will acquire the fundamentals of reading. Easy-to-read books or books for beginning readers make use of familiar words, word patterns, illustration clues, and, in some cases, rhyme to make the text easier to read. Often these books appear in series. It is important that books selected for beginning readers precisely match their interests and reading abilities so as not to bore or dishearten them. An outstanding example of books long enjoyed by 4- to 7-year-olds is the Frog and Toad series of easy-to-read books by Arnold Lobel. Cynthia Rylant's Henry and Mudge series is a more recent favorite.

Ages 7 to 9

Most 7- to 9-year-old children become readers, begin to understand and accept others' perspectives, recognize that life and people do not fit into neat "good" and "bad" categories, and develop an understanding of past and future time. They begin to assert their growing abilities to meet their own needs. With these skills they can read or listen to and enjoy books about the lives of other children of the past, present, and future in picture books for older readers, transitional books, and later in novels. Fittingly, books for children aged 7 to 9 often center on the adventures of young characters within their neighborhoods and communities. Two excellent older transitional books are Mary Stolz's *A Dog on Barkham Street* (1960) and its sequel, *The Bully of Barkham Street* (1963). For more recent examples, see the Ivy and Bean series by Annie Barrows.

Ages 9 to 12

With their rapidly developing physical and mental skills and abilities, 9- to 12-year-olds are ready for more complicated story plots, including such devices as flashback, symbolism, and dialects of earlier times or different cultures. Both historical fiction and science fiction, which are set in the distant past and the distant future, respectively, can be understood and enjoyed. Equally interesting to this age group are stories about their peers who are growing up, asserting themselves, using their new-found skills, moving toward independence, and experiencing growth through meeting challenges, as in survival stories. Because their moral development allows them to recognize the legitimacy of opinions, mores, and lifestyles different from their own, these young people can enjoy stories that present alternative points of view, nontraditional characters, and moral dilemmas. Some good examples include *Esperanza Rising* (historical fiction, Hispanic culture) by Pam Muñoz Ryan (2001), *The City of Ember* (science fiction) by Jeanne DuPrau (2003), and *Wringer* (moral dilemma) by Jerry Spinelli (1997).

Teachers and librarians who are consistently successful in helping children find books they like rapidly narrow the field of choices by first considering general factors such as age level and types of books appropriate for children of that general age level. Then they consider more personal factors such as the child's current reading interests and reading ability to select specific titles. Knowing children's general reading preferences provides some guidance in book selection, but there is no substitute for knowing the child.

Topics for Further Investigation

- Review theory and research on the effects of reading aloud to children at preschool, primary, or intermediate grade levels.
- In *Cushla and Her Books* Dorothy Butler chronicles the positive impact of literature on a child who is severely disabled. Read this book and reflect on the lessons it has for you and other teachers.
- Investigate the reading–writing connection. Why are young people who are good readers usually also good writers?

 See the companion website at www.ablongman.com/lynchbrown6e for further suggestions.

References

Anderson, R. C. (1996). Research foundations to support wide reading. In V. Greaney (Ed.), *Promoting reading: Views on making reading materials accessible to increase literacy levels* (pp. 55–77). Newark, DE: International Reading Association.

———, Hiebert, E. H., Scott, J. A., & Wilkinson, I. A. G. (1985). *Becoming a nation of readers: The report of the commission on reading.* Washington, DC: National Institute of Education.

Applebee, A. N. (1978). *The child's concept of story.* Chicago: University of Chicago.

Barrs, M. (2000). The reader in the writer. *Reading, 34*(2), 54–60.

Bogart, D. (Ed.). (2006). *Bowker annual: Library and book trade almanac.* Medford, NJ: Information Today.

Browning, E. B. (1902). Reading. In K. D. Wiggins & N. A. Smith (Eds.), *Golden numbers.* New York: Doubleday.

Butler, D. (1975). *Cushla and her books.* Boston: Horn Book.

Cantrell, S. C. (1999). The effects of literacy instruction on primary students' reading and writing achievement. *Reading Research and Instruction, 39*(1), 3–26.

Carlsen, G. R., & Sherrill, A. (1988). *Voices of readers: How we come to love books.* Urbana, IL: National Council of Teachers of English.

Children's books in print, 2006. (2005). New Providence, NJ: R. R. Bowker.

Dressel, J. H. (1990). The effects of listening to and discussing different qualities of children's literature on the narrative writing of fifth graders. *Research in the Teaching of English, 24*(4), 397–414.

Duprau, J. (2003). *The city of Ember.* New York: Random.

Durkin, D. (1966). *Children who read early.* New York: Columbia Teachers College Press.

Eldredge, J. L., & Butterfield, D. (1986). Alternatives to traditional reading instruction. *The Reading Teacher, 40*, 32–37.

Fielding, L. G., Wilson, P. T., & Anderson, R. C. (1986). A new focus on free reading: The role of trade books in reading instruction. In T. Raphael (Ed.), *The contexts of school-based literacy* (pp. 149–160). New York: Random House.

Henkes, K. (1993). *Owen.* New York: Greenwillow.

Hughes, S. (1982). *Alfie gets in first.* New York: Lothrop.

Ivey, G., & Broaddus, K. (2001). "Just plain reading": A survey of what makes students want to read in middle school classrooms. *Reading Research Quarterly, 36*(4), 350–377.

Jenkins, S., & Page, R. (2003). *What do you do with a tail like this?* New York: Houghton.

Kiefer, B. Z. (1994). *The potential of picturebooks: From visual literacy to aesthetic understanding.* Englewood Cliffs, NJ: Prentice Hall.

Kunhardt, D. (1962/2001). *Pat the bunny.* New York: Golden.

Lancia, P. J. (1997). Literary borrowing: The effects of literature on children's writing. *The Reading Teacher, 50*(6), 470–475.

Leinhardt, G., Zigmond, N., & Cooley, W. W. (1981). Reading instruction and its effects. *American Educational Research Journal, 18,* 343–361.

Levstik, L. (1986). The relationship between historical response and narrative in a sixth-grade classroom. *Theory and Research in Social Education, 14,* 1–15.

Morrow, L. M., Pressley, M., Smith, J. K., & Smith, M. (1997). The effect of a literature-based program integrated into literacy and science instruction with children from diverse backgrounds. *Reading Research Quarterly, 32*(1), 54–76.

National Reading Panel. (2000). *Teaching children to read.* NIH Publication No. 00-4769. Washington, DC: U.S. Government Printing Office.

Ryan, P. M. (2001). *Esperanza rising.* New York: Scholastic.

Spinelli, J. (1997). *Wringer.* New York: HarperCollins.

Stolz, M. (1960). *A dog on Barkham Street.* Illustrated by Leonard Shortall. New York: Harper.

———. (1963). *The bully of Barkham Street.* Illustrated by Leonard Shortall. New York: Harper.

VanSledright, B. A., & Kelley, C. A. (1996). *Reading American history: How do multiple text sources influence historical learning in fifth grade?* Reading Research Report 68 (ERIC Document Reproduction Service No. ED 400 525).

Waber, B. (1972). *Ira sleeps over.* Boston: Houghton.

Wilson, G. P., Martens, P., Arya, P., & Altwerger, B. (2004). Readers, instruction, and the NRP. *Phi Delta Kappan, 86*(3), 242–246.

Worthy, J., Patterson, E., Salas, R., Prater, S., & Turner, M. (2002). "More than just reading": The human factor in reaching resistant readers. *Reading Research and Instruction, 41*(2), 177–202.

Ziefert, H. (2002). *Who said moo?* Illustrated by S. Taback. Brooklyn, NY: Handprint Books.

chapter 2

Learning about Reading and Literature

My Book!
I did it!
I did it!
Come and look
At what I've done!
I read a book!
When someone wrote it
Long ago
For me to read,
How did he know
That this was the book
I'd take from the shelf
And lie on the floor
And read by myself?
I really read it!
Just like that!
Word by word,
From first to last!
I'm sleeping with
This book in bed,
This is the FIRST book
I've ever read!

—David L. Harrison

Beginning teachers are fully aware that reading is the most important skill for the future success of the children they teach. Yet many beginning teachers are unsure of literature's role in our schools and in the lives of their students. In Chapter 1 we discussed benefits to be found in literature, but given the current challenges in teaching students to read today, teachers worry that there is time for nothing else but instruction in reading.

What is the intersection between reading and literature? Reading courses provide teachers with instructional strategies that will help children learn how to read and understand what they are reading. Courses in children's literature will acquaint teachers with good-quality material for children to read and strategies to motivate children to read widely for practice of their reading skills and for developing into lifelong readers. Children need the reading strategies, the motivation, and the practice that literature provides to develop fully in the area of literacy. For these reasons, students in elementary education teacher preparation programs usually take coursework in reading and literature.

In this chapter we will discuss this intersection of reading and literature as it pertains to the reading process, literature in the reading curriculum, accountability and reading, independent reading, resistant readers, children's book choices, children's reading interests, difficulty of reading materials, and reading incentive programs.

Reading Process

Children learn to read at different ages and in different ways, depending on their early experiences with books, their innate abilities, and the quality of their early reading instruction. There is no absolute, lockstep method for learning to read, although some would claim otherwise and subscribe to one of the two prevailing approaches: phonics based and meaning based. Advocates of *phonics-based reading instruction* believe that children learn to read by progressing from letter names to letter sounds to words and, finally, to meaning. Emphasis is placed on decoding more than comprehension. Advocates of *meaning-based reading instruction* believe that children primarily use their oral language skills—including grammar, the structure of English, and knowledge of the world—to make meaning of written text, and resort to phonetic decoding when other meaning-making strategies fail.

We subscribe to an interactive model of reading that synthesizes aspects of both approaches. Generally, whether they are consciously taught or learn on their own, children come to know that stories can be found in books; that certain formalities, known as *concepts of print,* apply in reading (front-to-back, left-to-right, top-to-bottom); that letters represent sounds (sound–symbol relationships); that letters can be used to code spoken language (writing); that words convey meaning; and that finding meaning in the text (comprehension) is the goal of reading.

Literature in the Reading Curriculum

Teaching literature and teaching reading are similar in some respects. Both use similar materials—stories, poetry, plays, and informational texts; both have the purpose of making meaning from texts; and both have the ultimate goal of a greater or deeper understanding of and response to the written text. Because of these similarities, literature and reading can be, and often are, taught simultaneously in the elementary and middle grades. Inservice and preservice teachers will encounter two different approaches to literacy subscribed to in schools and teacher training institutions: the basal reader approach and the literature-based reading approach. (These two philosophies and how each may affect aspects of your teaching are outlined and described in Chapter 12.) Underlying the differences in these two approaches are the different learning theories on which each is based. Your approach to literacy development will depend on your own philosophy of teaching and learning, the ideas you believe in strongly enough to act on.

National Reading Panel Report

Using good, carefully selected literature in the classroom can support many of the findings of the National Reading Panel report (2000) that was discussed in Chapter 1. For example, use of nursery rhymes, pattern books, and poems can help children develop phonemic awareness. *Reading aloud by the teacher, paired reading, readers' theatre,* and *choral reading* can increase children's reading fluency by giving them models of fluent reading. *Shared reading,* with its emphasis on repeated oral reading, can teach children sound–symbol relationships and increase their reading fluency. Independent *silent reading* of good literature, especially if followed up with some reflection on what was read, can increase children's meaning vocabulary and conceptual knowledge, as well as develop their reading comprehension. For full descriptions and explanations of these strategies, see Chapter 13.

Overemphasis of any one component of reading instruction, such as phonics, to the exclusion of the others in beginning reading instruction would be detrimental to some, if not all, students who are learning to read. Programs advocating heavy emphasis on phonics but no daily teacher read-aloud or daily independent silent reading of excellent books of the students' own choosing should be viewed with suspicion. We strongly advocate daily read-alouds by the teacher and independent silent reading because they give students models of fluency, build meaning vocabulary and conceptual knowledge, offer reading practice, and improve students' attitudes toward reading. As students' reading ability grows, logic would suggest (despite the dictates of any scripted reading program teacher's manual) that teachers shift their emphasis from letter and word decoding toward strategies that involve reading actual stories, poems, and plays. It is important to note that reading aloud and independent silent reading are *not* substitutes for direct reading instruction, however. Primary- and intermediate-grade schedules should include all three every day.

Accountability and Reading

Accountability is a demand by government agencies and the public for school systems and teachers to improve students' school achievement as demonstrated by test scores in the areas of reading, writing, and mathematics. This trend began in the 1980s at the local school district level, then expanded to the state level in many locations, and, with the enactment of the No Child Left Behind Act (NCLB) in 2002, became an important part of federal policy in education. The NCLB Act expanded the original notion of accountability in two important ways: Annual testing of reading and mathematics achievement for all students in grades 3 to 8 became mandatory; and performance data had to be disaggregated according to race, gender, and other criteria to demonstrate progress in closing the achievement gap between disadvantaged students and other groups of students.

Under NCLB, each school is graded as Pass or Fail, depending on student achievement by averages for the grade and by subgroups. Schools that receive failing grades are given a period of time to improve student achievement. Failure of a school to do so can result in reduced federal and state funding for the school, vouchers for students to attend another public school or charter school in the case of repeated failures by the school, or replacement of administrators and teachers, depending on state and local policies. States develop the actual tests used, the procedures for implementation of the policy, and timetables for implementation according to federal requirements.

Although we question the reliability of a score on a single test as the predominant measure of a student's progress or of a teacher's success over the course of a school year, this is the reality educators currently face and within which they must operate. Because it directly affects students, teachers, schools, and school systems, accountability is a high priority issue in education. The curricular area that is of most concern to parents, teachers, and school administrators is reading, due to its importance for learning in all subjects and because reading scores have been in general decline across the nation for the last twenty years, especially at fourth grade through high school levels. Moreover, U.S. students do not compare favorably with those in other developed nations, as the recent Progress in International Reading Literacy Study (PIRLS) and Programme for International Student Assessment (PISA) reports have demonstrated. We believe that a major reason for the decline in reading scores is a decrease in voluntary reading among our students. Young people have lost the reading habit.

 ## Reading at Risk: A Survey of Literary Reading in America

The trend toward less voluntary reading of literature in the United States has been monitored by the Research Division of the United States Bureau of the Census since the 1980s. A report published in 2004 entitled *Reading at Risk: A Survey of Literary Reading in America* (Bradshaw & Nichols, 2004), produced by the National Endowment for the Arts and based on a survey of 17,000 adults, describes a startling transformation in this country away from books and reading toward electronic media as sources for entertainment and information. Of particular note for teachers and librarians are the following key findings:

- Less than half (46.7% in 2002) of the adult U.S. population now reads literature.
- The ten-year rate of decline in literary reading has accelerated from 5 percent to 14 percent since 1992.
- Literary reading is declining among all education levels and age groups, but the steepest decline in literary reading is in the youngest age groups of adults (28% decline from 1982 to 2002 in 18- to 24-year-olds).
- The decline in reading correlates with increased participation in a variety of electronic media, including the Internet, video games, and portable digital devices (Bradshaw & Nichols, 2004, pp. xi–xii).

The authors of the *Reading at Risk* study go on to state, "Indeed, at the current rate of loss, literary reading as a leisure activity will virtually disappear in half a century" (Bradshaw & Nichols, 2004, p. xiii).

More is at stake here than falling reading scores and a loss of accountability. In the words of Dana Gioia, Chairman of the National Endowment for the Arts, "Print culture affords irreplaceable forms of focused attention and contemplation that makes complex communications and insights possible. To lose such intellectual capacity—and the many sorts of human continuity it allows—would constitute a vast cultural impoverishment." He goes on to state that "readers play a more active and involved role in their communities. The decline in reading, therefore, parallels a larger retreat from participation in civic and cultural life. The long-term implications of this study not only affect literature but all of the arts—as well as social activities such as volunteerism, philanthropy, and even political engagement." Gioia concludes by saying, "Advanced literacy is a specific intellectual skill and social habit that depends on a great many educational, cultural, and economic factors. As more Americans lose this capability, our nation becomes less informed, active, and independent-minded. These are not qualities that a free, innovative, or productive society can afford to lose" (Bradshaw & Nichols, 2004, p. vii). It is little wonder that teachers feel pressured by the demands of accountability to improve their students' reading ability when the population in general is moving away from reading.

 ## Independent Reading and Societal Changes

Independent reading—that is, free-choice reading done voluntarily in and out of school—has been in decline among children and young adults in this country for several decades (Anderson, Tollefson, & Gilbert, 1985; Bradshaw & Nichols, 2004; Cline & Kretke, 1980; McKenna, Ellsworth, & Kear, 1995; Shapiro & White, 1991). Some national studies report that more than half of today's young people do not engage in independent reading (Bradshaw & Nichols, 2004). This trend is cause for concern, since research findings show that time spent reading correlates with reading achievement (Anderson, Wilson, & Fielding, 1988; Fielding, Wilson, & Anderson, 1986; Krashen, 1988; Moore, Bean, Birdyshaw, & Rycik, 1999; Postlethwaite & Ross, 1992). Research findings also show that reading practice helps to strengthen the skills learned through reading instruction and that the reading skills of those who do not engage in recreational reading, including good readers, often erode over time (Anderson et al., 1988; Mullis, Campbell, & Farstrup, 1993; Stanovich, 1986).

By the time they are in intermediate grades and middle-school grades, many children have turned off to reading. Most often, these students cite irrelevance of teacher-selected reading materials to their lives, disliked instructional practices, too little time, peer pressure, past failures, a preference for electronic media, and a perception of reading as hard work as reasons for not reading. Consequently, the greatest challenge for teachers and librarians who work in primary grades is to provide solid skills instruction and inspire children to love to read and to read voluntarily and regularly. Intermediate-grade teachers must continue these efforts and overcome students' resistance to reading by locating materials appealing to them and by finding ways to get them to read widely and intensively, both at school and at home. Teachers and parents need to convince young people of the importance of independent reading and be determined and persistent in guiding them to read better and read more. This determination is essential if we want students to become readers.

Resistant Readers

Children and adolescents resist or reject reading for many different reasons. The term we will use for young people who can read but choose not to read is *resistant readers.* We have identified five main groups of resistant readers.

Good to Average Readers Who Choose Not to Read

Some children who have good to excellent comprehension, few difficulties in decoding, and average reading rates by third or fourth grade rarely read or do not like to read. They include males and females of all ethnic, racial, and socioeconomic groups. With little or no reading practice, these children eventually lose their former reading achievement levels.

Reasons for this turn of events are multiple: Children perceive the books they must read in school to be irrelevant to their lives and therefore boring. They lack encouragement at home to read for recreational reasons. They seldom or never go to public or school libraries to select books for their reading enjoyment, since the emphasis by their teachers and parents is almost exclusively on improving their reading levels. Neither their parents nor their teachers serve as reading role models, nor do they persist in their efforts to foster a love of reading in these children. Tests and test scores take on tremendous importance to the detriment of other aspects of reading. Yet, in the long run, a passing test score is only a starting point, not an end goal.

Struggling Readers

Struggling readers are those children who struggled with reading from the earliest grades and became discouraged. Most of them can decode, but this skill remains a conscious cognitive act rather than an automatic process. The act of concentrating on decoding words slows the reading rate and fluency of these children, hampers their ability to recall what they have read to make sense of the text, and tires them mentally. Others in this group are fluent decoders who have difficulty comprehending what they read. Experiencing ridicule by their peers and embarrassment in class for their reading difficulties has taught them to avoid reading whenever possible. These are the children for whom regular reading practice is especially important to maintain and improve reading levels.

Ethnic and Racial Minorities Who Resist Reading

Some members of *ethnic and racial minorities* resist reading because of school instructional practices, teacher perceptions, low socioeconomic status, and self-perceptions molded by a cultural disbelief in the importance of intellectual development (Gilbert & Gilbert, 1998; Maynard, 2002; Tatum, 2005). The National Assessment for Educational Progress, since its inception in 1992, has reported a continuing reading achievement gap between whites and Asian Americans on the one hand and American Indians, Hispanics, and African Americans on the other. In 2005, the average reading scores for eighth-grade whites and Asian Americans was 271 versus 249 for American Indians, 246 for Hispanics, and 243 for African Americans (National Center for Education Statistics, 2005).

English Language Learners Who Resist Reading

Students learning English as a second language sometimes encounter difficulties in reading. Because they lack strong vocabularies and well-developed sentence structures in English to draw on when encountering English language texts, and because the texts they are asked to read often portray unfamiliar experiences and cultural norms, they have difficulty reading, so they avoid it whenever possible. This group is large and growing. In 2000, about three and a half million children between the ages of 5 and 17 in the United States spoke English less than "very well" (U.S. Census Bureau, 2000).

Boys Who Resist Reading

Boys who resist reading may do so in part because of the preponderance of female teachers in U.S. schools (75% in grades K–12) who tend to select reading materials that do not necessarily appeal to boys, according to Brozo (2005). Their resistance to reading also may stem from the perception that reading, because it is quiet and passive, is a female activity, or at least not macho. On average, boys exhibit more difficulty in reading and other language areas than girls (National Center for Education Statistics, 2005).

Not all young people who dislike reading school-based materials are resistant readers. Some, in fact, are avid readers, but of materials that schools do not traditionally recognize, such as magazines, Internet websites, and informational books (Taylor, 2004). Some boys, in particular, fit this profile. Two informative sources about boys and their reading are *Reading Don't Fix No Chevys: Literacy in the Lives of Young Men* (Smith & Wilhelm, 2002) and *Teaching Reading to Black Adolescent Males: Closing the Achievement Gap* (Tatum, 2005).

How do we inspire young people to love reading and to become aware of its power to inform, entertain, educate, and change? How do we instill in them the reading habit?

 ## Assisting Students in Book Selection

The aim of teachers, librarians, and publishers is to bring students to the reading habit by placing in their hands reading materials that will interest and not intimidate them. Publishers, aware of falling test scores in reading and the demand of the public and policymakers for schools to reverse this trend, have produced books written specifically for low-level readers. These include easy-to-read books for beginning readers and transitional books, generally short novels of about 100 pages with high-interest topics. Regardless of students' reading ability, promoting reading is partly a matter of helping students select appropriate and appealing reading materials. Note the success of various television programs, from *Reading Rainbow* to *Oprah Winfrey*, in convincing people to read recommended books. These programs and celebrities are saying, "I read this book and loved it. I recommend it to you." To be a successful promoter of reading, you yourself must be a reader. Recommending a book that you have enjoyed is an effective reading motivator.

The points made about quality and content of literature at the beginning of Chapter 1 definitely play a part in any book selection for children. In addition, you will want to consider the following suggestions.

Know the Books

Teachers and librarians who read children's books regularly, who are familiar with a wide variety of genres, and who are informed about recently published books are likely able to interest children in books. In Chapter 3, ways to interpret literature and the elements of fiction will be reviewed in order to assist you in thinking about and evaluating the books you are reading. It is advantageous to have read widely and to be able to share and compare your reactions to a book with children. Other ways to become familiar with a variety of genres include sharing information about books with your fellow teachers and reading book reviews. Chapter 3 lists the major book review journals.

Your own reading program can be made more effective by focusing on award-winning and notable books, as well as those selected for their appeal to individual children under your care. After you have read a number of books from a genre, particularly notable examples, you will develop a framework for thinking about books of that kind, whether or not you have read an individual title. You will, of course, want to have read any book you plan to read aloud to a class.

Know the Child

The best teachers know their students well. For instance, you will find it helpful to know your students—their long-term and short-term interests, their home environment (family makeup, siblings, pets), their friends and social activities, their hobbies, their skills (athletic, academic, artistic), their hopes or plans for the future, and the kind of books they are currently selecting in free-choice situations, such as during library visits and while perusing classroom collections of trade books. Children's interests have been shown to be one of the most powerful motivating forces available to teachers. Since there are now books on almost every topic conceivable and written at varying degrees of difficulty, you should be able to assemble a collection of books from which your students can make satisfying selections.

You will also want to have a grasp of your students' reading and listening levels. Often, children's abilities to read and listen are on different levels. Young children, in particular, are able to listen and comprehend more difficult material than they are able to read and comprehend. This difference is one that teachers accommodate by reading aloud more challenging books and providing a choice of easier reading material for students' independent reading.

Research on Children's Reading Interests

Research studies on reading interest, reading preference, and reading choice provide useful information to those who purchase books for children and those who encourage them to read the books. Although the terms to describe the various studies and the procedures used in conducting the studies may vary, the studies are trying to infer what students like to read. Generally, a ***reading interest*** suggests a feeling one has toward particular reading material; a ***reading preference*** implies making a choice from two or more options; a ***reading choice*** study investigates "print materials selected and read from a predetermined collection" (Chance, 1999, p. 65). The studies do not always provide an opportunity for students to express their interests. If, for example, the options do not include illustrated books, then students will not be able to select illustrated books. Although the findings from this body of research can be useful, it is important to realize that the results of these studies are based on group data or aggregated data and reflect the reading interests of groups of students, not individuals.

Many studies of children's reading interests have been conducted during the past fifty years. Differences in the choices offered to children and in the ways data were gathered from study to study make extensive generalization difficult, but a few patterns have emerged from these studies (Haynes, 1988):

- There are no significant differences between the reading preferences of boys and girls before age 9.
- The greatest differences in reading preferences of boys and girls occur between ages 10 and 13.
- Boys and girls in the middle grades (ages 10 to 13) share a pronounced preference for mystery and, to a lesser degree, humor, adventure, and animals.
- Preferences of boys in the middle grades include action and adventure stories and sports stories.
- Preferences of girls in the middle grades include fantasy stories, animal stories, and stories about people.

Certain characteristics of books may matter as much to a young reader as the topic. According to reports (Carter & Harris, 1982; Langerman, 1990; Worthy, 1996; Worthy, Moorman, & Turner, 1999; Worthy, Patterson, Salas, Prater, & Turner, 2002; Worthy, Turner, & Moorman, 1998) and our own observations in working with children, consideration needs to be given to the following characteristics:

- Short books or books with short sections or chapters
- Picture books, illustrated books, comic books, and novels in which illustrations are interspersed throughout the book
- Cover illustrations that suggest the topic of the story
- Episodic plots
- Progressive chronological plots that can be easily followed
- Quick start to the story with action beginning on the first or second page to hook the reader
- Rapid introduction to main characters and only a few main characters
- Characters the age of the reader or slightly older
- Books based on movies and television

In addition, trivia books such as the *Guinness Book of World Records*, sports statistics books, joke books, and game system guides for video and computer games are very appealing to some boys. Although you will want to motivate your students to enjoy books of excellent quality, the first step is to create in them an enthusiasm about books and reading. Once they are willing readers then you can find many opportunities to booktalk and read aloud excellent books that they will come to love and want to read independently.

A teacher or librarian might use the foregoing information to make general predictions about what types of books students of a certain age might enjoy. However, it is inadvisable to depend on the findings of reading interest studies as the sole guide in making specific book recommendations to individuals. General reading preferences do not capture individual reading interests. Knowledge of children's reading interests is personal and individual. Since most teachers and school librarians work with particular groups of children over an extended time, they can learn the interests of each child within the group. In doing this, they gain powerful, effective knowledge to use in successfully matching children and books.

 ## Discovering Reading Interests of Individual Students

Learning your students' reading interests can be accomplished in several ways. One effective method is observing your students' choices of books from the classroom collection or from the school library media center collection and then noting their choices by jotting down authors and titles of books selected. These notes can give you insight to their preferences. Getting to know your students by talking and listening to them in whole-class sharing and in one-to-one conferences are other effective means. All people like to talk about themselves and what interests them, and children are no exception. One or more of the following questions might start a productive dialogue between you and a student:

1. Who is in your family? Tell me about each family member.
2. What are your favorite things to do?
3. Are you very good at doing something? Tell me about it.
4. What would you like to learn more about?
5. What do you like to spend most of your free time doing?
6. Do you like fiction (stories) or nonfiction (information books) better?
7. What kinds of stories do you like to hear?
8. Which subjects do you enjoy reading about in information books?
9. Are there some kinds of books you don't enjoy reading? If so, why?
10. Tell me about a book that you especially enjoyed and why you enjoyed it.

You can also learn about children's interests through their free-choice writing. Journal writing is particularly helpful in this regard. A perfectly valid and more direct approach is to ask children to list their interests or the type of books they like to read. Many teachers keep such lists in their students' writing folders to use during individual conferences.

Yet another way for teachers and librarians to keep current on students' reading interests is to conduct their own *reading interest inventories* several times a year. The following steps show one way to conduct a classroom reading interest inventory:

1. Collect thirty to forty appropriate books that are new to your students and represent a wide variety of genres and topics.
2. Number the books by inserting paper markers with numbers at the top.

Figure 2.1   Sample Student Response Form for Reading Interest Inventory

Would You Like to Read This Book?

As you look at each book, answer this question by circling either YES or NO next to the appropriate book number. Be sure to match the book number and the item number before circling your answer. You will not be required to read the books, but your answers will help me select books for our classroom that you will like.

1. YES   NO
2. YES   NO
3. YES   NO
4. YES   NO
5. YES   NO

3. Note on a master list the number and genre of each book.
4. Design a response form for students, such as the one in Figure 2.1.
5. Place the books in numerical order on tables and shelves around the classroom or media center.
6. Give the students twenty to thirty minutes to make the circuit, peruse the books, and mark their response forms.
7. Collect and tally the students' responses and compare to your master list to arrive at the types of books in which your students are currently most interested.

Classroom reading interest inventories as demonstrated here not only provide teachers and librarians with helpful information about their students' current interests but they also have the added advantage of introducing children to new genres, topics, and actual titles. Many students will discover a book that they will want to read from the books set out in this manner. Teachers and librarians help accomplish the fundamental tasks of guiding students to good books and expanding their fields of interest and their knowledge bases.

Common sense tells us that children will apply themselves more vigorously to read or learn something that they are interested in than they will to read or learn something that they find uninteresting or boring. Interest generates motivation, and good teachers and librarians put that motivation to work by guiding students to good books on topics that satisfy their individual interests.

 ## Judging the Difficulty of Reading Materials

Two features of books for teachers and librarians to consider are the readability and conceptual difficulty of books. *Readability* is an estimate of a text's difficulty based on its vocabulary (common versus uncommon words) and sentence structure (short, simple sentences versus long, complex sentences). *Conceptual difficulty* pertains to the complexity of ideas treated in the work and how these ideas are presented. Symbolism, abstraction, and lengthy description contribute to the complexity of ideas, just as the use of flashback or shifting points of view contribute to the complexity of plot presentation.

Students' reading levels differ greatly in most classrooms, making it important to provide materials of varying difficulty. Being able to assess the difficulty of reading materials can be helpful to teachers and librarians, especially when locating lower-level materials. However, for independent, leisure reading, students should be encouraged to read books of interest to them regardless of the level, so long as they are capable of comprehending the material and want to read it. As adults, we do not decide to read a book because it is too easy for us; we should accord the same courtesy to young readers for their leisure reading if we wish to motivate them to be readers.

The long-standing system that has been used in education to assign reading levels to books has been readability formulas, such as the Fry Readability Graph (http://school.discovery.com/schrockguide/fry) and the Lexile Framework (www.lexile.com; Schnick, 2000). *Readability* is defined as "the ease of comprehension because of style of writing" (Harris & Hodges, 1995, p. 203). Syntactic length and vocabulary difficulty are usually measured by a variety of means that vary by readability formula. Generally, texts with shorter, less complex sentences and a predominance of common, high-frequency words, such as *because, little,* and *everyone,* are rated as easier to comprehend. Readability is expressed as a grade level (6.4 = sixth grade, fourth month) or as an age level (11.5 = eleven years and five months) and refers to the approximate grade or age at which an average individual will be able to read the text with comprehension. For example, using the Fry Readability Graph, we estimate that the well-known classic, *Charlotte's Web* (White, 1952), is written at a 5.3 grade level and a 10.4 age level. Using the same formula, we estimate that the Caldecott Award–winning picture book, *The Stray Dog* (Simont, 2001), is written at a 2.1 grade level and an 8.0 age level.

Publishers sometimes place readability information on book covers; some databases also include reading levels. Basal reading programs and reading incentive programs, such as *Accelerated Reader,* grade the books for student reading by such formulas. They tend to use different formulas, however, depending on the publisher.

A teacher who looks carefully at a book can assess its difficulty without using a formula, and most teachers do this with practice. Select a page of uninterrupted text, read the first sentence, count the words in the sentence, then look to see if this length appears to be typical of the rest of the page. Are the sentences generally short or long? Then read the page for word difficulty, noting words your students will likely not know. Are there many or few such words? Readers can, of course, figure out unknown words through context, if they are infrequent. You can estimate a book's difficulty in this way.

Readability formulas may be helpful to teachers, librarians, and parents in selecting books but they are not without their drawbacks. Different readability formulas give different estimates for the same book, so at best they give only a broad estimate of difficulty. Although the two factors of syntactic complexity and word choice are important, other factors make an important difference. A student's prior knowledge on a particular topic cannot be factored into any formula, nor can a student's interest in a topic be measured by formula. Yet we know that students' interest and background knowledge are central to their willingness to read and their ability to comprehend a text.

Conceptual difficulty is another factor not included in a readability formula. Conceptual difficulty pertains to the complexity of the ideas treated in the work and to how these ideas are presented. Symbolism, abstraction, and figurative language contribute to the complexity of ideas, just as the use of nonlinear plots or shifting points of view contribute to the complexity of plot presentation. Consider the work of magical realism, *Skellig* (Almond, 1999), in which two young persons become involved with an otherworldly being who is hidden in a garage. The text, having easy vocabulary and short sentences, has a readability of about grade 3.5. Yet the concepts of spirituality, faith, and prejudice cast the conceptual level of this novel at a much higher level, probably appropriate for students aged 11 to 15.

Readability is an issue only when the text is at such a high level that the reader cannot comprehend it. The challenge is to find materials for those students whose reading levels are lower. For this, we return to the experts, individual students, in determining what they can read. The teacher can help students decide whether books are too difficult for them by encouraging them to open a book they are considering reading to a middle page and reading through it while counting the number of words they do not understand or cannot read. If they count more than 5 or 6 words they cannot read or do not know out of every 100 words, they may want to choose a different book.

Reading Incentive Programs

Many elementary and middle schools have purchased commercially produced *reading incentive programs* to motivate students to read more widely. Generally these programs have computerized management components to track students' progress on the tests. These programs, such as *Accelerated Reader,* include a pretest for assigning a reading level to each student for a certain level of books that have a predetermined number of points according to their difficulty as determined by the program developers. After students finish reading a book silently, they complete a multiple-choice test to assess literal comprehension of the book and to earn points based on their score. Students earn prizes according to their performance.

Reports on the success of such programs are mixed. Many teachers and schools report disappointment in the programs. Teachers need to be cautious about whether such programs are having a positive impact on their students' interest in reading. Concerns include the following:

- Students' free choices of books for reading are limited.
- Students value only books in the program's database due to the reward system.
- Extrinsic rewards can diminish the desire of students to read for the pleasure of reading.
- Testing students' literal comprehension can undermine the importance of reading books for vicarious experiences.
- Tests of literal comprehension often emphasize inconsequential material to the detriment of the development of critical thinking in students.
- Many students find ways to gain the rewards without reading the books—for example, by asking other students for the answers, skimming the books for frequently tested details, and seeing the movie.
- Personal enjoyment of literature and reading is often deemphasized.
- These programs are very costly and could be replaced by simply purchasing ample trade books for classroom use and school libraries. The program selections can soon become dated, necessitating additional expenditures.

Teachers can design their own reading incentive programs that avoid these drawbacks and still help students develop as independent readers. In these teacher-developed programs, students usually keep a record of their own free-choice silent reading, have opportunities to respond to books in a variety of ways on a regular basis, and work to achieve individual silent reading goals set by the student and the teacher together. Rewards, such as a special celebration party, are provided for the class for reading, as a group, more total pages or books than were read during the last grading period. Such group rewards avoid the negative consequences of highly competitive programs.

Topics for Further Investigation

- Review studies on children's reading interests.
- As shown in this chapter, conduct a reading interest inventory of children in a class. Analyze your findings, then suggest to individual children appropriate titles for independent reading from books available in the school.
- Observe and document the reading habits and literary selections of three children over a period of several weeks. Select one avid reader, one typical reader, and one resistant reader for your observations.

 See the companion website at www.ablongman.com/lynchbrown6e for additional suggestions.

References

Almond, D. (1999). *Skellig.* New York: Delacorte.

Anderson, M. A., Tollefson, N. A., & Gilbert, E. C. (1985). Giftedness and reading: A cross-sectional view of differences in reading attitudes and behaviors. *Gifted Child Quarterly, 29*(4), 186–189.

Anderson, R., Wilson, P., & Fielding, L. (1988). Growth in reading and how children spend their time outside of school. *Reading Research Quarterly, 23*(3), 285–303.

Bradshaw, T., & Nichols, B. (2004). *Reading at risk: A survey of literary reading in America.* Research Division Report #46. Washington, DC: National Endowment for the Arts.

Brozo, W. G. (2005). Gender and reading literacy. *Reading Today, 22*(4), 18.

Carter, B., & Harris, K. (1982). What junior high students like in books. *Journal of Reading 26*(1), 42–46.

Chance, R. (1999). A portrait of popularity: An analysis of characteristics of novels from Young Adults' Choices for 1997. *The ALAN Review, 27*(1), 65–68.

Cline, R. K. L., & Kretke, G. L. (1980). An evaluation of long-term SSR in the junior high school. *Journal of Reading, 23*(6), 502–506.

Fielding, L. G., Wilson, P. T., & Anderson, R. C. (1986). A new focus on free reading: The role of trade books in reading instruction. In T. Raphael (Ed.), *The contexts of school-based literacy* (pp. 149–160). New York: Random House.

Gilbert, R., & Gilbert, P. (1998). *Masculinity goes to school.* New York: Routledge.

Harris, T. L., & Hodges, R. E. (1995). *The literacy dictionary: The vocabulary of reading and writing.* Newark, DE: International Reading Association.

Harrison, D. L. (1993). My book! In D. L. Harrison (Ed.), *Somebody catch my homework.* Illustrated by Betsy Lewin. Honesdale, PA: Boyds Mills.

Haynes, C. (1988). Explanatory power of content for identifying children's literature preferences. *Dissertation Abstracts International, 49—12A,* p. 3617 (University Microfilms No. DEW8900468).

Krashen, S. (1988). Do we learn to read by reading? The relationship between free reading and reading ability. In D. Tannen (Ed.), *Linguistics in context: Connecting observation and understanding* (pp. 269–298). Norwood, NJ: Ablex.

Langerman, D. (1990). Books and boys: Gender preferences and book selection. *School Library Journal 36*(3), 132–136.

Maynard, T. (2002). *Boys and literacy: Exploring the issues.* New York: Routledge.

McKenna, M., Ellsworth, R., & Kear, D. (1995). Children's attitudes toward reading: A national survey. *Reading Research Quarterly, 30*(4), 934–957.

Moore, D. W., Bean, T. W., Birdyshaw, D., & Rycik, J. A. (1999). *Adolescent literacy: A position statement.* Newark, DE: International Reading Association.

Mullis, I., Campbell, J., & Farstrup, A. (1993). *NAEP 1992: Reading report card for the nation and states.* Washington, DC: U.S. Department of Education.

National Center for Education Statistics. (2005). *The nation's report card: Reading 2005.* Retrieved from http://nces.ed.gov/nationsreportcard/pdf/main 2005.

National Reading Panel. (2000). *Teaching children to read.* NIH Publication No. 00-4769. Washington, DC: U.S. Government Printing Office.

Postlethwaite, T., & Ross, K. N. (1992). *Effective schools in reading: Implications for educational planners. An exploratory study.* The Hague: The International Association for the Evaluation of Educational Achievement.

Schnick, T. (2000). *The Lexile framework: An introduction for educators.* Durham, NC: MetaMetrics.

Shapiro, J., & White, W. (1991). Reading attitudes and perceptions in traditional and nontraditional reading programs. *Reading Research and Instruction, 30*(4), 52–66.

Simont, M. (2001). *The stray dog.* New York: Harper-Collins.

Smith, M. W., & Wilhelm, J. D. (2002). *Reading don't fix no Chevys: Literacy in the lives of young men.* Portsmouth, NH: Heinemann.

Stanovich, K. E. (1986). Matthew effects in reading: Some consequences of individual differences in the acquisition of literacy. *Reading Research Quarterly, 21*(4), 360–407.

Tatum, A. (2005). *Teaching reading to black adolescent males: Closing the achievement gap.* Portland, ME: Stenhouse.

Taylor, D. L. (2004). "Not just boring stories": Reconsidering the gender gap for boys. *Journal of Adolescent & Adult Literacy, 48*(4), 290–298.

United States Census Bureau. (2000). Retrieved from www.census.gov.

White, E. B. (1952). *Charlotte's web.* Illustrated by G. Williams. New York: Harper.

Worthy, J. (1996). Removing barriers to voluntary reading: The role of school and classroom libraries. *Language Arts, 73,* 483–492.

Worthy, J., Moorman, M., & Turner, M. (1999). What Johnny likes to read is hard to find in school. *Reading Research Quarterly, 34*(1), 12–27.

Worthy, J., Patterson, E., Salas, R., Prater, S., & Turner, M. (2002). "More than just reading": The human factor in reaching resistant readers. *Reading Research and Instruction, 41*(2), 177–202.

Worthy, J., Turner, M., & Moorman, M. (1998). The precarious place of free-choice reading. *Language Arts, 75,* 296–304.

chapter 3

Learning about Literature

A Book

I'm a strange contradiction; I'm new and I'm old,
I'm often in tatters, and oft deck'd in gold;
Though I never could read, yet letter'd I'm found;
Though blind, I enlighten; though loose, I am bound—
I am always in black, and I'm always in white;
I am grave and I'm gay, I am heavy and light.
In form too I differ—I'm thick and I'm thin,
I've no flesh, and no bones, yet I'm covered with skin;
I've more points than the compass, more stops than the flute—
I sing without voice, without speaking confute;
I'm English, I'm German, I'm French and I'm Dutch;
Some love me too fondly; some slight me too much;
I often die soon, though I sometimes live ages,
And no monarch alive has so many pages.

—Hannah More

This chapter provides background information on literature, including how to study and interpret literature, and reviews the elements of fiction useful in literary evaluation. Also discussed are sources available for identifying good books, including major children's book awards, review journals, and professional websites. The chapter ends with a discussion of the reasons to select a varied and balanced array of literature for use with children.

Approaches to Studying and Interpreting Literature

The scholarly study of literature generally focuses on the meaning found in a work of literature and how readers construct that meaning. When readers subject a work to deep analysis through exact and careful reading, it is referred to as *New Criticism* or *structural criticism.* In this approach, the analysis of the words and structure of a work is the focus; the goal is to find the "correct" interpretation.

Until the 1960s, structural criticism held sway in most literature classrooms. Many teachers continue to use this method today. Most teachers using this approach take the view that there is one correct interpretation of any work of literature. According to this view, reading is a process of taking from the text only what was put there by the author. Young readers' success with any work of literature is determined by how closely their interpretations match the "authorized" interpretation. Students' responses to literature are thus limited to naming (or guessing) the "right" answers to teachers' questions.

In 1938, Louise Rosenblatt introduced *reader response theory* or the *transactional view of reading.* She asserted that what the reader brings to the reading act—his or her world of experience, personality, and current frame of mind—is just as important in interpreting the text as what the author writes. According to this view, reading is a fusion of text and reader. Consequently, any text's meaning will vary from reader to reader and, indeed, from reading to reading of the same text by the same reader. Almost everyone has experienced reading a book only to discover that a friend has reacted to or interpreted the same book quite differently. Although Rosenblatt (1978) points out that the text of any book guides and constrains the interpretation that is made, an important corollary to her view of reading is that personal interpretations, within reason, are valid, permissible, and, in fact, desirable.

Beach and Marshall (1990) similarly point out the importance of students' worlds of experience, including (1) knowledge of various genres and literary forms gained from previous reading that can help them understand new, similar works; (2) social relationships that can help them understand and evaluate book characters' actions and motivations; (3) cultural knowledge that influences one's attitudes toward self and others (as in gender roles) and can help readers understand their responses to story events; and (4) topic knowledge or knowledge of the world that can deepen readers' understanding of a text and enrich their response to it.

Another interesting aspect of Rosenblatt's theory is that reading is done for two distinct purposes: to take knowledge from the text (*efferent reading*) and to live through a literary experience, in the sense of assuming the identity of a book character (*aesthetic reading*). Whether people read efferently or aesthetically depends on what they are reading (e.g., a want ad versus a mystery novel) and why they are reading it (e.g., for information versus for pleasure).

Rosenblatt's view of reading has important implications for the way teachers will encourage their students to respond to the literature they share with them. Reader response theory, in accepting different interpretations of the same literary work, accommodates both traditional, genre-specific works as well as genre-eclectic, nonlinear literature with its multiple perspectives and plots and its demands on the reader to act as coauthor. See Chapter 13 for a detailed discussion, suggestions, and explanations of literature-related response activities.

Reading is a merging of text and reader, and each reading of a particular literary work results in a different transaction. But if the transaction is unique each time a book is read, how can general assessments of literary merit be made? Rosenblatt believes that although the notion of a single, correct reading of a literary work is rejected, *"given agreed-upon criteria, it is possible to decide that some readings are more defensible than others"* (1985, p. 36). Although each reading of a given literary work will be different, there are certain generally agreed upon interpretations of that work by a community of educated readers.

Traditional literary elements are reviewed next in order to heighten your awareness of literary criticism and to provide a more precise vocabulary for you to express your responses to children's books. Literary terms may also be considered as tools that your students can use to initiate and sustain conversations about literature. In using these terms in the classroom you can help children acquire a literary vocabulary.

Elements of Fiction

Learning to evaluate children's books can best be accomplished by reading as many excellent books as possible. Gradually, your judgment on the merits of individual books will improve. Discussing your responses to these books with children, teachers, and other students and listening to their responses will also assist you in becoming a more appreciative critic. Understanding the different parts, or elements, of a piece of fiction and how they work together can help you become more analytical about literary works; and this, too, can improve your judgment of literature. The elements of fiction are discussed separately in the following sections, but it is the unity of all these elements that produces the story.

Plot

The events of the story and the sequence in which they are told constitute the ***plot*** of the story. In other words, the plot is what happens in the story. Plot is the most important element of fiction to the child reader. Often, adults believe that a story for children needs only to present familiar, everyday activities—the daily routines of life. Perhaps 2- and 3-year-olds will enjoy hearing narratives such as this, but by age 4, children want to find more excitement in books. A good plot produces conflict to build the excitement and suspense that are needed to keep the reader involved.

The nature of the *conflict* within the plot can arise from different sources. The basic conflict may be one that occurs within the main character, called ***person-against-self.*** In this type of story, the main character struggles against inner drives and personal tendencies to achieve some goal. Stories about adolescence will frequently have this conflict as the basis of the story problem. For example, in *Ghost Boy* (2000) by Iain Lawrence, 14-year-old Harold struggles to find himself and to accept himself and others.

A conflict usually found in survival stories is the struggle the character has with the forces of nature. This conflict is called ***person-against-nature.*** Worthy examples are *Ice Drift* (2004) by Theodore Taylor, *The Young Man and the Sea* (2004) by Rodman Philbrick, and *Hatchet* (1987) by Gary Paulsen.

In other children's stories, the source of the conflict is found between two characters. Conflicts with peers, problems with sibling rivalries, and stories of children rebelling against an adult are **person-against-person** conflicts. For example, in *Bucking the Sarge* (2004) by Christopher Paul Curtis, 15-year-old Luther's conflict is with his mother, whose views on right and wrong collide with his own.

Occasionally, a story for children presents the main character in conflict with society. This conflict in children's stories is most often either about the environment being destroyed by new technology or changing times or about children caught up in a political upheaval such as war. The conflict is then called **person-against-society.** *Shades of Gray* (1989) by Carolyn Reeder and *Yellow Star* (2006) by Jennifer Roy, both war stories, pose this type of conflict. In the mystery *Hoot* (2002) by Carl Hiaasen, the conflict is between those who want to develop and destroy natural areas and wildlife and those who want to preserve them.

In some stories, the protagonist faces **multiple conflicts** in which, for example, a character may be in conflict with society and also in a conflict with self. In Jean Craighead George's *Julie of the Wolves* (1972), protagonist Julie/Miyax rebels against the societal changes that threaten the wildlife in her native Alaska while at the same time seeks to resolve her own conflicting thoughts about her Inuit traditions and modern society.

Plots are constructed in many different ways. The most common plot structures found in children's stories are **chronological plots,** which cover a particular period of time and relate the events in order within the time period. For example, if a book relates the events of one week, then Monday's events will precede Tuesday's, and so on. *Lizzie Bright and the Buckminster Boy* (2004) by Gary D. Schmidt as well as the classic *Charlotte's Web* (1952) by E. B. White have chronological plots.

Two distinct types of chronological plots are progressive plots and episodic plots. In books with **progressive plots,** the first few chapters are the exposition, in which the characters, setting, and basic conflict are established. Following the expository chapters, the story builds through rising action to a climax. The climax occurs, a satisfactory conclusion (or dénouement) is reached, and the story ends. Figure 3.1 suggests how a progressive, chronological plot might be visualized.

An **episodic plot** ties together separate short stories or episodes, each an entity in itself with its own conflict and resolution. These episodes are typically unified by the same cast of characters and the same setting. Often, each episode comprises a chapter. Although the episodes are usually chronological, time relationships among the episodes may be nonexistent or loosely connected by "during that same year" or "later that month." Examples of short chapter books with an episodic plot structure are *Ramona Quimby, Age 8* (1981) by Beverly Cleary and *26 Fairmount Avenue* (1999) by Tomie dePaola. Because episodic plots are less complex, they tend to be easier to read

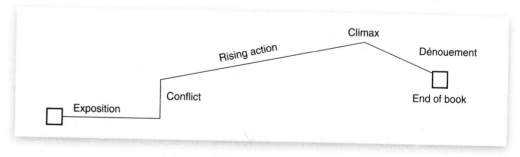

Figure 3.1   Diagram of a Progressive Plot

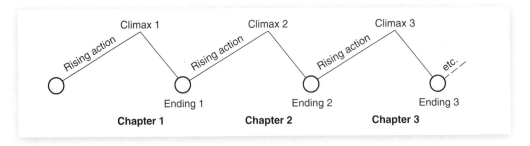

Figure 3.2   Diagram of an Episodic Plot

and lend themselves to the recounting of humorous escapades. Thus, the reader who is just making the transition from picture books to chapter books may find these plots particularly appealing. Many easy-to-read books for the beginning reader are also structured in this way. *Frog and Toad Are Friends* (1970) by Arnold Lobel and *Mr. Putter & Tabby Feed the Fish* (2001) by Cynthia Rylant are good examples of an episodic plot in an easy-to-read book. Figure 3.2 suggests how a chronological, episodic plot might be visualized.

Authors use a ***flashback*** to convey information about events that occurred earlier—for example, before the beginning of the first chapter. In this case, the chronology of events is disrupted, and the reader is taken back to an earlier time. Flashbacks can occur more than once and in different parts of a story. The use of a flashback permits authors to begin the story in the midst of the action but later fill in the background for full understanding of the present events. Flashbacks in children's books are mostly found in chapter books for older readers, since such plots can confuse children younger than age 8 or 9. Teachers can help students understand this plot structure by reading aloud good examples of this type of story, such as Jean Craighead George's *My Side of the Mountain* (1959) and *Chasing Redbird* (1997) by Sharon Creech. Class discussion can then focus on the sequence of events and why the author may have chosen to relate the events in this manner. Figure 3.3 illustrates the structure of a flashback in a book in which some events occurred before the beginning of the book.

With greater frequency, children's novels are appearing with new plot formulations such as ***complex multiple plots*** in which the traditional chronology is replaced by nonlinear plots that occur simultaneously. In Louis Sachar's *Holes* (1998), a humorous mystery and survival story, two apparently unrelated stories set in two different time periods are developed, yet are gradually revealed to be connected to one another through the unraveling of the mystery. Other stories are told through a multiplicity of protagonists each of whom has a vantage point from which to unfold some portion of the story being told. Paul Fleischman's *Bull Run* (1993) captures the events and context of the Civil War through various characters whose vignettes feature several aspects in the run-up to the first battle of the Civil War, events during the battle from different parts of the war theatre, and the aftermath of the battle, experienced by the various characters.

A stylistic plot device that prepares readers for coming events in a story is ***foreshadowing***. This device gives clues to a later event, possibly even the climax of the story. For example, in the first chapter of Kenneth Oppel's *Airborn* (2004), the cabin boy's chance meeting and rescue of a

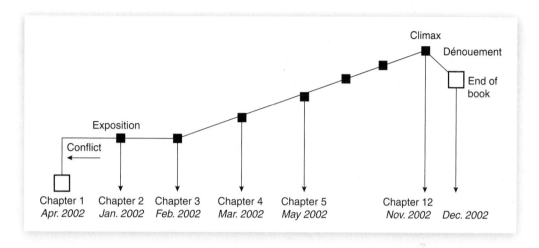

Figure 3.3   Diagram of a Flashback

dying balloonist who shares his tales of strange flying creatures foreshadows events to come a year later and prepares readers for the cabin boy's pivotal role in these events. Also, in the classic novel *Tuck Everlasting* (1975) by Natalie Babbitt, the detailed description of the long yellow road in the first chapter foreshadows the long journey the Tuck family members must travel in their lives. You can alert young readers to one of the subtle ways authors prepare them for the outcomes of stories by discussing foreshadowing.

Plot is an important element to all readers, but especially to young readers, who enjoy fast-moving, exciting stories. A well-constructed plot contributes substantially to children's acceptance and enjoyment of stories.

Characters

Memorable characters populate the world of children's literature. Ferdinand the bull, Charlotte the spider, Frances the badger, Little Toot the young tugboat, Karana the Native American girl, and Peter the African-American child with his dog, Willie, are all remembered fondly by generations of readers.

Characters, the "actors" in a story, are another element of fiction vital to the enjoyment of a story. A well-portrayed character can become a friend, a role model, or a temporary parent to a child reader. Although young readers enjoy exciting events, the characters involved in those events must matter to the reader, or the events no longer seem important. How characters are depicted and how they develop in the course of the story are important to the reader. Two aspects to consider in studying a character are characterization and character development.

Characterization refers to the way an author helps the reader know a character. The most obvious way an author can do this is to describe the character's physical appearance and personality. Portraying the character's emotional and moral traits or revealing her relationships with other characters are more subtle and effective techniques. In the most convincing characterizations, we see the character through a combination of her own actions and dialogue, the responses of other characters to her, and the narrator's descriptions.

Character development refers to the changes, good or bad, the character undergoes during the course of events in the story. If a character experiences significant, life-altering events, we, as readers, expect that the character will somehow be different as a result of those events. For example, Matt, a boy of 11, who was left alone for months in the Maine territory to take care of his family's new cabin, becomes a stronger, more independent young man by the end of *The Sign of the Beaver* (1973) by Elizabeth George Speare. Also, in Peggy Brooke's *Jake's Orphan* (2000), 12-year-old orphan Tree grows up as he struggles to find a home for himself and his younger brother on a North Dakota farm in 1926.

In a work of fiction for children there are usually one or two main characters and some minor characters. Ideally, each main character, sometimes called the *protagonist,* will be a fully described, complex individual who possesses both good and bad traits, like a real person. Such a character is called a *round character.* For example, in the historical fiction novel *Catherine, Called Birdy* (1994) by Karen Cushman, Birdy, the protagonist whose father is seeking a suitable husband for her, is presented as a complex character with many strengths and weaknesses. In the realistic fiction novel *A Step from Heaven* (2001) by An Na, young Ju, the protagonist whose Korean family immigrates to America, is presented as a round, complex character dealing with the many challenges an immigrant must face.

Minor, or *secondary, characters* may be described in a partial or less complete manner. The extent of description depends on what the reader needs to know about the character for a full understanding of the story. Some of the minor character's traits are described fully, whereas other facets of the character's personality may remain obscure. Because the purpose is to build the story and make it comprehensible, fragmentary knowledge of a minor character may suffice. In the novel *Under the Red-Blood Sun* (1994) by Graham Salisbury, Billy Wilson is portrayed as a loyal friend to Tomi, the protagonist, in this story about the treatment of Tomi's Japanese family in Hawaii during World War II. Occasionally, an author will insert a *flat character*—that is, a character described in a one-sided or underdeveloped manner. Although such people do not exist in real life, they may be justified within the story to propel the plot. Sometimes the character is shown as an all-evil or all-frivolous person; for instance, folktales present flat characters as symbols of good and evil. In some stories, a flat character plays the role of *character foil,* a person who is in direct juxtaposition to another character (usually the protagonist) and who serves to highlight the characteristics of the other individual. A character foil may occur as a flat or as a round character. For example, the neighborhood bully, Beans, who was pushing 10-year-old Palmer to participate in wringing the necks of pigeons as part of the town's annual Family Fest, is portrayed as a flat character in *Wringer* (1997) by Jerry Spinelli. The character or force that is in direct opposition to the main character is called the *antagonist.* In Avi's *The True Confessions of Charlotte Doyle* (1990), the ship's captain is a frightening antagonist to Charlotte. And in the sports story *Offsides* (2004) by Erik Eskilsen, protagonist Tom Gray, the star soccer player, challenges the school's mascot that stereotypes Native Americans and stands up to his coach, one of the antagonists.

The main characters in an excellent work of fiction for children are rounded, fully developed characters who undergo change in response to life-altering events. Because children generally prefer personified animals or children of their own age, or slightly older, as the main characters of their stories, authors of children's books often face a dilemma. Although in real life, children usually have restricted freedom of action and decision making within the confines of a family, the author can develop a more vivid and exciting story if the main characters are "on their own." Thus, in many children's stories, parents are absent, no longer living, or no longer functioning. Furthermore, by making up situations, authors are able to focus on just one aspect of life, thereby enabling young readers to see and understand this one facet of life more clearly.

Setting

The time when the story occurs and the place(s) where it occurs constitute the setting of a story. The setting has a more or less important function depending on the story. For example, in historical fiction the authentic re-creation of the period is essential to the comprehension of the story's events. In this situation, the setting, fully described in both time and place, is called an *integral setting.* The story could not be the same if placed in another setting. For example, in the historical novel *Bull Run* (1993) by Paul Fleischman, battle maps are included, and many of the sixteen characters whose points of view are presented discuss the battlegrounds.

By contrast, the setting in folktales is often vague and general. For example, "long ago in a cottage in the deep woods" is meant to convey a universal, timeless tale, one that could have happened anywhere and almost anytime except the present or very recent past. This type of setting is called a *backdrop setting.* It simply sets the stage and the mood.

Theme

The literary theme of a story is its underlying meaning or significance. The term *theme* should not be confused with topic or theme as used in the sense of a thematic unit. Although we sometimes think of the literary *theme* as the message or moral of the story, it can just as likely be an aesthetic understanding, such as an appreciation for nature or a viewpoint on a current societal issue. To identify the theme, you may ask yourself what the author's purpose was in writing the story or what the author is saying through this story.

A theme is better expressed by means of a complete sentence than by a single word. For example, students often suggest that a theme found in *Charlotte's Web* (1952) by E. B. White is friendship. A better statement of the theme is "Friendship is one of the most satisfying things in the world," as Wilbur the pig tells us in the story. The single word *friendship* may be a topic found in the story, but it is not an expression of the theme. Similarly, the phrase, "loss of a parent" incompletely expresses the theme of *Belle Prater's Boy* (1996) by Ruth White. "Facing the loss of a parent is slow and difficult, but reaching out to others can help" more clearly states the theme.

Themes in children's books should be worthy of children's attention and should convey truth to them. Furthermore, the themes should be based on high moral and ethical standards. A theme must not overpower the plot and characters of the story, however; children read fiction for enjoyment, not for enlightenment. If the theme is expressed in a heavy-handed, obvious fashion, then the pleasure of the reading experience is diminished. Likewise, overly "teachy" or didactic themes detract from a reader's enjoyment of a story. Certainly a well-written book may convey a moral message, but it should also tell a good story from which the message evolves. In this way the theme is subtly conveyed to the reader. For example, in the picture book *Heroes* (1995), written by Ken Mochizuki and illustrated by Dom Lee, Donnie's dad and uncle help Donnie and his friends discover that peaceful alternatives to war exist.

Often, adults write stories not for children's pleasure but to teach morality lessons. Although we think of stories of this sort as the thinly disguised religious tracts found in the early history of children's literature, we must be alert to a tendency for some current authors to use children's literature as a platform to preach about drug abuse, animal rights, and other issues of contemporary interest. If the literary quality of these so-called problem novels is weakened, then the story and characters become secondary to the issue or problem. However, when moral values are embedded within the fabric of a powerful story, children can be led to develop a sense of right and wrong without feeling as if they are being indoctrinated.

Style

Style is the way an author tells the story; it can be viewed as the writing itself, as opposed to the content of the book. However, the style must suit the content of the particular book; the two are intertwined.

Different aspects of style are considered in evaluating a work of fiction. Most obviously, you can look at the *words* chosen to tell the story. Are they long or short, common or uncommon, rhyming or melodic, boring and hackneyed or rich and challenging, unemotional or emotional, standard dialect or regional/minority dialect? The words should be appropriate to the story being told. As an evaluator of books for children, you will want to ask the following questions as you read: Why did the author choose these words? What effect was the author trying to achieve?

The *sentences* may also be considered. Do they read easily? Do they flow without the reader needing to reread to gain the meaning of the text? Sometimes an author chooses to limit the word choices to write a book that can be read by a beginning reader. Yet in the hands of a gifted writer, the sentences will remain no less melodic, varied in length and structure, and enjoyable to read and hear than sentences in the best books for the more advanced reader. Good examples of well-written books for beginning readers are Arnold Lobel's *Frog and Toad Are Friends* (1970) and *Power and Glory* (1996) by Emily Rodda.

The *organization* of the book may be considered by noting the paragraphs and transitions, length of chapters, headings and chapter titles, preface, endnotes, prologue, epilogue, and length of the book. For the beginning reader it is important whether a story is divided into chapters. After years of looking at, listening to, and reading books without chapters, it is quite an accomplishment for a 6-year-old to move up to so-called chapter books, even if each chapter is only three pages long.

Chapter titles can provoke interest in what will follow, as well as provide the reader with clues to predict story events. Some books provide the readers with a *prologue,* an introductory statement telling events that precede the start of the story. Some authors include an *epilogue,* a concluding statement telling events that occur after the story has ended. Adeline Yen Mah, author of *Chinese Cinderella: The True Story of an Unwanted Daughter* (1999), speaks directly to the reader in an informative prologue about the Chinese language. She invites the reader to become interested in a Chinese girl's language, history, and culture.

In *Kipling's Choice* (2005) by Geert Spillebeen, an epilogue has been included to provide information on the historical context of World War I in France. Other times, an epilogue resolves questions readers may have regarding what happened after the story's conclusion, as in Marion Dane Bauer's *A Bear Named Trouble* (2005), a story of companionship between a wild bear cub and a lonely boy.

Point of view is another aspect of an author's style. If the story is told through the eyes and voice of a ***third-person narrator*** (the use of *he, she, it*), then the reader can know whatever the narrator knows about the events of the story. In many stories, the narrator is ***omniscient*** and can see into the minds of all characters and be at many places at the same time. The reader of E. B. White's *Charlotte's Web* (1952) can understand and interpret the story from many different perspectives because of White's use of the omniscient point of view. In *Loser* (2002), Jerry Spinelli also draws on the omniscient narrative point of view to relate the story of Donald Zinkoff, whose enthusiasm and exuberance are unabated in spite of being seen as a loser by classmates.

Other stories are narrated from the perspective of only one character in the story. In this case, the story is still told in the third person, but the reader knows only what that particular character can see and understand. This latter technique is called ***limited omniscient*** point of view. Beverly Cleary's *Dear Mr. Henshaw* (1983) is a realistic story told from the perspective of Leigh, a boy troubled by family difficulties and changes at school, who corresponds with Mr. Henshaw, an author. In *Clay* (2006) by David Almond, disturbing events are told through the point of view of altar boy Davie, who becomes part of those events.

Other times, authors choose to tell the story through a ***first-person narrator*** (the use of *I*), generally the main character of the story. In such cases the reader gains a sense of closeness to the main character but is not privy to any information unavailable to this character. As you read, you will note that some authors have accomplished a first-person point of view by writing as though their main character were writing a diary or letters, as in *Flight to Freedom* (2002) by Ana Veciana-Suarez. Occasionally, a story is told in first person through the eyes of a minor character. For example, *Faith and the Electric Dogs* (1996) by Patrick Jennings is a humorous fantasy novel about 10-year-old Faith told through the first-person narration of Eddie, a stray dog.

A ***shifting point of view*** permits the reader to see events from different characters' points of view. This technique is demanding on young readers' skill. When the point of view shifts, the author must carefully cue readers to the changing point of view, as Avi does in *Nothing but the Truth* (1991) by identifying sender, receiver, or discussants at the beginning of each letter, memorandum, telephone call, or face-to-face conversation. Beverley Naidoo's *Web of Lies* (2006), a sequel to her award-winning *The Other Side of Truth* (2001) about Sade and her brother Femi, two Nigerian refugee children, relates the story of the children's school experiences in London by shifting between their two points of view.

Symbolism is an artistic invention that authors use to suggest invisible or intangible meanings by analogy to something else through association, resemblance, or convention. Often, a symbol—a person, object, or situation—represents an abstract or figurative meaning in the story in addition to its literal meaning. Some symbols are universal and can be found repeatedly in literary works; others may be particular to the story. For example, a farm usually represents love and security in works of literature. Children often read only on a literal level, but they can be helped by teachers to note more obvious symbols existing in the books they are reading. If the symbolic feature recurs in the story, it is referred to as a ***motif***. The number 3 is a common motif in folktales, for example.

A story for children must be more than a plot and a character study; a story integrates all the elements of fiction into a pleasing whole. In drawing together these elements, authors create new worlds for young readers.

 ## Changes in Traditional Fictional Forms

Following World War II, the traditional way of telling stories began to change; some works that no longer fit well-known and accepted patterns of fiction appeared and gained recognition, especially in adult fiction. The postmodern movement in literature emerged. According to *Merriam-Webster's Encyclopedia of Literature, postmodern* refers to "any of several artistic movements that have challenged the philosophy and practices of modern arts or literature since about the 1940s. In literature this has amounted to a reaction against fixed ideas about the form and meaning of texts" (Kuiper, 1995, p. 899). Although it began as a trend in adult literature, postmodernism in works for children and young adults is increasing.

Nikolajeva (1998) points out the defining characteristics of the postmodern literary work, the most recognized of which is genre eclecticism—writing that has aspects of more than one genre and ready acceptance of elements of popular culture such as film and television. Postmodern literature is also characterized by narrative structures that mirror life. That is, there are not necessarily distinct beginnings, middles, and endings; stories can be emotion driven rather than event driven; and stories may include multiple protagonists, perspectives, and narrators. Some postmodern stories include multiple plots or realities with parallel times and places. Authors of postmodern works encourage readers to take a more active role in the storytelling. Postmodernism has helped broaden the types of literature accepted into the mainstream, including graphic novels, novels in verse, docudramas, and novels of mixed genres.

 ## Book Format

Children's books are more than text or text and pictures combined. Other parts of a book contribute to the final product we call a book. The ***dust jacket*** is a removable paper cover wrapped around the book; it serves as protection against soiling. It also attracts purchasers and readers as well as informs them about the book, its author, and its illustrator. The *covers* of a book are usually made of two boards, which make the book more durable and allow it to stand on a shelf. When no dust jacket is on a book, the front cover provides the reader with a first impression of the story. The *title,* an important part of the text—usually first seen by the reader on the dust jacket or front cover—combines with the illustrations of the dust jacket or cover to communicate the nature of the story to young readers who choose books primarily by title and cover. Many titles suggest the topic of the story and can assist readers in deciding whether to read the book. Other titles and covers may not offer as much information about the story. In such cases, some explanation by a teacher or librarian in the form of a booktalk may prove invaluable to young readers seeking just such a book.

The *endpapers* are the pages glued to the inside front and back boards of the cover, and the *flyleaf* is the page facing each endpaper. In many fine, well-illustrated books, the endpaper and flyleaf are used to provoke curiosity in the reader for what follows, to set a mood, or to evoke an affective response in preparation for the story. Often, those first colors and first decorative touches are the visual introduction to the story. When readers turn the flyleaf, they are further prepared by the artist for the story by viewing the title page. The *title page* tells the book's full title and sub-title, if there is one; the names of the author(s) and illustrator(s); and the name and location of the publisher. Occasionally, a book will include a *frontispiece,* an illustration facing the title page, which is intended to establish the tone and to entice the reader to begin the story.

On the reverse side of the title page, often referred to as the *verso* of the title page, is the *publishing history* of the book. On this page is the copyright notice, a legal right giving only the holder permission to produce and sell the work. Others who wish to reproduce the work in any way must request permission from the copyright holder. The copyright is indicated by the international symbol ©. This symbol is followed by the name of the person(s) holding the copyright and the date it takes effect, which is the year the book is first published. Later publications are also listed. The country in which the book was printed, the number assigned to the book by the Library of Congress, the International Standard Book Number (ISBN), and the edition of the book are also included on this page. Many publishers now include on this page cataloguing information for libraries, a very brief annotation of the story, and a statement on the media and techniques used in the illustrations.

The title page typically presents the *typeface,* the style of print to be used throughout the book. The size and legibility of the typeface must be suited to the book's intended audience. In children's books this can be extremely important. Books for the young child who is just learning to read should have large, well-spaced print for easy eye scanning. The print style for an easy-to-read book should be a somewhat larger-than-average standard block print with easily distinguishable and recognizable uppercase and lowercase letters. Many children's trade books are now being produced in "big book" size for beginning reading activities with a whole class or group of children. In this case, the print needs to be large enough to be readily seen from a distance of 10 to 12 feet minimum. Legibility is diminished when background colors are used behind the text, leaving insufficient contrast for easy reading.

The size, shape, and darkness of the print type may vary from book to book. The lines may be heavy and strong or light and willowy. The choice of print type should enhance the overall visual message of the illustrations and fit with the illustrations in style and mood. Note also that the placement of the print on the pages in relation to the illustrations can subtly guide the reader and become a functional part of the story.

Unusual print styles are sometimes selected for a children's book. In a book with a diary format, the use of script print gives the impression of handwriting. In this case, the amount of script print is usually brief, and standard block print is used throughout most of the book for greater ease of reading. In place of print some illustrators choose to hand-letter the text. Classic examples of lettering as part of the illustrative component of a book are found in *Millions of Cats* (1928) by Wanda Gág and in *Fox* (2001) by Margaret Wild and illustrated by Ron Brooks.

The *page layout* is also worth observing. You will notice that illustrations are variously placed one on a page, on facing pages, on alternating pages, or on parts of pages. When the picture extends across the two facing pages, it is called a *doublespread.* A doublespread gives the effect of motion, since the eye is drawn to the next page. It can also give a feeling of grandeur, openness, and expansiveness. Sometimes, a picture will begin on a right-hand page and spill over to the following page, the reverse side. This offers a strong sense of continuity from one part of the story to the next. Some pictures have a *frame.* Framing of a picture can work to distance the reader from the action, lend a sense of order to the story, or make the mood more formal. The frame itself may be anything from a simple line to a broad, ornately decorated ribbon of information. Decorations on a frame may repeat certain images or symbols to reinforce the meaning of the story.

Pages are another part of the book makeup. In evaluating the pages, you should ask yourself, What is the quality of the paper? Is it thick, high quality? Is it glossy or textured, white or colored? Are the pages square, rectangular, or shaped in the form of a concrete object? Are they in keeping with the rest of the book? Are unique or unusual page formats, such as half-pages, see-through pages, engineered pages, or partial pages, appropriate and logical?

The *size* of the book is also worth noting. Large picture books are well suited for reading aloud to a class. Smaller picture books are usually not satisfactory choices for read-alouds, unless, of course, you are reading to only one child or to a small group of children.

Next, consider the *book binding.* Books may be bound in hard cover, paperback, or in some special-purpose material. For example, books for babies are frequently bound in sturdy cardboard or vinyl to withstand the dual role of toy and book. When buying a hardcover book, determine whether the binding is glued or sewn. Look for the stitching. Sewn bindings last much longer than glued ones. Durability relative to cost is the usual trade-off you must weigh in selecting paper or hardcover bindings for classroom or school libraries. Generally speaking, the cost of hardcover books is justified when you expect fairly heavy use.

Book Awards

Several book award programs have been established for the purposes of elevating and maintaining the literary and artistic standards of children's books and for honoring the authors whose work is judged by experts in the field to have the greatest merit. These awards provide teachers and librarians with one source for selecting excellent works of literature to share with children. Table 3.1 lists what are considered to be the major awards for children's books in the United States, Canada, and Great Britain. Lists of actual winners of these major children's book awards listed in Table 3.1 and other awards, such as awards for a specific genre or topic, can be found in Appendix A.

Review Journals

Journals that review children's books and feature current topics in the field of children's literature are an important source of information for teachers and librarians. Language-related professional teacher journals to which elementary teachers often subscribe, *The Reading Teacher* and *Language Arts,* have columns devoted to reviewing new children's books in each monthly issue. *The Journal of Children's Literature,* a journal dedicated solely to children's literature and those

Table 3.1   Major U.S., Canadian, and British Children's Book Awards

Award/Country	Period	For/Year Established
Newbery Medal/United States	Annual	The most distinguished contribution to children's literature published in the previous year. Given to a U.S. author. Established 1922.
Caldecott Medal/United States	Annual	The most distinguished picture book for children published in the previous year. Given to a U.S. illustrator. Established 1938.
Coretta Scott King Awards for writing and for illustration/United States	Annual, two awards	Outstanding inspirational and educational contribution to literature for children and young people by an African-American author/illustrator published in the previous year. Established 1970/1974.
Mildred L. Batchelder Award/United States	Annual	The most distinguished translated work for children published in the previous year. Given to a U.S. publisher. Established 1968.
Pura Belpré Awards for writing and illustration/United States	Biennial, two awards	Writing and illustration in a work of literature for youth published in the previous two years by a Latino writer and illustrator whose work best portrays, affirms, and celebrates the Latino cultural experience. Established 1996.
Governor General's Literature for Children Award for Writing/Canada	Annual	Best book for children published in the previous year. Separate prizes for works in English and French. Established 1987.
Governor General's Literature for Children Award for Illustration/Canada	Annual	Best illustration in a children's work published in the previous year. Separate prizes for works in English and French. Established 1987.
Carnegie Medal/Great Britain	Annual	The most distinguished contribution to children's literature first published in the United Kingdom the previous year. Given to an author. Established 1936.
Kate Greenaway Medal/Great Britain	Annual	The most distinguished picture book for children first published in the United Kingdom in the previous year. Given to an illustrator. Established 1956.

involved in it, also has review sections of newly published children's books. In addition, these journals contain articles discussing effective strategies for incorporating literature into reading and content-area instruction and for bringing children and books together.

The review journals listed here offer evaluative annotations and suggested grade-level ranges for books reviewed. These journals are readily available in most university libraries as well as some school and public libraries.

- *Booklist.* This journal reviews current print and nonprint materials for children and adults that are worthy of consideration for purchase by public libraries and school media centers.
- *The Bulletin of the Center for Children's Books.* This publication reviews current children's books with adverse as well as favorable reviews, assigning a recommendation code to each.
- *The Horn Book Magazine.* This magazine includes detailed reviews of children's books deemed worthy in children's literature. The Newbery and Caldecott acceptance speeches are features in the July/August issue.
- *Kirkus Reviews.* This publication annually reviews approximately 5,000 titles of prepublication books for adults and children with both adverse and favorable reviews.
- *School Library Journal for Children's, Young Adult, and School Librarians.* This journal prints both negative and positive reviews of most children's books published. It also includes articles of interest to school librarians.

 ## Professional Websites

The following websites are helpful in locating professional information about children's literature:

Association for Library Service to Children (ALSC) Site: www.ala.org/alsc
This professional association site includes the Newbery and Caldecott home pages. New awards are announced on this site.

Carol Hurst's Children's Literature Site: www.carolhurst.com
This educational consultant's site provides a collection of book reviews, curriculum ideas, themes, and professional topics for teachers.

Children's Book Council (CBC) Site: www.cbcbooks.org
This nonprofit association of children's book publishers offers book-related literacy materials for children. It also provides updates on National Children's Book Week.

Children's Literature Site: www.childrenslit.com
Founded in 1993, this independent review-media site includes information about authors and illustrators, special monthly features, recommended book lists, and announcements of book events.

Cooperative Children's Book Center Site: www.education.edu/ccbc
This children's literature examination and research library site provides information about its collections, upcoming events, and publications.

The Looking Glass: An Online Children's Literature Journal: www.the-looking-glass.net
 Founded in 1997, this electronic journal about children's literature is international in terms
 of topic and approach. Most contributors have a Canadian connection.

Balance and Variety in Book Selections

In addition to evaluating the various literary elements that are central to the issue of quality, the child's age and development and the balance and variety among books are also important considerations. Because children in any elementary-grade class have a wide range of reading abilities and reading interests, you need to provide many different types of books, including picture books, easy-to-read books, short chapter books, longer books, and books of prose, poetry, fiction, and nonfiction. Thus, balance among the *genres of literature* as well as *variety in topic* are essential.

Which stories teachers choose to read aloud to students is important. Varying choices for read-alouds will challenge students and enhance the resulting academic benefits for their language and cognitive development, as discussed in Chapter 1. In sharing books with students the *mood* of the books must also be varied to include stories that are sad, humorous, silly, serious, reflective, boisterous, suspenseful, or even a little scary. A steady diet of light, humorous books might appeal to students at first, but eventually, the sameness will become boring. For a teacher to read aloud over many months works of literature with the same predominant emotion is to ignore the rapid change and growth in personal lives and choices that are the hallmark of youth.

A balance between male and female main characters over the course of a year is necessary if you are to meet the needs of children of both sexes and to help members of each sex understand more fully the perspectives, problems, and feelings of members of the opposite sex. Classroom and school library collections need to have a wide range of topics with a balance of male and female main characters.

In addition, understanding and empathy for people with physical, emotional, mental, and behavioral disabilities can be gained through portrayals in books of children and adults with impairments. A positive image of people with disabilities needs to be conveyed in these books. Furthermore, children with disabilities need to see characters like themselves in books.

The representation of minorities as main characters is also essential if you are to present a realistic view of society and the world. Through well-written *multicultural literature,* children can see that someone from a different race, ethnic group, or religion has many of the same basic needs and feelings that they themselves have. Literature by and about people different from oneself can help develop an understanding and appreciation for all peoples. Minority children will enjoy reading books in which children from backgrounds similar to their own play the leading, and sometimes, heroic roles. Characters with whom one can identify permit a deeper involvement in literature and at the same time help children understand situations in their own lives.

International literature, literature from other nations and regions of the world, needs to be included in read-aloud choices and in classroom and library collections in order to guide students toward global understanding. Through reading or listening to the favorite books of children from other nations, your children will experience cultural literacy on a worldwide basis.

Classroom libraries are usually limited in scope; therefore, school libraries are necessary to provide adequate balance and variety of books for students' research needs and independent reading. Frequent visits to the library by the class and by individual students need to be arranged by the teacher and librarian.

 # Categories of Literature

In Chapters 4 to 11, the main categories of children's books will be defined and explained, followed by book titles recommended for reading in each of the categories. Chapters 4 and 6 through 10 focus on the literary genres, as presented in Table 3.2 (the number of the chapter in which each genre of literature is discussed is noted next to the genre). For the purposes of this textbook, a genre organization—a traditional, though admittedly imperfect, way of grouping literature—is the most practical choice. It is easy for teachers and librarians to organize learning and to demonstrate the wide spectrum of ideas and emotions that can be found in children's literature. Many students seek and select books for their independent reading by topics, such as mystery, adventure, sports, or friendships. For this reason we have also included subheadings of topics within each genre chapter and have arranged the recommended books by these genres and by the topical subheadings.

Understanding genre characteristics builds a frame of reference for readers of a particular genre and can ease the task of comprehension. Furthermore, as readers encounter postmodern works of literature, which go beyond the traditional boundaries of a genre, knowledge of the traditional literary forms may help them understand what the authors are doing and help them gain new understandings from this shift.

Authors of children's literature have been experimenting with works that blend characteristics of several genres, and, as a result, genre boundaries are increasingly blurred (Kaplan, 2005; Laminack & Bell, 2004). As discussed earlier in this chapter, novels and picture books for children written in the style of free verse and other verse forms are being seen with greater frequency. An example is Karen Hesse's *Out of the Dust* (1997), awarded the Newbery Medal and the Scott O'Dell Award for Historical Fiction in the same year. Novels in verse form are listed in this textbook under the particular narrative genre, such as historical fiction, rather than in the chapter about poetry. Works of magical realism, a literary mode that combines realism and fantasy, such as those of Virginia Hamilton (*Sweet Whispers, Brother Rush*, 1982) and David Almond (*Skellig*, 1999), offer the reader new ways to perceive the world. Works of magical realism appear and are discussed in Chapter 7. Historical fantasy blends historical fiction and modern fantasy, as Mary Hoffman does in *Stravaganza: City of Masks* (2002). These works also appear and are discussed in Chapter 7. Other blended genres include works of fictionalized biography and informational books that contain elements of both fiction and nonfiction, as in Russell Freedman's *Confucius: The Golden Rule* (2002) and David Macauley's *Mosque* (2003); these works appear in Chapter 10. These blended-genre works offer readers new ways to perceive the world and often provide heightened interest for readers.

Chapter 11 diverges from the organization of genre and presents books organized by culture. Although multicultural and international books have been placed in a separate chapter for emphasis and ready access, many multicultural and international titles are also recommended in the genre chapters.

Table 3.2 Genres and Topics of Children's Literature

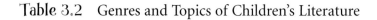

Poetry (4)	Plays (4)	Prose				
		FICTION				**NONFICTION (10)**
		FANTASY		**REALISM**		
		Traditional Literature (6)	*Modern Fantasy (7)*	*Realistic Fiction (8)*	*Historical Fiction (9)*	
Nursery rhymes Lyric poems Narrative poems	Original plays Adaptations	Myths Epics Legends and tall tales Folktales Fables Religious stories	Modern folktales Animal fantasy Personified toys and objects Unusual characters and situations Worlds of little people Supernatural events and mystery fantasy Historical fantasy Quest stories Science fiction and science fantasy	Families Peers Physical, emotional, mental, and behavioral challenges Communities Animals Sports Mysteries Moral choices Romance and sexuality Coming of age Adventure and survival	Beginnings of civilization Civilizations of the ancient world Civilizations of the medieval world Emergence of modern nations Development of industrial society World wars in the twentieth century Post–World War II	Biographies Informational books

An overview of the genres, subtopics, and their relationships to one another is displayed in Table 3.2. These genres can be used in making balanced choices for library and classroom reading collections and for choosing books to read aloud.

Topics for Further Investigation

- Review the history of children's book award programs.
- Find and read a book with each of the following characteristics: progressive chrono-logical plot, episodic plot, and plot with flashbacks. Describe each book's plot structure and the age-appropriate target audience for the book.
- Find and read a literary work written from one of the following points of view: third-person omniscient, limited omniscient, first person, or shifting. In your opinion, what effect does the point of view have on the literary work and on the reader? Describe the writing style and your response to the style as a reader.

 See the companion website at www.ablongman.com/lynchbrown6e for additional suggestions.

References

Almond, D. (1999). *Skellig.* New York: Delacorte.

———. (2006). *Clay.* New York: Delacorte.

Avi. (1990). *The true confessions of Charlotte Doyle.* New York: Orchard.

———. (1991). *Nothing but the truth.* New York: Orchard.

Babbitt, N. (1975). *Tuck everlasting.* New York: Farrar.

Bauer, M. D. (2005). *A Bear named Trouble.* New York: Clarion.

Beach, R. W., & Marshall, J. D. (1990). *Teaching literature in the secondary school.* Belmont, CA: Wadsworth.

Brooke, P. (2000). *Jake's orphan.* New York: DK Inc.

Cleary, B. (1981). *Ramona Quimby, age 8.* Illustrated by A. Tiegreen. New York: Morrow.

———. (1983). *Dear Mr. Henshaw.* Illustrated by P. O. Zelinsky. Orlando, FL: Harcourt.

Creech, S. (1997). *Chasing Redbird.* New York: Harper-Collins.

Curtis, C. P. (2004). *Bucking the Sarge.* New York: Random.

Cushman, K. (1994). *Catherine, called Birdy.* New York: Clarion.

dePaola, T. (1999). *26 Fairmount Avenue.* New York: Putnam.

Esckilsen, E. (2004). *Offsides.* Boston: Houghton.

Fleischman, P. (1993). *Bull Run.* New York: HarperCollins.

Freedman, R. (2002). *Confucius: The Golden Rule.* Illustrated by Frédéric Clément. New York: Arthur A. Levine.

Gág, W. (1928). *Millions of cats.* New York: Coward-McCann.

George, J. C. (1959). *My side of the mountain.* New York: Dutton.

———. (1972). *Julie of the wolves.* Illustrated by J. Schoenherr. New York: Harper.

Hamilton, V. (1982). *Sweet whispers, Brother Rush.* New York: Philomel.

Hesse, K. (1997). *Out of the dust.* New York: Scholastic.

Hiaasen, C. (2002). *Hoot.* New York: Knopf.

Hoffman, M. (2002). *Stravaganza: City of masks.* New York: Bloomsbury.

Jennings, P. (1996). *Faith and the electric dogs.* New York: Scholastic.

Kaplan, J. (2005). Young adult literature in the 21st century: Moving beyond traditional constraints and conventions. *The ALAN Review, 32*(2), 11–18.

Kuiper, K. (Ed.). (1995). *Merriam Webster's encyclopedia of literature.* Springfield, MA: Merriam-Webster.

Laminack, L. L., & Bell, B. H. (2004). Stretching the boundaries and blurring the lines of genre. *Language Arts 81*(3), 248–253.

Lawrence, I. (2000). *Ghost boy.* New York: Delacorte.

Lobel, A. (1970). *Frog and toad are friends.* New York: Harper.

Macaulay, D. (2003). *Mosque.* Boston: Houghton.

Mah, A. Y. (1999). *Chinese Cinderella: The true story of an unwanted daughter.* New York: Delacorte.

Mochizuki, K. (1995). *Heroes.* Illustrated by D. Lee. New York: Lee & Low.

More, H. (1961). A book. In W. Cole (Ed.), *Poems for seasons and celebrations.* Cleveland: World Publishing.

Na, A. (2001). *A step from heaven.* Asheville, NC: Front Street.

Naidoo, B. (2001). *The other side of truth.* New York: HarperCollins.

————. (2006). *Web of lies.* New York: HarperCollins.

Nikolajeva, M. (1998). Exit children's literature? *The Lion and the Unicorn, 22*(2), 221–236.

Oppel, K. (2004). *Airborn.* Toronto, ON: HarperCollins.

Paulsen, G. (1987). *Hatchet.* New York: Bradbury.

Philbrick, R. (2004). *The young man and the sea.* New York: Blue Sky Press.

Reeder, C. (1989). *Shades of gray.* New York: Macmillan.

Rodda, E. (1996). *Power and Glory.* Illustrated by Geoff Kelly. New York: Greenwillow.

Rosenblatt, L. (1978). *The reader, the text, the poem.* Carbondale, IL: Southern Illinois University.

————. (1985). The transactional theory of the literary work: Implications for research. In C. R. Cooper (Ed.), *Researching response to literature and the teaching of literature: Points of departure* (pp. 33–53). Norwood, NJ: Ablex.

Roy, J. (2006). *Yellow star.* New York: Marshall Cavendish.

Rylant, C. (2001). *Mr. Putter & Tabby feed the fish.* Illustrated by A. Howard. San Diego, CA: Harcourt.

Sachar, L. (1998). *Holes.* New York: Farrar.

Salisbury, G. (1994). *Under the red-blood sun.* New York: Delacorte.

Schmidt, G. D. (2004). *Lizzie Bright and the Buckminster boy.* New York: Clarion.

Speare, E. G. (1973). *The sign of the beaver.* Boston: Houghton.

Spillebeen, G. (2005). *Kipling's choice.* Illustrated by T. Edelstein. Boston: Houghton.

Spinelli, J. (2002). *Loser.* New York: HarperCollins.

————. (1997). *Wringer.* New York: HarperCollins.

Taylor, T. (2004). *Ice drift.* Orlando, FL: Harcourt.

Veciana-Suarez, A. (2002). *Flight to freedom.* New York: Orchard.

White, E. B. (1952). *Charlotte's web.* Illustrated by G. Williams. New York: Harper.

White, R. (1996). *Belle Prater's boy.* New York: Farrar.

Wild, M. (2001). *Fox.* Illustrated by R. Brooks. La Jolla, CA: Kane/Miller.

Categories of Literature

Part II presents a broad spectrum of the genres of literature as outlined in Table 3.2 in Chapter 3. We believe that the organization by genres, topics, and historical eras as found in Chapters 4 through 11 is the most convenient and helpful way for you and your students to locate books. However, from the outset, we acknowledge that literary genres defy absolute definitions. Furthermore, most books can be categorized within genres in more than one way because the stories address more than one topic. For example, stories about peers are often about families, too.

Special features in each chapter of Part II deserve your attention. The Milestones features give you the history of the development of each genre at a glance. The lists of Notable Authors will familiarize you with well-known creators of literature and help you make good choices for in-depth author studies, just as the Excellent Books to Read Aloud features provide help in selecting good read-alouds. The Topics for Further Investigation suggest aspects of each chapter's content for in-depth study and also a literature-related activity involving children.

In this edition, as in past editions, we have updated the important Recommended Books section at the end of each genre chapter. Our overall goal has been to include the best books from the recent past as well as some older titles that continue to hold wide appeal for today's children. Inevitably some titles must be dropped from edition to edition, just as libraries periodically remove books from their shelves to make room for newer books. Please note that titles in the Recommended Books lists are organized by the same topics or historical eras as presented in the body of the chapter to make finding specific types of books easier. Following each Recommended Books list is a brief list of films related to the genre. Chapter 11 features multicultural and international literature, the status of the field, and recommended books in this separate chapter in order to highlight the importance of these areas of literature. Please note that we have also integrated multicultural and international titles in the preceding genre chapters.

Other good children's literature titles may be found in Appendices A (Children's Book Awards) and D (Transitional Books). Appendix C lists good magazines available for children.

chapter 4

Poetry and Plays

What's a Poem?

A whisper,
a shout,
thoughts turned
inside out.

A laugh,
a sigh,
an echo
passing by.

A rhythm,
a rhyme,
a moment
caught in time.

A moon,
A star,
a glimpse
of who you are.

—Charles Ghigna

This chapter is presented in two sections. The first section focuses on poetry, information about poetry, and its uses in the classroom. The second section focuses on plays, information about plays, and their importance in a good language arts curriculum.

Poetry and plays represent two of the three major components of literature: prose, poetry, and plays. While poetry is an accepted, albeit underused, genre in the elementary classroom, the genre of plays is truly neglected. Because of their underuse and neglect we have chosen to discuss poetry and plays before other types of literature. We hope you will read and reread favorite poems to your students each day and bring plays and the theatre into your classroom on a regular basis.

Section One: Poetry

Poetry, in the form of nursery rhymes, is a natural beginning to literature for young children and an enjoyable literary form for all ages. In their earliest years, children acquire language and knowledge of the world around them through listening and observing. Poetry, primarily an oral form of literature that draws heavily on the auditory perceptions of the listeners, is ideally suited to children at this stage. Then, throughout the elementary- and middle-school years, poetry that relates to any and every subject can be found and shared orally during the school day, providing a flash of humor or a new perspective on the subject.

Definition and Description

Poetry is the concentrated expression of ideas and feelings through precise and imaginative words selected for their sonorous and rhythmical effects. Originally, poetry was oral, and as various minstrels traversed the countryside, they recited poetry and sang songs to groups of listeners of all ages. The musicality of poetry makes it an especially suitable literary form for teachers to read aloud and, at times, to put to music.

Children often believe that rhyme is an essential ingredient of poetry, yet some types of poetry do not rhyme. What, then, distinguishes poetry from prose? The concentration of thought and feeling expressed in succinct, exact, and beautiful language, as well as an underlying pulse or rhythm are the traits that most strongly set poetry apart from prose.

Not all rhyming, rhythmical language merits the label of poetry. *Verse* is a language form in which simple thoughts or stories are told in rhyme with a distinct beat or meter. Mother Goose and nursery rhymes are good examples of well-known, simple verses for children. And, of course, we are all too aware of the ***jingle,*** a catchy repetition of sounds heard so often in commercials. The most important feature of verses and jingles is their strong rhyme and rhythm. Content is light or even silly. Although verses and jingles can be enjoyable and have a place in the classroom, poetry can enrich children's lives by giving them new insights and fresh views on life's experiences and by bringing forth strong emotional responses.

The term *poetry* is used in this chapter both to refer to a higher quality of language—a form of language that can evoke great depth of feeling and provoke new insights through imaginative and beautiful language—and to refer to favorite verses of childhood.

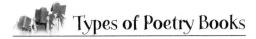 Types of Poetry Books

Poetry touches our minds and hearts through drawing on our five senses. Children, too, are reached by poetry, even though the subjects that move them may differ from those that move adults. A wide variety of poetry books is available today for use by students and teachers. Selecting books of poetry for use in the classroom as bridges between classroom activities, as materials for reading, and as literature for enjoyment will require teachers to review and evaluate the many types of poetry books: anthologies, Mother Goose and nursery rhyme books, nursery and folk songbooks, books of poems on special topics and by favorite poets, and single illustrated poems in picture book formats.

Mother Goose and Nursery Rhyme Books

Mother Goose and nursery rhyme books are heavily illustrated collections of traditional verse. *Tomie dePaola's Mother Goose,* collected and illustrated by Tomie dePaola, is a good example. Often, a familiar illustration is all a child needs to get her or him to recite one of these well-loved verses. Collected nursery rhymes first appeared in editions of Charles Perrault's *Tales of Mother Goose* in France in the early eighteenth century. These verses are now part of our children's literary heritage. Also, they have proven to be a wonderful introduction to the world of literature for young children. In societies in which countless allusions are made every day to the characters and situations found in nursery rhymes, knowledge of this literature is a mark of being culturally literate.

Because so many of these verses exist, the better collections include large numbers of them thoughtfully organized around themes or topics; they are indexed by titles or first lines. A favorite book of this kind is *The Book of Nursery and Mother Goose Rhymes,* collected and illustrated by Marguerite de Angeli. Some lesser-known traditional verses were collected and illustrated by Arnold Lobel in *The Random House Book of Mother Goose.*

Nursery and Folk Songbooks

Nursery and folk songbooks are heavily illustrated collections of both traditional and modern verses and their musical notation. *Songs from Mother Goose,* compiled by Nancy Larrick and illustrated by Robin Spowart, is a good example. Melody further emphasizes the innate musicality of these verses and turns some verses into games ("Ring around the Roses") and others into lullabies ("Rock-a-Bye Baby"). In choosing a songbook, teachers, librarians, and parents should ascertain that there is a good selection of songs and that the music is well arranged for young voices and playable. Those who plan to work with preschoolers and first- and second-graders will be wise to make these songs part of their repertoire.

Anthologies of Poetry

A large, comprehensive *anthology* of poetry for children is a must in every classroom. Anthologies should be organized by subject for easy retrieval of poems appropriate for almost any occasion. In addition, indices of poets and titles, or first lines, are usually provided in these texts.

Works by contemporary and traditional poets can be found in most of these anthologies; they appeal to a wide age range, providing nursery rhymes for toddlers as well as longer, narrative poems for the middle-grade student. An example is *A New Treasury of Children's Poetry: Old Favorites and New Discoveries,* selected by Joanna Cole.

Specialized Poetry Books

Specialized poetry books are also readily available in which the poems are all by one poet, on one topic, for one age group, or of one poetic form. These specialized collections become necessary adjuncts for a teacher and class who come to love certain kinds of poetry or specific poets. Beautifully illustrated collections are also available and seem to be especially enjoyed by children for independent reading of poetry. Examples include *Mathematickles* by Betsy Franco and *Doodle Soup* by John Ciardi.

Single Illustrated Poems

Single narrative poems of medium length are presented more frequently in picture book formats. These editions make poetry more appealing and accessible to many children, but in some cases the illustrations may remove the opportunity for children to form their own mental images from the language created by poets. The poetry section of your school library is worth perusing for interesting poetry books to use in the classroom.

 # Elements of Poetry

Just as with a work of fiction, the elements of a poem should be considered if the reader is to understand and evaluate the poem. Each of these parts—meaning, rhythm, sound patterns, figurative language, and sense imagery—is discussed in the following list.

■ *Meaning.* **Meaning** is the underlying idea, feeling, or mood expressed through the poem. As with other literary forms, poetry is a form of communication; it is the way a poet chooses to express emotions and thoughts. Thus, the meaning of the poem is the expressed or implied message the poet conveys.

■ *Rhythm.* **Rhythm** is the beat or regular cadence of the poem. Poetry, usually an oral form of literature, relies on rhythm to help communicate meaning. A fast rhythm is effected through short lines, clipped syllables, sharp, high vowel sounds, such as the sounds represented by the letters *a, e,* and *i,* and abrupt consonant sounds, such as the sounds represented by the letters *k, t, w,* and *p.* A fast rhythm can provide the listener with a feeling of happiness, excitement, drama, and even tension and suspense. A slow rhythm is effected by longer lines, multisyllabic words, full or low vowel sounds such as the sounds represented by the letters *o* and *u,* and resonating consonant sounds such as the sounds represented by the letters *m, n,* and *r.* A slow rhythm can evoke languor, tranquility, inevitability, and harmony, among other feelings. A change in rhythm during a poem signals the listener to a change in meaning.

In the poems that follow, "Song for a Blue Roadster" exhibits a fast rhythm that evokes the rapid speed of an automobile; "Slowly" proceeds more slowly in communicating the calm and quiet of summer.

SONG FOR A BLUE ROADSTER

Fly, roadster, fly!
The sun is high,
Gold are the fields
We hurry by,
Green are the woods
As we slide through
Past harbor and headland,
Blue on blue.

Fly, Roadster, fly!
The hay smells sweet,
And the flowers are fringing
Each village street,
Where carts are blue
And barns are red,
And the road unwinds
Like a twist of thread.

Fly, Roadster, fly!
Leave Time behind;
Out of sight
Shall be out of mind.
Shine and shadow
Blue sea, green bough,
Nothing is real
But Here and Now.

    —Rachel Field

SLOWLY

Slowly the tide creeps up the sand,
Slowly the shadows cross the land.
Slowly the cart-horse pulls his mile,
Slowly the old man mounts the stile.

Slowly the hands move round the clock,
Slowly the dew dries on the dock.
Slow is the snail—but slowest of all
The green moss spreads on the old brick wall.

    —James Reeves

■ *Sound Patterns.* **Sound patterns** are made by repeated sounds and combinations of sounds in the words. Words, phrases, or lines are sometimes repeated in their entirety. Also, parts of words may be repeated, as with **rhyme,** the sound device that children most recognize and enjoy. *Rhyme* occurs when the ends of words (the last vowel sound and any consonant sound that may follow it) have the same sounds. Examples of rhyming words are *vat, rat, that, brat,* and *flat,* as well as *hay, they, flay, stray,* and *obey.* **Assonance** is another pattern poets use for effect. In this case, the same vowel sound is heard repeatedly within a line or a few lines of poetry. Assonance is exemplified in these words: *hoop, gloom, moon, moot,* and *boots.* **Alliteration** is a pattern in which initial consonant sounds are heard frequently within a few lines of poetry. Examples are *ship, shy,* and *shape.* *Consonance* is similar to alliteration but usually refers to a close juxtaposition of similar final consonant sounds, as in fla*ck*e, chu*ck,* and stro*ck*e. *Onomatopoeia* is the device in which the sound of the word imitates the real-world sound. Examples are *buzz* for the sound of a bee and *hiss* for the sound a snake makes.

■ *Figurative Language.* **Figurative language** takes many different forms, but it involves comparing or contrasting one object, idea, or feeling with another one. A **simile** is a direct comparison, typically using *like* or *as* to point out the similarities. The familiar poem "The Star" includes a simile to compare a star to a diamond.

THE STAR

Twinkle, twinkle little star,
How I wonder what you are!
Up above the world so high,
Like a diamond in the sky.

　—Jane Taylor

A **metaphor** is an implied comparison without a signal word to evoke the similarities. In the poem "The Night Is a Big Black Cat," the metaphor implies a comparison between the night sky and a black cat.

THE NIGHT IS A BIG BLACK CAT

The Night is a big black cat
The Moon is her topaz eye,
The stars are the mice she hunts at night,
In the field of the sultry sky.

　—G. Orr Clark

Personification is the attribution of human qualities to animate, nonhuman beings or to inanimate objects for the purpose of drawing a comparison between the animal or object and human beings. In "The Crocus," the flower is personified by human actions and a personal pronoun.

THE CROCUS

The golden crocus reaches up
To catch a sunbeam in her cup.

　—Walter Crane

Hyperbole is an exaggeration to highlight reality or to point out ridiculousness. To show a boy's reluctance to go to school John Ciardi used hyperbole with good effect in the following stanza from "Speed Adjustments."

> Why does a boy who's fast as a jet
> Take all day—and sometimes two—
> To get to school?

Children often delight in hyperbole because it appeals to their strong sense of the absurd.

■ *Sense Imagery.* A poet will play on one or more of the five senses in descriptive and narrative language. *Sight* may be awakened through the depiction of beauty; *hearing* may be evoked by the sounds of a city street; *smell* and *taste* may be recalled through the description of a fish left too long in the sun; and finally, *touch* can be sensitized through describing the gritty discomfort of a wet swimsuit caked with sand from the beach. After listening to a poem, children can be asked to think about which of the senses the poet is appealing to.

These elements of poetry may be considered to select varied types of poems and to group them for presentation. However, little is gained by teaching each of these elements as a separate item to be memorized and/or analyzed. Poetic analysis has caused many students to dislike poetry. On the other hand, students whose teachers love poetry, select it wisely, read it aloud well, and share it often and in many enjoyable ways will come to appreciate poetry.

 ## Evaluation and Selection of Poetry

The criteria to keep in mind in evaluating a poem for use with children are as follows:

- The ideas and feelings expressed are worthy, fresh, and imaginative.
- The expression of the ideas and feelings is unique, often causing the reader to perceive ordinary things in new ways.
- The poem is appropriate to the experiences of children and does not preach to them or appeal to their baser instincts.
- The poem presents the world through a child's perspective and focuses on children's lives and activities as well as on activities to which people of all ages can relate.
- Poetry collections should be judged on the quality of the poetry choices first and illustrations and the appearance of the book second. Beautiful illustrations do not ensure a good collection of poems within the covers.
- Children report a preference for narrative poems. You will want to share narrative poems regularly.
- Although certain poets may be favored by your students, they will also enjoy the poetry of many other writers. Thus, be sure to share with your students poems by a variety of authors.

In selecting poems to read to students, the Golden Age poets listed in the Milestones feature in this chapter, the list of notable poets at the end of this chapter, and the list of poets who have won the National Council of Teachers of English (NCTE) Award are good starting points. The NCTE Award was established in 1977 in the United States to honor living U.S. poets whose poetry has contributed substantially to the lives of children. This award is given to a poet for the entire body of writing for children ages 3 through 13 and is now given every three years. In addition, a recent reference book, *Young Adult Poetry: A Survey and Theme Guide* (Schwedt & DeLong, 2002), can be a useful tool for students and teachers in upper elementary and middle grades for locating poems to support the curriculum and to address student interests. This bibliography annotates 198 poetry books and identifies themes in more than 6,000 poems.

NCTE Excellence in Poetry for Children Award Winners

1977	David McCord	1988	Arnold Adoff
1978	Aileen Fisher	1991	Valerie Worth
1979	Karla Kuskin	1994	Barbara Juster Esbensen
1980	Myra Cohn Livingston	1997	Eloise Greenfield
1981	Eve Merriam	2000	X. J. Kennedy
1982	John Ciardi	2003	Mary Ann Hoberman
1985	Lilian Moore	2006	Nikki Grimes

Although more poetry for children is being written and published and many teachers and their students are enjoying this genre of literature, some teachers report that they do not share poetry because of their uncertainty about selecting poems for their students. By learning about students' preferences in poetry and some of the best-loved poems and most respected poets, a teacher can become more skillful at selecting good and enjoyable poems for students. The next section will review research on children's preferences in poetry.

Children's Poetry Preferences

The findings from surveys of children's poetry preferences can be helpful to teachers in selecting poems for a new group of students. Fisher and Natarella (1982) surveyed primary-grade children and their teachers, and Terry (1974) studied intermediate-grade children. The two age groups were similar, although not identical, in their preferences.

- Both age groups preferred narrative poems over lyric poems.
- Limericks were the favored poetic form of both age groups; free verse and haiku were not well liked by either age group.
- Children of both age groups preferred poems that had pronounced sound patterns of all kinds, but especially enjoyed poems that rhymed.
- Rhythm was also an important element to students of both age groups; they preferred poems with regular, distinctive rhythm.
- Children of both age groups liked humorous poems, poems about animals, and poems about enjoyable familiar experiences.
- The subjects most preferred by primary-grade children were strange and fantastic events, animals, and other children; the older children preferred the realistic contents of humor, enjoyable familiar experiences, and animals.
- Children in both age groups often found figurative language in poetry confusing.

A study by Kutiper and Wilson (1993) was conducted to determine whether an examination of school library circulation records would confirm the findings of the earlier poetry preference studies. The findings of this library circulation study indicated that the humorous contemporary poetry of Shel Silverstein and Jack Prelutsky dominated the students' choices. The collections of poetry written by the NCTE award winners did not circulate widely; nor were they widely available in the school libraries studied, even though these poets reflect a higher quality of language and usage than is found in the light verse so popular with students. Kutiper and Wilson stated that real interest in poetry must go beyond Prelutsky and Silverstein. This interest needs to be developed by teachers who provide an array of poetry that builds on students' natural interests.

Children's appreciation of poetry can be broadened and deepened by a good teacher, but you may be wise to proceed with caution on less-liked aspects of poetry until your students become fans of poetry. Thus, a good selection of rhyming, narrative poems with distinct rhythms about humorous events, well-liked familiar experiences, and animals is a good starting point for students who have little experience with poetry.

 ## Historical Overview of Poetry

Poetry for children began centuries ago in the form of nursery rhymes that were recited to babies and toddlers by caregivers. These verses were passed along via the oral tradition. The earliest published collection of nursery rhymes that survives today is *Tommy Thumb's Pretty Song Book* (1744), which is housed in the British Museum (Gillespie, 1970). This songbook contains familiar rhymes such as "Hickory Dickory Dock" and "Mary Mary Quite Contrary." These rhymes and others like them came to be called *Mother Goose rhymes,* but the term *Mother Goose* was first used in France by Charles Perrault in his *Stories and Tales of Past Times with Morals; or, Tales of Mother Goose* (1697) to refer to his collection of fairy tales. Later editions contained nursery rhymes, which became so popular that Mother Goose became a general name for nursery rhymes. For many, nursery rhymes and other poems were the first forms of literature experienced; these poems symbolize the reassuring sounds of childhood.

Poems of a moral and religious bent were shared with obvious didactic intent, reflecting the strict attitude toward the rearing of children that held sway in the Western world from the Middle Ages to the late nineteenth century. Fear of death and punishment was instilled as a means of gaining obedience to authority. Ann and Jane Taylor's *Original Poems, for Infant Minds, by Several Young Persons* (1804) provided verse of this kind. Some titles of poems from this early collection are "The Idle Boy," "Greedy Richard," "Meddlesome Matty," and "The Church-Yard."

Poetry for children flourished from the middle of the nineteenth century through the 1920s, a period that can be considered the Golden Age of Poetry for Children. The accompanying Milestones feature lists the poets, countries, landmark works and dates, and characteristics. The Golden Age of Poetry moved away from moralistic poetry and instead provided children with poems describing the beauty of life and nature, with poems of humor, nonsense, and word fun, and with imaginative poems that interpreted life from the child's perspective. Much of the Golden Age poetry retains its appeal for today's children; for example, *A Child's Garden of Verses* (1885) by Robert Louis Stevenson remains a favorite collection of poems among parents and children. This positive shift in poetry for children remains the standard for poetry today.

In the 1960s and 1970s, the general trend toward realism in children's literature was also reflected in poetry. More topics considered suitable for the child audience resulted in protest

MILESTONES in Poetry during the Golden Age

Date	Poet	Landmark Work	Country	Characteristic
1846	Edward Lear	*A Book of Nonsense*	England	Father of nonsense poetry, limericks
1864	Lewis Carroll	"Jabberwocky"	England	Nonsense verses, such as those in *Alice's Adventures in Wonderland*
1872	Christina Rossetti	*Sing Song*	England	Poems on children and the small things around them
1885	Robert Louis Stevenson	*A Child's Garden of Verses*	England	Descriptive poems of childhood memories
1888	Ernest Thayer	"Casey at the Bat"	U.S.A.	Famous ballad on baseball
1890	Laura E. Richards	*In My Nursery*	U.S.A.	Poems with hilarious situations, wordplay, and strong rhythm
1896	Eugene Field	*Poems of Childhood*	U.S.A.	Poems reflecting on children and child life
1902	Walter de la Mare	*Songs of Childhood*	England	Musical and imaginative poetry
1920	Rose Fyleman	*Fairies and Chimneys*	England	Imaginative poems about fairies
1922	A. A. Milne	*When We Were Very Young*	England	Poems of fun in which the child's world is observed
1926	Rachel Field	*Taxis and Toadstools*	U.S.A.	Poems about city and country through the child's eyes

poetry, poems about girls in nontraditional roles, and irreverent poems. For example, parents, teachers, and other adults became fair game for ridicule and mockery. Minority poets were more frequently published, and their poetry gained in popularity.

Popularity of poetry in the classroom began in the 1980s and continues to the present day. Developments in the publishing industry attest to this popularity. For example, Boyds Mills Press has a division devoted to children's poetry, called Windsong. Publishers continue to present both single poems and collections of poems in beautifully illustrated book formats. In the 1980s, Nancy Willard's *A Visit to William Blake's Inn: Poems for Innocent and Experienced Travelers* and Paul Fleischman's *Joyful Noise: Poems for Two Voices* received Newbery Medals, indicating greater recognition of poetry for young people in the United States. An increase in the publication of anthologies of poems by and about minorities, such as *Pass It On,* edited by Wade Hudson, has been noted in the 1990s. This increased publication has also resulted in greater attention to earlier African-American poets, such as Paul Laurence Dunbar, Countee Cullen, and Langston Hughes.

 ## Poetry Types and Forms

Poetry can be classified in many ways; one way is to consider two main types that generally differ in purpose: lyric and narrative poetry. *Lyric poetry* captures a moment, a feeling, or a scene, and is descriptive in nature, whereas **narrative poetry** tells a story or includes a sequence of events. From this definition, you will recognize the following selection to be a lyric poem.

GIRAFFES

Stilted creatures,
Features fashioned as a joke,
Boned and buckled,
Finger painted,
They stand in the field
On long-pronged legs
As if thrust there.
They airily feed,
Slightly swaying,
Like hammer-headed flowers.

Bizarre they are,
Built silent and high,
Ornaments against the sky.
Ears like leaves
To hear the silken
Brushing of the clouds.

  —Sy Kahn

The next selection is an example of a narrative poem:

THE BROKEN-LEGG'D MAN

I saw the other day when I went shopping in the store
A man I hadn't ever ever seen in there before,

A man whose leg was broken and who leaned upon a crutch—
I asked him very kindly if it hurt him very much.
"Not at all!" said the broken-legg'd man.

I ran around behind him for I thought that I would see
The broken leg all bandaged up and bent back at the knee;
But I didn't see the leg at all, there wasn't any there,
So I asked him very kindly if he had it hid somewhere.
"Not at all!" said the broken-legg'd man.

"Then where," I asked him, "is it? Did a tiger bite it off?
Or did you get your foot wet when you had a nasty cough?
Did someone jump down on your leg when it was very new?
Or did you simply cut it off because you wanted to?"
"Not at all!" said the broken-legg'd man.

"What was it then?" I asked the man, and this is what he said:
"I crossed a busy crossing when the traffic light was red;
A big black car came whizzing by and knocked me off my feet."
"Of course you looked both ways," I said, "before you crossed the street."
"Not at all!" said the broken-legg'd man.

"They rushed me to a hospital right quickly," he went on,
"And when I woke in nice white sheets I saw my leg was gone;
That's why you see me walking now on nothing but a crutch."
"I'm glad," said I, "you told me, and I thank you very much!"
"Not at all!" said the broken-legg'd man.

> —John Mackey Shaw

Poetry can also be categorized by its *poetic form,* which refers to the way the poem is structured or put together. *Couplets, tercets, quatrains,* and *cinquains* refer to the number (two, three, four, and five) of lines of poetry in a stanza—a set of lines of poetry grouped together. Couplets, tercets, quatrains, and cinquains usually rhyme, though the rhyme scheme may vary; these poetic forms may constitute an entire poem, or a poem may be comprised of a few stanzas of couplets, tercets, and so on. "Higglety, Pigglety, Pop!" is an example of the cinquain poetic form found in a traditional nursery rhyme.

HIGGLETY, PIGGLETY, POP!

Higglety, pigglety, pop!
The dog has eaten the mop.
The pig's in a hurry,
The cat's in a flurry,
Higglety, pigglety, pop!

> —Traditional

Other specific poetic forms frequently found in children's poetry are limericks, ballads, haiku, free verse, and concrete poetry.

A *limerick* is a humorous, one-stanza, five-line verse form (usually a narrative), in which lines 1, 2, and 5 rhyme and are of the same length and lines 3 and 4 rhyme and are of the same length but shorter than the other lines. The following is an example of a limerick by Edward Lear, the poet who popularized this poetic form in the nineteenth century.

THERE WAS AN OLD PERSON WHOSE HABITS

There was an old person whose habits
Induced him to feed upon rabbits;
When he'd eaten eighteen,
He turned perfectly green,
Upon which he relinquished those habits.

    —Edward Lear

A *ballad* is a fairly long narrative poem of popular origin, usually adapted to singing. These traditional story poems are often romantic or heroic. "The Outlandish Knight," a thirteen-stanza ballad, tells the tale of the clever young woman who tricks the man who deceived her.

THE OUTLANDISH KNIGHT

An outlandish knight came out of the North,
    To woo a maiden fair,
He promised to take her to the North lands,
    Her father's only heir.

"Come, fetch me some of your father's gold,
    And some of your mother's fee;
And two of the best nags out of the stable,
    Where they stand thirty and three."

She fetched him some of her father's gold
    And some of her mother's fee;
And two of the best nags out of the stable,
    Where they stood thirty and three.

He mounted her on her milk-white steed,
    He on the dapple grey;
They rode till they came unto the sea-side,
    Three hours before it was day.

"Light off, light off thy milk-white steed,
    And deliver it unto me;
Six pretty maids have I drowned here,
    And thou the seventh shall be."

"Pull off, pull off thy silken gown,
    And deliver it unto me;
Methinks it looks too rich and too gay
    To rot in the salt sea."

"Pull off, pull off thy silken stays,
　　And deliver them unto me;
Methinks they are too fine and gay
　　To rot in the salt sea."

"Pull off, pull off the Holland smock
　　And deliver it unto me;
Methinks it looks too rich and gay
　　To rot in the salt sea."

"If I must pull off my Holland smock,
　　Pray turn thy back unto me,
For it is not fitting that such a ruffian
　　A woman unclad should see."

He turned his back towards her,
　　And viewed the leaves so green;
She catch'd him round the middle so small,
　　And tumbled him into the stream.

He dropped high, and he dropped low,
　　Until he came to the tide—
"Catch hold of my hand, my pretty maiden,
　　And I will make you my bride."

"Lie there, lie there, you false-hearted man,
　　Lie there instead of me;
Six pretty maidens have you drowned here,
　　And the seventh has drowned thee."

She mounted on her milk-white steed,
　　And led the dapple grey.
She rode til she came to her father's hall,
　　Three hours before it was day.

　　—Traditional

Haiku is a lyric, unrhymed poem of Japanese origin with seventeen syllables, arranged on three lines with a syllable count of five, seven, and five. Haiku is highly evocative poetry that frequently espouses harmony with and appreciation of nature. Here is an example.

　　Pigeons masquerade
As wildlife. They can't fool me.
　　We're all city folk.

　　—Nikki Grimes

Free verse is unrhymed poetry with little or light rhythm. Sometimes words within a line will rhyme. The subjects of free verse are often abstract and philosophical; they are always reflective.

AUTUMN LEAVES

gather in gutters,
pile on walks,
tumble
      from the tips
of toes,
crunching
fall hellos
to back-to-school feet.

—Rebecca Kai Dotlich

Concrete poetry is written and printed in a shape that signifies the subject of the poem. Concrete poems are a form of poetry that must be seen as well as heard to be fully appreciated. These poems do not usually have rhyme or definite rhythm; they rely mostly on the words, their meanings and shapes, and the way the words are arranged on the page to evoke images. In "Concrete Cat" you will note through the position of the word that the mouse appears to have met with an accident.

CONCRETE CAT

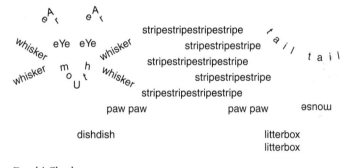

—Dorthi Charles

 # Poetry in the Classroom

Poetry is enjoyable for students of all ages. It enhances students' development of literacy. Teachers and librarians can entice students into a lifelong love for poetry through making available a well-balanced collection of poetry books and through providing many experiences with poetry.

Students' Listening to and Saying Poems

Teachers and librarians can begin by providing even very young students with many opportunities to hear and say poems. Later, when students have developed a love of poetry and an affinity for the language play in poems, students can read poetry by fine poets and poems by their classmates and can begin to write poems themselves. In other words, poetry needs to be shared in both oral and written forms.

Poetry should be introduced first and often to children in an oral form. As discussed earlier, poetry was in its origins an oral form of literature; it still relies heavily on the auditory perceptions of listeners. Moreover, children's oral language is the basis for their later acquisition of literacy. These two facts combine nicely to make listening to poems and saying poems a natural early introduction to literature for children. Some teachers report that they do not share poetry with their students because of their uncertainty about how to read it aloud. By practicing the poems ahead of time and by reading poetry frequently, a teacher can overcome this reluctance. The rewards to both students and teachers are worth the effort. The next section offers suggestions to help you become an effective reader of poetry.

Reading Poetry Aloud to Children

Poetry should be read aloud to students on a daily basis. Elster and Hanauer (2002), in examining how kindergarten to fourth-grade teachers shared poems with their students, found that reading poetry aloud expressively is effective in drawing children's attention to literate language. Brief, positive encounters with one to three poems at a time are best. Too many poems in one sitting may overwhelm students or make the reading tedious. Introduce the poem to the class before reading it aloud, either by tying the poem in with something else or by briefly telling why you chose to read this poem aloud. Then state the title of the poem and begin to read. After reading the poem, be sure to announce the name of the poet so that students discover the writers they especially enjoy. In addition, the following points will help you to read poetry well:

- Keep in mind that poetry should be read for its meaning. Stress the meaning elements of the poem just as you do when reading prose. The pauses must be determined by the meaning units of the poem, not by the end of the lines.

- A reader should not overemphasize the beat of the poem. Doing so results in an annoying singsong effect. Let the poetic language provide the rhythm.

- Poetry should be enunciated clearly. Each sound and each syllable of a poem are important and must be heard to be appreciated. You may need to slow down your normal reading pace to give full value to each sound.

- Poetry needs to be performed and dramatized. Take some chances and try out different effects (using different voices, elongating words, singing, shouting, whispering, pausing dramatically, and so on) as you read poems aloud. Your voice is a powerful tool: You may change it from louder to softer to only a whisper; you may start at a deep, low pitch and rise to a medium and eventually high pitch; you may speak very quickly in a clipped fashion and then slow down and drawl out the words. Sara Holbrook's *Wham! It's a Poetry Jam: Discovering Performance Poetry* (2002) offers good suggestions for performing poetry and even for running a poetry contest.

- Some poems may need to be read aloud a number of times for the meaning to be fully understood by listeners. Also, favorite poems can be enjoyed again and again, as teachers and students savor one more reading.

- Consider recording audiotapes of poems for the listening center and making them available along with the poem in print, on a chart or in a book, for the student to listen to and read.

Commercially made tapes with popular poets reading their works, accompanied by music, are available and are quite popular with children. Some teachers have asked parents to peruse a poetry anthology, select a favorite poem, and then read the poem on tape for use in the listening center.

■ After reading a poem aloud, some form of response is usually enjoyed. Some poems warrant discussion, and students can take the opportunity to tell how the poem made them feel or what it made them think about.

Choral Poetry

A time-honored technique for providing opportunities to say and hear poems over and over again is given by choral poetry. *Choral poetry* consists of interpreting and saying a poem together as a group activity. These poems may either be practiced and recited aloud or rehearsed and read aloud. Students enjoy this way of experiencing poetry because they have a participatory role in the activity. Most poetry, intended to be listened to, is suitable for choral presentation. The following sections explain how to select choral poems and teach them to students.

1. *Selection*

    At first, select a short poem (from one to four stanzas) until your students develop some skill in memorizing, reciting, and performing poems. Humorous narrative poems are good first choices. Later, you will want to experiment with longer poems.

2. *Memorization*

    For most choral presentations, the first step is for the teacher to select and read aloud a poem that is well liked by the students. Then each line or pair of lines is said by the teacher and repeated by the students until they know them. It is preferable for the students to repeat the lines after the teacher and for the teacher to avoid reciting with the class, so that the students will commit the poem to memory instead of waiting for the teacher's voice. Once the entire poem is learned in this way, variations can be added for performing the poem. Although students need to rehearse a poem to intone it similarly, some longer poems with older students who read well will not be memorized but will be practiced and read together as a group.

3. *Arrangements*

    Options for reading a poem chorally include unison, two- or three-part, solo voices, cumulative buildup, and simultaneous voices, as is now explained.

    ■ In unison choral speaking, the students learn the poem and recite it together as a group. Two-part or three-part choral poetry is usually based on arranging students into voice types (for example, high, medium, and low) to achieve different effects and by selecting lines of the poem for each group to recite or read.

    ■ Solo voices can be added to either of these presentations and are sometimes used for asking a question or making an exclamation.

    ■ Some poems lend themselves to cumulative buildup presentations. A cumulative buildup is effected by having, for example, only two voices say the first line, then two more join in on the second, and then two more, gradually building to a crescendo until the entire class says the last line or stanza.

    ■ Poems can be presented by simultaneous recitation, which forms a presentation similar to a musical round. In this case, group one begins the poem and recites it all the way through. When group one begins the third line, for example, then group two starts the first line, and the two groups recite simultaneously until the end. Other groups can, of course, be added.

- Poetry selected and arranged for dramatic choral readings on a particular theme infuses an interesting variation into choral poetry. Paul Fleischman's *Joyful Noise: Poems for Two Voices, I Am Phoenix: Poems for Two Voices,* and *Big Talk: Poems for Four Voices* are collections of poetry written in a manner that is already suitable for choral reading. These collections were written to be read aloud by two readers at once, one reading the left half of the page and one reading the right half, as well as certain lines simultaneously. Pairs of students may each take a different poem from the collection for presentation.

Many other variations can be developed for use in choral presentations. Let imagination be your guide. Words and lines can be spun into ghostly moans, or barked, or sung, or repeated. Choreography adds visual impact, as do simple props. As soon as children learn that poems do not have to be read sedately through exactly as written, they will begin to find excitement and deeper meaning in poetry.

4. *Performance*
   Incorporating action, gestures, body movements, and finger plays can produce more interesting and enjoyable presentations. Occasionally performing a well-honed choral poem for an audience can bring pride to young performers. Remember, the best audiences are close by—the class next door, the principal, the librarian, the custodian, or a visiting parent.

In addition to the group activity of performing choral poetry, teachers can encourage an individual student to learn a poem by heart, voluntarily, and then to recite the poem in a small group or as part of a group performance, perhaps around a theme. For example, a small group of interested students might each select a poem about weather as part of their study about weather in science. Jane Yolen's collection of weather poems, *Weather Report,* could be a resource for this activity.

Students' Reading and Writing Poems

Learning to Read Poetry

Children enjoy reading poetry silently and aloud to others. The classroom library corner should have one or two comprehensive poetry anthologies for students to browse through for general purposes. In addition, two or three specialized collections by a single poet, such as A *Pocketful of Poems* by Nikki Grimes, and another two or three books of poems on a single topic, such as *Around the World in Eighty Poems* edited by James Berry, are needed as well. Students can be encouraged to make copies of their favorite poems from these various collections to develop personal, individual anthologies. Many students choose to illustrate these and arrange the poems in new and inventive ways. Rotating the poetry books occasionally over the course of the school year will spark renewed interest in reading poetry.

Other activities to encourage the reading of poetry by students follow:

- Place students in pairs to take turns reading favorite poems to one another. Make videotapes or audiotapes of these readings and permit students to listen to or watch their own and other students' readings of poetry.
- Ask each student to select three poems by one poet (for example, a Golden Age poet or an NCTE poet) and find something out about the poet; then place students in small groups of

five or six to tell briefly about the poet and read the three poems aloud. Paul B. Janeczko's *The Place My Words Are Looking For: What Poets Say about and through Their Work* (1990) is an excellent resource for this purpose. Information about children's authors can also be found on many websites, including www.childrenslit.com.

- Have students find three poems on the same topic, such as trees, mice, or friendship; then read them aloud in small groups.
- Encourage students to find poems that are of the same poetic form—cinquains, limericks, and so forth; or that exhibit similar poetic elements—rhyme, alliteration, or onomatopoeia; or that have fast or slow rhythms. These poems can then comprise the poems for reading aloud that day or week.

Learning to Write Poetry

A rich poetry environment stimulates children's interest in writing their own poems. Children need to be very familiar with poetry of many kinds and by many poets before they should be expected to compose poems. The collection of poems *Inner Chimes: Poems on Poetry* (1992) may be a natural starting place for helping students to think about poetry and what it is. Poems by various renowned children's poets writing about creating poetry have been selected by Bobbye S. Goldstein for this volume. Other books that provide suggestions on how to include poetry in the classroom are *How to Write a Poem* (1996) by Margaret Ryan and *Give Them Poetry! A Guide for Sharing Poetry with Children K–8* (2003) by Glenna Sloan.

Teachers often start the writing of poetry as a collaborative effort. The class brainstorms for ideas, then composes the poem orally as the teacher writes it on the board or on chart paper. As students become comfortable with writing group poetry, they can branch off and begin composing poems in pairs or their own individual poems.

Children should be reminded that poetry is a form of communication and that they should think of an idea, feeling, or event to write about in their poems. They should be reminded that poetry does not have to rhyme and that they may write about something of interest to them. Children's poetry follows no absolute rules; perfection of form should not be a goal. Other suggestions to foster poetry writing include the following:

- Have students compile personal and class anthologies of their own poems or their favorite poems.
- Design bulletin boards with poetry displays of students' own poems as well as copies of poems by favorite poets. Students may also design posters, individually or in groups, to illustrate a favorite poem. Posters are then displayed around the school for a few weeks.
- Encourage students to model the works of professional poets by attempting imitation of a whole poem or of specific techniques.
- Read aloud many poems of one poetic form; then analyze the form with the students to reveal the characteristics of its structure. Quatrains, cinquains, haiku, concrete poems, and limericks can all be used as models with students once they have an appreciation for poetry and for the specific poetic form.

Some poets have suggested other models and patterns for students to follow in writing poetry. Kenneth Koch's *Rose, Where Did You Get That Red?* (1990) and *Wishes, Lies, and Dreams: Teaching Children to Write Poetry* (1999); M. K. Glover's *A Garden of Poets: Poetry Writing in the*

Elementary Classroom (1999); Myra Cohn Livingston's *Poem Making: Ways to Begin Writing Poetry* (1991); Paul Janeczko's *How to Write Poetry* (1999) and *Poetry from A to Z: A Guide for Young Writers* (1994); and Jack Prelutsky's *Read a Rhyme, Write a Rhyme* (2005) are useful resources for teachers who want to encourage students to compose poems.

Do	Don't
Read poetry aloud every day	Limit poetry choices to one or two poets or types of poems
Practice reading a poem before reading it aloud for the first time to students	Read poems in a singsong style
Choose poetry the students will like	Choose all poems from one anthology
Make a variety of excellent poetry anthologies and specialized poetry books available in the classroom	Have poetry marathon days or weeks to make up for not sharing poetry regularly
Encourage students to recite and write poems	Force students to memorize and recite poems
Direct choral poetry presentations	Make the analysis of poetry the focus of poetry study
Feature a notable poet each month	Have students copy poems for handwriting practice
Begin and end each day with a poem	Make the main emphasis of poetry be the writing of formula poems

Section Two: Plays

Plays should be included in a well-balanced literary curriculum for children. Children, when allowed to play freely, often dramatize their daily lives and fantasies. In playacting, children can act out in ways not normally allowed, giving expression to hidden feelings. Children's linguistic abilities can improve if they become actively engaged in the literature of the theatre by reading plays, performing plays, and watching others perform plays. And, of course, children delight in plays and playacting.

The use of the same word, *play,* for the main, natural activity of childhood is not a coincidence. The development and use of the imagination in the child's creation of play and in the creation of theatre are similar. The same human needs are met. In a play and in a child's own play, imagination transforms reality and endows ordinary objects with fantastic qualities. Imagination also helps the actor create a character for the enjoyment of the audience (Davis, 1981). The persons who long ago performed plays for the enjoyment of audiences were called players long before they were called actors.

Plays provide many of the same personal benefits to young readers as prose. Students enjoy reading plays and are able to experience a story vicariously quite readily through the play form. Plays can also help students develop their imaginations and ability to empathize with others (Smolkin, 1995). In addition, reading plays aloud and performing plays are natural ways to develop and demonstrate a child's oral reading fluency—the ability to read smoothly without hesitation and with good comprehension—a reading goal many teachers have for their students. McKean (2000–2001) offers practical acting tips for teachers and students to develop excellent oral reading interpretations. Plays provide a natural reason to develop these traits and put oral reading to use in a purposeful way.

 ## Definition and Description

Plays, as a literary genre, refers to written, dramatic compositions or scripts intended to be acted. A play may be divided into parts called *acts;* in turn, each act may be divided into *scenes.* The script usually has set, costume, and stage directions noted, as well as dialogue provided for each actor.

Plays are usually published in ***playbooks*** or ***acting editions,*** 4×8 paperback books, by publishers who specialize in plays. These playbooks are quite inexpensive and can be purchased directly from the publishers or ordered through bookstores. A teacher or school may purchase a set of playbooks for children's use in group reading situations. Generally, if the plays are for classroom use, no royalty need be paid. If they are being used in a school but for an audience beyond the classroom, there is usually a moderate royalty fee as indicated in the publisher's catalog.

Some other terms are worth clarifying:

- *Readers' theatre* is the oral presentation of literature by actors, and usually a narrator, reading from a script; it is a form of play reading, a dramatic reading that depends largely on voice and gestures to convey additional meaning. Generally no stage sets, costumes, or stage movements are involved in readers' theatre.

- *Creative drama* is informal drama that lends itself to the reenactment of story experiences. This form of drama is spontaneously generated by the participants who compose and act out their parts as the drama progresses. Generally no scripts are developed or lines read or memorized. Creative drama is a process-centered form of drama performed for the benefit of the participants.

- *Recreational drama* is a formal theatrical presentation where the development and experience of the performers is as important as the enjoyment by the audience. School and camp plays are examples of recreational drama.

- *Children's theatre,* sometimes referred to as theatre for young audiences, is a formal theatrical experience in which a play is presented for an audience of children. Usually the performers are skilled actors, and the production is overseen by trained directors (Goldberg, 1974).

In this chapter we address published plays found in books and magazines as a literary genre— that is, as material to be read by children, either independently or in small groups. Some of these same plays also may be performed in children's theatres. We recommend that teachers and librarians emphasize the informal reading of plays by children during the elementary school years. Recreational plays and formal play productions are better left to middle-school or older students. The dramatic processes of creative drama and readers' theatre, discussed in Chapter 13, are also suitable for elementary-grade students.

Evaluation and Selection of Plays

A good play has a subject that appeals to children, an interesting character or two, and a problem that thickens or worsens, but gets resolved satisfactorily in the end. Humor always appeals to children, and conflict between characters is needed for interest and drama. Dialogue must be natural and reflect the personality of the character speaking. One or more of the characters in the play must have child appeal; typically such a character is a child or a childlike figure; a personified animal, doll, or other creature; or an adult with magical traits. Many published plays are planned for more elaborate productions than time will permit in the classroom. Such details can be interesting for children to read about, even if they are not likely to be able to produce the play as suggested.

Children's plays in the United States have been viewed as the stepchild both in the field of theatre and in the field of children's literature. Although some writers have given substantial attention to the development of play scripts for children, their work has not always been as highly valued by theatre producers and critics as that of playwrights who write for adults. Locating and selecting plays can be a challenge.

Children's Book and Play Review, a professional journal that appears five times a year, provides reviews of ten or twelve children's plays in each issue and has feature articles occasionally about the publication status of children's plays. Other review journals, such as *School Library Journal, Booklist,* and *Horn Book* Magazine, occasionally review published plays as well. The International Association of Theatre for Children and Young People periodically publishes international bibliographies of plays organized by country and provides a synopsis of each play, as well as its length, type, number of characters, languages in which it is available, and source for ordering (Oaks, 1996).

Anthologies are a good source of plays for children's reading enjoyment. One publisher, Smith and Kraus, Inc., has many play anthologies available on a variety of topics, such as holidays, cultural diversity, and mythology. Some recent anthologies from Smith and Kraus have been included in the Recommended Books of Plays at the end of this chapter.

At the present time, eighteen to twenty publishing houses handle children's plays. Eleven publishers have specialized in plays for children and deserve special mention here:

Anchorage Press Plays, P.O. Box 2901, Louisville, KY 40201-2901, formerly Children's Theatre Press, one of the oldest publishing houses for children's plays, remains a major publisher of children's plays with a backlist of approximately 290 plays for children. www.applays.com

Baker's Plays, P.O. Box 699222, Quincy, MA 02269, is a general play publisher with a specialization in children's plays with both a backlist and recent titles. The current list has approximately 110 plays. www.bakersplays.com

Contemporary Drama Service, 885 Elkton Drive, Colorado Springs, CO 80907, publishes plays for middle-school and high school students, has approximately 500 plays, and publishes 25 new plays each year. www.contemporarydrama.com

Dramatic Publishing Company, 311 Washington Street, Woodstock, IL 60098, has a large list of approximately 180 children's and young adults' plays. www.dramaticpublishing.com

Eldridge Publishing, P.O. Box 1595, Venice, FL 34284, is one of the oldest children's play publishers with a large list of approximately 600 plays and publishes 30 or more new plays each year. www.histage.com

I. E. Clark, Inc., Box 246, Schulenberg, TX 78956, is a general publisher with over 60 children's plays, including some bilingual plays. www.ieclark.com

New Plays, Inc., New Plays for Children, P.O. Box 5074, Charlottesville, VA 22905, is a publisher that specializes in children's plays with 100 titles available, many for the middle-school level. www.newplaysforchildren.com

Pioneer Drama Service, P.O. Box 4267, Englewood, CO 80155, is a general publisher of plays with more than 130 plays for children. www.pioneerdrama.com

Samuel French, Inc., 45 W. 25th St., New York, NY 10010, is a large general publisher of plays with a large backlist of children's plays, but is publishing few new children's plays currently. www.samuelfrench.com

Smith and Kraus, Inc., c/o IDS, 300 Bedford Street, Building B, Suite 213, Manchester, NH 03101, is a publisher of plays and play anthologies for children. www.smithandkraus.com

Plays Magazine, P.O. Box 600160, Newton, MA 02460, publishes fifty to sixty royalty-free new plays for children each year in the moderately priced magazine, *Plays, the Drama Magazine for Young People*. Anthologies drawn from these plays are also available. www.playsmag.com

The American Alliance for Theatre and Education (AATE) gives two awards that are useful in identifying notable children's plays and playwrights. The Distinguished Play Award, established in 1983, is given annually to honor the playwright and publisher of the works voted as the best original plays for young people published during the preceding year in category A, for upper and secondary school age audiences, and category B, for elementary and middle-school age audiences. In 1997, category C was added for the best adaptation. (See Appendix A for the complete list of winners.) The Charlotte B. Chorpenning Playwright Award, first conferred in 1967, honors a body of work by a children's playwright. The award is given annually, if merited.

Charlotte B. Chorpenning Playwright Award Winners

1967	Aurand Harris	1985	Aurand Harris
1968	Martha Bennett King	1986	Virginia Glasgow Koste
1969	Marian Johnson	1987–1988	No award
1970	Madge Miller	1989	Brian Kral
1971	Joanna Halpert Kraus	1990–1993	No award
1972	Ed Graczxk	1994	James Still
1973	Alan Cullen	1995	Max Bush
1974	Rosemary Musil	1996–1998	No award
1975	Helen P. Avery	1999	Sandra Fenichel Asher
1976	Joseph Robinette	2000–2001	No award
1977	Flora B. Atkin	2002	Y York
1978	Suzan L. Zeder	2003	Laurie Brooks
1979	Jonathan Levy	2004	No award
1980	Moses Goldberg	2005	José Cruz González
1981–1984	No award	2006	Mary Hall Surface

 ## Historical Overview of Plays

Plays were seldom written exclusively for children prior to the twentieth century, yet for centuries plays were written and performed for a general audience that included children. Church dramas also have a long tradition that can be traced back to the Middle Ages when the Catholic Church

used such plays as a means of educating. Examples of plays appealing to children but intended for a general audience are *Gulliver's Travels, Huckleberry Finn,* and Shaw's *Androcles and the Lion,* among others. J. M. Barrie's *Peter Pan,* the most widely acknowledged classic of the genre of plays for children, has had great appeal to children during its long history of production beginning in 1904.

The main stimulus for writing plays has been the development and existence of children's theatres and theatre groups that have a need for material. Children's theatre in the United States has generally been independent of the adult professional theatre, is community based with substantial contributions by amateurs, has suffered from limited budgets, and yet has tenaciously survived. Programs by theatres specializing in productions for young people began in the early twentieth century when the influential, though short-lived, Children's Educational Theatre was founded in 1903 in New York.

Following the establishment of theatres for children, a small number of plays and collections of plays for children began to be written and published. Small children's theatres gradually arose in many communities.

With the spread of children's theatre groups there was an increase in the number of published scripts; for example, as early as 1921, *A Treasury of Plays for Children* by Montrose J. Moses appeared. An early children's playwright of exceptional note was Charlotte B. Chorpenning (1872–1955), who published with Anchorage Press Plays. She was artistic director of the Goodman Children's Theatre of the Art Institute of Chicago from 1931 until her death and wrote many plays for its use. Her contributions to juvenile dramatic literature were outstanding for both the quality and quantity of her work. Her observations of children's interests at each age level are still useful to playwrights (McCaslin, 1971).

During the 1960s and 1970s, professional theatre companies for young audiences began to appear. They encountered an extremely limited body of children's plays suitable to their needs. This lack was the major stimulus for a rapid increase in children's play publishing (Oaks, 1997). An outstanding children's playwright who wrote during this period was Aurand Harris, a playwright of children's plays from 1945 to the time of his death in 1996. He left behind a rich legacy of published plays that include original works as well as adaptations of folktales and modern literature. He is particularly noted for exploring different styles for children's theatre, including a vaudevillian show (*The Toby Show*), a melodrama (*Rags to Riches*), and even a serious drama that treats the topic of death (*The Arkansaw Bear*). He remained for many years the most produced children's playwright in the United States. He was the first winner of the Charlotte B. Chorpenning Award and the only playwright to win it twice, in 1967 and in 1985. Other children's playwrights who have been honored for a number of their children's plays include James Still, Edward Mast, and Suzan L. Zeder.

 ## Types of Plays

Traditionally, plays are categorized within types such as drama, comedy, farce, melodrama, and tragedy. Dramas and comedies are the most common play types found in children's plays. Some children's theatres produce **participation plays,** sometimes referred to as **interactive theatre.** A participation play is the presentation of a drama with an established storyline constructed to involve structured opportunities for active involvement by the audience.

In children's plays the distinction between adaptations and original plays is important. Many adaptations of traditional literature—generally folktales, fables, and Bible stories—have been

Notable Poets and Playwrights

Arnold Adoff, recipient of the National Council of Teachers of English (NCTE) Award for Excellence in Poetry for Children. Many poems about relating to people across racial groups. *All the Colors of the Race.* www.arnoldadoff.com

Sandra Fenichel Asher, a playwright whose plays focus on the real life struggles of young adults. *A Woman Called Truth; Blackbirds and Dragons, Mermaids and Mice.* http://usawrites4kids .drury.edu/authors/asher

Paul Fleischman, winner of the Newbery Medal for his *Joyful Noise: Poems for Two Voices;* in it and *Big Talk,* the poems are composed and printed for two or four readers to read lines in unison and solo. www.paulfleischman.net

Kristine O'Connell George, noted for several poetry collections of interest to children from preschool to middle school in which she uses many different poetic forms. *Little Dog Poems; Swimming Upstream: Middle School Poems; Fold Me a Poem.* www.kristinegeorge.com

Nikki Grimes, African-American poet whose poetry celebrates children and their friendships and families. 2006 recipient of the NCTE Award for Excellence in Poetry. *Meet Danitra Brown; A Pocketful of Poems; Thanks a Million.* www.nikkigrimes.com

Mary Ann Hoberman, recipient of the NCTE Award for Excellence in Poetry, is known for her humorous, colorful poetry. *Fathers, Mothers, Sisters, Brothers: A Collection of Family Poems; You Read to Me, I'll Read to You.* www.maryannhoberman.com.

Sara Holbrook, known as a poet and a performer of poetry that appeals especially to adolescents. *By Definition: Poems of Feelings; I Never Said I Wasn't Difficult.* www.saraholbrook.com

Paul B. Janeczko, contemporary poet and anthologist of poetry that especially appeals to young adults. *Dirty Laundry Pile: Poems in Different Voices; A Poke in the I: A Collection of Concrete Poems; Worlds Afire.* www.pauljaneczko.com

X. J. Kennedy, a favorite creator of nonsense and humorous verse about contemporary themes. *Fresh Brats; Exploding Gravy.* www .xjanddorothymkennedy.com

Naomi Shihab Nye, a poet and anthologist whose meditative poems offer global perspectives and whose edited collections include Mexican, Native American, and Middle Eastern poetry. *This Same Sky: A Collection of Poems from Around the World; 19 Varieties of Gazelle: Poems of the Middle East.*

Gary Soto, a writer whose poetry captures the experiences of growing up in a Mexican neighborhood in California's Central Valley. *Neighborhood Odes; Worlds Apart: Traveling with Fernie and Me.* www.garysoto.com

James Still, award-winning playwright noted for his highly original fantasy play, *In the Suicide Mountains,* and for cross-generational plays. *And Then They Came for Me: Remembering the World of Anne Frank; Amber Waves.*

Mary Hall Surface, a theatre artist who writes and directs plays for young audiences. *The Reluctant Dragon; Sing Down the Moon: Appalachian Wonder Tales, A Musical; The Sorcerer's Apprentice.*

David Wood, noted British playwright for children who has developed screenplays and musical plays from children's literature. *Babe, the Sheep-Pig; The Gingerbread Man.*

Suzan L. Zeder, experimental playwright who has written contemporary plays and musicals for a multigenerational audience. *Step on a Crack; Mother Hicks; The Taste of Sunrise.*

made and are readily available from most of the children's play publishers. Adaptations of modern children's literature, such as Mary Hoffman's *Amazing Grace* and Maurice Sendak's *Where the Wild Things Are,* are being published with increasing frequency.

Original plays—that is, stories originating in play form—represent fewer than one-third of the new plays published annually. According to Sather (1976), children indicate a preference for plays with stories never heard before. Perhaps in response to this, the publication of children's plays is growing rapidly. It has increased substantially from 10 or 12 a year in the early 1960s to more than 200 a year at the beginning of the twenty-first century.

The natural play of children and the theatre are "manifestations of the same human need to make concrete the intangible, to make explicable the inexplicable, to make accessible the incomprehensible, and to make memorable the significant" (Davis, 1981, p. 14). Plays help children come to terms with the unknown and the threatening and help to heighten their appreciation of the actual and the enjoyment of the human comedy. Make plays a vital part of your literary curriculum.

Topics for Further Investigation

- Design an attractive poetry file in which you include thirty to fifty of your favorite poems for children. Type or copy each poem in its entirety, list the poet and the source of the poem, and suggest classroom uses such as choral arrangements or movements to accompany a poem. (See Chapter 13 for ideas.)
- Research the history of Mother Goose, its origins, and uses with children.
- Research the history of plays for children. Consider the early roles of children in plays and the development of plays for a child audience.

 See the companion website at www.ablongman.com/lynchbrown6e for additional suggestions.

References

Charles, D. (1982). Concrete cat. In X. J. Kennedy & D. M. Kennedy (Eds.), *Knock at a star.* Illustrated by K. A. Weinhaus. Boston: Little, Brown.

Ciardi, J. (1996). *The monster den.* Philadelphia: Lippincott.

Clark, G. O. (1983). The night is a big black cat. In J. Prelutsky (Ed.), *The Random House book of poetry for children.* Illustrated by A. Lobel. New York: Random House.

Crane, W. (1983). The crocus. In J. Prelutsky (Ed.), *The Random House book of poetry for children.* Illustrated by A. Lobel. New York: Random House.

Davis, D. (1981). *Theater for young people.* New York: Beaufort.

Dotlich, R. K. (2003). Autumn leaves. In R. K. Dotlich (Ed.), *In the spin of things: Poetry of motion.* Illustrated by Karen Dugan. Honesdale, PA: Boyds Mills.

Elster, C. A., & Hanauer, D. I. (2002). Voicing texts, voices around texts: Reading poems in elementary school classrooms. *Research in the Teaching of English, 37*(1), 89–134.

Field, Rachel. (1957). Song for a Blue Roadster. In H. Ferris (Ed.), *Favorite poems, old and new.* Illustrated by Leonard Weisgard. New York: Doubleday.

Fisher, C. J., & Natarella, M. A. (1982). Young children's preferences in poetry: A national survey of first, second and third graders. *Research in the Teaching of English, 16*(4), 339–354.

Ghigna, C. (2003). What's a poem? In C. Ghigna (Ed.), *A fury of motion: Poems for boys.* Honesdale, PA: Boyds Mills.

Gillespie, M. C. (1970). *Literature for children: History and trends.* Dubuque, IA: Wm. C. Brown.

Glover, M. K. (1999). *A garden of poets: Poetry writing in the elementary classroom.* Urbana, IL: National Council of Teachers of English.

Goldberg, M. (1974). *Children's theatre: A philosophy and a method.* Englewood Cliffs, NJ: Prentice Hall.

Grimes, N. (2001). Pigeons masquerade. In N. Grimes (Ed.), *A pocketful of poems.* Illustrated by J. Steptoe. New York: Clarion.

Holbrook, S. (2002). *Wham! It's a poetry jam: Discovering performance poetry.* Honesdale, PA: Boyds Mills.

Janeczko, P. B., Selector. (1990). *The place my words are looking for: What poets say about and through their work.* New York: Bradbury.

———. (1994). *Poetry from A to Z: A guide for young writers.* New York: Bradbury.

———. (1999). *How to write poetry.* New York: Scholastic.

Kahn, S. (1967). Giraffes. In S. Dunning, E. Lueders, & H. Smith (Eds.), *Reflections on a gift of watermelon pickle.* New York: Lothrop, Lee and Shepard.

Koch, K. (1990). *Rose, where did you get that red?* New York: Random.

———. (1999/1970). *Wishes, lies, and dreams: Teaching children to write poetry.* New York: Random.

Kutiper, K., & Wilson, P. (1993). Updating poetry preferences: A look at the poetry children really like. *The Reading Teacher, 47*(1), 28–35.

Lear, E. (1946). *The complete nonsense book.* New York: Dodd, Mead.

Livingston, M. C. (1991). *Poem making: Ways to begin writing poetry.* New York: HarperCollins.

McCaslin, N. (1971). *Theatre for children in the United States.* Norman: University of Oklahoma Press.

McKean, B. (2000–2001). Speak the speech, I pray you! Preparing to read aloud dramatically. *The Reading Teacher, 54*(4), 358–360.

Moses, M. J. (Ed.). (1921). *A treasury of plays for children.* Boston: Little, Brown.

Oaks, H. (Ed.). (1996). *Outstanding plays for young audiences: International bibliography,* vol. 5. Seattle, WA: United States Center for the International Association of Theatre for Children and Young People.

———. (1997). Collections of plays for young audiences. *Children's Book and Play Review, 17*(4), 1–3.

Prelutsky, J. (2005). *Read a rhyme, write a rhyme.* Illustrated by Meilo So. New York: Knopf.

Reeves, J. (1963). Slowly. In E. Blishen (Ed.), *Oxford book of poetry for children.* Illustrated by B. Wildsmith. Oxford: Oxford University Press.

Ryan, M. (1996). *How to write a poem.* New York: Watts.

Sather, S. P. (1976). A critical assessment of children's plays. *Children's Theatre Review, 25*(1), 2–5.

Schwedt, R., & DeLong, J. (2002). *Young adult poetry: A survey and theme guide.* Westport, CT: Greenwood.

Shaw, J. M. (1967). The broken-legg'd man. In J. M. Shaw (Ed.), *The things I want: Poems for two children.* Tallahassee, FL: Florida State University Library.

Sloan, G. (2003). *Give them poetry: A guide for sharing poetry with children K–8.* New York: Teachers College Press.

Smolkin, L. B. (1995). The literature of the theatre and aesthetic response: Welcoming plays into the world of children's literature. *The New Advocate, 8*(2), 109–123.

Taylor, J. (1983). The star. In J. Prelutsky (Ed.), *The Random House book of poetry for children.* Illustrated by A. Lobel. New York: Random House.

Terry, A. C. (1974). *Children's poetry preferences: A national survey of upper elementary grades.* Urbana, IL: National Council of Teachers of English.

Recommended Poetry Books

Because poetry is usually of interest to a broad age group, entries of poetry books indicate age only for books mainly suitable for older readers.

Mother Goose and Nursery Rhyme Books

Arenson, Roberta. *One, Two, Skip a Few! First Number Rhymes.* Barefoot, 1998. Illustrated.

Crews, Nina. *The Neighborhood Mother Goose.* Greenwillow, 2004. Illustrated with photographs in a city setting.

de Angeli, Marguerite. *Marguerite de Angeli's Book of Nursery and Mother Goose Rhymes.* Doubleday, 1954.

dePaola, Tomie, compiler. *Tomie dePaola's Mother Goose.* Putnam, 1985.

Engelbreit, Mary. *Mary Engelbreit's Mother Goose.* HarperCollins, 2004. Illustrated.

Foreman, Michael. *Michael Foreman's Playtime Rhymes.* Candlewick, 2002. Includes activities and motions to accompany rhymes.

Lobel, Arnold, selector. *The Random House Book of Mother Goose.* Random, 1986.

Millen, C. M. *Blue Bowl Down: An Appalachian Rhyme.* Illustrated by Holly Meade. Candlewick, 2004.

Moses, Will. *Will Moses' Mother Goose.* Philomel, 2003.

Opie, Iona, editor. *Here Comes Mother Goose.* Illustrated by Rosemary Wells. Candlewick, 1999.

Rojankovsky, Feodor. *The Tall Book of Mother Goose.* Harper, 1942.

Zemach, Margot, compiler. *Some from the Moon, Some from the Sun: Poems and Songs for Everyone.* Farrar, 2001.

Nursery and Folk Songbooks

Baum, Maxie. *I Have a Little Dreidel.* Illustrated by Julie Paschkis. Scholastic, 2006.

Eddleman, David, editor. *The Great Children's Songbook.* Illustrated by Andrew J. Dowty. Carl Fischer, 1998.

Guthrie, Woody. *This Land Is Your Land.* Illustrated by Kathy Jakobsen. Little, 1998.

Higgensen, Vy, selector. *This Is My Song!: A Collection of Gospel Music for the Family.* Illustrated by Brenda Joysmith. Crown, 1995.

Katz, Alan. *Where Did They Hide My Presents? Silly Dilly Christmas Songs.* Illustrated by David Katrow. McElderry, 2004.

Krull, Kathleen, editor. *Gonna Sing My Head Off! American Folk Songs for Children.* Illustrated by Allen Garns. Knopf, 1992.

Larrick, Nancy, compiler. *Songs from Mother Goose: With the Traditional Melody for Each.* Illustrated by Robin Spowart. Harper, 1989.

Nelson, Kadir. *He's Got the Whole World in His Hands.* Dial, 2005.

Anthologies of Poetry

Booth, David, editor. *'Til All the Stars Have Fallen.* Illustrated by Kady Denton. Viking, 1990. Ages 10–13.

Cole, Joanna, compiler. *A New Treasury of Children's Poetry: Old Favorites and New Discoveries.* Illustrated by Judith Gwyn Brown. Doubleday, 1984.

Driscoll, Michael. *A Child's Introduction to Poetry.* Illustrated by Meredith Hamilton. Black Dog & Leventhal, 2003. Ages 9–14. Discusses poetic forms and individual poets, with examples.

Ferris, Helen, compiler. *Favorite Poems Old and New.* Illustrated by Leonard Weisgard. Doubleday, 1957.

Hall, Donald, editor. *The Oxford Illustrated Book of American Children's Poems.* Oxford University, 1999.

Harrison, Michael, and Christopher Stuart-Clark, editors. *The New Oxford Treasury of Children's Poems.* Oxford, 1987. Ages 9–12.

———, editors. *The Oxford Treasury of Classic Poems.* Oxford, 1996. Ages 11–16.

Hopkins, Lee Bennett, editor. *Climb into My Lap: First Poems to Read Together.* Illustrated by Kathryn Brown. Simon & Schuster, 2000.

———. *My America: A Poetry Atlas of the United States.* Simon & Schuster, 2000.

Kennedy, X. J., and Dorothy Kennedy, editors. *Knock at a Star: A Child's Introduction to Poetry,* rev. ed. Illustrated by Karen Lee Baher. Little, Brown, 1999.

Philip, Neil, editor. *A New Treasury of Poetry.* Illustrated by John Lawrence. Stewart, Tabori & Chang, 1990. Ages 11–15.

Prelutsky, Jack, editor. *The Random House Book of Poetry for Children.* Illustrated by Arnold Lobel. Random House, 1983.

———, editor. *The 20th Century Children's Poetry Treasury.* Illustrated by Meilo So. Knopf, 1999.

Rosenberg, Liz, editor. *The Invisible Ladder: An Anthology of Contemporary American Poems for Young Readers.* Holt, 1996. Ages 11–15.

Specialized Poetry Books

Poetry books by a single poet and thematic poetry books are included.

Adoff, Arnold. *All the Colors of the Race.* Illustrated by John Steptoe. Lothrop, 1982.

———, editor. *I Am the Darker Brother: An Anthology of Modern Poems by African Americans.* Drawings by Benny Andrews. Simon & Schuster, 1997/1968. Ages 13–18. This revised edition includes 21 new poems and 19 additional poets.

———. *Slow Dance Heartbreak Blues.* Illustrated by William Cotton. Lothrop, 1995. Ages 12–16.

———. *Touch the Poem.* Illustrated by Lisa Desimini. Scholastic, 2000.

Agard, John. *Half-Caste and Other Poems.* Hodder, 2005. Ages 14–18.

Appelt, Kathi. *Poems from Homeroom: A Writer's Place to Start.* Holt, 2002. Ages 12–18. Includes a bibliography of adult books on writing poems and stories.

Ashman, Linda. *The Essential Worldwide Monster Guide.* Illustrated by David Small. Simon & Schuster, 2003.

Berry, James. *A Nest Full of Stars: Poems.* Pictures by Ashley Bryan. New York: Greenwillow, 2004. Everyday Caribbean language and culture.

———, editor. *Around the World in Eighty Poems.* Illustrated by Katherine Lucas. Chronicle, 2002. Fifty countries represented and many narrative poems.

Ciardi, John. *Doodle Soup.* Illustrated by Merle Nacht. Houghton, 1985.

Clinton, Catherine, *I, Too, Sing America: Three Centuries of African-American Poetry.* Illustrated by Stephen Alcorn. Houghton, 1998.

———, editor. *A Poem of Her Own: Voices of American Women Yesterday and Today.* Illustrated by Stephen Alcorn. Abrams, 2003. Ages 10–16.

Cullinan, Bernice E., editor. *A Jar of Tiny Stars: Poems by NCTE Award–Winning Poets.* Boyds Mills, 1995.

Dunbar, Paul Laurence. *Jump Back, Honey: The Poems of Paul Laurence Dunbar.* Hyperion, 1999.

Fleischman, Paul. *Big Talk: Poems for Four Voices.* Illustrated by Beppe Giacobbe. Candlewick, 2000. Ages 9–14.

———. *I Am Phoenix: Poems for Two Voices.* Illustrated by Eric Beddows. Harper, 1985.

———. *Joyful Noise: Poems for Two Voices.* Illustrated by Eric Beddows. Harper, 1988.

Florian, Douglas. *Autumnblings.* Greenwillow, 2003. One of his cycles of seasons, including *Handsprings,* 2006; *Summersaults,* 2002; and *Winter Eyes,* 1999.

———. *Lizards, Frogs, and Polliwogs: Poems and Paintings.* Harcourt, 2001.

———. *Mammalabilia.* Illustrated. Harcourt, 2000.

Franco, Betsy. *Mathematickles.* Illustrated by Steven Salerno. Simon & Schuster, 2003.

George, Kristine O'Connell. *Fold Me a Poem.* Illustrated by Lauren Stringer. Harcourt, 2005.

———. *The Great Frog Race and Other Poems.* Illustrated by Kate Kiesler. Clarion, 1997.

———. *Hummingbird Nest: A Journal of Poems.* Illustrated by Barry Moser. Harcourt, 2004.

———. *Little Dog Poems.* Illustrated by June Otani. Clarion, 1999.

———. *Old Elm Speaks: Tree Poems.* Illustrated by Kate Kiesler. Clarion, 1998.

———. *Swimming Upstream: Middle School Poems.* Clarion, 2002. Ages 10–14.

———. *Toasting Marshmallows: Camping Poems.* Illustrated by Kate Kiesler. Clarion, 2001.

———. *Up!* Illustrated by Hiroe Nakata. Clarion, 2005.

Ghigna, Charles. *A Fury of Motion: Poems for Boys.* Boyds Mills, 2003. Ages 12–18.

Giovanni, Nikki, editor. *Grand Fathers: Poems, Reminiscences, Poems, Recipes, and Photos of the Keepers of Our Traditions.* Holt, 1999. Ages 13–18. Also *Grand Mothers: Reminiscences, Poems, Recipes, and Photos of the Keepers of Our Traditions.* Holt, 1994.

Glaser, Isabel Joshlin, editor. *Dreams of Glory: Poems Starring Girls.* Simon & Schuster, 1995.

Goldstein, Bobbye S., editor. *Inner Chimes: Poems on Poetry.* Illustrated by Jane Breskin Zalben. Wordsong/Boyds Mills, 1992.

Grandits, John. *Technically, It's Not My Fault: Concrete Poems.* Clarion, 2004. Ages 9–13.

Greenberg, Jan. *Heart to Heart: New Poems Inspired by Twentieth Century American Art.* Abrams, 2001. Ages 11–15.

———. *It's Raining Laughter.* Photos by Myles C. Pinkney. Dial, 1997.

———. *Meet Danitra Brown.* Illustrated by Floyd Cooper. Morrow, 1994.

———. *A Pocketful of Poems.* Illustrated by Javaka Steptoe. Clarion, 2001.

———. *Stepping Out with Grandma Mac.* Orchard, 2001.

———. *Thanks a Million.* Illustrated by Cozbi A. Cabrera. Greenwillow/Amistad, 2006.

Hoberman, Mary Ann. *Fathers, Mothers, Sisters, Brothers: A Collection of Family Poems.* Illustrated by Marylin Hafner. Little, 1991.

Holbrook, Sara. *By Definition: Poems of Feelings.* Illustrated by Scott Mattern. Boyds Mills, 2003.

———. *I Never Said I Wasn't Difficult.* Boyds Mills, 1996. Ages 10–14.

———. *Nothing's the End of the World.* Illustrated by J. J. Smith-Moore. Boyds Mills, 1995. Ages 10–14.

———. *Walking on the Boundaries of Change.* Boyds Mills, 1998. Ages 11–18.

Hopkins, Lee Bennett, compiler. *Hand in Hand: An American History through Poetry.* Illustrated by Peter M. Fiore. Simon & Schuster, 1994.

———, editor. *My America: A Poetry Atlas of the United States.* Illustrated by Stephen Alcorn. Simon & Schuster, 2000. Ages 9–14. Poems evocative of seven geographical regions of the United States.

————, selector. *Opening Days: Sports Poems.* Illustrated by Scott Medlock. Harcourt, 1996.

Hudson, Wade, editor. *Pass It On: African American Poetry for Children.* Illustrated by Floyd Cooper. Scholastic, 1993.

In Daddy's Arms I Am Tall: African Americans Celebrating Fathers. Illustrated by Javaka Steptoe. Lee & Low, 1997.

James, Simon, editor. *Days Like This: A Collection of Small Poems.* Illustrated. Candlewick, 2000.

Janeczko, Paul B., editor. *Dirty Laundry Pile: Poems in Different Voices.* Illustrated by Melissa Sweet. HarperCollins, 2001.

————, selector. *A Kick in the Head: An Everyday Guide to Poetic Forms.* Illustrated by Chris Raschka. Candlewick, 2005. Ages 9–14. Poems of various forms with brief explanations of each form.

————, editor. *Looking for Your Name: A Collection of Contemporary Poems.* Orchard, 1993. Ages: 10–14.

————, editor. *A Poke in the I: A Collection of Concrete Poems.* Illustrated by Chris Raschka. Candlewick, 2000.

————. *That Sweet Diamond: Baseball Poems.* Atheneum, 1998. Ages 10–14.

————. *We, the People.* Illustrated by Nina Crews. Greenwillow, 2000. First-person poems focused on U.S. history; could be used as dramatic monologues.

————. *Worlds Afire.* Candlewick, 2004. Ages 10–15.

Katz, Bobbi, editor. *Pocket Poems.* Illustrated by Marylin Hafner. Dutton, 2004.

Katz, Susan. *Looking for Jaguar and Other Rainforest Poems.* Illustrated by Lee Christiansen. Greenwillow, 2005.

————. *Mrs. Brown on Exhibit: And Other Museum Poems.* Illustrated by R. W. Alley. Simon & Schuster, 2002. Includes a list of "amazing museums" around the United States.

Kennedy, Caroline, editor. *My Favorite Poetry for Children.* Illustrated by Jon J. Muth. Hyperion, 2005.

Kennedy, X. J. *Exploding Gravy.* Little Brown, 2002. Ages 6–12.

————. *Fresh Brats.* Illustrated by James Watts. Macmillan, 1990.

Kurtz, Jane. *River Friendly, River Wild.* Illustrated by Neil Brennan. Simon & Schuster, 2000.

Kuskin, Karla. *Green as a Bean.* Illustrated by Melissa Iwai. HarperCollins, 2007.

Lewis, J. Patrick. *Doodle Dandies: Poems That Take Shape.* Illustrated by Lisa Desimini. Simon & Schuster, 1998.

————. *Freedom Like Sunlight: Praisesongs for Black Americans.* Creative Editions, 2000.

————. *Vherses: A Celebration of Outstanding Women.* Illustrated by Mark Summers. Creative, 2005. Ages 9–14.

Lillegard, Dee. *Wake up House! Rooms Full of Poems.* Illustrated by Don Carter. Knopf, 2000.

Liu, Siyu, and Orel Protopopescu. *A Thousand Poems: Poems from China.* Illustrated by Siyu Liu. Pacific View Press, 2001. Ages 10–18.

Mak, Kam. *My Chinatown.* Illustrated by Kam Mak. HarperCollins, 2002.

Morrison, Lillian, compiler. *It Rained All Day That Night: Autographs, Rhymes & Inscriptions.* Illustrations by Christy Hale. August House, 2003.

Myers, Walter Dean. *Blues Journey.* Illustrated by Christopher Myers. Holiday, 2003. Ages 10–15.

————. *Harlem.* Illustrated by Christopher Myers. Scholastic, 1997. Ages 11–16.

————. *Here in Harlem: Poems in Many Voices.* Holiday, 2004. Ages 12–18.

————. *Jazz.* Illustrated by Christopher Myers. Holiday, 2006.

Nye, Naomi Shihab, editor. *A Maze Me: Poems for Girls.* Illustrated by Terre Maher. Greenwillow, 2005. Ages 11–18.

————. *Come with Me: Poems for a Journey.* Illustrated by Dan Yaccarino. Greenwillow, 2000.

————, editor. *19 Varieties of Gazelle: Poems of the Middle East.* HarperCollins, 2002. Ages 11–18.

————, editor. *The Space Between Our Footsteps: Poems and Paintings from the Middle East.* Simon & Schuster, 1998.

————, editor. *This Same Sky: A Collection of Poems from around the World.* Four Winds, 1992. Ages: 11–18.

Nye, Naomi, and Paul B. Janeczko, editors. *I Feel a Little Jumpy around You: A Book of Her Poems and His Poems Collected in Pairs.* Simon & Schuster, 1996. Ages 12–18.

Panzer, Nora, editor. *Celebrate America: In Poetry and Art.* Hyperion, 1994. Ages 12–16. Poems celebrating America's diversity and cultural heritage.

Pearson, Susan. *The Drowsy Hours: Poems for Bedtime.* Illustrated by Peter Malone. HarperCollins, 2002.

Peters, Lisa Westberg. *Earthshake: Poems from the Ground Up.* Illustrated by Cathie Felstead. Greenwillow, 2003. Ages 9–12. Poems about geology.

Prelutsky, Jack. *Behold the Bold Umbrellaphant and Other Poems.* Illustrated by Carin Berger. Harper-Collins, 2006.

———. *If Not for the Cat.* Illustrated by Ted Rand. Greenwillow, 2004. Different animals described in haiku.

———. *A Pizza the Size of the Sun.* Illustrated by James Stevenson. Greenwillow, 1996.

———, editor. *Read a Rhyme, Write a Rhyme.* Illustrated by Meilo Su. Knopf, 2005.

Rochelle, Belinda. *Words with Wings: A Treasury of African-American Poetry and Art.* HarperCollins/ Amistad, 2001.

Roessel, David, and Arnold Rampersad, editors. *Langston Hughes.* Illustrated by Benny Andrews. Sterling, 2006. Ages 10–18.

Scieszka, Jon. *Science Verse.* Illustrated by Lane Smith. Viking, 2004.

Sidman, Joyce. *Song of the Water Boatman and Other Pond Poems.* Illustrated by Beckie Prange. Houghton, 2005.

Siebert, Diane. *Tour America: A Journey Through Poems and Art.* Illustrated by Stephen T. Johnson. Chronicle, 2006. Ages 9–13.

Silverstein, Shel. *Where the Sidewalk Ends: The Poems and Drawings of Shel Silverstein.* Harper, 1974.

Singer, Marilyn. *Central Heating: Poems about Fire and Warmth.* Illustrated by Meilo Su. Knopf, 2005. Ages 9–14.

Smith, Hope Anita. *The Way a Door Closes.* Illustrated by Shane Evans. Holt, 2003. Ages 11–15. Snapshots of a contemporary African-American family.

Soto, Gary. *Neighborhood Odes.* Illustrated by David Diaz. Harcourt, 1992. Ages 10–15. Life in a Mexican-American neighborhood.

———. *Worlds Apart: Traveling with Fernie and Me.* Illustrated by Greg Clarke. Putnam, 2005. Ages 9–13.

Stevenson, James. *Popcorn.* Greenwillow, 1998.

Strickland, Dorothy S., and Michael R., editors. *Families: Poems Celebrating the African American Experience.* Illustrated by John Ward. Wordsong/ Boyds Mills, 1994.

Tadjo, Véronique, editor. *Talking Drums: A Selection of Poems from Africa South of the Sahara.* New York: Bloomsbury, 2004. Ages 9–14. A collection of 75 poems from 16 African countries arranged by themes.

Thomas, Joyce Carol. *Crowning Glory: Poems.* Illustrated by Brenda Joysmith. Joanna Cotler, 2002.

Updike, John. *A Child's Calendar.* Illustrated by Trina Schart Hyman. Holiday, 1999.

Vecchione, Patrice, editor. *Truth and Lies.* Holt, 2000. Ages 12–18. A multicultural anthology of 70 poems.

Weatherford, Carole Boston. *Remember the Bridge: Poems of a People.* New York: Philomel, 2002. Ages 10–16.

Whipple, Laura, editor. *Celebrating America: A Collection of Poems and Images of the American Spirit.* Putnam/Philomel, 1994. Age: 10–15.

Wilbur, Richard. *The Disappearing Alphabet.* Illustrated by David Diaz. Harcourt, 1998.

Yolen, Jane, editor. *Weather Report.* Illustrated by Annie Guzman. Boyds Mills, 1993. Fifty poems to capture all kinds of weather.

Zolotow, Charlotte. *Seasons: A Book of Poems.* Illustrated by Erik Blegvad. HarperCollins, 2002. Easy-to-read book.

Single Illustrated Poems

Note the distinction between *poems* and *stories told in verse.* Heavily illustrated poems are listed here. Illustrated stories told in verse are included under the heading of Picture Storybooks in Chapter 5.

Bates, Katharine Lee. *America the Beautiful.* Illustrated by Chris Gall. Little, Brown, 2004.

Burleigh, Robert. *Hoops.* Illustrated by Stephen T. Johnson. Harcourt, 1997.

Johnson, James Weldon. *The Creation.* Illustrated by James Ransome. Holiday, 1994.

Longfellow, Henry Wadsworth. *Paul Revere's Ride: The Landlord's Tale.* Illustrated by Charles Santore. HarperCollins, 2003. Ages 9–14. Dramatic illustrations accompany this classic poem.

Myers, Walter Dean. *Harlem.* Illustrated by Christopher Myers. Scholastic, 1997. Ages 11–15. A poem celebrating Harlem.

Nelson, Marilyn. *Fortune's Bones: The Manumission Requiem.* Front Street, 2004. Ages 12–16. An illustrated poetic memorial of an enslaved man who died in 1798.

———. *A Wreath for Emmett Till.* Illustrated by Philippe Lardy. Houghton, 2005. Ages 12–18. An illustrated memorial to the lynched teen through interlocking sonnets.

Ryder, Joanne. *Earthdance.* Illustrated by Norman Gorbaty. Holt, 1996.

Shange, Ntozake. *Ellington Was Not a Street.* Illustrated by Kadir Nelson. Simon & Schuster, 2004. Ages 9–13. Memories of a Harlem childhood.

Siebert, Diane. *Heartland.* Illustrated by Wendell Minor. HarperCollins, 1989.

———. *Mojave.* Illustrated by Wendell Minor. Crowell, 1988. Ages 10–14.

———. *Sierra.* Illustrated by Wendell Minor. HarperCollins, 1991.

Thayer, Ernest L. *Casey at the Bat.* Illustrated by Joe Morse. Kids Can, 2006. Ages 9–13. An urban setting.

———. *Casey at the Bat: A Ballad of the Republic Sung in the Year 1888.* Illustrated by C. F. Payne. Simon & Schuster, 2003.

Thomas, Joyce Carol. *Cherish Me!* Illustrated by Nneka Bennett. HarperFestival, 1998.

Willard, Nancy. *The Tale I Told Sasha.* Illustrated by David Christiana. Little, Brown, 1999.

Recommended Books of Plays

Anthologies of Plays

Bany-Winters, Lisa. *On Stage!* Chicago Press, 1997. Ages 9–12. Several play scripts and an assortment of theatre games.

Bruchac, Joseph. *Pushing Up the Sky: Seven Native American Plays for Children.* Dial, 2000. Ages 7–11.

Bush, Max. *Plays for Young Audiences.* Edited by Roger Ellis. Meriwether, 1995. Ages 9–13. Ten full-length plays by award-winning playwrights.

Carlson, Lori Marie, selector. *You're On! Seven Plays in English and Spanish.* Morrow, 1999. Ages 9–15.

Ellis, Roger, editor. *Audition Monologues for Student Actors: Selections from Contemporary Plays.* Meriwether, 1999. Ages 13–16.

———, editor. *International Plays for Young Audiences: Contemporary Works from Leading Playwrights.* Meriwether, 2000. Ages 12–16.

———. *New International Plays for Young Audiences: Plays of Cultural Conflict.* Meriwether, 2002. Ages 12–16.

———, and Ted Zapel, editors. *Multicultural Theatre II: Contemporary Hispanic, Asian, and African American Plays.* Meriwether, 1998. Ages 12–16.

Espinosa, Resurrección. *Don Quixote in America: Plays in English and Spanish, Grades 1–6.* Libraries Unlimited, 2002. Ages 6–12.

Gerke, Pamela. *Multicultural Plays for Children, vol. 1: Grades K–3.* Smith and Kraus, 1996. Ages 5–8.

———. *Multicultural Plays for Children, vol. 2: Grades 4–6.* Smith and Kraus, 1996. Ages 9–12.

Halligan, Terry. *Funny Skits and Sketches.* Illustrated by Joyce Behr. Players Press, 1999. Ages 6–12. Primarily related to holidays and appropriate for schools and community functions.

Jennings, Coleman A., editor. *Theatre for Young Audiences.* St. Martin's Press, 1998. Ages 9–12. Mostly recent short plays.

Kamerman, Sylvia E. *Thirty Plays from Favorite Stories.* Plays, Inc., 1998. Ages 7–12.

McCaslin, Nellie. *Legends in Action: Ten Plays of Ten Lands.* Players Press, 2001. Ages 8–12.

McCullough, L. E. *"Now I Get It!": 12 Ten-Minute Classroom Drama Skits for Science, Math, Language, and Social Studies.* Smith and Kraus, 2000. Vol. 1 for ages 5–8; Vol. 2 for ages 9–12.

———. *Plays from Fairy Tales: Grades K–3.* Also, *Plays from Mythology: Grades 4–6.* Smith and Kraus, 1998. Ages 5–8.

———. *Plays of Exploration and Discovery, Grades 4–6.* Smith and Kraus, 1999. Ages 9–12. The 12 plays depict moments of discovery in science and geography.

McDonnell, Kathleen. *Putting on a Show: Theater for Young People.* Second Story Press, 2004. Ages 10–14. Four original plays included with theatre background and history.

Stevens, Chambers. *Magnificent Monologues for Kids.* Sandcastle, 1999. Ages 6–11. Includes 51 brief monologues.

Surface, Mary Hall. *Most Valuable Player: And Four Other All-Star Plays for Young Audiences.* Smith and Kraus, 1999. Ages 13–16.

———. *Short Scenes and Monologues for Middle School Actors.* Smith and Kraus, 2000. Ages 11–14. Includes monologues and scenes for two actors.

Swortzell, Lowell, editor. *Theatre for Young Audiences: Around the World in 21 Plays.* Applause Theatre Book Publishers, 1997. Ages 13–18.

Thistle, Louise. *Dramatizing Aesop's Fables: Grades K–6.* Smith and Kraus, 1997. Ages 5–12.

———. *Dramatizing Mother Goose: Introducing Students to Classic Literature through Drama.* Smith and Kraus, 1998. Ages 5–12.

Ullom, Shirley. *Tough Acts to Follow: Seventy-Five Monologs for Teens.* Meriweather, 2000. Ages 11–18. A collection of new and original short character sketches.

Williams, Marcia, adapter. *Tales from Shakespeare: Seven Plays.* Illustrated. Candlewick, 1998. Ages 7–11.

Winther, Barbara. *Plays from Hispanic Tales: One Act, Royalty-Free Dramatizations for Young People from Hispanic Stories and Folktales.* Plays, Inc., 1998. Ages 10–16.

Single Plays

Almond, David. *Two Plays.* Delacorte, 2005. Ages 10–14. The novel, *Skellig,* is dramatized and presented along with a shorter play, *Wild Girl, Wild Boy.*

Asher, Sandra Fenichel. *In the Garden of the Selfish Giant.* Dramatic Publishing, 2004. Ages 6–12.

———. *The Wolf and Its Shadow.* Anchorage, 2000. Ages 6–9.

Burdett, Lois. *Hamlet for Kids.* Firefly, 2000. Ages 8–12. (Also, *The Tempest for Kids,* Firefly, 1999. Ages 6–10.)

Bush, Max. *Ghost of the Riverhouse.* Anchorage, 1997. Ages 9–12.

Butterfield, Moira. *Hansel and Gretel.* Playtales Series. Heinemann, 1997. Also, *Sleeping Beauty.* Ages 7–10.

Creech, Sharon. *Replay.* Joanna Cotler, 2005. Ages 9–13. A novel with a play included at the end.

DeVita, James. *Bambi, a Life in the Woods.* Anchorage, 1995. Ages 9–12.

———. *Excavating Mom.* Dramatic Publishing, 1998. Ages 12–14.

Fleischman, Paul. *Zap.* Candlewick, 2005. Ages 12–18. Seven storylines in one innovative play.

Goldberg, Moses. *Puss in Boots* (a participation play). Anchorage, 1992. His plays are especially appealing for children in early childhood, ages 3–8.

Hezlip, William. *Kokopelli's Cave.* Players, 2002. Ages 10–15. (Part of a series of time travel plays including *Trouble in the Mountains.* Players Press, 2003.)

Ledoux, Paul. *Anne.* Playwrights Canada Press, 1999. Ages 8–12.

Mast, Edward. *Wolf Child: The Correction of Joseph.* Anchorage, 1999. Ages 6–10.

Myers, Walter Dean. *Monster.* HarperCollins, 1998. Ages 13–18. A novel written as a television script.

Robinette, Joseph, playwright. *Sarah Plain and Tall.* (Adapted from the book by Patricia MacLachlan.) Dramatic Publishing, 2003. Ages 7–12.

Shapiro, Jacqui. *Joshua's Egg: A Play for Children.* Samuel French, 1999. Ages 5–9.

Soto, Gary. *Nerdlandia: A Play.* Penguin, 1999. Ages 13–16. Some Spanish dialogue.

Still, James. *And Then They Came for Me: Remembering the World of Anne Frank.* Dramatic Publishing, 1999. Ages 12–16.

Surface, Mary Hall. *Blackbirds and Dragons, Mermaids and Mice.* Dramatic Publishing, 2005. Ages 5–10. A collection of five plays.

———. *The Sorcerer's Apprentice* (playscript). Anchorage, 1994. Ages 8–12. Adaptation of the folktale.

Wing, Paula. *Naomi's Road.* PUC Play Service, 1999. (Based on a novel by Joy Kogawa with the same name.) Ages 11–15.

Wood, David, adapter. *Babe, the Sheep-Pig: A Play.* Samuel French, 1997. Ages 6–10.

———, playwright. *Spot's Birthday Party.* (Based on the book by Eric Hill.) Samuel French, 2002. Ages 4–8.

York, Y, adapter. *Afternoon of the Elves.* Dramatic Publishing, 2000. Ages 9–12.

———, adapter. *The Garden of Rikki Tikki Tavi.* Dramatic Publishing, 1999. Ages 8–12.

Zeder, Suzan L. *Mother Hicks, Playscript.* Anchorage, 1986. Ages 5–8.

———. *Step on a Crack.* Anchorage, 1976. Ages 6–12.

———. *The Taste of Sunrise* (prequel to *Mother Hicks*). Anchorage, 1999. Ages 5–9.

Guide to Illustrations

Source of Book Illustration	Artistic Style; Medium	Visual Elements	Elements of Fiction
1 Siebert, Diane. *Heartland.* Illustrated by Wendell Minor. Crowell, 1989.	Realistic; watercolors	Line, composition	Setting, theme, author's style
2 Rawlinson, Julia. *Fletcher and the Falling Leaves.* Illustrated by Tiphanie Beeke. Greenwillow, 2006.	Impressionistic; pastels	Color, line, texture	Setting, character, mood
3 Juster, Norton. *The Hello, Goodbye Window.* Illustrated by Chris Raschka. Hyperion, 2005.	Impressionistic; watercolors, oil pastels, pen and ink, charcoals	Composition, color, line	Character, setting, mood, style
4 Raschka, Chris. *Yo! Yes?* Orchard, 1993.	Expressionistic; watercolors, charcoals	Shape/space	Plot, character, theme
5 Thompson, Lauren. *Polar Bear Night.* Illustrated by Stephen Savage. Scholastic, 2004.	Abstract; linocut prints	Color, shape, composition	Setting, characters, theme
6 Browne, Anthony. *Changes.* Knopf, 1986.	Surrealistic; watercolors	Composition, mood	Plot, theme

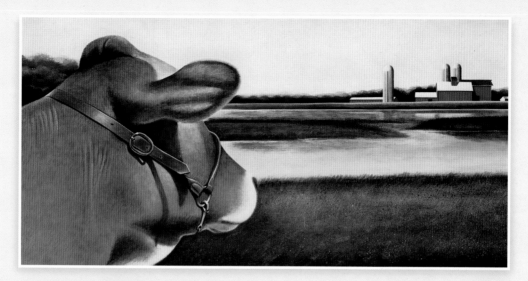

1

2

3

4

5

6

7

8

9

10

11

12

Guide to Illustrations

	Source of Book Illustration	Artistic Style; Medium	Visual Elements	Elements of Fiction
7	Garza, Carmen L. *Family Pictures/Cuadros de familia.* Spanish version by Rosalma Zubizaretta. Children's Book Press, 1990.	Primitive/folk; oil	Composition	Setting, theme
8	Henkes, Kevin. *Chrysanthemum.* Greenwillow, 1991.	Cartoon; watercolors, black pen	Shape/space, line, color, mood	Character, setting, theme
9	Rathmann, Peggy. *Officer Buckle and Gloria.* Putnam, 1995.	Cartoon; watercolors, pen and ink	Line, composition, mood	Plot, character, theme
10	Reid, Barbara. *The Subway Mouse.* Scholastic, 2003.	Cartoon; collage	Texture, color, mood	Character, setting, style
11	Sidman, Joyce. *Song of the Water Boatman & Other Pond Poems.* Illustrated by Beckie Prange. Houghton, 2005.	Woodcut; watercolors	Composition, line, color, mood	Setting, theme
12	Wick, Walter. *A Drop of Water: A Book of Science and Wonder.* Scholastic, 1997.	Realistic; photography	Composition, space	Style, theme

chapter 5

Picture Books

In the Library

Youre right:
I am too old for THIS.
But I like pictures in my book,
And lots of color, easy words—
You needn't give me such a look!
You're wrong:
I am too young for THAT.
The words are long, the type's too small.
I don't find any pictures there—
I'd never get through that at all!

—Michael Patrick Hearn

In an era when picture books abound and provide many children with a delightful introduction to the world of books, it is difficult to imagine a time when books had no illustrations. Nonetheless, the picture book as we know it is a product of the twentieth century. The development of different types of picture books over the last three-quarters of a century can be seen as a response to our developing awareness of the importance of early learning.

Definition and Description

Picture books are profusely illustrated books in which both words and illustrations contribute to the story's meaning. In a true picture book, the story would be diminished, and in some cases confusing, without the illustrations, and so we say that illustrations in picture books are integral, or essential, to the story. Picture books are written in all genres; they have illustrations on every page or every other page; and, as a general rule, they are thirty-two pages long. A good example of a picture book is *Officer Buckle and Gloria* by Peggy Rathmann.

Books with occasional illustrations that serve to break up or decorate the text, add interest, or depict isolated incidents are called ***illustrated books.*** Illustrations in these books are said to be incidental, or nonessential, to the content. Illustrated books are not picture books. In *Sister Tricksters: Rollicking Tales of Clever Females,* retold by Robert D. San Souci and illustrated by Daniel San Souci, an illustration introduces each story, but no other illustrations occur elsewhere in the sixty pages of text. This is an example of an illustrated book.

 ## Evaluation and Selection of Picture Books

Children's first experiences with books must be enjoyable or they will soon not want to be involved with books. Negative experiences could mean that they may never learn to read or to enjoy reading. Over a period of time, evaluation and selection of picture books become a matter of achieving a good balance between what children naturally enjoy and what you want to lead them to enjoy.

The following criteria will help you to identify the best picture books:

- The ideas in picture books should be original or presented in an original way. Picture books on topics that children enjoy and find interesting are preferable to books about childhood, in the sense of nostalgia for or reminiscence of childhood. Books of the latter sort are for adults, not children.
- Picture books should avoid racial, ethnic, or sexual stereotyping in text and illustrations.
- Language and writing style should be rich and varied but not so complicated as to be incomprehensible to the child. It is desirable to feature new or unusual vocabulary within the context of interesting situations and complementary illustrations. Avoid books with overly sentimental and trite language.
- Illustrations should be appropriate in complexity to the age of the intended audience. In picture books for infants, look for relatively uncomplicated pages showing outlined figures against a plain background. Unusual perspectives or page designs in which only parts of a figure are shown may not be readily understood or appreciated by children younger than age 2.
- Children prefer color in illustrations, but color is not essential in picture book illustrations. The more important point to consider is whether color or black and white is right for the story.
- When a book is to be shared with a large group, the illustrations must be large enough to be seen from a distance.
- Picture books selected for reading aloud to children by adults, especially parents and preschool and kindergarten teachers, should offer something to both listener and reader and

Excellent Picture Books to Read Aloud

Agee, Jon. *Terrific.* Ages 5–8.
Alborough, Jez. *Where's My Teddy?* Ages 5–8.
Kasza, Keiko. *The Dog Who Cried Wolf.* Ages 4–7.
Mayo, Margaret. *Choo Choo Clickety Clack!* Illustrated by Alex Ayliffe. Ages 2–5.
McCarthy, Meghan. *Aliens Are Coming! The True Account of the 1938 War of the Worlds Radio Broadcast.* Ages 8–12.
Rathman, Peggy. *Officer Buckle and Gloria.* Ages 5–8.
Steig, William. *The Amazing Bone.* Ages 7–10.
Waddell, Martin. *Farmer Duck.* Illustrated by Helen Oxenbury. Ages 5–8.
Willems, Mo. *Knuffle Bunny: A Cautionary Tale.* Ages 3–5.
————. *Leonardo, the Terrible Monster.* Ages 4–6.
Willis, Jeanne. *Tadpole's Promise.* Illustrated by Tony Ross. Ages 5–9.
Yorinks, Arthur. *Hey, Al.* Illustrated by Richard Egielski. Ages 8–11.

promote interactive discussion between them (Brabham & Lynch-Brown, 2002). Multiple layers of meaning, child and adult perspectives, and humor are sources of enjoyment found in books that adults willingly read and reread to children. Generally, picture storybooks lend themselves to being read aloud. The titles in the Excellent Picture Books to Read Aloud list provide examples of the sort of book that works well as a read-aloud.

■ The amount of text on the pages of a picture book determines how long it will take to read the book aloud or for a child to read the book to herself or himself. Generally, the longer the text, the older the intended audience. Note that children's willingness to listen to stories grows with experience, which may result in a younger child who has been read to regularly having a much longer attention span than an older child with no story experience.

Teachers and librarians often rely on the professional judgment of committees that choose what they consider to be the most outstanding picture books published each year in this country and abroad. The most prestigious picture book award in the United States is the Caldecott Medal, sponsored by the Association for Library Service to Children division of the American Library Association. The equivalent award in Great Britain is the Kate Greenaway Medal, in Canada, the Governor General's Award for Illustration, and in Australia, the Picture Book of the Year Award. (See Appendix A for lists of award winners.) Another reliable source of information about good quality picture books is "The New York Times Best Illustrated Children's Books of the Year," published in early November as a part of *The New York Times Book Review Supplement.*

 ## Visual Elements

In many children's books the story is told through both text and pictures. This is particularly true of picture books but is also true of other books for children in which pictures serve an important function. Understanding and assessing the contributions of illustrations in books for children begin with knowing the *visual elements,* or basic elements with which artists and illustrators work. These visual elements are line, color, shape, texture, and composition. Understanding them will help you become more observant of illustrations and more discerning in your selection of picture books to share with children.

Line

The stroke marks that form part of a picture and often define its outline are the *lines.* The line of a picture generally defines the objects within the picture. Artists may choose to use lines that are dark or pale, heavy or light, solid or broken, wide or thin, straight or curved, or have combinations of these elements. The lines may be mostly vertical, horizontal, or on a diagonal. In pictures of the ocean and open prairies, the lines are predominantly horizontal; the impression is one of calm and tranquility. If the ocean is stormy, then the lines are more likely diagonal and upward moving, suggesting action or emotion or both. Each of these choices results in a different visual effect and can help to set a different mood. In evaluating the element of line within a picture, you may ask yourself whether the lines of the picture help to create and convey both the meaning and the feeling of the story. David Shannon's jagged, diagonal lines in his *No, David!* convey the constant motion of an exuberant male toddler and the resulting chaos. David Small's use of line in *The Gardener* by Sarah Stewart subtly contrasts the openness and tranquility of the countryside (horizontal lines) with the oppressive, crowded city (vertical lines). See Illustrations 1, 2, 3, 8, and 9 in the color insert.

Color

Color, another visual element of a book, may be observed for its hue, lightness, and saturation. Colors may be considered for the actual part of the color spectrum they represent or for their hue. The predominant colors may be from the cool end of the spectrum (the blues, greens, and gray-violets) or from the warm end of the color chart (the reds, oranges, and yellows). The colors may be intense or pale (that is, more or less saturated) and may range from diaphanous to opaque. The colors used must first complement the text. For example, if the mood of the story is that of calm and contentment, the illustrator may choose soft, warm tones that strengthen the emotional warmth of the story. If the events and mood of the text change during the course of the story, then the colors will change to reflect and signal the shift occurring in the story. In Molly Bang's *When Sophie Gets Angry—Really, Really Angry,* the colors explode in violent, saturated shades of red, orange, and yellow to communicate Sophie's rage, but gradually shift to cool greens, blues, and whites as her anger subsides and then to warm browns, pinks, and reds as she returns to her loving and forgiving family. See Illustrations 2, 3, 5, 8, 10, and 11 in the color insert. Sometimes an illustrated book will be noteworthy for its lack of color, which can be very appropriate and effective, as in *A Day, A Dog* (1999) by Gabrielle Vincent.

Shape

Shape, or the spatial forms of a picture, is produced by areas of color and by lines joining and intersecting to suggest outlines of forms. Shapes can be evaluated for their simplicity or complexity, their definition or lack of definition, their rigidity (as in geometric shapes) or suppleness (as in organic shapes), and their size. It is easy to see how this visual element can help to create a

Notable Authors and Illustrators of Picture Books

Eric Carle, author/illustrator. Unusually formatted picture storybooks and concept books about insects and animals. *The Grouchy Ladybug; The Very Busy Spider.* www.eric-carle.com

Lois Ehlert, author/illustrator. Bold color, use of collage, and engineered pages characterize her informational and concept books. *Color Zoo; Leaf Man.*

Denise Fleming, author/illustrator. Creates pattern books of handmade paper. *In the Small, Small Pond; Mama Cat Has Three Kittens.* www.denisefleming.com

Stephen Gammell, illustrator. Uses colored pencil in an informal, airy style. *The Relatives Came* (by Cynthia Rylant).

Kevin Henkes, author/illustrator. Creator of family situation animal fantasies featuring mice. *Chrysanthemum; Julius, the Baby of the World; Owen.* www.kevinhenkes.com

Steven Kellogg, author/illustrator. Uses animals as characters in picture storybooks. *Island of the Skog.* www.stevenkellogg.com

Bill Martin Jr., author. Pattern and rhyming stories for the beginning reader. *Brown Bear, Brown Bear, What Do You See?* (illustrated by Eric Carle). www.billmartinjr.com

Patricia McKissack, author. Picture storybooks with African-American characters and themes. *Nettie Jo's Friends* (illustrated by Scott Cook).

Helen Oxenbury, author/illustrator. British. Board books for babies. *Dressing; Say Goodnight.*

Brian Pinkney, illustrator. Uses distinctive scratchboard technique in folktales and biographies featuring African Americans. *Duke Ellington: The Piano Prince and His Orchestra* (by Andrea Davis Pinkney).

Chris Raschka, illustrator. Spare, expressionist watercolors and brief texts elegantly capture mood. *Yo! Yes?; Mysterious Thelonious.*

Jon Scieszka, author. Fractured folktales and books for reluctant readers. *The Stinky Cheese Man and Other Fairly Stupid Tales.*

Maurice Sendak, author/illustrator. Explores the dreams and imagination of children in complex picture storybooks. *Where the Wild Things Are; Outside Over There.*

Uri Shulevitz, author/illustrator. Rich but subtle watercolor illustrations create long-ago settings and exemplify interplay between text and pictures. *The Fool of the World and the Flying Ship: A Russian Tale; Snow; The Treasure.*

Peter Sís, author/illustrator. Noted for intricate, pen and ink and watercolor illustrations in picture book biographies for older readers. *Starry Messenger; Tibet through the Red Box.* www.petersis.com

David Small, illustrator. Two-time Caldecott medalist known for his loose style and narrative-rich watercolors. *The Gardener; So You Want to Be President?*

Simms Taback, author/illustrator. Noted for folk art style and effective use of paper engineering in engaging interpretations of poems. *Joseph Had a Little Overcoat.*

Chris Van Allsburg, author/illustrator. Uses shadow and unusual perspectives to create mysterious moods in picture storybooks for intermediate-grade readers. *Jumanji; The Garden of Abdul Gasazi.* www.chrisvanallsburg.com/flash.html

David Wiesner, author/illustrator. Creator of wordless fantasy stories. *Tuesday; Sector 7.* www.houghtonmifflinbooks.com/authors/wiesner/home.html

Mo Willems, author/illustrator. Creator of picture books for preschoolers featuring minimalist, childlike art, much humor, and action. *Don't Let the Pigeon Drive the Bus!; Knuffle Bunny: A Cautionary Tale.* www.mowillems.com

Vera B. Williams, author/illustrator. Expressive artistic style used to depict nontraditional families in picture storybooks. *A Chair for My Mother; Amber Was Brave, Essie Was Smart.*

David Wisniewski, author/illustrator. Uses intricate cut paper and layering technique to illustrate ancient stories and legends. *Golem; Rain Player.* www.davidwisniewski.com

mood or carry a message. In looking at shapes in a picture, the proportion of one object to another and the spaces surrounding the shapes are noteworthy for the nonverbal messages they carry (the bigger, the more important). The use of negative space or blank space may also be observed for its ability to highlight an object or to show isolation or loneliness. Chris Raschka effectively uses space on successive doublespreads to demonstrate a developing friendship between two boys in his book, *Yo! Yes?* See Illustrations 4, 5, 8, and 12 in the color insert.

Texture

The tactile surface characteristics of pictured objects comprise the *texture* of a picture. More simply, the impression of how a pictured object feels is its texture. Textures may be rough or slick, firm or spongy, hard or soft, jagged or smooth. Textural effects generally offer a greater sense of reality to a picture, as happens in Barbara Reid's illustrations for *The Subway Mouse*, which feature slightly rounded and textured plasticine for the mice's furry bodies and found objects such as a feather, scraps of newspaper, buttons, and old food labels in their nests. See Illustrations 2 and 10 in the color insert.

Composition

Composition includes the arrangement of the visual elements within a picture and the way in which these visual elements relate one to the other and combine to make the picture. Many artists arrange each illustration around a single focal point, which is often a key to understanding composition. The artist decides on proportion, balance, harmony, and disharmony within the various elements to produce the desired visual impact. The total effect should not overpower the story but rather extend and enrich the meaning and mood of the text. In *The Gardener,* by Sarah Stewart, illustrator David Small shows Sarah, the protagonist, in Grand Central Station the moment she arrives in New York City. He places her in a corner of a double-page spread, isolates her in a pool of white, and contrasts her small size with the huge interior of the station and her pastel clothes with the gloomy gray and black of the station. This composition conveys to the reader the girl's feelings of loneliness and intimidation. See Illustrations 1, 3, 5, 6, 7, 9, 11, and 12 in the color insert.

Obviously, the details in the illustrations must not conflict with those in the text. Surprisingly, many examples can be cited in which the illustrator was not true to the text in all details. Children are keenly observant of these contradictions and find them distracting. Although children accept illustrations that are varied in all visual elements and artistic styles, they have little tolerance for inaccuracies.

 ## Artistic Styles

Children come to note the distinctive features that identify the work of their favorite illustrators. Although the style of a picture is individual to each artist, artwork in general can be grouped by style similarities. Five broad categories of artistic styles are realistic, impressionistic, expressionistic, abstract, and surrealistic. Although an artist's works seldom fit neatly into one single art style, facets of these styles may be merged into the artist's personal expression of the world.

Realistic art represents natural forms and provides accurate representations without idealization. Wendell Minor's illustrations in *Heartland* by Diane Siebert are examples of realistic art, as is Henri Silberman's photographic rendering of the haiku collection *Stone Bench in an Empty Park,* selected by Paul B. Janeczko. See Illustrations 1 and 12 in the color insert.

Impressionistic art depicts natural appearances of objects by rendering fleeting visual impressions with an emphasis on light. Illustrator Tiphanie Beeke's pastel illustrations in *Fletcher and the Falling Leaves* by Julia Rawlinson emphasize the play of light in nature. See Illustrations 2 and 3 in the color insert.

Expressionistic art communicates an inner feeling or vision by distorting external reality. Examples can be found in *A Chair for My Mother* by Vera B. Williams and *Yo! Yes?* by Chris Raschko. Graphic art, used heavily in advertising and billboards, can be considered a form of expressionistic art. The intent of the artist is to draw attention to the central message by eliminating competing details. Donald Crews has successfully developed this art style into concept books for the very young child in *Truck* and *Freight Train.* See Illustration 4 in the color insert.

Abstract art emphasizes intrinsic geometric forms and surface qualities with little direct representation of objects but rather an emphasis on mood and feeling. Stephen Savage's restrained abstract drawings and cool blues and grays in *Polar Bear Night* by Lauren Thompson perfectly suit the barren landscapes and frigid climate of the Arctic. See Illustration 5 in the color insert.

In emphasizing the unconscious, *surrealistic art* often presents incongruous dream and fantasy images juxtaposed with very realistic ones. Anthony Browne uses a surrealistic artistic style in all of his picture books, juxtaposing almost photographically realistic settings with humanlike chimpanzee characters, as in *Willy the Dreamer,* or incongruous objects, as in *Changes.* See Illustration 6 in the color insert.

Primitive art and *folk art* styles are seen in books about a particular era or culture. The style of art is reminiscent of the style prevalent at the time the story events occurred. In illustrating *Ox-Cart Man* by Donald Hall, Barbara Cooney uses features of Early American art in order to express the culture of early nineteenth-century New England. Folktales from tribal societies also present occasions for artists to choose a folk art style reminiscent of the art from earlier cultures.

Primitive art is sometimes referred to as *naïve,* in the sense of "untrained." Illustrations that seem to have been done by a child, thus adding to the child narrator's voice or giving the story a child's perspective, are usually in this style. Chris Raschka's illustrations in *The Hello, Goodbye Window* by Norton Juster have this quality. See Illustrations 3 and 7 in the color insert.

Because *cartoons* are popular with children, many artists select this style for their children's books. This artistic style features rounded figures, exaggerated action, and simplified backgrounds. Old favorites such as Dr. Seuss's *The Cat in the Hat* and William Steig's *Sylvester and the Magic Pebble* are illustrated in cartoon style. Peggy Rathmann's humorous illustrations for *Officer Buckle and Gloria* are reminiscent of those found in comic books. See Illustrations 8, 9, and 10 in the color insert.

 ## Artistic Media

The *artistic media* refer to the materials and technical means used by artists to create pictures. Although the variety of techniques and materials used by book illustrators is virtually unlimited, some of the more common media found in children's books are listed here.

- *Drawing:* Pen and ink, colored pencils, pastels (colored chalk), charcoal pencils
  Stephen Gammell offers outstanding examples of the use of pencils, both colored and charcoal, in his books, such as the enduring *Song and Dance Man* by Karen Ackerman, in which he blends colors for vibrant effects and uses the pencil stroke to suggest motion. See Illustrations 2 and 3 in the color insert.

- *Collage:* An assemblage of different forms such as real objects and pieces of cut or torn paper to construct an illustration
  Illustrations in Barbara Reid's *The Subway Mouse* include found objects. Simms Taback uses pictures cut from magazines and pieces of fabric in his *Joseph Had a Little Overcoat.* See Illustration 10 in the color insert.

- *Print making:* Woodcuts, linoleum prints, block prints, lithography
  Beckie Prange's hand-colored woodcuts in *Song of the Water Boatman & Other Pond Poems* by Joyce Sidman perfectly capture the woodsy spirit of nature and wetland wildlife. See Illustrations 5 and 10 in the color insert.

- *Photography:* Black and white, color
  The large, close-up photographs Walter Wick uses to illustrate his book, *A Drop of Water: A Book of Science and Wonder,* support the factual nature of its contents by saying, in effect, "This is real." See Illustration 12 in the color insert.

- *Painting:* Oils, acrylics, watercolors, gouache, tempera
  Paul O. Zelinsky's Italian Renaissance-style oil paintings in *Rapunzel* establish a distant setting and a somber tone for this intriguing folktale. See Illustrations 1, 3, 4, 6, 7, 8, 9, and 11 in the color insert. Of course, the tools with which the artist applies the paint will affect its look. Tools as varied as brushes, air brushes, and sponges are used for applying paint.

Artists will generally use one predominant medium in a picture book, drawing from other media for special effects. Occasionally, an artist will choose to combine media more liberally to achieve the desired effect. Mo Willems, for example, in his *Knuffle Bunny: A Cautionary Tale,* uses muted, sepia-toned photographs of an urban neighborhood to provide the setting of his story and superimposes his bright cartoon drawings of characters over them. Brief explanations of the artist's techniques and materials have recently begun to be included on the publishing history page of children's picture books; at other times they appear at the end of illustrated books.

 ## Observing the Role of Illustrations in Picture Books

The role of illustrations in picture books can best be understood in terms of the literary elements, as defined in Chapter 3, and the visual elements, artistic styles, and artistic media as discussed earlier in this chapter. These roles vary in importance, depending on the type of picture book: In wordless picture books, the illustrations tell the whole story; in picture storybooks, they tell part of the story; in illustrated books, they may serve as mere breaks in the narrative and decoration. The key to understanding and appreciating the role of illustrations in picture books is to observe them carefully. Look at the illustrations for the messages they contain, in the way children who cannot read words "read" illustrations. Table 5.1 offers tips in what to look for as you read picture storybooks.

Table 5.1   How Illustrations Contribute to Picture Book Stories:
A Summary

Artistic and Literary Aspects		Examples of Illustrations' Contributions to Stories
Literary Elements	Plot	Convey story events not included in the text.
	Character	Show characters not mentioned in the text; contribute to characterization by showing characters' physical descriptions and actions not mentioned in the text.
	Setting	Show the setting (e.g., era as indicated by clothes, cars, architecture). Indicate the passing of time (time of day, seasons, etc.).
	Theme	Underscore the book's theme. Indicate the book's theme (in wordless books).
	Style	Show the author's stance toward the protagonist by viewing the world from the protagonist's perspective. Support a book's literary style to faithfully represent an era or culture.
Visual Elements	Line	Indicate motion or action, story mood (e.g., calm vs. agitated), aspects of plot (e.g., real vs. dreamed), and character (e.g., fragile vs. strong).
	Color	Indicate characters' emotions and personalities, story mood, aspects of setting (e.g., lush vs. arid, cold vs. warm).
	Shape	Indicate what is most important by relative size. Emphasize contrast by juxtaposing large and small objects.
	Texture	Intensify a sense of character or setting by indicating the feel of objects or surroundings.
	Composition	Focus the eye on what is most important (usually in the center). Indicate a character's perspective (how the character sees the world).
Artistic Styles	Realistic	Emphasize the idea that information in works of nonfiction is factual and that realistic works of fiction could be true or based on fact.
	Impressionistic	Contribute to settings through light-filled scenes of nature.
	Expressionistic	Express characters' feelings and emotions through exaggeration.
	Abstract	Emphasize basic, shared traits of characters; create a nonspecific setting, whether primitive or futuristic.
	Surrealistic	Help connect characters' imaginations, dreams, and fears to their real worlds.
	Primitive or folk	Establish and develop settings in the past.
	Cartoon	Provide humor through exaggeration of characters' physical appearance and actions.
Artistic Media	Pen and ink	Help define outlines and distinguish figure from ground in books for the very young; underscore the simplicity of some stories by simplicity of line and absence of color; help explain complicated scientific and technological concepts.

Pastels	Contribute to the creation of strong emotions and lush settings with saturated colors.
Graphite pencils	Focus attention on characters, mood, and actions due to absence of color.
Colored pencils	Help create a lighter mood due to transparency of the medium.
Wax crayons	Lend a childlike perspective by using an artistic medium popular with children.
Collages	Contribute to settings and characterization through use of objects with tactile feel; lend a sense of reality through the use of real-world objects.
Woodcuts	Help establish outdoor settings with rough-hewn look; lend a sense of character strength through bold lines.
Photographs	Create a sense of the real world with contemporary photographs; create a sense of the past with period photographs.
Oil paints Gouache	Establish a somber or serious mood due to opaqueness of the medium.
Watercolors	Establish a lighter mood because of transparency of the medium and consequent amount of light reflected.

Historical Overview of Picture Books

Orbis Pictus (The World in Pictures), an ABC book written and illustrated by John Amos Comenius in Moravia and published in 1657, is considered to be the first children's picture book. Comenius's emphasis on using pictures to explain and expand the meaning of the text in books for young people was an important first. But since early books were rare and prohibitively expensive, they were seen by very few children. Moreover, until well into the nineteenth century, Europeans and Americans believed that books were for the serious business of educating and soul saving, not for enjoyment! Today's full-color, extravagantly illustrated, highly amusing picture book is the product of the following important developments.

- Technological advances in color printing made high-quality illustrations in books more affordable.
- A more understanding attitude toward childhood evolved. During the nineteenth century, society began to accept the notion of childhood as a time for playing and learning. At the same time, the general economy began to be able to afford the average child the leisure time these activities require.
- Higher standards of excellence in picture book illustrations developed. The beauty, charm, and humor of the illustrations of nineteenth-century illustrators Randolph Caldecott, Kate Greenaway, and Walter Crane brought children's book art to the attention of the general public.
- The establishment of national awards for excellence in children's book illustration in the twentieth century encouraged more artists to enter the children's book field.

MILESTONES in the Development of the Picture Book

Date	Event	Significance
1484	Publication of *Aesop's Fables,* illustrated by William Caxton.	One of the first-known illustrated books enjoyed by children.
1657	Publication of *Orbis Pictus,* written and illustrated by John Amos Comenius.	Considered to be the first picture book for children.
1860–1900	Golden Age of children's book illustration in Great Britain, led by Randolph Caldecott, Walter Crane, and Kate Greenaway.	Increased awareness, stature, popularity, and appreciation of children's picture books.
1902	Publication of *The Tale of Peter Rabbit* by Beatrix Potter.	Early important modern picture storybook in English.
1928	Publication of *Millions of Cats* by Wanda Gág.	Early important modern American picture storybook.
1938	Establishment of the Caldecott Award for illustration in children's books in the United States.	Promoted excellence in illustrating for children and encouraged talented artists to illustrate children's books.
1940	Publication of *Pat the Bunny* by Dorothy Kunhardt.	One of the first books for babies. Began the move to supply different types of picture books for different child audiences.
1957	Publication of *The Cat in the Hat,* written and illustrated by Dr. Seuss, and *Little Bear,* written by Else Minarik and illustrated by Maurice Sendak.	Introduced the easy-to-read genre of picture books.
1962	Publication of *A Snowy Day,* written and illustrated by Ezra Jack Keats.	One of the first picture books with a minority character as the protagonist to win the Caldecott Medal.
1967	Publication of *A Boy, a Dog, and a Frog,* illustrated by Mercer Mayer.	Popularized the wordless book genre.
1972	Publication of *Push Pull, Empty Full* by Tana Hoban.	Signaled the growing popularity of the concept picture book.
1974	Publication of *Arrow to the Sun: A Pueblo Indian Tale* by Gerald McDermott.	Signaled the emergence of picture books for older readers as a distinct type of picture book.
1981	Publication of "The Baby Board Books" by Helen Oxenbury.	Baby books were established as a distinct and important type of picture book.
1990	*Color Zoo* by Lois Ehlert wins a Caldecott Honor Award.	Recognition of the engineered book genre.
1991	*Black and White* by David Macaulay wins Caldecott Medal.	Denoted influence of postmodernism and acceptance of nontraditional picture book formats.
2006	*Henry and Mudge and the Great Grandpas* by Cynthia Rylant, illustrated by Suçie Stevenson, wins the first Theodor Seuss Geisel Award for Beginning Reader Books.	Affirmed the importance of good literature in motivating children to learn to read. Promoted excellence in books for beginning readers.

■ The demand for books grew. Growth of public school systems and public and school library systems accounted for much of this increase in the number of books for children. In addition, reading came to be recognized as one of the child's best tools for learning and for gaining a worthy source of entertainment.

Today, the picture book genre is well established with an ever-widening audience, more multicultural themes, a greater number of bilingual picture books (especially English–Spanish), and more realistic themes such as the effects of war, poverty, immigration, and disabilities on the lives of children. Greater diversity in formats and more illustrated retellings of folktales are available. A trend of the 1990s was to publish picture books with high levels of conceptual difficulty and artistic sophistication intended for middle-grade students. The twenty-first century has witnessed the growth of the graphic novel, a novel-length comic book, originally created for adults, that includes books for elementary- and middle-grade students.

 ## Types of Picture Books

Today's picture books differ in intended audience, purpose, format, and relative amount of text and illustration. These differences are not absolute, however; quite often, one will find a picture book having characteristics of several specific types. With the understanding that overlap between types is inevitable, you will want to learn to recognize the following kinds of picture books (organized by the intended age of the audience from youngest to oldest). Poems, nursery rhymes, and songbooks in picture book format are detailed in Chapter 4, folktales in picture book format are discussed in Chapter 6, and informational picture books are covered in Chapter 10.

Baby Books

Baby books are simply designed, brightly illustrated, durable picture books that are intended for use with children aged 0 to 2. Safety is ensured by rounded corners, nontoxic materials, washable pages, and no loose attachments. An example is *Baby Radar* by Naomi Shihab Nye. The types of baby books actually denote the material used in their construction. *Board books* are constructed of heavy, laminated cardboard and are either bound as a book with pages or made to fold out in an accordion fashion. *Vinyl books* and *cloth books* are also types of baby books. These books have little or no text. Their content, which deals with the objects and routines that are familiar to the infant and toddler, is presented mainly by the illustrations. The best baby books, such as those produced by Helen Oxenbury, are intelligently designed to emphasize patterns and associations to promote dialogue between the caregiver and the young child, who will often look at these books together.

Interactive Books

Interactive books are picture books that stimulate a child's verbal or physical participation as the book is read. These books ask the child direct questions, invite unison recitation of chants or repeated lines, encourage clapping or moving to the rhythm of the words, or require the child to touch or manipulate the book or find objects in the illustrations. The intended audience is usually children aged 2 to 6, and the books are seen as an extension of their world of play. One classic example of this type of book that is still greatly enjoyed by toddlers today is Dorothy Kunhardt's *Pat the Bunny*.

Author Karen Beaumont's use of rhyme and illustrator David Catrow's visual clues invite young listeners to participate in the reading of the humorous, rollicking *I Ain't Gonna Paint No More!*

Toy Books

Sometimes called *engineered* or *mechanical books, toy books* use paper that has been engineered (i.e., cut, folded, constructed) to provide pop-up, see-through, movable, changeable, or three-dimensional illustrations. Toy books can be found for all ages, but only those that have the simpler types of engineering, such as pages of varying widths or drilled holes for see-through effects (as in Eric Carle's *The Very Hungry Caterpillar*), would be appropriate for most young children. Toy books with fragile or elaborate pop-up features, such as Robert Sabuda's amazing pop-up version of *Alice in Wonderland,* would not last in the hands of a very young child, but would delight older children (and adults).

Wordless Books

The *wordless book* depends entirely on carefully sequenced illustrations to present the story. There is no text, or the text is limited to one or two pages in the book, so the illustrations must be highly narrative. An outstanding example is Barbara Lehman's *The Red Book,* a fantasy about finding friends in books—literally. Wordless books are generally intended for prereaders, usually children aged 4 to 6. More sophisticated wordless books for older readers, such as David Weisner's *Sector 7,* are also available. When children "read" these illustrations in their own words, they benefit from the book's visual story structure in several ways:

- They develop a concept of story as a cohesive narrative with a beginning and an end.
- They use language inventively, which promotes language development.
- They learn the front-to-back, left-to-right page progression in reading.
- They begin to understand that stories can be found not only in books but in themselves.

Alphabet Books

The *alphabet,* or *ABC, book* presents the alphabet letter by letter to acquaint young children with the shapes, names, and, in some cases, the sounds of the twenty-six letters. For example, see *ABC: A Child's First Alphabet Book* by Alison Jay. Almost all ABC book authors and illustrators choose a theme (animals, elves, fruit, etc.) or device (finding the many objects in the accompanying illustration beginning with the featured letter) to give their books cohesion. In choosing an ABC book, consider the appropriateness of the theme or device for students, whether both uppercase and lowercase letters are displayed, and the use of a simple, easy-to-read style of print.

Most ABC books are intended for the nonreader or beginning reader. Some authors and illustrators use the alphabet itself as a device for presenting information or wordplay. In these cases, the intended audience already knows the alphabet. In *Superhero ABC,* Bob McLeod presents imaginative and wacky superheroes whose names and descriptions begin with the featured letter, inviting readers to invent such characters of their own.

Counting Books

The *counting book* presents numbers, usually 1 through 10, to acquaint young children with the numerals and their shapes (1, 2, 3, . . .), the number names (one, two, three, . . .), the sense of what quantity each numeral represents, and the counting sequence. *Teeth, Nails, & Tentacles: An Animal Counting Book* by Christopher Wormell, with its bold linocut prints clearly depicting the numerals and the objects to be counted, presents lessons in counting and zoology simultaneously. As with alphabet books, authors and illustrators of counting books employ themes or devices to make them more cohesive and interesting. Specific considerations in evaluating a counting book include the appeal to children of the theme and objects chosen to illustrate the number concepts, and the clarity with which the illustrator presents the concept of number.

Illustrators often fill their alphabet and counting books with unusual and intriguing objects for children to name and count, such as aardvarks, barracudas, and chameleons. Children pick up a great deal of interesting information and vocabulary in this way. You will be in the best position to decide whether the novelty of these objects will be motivating or confusing to your students.

Concept Books

A *concept book* is a picture book that explores or explains an idea or concept (e.g., opposites), an object (e.g., a train), or an activity (e.g., working) rather than telling a story. Many concept books have no plot but use repeated elements in the illustrations and text to tie the book together. Laura Seeger combines a simple format, well-known but unexpected objects, and paper cut-outs to create an interesting book about color in her *Lemons Are Not Red*. Limited text and clearly understood illustrations in the best concept books stimulate children's exploratory talk about the concepts, objects, and activities presented.

Alphabet and counting books are considered types of concept books. Another variety of the concept book that is popular with 2- to 4-year-olds is the *naming book,* which presents simple, labeled pictures of people, animals, and objects for young children to identify. *My First Word Book* by Angela Wilkes is an example of a naming book.

Picture Storybooks

The *picture storybook* is a book in which a story is told through both the words and pictures. Text and illustration occur with equal frequency in these books, and on most double spreads, both are in view. This is the type of book most people associate with the term *picture book*. Two good examples are *Officer Buckle and Gloria* by Peggy Rathmann and *Lilly's Purple Plastic Purse* by Kevin Henkes. The picture storybook is the most common type of picture book.

The text of most picture storybooks is meant to be read aloud to the intended audience of 4- to 7-year-olds, at least for the first time or two, and often includes challenging vocabulary. Many of the best picture storybooks are also read and enjoyed independently by children 8 years old and up.

Pattern Books

Picture books that strongly emphasize word patterns are called *pattern books.* They are also called *decodable books* because of their language regularities in which certain phonological features are repeated, as is the line, "Is this the bus for us, Gus?" in Suzanne Bloom's *The Bus for Us.* In addition, *predictable books,* such as Bill Martin Jr. and Eric Carle's perennial favorite *Brown Bear,*

Brown Bear, What Do You See? and its companion books, *Polar Bear. . . .* and *Panda Bear. . . .* , are sometimes included in this category because of meaning and illustration clues.

Easy-to-Read Books

Easy-to-read books are created to help the beginning reader read independently with success. These books have limited text on each page, large print, double spacing, short sentences, and often occur in series. There is usually an illustration on about every other page. Language is often, but not always, controlled, and words are short and familiar. Laura Kvasnosky's *Zelda and Ivy: The Runaways*, with its emphasis on familiar family situations and gentle humor, is a good example. Easy-to-read books can be used with children whenever they want to learn to read, but the audience for this type of book is usually 5- to 7-year-olds.

The easy-to-read book differs in appearance from the picture storybook in several obvious ways. Because they are intended for independent reading, they do not have to be seen from a distance and may be smaller, the text takes up a greater proportion of each page, and the text is often divided into short chapters.

Picture Books for Older Readers

Picture books for older readers are generally more sophisticated, abstract, or complex in themes, stories, and illustrations and are suitable for children aged 10 and older. This type of picture book began to appear in the 1970s, perhaps in response to our increasingly visual modes of communication, and now artists such as Anthony Browne, D. B. Johnson, David Macaulay, and the team of Jörg Müller and Jörg Steiner are known for their work in this area. Peter Sís's *Tibet through the Red Box*, with its mixed genres and intricate, symbolic illustrations, is a worthy challenge for older readers and adults alike.

Picture books for older readers lend themselves well to use across the middle-school curriculum, including social studies, science, language arts, mathematics, art, music, and physical education. Consider the advantages of using picture books for older readers in middle and secondary schools:

- They can be used as teacher read-alouds for introductions and supplements to textbook-based units of instruction.
- They can be used in text sets (several books on the same topic) for small group in-class reading, analysis, and discussion.
- They can be used by individual students as models of excellent writing.
- They can inject humor and stimulate interest in a topic, and possibly provoke discussion, which would result in a deeper understanding of the content (Albright, 2000, 2002), as Jorge Diaz's *The Rebellious Alphabet* does for the topic of First Amendment rights.
- They can demonstrate practical applications of concepts (Alvermann & Phelps, 1998), as D. B. Johnson's *Henry Climbs a Mountain* does for the concept of civil disobedience.
- They often have factual content that reinforces or adds to that found in textbooks, as Brett Harvey's *Cassie's Journey: Going West in the 1860s*, illustrated by Deborah Kogan Ray, does for a unit of instruction about pioneer life in the mid-nineteenth century by adding a wealth of detail about daily life in a wagon train.
- They offer different perspectives on issues, such as the African-American perspective on the Civil War in Patricia Polacco's *Pink and Say*.

The traditional notion that picture books are only for younger children no longer applies. Although some adults may persist in guiding older children away from picture books, as Gontarski (1994) found, today's teachers and librarians would be wise to make picture books for older readers an option in any learning situation.

Graphic Novels

The last decade has seen the emergence of **graphic novels** as a book format related to picture books. These novel-length books feature text written in speech bubbles or as captions similar to comic-book illustrations. The term *graphic* refers to stories told through images and does not refer to the nature of the content. Features of graphic novels that appeal to young people and especially to reluctant readers are that they are visually oriented, emphasize dialogue, often occur in series, and have close ties to popular culture such as films and comic-book superheroes. A graphic novel appropriate for intermediate-graders is *Babymouse: Queen of the World!* by Jennifer Holm and illustrated by Matthew Holm.

Transitional Books

Transitional books are a special type of book for the child who can read but has not yet become a fluent reader. They are not picture books, but lie somewhere between picture books and full-length novels. Characteristics of transitional books are an uncomplicated writing style and vocabulary, illustrations on about every third page, division of text into chapters, slightly enlarged print, and an average length of 100 pages. A good example of a transitional book is *Ruby Lu, Brave and True* by Lenore Look, illustrated by Anne Wilsdorf. Often, books for the transitional reader occur in series, as Donald Sobol's much-loved Encyclopedia Brown books and the more recent Ivy and Bean series by Annie Barrows and Martin Bridge series by Jessica Kerrin.

The Center for Children's Books and the Graduate School of Library and Information Science of the University of Illinois at Urbana–Champaign established the Gryphon Award for transitional books in 2004. The $1,000 prize is given annually to the author of the English-language work of fiction or nonfiction published in the preceding year that best exemplifies qualities that successfully bridge the gap in difficulty between picture books and full-length books. Gryphon Award winners to date include:

2004	*Bow Wow Meow Meow: It's Rhyming Cats and Dogs* by Douglas Florian. Harcourt.
2005	*Little Rat Rides* by Monika Bang-Campbell. Harcourt.
2006	*Stinky Stern Forever* by Michelle Edwards. Harcourt.

See Appendix D for a list of more good transitional books.

During the twentieth century the picture book was begun and developed as a genre, diversified to meet the demands of an ever-expanding audience and market, and improved as a result of new and refined printing technology. As researchers came to realize the connections between positive early experiences with good literature, reading, and school success, new types of picture books were developed. Today, high-quality picture books on nearly every imaginable topic can enrich the lives and imaginations of young children and the classrooms and libraries where they learn.

Topics for Further Investigation

- Select a classic picture book such as *Where the Wild Things Are* (Sendak), *The Tale of Peter Rabbit* (Potter), or *Millions of Cats* (Gág). Read articles of literary criticism on the book and then present your perspective on this work. Give your thoughts on why this book became a classic and whether this book would be of interest to children today.
- Investigate the topic of visual literacy as it applies to readers of picture books.
- Investigate the topic of graphic novels for elementary- and middle-grade students in such articles as Brenner's (2006) "Graphic Novels 101: FAQ" and Rudiger's (2006) "Graphic Novels 101: Reading Lessons," both in *The Horn Book Magazine*.

 See the companion website at www.ablongman.com/lynchbrown6e for further suggestions.

References

Albright, L. K. (2000). "The effects on attitudes and achievement of reading aloud picture books in seventh-grade social studies classes." Unpublished doctoral dissertation, Ohio University, Athens.

———. (2002). Bringing the Ice Maiden to life: Engaging adolescents in learning through picture book read-alouds in content areas. *Journal of Adolescent and Adult Literacy, 45*(5), 418–428.

Alvermann, D. E., & Phelps, S. F. (1998). *Content reading and literacy: Succeeding in today's diverse classrooms* (2nd ed.). Boston: Allyn and Bacon.

Brabham, E. G., & Lynch-Brown, C. (2002). Effects of teachers' reading aloud styles on vocabulary acquisition and comprehension of students in the early elementary grades. *Journal of Educational Psychology, 94*(3), 465–474.

Brenner, R. (2006). Graphic novels 101: FAQ. *Horn Book Magazine, 82*(2), 123–125.

Gontarski, M. (1994). "Visual literacy as it relates to picture book use by selected fifth grade students." Unpublished doctoral dissertation, The Florida State University, Tallahassee, FL.

Hearn, M. P. (1984). In the library. In J. Cole (Ed.), *A new treasury of children's poetry.* New York: Doubleday.

Rudiger, H. M. (2006). Graphic novels 101: Reading lessons. *Horn Book Magazine, 82*(2), 126–134.

Recommended Picture Books

Ages indicated refer to approximate concept and interest levels.

Baby Books

Ashman, Linda. *Babies on the Go.* Illustrated by Jane Dyer. Harcourt, 2003. Ages 2–4.

Burningham, John. *Hushabye.* Knopf, 2001. Ages 1–3.

Frazee, Marla. *Walk On! A Guide for Babies of All Ages.* Harcourt, 2006. Ages 1–2.

Henkes, Kevin. *Owen's Marshmallow Chick.* HarperCollins, 2002. Ages 2–5. (Board book.)

Nye, Naomi Shihab. *Baby Radar.* Illustrated by Nancy Carpenter. Greenwillow, 2003. Ages 2–4.

Oxenbury, Helen. "The Baby Board Books." *Dressing.* Simon & Schuster, 1981. Ages 0–2. (Others in this series: *Family; Friends; Playing; Working.*)

Suen, Anastasia. *Toddler Two.* Illustrated by Winnie Cheon. Lee & Low, 2002. Ages 1–3. Also available in Spanish (*Dos años*) and English/Spanish editions. (Board book.)

Uff, Caroline. *Lulu's Busy Day.* Walker, 2000. Ages 0–2. (See also *Happy Birthday, Lulu.*)

Wells, Rosemary. "Very First Books." *Max's Bath.* Dial, 1985. Ages 0–2.

Ziefert, Harriet. *Who Said Moo?* Illustrated by Simms Taback. Handprint Books, 2002. Ages 1–3. (Board book.)

Interactive Books

Ahlberg, Janet, and Allen Ahlberg. *Each Peach Pear Plum: An I-Spy Story.* Viking, 1978. Ages 2–4.

Beaumont, Karen. *I Ain't Gonna Paint No More!* Illustrated by David Catrow. Harcourt, 2005. Ages 3–7.

Blake, Quentin. *All Join In.* Little, Brown, 1991. Ages 4–8.

Fleming, Denise. *The Cow Who Clucked.* Holt, 2006. Ages 3–6.

Hill, Eric. *Where's Spot?* Putnam, 1980. (Others in this series: *Spot's First Walk; Spot's Birthday Party; Spot's First Christmas.*) Ages 3–5.

Kunhardt, Dorothy. *Pat the Bunny.* Golden, 2001 (1940). Ages 2–4.

Schwartz, Amy. *What James Likes Best.* Simon & Schuster, 2003. Ages 3–5.

Slater, Dashka. *Baby Shoes.* Illustrated by Hiroe Nakata. Bloomsbury, 2006. Ages 1–3.

Whybrow, Ian. *The Noisy Way to Bed.* Illustrated by Tiphanie Beeke. Scholastic, 2004. Ages 2–4.

Williams, Vera B. *"More More More," Said the Baby.* Greenwillow, 1990. Ages 2–4.

Yolen, Jane, editor. *This Little Piggy: Lap Songs, Finger Plays, Clapping Games, and Pantomime Rhymes.* Illustrated by Will Hillenbrand. Candlewick, 2006. Ages 2–4.

Zane, Alexander. *The Wheels on the Race Car.* Illustrated by James Warhola. Orchard, 2005. Ages 4–7.

Toy Books

Baum, L. Frank. *The Wonderful World of Oz: A Commemorative Pop-Up.* Illustrated by Robert Sabuda. Simon & Schuster, 2000. Ages 6–9.

Carle, Eric. *The Very Hungry Caterpillar.* World, 1968. Ages 4–6.

———. *The Very Quiet Cricket.* Putnam, 1990. Ages 2–6.

Ehlert, Lois. *Leaf Man.* Harcourt, 2005. Ages 5–8. (Engineered.)

Hill, Eric. *Where's Spot?* Putnam, 1980. Ages 3–5.

Sabuda, Robert. *Alice's Adventures in Wonderland.* Simon & Schuster, 2003. Ages 8–12.

———, and Matthew Reinhart. *Encyclopedia Prehistorica: Dinosaurs.* Candlewick, 2005. Ages 5–9. (Pop-up.)

Taback, Simms. *There Was an Old Lady Who Swallowed a Fly.* Viking, 1997. Ages 5–7. (See also Pattern Books.)

Yorinks, Arthur. *Mommy?* Illustrated by Maurice Sendak. Paper engineering by Matthew Reinhart. Scholastic, 2006. Ages 5–10. (Pop-up.)

Zelinsky, Paul O., adapter. *Knick-Knack Paddywhack! A Moving Parts Book.* Dutton, 2002. Ages 5–8.

Wordless Books

Baker, Jeannie. *Window.* Greenwillow, 1991. Ages 7–12.

Blake, Quentin. *Clown.* Holt, 1996. Ages 3–8.

Faller, Régis. *The Adventures of Polo.* Roaring Brook, 2006. Ages 4–8. (International/France)

Feelings, Tom. *The Middle Passage: White Ships/Black Cargo.* Dial, 1995. Ages 9–14.

Fleischman, Paul. *Sidewalk Circus.* Illustrated by Kevin Hawkes. Candlewick, 2004. Ages 5–10.

Geisert, Arthur. *Lights Out.* Houghton, 2005. Ages 5–10.

Lehman, Barbara. *Museum Trip.* Houghton, 2006. Ages 5–8.

———. *The Red Book.* Houghton, 2004. Ages 4–9.

Mayer, Mercer. *A Boy, a Dog, and a Frog.* Dial, 1967. Ages 3–6. (Others in this series: *Frog, Where Are You?; A Boy, a Dog, and a Friend; Frog on His Own; Frog Goes to Dinner; One Frog Too Many,* with Marianna Mayer.)

McCully, Emily Arnold. *Four Hungry Kittens.* Dial, 2001. Ages 4–7.

Rohmann, Eric. *Time Flies.* Crown, 1994. Ages 7–12.

Varon, Sara. *Chicken and Cat.* Scholastic, 2006. Ages 4–7.

Vincent, Gabrielle. *A Day, a Dog.* Front Street, 1999. Ages 6–8.

Wiesner, David. *Flotsam.* Clarion, 2006. Ages 4–7.

———. *Free Fall.* Lothrop, 1988. Ages 6–10.

———. *Sector 7.* Clarion, 1999. Ages 6–10.

———. *Tuesday.* Clarion, 1991. Ages 6–10.

Alphabet Books

Cronin, Doreen. *Click, Clack, Quackity-Quack: An Alphabetical Adventure.* Illustrated by Betsy Lewin. Atheneum, 2005. Ages 3–6.

Ehlert, Lois. *Eating the Alphabet: Fruits and Vegetables from A to Z.* Harcourt, 1989. Ages 3–6.

Ernst, Lisa Campbell. *The Turn-Around, Upside-Down Alphabet Book.* Simon & Schuster, 2004. Ages 3–6.

Fleming, Denise. *Alphabet under Construction.* Holt, 2002. Ages 4–7.

Holtz, Lara Tankel. *DK Alphabet Book.* Illustrated by Dave King. DK, 1997. Ages 5–8.

Inkpen, Mick. *Kipper's A to Z: An Alphabet Adventure.* Harcourt, 2001. Ages 5–7.

Jay, Alison. *ABC: A Child's First Alphabet Book.* Dutton, 2003. Ages 4–7.

Kalman, Maira. *What Pete Ate from A to Z (Really!).* Putnam, 2001. Ages 5–8.

Lear, Edward, and Suse MacDonald, adapter. *A Was Once an Apple Pie.* Illustrated by Suse MacDonald. Orchard, 2005. Ages 3–7.

Martin, Bill, Jr., and John Archambault. *Chicka Chicka Boom Boom.* Illustrated by Lois Ehlert. Simon & Schuster, 1989. Ages 3–6.

McLeod, Bob. *Superhero ABC.* HarperCollins, 2006. Ages 4–8.

Mullins, Patricia. *V for Vanishing: An Alphabet of Endangered Animals.* HarperCollins, 1993. Ages 6–8.

Musgrove, Margaret. *Ashanti to Zulu: African Traditions.* Illustrated by Leo and Diane Dillon. Dial, 1976. Ages 8–12.

Pelletier, David. *The Graphic Alphabet.* Orchard, 1996. Ages 9–12.

Seeger, Laura Vaccaro. *The Hidden Alphabet.* Roaring Brook, 2003. Ages 4–7.

Shannon, George. *Tomorrow's Alphabet.* Illustrated by Donald Crews. Greenwillow, 1996. Ages 6–8.

Spirin, Gennady. *A Apple Pie.* Philomel, 2005. Ages 4–7.

Wood, Audrey. *Alphabet Mystery.* Illustrated by Bruce Wood. Scholastic, 2003. Ages 3–6.

Counting Books

Alda, Arlene. *Arlene Alda's 1 2 3: What Do You See?* Tricycle, 1998. Ages 3–7.

Carle, Eric. *10 Little Rubber Ducks.* HarperCollins, 2005. Ages 3–6.

Falwell, Cathryn. *Turtle Splash! Countdown at the Pond.* Greenwillow, 2001. Ages 3–6.

Hoban, Tana. *Let's Count.* Greenwillow, 1999.

McMullen, Kate. *I'm Dirty.* Illustrated by Jim McMullen. HarperCollins, 2006. Ages 4–7.

Moss, Lloyd. *Zin! Zin! Zin! A Violin.* Illustrated by Marjorie Priceman. Simon & Schuster, 1995. Ages 4–7.

Reiser, Lynn. *Hardworking Puppies.* Harcourt, 2006. Ages 3–7.

Shea, Pegi Deitz, and Cynthia Weill. *Ten Mice for Tet!* Illustrated by Tô Ngoc Trang and Pham Viét Đinh. Chronicle, 2003. Ages 5–8.

Sturges, Philemon. *Ten Flashing Fireflies.* Illustrated by Anna Vojtech. North-South, 1995. Ages 4–6.

Wormell, Christopher. *Teeth, Nails, & Tentacles: An Animal Counting Book.* Running Press, 2004. Ages 3–8.

Concept Books

Bang, Molly. *When Sophie Gets Angry—Really, Really Angry . . .* Scholastic, 1999. Ages 3–6.

Barton, Byron. *My Car.* Greenwillow, 2001. Ages 2–4.

Cabrera, Jane. *Cat's Colors.* Dial, 1997. Ages 1–4.

Crews, Donald. *Freight Train.* Greenwillow, 1978. Ages 3–5.

————. *Truck.* Greenwillow, 1980. Ages 3–5.

Ehlert, Lois. *Growing Vegetable Soup.* Harcourt, 1987.

Fox, Mem. *Where Is the Green Sheep?* Illustrated by Judy Horacek. Harcourt, 2004. Ages 2–5.

Freymann, Saxton, and Joost Elffers. *Fast Food.* Illustrated by Saxton Freymann. Scholastic, 2006. Ages 3–7.

————. *Food for Thought: The Complete Book of Concepts for Growing Minds.* Scholastic, 2005. Ages 3–5.

Hoban, Tana. *Color Everywhere.* Morrow, 1995. Ages 3–5.

Jenkins, Emily. *Five Creatures.* Illustrated by Tomek Bogacki. Farrar, 2001. Ages 4–7.

Mayo, Margaret. *Choo Choo Clickety Clack!* Illustrated by Alex Ayliffe. Carolrhoda, 2005. Ages 2–5.

Meyers, Susan. *Everywhere Babies.* Illustrated by Marla Frazee. Harcourt, 2001. Ages 3–5.

————. *Puppies! Puppies! Puppies!* Illustrated by David Walker. Abrams, 2005. Ages 3–7.

Prince, April Jones. *What Do Wheels Do All Day?* Illustrated by Giles Laroche. Houghton, 2006. Ages 3–7.

Rosenthal, Amy Krouse. *Cookies! Bite Size Life Lessons.* Illustrated by Jane Dyer. HarperCollins, 2006. Ages 4–7.

Scarry, Richard. *My First Word Book.* Random House, 1986. Ages 3–5.

———. *Richard Scarry's Biggest Word Book Ever!* Random House, 1985. Ages 3–5.

Seeger, Laura Vaccaro. *Black? White! Day? Night!* Roaring Brook, 2006. Ages 3–7. (Also a toy book.)

———. *Lemons Are Not Red.* Roaring Brook, 2004. Ages 3–7. (Also a toy book.)

Serfozo, Mary. *What's What: A Guessing Game.* Illustrated by Keiko Narahashi. McElderry, 1996. Ages 2–5.

Sís, Peter. *Fire Truck.* Greenwillow, 1998. Ages 1–3. (Also a counting book.)

———. *Trucks, Trucks, Trucks.* Greenwillow, 1999. Ages 1–3.

Wilkes, Angela. *My First Word Book.* DK, 1999. Ages 3–5.

Picture Storybooks

Ackerman, Karen. *Song and Dance Man.* Illustrated by Stephen Gammell. Knopf, 1988. Ages 7–10.

Agee, Jon. *Milo's Hat Trick.* Hyperion, 2001. Ages 5–8.

———. *Terrific.* Hyperion, 2005. Ages 5–8.

Alarcón, Karen B. *Louella Mae, She's Run Away.* Illustrated by Roseann Litzinger. Holt, 1997. Ages 3–5.

Alborough, Jez. *Where's My Teddy?* Candlewick, 1992. Ages 5–8.

Allard, Harry. *Miss Nelson Is Missing.* Illustrated by James Marshall. Houghton, 1977. Ages 6–8.

Arnosky, Jim. *Grandfather Buffalo.* Putnam, 2006. Ages 5–8.

Baker, Jeannie. *Where the Forest Meets the Sea.* Greenwillow, 1988. Ages 8–10.

Baker, Olaf. *Where the Buffaloes Begin.* Illustrated by Stephen Gammell. Warne, 1981. Ages 8–10.

Bemelmans, Ludwig. *Madeline.* Viking, 1939. Ages 5–7.

Best, Cari. *Three Cheers for Catherine the Great!* Illustrated by Giselle Potter. DK Ink, 1999. Ages 6–9.

Bloom, Suzanne. *A Splendid Friend, Indeed.* Boyds Mills, 2005. Ages 2–5.

Brown, Margaret Wise. *Goodnight Moon.* Illustrated by Clement Hurd. Harper, 1947. Ages 4–6.

Browne, Anthony. *Changes.* Knopf, 1986. Ages 5–8.

———. *Gorilla.* Knopf, 1985. Ages 7–9.

———. *Voices in the Park.* DK Ink, 1998. Ages 6–10.

———. *Willy the Dreamer.* Candlewick, 1998. Ages 7–10.

Bunting, Eve. *Train to Somewhere.* Illustrated by Ronald Himler. Clarion, 1996. Ages 7–10.

———. *The Wall.* Illustrated by Ronald Himler. Clarion, 1990. Ages 7–9.

———. *The Wednesday Surprise.* Illustrated by Donald Carrick. Clarion, 1989. Ages 6–10.

Burton, Virginia Lee. *The Little House.* Houghton, 1942. Ages 5–7.

———. *Mike Mulligan and His Steam Shovel.* Houghton, 1939. Ages 5–7.

Carle, Eric. *The Grouchy Ladybug.* Crowell, 1971. Ages 5–7.

———. *The Very Busy Spider.* Philomel, 1984. Ages 5–7.

Caudill, Rebecca. *A Pocketful of Cricket.* Illustrated by Evaline Ness. Holt, 1964. Ages 6–8.

Child, Lauren. *But Excuse Me That Is My Book.* Dial, 2006. Ages 4–6.

Chodos-Irvine, Margaret. *Best Best Friends.* Harcourt, 2006. Ages 3–6.

Cohen, Miriam. *My Big Brother.* Illustrated by Ronald Himler. Star Bright, 2004. Ages 4–7.

Cooney, Barbara. *Miss Rumphius.* Viking, 1982. Ages 6–10.

Cooper, Elisha. *A Good Night Walk.* Orchard, 2005. Ages 3–6.

Cordsen, Carol Foskett. *The Milkman.* Illustrated by Douglas B. Jones. Dutton, 2005. Ages 3–7.

Crews, Donald. *Bigmama's.* Greenwillow, 1991. Ages 4–7.

Cronin, Doreen. *Click, Clack, Moo: Cows That Type.* Illustrated by Betsy Lewin. Simon & Schuster, 2000. Ages 4–7.

———. *Duck for President.* Illustrated by Betsy Lewin. Simon & Schuster, 2004. Ages 4–7.

———. *Wiggle.* Illustrated by Scott Menchin. Simon & Schuster, 2005. Ages 2–5.

Cunnane, Kelly. *For You Are a Kenyan Child.* Illustrated by Ana Juan. Atheneum, 2006. Ages 5–8.

D'Amico, Carmela. *Ella Takes the Cake.* Illustrated by Steven D'Amico. Scholastic, 2005. Ages 4–6.

Deacon, Alexis. *Beegu.* Farrar, 2003. Ages 3–6.

de Brunhoff, Jean. *The Story of Babar.* Random House, 1933. Ages 6–8.

dePaola, Tomie. *Strega Nona.* Prentice Hall, 1975. Ages 5–7.

Dorros, Arthur. *Abuela.* Illustrated by Elisa Kleven. Dutton, 1991. Ages 5–7.

Duval, Kathy. *The Three Bears' Christmas.* Illustrated by Paul Meisel. Holiday, 2005. Ages 3–6.

Falconer, Ian. *Olivia..* Atheneum, 2000. Ages 4–7.

———. *Olivia Saves the Circus.* Atheneum, 2001. Ages 3–7.

Feiffer, Jules. *Bark, George.* HarperCollins, 1999. Ages 3–5.

Flack, Marjorie. *The Story about Ping.* Illustrated by Kurt Wiese. Viking, 1933. Ages 7–9.

Flatharta, Antoine Ó. *Hurry and the Monarch.* Illustrated by Meilo So. Knopf, 2005. Ages 4–7.

Fleming, Candace. *Muncha! Muncha! Muncha!* Illustrated by Brian Karas. Simon & Schuster, 2002. Ages 3–7.

Ford, Bernette. *First Snow.* Illustrated by Sebastian Braun. Holiday, 2005. Ages 3–7.

Fox, Mem. *Wilfrid Gordon McDonald Partridge.* Illustrated by Julie Vivas. Kane/Miller, 1985. Ages 6–8.

Frazee, Marla. *Roller Coaster.* Harcourt, 2003. Ages 4–7.

———. *Santa Claus: The World's Number One Toy Expert.* Harcourt, 2005. Ages 5–7.

Freeman, Don. *Corduroy.* Viking, 1968. Ages 3–5.

———. *A Pocket for Corduroy.* Viking, 1978. Ages 3–5.

Gág, Wanda. *Millions of Cats.* Coward-McCann, 1928. Ages 4–6.

George, Kristine O'Connell. *Up!* Illustrated by Niroe Nakata. Clarion, 2005. Ages 1–4.

Gerstein, Mordecai. *The Man Who Walked Between the Towers.* Millbrook, 2003. Ages 5–8.

Goode, Diane. *The Most Perfect Spot.* HarperCollins, 2006. Ages 5–7.

Graham, Bob. *Benny, An Adventure Story.* Candlewick, 1999. Ages 5–8.

———. *"Let's Get a Pup!" Said Kate.* Candlewick, 2001. Ages 3–6.

———. *Max.* Candlewick, 2000. Ages 4–7.

Gravett, Emily. *Wolves.* Simon & Schuster, 2006. Ages 6–8.

Grey, Mini. *Traction Man Is Here!* Knopf, 2005. Ages 5–7.

Haas, Irene. *Bess and Bella.* Simon & Schuster, 2006. Ages 4–7.

Hall, Donald. *Ox-Cart Man.* Illustrated by Barbara Cooney. Viking, 1979. Ages 7–9.

Heide, Florence Parry, and Judith Heide Gilliland. *The Day of Ahmed's Secret.* Illustrated by Ted Lewin. Lothrop, 1990. Ages 6–10.

Henkes, Kevin. *Chrysanthemum.* Greenwillow, 1991. Ages 5–7.

———. *Julius, the Baby of the World.* Greenwillow, 1990. Ages 5–7.

———. *Kitten's First Full Moon.* Greenwillow, 2004. Ages 3–5.

———. *Lilly's Big Day.* Greenwillow, 2006. Ages 4–7.

———. *Lilly's Purple Plastic Purse.* Greenwillow, 1996. Ages 5–7.

———. *Owen.* Greenwillow, 1993. Ages 2–4.

———. *Sheila Rae the Brave.* Greenwillow, 1987. Ages 5–7.

———. *So Happy!* Illustrated by Anita Lobel. Greenwillow, 2005. Ages 6–9.

———. *Wemberley Worried.* Greenwillow, 2000. Ages 5–8.

Ho, Minfong. *Hush!: A Thai Lullaby.* Illustrated by Holly Meade. Orchard, 1996. Ages 4–6.

Hoban, Russell. *A Baby Sister for Frances.* Illustrated by Lillian Hoban. Harper, 1964. (Others in this series: *Bedtime for Frances,* illustrated by Garth Williams, 1969; *Best Friends for Frances,* illustrated by Lillian Hoban, 1969; *A Bargain for Frances,* illustrated by Lillian Hoban. Harper, 1970.) Ages 4–6.

Hoffman, Mary. *Amazing Grace.* Illustrated by Caroline Binch. Dial, 1991. Ages 5–7.

Isaacs, Anne. *Swamp Angel.* Illustrated by Paul O. Zelinsky. Dutton, 1994. Ages 4–8.

Jacobson, Jennifer Richard. *Andy Shane and the Very Bossy Dolores Starbuckle.* Illustrated by Abby Carter. Candlewick, 2005. Ages 5–8.

Jenkins, Emily. *That New Animal.* Illustrated by Pierre Pratt. Farrar, 2005. Ages 3–7.

Johnson, Angela. *Tell Me a Story, Mama.* Illustrated by David Soman. Orchard, 1989. Ages 6–8.

Johnson, Crockett. *Harold and the Purple Crayon.* Harper, 1955. Ages 5–7.

Joyce, William. *Bently and Egg.* HarperCollins, 1992. Ages 4–8.

Juan, Ana. *The Night Eater.* Scholastic, 2004. Ages 4–7.

Jukes, Mavis. *Like Jake and Me.* Illustrated by Lloyd Bloom. Knopf, 1984. Ages 6–8.

Juster, Norton. *The Hello, Goodbye Window.* Illustrated by Chris Raschka. Hyperion, 2005. Ages 4–7.

Kasza, Keiko. *The Dog Who Cried Wolf.* Putnam, 2005. Ages 4–7.

Keats, Ezra Jack. *The Snowy Day.* Viking, 1962. Ages 4–6.

———. *Whistle for Willie.* Viking, 1964. Ages 5–7.

Kinsey-Warnock, Natalie. *Nora's Ark.* Illustrated by Emily Arnold McCully. HarperCollins, 2005. Ages 5–8.

Kloske, Geoffrey. *Once Upon a Time, the End (Asleep in 60 Seconds).* Illustrated by Barry Blitt. Simon & Schuster, 2005. Ages 5–8.

Knudsen, Michelle. *Library Lion.* Illustrated by Kevin Hawkes. Candlewick, 2006. Ages 4–7.

Krensky, Stephen. *How Santa Got His Job.* Illustrated by S. D. Schindler. Simon & Schuster, 1998. Ages 5–8.

Kvasnosky, Laura McGee. *Zelda and Ivy.* Candlewick, 1998. Ages 6–8.

———. *Zelda and Ivy One Christmas.* Candlewick, 2000. Ages 6–8.

Leaf, Munro. *The Story of Ferdinand.* Illustrated by Robert Lawson. Viking, 1936. Ages 7–9.

Lee, Ho Baek. *While We Were Out.* Kane/Miller, 2003. Ages 4–7.

Lester, Helen. *Hooway for Wodney Wat.* Illustrated by Lynn Munsinger. Houghton, 1999. Ages 4–7.

Lionni, Leo. *Alexander and the Wind-Up Mouse.* Pantheon, 1967. Ages 6–8.

———. *The Biggest House in the World.* Pantheon, 1968. Ages 5–7.

———. *Inch by Inch.* Astor-Honor, 1960. Ages 5–7.

———. *Swimmy.* Pantheon, 1963. Ages 6–8.

Long, Melinda. *How I Became a Pirate.* Illustrated by David Shannon. Harcourt, 2003. Ages 5–8.

Loomis, Christine. *Astro Bunnies.* Illustrated by Ora Eitan. Putnam, 2001. Ages 4–7.

Lum, Kate. *What? Cried Granny: An Almost Bedtime Story.* Illustrated by Adrian Johnson. Dial, 1999. Ages 5–8.

MacDonald, Ross. *Bad Baby.* Roaring Brook, 2005. Ages 5–8.

Markes, Julie. *Shhhhh! Everybody's Sleeping.* Illustrated by David Parkins. HarperCollins, 2005. Ages 4–6.

McCarty, Peter. *Moon Plane.* Holt, 2006. Ages 3–5.

McClintock, Barbara. *Adèle and Simon.* Farrar, 2006. Ages 5–8.

———. *Dahlia.* Farrar, 2002. Ages 5–7.

McCloskey, Robert. *Make Way for Ducklings.* Viking, 1941. Ages 5–7.

McDonald, Megan. *Insects Are My Life.* Illustrated by Paul B. Johnson. Orchard, 1995. Ages 5–8.

McElmurry, Jill. *I'm Not a Baby!* Random, 2006. Ages 4–7.

McFarland, Lyn Rossiter. *Widget.* Illustrated by Jim McFarland. Farrar, 2001. Ages 4–6.

McMillan, Bruce. *The Problem with Chickens.* Illustrated by Gunnella. Houghton, 2005. Ages 4–8.

McMullan, Kate. *I Stink!* Illustrated by Jim McMullan. HarperCollins, 2002. Ages 4–7.

McNulty, Faith. *If You Decide to Go to the Moon.* Illustrated by Steven Kellogg. Scholastic, 2005. Ages 5–8.

Meddaugh, Susan. *Martha Blah Blah.* Houghton, 1996. Ages 5–7.

———. *Martha Speaks.* Houghton, 1992. Ages 4–8.

———. *The Witch's Walking Stick.* Houghton, 2005. Ages 5–7.

Mochizuki, Ken. *Baseball Saved Us.* Illustrated by Dom Lee. Lee & Low, 1993. Ages 7–9.

———. *Heroes.* Illustrated by Dom Lee. Lee & Low, 1995. Ages 7–9.

Mosel, Arlene, adapter. *The Funny Little Woman.* Illustrated by Blair Lent. Dutton, 1972. Ages 6–8.

Napoli, Donna Jo. *Albert.* Illustrated by Jim LaMarche. Harcourt, 2001. Ages 5–8.

Ogburn, Jacqueline. *The Bake Shop Ghost.* Illustrated by Marjorie Priceman. Houghton, 2005. Ages 5–8.

Palatini, Margie. *Three French Hens.* Illustrated by Richard Egielski. Hyperion, 2005. Ages 5–7.

Perl, Erica S. *Chicken Bedtime Is Really Early.* Illustrated by George Bates. Abrams, 2005. Ages 3–5.

Peters, Lisa Westberg. *Cold Little Duck, Duck, Duck.* Illustrated by Sam Williams. Greenwillow, 2000. Ages 1–4.

Pilkey, Dav. *The Paperboy.* Orchard, 1996. Ages 6–9.

Pitzer, Susanna. *Not Afraid of Dogs.* Illustrated by Larry Day. Walker, 2006. Ages 5–8.

Polacco, Patricia. *Chicken Sunday.* Putnam, 1992. Ages 4–9.

———. *Thunder Cake.* Putnam, 1990. Ages 6–8.

Potter, Beatrix. *The Tale of Peter Rabbit.* Warne, 1902. (See 20 other titles in the series.) Ages 5–7.

Priceman, Marjorie. *How to Make an Apple Pie and See the World.* Knopf, 1994. Ages 6–8.

Provensen, Alice, and Martin Provensen. *The Glorious Flight: Across the Channel with Louis Blériot.* Viking, 1983. Ages 8–10.

Ransome, Arthur. *The Fool of the World and the Flying Ship.* Illustrated by Uri Shulevitz. Farrar, 1968. Ages 6–8.

Rathmann, Peggy. *The Day the Babies Crawled Away.* Putnam, 2003. Ages 4–7.

———. *Officer Buckle and Gloria.* Putnam, 1995. Ages 6–8.

———. *10 Minutes till Bedtime.* Putnam, 1998. Ages 3–6.

Rawlinson, Julia. *Fletcher and the Falling Leaves.* Illustrated by Tiphanie Beeke. Greenwillow, 2006. Ages 4–8.

Reid, Barbara. *The Subway Mouse.* Scholastic, 2005. Ages 5–7.

Rey, Hans A. *Curious George.* Houghton, 1941. (See others in the Curious George series.) Ages 5–7.

Richards, Beah E. *Keep Climbing, Girls.* Illustrated by R. Gregory Christie. Simon & Schuster, 2006. Ages 5–8.

Richardson, Justin, and Peter Parnell. *And Tango Makes Three.* Illustrated by Henry Cole. Simon & Schuster, 2005. Ages 5–8.

Riley, Linnea. *Mouse Mess.* Scholastic, 1997. Ages 4–6.

Ringgold, Faith. *Tar Beach.* Crown, 1991. Ages 8–10.

Rodman, Mary Ann. *My Best Friend.* Illustrated by E. B. Lewis. Viking, 2005. Ages 5–7.

Rylant, Cynthia. *The Relatives Came.* Illustrated by Stephen Gammell. Bradbury, 1985. Ages 6–10.

———. *When I Was Young in the Mountains.* Illustrated by Diane Goode. Dutton, 1982. Ages 7–9.

Sakai, Komako. *Emily's Balloon.* Chronicle, 2006. Ages 2–4.

Samuels, Barbara. *Happy Valentine's Day, Delores.* Farrar, 2005. Ages 5–7.

Say, Allen. *Tree of Cranes.* Houghton, 1991. Ages 7–9.

Schotter, Roni. *The Boy Who Loved Words.* Illustrated by Giselle Potter. Random, 2006. Ages 6–10.

Scieszka, Jon. *Math Curse.* Illustrated by Lane Smith. Viking, 1995. Ages 8–10.

———. *The Stinky Cheese Man and Other Fairly Stupid Tales.* Illustrated by Lane Smith. Viking, 1992. Ages 7–10.

Sendak, Maurice. *In the Night Kitchen.* Harper, 1970. Ages 7–9.

———. *Where the Wild Things Are.* Harper, 1963. Ages 5–7.

Seuss, Dr. (pseudonym of Theodor S. Geisel). *And to Think That I Saw It on Mulberry Street.* Vanguard, 1937. Ages 5–7.

———. *The 500 Hats of Bartholomew Cubbins.* Vanguard, 1938. Ages 5–7.

———. *Horton Hatches the Egg.* Random, 1940. Ages 6–8.

Shannon, David. *David Gets in Trouble.* Scholastic, 2002. Ages 4–6.

———. *Duck on a Bike.* Scholastic, 2002. Ages 3–6.

Shannon, George. *Tippy-Toe Chick, Go!* Illustrated by Laura Dronzek. Greenwillow, 2003. Ages 4–6.

Shulevitz, Uri. *Snow.* Farrar, 1998. Ages 3–6.

———. *So Sleepy Story.* Farrar, 2006. Ages 2–6.

———. *The Stray Dog: From a True Story by Reiko Sassa.* HarperCollins, 2001. Ages 4–7.

Sís, Peter. *Madlenka.* Farrar, 2000. Ages 5–8.

———. *Madlenka's Dog.* Farrar, 2002. Ages 3–7.

Slobodkina, Esphyr, *Caps for Sale.* Addison-Wesley, 1947. Ages 4–6.

Soto, Gary. *Chato's Kitchen.* Illustrated by Susan Guevara. Putnam, 1995. Ages 4–7.

———. *Too Many Tamales.* Illustrated by Ed Martinez. Putnam, 1993. Ages 4–7.

Steen, Sandra and Susan. *Car Wash.* Illustrated by Brian Karas. Putnam, 2001. Ages 3–7.

Steig, William. *The Amazing Bone.* Farrar, 1976. Ages 7–9.

———. *Doctor De Soto.* Farrar, 1982. Ages 7–9.

———. *Sylvester and the Magic Pebble.* Simon & Schuster, 1969. Ages 7–9.

Steptoe, John. *Stevie.* Harper, 1969. Ages 5–7.

Stevens, Janet, and Susan Stevens Crummel. *The Great Fuzz Frenzy.* Illustrated by Janey Stevens. Harcourt, 2005. Ages 4–7.

Stewart, Sarah. *The Gardener.* Illustrated by David Small. Farrar, 1997. Ages 4–7.

Stock, Catherine. *Where Are You Going, Manyoni?* Morrow, 1993. Ages 4–8.

Stuve-Bodeen, Stephanie. *Elizabeti's Doll.* Illustrated by Christy Hale. Lee & Low, 1998. Ages 3–7.

Thompson, Lauren. *Polar Bear Night.* Illustrated by Stephen Savage. Scholastic, 2004. Ages 2–5.

Udry, Janice May. *The Moon Jumpers.* Illustrated by Maurice Sendak. Harper, 1959. Ages 5–7.

Van Allsburg, Chris. *Jumanji.* Houghton, 1981. Ages 6–10.

———. *The Sweetest Fig.* Houghton, 1993. Ages 8–11.

———. *Two Bad Ants.* Houghton, 1988.

———. *The Wretched Stone.* Houghton, 1991. Ages 8–11.

Van Leeuwen, Jean. *Benny & Beautiful Baby Delilah.* Illustrated by LeUyen Pham. Dial, 2006. Ages 3–5.

Viorst, Judith. *Alexander and the Terrible, Horrible, No Good, Very Bad Day.* Illustrated by Ray Cruz. Atheneum, 1972. Ages 5–7.

———. *Alexander, Who's Not (Do You Hear Me? I Mean It!) Going to Move.* Illustrated by Robin Glasser. Atheneum, 1995. Ages 4–8.

———. *Alexander Who Used to Be Rich Last Sunday.* Illustrated by Ray Cruz. Atheneum, 1978. Ages 6–8.

———. *I'll Fix Anthony.* Illustrated by Arnold Lobel. Harper, 1969. Ages 4–6.

Waber, Bernard. *Ira Says Goodbye.* Houghton, 1988. Ages 6–8.

———. *Ira Sleeps Over.* Houghton, 1972. Ages 6–8.

Waddell, Martin. *Farmer Duck.* Illustrated by Helen Oxenbury. Candlewick, 1992. Ages 4–6.

———. *Hi, Harry! The Moving Story of How One Slow Tortoise Slowly Made a Friend.* Illustrated by Barbara Firth. Candlewick, 2003. Ages 3–5.

———. *Tiny's Big Adventure.* Illustrated by John Lawrence. Candlewick, 2004. Ages 4–7.

Wells, Rosemary. *Bunny Cakes.* Dial, 1997. Ages 2–6.

Wheeler, Lisa. *Castaway Cats.* Illustrated by Ponder Goembel. Atheneum, 2006. Ages 4–7.

Wiesner, David. *June 29, 1999.* Clarion, 1992. Ages 6–9.

Wild, Margaret. *The Very Best of Friends.* Illustrated by Julie Vivas. Harcourt, 1990. Ages 6–8.

Willems, Mo. *Don't Let the Pigeon Drive the Bus!* Hyperion, 2003. Ages 4–7.

———. *Don't Let the Pigeon Stay Up Late!* Hyperion, 2006. Ages 3–7.

———. *Knuffle Bunny: A Cautionary Tale.* Hyperion, 2004. Ages 3–5.

———. *Leonardo, the Terrible Monster.* Hyperion, 2005. Ages 4–6.

Williams, Karen Lynn. *Galimoto.* Illustrated by Catherine Stock. HarperCollins, 1990. Ages 6–8.

———. *Painted Dreams.* Illustrated by Catherine Stock. HarperCollins, 1998. Ages 5–8.

Williams, Margery. *The Velveteen Rabbit.* Illustrated by William Nicholson. Doubleday, 1922. Ages 6–8.

Williams, Sherley Anne. *Working Cotton.* Illustrated by Carole Byard. Harcourt, 1992. Ages 5–7.

Williams, Vera B. *A Chair for My Mother.* Greenwillow, 1982. Ages 6–8.

———. *Stringbean's Trip to the Shining Sea.* Illustrated by author and Jennifer Williams. Greenwillow, 1988. Ages 7–9.

Willis, Jeanne. *Tadpole's Promise.* Illustrated by Tony Ross. Atheneum, 2005. Ages 5–9.

Winthrop, Elizabeth. *Squashed in the Middle.* Illustrated by Pat Cummings. Holt, 2005. Ages 5–8.

Wong, Janet S. *Buzz.* Harcourt, 2000. Ages 3–5.

Yaccarino, Dan. *Deep in the Jungle.* Atheneum, 2000. Ages 5–9.

Yorinks, Arthur. *Hey, Al.* Illustrated by Richard Egielski. Farrar, 1986. Ages 7–9.

Young, Ed. *Seven Blind Mice.* Philomel, 1992. Ages 6–10. (Modern folktale.)

Zion, Gene. *Harry, the Dirty Dog.* Illustrated by Margaret B. Graham. HarperTrophy, 1976 (1956). Ages 4–6.

Zolotow, Charlotte. *Mr. Rabbit and the Lovely Present.* Illustrated by Maurice Sendak. Harper, 1962. Ages 5–7.

Pattern Books

Arnold, Marsha Diane. *Roar of a Snore.* Illustrated by Pierre Pratt. Dial, 2006. Ages 2–4.

Bloom, Suzanne. *The Bus for Us.* Boyds Mills, 2001. Ages 3–6.

Chodos-Irvine, Margaret. *Ella Sarah Gets Dressed.* Harcourt, 2003. Ages 2–5.

Fleming, Denise. *The Cow Who Clucked.* Holt, 2006. Ages 3–6.

———. *Mama Cat Has Three Kittens.* Holt, 1998. Ages 2–5.

Guarino, Deborah. *Is Your Mama a Llama?* Illustrated by Stephen Kellogg. Scholastic, 1989. Ages 3–7.

Martin, Bill, Jr. *Brown Bear, Brown Bear, What Do You See?* Illustrated by Eric Carle. Holt, 1983. Ages 3–6.

———. *Panda Bear, Panda Bear, What Do You See?* Illustrated by Eric Carle. Holt, 2003. Ages 3–6.

———. *Polar Bear, Polar Bear, What Do You Hear?* Illustrated by Eric Carle. Holt, 1991. Ages 3–6.

Shannon, David. *No, David!* Scholastic, 1998. Ages 2–5.

Smee, Nicola. *Clip-Clop.* Boxer, 2006. Ages 3–5.

Taback, Simms. *Joseph Had a Little Overcoat.* Viking, 1999. Ages 3–6.

———. *There Was an Old Lady Who Swallowed a Fly.* Viking, 1997. Ages 5–7. (See also Toy Books.)

Williams, Sue. *I Went Walking.* Illustrated by Julie Vivas. Harcourt, 1990. Ages 3–6.

Easy-to-Read Books

Adler, David A. *Young Cam Jansen and the Double Beach Mystery.* Illustrated by Susanna Natti. Viking, 2002. Ages 5–7.

Ahlberg, Allan. *The Children Who Smelled a Rat.* Illustrated by Katharine McEwen. Candlewick, 2005. Ages 7–10.

Arnold, Tedd. *Hi! Fly Guy.* Cartwheel Books/Scholastic, 2005. Ages 5–7.

Bloom, Suzanne. *A Splendid Friend, Indeed.* Boyds Mills, 2005. Ages 5–7.

Brown, Marc T., creator, and Stephen Krensky. *Arthur and the Big Blow-Up.* Illustrated by Marc Brown. Little Brown, 2000. (Representative of others in the lengthy Arthur chapter book series: *Arthur and the Perfect Big Brother; Francine, the Superstar.*) Ages 5–7.

Brown, Margaret Wise. *The Runaway Bunny.* Illustrated by Clement Hurd. Harper, 1991 (1942). Ages 2–5.

Byars, Betsy. *Ant Plays Bear.* Illustrated by Marc Simont. Viking, 1997. Ages 6–8.

———. *My Brother, Ant.* Illustrated by Marc Simont. Viking, 1996. Ages 6–8.

Calmenson, Stephanie, and Joanna Cole. *The Gator Girls.* Illustrated by Lynn Munsinger. Morrow, 1995. Ages 5–7.

Cole, Joanna, and Stephanie Calmenson, compilers. *Ready . . . Set . . . Read! The Beginning Reader's Treasury.* Illustrated by Anne Burgess and Chris Demarest. Doubleday, 1990.

Danziger, Paula. *Get Ready for Second Grade, Amber Brown.* Illustrated by Tony Ross. Putnam, 2002. Ages 5–7.

———. *It's a Fair Day, Amber Brown.* Illustrated by Tony Ross. Putnam, 2002. Ages 5–7.

dePaola, Tomie. *Hide-and-Seek All Week.* Grosset and Dunlap, 2001. Ages 5–7.

de Regniers, Beatrice Schenk. *May I Bring a Friend?* Illustrated by Beni Montresor. Atheneum, 1964. Ages 4–7.

DiCamillo, Kate. *Mercy Watson to the Rescue.* Illustrated by Chris Van Dusen. Candlewick, 2005. Ages 5–7. (Part of a series.)

Dunrea, Olivier. *Gossie.* Houghton, 2002. Ages 3–5. Also *Gossie and Gertie.*

Edwards, Michelle. *Stinky Stern Forever.* Harcourt, 2005. Ages 6–9.

Fenner, Carol. *Snowed in with Grandmother Silk.* Illustrated by Amanda Harvey. Dial, 2003. Ages 5–7.

Fine, Anne. *The Jamie and Angus Stories.* Illustrated by Penny Dale. Candlewick, 2002. Ages 5–7.

Fleming, Denise. *Buster.* Holt, 2003. Ages 5–7.

Greene, Stephanie. *Owen Foote, Frontiersman.* Illustrated by Martha Weston. Clarion, 1999. Ages 5–7.

Guest, Elissa Haden. *Iris and Walter.* Illustrated by Christine Davenier. Harcourt/Gulliver, 2000. Ages 6–8.

———. *Iris and Walter: The Sleepover.* Illustrated by Christine Davenier. Harcourt, 2002. Ages 5–7.

Haskins, Lori. *Ducks in Muck.* Illustrated by Valeria Petrone. Random, 2000. Ages 5–7.

Hoberman, Mary Ann. *You Read to Me, I'll Read to You. Very Short Stories to Read Together.* Illustrated by Michael Emberley. Little, Brown, 2001. Ages 5–7.

Holub, Joan. *The Garden That We Grew.* Illustrated by Hiroe Nakata. Viking, 2001. Ages 5–7.

Horowitz, Ruth. *Breakout at the Bug Lab.* Illustrated by Joan Holub. Dial, 2001. Ages 5–8.

Howe, James. *Pinky and Rex and the Just-Right Pet.* Illustrated by Melissa Sweet. Simon & Schuster, 2001. Ages 6–8.

Hutchins, Pat. *Rosie's Walk.* Macmillan, 1968. Ages 3–6.

Koss, Amy Goldman. *Where Fish Go in Winter and Other Great Mysteries.* Illustrated by Laura J. Bryant. Dial, 2000. Ages 5–7.

Kraus, Robert. *Leo the Late Bloomer.* Illustrated by José Aruego. Dutton, 1971. Ages 4–7.

Kvasnosky, Laura McGee. *Zelda and Ivy: The Runaways.* Candlewick, 2006. Ages 5–8.

Livingstone, Star. *Harley.* Illustrated by Molly Bang. North-South, 2001. Ages 5–7.

Lobel, Arnold. "Frog and Toad Series." *Frog and Toad Are Friends.* Harper, 1970. Ages 4–8. (Others in this series: *Frog and Toad Together,* 1972; *Frog and Toad All Year,* 1976; *Days with Frog and Toad,* 1979.)

McDonough, Yona Zeldis. *The Dollhouse Magic.* Illustrated by Diane Palmisciano. Holt, 2000. Ages 7–9.

Minarik, Else Holmelund. *Little Bear.* Illustrated by Maurice Sendak. Harper, 1957. Ages 4–7. (Others in the Little Bear series: *Father Bear Comes Home,* 1959; *Little Bear's Friend,* 1960; *Little Bear's Visit,* 1961; *A Kiss for Little Bear,* 1968.)

Numeroff, Laura Joffe. *If You Give a Mouse a Cookie.* Harper, 1985. Ages 4–7.

Parish, Peggy. *Amelia Bedelia.* Illustrated by Lynn Sweat. Econo-Clad, 1999 (originally published by Greenwillow, 1985). Ages 5–7. (Others in this series: *Amelia Bedelia Helps Out; Amelia Bedelia Goes Camping; Amelia Bedelia and the Baby; Amelia Bedelia's Family Album.*)

Paterson, Katherine. *Marvin One Too Many.* Illustrated by Jane Clark Brown. HarperCollins, 2001. Ages 5–7.

Porte, Barbara Ann. *If You Ever Get Lost: The Adventures of Julia and Evan.* Illustrated by Nancy Carpenter. Greenwillow, 2000. Ages 5–7.

Raschka, Chris. *Yo! Yes?* Orchard, 1993. Ages 4–7. (See also *Ring! Yo?*)

Rodowsky, Colby. *Not My Dog.* Illustrated by Thomas F. Yezerski. Farrar, 1999. Ages 5–7.

Root, Phyllis. *Mouse Goes Out.* Illustrated by James Croft. Candlewick, 2002. Ages 4–6.

Rylant, Cynthia. *Henry and Mudge.* Illustrated by Suçie Stevenson. Bradbury, 1987. Ages 4–7. (See others in this series.)

———. *Henry and Mudge and the Great Grandpas.* Illustrated by Suçie Stevenson. Simon & Schuster, 2005. Ages 5–7. (part of a series)

———. *Mr. Putter & Tabby Feed the Fish.* Illustrated by Arthur Howard. Harcourt, 2001. Ages 5–7.

———. *Mr. Putter & Tabby Make a Wish.* Illustrated by Arthur Howard. Harcourt, 2005. Ages 5–7. (Part of a series)

Sachar, Louis. *Marvin Redpost: A Flying Birthday Cake?* Illustrated by Amy Wummer. Random House, 1999. Ages 5–7. (Part of a series.)

Seuss, Dr. (pseudonym of Theodor S. Geisel). *The Cat in the Hat.* Random, 1957. Ages 4–7.

———. *Fox in Sox.* Random, 1965. Ages 4–7.

Silverman, Erica. *Cowgirl Kate and Cocoa.* Illustrated by Betsy Lewin. Harcourt, 2005. Ages 5–7.

Stevenson, James. *The Mud Flat Mystery.* Greenwillow, 1997. Ages 5–7.

Thomas, Shelley Moore. *Good Night, Good Knight.* Illustrated by Jennifer Plecas. Dutton, 2000. Ages 5–8.

Van Leeuwen, Jean. *Amanda Pig and the Really Hot Day.* Illustrated by Ann Schweninger. Dial, 2005. Ages 5–7.

Wallace, Karen. *Wild Baby Animals.* Dorling Kindersley, 2000. Ages 5–8.

Wood, Audrey. *The Napping House.* Illustrated by Don Wood. Harcourt, 1984. Ages 4–8.

Picture Books for Older Readers

Avi. *Silent Movie.* Illustrated by C. B. Mordan. Atheneum, 2003. Ages 8–12.

Bang, Molly. *Goose.* Scholastic, 1996. Ages 8–10.

———. *The Paper Crane.* Greenwillow, 1985. Ages 8–10.

Briggs, Raymond. *The Man.* Random House, 1995. Ages 9–14.

———. *Ug: Boy Genius of the Stone Age.* Knopf, 2002. Ages 8–12.

Browne, Anthony. *Piggybook.* Knopf, 1986. Ages 9–14.

———. *The Tunnel.* Knopf, 1990. Ages 8–12.

———. *Zoo.* Knopf, 1993. Ages 8–14.

Bunting, Eve. *Riding the Tiger.* Illustrated by David Frampton. Clarion, 2001. Ages 8–11.

Collington, Peter. *The Coming of the Surfman.* Knopf, 1994. Ages 8–14.

Crew, Gary. *The Watertower.* Illustrated by Steven Woolman. Kane/Miller, 1995. Ages 10–14.

Diaz, Jorge. *The Rebellious Alphabet.* Illustrated by Øivind S. Jorfald. Translated by Geoffrey Fox. Holt, 1993. Ages 9–12.

Gallaz, Christophe, and Roberto Innocenti. *Rose Blanche.* Illustrated by Roberto Innocenti. Creative Education, 1985. Ages 9–14.

Harvey, Brett. *Cassie's Journey: Going West in the 1860s.* Illustrated by Deborah Kogan Ray. Holiday, 1988. Ages 8–10.

Hooks, William H. *The Ballad of Belle Dorcas.* Illustrated by Brian Pinkney. Knopf, 1990. Ages 10–12.

Johnson, D. B. *Henry Builds a Cabin.* Houghton, 2002. Ages 9–13.

———. *Henry Climbs a Mountain.* Houghton, 2003. Ages 9–13.

———. *Henry Hikes to Fitchburg.* Houghton, 2000. Ages 9–13.

Kerley, Barbara. *The Dinosaurs of Waterhouse Hawkins.* Illustrated by Brian Selznick. Scholastic, 2001. Ages 8–12.

Maruki, Toshi. *Hiroshima No Pika.* Lothrop, 1980. Ages 9–14.

McCarthy, Meghan. *Aliens Are Coming! The True Account of the 1938 War of the Worlds Radio Broadcast.* Knopf, 2006. Ages 8–12.

McKissack, Patricia C., and Fredrick L. *Christmas in the Big House, Christmas in the Quarters.* Illustrated by John Thompson. Scholastic, 1994. Ages 8–12.

Moss, Marissa. *Brave Harriet: The First Woman to Fly the English Channel.* Illustrated by C. F. Payne. Harcourt, 2001. Ages 8–10.

Myers, Walter Dean. *Blues Journey.* Illustrated by Christopher Myers. Holiday, 2003. Ages 10–14.

Polacco, Patricia. *Pink and Say.* Philomel, 1994. Ages 8–11.

Popov, Nikolai. *Why?* North-South, 1996. Ages 8–12. (Wordless.)

Rogers, Gregory. *The Boy, the Bear, the Baron, the Bard.* Roaring Brook, 2004. Ages 8–12. (Wordless.)

Rosen, Michael. *Michael Rosen's Sad Book.* Illustrated by Quentin Blake. Candlewick, 2005. Ages 12–14. (England)

Scieszka, Jon. *The True Story of the 3 Little Pigs By A. Wolf.* Illustrated by Lane Smith. Viking, 1989. Ages 8–11.

Sidman, Joyce. *Song of the Water Boatman: And Other Pond Poems.* Illustrated by Beckie Prang. Houghton, 2005. Ages 7–12.

Sís, Peter. *Starry Messenger.* Farrar, 1996. Ages 9–14.

———. *Tibet through the Red Box.* Farrar, 1998. Ages 9–16.

Walter, Mildred Pitts. *Alec's Primer.* Illustrated by Larry Johnson. Vermont Folklife Center, 2004. Ages 7–10.

Ward, Lynd. *The Biggest Bear.* Houghton, 1952. Ages 7–9.

Wisniewski, David. *Rain Player.* Houghton, 1991. Ages 8–10.

Graphic Novels

Atagan, Patrick. *The Yellow Jar: Volume I: Two Tales from Japanese Tradition.* NBM, 2002. Ages 11–14.

Crilley, Mark. *Akiko on the Planet Smoo.* Random, 2000. Ages 9–14.

Czekaj, Jef. *Grampa and Julie: Shark Hunters.* Top Shelf, 2004. Ages 9–14.

Dini, Paul. *Wonder Woman: Spirit of Truth.* Illustrated by Alex Ross. DC Comics, 2001. Ages 9–11.

Eisner, Will. *Sundiata: A Legend of Africa.* NBM, 2003. Ages 10–14.

Gaiman, Neil. *The Wolves in the Walls.* Illustrated by Dave McKean. HarperCollins, 2003. Ages 9–12.

Gownley, Jimmy. *Amelia Rules! What Makes You Happy.* ibooks, 2004. Ages 8–12.

———. *Amelia Rules! The Whole World's Crazy.* ibooks, 2003. Ages 8–11.

Harper, Charisse Mericle. *Fashion Kitty.* Hyperion, 2005. Ages 9–13.

Hartman, Rachel. *Amy Unbounded: Belondweg Blossoming.* Pug House, 2002. Ages 9–14.

Hergé. *The Adventures of Tintin: Volume I.* Translated from the French by Leslie Lonsdale-Cooper and Michael Turner. Little, Brown, 1994. Ages 9–12.

Holm, Jennifer L. *Babymouse: Queen of the World!* Illustrated by Matthew Holm. Random, 2005. Ages 9–12. (Part of the Babymouse series.)

Hosler, Jay. *Clan Apis.* Active Synapse, 2000. Ages 10–14.

Irwin, Jane, and Jeff Verndt. *Vögelein: A Clockwork Faerie.* Fiery Studio, 2003. Ages 12–16.

Kochalka, James. *Monkey vs. Robot.* Top Shelf, 2000. Ages 8–12.

———. *Monkey vs. Robot and the Crystal of Power.* Top Shelf, 2003. Ages 8–12.

———. *Pinky & Stinky.* Top Shelf, 2002. Ages 8–11.

Lat. *Kampung Boy.* First Second, 2006. Ages 9–14. (Autobiography; set in Malaysia; Muslim.)

Rodi, Rob. *Crossovers.* CrossGeneration, 2003. Ages 11–16.

Roman, Dave, and John Green. *Jax Epoch and the Quicken Forbidden.* Ait/Planet Lar, 2002. Ages 9–14.

Runton, Andy. *Owly, Volume I: The Way Home & the Bittersweet Summer.* Top Shelf, 2004. Ages 5–9.

———. *Owly, Volume II: Just a Little Blue.* Top Shelf, 2005. Ages 5–9.

Sfar, Joann. *Little Vampire Does Kung Fu!* Translated from the French by Mark and Alexis Siegel. Simon & Schuster, 2003. Ages 9–13.

Siegel, Siena Cherson. *To Dance: A Ballerina's Graphic Novel.* Illustrated by Mark Siegel. Simon & Schuster, 2006. Ages 10–14.

Smith, Jeff. *Bone: Out from Boneville.* Graphix, 2005. Ages 9–14.

Spiegelman, Art. *Little Lit: Folklore & Fairy Tale Funnies.* HarperCollins, 2000. Ages 9–14.

Stamaty, Mark Alan. *Alia's Mission: Saving the Books of Iraq.* Knopf, 2004. Ages 9–13.

Torres, J. *The Collected Alison Dare: Little Miss Adventures.* Illustrated by J. Bone. Oni, 2002. (Vol. 2, 2005). Ages 9–11.

Weigel, Jeff. *Atomic Ace (He's Just My Dad).* Albert Whitman, 2004. Ages 9–12.

Yang, Gene L. *American Born Chinese.* First Second, 2006. Ages 12–16. (Also multicultural.)

Illustrated Books of Poetry

See Chapter 4 recommended books list.

Illustrated Nursery Rhymes and Folk Songbooks

See Chapter 4 recommended books list.

Illustrated Traditional Folktales

See Chapter 6 recommended books list.

Illustrated Modern Folktales

See Chapter 7 recommended books list.

Related Films, Videos, and DVDs

Antarctic Antics. (2000). Author: Judy Sierra. Illustrators: Jose Aruego and Ariane Dewey. 32 minutes.

The Dot. (2004). Author/Illustrator: Peter H. Reynolds. 7 1/2 minutes.

Giggle, Giggle, Quack. (2003). Author: Doreen Cronin. Illustrator: Betsy Lewin. 9 1/2 minutes.

I Stink! (2004). Authors/Illustrators: Kate and Jim McMullan. 9 minutes.

Jumanji. (1995). Author/Illustrator: Chris Van Allsburg. 104 minutes.

The Man Who Walked between the Towers. (2005). Author/Illustrator: Mordicai Gerstein. 60 minutes.

Miss Nelson Has a Field Day. (1999). Author: Harry Allard. Illustrator: James Marshall. 13 minutes.

Notes Alive! On the Day You Were Born. (1996). Author/Illustrator: Debra Frasier. 30 minutes.

Owen. (1995). Author/Illustrator: Kevin Henkes. 9 minutes.

So You Want to Be President? (2002). Author: Judith St. George. Illustrator: David Small. 26 minutes.

Sources for Films, Videos, and DVDs

The Video Source Book. Syosset, NY: National Video Clearinghouse, 1979–. Published by Gale Research, Detroit, MI.

An annual reference work that lists media and provides sources for purchase and rental.

Websites of large video distributors:

www.libraryvideo.com

http://teacher.scholastic.com/products/westonwoods

chapter 6

Traditional Literature

Listen!
Quiet your faces; be crossed every thumb;
Fix on me deep your eyes . . .
And out of my mind a story shall come—
Old, and lovely, and wise.

—Walter de la Mare

Visual narratives told by ancient cave paintings in Europe, Asia, and Australia show us that prehistoric humans had stories to tell long before they had a written language. For thousands of years before writing was discovered, the best of these stories were preserved through the art of storytelling from one generation to the next. Surely these stories survived because people enjoyed hearing them.

Even today, their entertainment value cannot be denied. In folk literature we have our most ancient stories and a priceless literary heritage that links us to our beginnings as thinking beings.

Definition and Description

Traditional literature is the body of ancient stories and poems that grew out of the oral tradition of storytelling before being eventually written down. Having no known or identifiable authors, these stories and poems are attributed to entire groups of people or cultures. Although in ancient times some traditional stories may have been told as truths or may have been thought to contain elements of truth, today we consider them to be mostly or wholly fantasy.

Traditional literature includes several different types of stories, but because they were all shared orally for so long, they have many features in common:

- *Plots* are shorter than in other genres of literature; all but the essentials disappeared during countless retellings.
- *Action* is concentrated and fast paced, adding interest.
- *Characters* are two-dimensional and easily identified as good or bad.
- *Settings* are unimportant and vague ("In the beginning . . ." or "Long ago in a land far away . . .").
- *Literary style* is characterized by stock beginnings and endings ("Once upon a time . . ."), *motifs* (recurring features such as the number 3), and repeated refrains ("Mirror, mirror, on the wall . . .").
- *Themes* are limited (e.g., good overcomes evil, perseverance is a powerful tool, and explanations for the ways of the world).
- *Endings* are almost always happy (". . . and they lived happily ever after.").

Folklore is still being created, particularly in some of the developing countries where the oral tradition remains the chief means of communication. In the United States, urban legends, jokes, and jump-rope rhymes are all part of the constantly evolving body of folklore. These stories and rhymes are of unknown origin, but because they are certainly not ancient, they will not be treated in this chapter.

Evaluation and Selection of Traditional Literature

For thousands of years, people of all ages were the intended audience for traditional stories. In our scientifically enlightened times, these stories have come to be seen as childlike in their use of the supernatural and magic but nonetheless charming and entertaining. The following list of evaluation criteria was developed with a general child audience in mind:

- A traditional tale, even though written down, should preserve the narrative, or storytelling, style and should sound as though it is being told.
- A traditional tale should preserve the flavor of the culture or country of its origin through the use of colloquialisms, unusual speech patterns, a few easily understood foreign terms, or proper names that are common to the culture.

- In illustrated versions of traditional literature, text and illustrations must be of high quality, and illustrations must match the tone of the text and help to capture the essence of the culture of origin.
- Although simple in other respects, traditional tales employ a rich literary style. Even very young children are fascinated by the chants, stylistic flourishes, and colorful vocabulary that are characteristic of masterful storytelling.
- In evaluating collections of traditional literature, consider the number and variety of tales in the collection and the quality of reference aids, such as tables of contents and indexes.

Some adults raise concerns that the gruesome violence that is sometimes found in traditional stories harms or traumatizes children. In recent times, many traditional stories have been rewritten to omit the violence, as in the Disney versions of folktales. In a "softened" version of "Snow White," the evil stepmother is either forgiven by the heroine or banished from the kingdom. Earlier versions of the tale end like this:

> Then she [the stepmother] railed and cursed, and was beside herself with disappointment and anger. First she thought she would not go to the wedding; but then she felt she should have no peace until she went and saw the bride. And when she saw her she knew her for Snow-white, and could not stir from the place for anger and terror. For they had ready red-hot iron shoes, in which she had to dance until she fell down dead. (From Jakob Grimm and Wilhelm Grimm, *Household Stories,* translated by Lucy Crane [Macmillan, 1886].)

Critics of the softened versions of traditional tales claim that altering the stories robs them of their power, their appeal, and their psychological benefit to children, who are reassured that the evil force is gone forever and cannot come back to hurt them. We believe that young children who have heard "softened" versions of folktales have a right to know the earlier, unaltered versions when they are old enough to cope with the violence or harsh justice they contain. Likewise, as children enter the upper intermediate and middle grades, they should be made aware of the male chauvinism and poor feminine role models, from ever-sinister stepmothers to ever-helpless princesses, rampant in folktales.

 ## Historical Overview of Traditional Literature

Perhaps the world's first stories grew out of the dreams, wishes, ritual chants, or retellings of the notable exploits of our earliest ancestors. No one knows. Little can be said about the early history of this genre except that these stories existed only in oral form for thousands of years.

Folklorists are intrigued by the startling similarity of traditional tales around the world. Cinderella-type tales, for example, can be found in every culture. One explanation for this is that the first humans created these stories and took them along as they populated the globe. We call this theory *monogenesis,* or "single origin." Another theory credits the fundamental psychological similarity of humans for the similarity of their stories. *Polygenesis,* or "many origins," holds that early humans had similar urges and motives; asked similar, fundamental questions about themselves and the world around them; and, logically, created similar stories in response. Both theories have merit, and since the answer lies hidden in ancient prehistory, neither theory has prevailed over the other.

Excellent Traditional Literature to Read Aloud

Aliki. ***The Gods and Goddesses of Olympus.*** Ages 10–14. Myths.

dePaola, Tomie. ***Strega Nona.*** Ages 5–8. Folktale.

Hamilton, Virginia. ***The Girl Who Spun Gold.*** Illustrated by Leo and Diane Dillon. Ages 5–8. Folktale. Rumpelstiltskin variant.

Hennessy, B. G., reteller. ***The Boy Who Cried Wolf.*** Illustrated by Boris Kulikov. Ages 4–7. Fable.

Hodges, Margaret. ***The Hero of Bremen.*** Illustrated by Charles Mikolaycak. Ages 8–11. Folktale.

———. ***Merlin and the Making of the King.*** Illustrated by Trina Schart Hyman. Ages 8–12. Legend.

Mora, Pat. ***Doña Flor: A Tall Tale about a Giant Woman with a Great Big Heart.*** Illustrated by Raúl Colón. Ages 4–7. Tall tale.

San Souci, Robert D. ***The Faithful Friend.*** Illustrated by Brian Pinkney. Ages 11–14. Folktale.

Steptoe, John. ***Mufaro's Beautiful Daughters: An African Tale.*** Ages 6–8. Folktale. Cinderella variant.

Stevens, Janet. ***Tops and Bottoms.*** Ages 5–8. Folktale.

The popularity of traditional literature with children has continued to grow in the twenty-first century, owing in part to a renewed interest in storytelling. Other trends contributing to the popularity of this genre are the publication of single illustrated retellings of works of traditional literature, publication of cultural variants of traditional tales from around the world, and publication of newly discovered ethnic folk literature of many Canadian and U.S. minorities in collections and single illustrated works.

Types of Traditional Literature

Classification of traditional literature can be confusing. For instance, not everyone uses the same terms when referring to certain types of traditional stories. Also, modern stories that were written by known authors in the style of the traditional ones but are not of ancient and unknown origin are therefore not "traditional" in the strict sense.

The following terms are commonly used when referring to traditional literature:

- ***Traditional Literature.*** The entire body of stories passed down from ancient times by the oral tradition. The term *folktales* is sometimes used synonymously with traditional literature, but not in this textbook.
- ***Retold Tale.*** A version of a tale written in a style that will appeal to a contemporary audience but otherwise remaining true to the ancient tale.
- ***Variant.*** A story that shares elements of plot or character with other stories and is therefore in the same "story family" but differs mainly by culture. There are hundreds of variants of "Cinderella," for example, from all over the world, and all originated in the ancient past.

Myths

Myths are stories that recount and explain the origins of the world and the phenomena of nature. They are sometimes referred to as *creation stories.* The characters in these stories are mainly gods and goddesses, with occasional mention of humans, and the setting is high above earth in the home of the gods. Although often violent, myths nonetheless mirror human nature and the essence of our sometimes primitive emotions, instincts, and desires. Some folklorists believe that myths are the foundation of all other ancient stories. The best-known mythologies are of Greek, Roman, and Norse origin.

The complexity and symbolism often found in myths make them appropriate for an older audience (9 years and up) than is usual with traditional literature. Some myths have been simplified for a younger audience, but oversimplification robs these stories of their power and appeal.

Epics

Epics are long stories of human adventure and heroism recounted in many episodes, sometimes in verse. Epics are grounded in mythology, and their characters can be both human and divine. However, the hero is always human or, in some cases, superhuman, as was Ulysses in the *Odyssey,* Beowulf in the epic of that name, and Roland in *The Song of Roland.* The setting is earthly but not always realistic. Because of their length and complexity, epics are perhaps more suitable for students in high school or college, but on the strength of their compelling characters and events, some epics have been successfully adapted and shortened for younger audiences. *Dragonslayer,* an adaptation of *Beowulf* by Rosemary Sutcliff, is a good example.

Legends and Tall Tales

Legends are stories based on either real or supposedly real individuals and their marvelous deeds. Legendary characters such as King Arthur and Robin Hood and legendary settings such as Camelot are a tantalizing mix of realism and fantasy. Although the feats of the heroes of legend defy belief today, in ancient times these stories were considered factual. Legends, in general, are austere in tone, and, because of their length, seriousness, and complexity, are often suitable for middle-graders.

Tall tales are highly exaggerated accounts of the exploits of persons, both real and imagined, so they may be considered a subcategory of legends. In the evolution of the tall tale, as each teller embroidered on the hero's abilities or deeds, the tales became outlandishly exaggerated and were valued more for their humor and braggadocio than for their factual content. Well-known North American tall-tale heroes are Pecos Bill, Paul Bunyan, John Henry, and Johnny Appleseed. Lesser known but equally amazing are such tall-tale heroines as Annie Christmas and Sally Ann Thunder Ann Whirlwind Crockett. Tall tales can be enjoyed by children aged 7 and up.

Folktales

Folktales are stories that grew out of the lives and imaginations of the people, or folk. Folktales have always been children's favorite type of traditional literature and are enjoyed by children from about age 3 and up.

MILESTONES in the Development of Traditional Literature

Date	Event	Significance
Prehistory–1500s	Oral storytelling	Kept ancient stories alive and provided literature to common people
500 B.C.	Aesop, a supposed Greek slave, wrote classic fables	Established the fable as a type of traditional literature
1484	*Aesop's Fables* published by William Caxton in England	First known publication of traditional literature
1500–1700	Puritan Movement	Prevented the publication of traditional literature by the legitimate press
	Chapbooks emerge	Helped keep interest in traditional heroes alive during Puritan Movement
Late 1600s	Jean de La Fontaine of France adapted earlier fables in verse form	Popularized the fable
1697	*Tales of Mother Goose* published by Charles Perrault in France	First written version of folktales
1700s	Romantic Movement	Traditional fantasy promoted and embraced in Europe
1812	Wilhelm and Jakob Grimm collected and published *Nursery and Household Tales* in Germany	Helped popularize folk literature
1851	Asbjörnsen and Moe collected and published *The Norwegian Folktales* in Norway	Helped popularize folk literature
1894	Joseph Jacobs collected and published *English Fairy Tales* in England; adapted many tales for a child audience	Helped popularize folk literature
1889–1894	Andrew Lang collected and published four volumes of folktales from around the world	Growing popularity and knowledge of folktales worldwide helped popularize folk literature

Folktales vary in content as to their original intended audiences. Long ago, the nobility and their courtiers heard stories of the heroism, valor, and benevolence of people like themselves—the ruling classes. In contrast, the stories heard by the common people portrayed the ruling classes as unjust or hard taskmasters whose riches were fair game for those common folk who were quick-witted or strong enough to acquire them. These class-conscious tales are sometimes referred to as *castle* and *cottage* tales, respectively.

Some people use the terms *folktale* and *fairy tale* interchangeably. In fact, the majority of these stories have no fairies or magic characters in them, so to use one term in place of the other can be confusing and erroneous. We categorize fairy tales under *magic tales,* a kind of folktale having magic characters such as fairies.

The following is a list of the most prevalent kinds of folktales. Note that some folktales have characteristics of two or more folktale categories.

Cumulative

The *cumulative tale* uses repetition, accumulation, and rhythm to make an entertaining story out of the barest of plots. Because of its simplicity, rhythm, and humor, the cumulative tale has special appeal to 3- to 5-year-olds. "The Gingerbread Man," with its runaway cookie and his growing host of pursuers, is a good example of this kind of tale.

Humorous

The *humorous tale* revolves around a character's incredibly stupid and funny mistakes. These tales are also known as *noodleheads, sillies, drolls,* and *numbskulls.* They have endured, no doubt, for their comic appeal and the guaranteed laughter they evoke. Some famous noodleheads are the Norwegian husband who kept house (and nearly demolished it) and Clever Elsie, who was so addle-brained that she got herself confused with someone else and was never heard from again.

Beast

Beast tales feature talking animals and overstated action. Human characters sometimes occur. Young children accept and enjoy these talking animals, and older children can appreciate the fact that the animals symbolize humans. "Goldilocks and the Three Bears" is a good example of a beast tale.

Magic

Magic tales, also known as *wonder tales* or *fairy tales,* contain elements of magic or enchantment in characters, plots, or settings. Fairies, elves, pixies, brownies, witches, magicians, genies, and fairy godparents are pivotal characters in these stories, and they use magic objects or words to weave their enchantments. Talking mirrors, hundred-year naps, glass palaces, enchanted forests, thumb-sized heroines, and magic kisses are the stuff of magic tales. "Aladdin and the Wonderful Lamp" is a well-loved magic tale.

Pourquoi

Pourquoi tales explain phenomena of nature. The word *pourquoi* is French for *why,* and these tales can be understood as primitive explanations for the many "why" questions early humans asked. The strong connection between these tales and myths is obvious, which is why some folklorists identify pourquoi tales as the simplest myths. Note, however, that deities play no role in pourquoi tales as they do in myths. Moreover, the setting in pourquoi tales is earthly, whereas the setting in myths is the realm of the gods. An example of a pourquoi tale is "Why the Sun and the Moon Live in the Sky."

Realistic

Realistic tales are those whose characters, plot, and setting could conceivably have occurred. There is no magic in these tales, and any exaggeration is limited to the possible. Only a few realistic tales exist. "The Hero of Bremen" is a good example.

Fables

The *fable* is a simple story that incorporates characters—typically animals—whose actions teach a moral lesson or universal truth. Often, the moral is stated at the end of the story. Throughout history, fables have appealed to adults as well as to children, for the best of these stories are both simple and wise. Moreover, their use of animals as symbols for humans have made them safe, yet effective, political tools. Perhaps because of their adult appeal, fables were put into print far earlier than other forms of traditional literature.

Aesop's fables compose the best-known collection of fables in the Western world, but other collections deserve our notice. From Persia, there are the *Panchatantra Tales;* from India, the *Jataka Tales;* and from France, the collected fables of Jean de La Fontaine.

Religious Stories

Stories based on religious writings or taken intact from religious manuscripts are considered to be *religious stories.* These stories may recount milestones in the development of a religion and its leadership, or they may present a piece of religious doctrine in narrative form. Stories of the latter sort are usually called *parables.*

Scholars of religion, language, and mythology have found a definite thread of continuity from myth and folk narrative to early religious thinking and writing. Many of the stories, figures, and rituals described in the sacred scriptures of Christianity, Hinduism, and Buddhism, among other religions, have their roots in ancient mythology.

Regardless of whether one considers the religious stories to be fact or fiction, the important point is that these wonderful stories should be shared with children. Because religion in the classroom is potentially controversial, however, many teachers and librarians do not feel comfortable sharing stories with any religious connection. This is unfortunate, since many wonderful stories and some superlative literature, as well as characters, sayings, and situations essential to the culturally literate person, are therefore missed.

Traditional literature, the wealth of ancient stories accumulated over the course of human existence, is one of the treasures of our species. We listen to these endlessly fascinating stories, we reflect on them, and they help to tell us who we are. Good companions of our childhood, they easily become part of us and stay with us throughout our lives. Every child deserves access to this wonderful literary heritage.

Notable Retellers and Illustrators of Traditional Literature

Tomie dePaola, author/illustrator. Droll characters and formal, balanced illustrations in cartoon style characterize his picture books. *Strega Nona: An Old Tale; The Legend of the Bluebonnet.* www.tomie.com

Paul Goble, author and illustrator. Reteller and illustrator of folktales and legends of the North American Indian. *Beyond the Ridge.*

Trina Schart Hyman, reteller and illustrator of classic folktales. *Little Red Riding Hood; The Sleeping Beauty.*

Julius Lester, reteller of African-American folktales and creation stories. *When the Beginning Began: Stories about God, the Creatures, and Us; John Henry.*

Gerald McDermott, reteller and illustrator of Native American myths and folktales. *Raven: A Trickster Tale from the Pacific Northwest.* www.geraldmcdermott.com

Jerry Pinkney, Caldecott medalist whose realistic watercolors invigorate folktales, many from the African-American tradition. *Noah's Ark; John Henry; The Ugly Duckling.*

Robert D. San Souci, adapter of obscure or almost-forgotten stories from many different places and ethnic groups. *The Faithful Friend; The Talking Eggs.* www.rsansouci.com

Janet Stevens, reteller and illustrator of humorous beast tales from around the world. *Tops & Bottoms;* various *Anansi* tales from Africa. www.janetstevens.com

Paul O. Zelinsky, illustrator whose realistic oil paintings provide insights into the meaning of folktales. *Hansel and Gretel; Rapunzel.* www.paulozelinsky.com/paul.html

Topics for Further Investigation

- Explore sexism in traditional literature and the subtle messages it conveys to children.
- Investigate the differences in early (eighteenth and nineteenth century) written versions of folktales and modern variants.
- Are folktales just for the elementary grades? Assess the messages for older students in tales such as "Rapunzel" and "Little Red Ridinghood."
- Select, learn, and tell (not read) a folktale to a group of children. Develop and use props, if appropriate. Note the differences in telling and reading a story to a young audience.

 See the companion website at www.ablongman.com/lynchbrown6e for further suggestions.

References

de la Mare, Walter. (1930). Listen! In W. de la Mare (Ed.), *Poems for children.* New York: Holt.

Grimm, J., & Grimm, W. (1886). *Household stories.* Translated by L. Crane. New York: Macmillan.

Recommended Traditional Literature

Ages refer to concept and interest levels. Formats other than novels will be coded as follows:
  (**PI**) Picture book
  (**COL**) Short story collection

Myths

Aliki, reteller. *The Gods and Goddesses of Olympus.* HarperCollins, 1994. (**PI**) Ages 8–12.

Burleigh, Robert. *Pandora.* Illustrated by Raúl Colón. Silver Whistle, 2002. (**PI**) Ages 8–11.

Byrd, Robert, reteller. *The Hero and the Minotaur: The Fantastic Adventures of Theseus.* Dutton, 2005. (**PI**) Ages 8–12.

d'Aulaire, Ingri, and Edgar Parin d'Aulaire. *Book of Greek Myths.* Doubleday, 1962. (**COL**) Ages 8–10.

———. *Norse Gods and Giants.* Doubleday, 1967. (**COL**) Ages 8–10.

Fisher, Leonard Everett. *Cyclops.* Holiday, 1991. (**PI**) Ages 8–10.

———. *Jason and the Golden Fleece.* Holiday, 1990. (**PI**) Ages 9–12.

———. *Theseus and the Minotaur.* Holiday, 1988. (**PI**) Ages 8–10.

Hamilton, Virginia, reteller. *In the Beginning: Creation Stories from Around the World.* Illustrated by Barry Moser. Harcourt, 1988. (**COL**) Ages 9–12.

Heaney, Marie. *The Names Upon the Harp: Irish Myth and Legend.* Illustrated by P. J. Lynch. Scholastic, 2000. (**COL**) Ages 10–13.

Hofmeyr, Diane. *The Star-Bearer: A Creation Myth from Ancient Egypt.* Illustrated by Judy Daly. Farrar, 2001. (**PI**) Ages 8–12.

McCaughrean, Geraldine. *The Golden Hoard: Myths and Legends of the World.* Illustrated by Bee Willey. McElderry, 1996. (**COL**) Ages 8–12.

McDermott, Gerald. *Creation.* Dutton, 2003. (**PI**) Ages 8–12.

Menchú, Rigoberta, and Dante Liano. *The Honey Jar.* Translated from the Spanish by David Unger. Illustrated by Domi. Groundwood, 2006. (**COL**) Ages 9–12. (Guatemala/Mayan)

Tchana, Katrin Hyman, reteller. *Changing Woman and Her Sisters.* Illustrated by Trina Schart Hyman. Holiday, 2006. (**COL**) Ages 10–14.

Zeitlain, Steve. *The Four Corners of the Sky: Creation Stories and Cosmologies from Around the World.* Illustrated by Chris Raschka. Holt, 2000. (**COL**) Ages 12–15.

Epics

McCaughrean, Geraldine. *Gilgamesh the Hero.* Illustrated by David Parkins. Eerdmans, 2003. (**PI**) Ages 10–14.

Sutcliff, Rosemary. *Black Ships before Troy: The Story of the Iliad.* Illustrated by Alan Lee. Delacorte, 1993. Ages 11–14.

———. *Dragonslayer: The Story of Beowulf.* Puffin, 1986 (1966). Ages 10–14.

———. *The Wanderings of Odysseus: The Story of the Odyssey.* Illustrated by Alan Lee. Delacorte, 1996. Ages 10–13.

Verma, Jatinder, reteller. *Rama, Sita, and the Story of Divaali.* Illustrated by Nilesh Mistry. Barefoot Books, 2002. (**PI**) Ages 8–14.

Legends and Tall Tales

Bertrand, Lynne. *Granite Baby.* Illustrated by Kevin Hawkes. Farrar, 2005. (**PI**) Ages 5–7. (New Hampshire)

dePaola, Tomie. *The Legend of the Poinsettia.* Putnam, 1994. (**PI**) Ages 6–8.

Goble, Paul. *The Girl Who Loved Wild Horses.* Bradbury, 1978. (**PI**) Ages 7–9.

Henderson, Kathy, reteller. *Lugalbanda: The Boy Who Got Caught Up in a War.* Illustrated by Jane Ray. Candlewick, 2006. (**PI**) Ages 8–14. (Iraq)

Hodges, Margaret. *Merlin and the Making of the King.* Illustrated by Trina Schart Hyman. Holiday, 2004. (**PI**) Ages 8–12. (England)

———. *Saint George and the Dragon.* Illustrated by Trina Schart Hyman. Little, Brown, 1984. (**PI**) Ages 8–10.

Hurston, Zora Neale. *Lies and Other Tall Tales.* Illustrated by Christopher Myers. HarperCollins, 2005. (**PI**) Ages 7–10. (Southern United States)

Kellogg, Steven, reteller. *Johnny Appleseed.* Morrow, 1988. (**PI**) Ages 6–8.

————, reteller. *Paul Bunyan.* Morrow, 1984. Ages 6–8.

————, reteller. *Pecos Bill.* Morrow, 1986. (**PI**) Ages 6–8.

Kimmel, Eric A., reteller. *Gershon's Monster: A Story for the Jewish New Year.* Illustrated by Jon J. Muth. Scholastic, 2000. (**PI**) Ages 6–11.

Lester, Julius. *John Henry.* Illustrated by Jerry Pinkney. Dial, 1994. (**PI**) Ages 8–10.

Lindbergh, Reeve. *Johnny Appleseed.* Illustrated by Kathy Jacobsen. Little, Brown, 1990. (**PI**) Ages 6–8.

Lister, Robin. *The Legend of King Arthur.* Illustrated by Alan Baker. Doubleday, 1990. Ages 8–12.

Maggi, María Elena, reteller. *The Great Canoe: A Kariña Legend.* Translated by Elisa Amado. Illustrated by Gloria Calderón. Groundwood, 2001. (**PI**) Ages 6–11.

Martin, Rafe. *The World Before This One: A Novel Told in Legend.* Illustrated by Calvin Nicholls. Scholastic, 2002. Ages 12–14. (Seneca Indian)

McCully, Emily Arnold. *Beautiful Warrior: The Legend of the Nun's Kung Fu.* Scholastic, 1998. (**PI**) Ages 5–9.

Mora, Pat. *Doña Flor: A Tall Tale about a Giant Woman with a Great Big Heart.* Illustrated by Raúl Colón. Knopf, 2005. (**PI**) Ages 4–7. (American Southwest)

Nolen, Jerdine. *Big Jabe.* Illustrated by Kadir Nelson. HarperCollins, 2000. (**PI**) Ages 6–10. (African-American; American South)

Osborne, Mary Pope. *American Tall Tales.* Illustrated by Michael McCurdy. Knopf, 1991. (**COL**) Ages 8–11.

————. *New York's Bravest.* Illustrated by Steve Johnson and Lou Fancher. Knopf, 2002. (**COL**) Ages 5–8.

Pyle, Howard. *The Merry Adventures of Robin Hood.* Scribner's, 1946 (1883). Ages 9–12. (Novel)

San Souci, Robert D. *Cut from the Same Cloth: American Women of Myth, Legend, and Tall Tale.* Illustrated by Brian Pinkney. Philomel, 1993. (**COL**) Ages 8–12.

————. *Young Merlin.* Illustrated by Daniel Horne. Doubleday, 1990. (**PI**) Ages 9–12.

Willey, Margaret. *Clever Beatrice: An Upper Peninsula Conte.* Illustrated by Heather Solomon. Atheneum, 2001. (**PI**) Ages 5–9. (Michigan)

Folktales

(Note country, continent, or culture of origin after each entry.)

Aardema, Verna, reteller. *Why Mosquitoes Buzz in People's Ears.* Illustrated by Leo and Diane Dillon. Dial, 1975. (**PI**) Ages 5–7. (Kenya)

Aylesworth, Jim, reteller. *The Tale of Tricky Fox: A New England Trickster Tale.* Illustrated by Barbara McClintock. Scholastic, 2001. (**PI**) Ages 5–8. (United States, New England)

Beneduce, Ann K., reteller. *Jack and the Beanstalk.* Illustrated by Gennady Spirin. Philomel, 1999. (**PI**) Ages 6–9. (England)

Brown, Marcia. *Stone Soup.* Scribner's, 1975 (1947). (**PI**) Ages 6–8. (France)

Bruchac, Joseph. *The First Strawberries: A Cherokee Story.* Illustrated by Anna Vojtech. Dial, 1993. (**PI**) Ages 7–9. (Native American)

————, & James Bruchac, retellers. *How Chipmunk Got His Stripes: A Tale of Bragging and Teasing.* Illustrated by Jose Aruego and Ariane Dewey. Dial, 2001. (**PI**) Ages 5–8. (Native American: Abenaki, Cherokee, Mohawk)

Bryan, Ashley, adapter. *Beautiful Blackbird.* Atheneum, 2003. (**PI**) Ages 5–7. (Zambia)

Casanova, Mary. *The Hunter: A Chinese Folktale.* Illustrated by Ed Young. Atheneum, 2000. (**PI**) Ages 5–8. (China)

Climo, Shirley. *The Egyptian Cinderella.* Illustrated by Ruth Heller. Crowell, 1989. (**PI**) Ages 7–9. (Egypt)

————. *The Korean Cinderella.* Illustrated by Ruth Heller. HarperCollins, 1993. (**PI**) Ages 7–9. (Korea)

Cohn, Amy L., editor. *From Sea to Shining Sea: A Treasury of American Folklore and Folk Songs.* Scholastic, 1993. (**COL**) Ages 4–10. (United States)

Corrin, Sara and Stephen, retellers. *The Pied Piper of Hamelin.* Illustrated by Errol Le Cain. Harcourt, 1989. (**PI**) Ages 7–9. (Germany)

Cummings, Pat. *Ananse and the Lizard: A West African Tale.* Holt, 2002. (**PI**) Ages 4–8. (Ghana)

Demi. *One Grain of Rice.* Scholastic, 1997. (**PI**) Ages 8–11. (India)

dePaola, Tomie. *Strega Nona.* Prentice Hall, 1975. (**PI**) Ages 5–8. (Italy)

Disney, Walt. *Walt Disney's Snow White and the Seven Dwarfs.* Western, 1984. (**PI**) Ages 5–8. (Germany)

Emberley, Rebecca, reteller. *Three Cool Kids.* Little, Brown, 1995. (**PI**) Ages 4–7. (Norway)

Galdone, Paul. *The Gingerbread Man.* Clarion, 1975. (**PI**) Ages 4–6. (England)

————. *The Little Red Hen.* Seabury, 1973. (**PI**) Ages 5–7. (England)

————. *The Three Billy Goats Gruff.* Seabury, 1973. (**PI**) Ages 5–7. (Norway)

Garland, Sherry. *Children of the Dragon; Selected Tales from Vietnam.* Illustrated by Trina Schart Hyman. Harcourt, 2001. (**COL**) Ages 8–12. (Vietnam)

Gerson, Mary-Joan. *Fiesta Femenina: Celebrating Women in Mexican Folktales.* Barefoot, 2001. (**COL**) Ages 10–13. (Mexico)

Glass, Andrew, reteller. *Folks Call Me Appleseed John.* Doubleday, 1995. (**PI**) Ages 7–10. (United States)

Gobel, Paul. *Beyond the Ridge.* Bradbury, 1989. (**PI**) Ages 8–10. (Native American)

———, reteller. *Iktomi and the Berries: A Plains Indian Story.* Orchard, 1989. (**PI**) Ages 7–9. (Native American)

———. *Storm Maker's Tipi.* Atheneum, 2001. (**PI**) Ages 7–12. (Native American: Siksika)

Grimm, Jakob, and Wilhelm Grimm. *The Bremen Town Musicians.* Illustrated by Joseph Palecek. Translated by Anthea Bell. Picture Book Studio, 1988. (**PI**) Ages 6–8. (Germany)

———. *Hansel and Gretel.* Illustrated by Anthony Browne. Knopf, 1998 (1981). (**PI**) Ages 8–14. (Germany)

———. *Little Red Riding Hood.* Illustrated by Trina Schart Hyman. Holiday, 1982. (**PI**) Ages 6–8. (Germany)

———. *Rumpelstiltskin.* Retold and illustrated by Paul O. Zelinsky. Dutton, 1986. (**PI**) Ages 7–9. (Germany)

———. *Snow-White and the Seven Dwarfs.* Translated by Randall Jarrell. Illustrated by Nancy Ekholm Burkert. Farrar, 1972. (**PI**) Ages 8–10. (Germany)

Hamilton, Virginia. *Bruh Rabbit and the Tar Baby Girl.* Illustrated by James Ransome. Scholastic, 2003. (**PI**) Ages 5–7. (Gullah, South Carolina)

———. *The Girl Who Spun Gold.* Illustrated by Leo and Diane Dillon. Blue Sky, 2000. (**PI**) Ages 5–8. (West Indian)

———. *Her Stories: African American Folktales, Fairy Tales, and True Tales.* Illustrated by Leo and Diane Dillon. Scholastic, 1995. (**COL**) Ages 9–15. (United States)

———. *The People Could Fly: American Black Folktales.* Illustrated by Leo and Diane Dillon. Knopf, 1985. (**COL**) Ages 8–10. (African-American)

Heo, Yumi, reteller. *The Green Frogs: A Korean Folktale.* Houghton, 1996. (**PI**) Ages 4–7. (Korea)

Hodges, Margaret. *The Hero of Bremen.* Illustrated by Charles Mikolaycak. Holiday, 1993. (**PI**) Ages 8–11. (Germany)

Hooks, William H. *The Ballad of Belle Dorcas.* Illustrated by Brian Pinkney. Knopf, 1990. (**PI**) Ages 8–10. (United States)

———, reteller. *Moss Gown.* Illustrated by Donald Carrick. Clarion, 1987. (**PI**) Ages 7–9. (United States; a Cinderella variant)

Huck, Charlotte. *The Black Bull of Norroway: A Scottish Tale.* Illustrated by Anita Lobel. Greenwillow, 2001. (**PI**) Ages 7–12. (Scotland)

———. *Princess Furball.* Illustrated by Anita Lobel. Greenwillow, 1989. (**PI**) Ages 6–8. (Germany; a Cinderella variant)

Hughes, Shirley, reteller. *Ella's Big Chance: A Jazz-Age Cinderella.* Simon & Schuster, 2004. (**PI**) Ages 6–9. (England)

Hurston, Zora Neale. *The Six Fools.* Adapted by Joyce Carol Thomas. Illustrated by Ann Tanksley. HarperCollins, 2005. (**PI**) Ages 5–10. (United States)

Hyman, Trina Schart. *The Sleeping Beauty.* Little, Brown, 1977. (**PI**) Ages 5–8. (Germany)

Johnson-Davies, Denys. *Goha the Wise Fool.* Illustrated by Hany El Saed Ahmed and Hag Hamdy Mohamed Fattouh. Philomel, 2005. (**COL**) Ages 6–12. (Middle East)

Kajikawa, Kimiko, adaptor. *Yoshi's Feast.* Illustrated by Yumi Heo. DK Ink, 2000. (**PI**) Ages 5–9. (Japan)

Kellogg, Steven. *Jack and the Beanstalk.* Morrow, 1991. (**PI**) Ages 5–8. (England)

Kimmel, Eric A. *Anansi and the Talking Melon.* Illustrated by Janet Stevens. Holiday, 1994. (**PI**) Ages 5–7. (Africa)

———. *Iron John.* Illustrated by Trina Schart Hyman. Holiday, 1994. (**PI**) Ages 8–10. (Germany)

———. *The Three Princes.* Illustrated by Leonard Everett Fisher. Holiday, 1995. (**PI**) Ages 5–9. (Middle East)

———. *Three Sacks of Truth: A Story from France.* Illustrated by Robert Rayevsky. Holiday, 1993. (**PI**) Ages 5–8.

Knutson, Barbara. *Love and Roast Chicken: A Trickster Tale from the Andes Mountains.* Carolrhoda, 2004. (**PI**) Ages 4–7. (Peru, Bolivia)

Lester, Julius, reteller. *The Tales of Uncle Remus: The Adventures of Brer Rabbit.* Illustrated by Jerry Pinkney. Dial, 1987. (**COL**) (See also: *More Tales of Uncle Remus: Further Adventures of Brer Rabbit, His Friends, Enemies, and Others.* Dial, 1988.) Ages 7–9. (African-American)

Louie, Ai-Ling. *Yeh-Shen: A Cinderella Story from China.* Illustrated by Ed Young. Philomel, 1982. (**PI**) Ages 7–9. (China)

Lunge-Larsen, Lise. *The Hidden Folk: Stories of Fairies, Dwarves, Selkies, and Other Secret Beings.* Illustrated by Beth Krommes. Houghton, 2004. (**COL**) Ages 6–12. (Northern Europe; includes modern folktales)

———, reteller. *The Troll with No Heart in His Body: And Other Tales of Trolls from Norway.* Illustrated by Betsy Bowen. Houghton, 1999. (**COL**) Ages 7–11. (Norway)

Marcantonio, Patricia Santos. *Red Ridin' in the Hood, and Other "Cuentos."* Illustrated by Renato Alarcão. Farrar, 2005. (**COL**) Ages 7–12.

Marshall, James. *Goldilocks and the Three Bears.* Dial, 1988. (**PI**) Ages 5–7. (England)

———. *Red Riding Hood.* Dial, 1987. (**PI**) Ages 6–8. (Germany)

———. *The Three Little Pigs.* Dial, 1989. (**PI**) Ages 5–7. (England)

Martin, Rafe, reteller. *Foolish Rabbit's Big Mistake.* Illustrated by Ed Young. Putnam, 1985. (**PI**) Ages 6–8. (India)

———. *The Rough-Face Girl.* Illustrated by David Shannon. Putnam, 1992. (**PI**) Ages 8–10. (Native American)

McClintock, Barbara, reteller. *Cinderella.* Scholastic, 2005. (**PI**) Ages 5–9. (France)

McDermott, Gerald. *Anansi the Spider.* Holt, 1972. (**PI**) Ages 6–8. (Africa)

———. *Arrow to the Sun.* Viking, 1974. (**PI**) Ages 8–10. (Native American)

———. *Raven: A Trickster Tale from the Pacific Northwest.* Harcourt, 1993. (**PI**) Ages 5–9. (Native American)

McKissack, Patricia C. *Flossie and the Fox.* Illustrated by Rachel Isadora. Dial, 1986. (**PI**) Ages 7–9. (American South)

Milligan, Bryce. *The Prince of Ireland and the Three Magic Stallions.* Illustrated by Preston McDaniels. Holiday, 2003. (**PI**) Ages 6–8. (Ireland)

Mollel, Tololwa. *Subira Subira.* Illustrated by Linda Saport. Clarion, 2000. (**PI**) Ages 5–10. (Tanzania)

Montresor, Beni, adapter. *Little Red Riding Hood.* Doubleday, 1991. (**PI**) Ages 10–14. (Germany)

Morimoto, Junko. *The Two Bullies.* Translated from Japanese by Isao Morimoto. Crown, 1999. (**PI**) Ages 5–7. (Japan)

Orgel, Doris, reteller. *The Bremen Town Musicians and Other Animal Tales from Grimm.* Illustrated by Bert Kitchen. Roaring Brook, 2004. (**COL**) Ages 6–9. (Germany)

Parks, Van Dyke, and Malcolm Jones, adaptors and retellers. (Original story by Joel Chandler Harris.) *Jump!: The Adventures of Brer Rabbit.* Illustrated by Barry Moser. Harcourt, 1986. (**COL**) Ages 7–9. (African-American)

Paterson, Katherine. *The Tale of the Mandarin Ducks.* Illustrated by Leo and Diane Dillon. Lodestar, 1990. (**PI**) Ages 7–9. (Japan)

Paulson, Timothy. *Jack and the Beanstalk and the Beanstalk Incident.* Illustrated by Mark Corcoran. Birch Lane, 1990. (**PI**) Ages 7–9. (England) (Note: second half of this flip book is a modern folktale.)

Perrault, Charles. *Cinderella.* Illustrated by Marcia Brown. Scribner's, 1954. (**PI**) Ages 6–8. (France)

———. *Little Red Riding Hood.* Illustrated by Sarah Moon. Creative Education, 1983. (**PI**) Ages 10–14. (France)

———. *Puss in Boots.* Illustrated by Fred Marcellino. Farrar, 1990. (**PI**) Ages 6–8. (France)

Polacco, Patricia. *Babushka Baba Yaga.* Philomel, 1993. (**PI**) Ages 7–9. (Russia)

Powell, Patricia H. *Frog Brings Rain/Ch'at Tó Yinílo'.* Translation by Peter A. Thomas. Illustrated by Kendrick Benally. Salina Bookshelf, 2006. (**PI**) Ages 5–8. (Bilingual English/Navajo)

Reneaux, J. J. *How Animals Saved the People: Animal Tales from the South.* Illustrated by James Ransome. Morrow, 2001. (**COL**) Ages 9–14. (Rural Southern United States: African-American, Appalachian, Native American)

San Souci, Robert D., reteller. *Cendrillon: A Caribbean Cinderella.* Illustrated by Brian Pinkney. Simon & Schuster, 1998. (**PI**) Ages 5–7. (The Caribbean)

———. *The Faithful Friend.* Illustrated by Brian Pinkney. Simon & Schuster, 1995. (**PI**) Ages 11–14. (Martinique)

———, reteller. *Sister Tricksters: Rollicking Tales of Clever Females.* Illustrated by Daniel San Souci. August House, 2006. (**COL**) Ages 8–12. (Rural Southern United States)

———. *The Talking Eggs: A Folktale from the American South.* Illustrated by Jerry Pinkney. Dial, 1989. (**PI**) Ages 7–9. (African-American)

Sanderson, Ruth, reteller. *Cinderella.* Little, Brown, 2002. (**PI**) Ages 4–8. (Germany)

———. *The Golden Mare, the Firebird, and the Magic Ring.* Little, Brown, 2001. (**PI**) Ages 8–12. (Russia)

Sierra, Judy, selector and reteller. *Can You Guess My Name? Traditional Tales Around the World.* Illustrated by Stefano Vitale. Clarion, 2002. (**COL**) Ages 8–10.

———. *The Gift of the Crocodile: A Cinderella Story.* Illustrated by Reynold Ruffins. Simon & Schuster, 2000. (**PI**) Ages 5–9. (Indonesia/Spice Islands)

———. *Tasty Baby Belly Buttons: A Japanese Folktale.* Illustrated by Meilo So. Knopf, 1999. (**PI**) Ages 4–7. (Japan)

Simonds, Nina, Leslie Swartz, and the Children's Museum, Boston. *Moonbeams, Dumplings and Dragon Boats: A Treasury of Chinese Holiday Tales, Activities and Recipes.* Illustrated by Meilo So. Harcourt, 2002. (**COL**) Ages 9–12. (China)

Singer, Isaac Bashevis. *When Shlemiel Went to Warsaw and Other Stories.* Translated by the author and Elizabeth Shub. Illustrated by Margot Zemach. Farrar, 1968. (**COL**) Ages 8–10. (Jewish)

Snyder, Diane. *The Boy of the Three-Year Nap.* Illustrated by Allen Say. Houghton, 1988. (**PI**) Ages 7–9. (Japan)

Steptoe, John. *Mufaro's Beautiful Daughters: An African Tale.* Lothrop, 1987. (**PI**) Ages 6–8. (Africa)

———. *The Story of Jumping Mouse.* Lothrop, 1984. (**PI**) Ages 7–9. (Native American)

Stevens, Janet, adaptor. *Tops and Bottoms.* Harcourt, 1995. (**PI**) Ages 5–8. (Europe and American South)

Sweet, Melissa, reteller. *Carmine: A Little More Red.* Houghton, 2005. (**PI**) Ages 4–8. (Germany; also an ABC book)

Taback, Simms, reteller. *Kibitzers and Fools: Tales My Zayda Told Me.* Viking, 2005. (**PI**) Ages 7–12. (Eastern Europe)

———. *This Is the House That Jack Built.* Putnam, 2002. (**PI**) Ages 5–7. (Hebrew)

Tchana, Katrin. *The Serpent Slayer and Other Stories of Strong Women.* Illustrated by Trina Schart Hyman. Little, Brown, 2000. (**COL**) Ages 7–12. (World)

Tejima. *Ho-Limlim: A Rabbit Tale from Japan.* Philomel, 1990. (**PI**) Ages 6–8. (Japan)

Van Laan, Nancy. *With a Whoop and a Holler: A Bushel of Lore from Way Down South.* Illustrated by Scott Cook. Atheneum, 1998. (**COL**) Ages 9–12. (American South)

Wattenberg, Jane. *Henny-Penny.* Scholastic, 2000. (**PI**) Ages 7–12. (England)

Yolen, Jane. *Not One Damsel in Distress: World Folktales for Strong Girls.* Illustrated by Susan Guevara. Silver Whistle, 2000. (**COL**) Ages 8–13.

Young, Ed. *Lon Po Po: A Red Riding-Hood Story from China.* Philomel, 1989. (**PI**) Ages 7–9. (China)

———. *What About Me?* Putnam, 2002. (**PI**) Ages 5–8. (Sufi)

Zelinsky, Paul O., reteller. *Rapunzel.* Dutton, 1997. (**PI**) Ages 5–8. (Germany)

———, reteller. *Rumpelstiltskin.* Dutton, 1986. (**PI**) Ages 6–8. (Germany)

Zemach, Harve. *Duffy and the Devil.* Illustrated by Margot Zemach. Farrar, 1973. (**PI**) Ages 6–8. (England)

Zemach, Margot. *It Could Always Be Worse.* Farrar, 1977. (**PI**) Ages 6–8. (Jewish)

Fables

Aesop's Fables. Illustrated by Jerry Pinkney. North-South/Sea Star, 2000. (**COL**) Ages 5–9.

Brown, Marcia. *Once a Mouse.* Scribner's, 1961. (**PI**) Ages 6–8.

Goodall, Jane. *The Eagle and the Wren.* Illustrated by Alexander Reichstein. North-South, 2000. (**PI**) Ages 5–8.

Hennessy, B. G., reteller. *The Boy Who Cried Wolf.* Illustrated by Boris Kulikov. Simon & Schuster, 2006. (**PI**) Ages 4–7.

Oberman, Sheldon. *The Wisdom Bird: A Tale of Solomon and Sheba.* Illustrated by Neil Waldman. Boyds Mills, 2000. (**PI**) Ages 5–9. (Also religious story)

Stevens, Janet. *The Town Mouse and the Country Mouse: An Aesop Fable.* Holiday, 1987. (**PI**) Ages 6–8.

Uribe, Verónica, reteller. *Little Book of Fables.* Translated from the Spanish by Susan Ouriou. Illustrated by Constanza Bravo. Groundwood, 2004. (**COL**) Ages 6–12.

Ward, Helen, adapter. *The Hare and the Tortoise: A Fable from Aesop.* Millbrook, 1999. (**PI**) Ages 4–8.

Wormell, Christopher. *Mice, Morals, & Monkey Business: Lively Lessons from Aesop's Fables.* Running Press, 2005. (**PI, COL**) Ages 5–8.

Religious Stories

Demi. *Buddha.* Holt, 1996. (**PI**) Ages 8–12.

———. *Buddha Stories* (Jataka tales). Holt, 1997. (**COL**) Ages 7–10.

Goldin, Barbara Diamond. *Journeys with Elijah: Eight Tales of the Prophet.* Illustrated by Jerry Pinkney. Harcourt, 1999. (**COL**) Ages 7–14.

Goodhart, Pippa. *Noah Makes a Boat.* Illustrated by Bernard Lodge. Houghton, 1997. (**PI**) Ages 4–6.

Hao, K. T. *Little Stone Buddha.* Translated from the Chinese by Annie Kung. Illustrated by Giuliano Ferri. Purple Bear, 2005. (**PI**) Ages 4–7.

Johnson, James Weldon. *The Creation.* Illustrated by James E. Ransome. Holiday, 1994. (**PI**) Ages 6–8.

Kimmel, Eric A., reteller. *The Spotted Pony: A Collection of Hanukkah Stories.* Illustrated by Leonard Everett Fisher. Holiday, 1992. (**COL**) Ages 6–12.

Lester, Julius. *When the Beginning Began: Stories about God, the Creatures, and Us.* Illustrated by Emily Lisker. Harcourt, 1999. (**COL**) Ages 11–14.

Muth, Jon J. *Zen Shorts.* Scholastic, 2005. (**PI, COL**) Ages 5–9. (Buddhist)

Pinkney, Jerry. *Noah's Ark.* North-South, 2002. (**PI**) Ages 5–8.

Root, Phyllis. *Big Momma Makes the World.* Illustrated by Helen Oxenbury. Candlewick, 2003. (**PI**) Ages 4–7.

Schwartz, Howard. *Invisible Kingdoms: Jewish Tales of Angels, Spirits, and Demons.* Illustrated by Stephen Feiser. HarperCollins, 2002. (**COL**) Ages 8–12. (World)

Vivas, Julie. *The Nativity.* Harcourt, 1988. (**PI**) Ages 6–10.

Wisniewski, David. *Golem.* Clarion, 1996. (**PI**) Ages 6–12.

Young, Ed. *Monkey King.* HarperCollins, 2001. (**PI**) Ages 5–8. (Buddhist)

Related Films, Videos, and DVDs

American Tall Tales (includes *John Henry, Swamp Angel*). (2006). Retellers: Julius Lester and Paul O. Zelinsky. Illustrators: Jerry Pinkney and Paul O. Zelinsky. 32 minutes.

Favorite Fairy Tales, Volume II (includes *Rapunzel, Princess Furball*). (2006). Retellers: Paul O. Zelinsky and Charlotte Huck. Illustrators: Paul O. Zelinsky and Anita Lobel. 32 minutes.

Hansel and Gretel. (2005). Reteller/Illustrator: James Marshall. 16.5 minutes.

James Marshall's Favorite Fairy Tales (includes *Goldilocks and the Three Bears, Little Red Riding Hood, The Three Little Pigs*). (2001). Reteller/Illustrator: James Marshall. 33 minutes.

The Tale of the Mandarin Duck. (1998). Reteller: Katherine Paterson. Illustrators: Leo and Diane Dillon. 16 minutes.

There Was an Old Lady Who Swallowed a Fly. (2002). Illustrator: Simms Tabeck. 8 minutes.

Why Mosquitoes Buzz in People's Ears and Other Caldecott Classics (includes *Why Mosquitoes Buzz in People's Ears, The Village of Round and Square Houses, A Story, A Story: An African Tale*). (2002). Retellers: Verna Aardema, Ann Grifalconi, and Gail E. Haley. Illustrators: Leo and Diane Dillon, Ann Grifalconi, and Gail E. Haley. 32 minutes.

Sources for Films, Videos, and DVDs

The Video Source Book. Syosset, NY: National Video Clearinghouse, 1979–. Published by Gale Research, Detroit, MI.

An annual reference work that lists media and provides sources for purchase and rental.

Websites of large video distributors:

www.libraryvideo.com

http://teacher.scholastic.com/products/ westonwoods

chapter 7

Modern Fantasy

Ladder to the Sky
Do you know
If you try
You really can
Touch the sky?

Lean a ladder
Against the moon
And climb, climb high
Talk to the stars
And leave your handprints
All across the sky

Jump on a cloud
And spend the day
Trampoline-jumping
Through the air
Climb a rainbow
And watch the world
From way up there
Then ride that rainbow slide

Back home.

—Sheree Fitch

Modern fantasy has its roots in traditional fantasy from which motifs, characters, stylistic elements, and, at times, themes have been drawn. Many of the most revered works of children's literature fall into the genre of modern fantasy. *The Adventures of Pinocchio, Alice's Adventures in Wonderland, The Wonderful Wizard of Oz, The Wind in the Willows, Winnie-the-Pooh, Pippi*

Longstocking, and *Charlotte's Web* immediately come to mind. The creation of stories that are highly imaginative—yet believable—is the hallmark of this genre.

Definition and Description

Modern fantasy refers to the body of literature in which the events, the settings, or the characters are outside the realm of possibility. A fantasy is a story that cannot happen in the real world, and for this reason this genre has been called the literature of the fanciful impossible. In these stories, animals talk, inanimate objects come to life, people are giants or thumb-sized, imaginary worlds are inhabited, and future worlds are explored, just to name a few of the possibilities. Modern fantasies are written by known authors, and this distinguishes the genre from traditional literature, in which the tales are handed down through the oral tradition and have no known author. Although the events could not happen in real life, modern fantasies often contain truths that help the reader understand today's world.

The *cycle format,* in which one book is linked to another through characters, settings, or both, is especially prevalent in modern fantasy. Elleman (1987) states, "Events in [fantasy] cycle books are often strung out over three or four volumes. Authors attempt to make each novel self-contained, with varying degrees of success, but usually readers need the entire series for full impact" (p. 418). The cycle format appeals to readers who become attached to certain characters and then delight in reading the next book in the series. An example of the cycle format can be found in the chronicles of the creatures of Redwall Abbey, a series of animal fantasies by Brian Jacques.

Evaluation and Selection of Modern Fantasy

The usual standards for fine fiction must also be met by authors of modern fantasy. Believable and well-rounded characters who develop and change, well-constructed plots, well-described settings with internal consistency, a style appropriate to the story, and worthy themes are elements to be expected in all fiction. In addition, the following criteria apply specifically to modern fantasy:

- Authors of modern fantasy have the challenge of persuading readers to open themselves up to believing that which is contrary to reality, strange, whimsical, or magical, yet has an internal logic and consistency. Sometimes, authors will accomplish this through beginning the story in a familiar and ordinary setting with typical, contemporary human beings as characters. A transition is then made from this realistic world to the fantasy world. An example of this literary device is found in C. S. Lewis's *The Lion, the Witch, and the Wardrobe,* in which the children in the story enter a wardrobe in an old house only to discover that the back of the wardrobe leads into the land of Narnia, a fantasy world with unusual characters. Other fantasies begin in the imagined world but manage, through well-described settings and consistent well-rounded characters, to make this new reality believable. Either way, the plot, characters, and setting must be so well developed that the child reader is able to suspend disbelief and to accept the impossible as real.

Excellent Modern Fantasy to Read Aloud

Almond, David. *Skellig.* Ages 9–12.
Anderson, M. T. *Whales on Stilts!* Ages 9–13.
Avi. *Strange Happenings: Five Tales of Transformations.* Ages 10–15.
Bunting, Eve. *Riding the Tiger.* Illustrated by David Frampton. Ages 8–11.
Clements, Andrew. *Things Not Seen.* Ages 10–14.
DiCamillo, Kate. *The Miraculous Journey of Edward Tulane.* Ages 8–12.
Grey, Mini. *The Adventures of the Dish and the Spoon.* Ages 5–9.
Jennings, Richard W. *Orwell's Luck.* Ages 9–12.
Pullman, Philip. *The Scarecrow and His Servant.* Ages 9–13.
Rodda, Emily. *Rowan of Rin.* Ages 8–11.
Waugh, Sylvia. *Space Race.* Ages 9–12.

■ For a modern fantasy to be truly imaginative, the author must provide a unique setting. In some stories, the setting may move beyond the realistic in both time (moving to the past, future, or holding time still) and place (imagined worlds); in other stories, only one of these elements (place or time) will go beyond reality. Moreover, a modern fantasy author's creation must be original.

Historical Overview of Modern Fantasy

Imaginative literature did not appear until the eighteenth century. These stories were not intended primarily for children but were political satires that came to be enjoyed by children as well as adults. *Gulliver's Travels* (1726) by the Irish clergyman Jonathan Swift is the most noteworthy of such books. In this adult satire ridiculing the antics of the English court and its politics, the hero, Gulliver, travels to strange, imaginary places—one inhabited by six-inch Lilliputians, another inhabited by giants. These imaginary worlds are described in fascinating detail and with sufficient humor to appeal to a child audience.

In England in 1865, Charles Lutwidge Dodgson, an Oxford don who used the pen name Lewis Carroll, wrote *Alice's Adventures in Wonderland,* which tells of a fantastic journey Alice takes to an imaginary world. The total absence of didacticism—replaced by humor and fantasy—resulted in the book's lasting appeal and world fame. Other fantasies that originated in England shortly after the appearance of *Alice* include *The Light Princess* (1867) and *At the Back of the North Wind* (1871) by George MacDonald, and *Just So Stories* (1902) by Rudyard Kipling. This early development of modern fantasy for children in England was unrivaled by any other country and established the standard for the genre worldwide.

Modern fantasy has continued to thrive in England. Noteworthy contributions from England include *The Tale of Peter Rabbit* (1902) by Beatrix Potter, *The Wind in the Willows* (1908) by Kenneth Grahame, *The Velveteen Rabbit* (1922) by Margery Williams, *Winnie-the-Pooh* (1926) by A. A. Milne, *Mary Poppins* (1934) by Pamela Travers, *The Hobbit* (1937) by J. R. R. Tolkien, *The Lion, the Witch, and the Wardrobe* (1950) by C. S. Lewis, *The Borrowers* (1953) by Mary Norton, and *The Children of Green Knowe* (1955) by Lucy M. Boston.

Early books of modern fantasy from other countries include *The Adventures of Pinocchio* (1881) by Carlo Collodi (Carlo Lorenzini) from Italy and *Journey to the Center of the Earth* (1864), *Twenty Thousand Leagues under the Sea* (1869), and *Around the World in Eighty Days* (1872) by the Frenchman Jules Verne. Verne's works are considered the first science fiction novels and remain popular today with adults and children. Later in France, Jean de Brunhoff wrote an internationally popular series of animal fantasies about a family of elephants. The first of these was *The Story of Babar* (1937).

Some works of fantasy from Scandinavia also deserve recognition. Hans Christian Andersen, a Dane, published many modern folktales, stories that were very similar in literary elements to the traditional tales. However, Andersen was the originator of most of his tales, for which his own life experiences were the inspiration. "The Ugly Duckling," "The Emperor's New Clothes," and "Thumbelina" are three of the most loved of Andersen's stories. His tales were published in 1835 and are considered the first modern fairy tales. A century later, Swedish author Astrid Lindgren produced *Pippi Longstocking* (1945). Pippi, a lively, rambunctious, and very strong heroine who throws caution to the wind, lives an independent life of escapades that are envied by children the world over.

The United States also produced some outstanding early modern fantasies, beginning with *The Wonderful Wizard of Oz* (1900) by L. Frank Baum, which is considered to be the first classic U.S. modern fantasy for children. Other landmark U.S. works of modern fantasy are the memorable animal fantasy *Rabbit Hill* (1944) by Robert Lawson; *Charlotte's Web* (1952) by E. B. White, the best-known and best-loved U.S. work of fantasy; *The Book of Three* (1964), the first of the Prydain Chronicles by Lloyd Alexander; and *A Wrinkle in Time* (1962) by Madeleine L'Engle, which is considered a modern classic in science fiction for children.

Science fiction, the most recent development in modern fantasy, is said to owe its birth to the aforementioned nineteenth-century novels of Jules Verne and H. G. Wells (*Time Machine*, 1895). Adults, not children, were the primary audience for these novels, however. It was not until the twentieth century that science fiction began to be aimed specifically at children. The Tom Swift series by Victor Appleton (collective pseudonym for the Stratemeyer Syndicate), although stilted in style and devoid of female characters, can be considered the first science fiction for children. The first Tom Swift book appeared in 1910 (*Tom Swift and His Airship*), with additional titles of the series appearing in rapid succession. The success of the science fiction magazine *Amazing Stories*, launched in 1926, brought formal recognition to the genre of science fiction.

In 1963, Madeleine L'Engle's novel *A Wrinkle in Time* was awarded the Newbery Medal. From this point forward, many science fiction novels for children began to appear. In the late 1960s and 1970s, the theme of mind control was popular. John Christopher's Tripods trilogy and William Sleator's *House of Stairs* (1974) are good examples. Space travel and future worlds were frequent science fiction topics in the 1980s. The accompanying Milestones feature highlights the development of modern fantasy.

Modern fantasy for children remains strong, especially in Great Britain and other English-speaking countries. Although personified toys and animals remain popular and prevalent in children's books, growth in this genre appears to be in stories in which fantasy is interwoven into other genres—science fiction, science fantasy, and historical fantasy. Fractured folktales, traditional tales with a contemporary twist or a tale told from a new perspective, took on new popularity with the publication of Jon Scieszka's *The True Story of the 3 Little Pigs by A. Wolf*,

MILESTONES in the Development of Modern Fantasy

Date	Event	Significance
1726	*Gulliver's Travels* by Jonathan Swift (England)	An adult novel prototype for children's fantasy adventures
1835	*Fairy Tales* by Hans Christian Andersen (Denmark)	First modern folktales
1864	*Journey to the Center of the Earth* by Jules Verne (France)	First science fiction novel (for adults)
1865	*Alice's Adventures in Wonderland* by Lewis Carroll (England)	First children's masterpiece of modern fantasy
1881	*The Adventures of Pinocchio* by Carlo Collodi (Italy)	Early classic personified toy story
1900	*The Wonderful Wizard of Oz* by L. Frank Baum (United States)	First classic U.S. modern fantasy for children
1908	*The Wind in the Willows* by Kenneth Grahame (England)	Early classic animal fantasy
1910	*Tom Swift and His Airship* by Victor Appleton (United States)	First science fiction novel for children
1926	*Winnie-the-Pooh* by A. A. Milne (England)	Early classic personified toy story
1937	*The Hobbit* by J. R. R. Tolkien (England)	Early quest adventure with a cult following
1950	*The Lion, the Witch, and the Wardrobe* by C. S. Lewis (England)	Early classic quest adventure for children; first of the Narnia series
1952	*Charlotte's Web* by E. B. White (United States)	Classic U.S. animal fantasy
1953	*The Borrowers* by Mary Norton (England)	Classic little people fantasy
1962	*A Wrinkle in Time* by Madeleine L'Engle (United States)	Classic U.S. science fiction novel for children
1993	*The Giver* by Lois Lowry (United States)	Popular futuristic fiction novel; Newbery Medal winner
1998	*Harry Potter and the Sorcerer's Stone* by J. K. Rowling (England)	First book in the best-selling quest fantasy series

illustrated by Lane Smith and published in 1989. This blurring of traditional genres can also be seen in the interesting mixture of the logic of realistic mystery stories with supernatural elements, as in the popular mysteries of John Bellairs and Mary Downing Hahn. Modern fantasy is likely to continue to be a popular genre with children and authors, as evidenced by the extraordinary popularity of the best-selling Harry Potter quest series by J. K. Rowling, whose first novel in the series was published in 1998.

Types of Modern Fantasy

In modern fantasy, as in other genres, the distinctions between types are not totally discrete. The types of modern fantasy in the sections that follow are a starting point for thinking about the variety of fantastic stories, motifs, themes, and characters that gifted authors have created. Additional categories could be listed, and you will find that some stories may fit appropriately in more than one category. For example, Terry Pratchett's *The Wee Free Men*, categorized as a "little people" story, could also be considered a *quest fantasy.*

Modern Folktales

Modern folktales, or *literary folktales* as they are also called, are tales told in a form similar to that of a traditional tale with the accompanying typical elements: little character description, strong conflict, fast-moving plot with a sudden resolution, vague setting, and, in some cases, magical elements. But these modern tales have a known, identifiable author who has written the tale in this form. In other words, the tales do not spring from the cultural heritage of a group of people through the oral tradition but rather from the mind of one creator. However, this distinction does not matter at all to children, who delight in these tales as much as they do in the old folktales.

The tales of Hans Christian Andersen are the earliest and best known of these modern tales. More recently, other authors, including Robin McKinley (*Beauty* and *Spindle's End*) and Donna Jo Napoli (*Crazy Jack* and *Bound*) have become known for their modern folktales.

Fractured folktales are a recent addition to the modern folktale genre, popularized by Jon Scieszka's picture book, *The True Story of the 3 Little Pigs by A. Wolf* in 1989. *Fractured folktales* can be defined as traditional folktales with a contemporary twist or a tale told from a new perspective. A humorous example in which the characters of the well-known nursery rhyme run away to become vaudeville stars is *The Adventures of the Dish and the Spoon* by Mini Grey.

Modern folktales are an important counterbalance to traditional tales. As was noted in Chapter 6, many of the traditional tales present an old-fashioned, stereotypic view of male and female characters. Many of the modern tales present more assertive female characters who are clearly in charge of their own destinies. Examples are *Swamp Angel* by Anne Isaacs and *Kate and the Beanstalk* by Mary Pope Osborne.

Animal Fantasy

Animal fantasies are stories in which animals behave as human beings in that they experience emotions, talk, and have the ability to reason. Usually, the animals in fantasies will (and should) retain many of their animal characteristics. In the best of these animal fantasies, the author will interpret the animal for the reader in human terms without destroying the animal's integrity or removing it from membership in the animal world. For example, a rabbit character in an animal fantasy will retain her natural abilities of speed and camouflage to outsmart her adversaries. At the same time, however, the author will permit the reader to see human qualities such as caring and love by having the rabbit carry on conversations with family members.

Animal fantasies can be read to very young children who enjoy the exciting but reassuring adventures in books. Examples are *The Tale of Peter Rabbit* by Beatrix Potter and *Bad Bear Detectives* by Daniel Pinkwater. Books for children in primary grades include somewhat longer stories, often in a humorous vein, such as Beverly Cleary's mouse stories, including *The Mouse and the Motorcycle,* Deborah and James Howe's humor-filled books, *Bunnicula* and *Howliday Inn,* and *The Nine Lives of Aristotle* by Dick King-Smith. Enjoyable animal fantasies for the young reader often have easy-to-follow, episodic plots.

Fully developed novels of modern fantasy with subtle and complex characterizations and a progressive plot are especially suitable for reading aloud to children in their elementary school years. *Charlotte's Web* by E. B. White remains a favorite read-aloud book; *The Tale of Despereaux* by Kate DiCamillo and *Poppy* by Avi are also popular. A beautifully written book with richly drawn characterizations is *The Wind in the Willows* by Kenneth Grahame, who describes in artistic detail the life of animal friends along a riverbank. This book features an episodic plot structure but has a challenging style that is appropriate to intermediate-grade students. In *A Coyote's in the House* by Elmore Leonard, the humorous story of a coyote in Hollywood satirizes the movie industry with a style that will be appreciated by many students age 10 and older. *Orwell's Luck* by Richard W. Jennings, a novel with a progressive plot, is also appreciated by intermediate-grade students who enjoy reflecting on what separates reality from fantasy.

Although the interest in animal fantasy peaks at age 8 or 9, many children and adults continue to enjoy well-written animal fantasies. In animal fantasies for older readers, an entire animal world is usually created, with all of the relationships among its members that might be found in a novel portraying human behavior. *Redwall* by Brian Jacques and *The Amazing Maurice and His Educated Rodents* by Terry Pratchett are examples of complex, fully developed animal fantasy novels for readers in fifth grade through adulthood.

Personified Toys and Objects

Stories in which admired objects or beloved toys are brought to life and believed in by a child or adult character in the story are the focus of this type of fantasy. An early classic example of these stories is *The Adventures of Pinocchio* by Carlo Collodi (Carlo Lorenzini), in which a mischievous puppet comes to life, runs away from his maker, and has many exciting and dangerous escapades. In these stories, the object, toy, or doll becomes real to the human protagonist and, in turn, becomes real to the child reader (who has perhaps also imagined a toy coming to life). Close family relationships are also demonstrated in *The Mennyms* by Sylvia Waugh. This motif of family is also found in *The Doll People* and *The Meanest Doll in the World* by Ann M. Martin and Laura Godwin. In Kate DiCamillo's *The Miraculous Journey of Edward Tulane,* a vain china rabbit learns the power of love in this story suitable for intermediate grade students. Personified toy and object stories appeal to children from preschool through upper elementary grades.

Unusual Characters and Strange Situations

Some authors approach fantasy through reality but take it beyond reality to the ridiculous or exaggerated. Generally, those stories can be best described as having unusual characters or strange situations. Without doubt, *Alice's Adventures in Wonderland* by Lewis Carroll is the best known of

Notable Authors of Modern Fantasy

Lloyd Alexander, author of quest fantasies based on Welsh mythology, including the Prydain series comprised of *The Book of Three* and four other titles; *The Xanadu Adventure.*

David Almond, British writer noted for magical realism novels for young adults. *Skellig,* Carnegie Medal winner; *Kit's Wilderness; Clay.* www.davidalmond.com

Jane Louise Curry, author known for her historical novels for children, especially historical fantasies. *Dark Shade; Black Canary.* www.janelouisecurry.com

Kate DiCamillo, author of fantasies and realistic stories for children in primary and intermediate grades. *The Tale of Despereaux,* winner of the Newbery Medal, and *The Miraculous Journey of Edward Tulane.* www.katedicamillo.com

Peter Dickinson, British author of modern fantasies including science fiction novels. *The Ropemaker.* www.peterdickinson.com

Nancy Farmer, author of young adult novels including *The House of the Scorpion,* National Book Award winner for young people's literature. Also, *The Ear, the Eye, and the Arm,* Newbery Honor Book.

Brian Jacques, author of the Redwall Abbey animal fantasy series. *Lord Brocktree; Mossflower.* www.redwall.org

Dick King-Smith, British author of animal fantasies. *Pigs Might Fly; Babe: The Gallant Pig.*

Gail Carson Levine, author of modern folktales. *Ella Enchanted; Fairest.*

Lois Lowry, winner of the 1994 Newbery Medal for *The Giver,* a popular work of science fiction. www.loislowry.com

Robin McKinley, author of quest tales and modern folktales with female protagonists. *The Hero and the Crown; Beauty; Spindle's End.* www.robinmckinley.com

Donna Jo Napoli, author of novels for young readers in many genres, especially recognized for her use of myth in modern folktales. *Bound; Crazy Jack; Beast.* www.donnajonapoli. com

Terry Pratchett, British author of the Discworld series that includes *The Wee Free Men.* Winner of the Carnegie Medal for *The Amazing Maurice and His Educated Rodents,* a work of humorous fantasy. www.terrypratchettbooks. com

Philip Pullman, British creator of His Dark Materials fantasies, a trilogy comprised of *The Golden Compass, The Subtle Knife,* and *The Amber Spyglass.* www.philip-pullman.com

J. K. Rowling, British author of the popular, best-selling series about Harry Potter, a child wizard. *Harry Potter and the Sorcerer's Stone.* www.jkrowling.com

Sylvia Waugh, British author of the Mennyms series about a family of life-sized rag dolls. Also, author of a science fantasy series that includes *Space Race; Earthborn.*

this type of modern fantasy. Writers of modern fantasy have described such strange situations as a boy sailing across the Atlantic Ocean in a giant peach (*James and the Giant Peach* by Roald Dahl) and the daily events of an unlikely school in *Wayside School Gets a Little Stranger* by Louis Sachar.

Modern fantasy appeals to readers of all ages. Florence Parry Heide's *The Shrinking of Treehorn* portrays a young boy who, one day, starts to shrink, but no one notices. The story is fascinating to middle-school students. In *Tuck Everlasting,* Natalie Babbitt explores the theme of immortality and its consequences, a provocative theme for children and adults.

Worlds of Little People

Some authors have written about worlds inhabited by miniature people who have developed a culture of their own in this world or who live in another world. In Mary Norton's *The Borrowers,* small people live in our world but take our discards to create their own world. It is, of course, eventually human beings who threaten their existence and cause them to seek safety elsewhere. In *The Dark Ground* and *The Black Room,* the first books of a new series by Gillian Cross, ant-sized people face psychological adventures, fantasies appealing to students age 11 and older. Stories of little people delight children because they can identify with the indignities foisted on little and powerless people and because the big people in these stories are invariably outdone by the more ingenious little people.

Supernatural Events and Mystery Fantasy

Many recent fantasies evoke the supernatural. One common form of supernatural literature found in children's books is the ghost story. Some ghost stories intrigue younger children, especially when the topic is treated humorously and reassuringly. The goblins of Hilari Bell's *The Goblin Wood* eventually become allies of the protagonist. Ghosts in children's books can be fearful threats or helpful protectors. The ghost of the priest in John Bellairs's *The Curse of the Blue Figurine* is the very soul of evil, whereas the ghost of Cynthia DeFelice's *The Ghost of Fossil Glen* is seeking revenge for a murder. Many authors write mysteries for children in which the solution is partially supernatural or arrived at with supernatural assistance.

Witchcraft and other aspects of the occult sometimes play a role in children's fantasy books. Witches are often portrayed as the broom-wielding villains of both traditional and modern tales, such as the Russian stories of Baba Yaga. Halloween and its traditions are also frequently presented in children's stories. Witchcraft has recently been the focus of criticism because of an upsurge of sects whose members refer to themselves as witches. Also, some parents' groups have attempted to censor children's books featuring witches, Halloween, and other elements of the occult. Chapter 12 has a full discussion on censorship and schools' responsibilities in these situations.

Magical realism, a blend of fantasy and realism, has the appearance of a work of realism but gradually introduces the fantastic as an integral, and necessary, part of the story. The fantastic is merged into these stories such that the distinction between realism and fantasy is blurred, often leaving the reader in some doubt as to what is real and what is fantasy. Magical realism with its origins in Latino literature has stories with the feel of realism, but the magical elements cause them to fall outside of the definition of realistic fiction. Examples are David Almond's works, such as *Skellig, The Fire-Eaters,* and *Clay,* among others. For a discussion on David Almond's works and magical realism, see Latham (2006). These stories of magical realism are placed in the Recommended Books list under Supernatural Events and Mystery Fantasy.

Historical Fantasy

Historical fantasy, sometimes called *time-warp fantasy,* is a story in which a present-day protagonist goes back in time to a different era. A contrast between the two time periods is shown to readers through the modern-day protagonist's discoveries of and astonishment with earlier customs. Historical fantasies must fully and authentically develop the historical setting, both time and place, just as in a book of historical fiction. Mary Hoffman, in *Stravaganza: City of Masks,* succeeds in producing this type of mixed-genre story. Thea Beckman, in *Crusade in Jeans,* also presents an interesting historical fantasy that will appeal to middle-grade students and older.

Quest Stories

Quest stories are adventure stories with a search motif. The quest may be pursuit for a lofty purpose, such as justice or love, or for a rich reward, such as a magical power or a hidden treasure. Quest stories that are serious in tone are called *high fantasy.* Many of these novels are set in medieval times and are reminiscent of the search for the holy grail. In these high fantasies, an imaginary otherworld fully portrays the society, its history, family trees, geographic location, population, religion, customs, and traditions. The conflict in these tales usually centers on the struggle between good and evil. Often, characters are drawn from myth and legend. The protagonist is engaged in a struggle against external forces of evil and internal temptations of weakness. Thus, the quest usually represents a journey of self-discovery and personal growth for the protagonist, in addition to the search for the reward. *The Hobbit,* written by J. R. R. Tolkien in 1937, is one of the first of these high fantasies; it retains a cult of followers even today. Because of the greater complexity of these novels, their allure is for children in fifth grade and higher, including adults, of course. Good examples are C. S. Lewis's Narnia series starting with *The Lion, the Witch, and the Wardrobe,* Philip Pullman's *His Dark Materials* trilogy, and J. K. Rowling's *Harry Potter* series.

Science Fiction and Science Fantasy

Science fiction is a form of imaginative literature that provides a picture of something that could happen based on real scientific facts and principles. Therefore, story elements in science fiction must have the appearance of scientific plausibility or technical possibility. Hypotheses about the future of humankind and the universe presented in science fiction appear plausible and possible to the reader because settings and events are built on extensions of known technologies and scientific concepts.

In novels of science fiction, such topics as mind control, genetic engineering, space technologies and travel, visitors from outer space, and future political and social systems all seem possible to the readers. These novels especially fascinate many young people because they feature characters who must learn to adjust to change and to become new people, two aspects of living that adolescents also experience. In addition, science fiction stories may portray the world, or one very much like it, that young people will one day inhabit; for this reason, science fiction has sometimes been called *futuristic fiction.*

Science fiction is a type of fiction that you will want to know about because of its growing popularity among children and adolescents. If you are reluctant to read science fiction or have never read it, you may want to start with some books by Nancy Farmer (*The House of the Scorpion*), John Christopher (*The White Mountains*), or Lois Lowry (*The Giver; Messenger*).

The distinction between science fiction and science fantasy is not clearly defined or universally accepted. *Science fantasy* is a popularized type of science fiction in which a scientific explanation, though not necessarily plausible, is offered for imaginative leaps into the unknown. Science fantasy presents a world that often mixes elements of mythology and traditional fantasy with scientific or technological concepts, resulting in a setting that has some scientific basis but never has existed or never could exist. A worthy example is Sylvia Waugh's *Earthborn,* in which the protagonist discovers her parents are space aliens. Science fantasy novels, which usually appear in series, appeal to adolescents and young adults and, like many series, are sometimes formulaic and of mixed quality.

Modern fantasy has appeal for persons with nonliteral minds, for people who go beyond the letter of a story to its spirit. Children, with their lively imaginations, are especially open to reading fantasies. The many types and topics within this genre—animal fantasies, little people stories, tales of personified toys, mystery fantasies, stories of unusual people and situations, quest tales, science fiction, and so on—offer children a breadth of inspiring and delightful entertainment. Since the level of conceptual difficulty varies considerably in this genre, modern fantasy offers many excellent stories for children, from the youngest to the oldest.

Topics for Further Investigation

- Science fiction for younger students is rare. Select three works of science fiction from the recommended booklist that are appropriate for children from ages 7 to 10 and evaluate the books for use with children of this age group.
- Select a classic work of modern fantasy for children, such as *Alice's Adventures in Wonderland, Charlotte's Web, The Wonderful Wizard of Oz,* or *The Wind in the Willows.* Read the work and review articles of literary criticism about the work. Then present your perspectives on the book. Consider whether it remains a valuable book for today's children.
- Select the device of time travel commonly found in historical fantasies. Read two historical fantasies that include time travel, then compare how different authors use this device in telling the story.

 See the companion website at www.ablongman.com/lynchbrown6e for additional suggestions.

References

Elleman, B. (1987). Current trends in literature for children. *Library Trends, 35*(3): 413–426.

Fitch, S. (1998). Ladder to the sky. In J. Prelutsky (Ed.), *Imagine that!* Illustrated by Kevin Hawkes. New York: Knopf.

Latham, D. (2006). *David Almond: Memory and magic.* Lanham, MD: Scarecrow.

Recommended Modern Fantasy Books

Ages indicated refer to concept and interest levels. Formats other than novels will be coded as follows:
> (PI) Picture book
> (COL) Short story collection

Modern Folktales

Andersen, Hans Christian. *The Emperor's New Clothes.* Illustrated by Angela Barrett. Translated by Naomi Lewis. Candlewick, 1997. Ages 7–9.

————. *The Pea Blossom.* Retold and illustrated by Amy Lowry Poole. Holiday, 2005. Ages 5–8.

Datlow, Ellen, and Terri Windling, editors. *A Wolf at the Door and Other Retold Fairy Tales.* Simon & Schuster, 2000. (COL) Ages 11–16.

Grey, Mini. *The Adventures of the Dish and the Spoon.* Knopf, 2006. Ages 5–9.

Gruber, Michael. *The Witch's Boy.* HarperCollins, 2005. Ages 11–14.

Hale, Shannon. *Goose Girl.* Bloomsbury, 2003. Ages 11–15.

Hopkinson, Deborah. *Apples to Oregon: Being the (Slightly) True Narrative of How a Brave Pioneer Father Brought Apples, Peaches, Pears, Plums, Grapes, and Cherries (and Children) Across the Plains.* Illustrated by Nancy Carpenter. Atheneum, 2004. (PI) Ages 6–10.

Isaacs, Anne. *Pancakes for Supper.* Illustrated by Mark Teague. Scholastic, 2006. (PI) Ages 4–8.

————. *Swamp Angel.* Illustrated by Paul Zelinsky. Dutton, 1994. Ages 7–10.

Lester, Julius. *The Old African.* Illustrated by Jerry Pinkney. Dial, 2005. (PI) Ages 9–12.

Levine, Gail Carson. *Ella Enchanted.* HarperCollins, 1997. Ages 10–13.

————. *Fairest.* HarperCollins, 2006. Ages 11–16.

————. *Fairy Dust and the Quest for the Egg.* Illustrated by David Christiana. Disney, 2005. Ages 8–11.

McKinley, Robin. *Rose Daughter.* Greenwillow, 1997. Ages 11–18.

————. *Spindle's End.* Putnam, 2000. Ages 12–18.

McKissack, Patricia C. *Porch Lies: Tales of Slickers, Tricksters, and Other Wily Creatures.* Illustrated by Andre Carilho. Random, 2006. (COL) Ages 8–11.

Napoli, Donna Jo. *Beast.* Atheneum, 2000. Ages 11–16.

————. *Bound.* Simon & Schuster, 2004. Ages 10–18.

————. *Crazy Jack.* Delacorte, 1999. Ages 11–15.

————. *Zel.* Dutton, 1996. Ages 13–18.

Osborne, Mary Pope. *Kate and the Beanstalk.* Illustrated by Giselle Potter. Schwartz/Atheneum, 2000. Ages 5–8.

Pattou, Edith. *East.* Harcourt, 2003. Ages 12–16.

Pinkney, Andrea Davis. *Peggony-Po: A Whale of a Tale.* Illustrated by Brian Pinkney. Hyperion, 2006. (PI) Ages 5–9.

Pullman, Philip. *The Scarecrow and His Servant.* Illustrated by Peter Bailey. Knopf, 2005. Ages 9–13.

Pyle, Howard. *Bearskin.* Illustrated by Trina Schart Hyman. Morrow, 1997. Ages 7–9.

Sandburg, Carl. *The Huckabuck Family: And How They Raised Popcorn in Nebraska and Quit and Came Back.* Illustrated by David Small. Farrar, 1999. Ages 5–8.

Scieszka, Jon. *The True Story of the 3 Little Pigs by A. Wolf.* Illustrated by Lane Smith. Viking, 1989. Ages 7–12.

Stanley, Diane. *Bella at Midnight: The Thimble, the Ring, and the Slippers of Glass.* Illustrated by Bagram Ibatoulline. HarperCollins, 2006. Ages 10–14.

————. *Rumpelstiltskin's Daughter.* Morrow, 1997. Ages 5–9.

Animal Fantasies

Anderson, M. T. *Whales on Stilts!* Harcourt, 2005. Ages 9–13. Sequel: *The Clue of the Linoleum Lederhosen,* 2006. Humor.

Arkin, Alan. *Cassie Loves Beethoven.* Hyperion, 2000. Ages 9–12. Humorous.

Armstrong, Alan. *Whittington.* Illustrated by S. D. Schindler. Random, 2005. Ages 9–13.

Avi. *Poppy.* Illustrated by Brian Floca. Orchard, 1995. Ages 8–11.

Bruchac, Joseph. *Wabi: A Hero's Tale.* Dial, 2006. Ages 10–15.

Cleary, Beverly. *The Mouse and the Motorcycle.* Illustrated by Louis Darling. Morrow, 1965. Ages 7–11.

DiCamillo, Kate. *The Tale of Despereaux.* Illustrated by Timothy B. Ering. Candlewick, 2003. Ages 7–10.

Dickinson, Peter. *Chuck and Danielle.* Delacorte, 1996. Ages 8–11.

Grahame, Kenneth. *The Wind in the Willows.* Illustrated by E. H. Shepard. Scribner's, 1908. Ages 8–12.

Howe, Deborah, and James Howe. *Bunnicula: A Rabbit-Tale of Mystery.* Illustrated by Alan Daniel. Atheneum, 1979. Ages 8–11.

Howe, James. *Howliday Inn.* Atheneum, 1982. Ages 8–11.

Jacques, Brian. *Redwall.* Illustrated by Gary Chalk. Philomel, 1987. Ages 11–14. Others in the Redwall series are *Mossflower, Mattimeo, Mariel of Redwall, Salamandastron, The Bellmaker, Lord Brocktree.*

Jennings, Patrick. *Faith and the Electric Dogs.* Scholastic, 1996. Ages 8–11.

Jennings, Richard W. *Orwell's Luck.* Houghton, 2000. Ages 9–12.

Johnson, D. B. *Henry Builds a Cabin.* Houghton, 2002. (PI) Ages 9–13. Others in these picture books for older readers: *Henry Climbs a Mountain* and *Henry Hikes to Fitchburg.*

King-Smith, Dick. *Babe: The Gallant Pig.* Illustrated by Mary Rayner. Crown, 1985. Ages 7–11.

———. *The Nine Lives of Aristotle.* Candlewick, 2003. Ages 6–9.

———. *Pigs Might Fly.* Illustrated by Mary Rayner. Viking, 1982. Ages 8–11.

Labatt, Mary. *Aliens in Woodford.* Kids Can Press, 2000. Ages 7–10. Humorous.

Leonard, Elmore. *A Coyote's in the House.* Harper-Entertainment, 2004. Ages 9–13.

Palatini, Marge. *The Web Files.* Illustrated by Richard Egielski. Hyperion, 2001. (PI) Ages 9–12. Humor.

Pinkwater, Daniel. *Bad Bear Detectives.* Illustrated by Jill Pinkwater. Houghton, 2006. (PI) Ages 4–8.

———. *Mush, A Dog from Space.* Simon & Schuster, 1995. Ages 7–9.

Potter, Beatrix. *The Tale of Peter Rabbit.* Warne, 1902. (PI) Ages 5–9.

Pratchett, Terry. *The Amazing Maurice and His Educated Rodents.* HarperCollins, 2001. Ages 12–16.

Said, S. F. *Varjak Paw.* Illustrated by Dave McKean. Knopf, 2003. Ages 9–12.

Seidler, Tor. *Mean Margaret.* Illustrated by Jon Agee. HarperCollins, 1997. Ages 8–11.

White, E. B. *Charlotte's Web.* Illustrated by Garth Williams. Harper, 1952. Ages 8–11.

Personified Toys and Objects

Collodi, Carlo (pseudonym of Carlo Lorenzini). *The Adventures of Pinocchio.* Illustrated by Attilio Mussino. Translated by Carol Della Chiesa. Macmillan, 1881. Ages 8–10.

DiCamillo, Kate. *The Miraculous Journey of Edward Tulane.* Illustrated by Bagram Ibatoulline. Candlewick, 2006. Ages 8–12.

Fine, Anne. *Jamie and Angus Stories.* Illustrated by Penny Dale. Candlewick, 2000. (COL) Ages 5–8.

Jenkins, Emily. *Toys Go Out: Being the Adventures of a Knowledgeable Stingray, a Toughy Little Buffalo, and Someone Called Plastic.* Illustrated by Paul O. Zelinsky. Random, 2006. Ages 5–8.

Martin, Ann M., and Laura Godwin. *The Doll People.* Illustrated by Brian Selznick. Hyperion, 2000. Ages 8–12.

———. *The Meanest Doll in the World.* Illustrated by Brian Selznick. Hyperion, 2003. Ages 7–11. Sequel to *The Doll People.*

Waugh, Sylvia. *The Mennyms.* Morrow, 1994. Ages 8–12.

———. *Mennyms in the Wilderness.* Greenwillow, 1995. Ages 8–11.

Winthrop, Elizabeth. *The Battle for the Castle.* Holiday, 1993. Ages 8–12.

Unusual Characters and Strange Situations

Ahlberg, Allan. *The Giant Baby.* Illustrated by Fritz Wegner. Viking, 1995. Ages 7–11.

Aiken, Joan. *Cold Shoulder Road.* Delacorte, 1996. Ages 10–13.

Avi. *Strange Happenings: Five Tales of Transformations.* Harcourt, 2006. (COL) Ages 10–15.

Babbitt, Natalie. *Tuck Everlasting.* Farrar, 1975. Ages 10–14.

Billingsley, Franny. *The Folk Keeper.* Simon & Schuster, 1999. Ages 10–13.

———. *Well Wished.* Simon & Schuster, 1997. Ages 10–12.

Carroll, Lewis (pseudonym of Charles Lutwidge Dodgson). *Alice's Adventures in Wonderland* and *Through the Looking Glass.* First published in 1865. A recent edition is illustrated by Anthony Browne. Knopf, 1988. Ages 9–13.

Dahl, Roald. *Charlie and the Chocolate Factory.* Illustrated by Joseph Schindelman. Knopf, 1964. Ages 8–11.

———. *James and the Giant Peach.* Illustrated by Nancy E. Burkert. Knopf, 1961. Ages 8–11.

———. *Matilda.* Illustrated by Quentin Blake. Viking, 1988. Ages 8–11.

Farmer, Nancy. *The Ear, the Eye, and the Arm.* Orchard, 1994. Ages 11–14. Humorous.

Gonzalez, Julie. *Wings.* Delacorte, 2005. Ages 12–16.

Heide, Florence Parry. *The Shrinking of Treehorn.* Illustrated by Edward Gorey. Holiday, 1971. Ages 7–10.

McGraw, Eloise. *The Moorchild.* Simon & Schuster, 1996. Ages 9–12.

Pullman, Philip. *I Was a Rat!* Illustrated by Kevin Hawkes. Knopf, 2000. Ages 8–12.

Sachar, Louis. *Wayside School Gets a Little Stranger.* Morrow, 1995. Ages 8–12. Humorous.

Worlds of Little People

Briggs, Raymond. *The Man*. Random, 1995. (PI) Ages 9–14.

———. *Ug: Boy Genius of the Stone Age*. Knopf, 2002. (PI) Ages 9–16.

Cross, Gillian. *The Dark Ground: Book One of the Dark Ground Trilogy*. Dutton, 2004. Also *The Black Room: Book Two*, 2006. Ages 11–15.

Dahl, Roald. *The Minpins*. Illustrated by Patrick Benson. Viking, 1991. Ages 5–8.

Kendall, Carol. *The Gammage Cup*. Illustrated by Erik Blegvad. Harcourt, 1959. Ages 8–12.

Norton, Mary. *The Borrowers*. Illustrated by Beth and Joe Krush. Harcourt, 2003 (1953). Ages 8–11. This is the first of a series of little people fantasies.

Pratchett, Terry. *The Wee Free Men*. HarperCollins, 2003. Ages 10–15. Sequels are *A Hat Full of Sky*, 2004, and *Wintersmith*, 2006.

Swift, Jonathan. *Gulliver in Lilliput*. Retold by Margaret Hodges. Illustrated by Kimberly Bulcken Root. Holiday, 1995. Ages 8–11. Nine-chapter, illustrated retelling.

Ullman, Barb Bentler. *The Fairies of Nutfolk Wood*. HarperCollins, 2006. Ages 8–11.

Supernatural Events and Mystery Fantasy

Almond, David. *Clay*. Delacorte, 2006. Ages 11–18.

———. *Heaven Eyes*. Delacorte, 2001. Ages 10–13.

———. *Kit's Wilderness*. Delacorte, 2000. Ages 12–18.

———. *Skellig*. Delacorte, 1999. Ages 9–12.

———. *The Fire-Eaters*. Delacorte, 2004. Ages 11–18.

Barry, Dave, and Ridley Pearson. *Peter and the Starcatchers*. Hyperion, 2004. Ages 9–13. Humor.

Bell, Hilari. *Flame*. Simon & Schuster, 2003. Ages 11–16.

———. *The Goblin Wood*. HarperCollins, 2003. Ages 11–16.

Bellairs, John. *The Curse of the Blue Figurine*. Dial, 1983. Ages 10–14.

Bunting, Eve. *The Presence: A Ghost Story*. Clarion, 2003. Ages 12–16.

Constable, Kate. *The Singer of All Songs*. Scholastic, 2004. Ages 12–16.

Coville, Bruce, editor. *A Glory of Unicorns*. Scholastic, 1998. (COL) Ages 10–13. Other fantasy collections edited by Coville: *The Skull of Truth,* 1997, and *Older Than Ever,* 1999.

Crutcher, Chris. *The Sledding Hill*. Greenwillow, 2005. Ages 11–18.

DeFelice, Cynthia. *The Ghost of Fossil Glen*. Farrar, 1998. Ages 9–12.

Delaney, Joseph. *Revenge of the Witch : The Last Apprentice, Book One*. Illustrated by Patrick Arrasmith. Greenwillow, 2005. Ages 10–14.

Dickinson, Peter. *The Lion Tamer's Daughter and Other Stories*. Delacorte, 1997. (COL) Ages 12–18.

———. *The Ropemaker*. Delacorte, 2001. Ages 11–18.

———. *The Tears of the Salamander*. Random, 2003. Ages 11–15.

Farmer, Nancy. *A Girl Named Disaster*. Orchard, 1996. Ages 12–18.

———. *A Sea of Trolls*. Atheneum, 2004. Ages 9–14.

Funke, Cornelia. *The Dragon Rider*. Translated from the German by Anthea Bell. Scholastic, 2004. Ages 9–14.

———. *Inkheart*. Translated from the German by Anthea Bell. Scholastic, 2003. Ages 12–18. *Inkspell,* 2005, is a sequel.

———. *The Thief Lord*. Translated from the German by Oliver Latsch. Scholastic, 2002. Ages 10–14.

Hahn, Mary Downing. *The Old Willis Place: A Ghost Story*. Clarion, 2004. Ages 10–13.

Hale, Shannon. *Princess Academy*. Bloomsbury, 2005. Ages 10–14.

———. *River Secrets*. Bloomsbury, 2006. Ages 10–15.

Hurston, Zora Neale. *The Skull Talks Back and Other Haunting Tales*. Adapted by Joyce Carol Thomas. Illustrated by Leonard Jenkins. HarperCollins, 2004. (COL, PI) Ages 9–13.

Ibbotson, Eva. *Island of the Aunts*. Illustrated by Kevin Hawkes. Dutton, 2000. Ages 9–12.

Jones, Diana Wynne. *Dark Lord of Derkholm*. Greenwillow, 1998. (Also its sequel, *Year of the Griffin.* Greenwillow, 2000.) Ages 12–16.

Lowry, Lois. *Gossamer*. Houghton, 2006. Ages 9–12.

Lubar, David. *Punished!* Darby Creek, 2006. Ages 8–11.

McBratney, Sam. *The Ghosts of Hungryhouse Lane*. Holt, 1989. Ages 7–10.

McKinley, Robin. *The Stone Fey*. Illustrated by John Clapp. Harcourt, 1998. (PI) Ages 13–18.

———, and Peter Dickinson. *Water: Tales of Elemental Spirits*. Putnam, 2002. (COL) Ages 11–16.

McKissack, Patricia C. *The Dark-Thirty: Southern Tales of the Supernatural*. Illustrated by Brian Pinkney. Knopf, 1992. Ages 9–12.

Melling, O. R. *The Hunter's Moon.* Abrams/Amulet, 2005. Ages 12–18. Beginning of a trilogy.

Noyes, Deborah, editor. *Gothic!: Ten Original Dark Tales.* Candlewick, 2004. (COL) Ages 12–18.

Pierce, Tamora. *Sandry's Book.* Scholastic, 1997. Ages 11–15. Four misfits, friendships, and magical powers. Others in the series include *Daja's Book, Tris's Book,* and *Briar's Book.*

Prue, Sally. *Cold Tom.* Scholastic, 2003. Ages 10–13.

Pullman, Philip. *Clockwork.* Illustrated by Leonid Gore. Scholastic, 1998. Ages 9–13.

Slade, Arthur. *Dust.* Random, 2003. Ages 12–16.

Stine, R. L., editor. *Beware!: R. L. Stine Picks His Favorite Scary Stories.* HarperCollins, 2002. (COL) Ages 9–14.

Turner, Megan Whelan. *Instead of Three Wishes.* Greenwillow, 1995. (COL) Ages 9–12.

Historical Fantasy

Beckman, Thea. *Crusade in Jeans.* Front Street, 2003. Ages 11–16. Time travel to Middle Ages.

Branford, Henrietta. *Fire, Bed, and Bone.* Candlewick, 1998. Ages 10–13. Set in late fourteenth-century England; told from a hunting hound's point of view.

Buckley-Archer, Linda. *Gideon the Cutpurse: Being the First Part of the Gideon Trilogy.* Simon & Schuster, 2006. Ages 10–14.

Cooney, Caroline B. *Both Sides of Time.* Delacorte, 1995. Ages 12–16.

Cooper, Susan. *King of Shadows.* Simon & Schuster, 1999. Ages 10–13.

Curry, Jane Louise. *The Black Canary.* Simon & Schuster, 2005. Ages 11–14.

———. *Dark Shade.* McElderry, 1998. Ages 11–14.

Dickinson, Peter. *A Bone from a Dry Sea.* Delacorte, 1993. Ages 12–16.

Gardner, Sally. *I, Coriander.* Dial, 2005. Ages 11–14.

Hoffman, Mary. *Stravaganza: City of Masks.* Bloomsbury, 2002. Ages 12–16. Sixteenth-century Venice. (Also a sequel, *Stravaganza II: City of Stars.* Bloomsbury, 2003. Sixteenth-century Italy.)

McKay, Hillary. *The Amber Cat.* Simon & Schuster, 1997. Ages 9–12.

Meyer, Kai. *The Water Mirror.* Translated from the German by Elizabeth D. Crawford. Simon & Schuster, 2005. Ages 10–14.

Myers, Laurie. *Lewis and Clark and Me.* Illustrated by Michael Dooling. Holt, 2002. Ages 8–12. The 1803 exploration of Lewis and Clark told by Seaman, a Newfoundland dog.

Smith, Roland. *The Captain's Dog: My Journey with the Lewis and Clark Tribe.* Harcourt, 1999. Ages 12–16.

Thal, Lilli. *Mimus.* Translated from the German by John Brownjohn. Annick, 2005. Ages 11–15. Humor.

Yolen, Jane. *The Devil's Arithmetic.* Viking, 1988. Ages 10–13.

Quest Stories

Alexander, Lloyd. *The Book of Three.* Holt, 1964. Ages 10–15. The first of the Prydain Chronicles, a series of five quest fantasies, including *The Black Cauldron, The Castle of Llyr, The High King,* and *Taran Wanderer.*

———. *The Xanadu Adventure.* Dutton, 2005. Ages 10–14.

Bass, L. G. *Sign of the Qin.* Hyperion, 2004. Ages 13–15.

Collins, Suzanne. *Gregor the Overlander.* Scholastic, 2003. Ages 9–14.

Cornish, D. M. *Foundling.* Putnam, 2006. Ages 12–16.

Crossley-Holland, Kevin. *The Seeing Stone: Arthur Trilogy, Book One.* Scholastic, 2001. Ages 12–16. King Arthur and the Crusades, Middle Ages. Others in the series include *At the Crossing Places,* 2002, and *King of the Middle March,* 2004.

Divakaruni, Chitra Banerjee. *The Conch Bearer.* Millbrook, 2003. Ages 10–14.

Fisher, Catherine. *Day of the Scarab: Book Three of the Oracle Prophecies.* Greenwillow, 2006. Ages 10–14. Also in this trilogy: *The Oracle Betrayed,* 2004, and *The Sphere of Secrets,* 2005.

Flanagan, John. *The Ruins of Gorlan.* Philomel, 2005. Ages 11–15.

Gavin, Jamila. *The Blood Stone.* Farrar, 2005. Ages 12–16.

Hodges, Margaret. *Merlin and the Making of the King.* Illustrated by Trina Schart Hyman. Holiday, 2004. (PI) Ages 9–12.

Ibbotson, Eva. *The Secret of Platform 13.* Dutton, 1998. Ages 9–13.

———. *Which Witch?* Dutton, 1999. Ages 10–14.

Le Guin, Ursula K. *A Wizard of Earthsea.* Parnassus, 1968. Ages 11–16. Other books in this series are *The Farthest Shore, The Tombs of Atuan,* and *Tehanu: The Last Book of Earthsea.*

————. *Gifts.* Harcourt, 2004. Ages 11–16.

————. *Voices.* Harcourt, 2006. Ages 11–16.

Lee, Tanith. *Wolf Tower.* Dutton, 2000. Ages 10–13. First in the Claidi Journals series.

Lewis, Clive Staples. *The Lion, the Witch, and the Wardrobe.* Illustrated by Pauline Baynes. Macmillan, 1950. Ages 9–12. The first in a series of quest fantasies, including *The Horse and His Boy, The Last Battle, The Magician's Nephew, Prince Caspian, The Silver Chair,* and *The Voyage of the Dawn Treader.*

McCaffrey, Anne. *Black Horses for the King.* Harcourt, 1996. Ages 11–14.

————. *Dragonsinger.* Atheneum, 1977. Ages 13–16.

————. *Dragonsong.* Atheneum, 1976. Ages 13–16.

McKinley, Robin. *The Hero and the Crown.* Greenwillow, 1984. Ages 11–15.

Morpurgo, Michael. *Sir Gawain and the Green Knight.* Illustrated by Michael Foreman. Candlewick, 2004. Ages 10–14.

Oppel, Kenneth. *Airborn.* HarperCollins, 2004. Ages 11–14.

Paterson, Katherine. *Parzival: The Quest of the Grail Knight.* Lodestar, 1998. Ages 10–14.

Pierce, Meredith Ann. *Treasure at the Heart of the Tanglewood.* Viking, 2001. Ages 12–16.

Pullman, Philip. *The Golden Compass.* Knopf, 1996. Ages 12–16. First of His Dark Materials trilogy. Also *The Subtle Knife,* Knopf, 1998, and *The Amber Spyglass,* Knopf, 1999.

Riordan, Rick. *The Lightning Thief.* Hyperion, 2005. Ages 10–15. Humor.

Rodda, Emily. *Rowan of Rin.* Greenwillow, 2002. Ages 8–11. Others in the series include *Rowan and the Zebak,* 2002, and *Rowan and the Travelers,* 2001.

Rowling, J. K. *Harry Potter and the Sorcerer's Stone.* Scholastic, 1998. Ages 9–13. The first in a series of quest fantasies, including *Harry Potter and the Chamber of Secrets,* 1999; *Harry Potter and the Prisoner of Azkaban,* 1999; *Harry Potter and the Goblet of Fire,* 2000; *Harry Potter and the Order of the Phoenix,* 2003; and *Harry Potter and the Half-Blood Prince,* 2005.

Stroud, Jonathan. *The Amulet of Samarkand.* Hyperion, 2003. Ages 11–18. Others in the Bartimaeus Trilogy are *The Golem's Eye,* 2004, and *Ptolemy's Gate,* 2006.

Turner, Megan Whalen. *The King of Attolia.* Greenwillow, 2006. Ages 11–18. Also *The Queen of Attolia,* 2005.

————. *The Thief.* Greenwillow, 1996. Ages 11–16.

Yolen, Jane. *Sword of the Rightful King: A Novel of King Arthur.* Harcourt, 2003. Ages 11–15.

Science Fiction and Science Fantasy

Adlington, L. J. *The Diary of Pelly D.* Greenwillow, 2005. Ages 12–18.

Anderson, M. T. *Feed.* Candlewick, 2002. Ages 12–18.

Atwater-Rhodes, Amelia. *Hawksong.* Delacorte, 2003. Ages 12–16.

Bawden, Nina. *Off the Road.* Clarion, 1998. Ages 9–13.

Bechard, Margaret. *Star Hatchling.* Viking, 1995. Ages 9–12.

Bell, Hilari. *A Matter of Profit.* HarperCollins, 2001. Ages 11–16.

Brittain, Bill. *Shape-Changer.* HarperCollins, 1994. Ages 8–16.

Cart, Michael, editor. *Tomorrowland: Ten Stories about the Future.* Scholastic, 1999. (COL) Ages 11–18.

Christopher, John. *The White Mountains.* Macmillan, 1967. Ages 11–16. (Also included in the Tripods series: *The City of Gold and Lead,* 1967, and *The Pool of Fire,* 1968.)

Clements, Andrew. *Things Not Seen.* Philomel, 2002. Ages 10–14.

Conly, Jane Leslie. *Racso and Rats of NIMH.* Illustrated by Leonard Lubin. Harper, 1986. Ages 9–12.

————. *R. T., Margaret, and the Rats of NIMH.* HarperCollins, 1990. Ages 9–12.

Crew, Gary. *The Watertower.* Illustrated by Steven Woolman. Crocodile, 1998. (PI) Ages 10–14.

DuPrau, Jeanne. *City of Ember.* Random, 2003. Ages 10–14. Sequel: *The People of Sparks,* 2004.

Engdahl, Sylvia. *Enchantress from the Stars.* Atheneum, 1970. Ages 11–16.

Etchemendy, Nancy. *The Power of Un.* Front Street, 2000. Ages 10–14.

Farmer, Nancy. *The House of the Scorpion.* Simon & Schuster, 2002. Ages 12–18.

Hughes, Ted. *The Iron Giant: A Story in Five Nights.* Knopf, 1999/1968. Ages 9–12.

L'Engle, Madeleine. *A Wrinkle in Time.* Farrar, 1962. Ages 11–15.

Lowry, Lois. *Gathering Blue.* Houghton, 2000. Ages 10–15.

———. *The Giver.* Houghton, 1993. Ages 11–15.

———. *Messenger.* Houghton, 2004. Ages 11–15.

Mackel, Kathy. *Can of Worms.* Avon, 1999. Ages 10–14. Humor.

Nix, Garth. *Shade's Children.* HarperCollins, 1997. Ages 12–16.

O'Brien, Robert C. *Mrs. Frisby and the Rats of NIMH.* Illustrated by Zena Bernstein. Atheneum, 1971. Ages 9–12. (See sequels by Conly.)

Reeve, Philip. *Larklight: A Rousing Tale of Dauntless Pluck in the Farthest Reaches of Space.* Ages 10–15. Humor.

———. *Mortal Engines.* HarperCollins, 2003. Ages 12–18. First of the Hungry Cities Chronicles.

Sleator, William. *The Boy Who Reversed Himself.* Dutton, 1986. Ages 10–15.

———. *The Duplicate.* Dutton, 1988. Ages 11–16.

———. *House of Stairs.* Dutton, 1974. Ages 11–16.

Waugh, Sylvia. *Earthborn.* Delacorte, 2002. Ages 9–13.

———. *Space Race.* Delacorte, 2000. Ages 9–12.

Related Films, Videos, and DVDs

The Black Cauldron. (1985). Author: Lloyd Alexander (1965). 80 minutes.

Borrowers. (1998). Author: Mary Norton (1953). 86 minutes.

Charlotte's Web. (2006). Author: E. B. White (1952). 113 minutes.

The Chronicles of Narnia: The Lion, the Witch, and the Wardrobe. (2005). Author: C. S. Lewis (1955). 140 minutes.

Ella Enchanted. (2004). Author: Gail Carson Levine (1997). 96 minutes.

Eragon. (2006). Author: Christopher Paolini (2003). 120 minutes

Escape to Witch Mountain. (1995). Author: Alexander Key (1968). 97 minutes.

Harry Potter and the Sorcerer's Stone. (2001). Author: J. K. Rowling (1998). 152 minutes. Four others in the series also available.

The Hobbit. (1991). J. R. R. Tolkien (1938). 76 minutes.

The Iron Giant. (1999). Author: Ted Hughes. (1999/ 1968). 86 minutes.

Redwall: Friends or Foes? (1999). Author: Brian Jacques (1987). 90 minutes.

Shrek. (2001). Author: William Steig (1990). 90 minutes.

Tuck Everlasting. (2002). Author: Natalie Babbitt. (1975). 88 minutes.

A Wrinkle in Time. (2003). Author: Madeleine L'Engle (1962). 128 minutes.

Sources for Films, Videos, and DVDs

The Video Source Book. Syosset, NY: National Video Clearinghouse, 1979–. Published by Gale Research, Detroit, MI.

An annual reference work that lists media and provides sources for purchase and rental.

Websites of large video distributors:

www.libraryvideo.com

www.knowledgeunlimited.com

chapter 8

Realistic Fiction

Listening to Grownups Quarreling,
standing in the hall against the
wall with my little brother, blown
like leaves against the wall by their
voices, my head like a pingpong ball
between the paddles of their anger:
I knew what it meant
to tremble like a leaf.

Cold with their wrath, I heard
the claws of the rain
pounce. Floods
poured through the city,
skies clapped over me,
and I was shaken, shaken
like a mouse
between their jaws.

—Ruth Whitman

Children's lives are sometimes sad and harsh. Realistic stories of today openly address these situations as well as the happy and humorous situations of life. Children of all ages appreciate stories about people who seem like themselves or who are involved in familiar activities. These realistic fiction stories have appealed to children for many years and continue to do so today.

Definition and Description

Realistic fiction refers to stories that could indeed happen to people and animals; that is, it is within the realm of possibility that such events could occur or could have occurred. The protagonists of these stories are fictitious characters created by the author, but their actions and reactions are quite like those of real people or real animals. Sometimes, events in these stories are exaggerated or outlandish—hardly probable but definitely possible. These stories, too, fit under the definition of realistic fiction.

Realism in literature is a complex, multifaceted concept. Marshall (1988) considers various components of realism in literature, including factual, situational, emotional, and social. *Factual realism* is provided by the description of actual people, places, and events in a book. When this occurs, the facts need to be recorded accurately. For example, usually in historical fiction and occasionally in realistic fiction, the names and locations of actual places are included in the story, with accurate and complete descriptions. *Situational realism* is provided by a situation that is not only possible but also quite likely, often in an identifiable location with characters of an identifiable age and social class, making the whole treatment believable. Family stories are often examples of stories built on situational realism. *Emotional realism* is provided by the appearance of believable feelings and relationships among characters. Rite-of-passage or growing-up stories often employ emotional realism. *Social realism* is provided by an honest portrayal of society and its conditions of the moment. In almost all good realistic stories, several of these components of realism occur, with varying degrees of emphasis.

Contemporary realism is a term used to describe stories that take place in the present time and portray attitudes and mores of the present culture. Unlike realistic books of several decades ago that depicted only happy families and were never controversial, today's contemporary realism often focuses on current societal issues, such as alcoholism, racism, poverty, and homelessness. Contemporary books still tell of the happy, funny times in children's lives, but they also include the harsh, unpleasant times that are, sadly, a part of many children's lives.

Authors of contemporary realistic fiction set their stories in the present or recent past. But, in time, features of these stories, such as dialogue and allusions to popular culture, customs, and dress become dated and the stories are therefore no longer contemporary, though they may still be realistic. Older stories that obviously no longer describe today's world, though they may have once been contemporary realistic fiction, are now simply realistic fiction. Older realistic fiction stories that are considered modern classics are included in this chapter.

 ## Evaluation and Selection of Realistic Fiction

The criteria for evaluating realistic fiction are the same as those for any work of fiction. Well-developed characters who manifest change as a result of significant life events, a well-structured plot with sufficient conflict and suspense to hold the reader's interest, a time and place suitable to the storyline, and a worthy theme are basic literary elements expected of any work of fiction, including works of realistic fiction.

Excellent Realistic Fiction to Read Aloud

Balliett, Blue. *Chasing Vermeer*. Ages 9–14.

Cameron, Ann. *Colibrí*. Ages 10–14. Set in Guatemala.

Couloumbis, Audrey. *The Misadventures of Maude March, or, Trouble Rides a Fast Horse*. Ages 10–13. Humorous.

Creech, Sharon. *Ruby Holler*. Ages 8–11.

DiCamillo, Kate. *Because of Winn-Dixie*. Ages 8–11.

Ellis, Sarah. *The Several Lives of Orphan Jack*. Illustrated by Bruno St.-Aubin. Ages 7–11.

Gantos, Jack. *Joey Pigza Swallowed the Key*. Ages 9–12.

Horvath, Polly. *Everything on a Waffle*. Ages 9–12.

Howe, James. *The Misfits*. Ages 10–14.

Lowry, Lois. *Anastasia Krupnik*. Illustrated by Diane De Groat. Ages 8–11. Humorous.

Lupica, Mike. *Travel Team*. Ages 10–14.

Myers, Walter Dean. *Monster*. Ages 12–18.

O'Connor, Barbara. *Moonpie and Ivy*. Ages 10–13.

Ritter, John H. *The Boy Who Saved Baseball*. Ages 10–13.

Rodman, Philbrick. *The Young Man and the Sea*. Ages 9–14.

Stauffacher, Sue. *Donuthead*. Ages 9–12. Humorous.

Woodson, Jacqueline. *Locomotion*. Ages 9–12. Told through a series of poems.

- Even stories that portray adverse and discouraging social situations should permit some cause for optimism. Children need to trust that problems can be overcome or ameliorated and that the world can be a good place in which to live.

- Themes in realistic stories often convey moral values, such as the rewards of kindness and generosity to others. However, these moral values must not be the main reason for the story. At times, adults write books for children with the sole intent of teaching or preaching, and the story itself is nothing more than a thin disguise for a heavy-handed moral lesson. The moral must not overwhelm the story but may be its logical outcome.

- A novel of realistic fiction must be believable, and the events must be possible, even though all aspects may not be probable. Sometimes, an author goes closer to the edge of the believable range to produce a more exciting, suspense-filled story.

- Controversy involving children's books often centers on topics that are found in realistic fiction novels, such as premarital sex, pregnancy, homosexuality, and the use of profanity. Many of these controversial books fall within the types of realism labeled "Moral Choices" and "Romance and Sexuality" in the recommended reading list at the end of this chapter. Chapter 12 provides a full discussion of issues surrounding censorship and selection.

- An aspect of writing style that students greatly appreciate is humor. Although humor may be found in stories of any genre, it is more often found in realistic fiction. Humorous stories feature characters caught up in silly situations or involved in funny escapades. *Anastasia Krupnik* by Lois Lowry and *The Schwa Was Here* by Neal Schusterman are good examples of humorous stories.

Selection of realistic fiction for classroom and library collections and for read-alouds should be balanced among the different types of realistic stories. A steady diet of humorous read-alouds does not offer the richness of experience to children that they deserve, nor does it provide for the varied reading interests of a group of children. The Edgar Allan Poe Award for Juvenile Mystery Novels can be helpful to you in selecting good mysteries. This award was established in 1961 by the Mystery Writers of America and is awarded annually in order to honor U.S. authors of mysteries for children. The list of winners is included in Appendix A. Intermediate-grade children report on reading interest surveys that realistic fiction is their favorite genre. Of course, some children may prefer other categories, but realistic fiction does hold high appeal for many children at all grade levels.

Historical Overview of Realistic Fiction

The earliest realistic stories were didactic ones that were intended to teach morality and manners to young readers. The characters of the children's stories of the 1700s were usually wooden, lifeless boys and girls whose lives were spent in good works; however, in England during this period, two significant events affecting the future of children's literature occurred. *Robinson Crusoe* by Daniel Defoe, an exciting survival story, was published in 1719 for adults but became a popular book among children. Then in 1744, John Newbery began to publish, expressly for a child audience, books of realistic fiction intended to entertain as well as to educate. These two events laid the groundwork for establishing children's literature as a separate branch of literature. The accompanying Milestones feature highlights the development of realistic fiction.

The first type of realistic fiction for children that avoided the heavy didactic persuasion was the adventure story. Imitators of *Robinson Crusoe* were many, including the very popular *Swiss Family Robinson* by Johann Wyss of Switzerland in 1812. Later adventure stories of renown from England were *Treasure Island* (1883) and *Kidnapped* (1886) by Robert Louis Stevenson; and from the United States, *The Adventures of Tom Sawyer* (1876) and *The Adventures of Huckleberry Finn* (1884) by Mark Twain (pseudonym of Samuel Clemens).

Realistic family stories also came on the scene during the 1800s with *Little Women* (1868) by Louisa May Alcott. The family story remained a favorite in the twentieth century, with early memorable books such as the series *Anne of Green Gables* (1908) by Canadian Lucy Maud Montgomery and *The Secret Garden* (1911) by Frances Hodgson Burnett. Since Anne of *Anne of Green Gables* and Mary of *The Secret Garden* were orphans, the books by Burnett and Montgomery can be considered precursors of adjustment stories that addressed the special needs of children with problems. Stories of happy and often large families continued to thrive and peaked in the 1940s and 1950s in family story series about the Moffat family by Eleanor Estes and about the Melendy family by Elizabeth Enright. These *happy family* stories compared with much of today's contemporary realism for children seem almost lighthearted.

Children from other lands is another theme that can be found in many realistic stories for children. *Hans Brinker, or The Silver Skates* (1865) by Mary Mapes Dodge and *Heidi* (1880) by Johanna Spyri of Switzerland are set in Holland and Switzerland, respectively, and were two of the earliest *other lands* books.

Realistic animal stories for children began to appear in the latter half of the nineteenth century. *Black Beauty* (1877) by Anna Sewell was a plea for humane treatment of animals, and

MILESTONES in the Development of Realistic Fiction

Date	Event	Significance
1719	*Robinson Crusoe* by Daniel Defoe (England)	Early survival/adventure on a desert island; many imitators
1812	*Swiss Family Robinson* by Johann Wyss (Switzerland)	Most successful imitation of *Robinson Crusoe*
1868	*Little Women* by Louisa May Alcott (United States)	An early family story of great popularity
1876	*The Adventures of Tom Sawyer* by Mark Twain (United States)	Classic adventure story set along the Mississippi
1877	*Black Beauty* by Anna Sewell (England)	Early horse story deploring inhumane treatment of animals
1880	*Heidi* by Johanna Spyri (Switzerland)	An early international story popular in the United States
1883	*Treasure Island* by Robert Louis Stevenson (England)	Classic adventure story with pirates
1908	*Anne of Green Gables* by Lucy Maud Montgomery (Canada)	Early family story about an orphan and her new family
1911	*The Secret Garden* by Frances Hodgson Burnett (United States)	A classic sentimental novel of two children adjusting to life
1938	*The Yearling* by Marjorie Kinnan Rawlings (United States)	Classic animal story and coming-of-age story
1945	*Strawberry Girl* by Lois Lenski (United States)	Regional story set in Florida
1964	*Harriet the Spy* by Louise Fitzhugh (United States)	The beginning of the new realism movement
1970	*Are You There, God? It's Me, Margaret* by Judy Blume (United States)	Early book with frank treatment of sex
2000	*Monster* by Walter Dean Myers (United States)	First winner of the Michael L. Printz Award for Excellence in Literature for Young Adults

although quite sentimental in places and completely personified (i.e., the animal is given human qualities), it is still appreciated by some readers. Animal stories showing the maturing of the young human protagonist who assists the animal in the story remain popular today.

Regional stories and stories about children of minority groups began to appear with more frequency in the 1940s. *Strawberry Girl* (1945) by Lois Lenski featured rural Florida and was one of the first regional stories. It was only in the 1960s and 1970s that books written by minorities began to achieve national recognition. *Zeely* (1967) by Virginia Hamilton and *Stevie* (1969) by

John Steptoe portray African-American childhood experiences and are two of the earliest and most noteworthy books representing this trend toward increased minority authorship—a trend that continues today.

A new era in realistic fiction for children was ushered in with the publication of *Harriet the Spy* by Louise Fitzhugh in 1964. This story of an unhappy and, at times, unpleasant girl depicted Harriet, her parents, and her classmates as anything but ideal or sympathetic human beings. This trend toward a more graphic and explicitly truthful portrayal of life and the inclusion of many topics that were previously considered taboo continued in children's books in the 1970s and 1980s and still prevails today. Controversial topics such as death, divorce, drugs, alcoholism, and disabilities, which have always been a part of childhood, became permissible topics in children's books. Parents and other adults began to be portrayed as they truly are, not as one might believe they should be. This newer, franker brand of realism, sometimes referred to as the *new realism,* changed the world of children's books. The *new realism* books may be less lighthearted than their predecessors, but they are also more truthful and more real. At the present time, censorship of materials for children, including children's trade books, is rampant, in part, because of this trend toward more graphic and explicit writing in children's books.

 ## Types of Realistic Fiction

The subject matter of realistic fiction includes the child's whole world of relationships with self and others: the joys, sorrows, challenges, adjustments, anxieties, and satisfactions of human life. Realistic books will often treat more than one aspect of human life; thus, some realistic fiction books can be categorized by more than one of the following topics.

Families

Stories about the *nuclear family*—children and their relationships with parents and siblings—are a natural subject of books for children. Childhood for most children is spent in close contact with family members. Family stories for younger children often portray a happy child with loving parents. In these stories the everyday activities are shown—from brushing teeth to cooking dinner. Easy chapter books appealing to newly independent readers can be found within this type. These stories often show the child at play and sometimes explore sibling relationships as well. *The Quigleys in a Spin* by Simon Mason and *Roxie and the Hooligans* by Phyllis Reynolds Naylor are good examples of this type of book.

Extended families can also be found in children's books. Aunts, uncles, grandparents, and cousins are important in the real lives of many children and may also be enjoyed in stories written for children. See *The Same Stuff as Stars* by Katherine Paterson and *Dillon Dillon* by Kate Banks.

The *alternative family* of today's world is also depicted in family stories. Not all family stories present the safe and secure world of healthy, intact families. Separation, divorce, single-parent families, adoptive families, foster families, and reconstructed families of stepparents and stepchildren are often the backdrop of stories today. For example, see *Pictures of Hollis Woods* by Patricia

Reilly Giff and *Ruby Holler* by Sharon Creech. The difficulty children and adults encounter in adjusting to these new family situations becomes the primary conflict in some stories. It is important for children to see families other than the typical mother, father, and two children portrayed positively in books.

Peers

In addition to adapting to one's family situation, children must also learn to cope with their peers. Many realistic stories show children struggling for **acceptance by peers** in a group situation. School settings are common in these stories. Examples include *Donuthead* by Sue Stauffacher and *Fame and Glory in Freedom, Georgia* by Barbara O'Connor.

Bullying by peers can be damaging to the self-esteem of those targeted. Angry outbursts by those being humiliated is not infrequent and, at times, can be frightening. Literature can provide an opportunity to address these issues, by developing an awareness and understanding of the harm caused and by encouraging more compassion toward those who are targeted for some real or perceived difference. In Wendelin Van Draanen's *Secret Identity*, Nolan, a fifth-grade outsider, becomes fed up with the school bully and finds an ingenious way to expose the bully's misdeeds. Although the treatment is humorous and lighthearted, the problem can be raised in discussion of the book.

Developing **close friendships** is another focus of stories about peer relationships. Friends may be of the same sex or the opposite sex, of the same age or a very different age, or of the same culture or a different culture. A concern for friendship and how to be a good friend to someone are shared traits of these stories. *The Misfits* by James Howe and *Granny Torrelli Makes Soup* by Sharon Creech are good examples of this type of book.

Physical, Emotional, Mental, and Behavioral Challenges

Many children must deal with difficult challenges in their lives. Some children have disabilities; others have a family member or a friend with a disability. These disabilities may be physical, such as scoliosis; emotional, such as bipolar disorder; mental, such as mental retardation or learning disabilities; behavioral, such as hyperactivity; or multiple. Yet children do not like to appear different or strange to others. Authors of children's books are becoming increasingly sensitive to the need for positive portrayals of individuals with special challenges. Well-written, honest stories of such individuals in children's books can help other children gain an understanding of disabilities and empathize with people who have disabilities. As inclusion of special education students into regular classrooms becomes a more common practice, this trend in children's literature can be an important educational resource. As examples, Jane Leslie Conly's Newbery Honor Book winner, *Crazy Lady!*, deals with physical disabilities and mental retardation, and Sarah Weeks's *So B. It* addresses a developmental disability and agoraphobia.

Communities

Part of growing up involves the discovery of one's membership in a **community**, a group extending beyond the family. In some children's books we find school settings in which students, teachers, administrators, and, at times, parents comprise the community. Helen Frost's novel told through 22 poetic forms, *Spinning through the Universe: A Novel in Poems from Room 214,* shows students, the teacher, and the custodian writing their thoughts about the school and other topics.

In other books the community setting is the neighborhood. An example is Paul Fleischman's *Seedfolks* in which neighbors join together to turn a vacant lot into a garden. Janet McDonald's novels, *Chill Wind, Twists and Turns,* and *Spellbound,* are about a community of teens living in urban housing projects, a community not often featured in juvenile novels.

Community extends beyond country to communities around the world. With increasing interdependence among countries, young people will likely be more connected to an international community than ever before. Books set in foreign countries about life in another culture can help children and adolescents develop an awareness of and kinship toward people from other countries and an appreciation for people whose lives differ from their own. Examples include *Colibrí* by Ann Cameron, *Shabanu: Daughter of the Wind* by Suzanne Fisher Staples, and *Chanda's Secrets* by Allan Stratton.

Animals

Animal stories remain an ever-popular genre with children, dog and horse stories being the most popular. In realistic animal stories the animal protagonist behaves like an animal and is not personified. Usually, a child is also a protagonist in these stories. Examples are *Because of Winn-Dixie* by Kate DiCamillo and *Shiloh* by Phyllis Reynolds Naylor.

Sports

Sports stories often present a story in which a child protagonist struggles to become accepted as a member of a team and does eventually succeed through determination and hard work. *The Boy Who Saved Baseball* by John H. Ritter is a good example of a sports story. Although traditionally written with boys as the main characters, some sports stories are now available that feature girls as protagonists.

Mysteries

Mysteries, popular with boys and girls, range from simple "whodunits" to complex character stories. The element of suspense is a strong part of the appeal of these stories. Mysteries have won more state children's choice awards than any other type of story, a fact that suggests that mysteries are truly favorites of many children. See *Chasing Vermeer* by Blue Balliett and *Sammy Keyes and the Dead Giveaway* by Wendelin Van Draanen.

Moral Choices

Characters in many realistic fiction novels face moments of crisis, situations of great difficulty, or events in which a decision may change someone's life. These situations are often similar to those that children will face in their lives. Through these stories children can understand the difficult decisions the character is faced with and can discuss the consequences that may result from the choice made. Teachers often select these books for class study with intermediate- and middle-grade students. Using a book in which a character is faced with a difficult moral choice

Notable Authors of Realistic Fiction

Ann Cameron, U.S. author who lives in Guatemala and is known for *The Stories Julian Tells* and its sequels. Also has written the novel *Colibrí,* set in Guatemala.

Beverly Cleary, author of humorous family stories about everyday happenings. *Ramona Quimby, Age 8; Dear Mr. Henshaw.* www.beverlycleary.com

Sharon Creech, author of novels about girls seeking their families to find themselves. *Walk Two Moons; Ruby Holler; The Wanderer.* www.sharoncreech.com

Jack Gantos, author of Joey Pigza novels about a boy with attention deficit disorder and autobiographical books. *Heads or Tails: Stories from the Sixth Grade; Joey Pigza Swallowed the Key.* www.jackgantos.com

Jean Craighead George, author of ecological fiction and survival in nature stories. *Julie of the Wolves; My Side of the Mountain.* www.jeancraigheadgeorge.com

Will Hobbs, author of wilderness-based adventure novels, many set in the Southwest and Mexico, Alaska, and western United States. *Crossing the Wire; The Maze; Jackie's Wild Seattle.* www.willhobbsauthor.com

Walter Dean Myers, author of novels about African-American adolescents in city settings. *Scorpions; Monster; Slam!* www.walterdeanmyers.com

Phyllis Reynolds Naylor, author of eight books about Alice and her family, including *Alice in April.* Also noted for Newbery Medal winner *Shiloh* and its sequels.

Katherine Paterson, author of stories featuring relationships with peers and family. *The Great Gilly Hopkins; Bridge to Terabithia.* www.katherinepaterson.com

Gary Paulsen, author of nature survival adventures often set in northern United States or Canada. *Hatchet; The River.* www.garypaulsen.com

Cynthia Rylant, author of introspective realistic stories often set in Appalachia. *Every Living Thing; Missing May.*

Louis Sachar, author of *Holes,* a warm and humorous novel that intertwines past and present events to solve a mystery. (Also *Wayside School Is Falling Down,* a light, humorous modern fantasy series.) *Small Steps.* www.louissachar.com

Jerry Spinelli, author of realistic novels of peers and their escapades, including Newbery Medal winner *Maniac Magee* and Newbery Honor book *Wringer.* www.jerryspinelli.com

Suzanne Fisher Staples, author of the Newbery Honor books *Shabanu* and its sequel *Haveli,* set in the Cholistan Desert of Pakistan; *Under the Persimmon Tree.* Her stories present conflicts within and between diverse cultures. www.suzannefisherstaples.com

Wendelin Van Draanen, author of the popular Sammy Keyes mystery series featuring a funny and clever heroine who has to extricate herself from difficult situations. *Sammy Keyes and the Dead Giveaway,* and a romantic comedy, *Flipped.* www.randomhouse.com/kids/vandraanen

Nancy Werlin, author of suspenseful mysteries that address difficult situations with sensitivity. *Killer's Cousin; Black Mirror; The Rules of Survival.* www.nancywerlin.com

Jacqueline Woodson, African-American author whose novels often treat sensitive issues of sexuality, abuse, and race. *Locomotion; Hush.* www.jacquelinewoodson.com

can stimulate lively discussions. An example is Paul Fleischman's *Whirligig,* in which the main character must face the devastating consequences of his choice.

Romance and Sexuality

Romance stories are popular with preteens and teens, especially girls. Some stories depict boy–girl friendships, as in *Flipped* by Wendelin Van Draanen. Other novels portray physical attraction, as in Iain Lawrence's *Ghost Boy.* Since the 1990s, more stories of characters dealing with pregnancy and teenage parenting have appeared; some realistic examples are Virginia Euwer Wolff's *Make Lemonade* and *True Believer.*

Children become aware of their *growing sexuality* during preteen and teen years as they begin to mature. Some stories for older teens show attraction between members of the opposite sex as well as members of the same sex, with the beginning of sexual activity sometimes depicted in relationships. Stories that portray the struggle of young people coming to terms with a homosexual or lesbian sexual orientation are seen more frequently than they were in the past; other stories show the cruelty of society toward young homosexuals or lesbians. See *Deliver Us from Evie* by M. E. Kerr and *Geography Club* by Brent Hartinger.

Coming of Age

From birth to age 10, most children's lives revolve around family, friends, and classmates, but during the preteen and teen years a shift toward self-discovery and independence occurs. Rapid growth and change are seen in the physical, emotional, moral, and intellectual domains of life. These changes are reflected in books for adolescents and are referred to as **coming-of-age stories.** Sometimes books that deal with the trials and tribulations encountered during growth from childhood to adulthood are called **rite-of-passage** books. A **rite of passage** refers to an event in one's life that signals a change from child to adult. Examples of rite-of-passage books are *Olive's Ocean* by Kevin Henkes and *A Fine White Dust* by Cynthia Rylant.

Adventure and Survival

Facing physical danger, an external force, also contributes to the maturing process. Stories of **survival and adventure** are ones in which the young protagonist must rely on will and ingenuity to survive a life-threatening situation. Although most survival stories are set in isolated places, a growing number are being set in cities where gangs, drug wars, and abandonment are life threatening. Adventure stories may be set in any environment where the protagonist has freedom of action. *Hatchet* by Gary Paulsen and *The Maze* by Will Hobbs are examples of this type of book.

Stories in the realistic fiction genre present familiar situations with which children can readily identify, often reflect contemporary life, and portray settings not so different from the homes, schools, towns, and cities known to today's children. The protagonists of these stories are frequently testing themselves as they grow toward adulthood; young readers can therefore empathize and gain insight into their own predicaments. Your challenge will be to stay abreast of good realistic stories in order to provide a wide range of books that will entertain, encourage, and inspire your students.

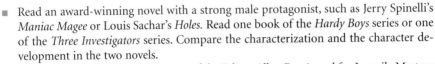

Topics for Further Investigation

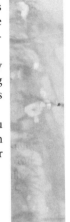

- Read an award-winning novel with a strong male protagonist, such as Jerry Spinelli's *Maniac Magee* or Louis Sachar's *Holes*. Read one book of the *Hardy Boys* series or one of the *Three Investigators* series. Compare the characterization and the character development in the two novels.
- Select and read three to five winners of the Edgar Allan Poe Award for Juvenile Mystery Novels. (See Appendix A for the list.) Compare and contrast these novels, considering the source and type of mystery, the devices used to cause suspense, and the elements of realism and fantasy in each story.
- Select fifteen realistic fiction novels suitable for a particular grade level in which you are participating. Booktalk and display these novels for a group of eight students, then ask them to complete an interest ballot on them. What did you discover about their reading preferences from this activity?

 See the companion website at www.ablongman.com/lynchbrown6e for additional suggestions.

References

Marshall, M. R. (1988). *An introduction to the world of children's books* (2nd ed.). Brookfield, VT: Gower.

Whitman, R. (1968). Listening to grownups quarreling. In R. Whitman (Ed.), *The marriage wig and other stories.* Orlando, FL: Harcourt.

Recommended Realistic Fiction Books

Ages indicated refer to content appropriateness and conceptual and interest levels. Formats other than novels will be coded as follows:

   (PI) Picture book
   (COL) Short story collection

Families

Acampora, Paul. *Defining Dulcie.* Dial, 2006. Ages 12–15.

Banks, Kate. *Dillon Dillon.* Farrar, 2002. Ages 10–13.

———. *Walk Softly, Rachel.* Farrar, 2003. Ages 12–15.

Baskin, Nora Raleigh. *What Every Girl (Except Me) Knows.* Little, Brown, 2001. Ages 10–13.

Bauer, Marion Dane. *A Question of Trust.* Scholastic, 1994. Ages 10–13.

Birdsall, Jeanne. *The Penderwicks: A Summer Tale of Four Sisters, Two Rabbits, and a Very Interesting Boy.* Knopf, 2005. Ages 8–12.

Bredsdorff, Bodil. *The Crow-Girl: The Children of Crow Cove.* Translated from the Danish by Faith Ingwersen. Farrar, 2004. Ages 9–12.

Budhos, Marina. *Ask Me No Questions.* Simon & Schuster, 2006. Ages 12–16.

Cameron. Ann. *The Stories Julian Tells.* Illustrated by Ann Strugnell. Random, 1989 (1981). Ages 8–11.

Choldenko, Gennifer. *Notes from a Liar and Her Dog.* Putnam, 2001. Ages 10–13.

Cleary, Beverly. *Dear Mr. Henshaw.* Illustrated by Paul Zelinsky. Morrow, 1983. Ages 9–12.

Cohn, Rachel. *The Steps.* Simon & Schuster, 2003. Ages 9–13.

Conly, Jane Leslie. *While No One Was Watching.* Holt, 1998. Ages 10–14.

Creech, Sharon. *Chasing Redbird.* HarperCollins, 1997. Ages 11–14.

————. *Heartbeat.* HarperCollins, 2004. Ages 9–14. Free verse.

————. *Replay.* HarperCollins, 2005. Ages 9–13. Includes a short play featured in the story.

————. *Ruby Holler.* HarperCollins, 2002. Ages 8–11.

————. *Walk Two Moons.* HarperCollins, 1994. Ages 10–13.

Danziger, Paula. *Amber Brown Goes Fourth.* Harper-Collins, 1995. Ages 7–10.

————. *Forever Amber Brown.* Illustrated by Tony Ross. Putnam, 1996. Ages 7–10.

Delacre, Lulu. *Salsa Stories.* Scholastic, 2000. (COL) Ages 11–14.

Fine, Anne. *Step by Wicked Step.* Little, Brown, 1996. Ages 9–12.

Fogelin, Adrian. *Anna Casey's Place in the World.* Peachtree, 2001. Ages 10–13.

————. *The Big Nothing.* Peachtree, 2004. Ages 11–14.

————. *Sister Spider Knows All.* Peachtree, 2003. Ages 11–14.

Fusco, Kimberly Newton. *Tending to Grace.* Knopf, 2004. Ages 12–15.

Gantos, Jack. *What Would Joey Do?* Farrar, 2002. Ages 9–12.

Giff, Patricia Reilly. *Pictures of Hollis Woods.* Wendy Lamb, 2002. Ages 10–12.

Gonzalez, Julie. *Wings.* Delacorte, 2005. Ages 12–16. Two parallel narrators.

Goscinny, René. *Nicholas Again.* Illustrated by Jean Jacques Sempé. Translated from the French by Anthea Bell. Phaidon, 2006. Ages 9–12. Humor.

Griffin, Adele. *The Other Shepards.* Hyperion, 1998. Ages 10–14.

Grimes, Nikki. *Dark Sons.* Hyperion, 2005. Ages 11–16.

Hannigan, Katherine. *Ida B: . . . and her Plans to Maximize Fun, Avoid Disaster, and (Possibly) Save the World.* Greenwillow, 2004. Ages 9–12.

Henkes, Kevin. *Sun and Spoon.* Greenwillow, 1997. Ages 8–11.

Hicks, Betty. *Out of Order.* Roaring Brook, 2005. Ages 9–12.

Horvath, Polly. *The Canning Season.* Farrar, 2003. Ages 12–16.

————. *Everything on a Waffle.* Farrar, 2001. Ages 9–12.

Johnson, Angela. *The First Part Last.* Simon & Schuster, 2003. Ages 12–18.

Jones, Kimberly K. *Sand Dollar Summer.* Simon & Schuster, 2006. Ages 10–14.

Koss, Amy Goldman. *The Ashwater Experiment.* Dial, 1999. Ages 9–13.

Leavitt, Martine. *Heck Superhero.* Front Street, 2004. Ages 12–15.

Lowry, Lois. *Anastasia Krupnik.* Houghton, 1985. Ages 8–11. Humorous.

Mackler, Carolyn. *The Earth, My Butt, and Other Big, Round Things.* Candlewick, 2003. Ages 12–16.

Mason, Simon. *The Quigleys in a Spin.* Illustrated by Helen Stephens. Random, 2006. Ages 8–11. Humor.

McKay, Hilary. *The Exiles in Love.* Simon & Schuster, 1998. Ages 9–12.

————. *Indigo's Star.* Simon & Schuster, 2004. Ages 11–14. Humor.

————. *Saffy's Angel.* Simon & Schuster, 2002. Ages 9–12.

Naylor, Phyllis Reynolds. *Alice in April.* Atheneum, 1993. Ages 9–13. Humorous.

————. *Roxie and the Hooligans.* Atheneum, 2006. Ages 7–10. Humorous transitional chapter book.

Nelson, Theresa. *Ruby Electric.* Simon & Schuster, 2003. Ages 10–13.

O'Connor, Barbara. *Moonpie and Ivy.* Farrar, 2001. Ages 10–13.

Paterson, Katherine. *The Great Gilly Hopkins.* Crowell, 1978. Ages 9–12.

————. *The Same Stuff as Stars.* Clarion, 2002. Ages 10–13.

Pennypacker, Sara. *Clementine.* Illustrated by Marla Frazee. Hyperion, 2006. Ages 7–9. Humor.

Rylant, Cynthia. *Missing May.* Orchard, 1992. Ages 10–14.

Scieszka, Jon, editor. *Guys Write for Guys Read: Boys' Favorite Authors Write about Being Boys.* Viking, 2005. (COL) Ages 10–14.

Stolz, Mary. *The Bully of Barkham Street.* Illustrated by Leonard Shortall. Harper, 1963. Ages 8–11.

————. *A Dog on Barkham Street.* Harper, 1960. Ages 8–11.

Tolan, Stephanie S. *Surviving the Applewhites.* Harper-Collins, 2002. Ages 10–14.

Van Draanen, Wendelin. *Runaway.* Knopf, 2006. Ages 12–16.

Werlin, Nancy. *The Rules of Survival.* Dial, 2006. Ages 12–18.

White, Ruth. *Belle Prater's Boy.* Farrar, 1996. Ages 10–13.

Williams, Vera B. *Amber Was Brave, Essie Was Smart: The Story of Amber and Essie Told Here in Poems and Pictures.* Greenwillow, 2001. Ages 6–10.

Peers

Clements, Andrew. *Frindle.* Illustrated by Brian Selznick. Simon & Schuster, 1996. Ages 8–12. Humorous.

Creech, Sharon. *Granny Torrelli Makes Soup.* Illustrated by Chris Raschka. HarperCollins, 2003. Ages 9–13.

———. *Love That Dog.* HarperCollins, 2001. Ages 9–14.

Dowell, Frances O'Roark. *Chicken Boy.* Atheneum, 2005. Ages 9–13.

Fine, Anne. *The Tulip Touch.* Little, Brown, 1997. Ages 10–14.

———. *Up on Cloud Nine.* Delacorte, 2002. Ages 10–13.

Gantos, Jack. *Heads or Tails: Stories from the Sixth Grade.* Farrar, 1994. (COL) Ages 10–14. Humorous.

———. *Jack's New Power: Stories from a Caribbean Year.* Farrar, 1995. (COL) Ages 11–15. Humor.

Grindley, Sally. *Dear Max.* Illustrated by Tony Ross. Simon & Schuster, 2006. Ages 7–10.

Grove, Vicki. *Reaching Dustin.* Putnam, 1998. Ages 10–13.

Gutman, Dan. *The Homework Machine.* Simon & Schuster, 2006. Ages 9–12.

Howe, James. *The Misfits.* Simon & Schuster, 2001. Ages 10–13.

Lombard, Jenny. *Drita, My Homegirl.* Putnam, 2006. Ages 8–11.

Look, Lenore. *Ruby Lu, Empress of Everything.* Illustrated by Anne Wilsdorf. Simon & Schuster, 2006. Ages 7–9.

Lubar, David. *Sleeping Freshmen Never Lie.* Dutton, 2005. Ages 12–15. Humor.

O'Connor, Barbara. *Fame and Glory in Freedom, Georgia.* Farrar, 2003. Ages 11–14.

Paterson, Katherine. *Bridge to Terabithia.* Illustrated by Donna Diamond. Crowell, 1977. Ages 9–13.

Perkins, Lynne Rae. *All Alone in the Universe.* Greenwillow, 1999. Ages 10–14.

———. *Criss Cross.* Greenwillow, 2005. Ages 11–15.

Soto, Gary. *Baseball in April and Other Stories.* Harcourt, 1991. (COL) Ages 10–14.

Spinelli, Jerry. *Wringer.* HarperCollins, 1997. Ages 9–12.

Stauffacher, Sue. *Donuthead.* Knopf, 2003. Ages 9–12.

Van Draanen, Wendelin. *Secret Identity.* Illustrated by Brian Biggs. Knopf, 2004. Ages 8–12.

Voigt, Cynthia. *Bad Girls.* Scholastic, 1996. Ages 8–12. See also sequel: *Bad, Badder, Baddest.* 1997.

Physical, Emotional, Mental, and Behavioral Challenges

Anderson, Rachel. *The Bus People.* Holt, 1992. Ages 10–14. Character portrayals, different disabilities.

Conly, Jane Leslie. *Crazy Lady!* HarperCollins, 1993. Ages 10–14. Mental retardation.

Duncan, Lois, editor. *On the Edge: Stories at the Brink.* Simon & Schuster, 2000. (COL) Ages 12–18.

Fleming, Virginia. *Be Good to Eddie Lee.* Illustrated by Floyd Cooper. Philomel, 1993. (PI) Ages 6–8. Down syndrome.

Gantos, Jack. *Joey Pigza Loses Control.* Farrar, 2000. Ages 9–12. Attention deficit/hyperactivity.

———. *Joey Pigza Swallowed the Key.* Farrar, 1998. Ages 9–13. AD/HD.

———. *What Would Joey Do?* Farrar, 2002. Ages 10–12.

Hobbs, Valerie. *Defiance.* Farrar, 2005. Ages 10–14.

Konigsburg, E. L. *Silent to the Bone.* Simon & Schuster, 2000. Ages 11–15. Mutism.

Mazer, Harry. *The Wild Kid.* Simon & Schuster, 1998. Ages 9–13. Down syndrome.

Philbrick, Rodman. *Freak the Mighty.* Blue Sky, 1993. Ages 12–16. Learning disability.

Schusterman, Neal. *The Schwa Was Here.* Dutton, 2004. Ages 12–15. Humor.

Sones, Sonya. *Stop Pretending: What Happened When My Big Sister Went Crazy.* HarperCollins, 1999. Ages 12–16. Free verse.

Trueman, Terry. *Stuck in Neutral.* HarperCollins, 2000. Ages 11–16. Cerebral palsy.

Weeks, Sarah. *So B. It.* HarperCollins, 2004. Ages 10–14.

Wilson, Nancy Hope. *The Reason for Janey.* Macmillan, 1994. Ages 10–13. Mental retardation.

Wood, June Rae. *About Face.* Putnam, 1999. Ages 9–12. Birthmark.

Communities

Beake, Lesley. *The Song of Be.* Holt, 1993. Ages 12–18.

Bunting, Eve. *Smoky Night.* Illustrated by David Diaz. Harcourt, 1995. (PI) Ages 9–12.

Cameron, Ann. *Colibrí.* Farrar, 2003. Ages 10–16. Set in Guatemala.

Canales, Viola. *The Tequila Worm.* Wendy Lamb, 2005. Ages 11–15.

Cofer, Judith Ortiz. *Call Me Maria.* Orchard, 2004. Ages 11–14.

Creech, Sharon. *Love that Dog.* HarperCollins, 2001. Ages 9–12. Free verse.

Danticat, Edwidge. *Behind the Mountains.* Orchard, 2002. Ages 11–14. Set in Haiti and Brooklyn, NY.

Dorris, Michael. *The Window.* Hyperion, 1997. Ages 11–14.

Fleischman, Paul. *Seedfolks.* HarperCollins, 1997. Ages 11–15.

Fogelin, Adrian. *Crossing Jordan.* Peachtree, 2000. Ages 11–14.

Frost, Helen. *Spinning through the Universe: A Novel in Poems from Room 214.* Farrar, 2004. Ages 11–14.

Grimes, Nikki. *Bronx Masquerade.* Dial, 2002. Ages 12–18.

Johnston, Tony. *Any Small Goodness: A Novel of the Barrio.* Illustrated by Raoúl Colón. Scholastic, 2001. Ages 9–12. A Mexican family in Los Angeles.

Kurtz, Jane. *The Storyteller's Beads.* Harcourt, 1998. Ages 10–13.

Mah, Adeline Yen. *Chinese Cinderella: The True Story of an Unwanted Daughter.* Delacorte, 1999. Ages 11–15. Set in China in latter part of twentieth century.

Marsden, Carolyn. *Silk Umbrellas.* Candlewick, 2004. Ages 8–12.

McDonald, Janet. *Chill Wind.* Farrar, 2002. Ages 12–18.
———. *Spellbound.* Farrar, 2001. Ages 12–18. Humor.
———. *Twists and Turns.* Farrar, 2003. Ages 12–18.

Myers, Walter Dean. *145th Street.* Delacorte, 2000. Ages 12–18. (**COL**) Harlem in New York City.

Na, An. *A Step from Heaven.* Front Street, 2001. Ages 13–18.

Naidoo, Beverley. *No Turning Back: A Novel of South Africa.* HarperCollins, 1997. Ages 10–13.
———. *The Other Side of Truth.* HarperCollins, 2001. Ages 11–14. Set in Nigeria, then in London.
———. *Out of Bounds: Seven Stories of Conflict and Hope.* HarperCollins, 2003. Ages 10–14. Set in South Africa in the period 1940–2000.
———. *Web of Lies.* HarperCollins, 2006. Ages 12–16.

Nye, Naomi Shihab. *Habibi.* Simon & Schuster, 1997. Ages 12–16.

Ochoa, Annette, Betsy Franco, and Tracy L. Gourdine, editors. *Night Is Gone, Day Is Still Coming: Stories and Poems by American Indian Teens and Young Adults.* Candlewick, 2003. (**COL**) Ages 12–18.

Polacco, Patricia. *Mr. Lincoln's Way.* Philomel, 2001. Ages 5–9.

Resau, Laura. *What the Moon Saw.* Delacorte, 2006. Ages 10–15.

Saldaña, René. *The Jumping Tree: A Novel.* Delacorte, 2001. Ages 11–16. Set in a Texas town near the Mexican border.

Smith, Hope Anita. *The Way a Door Closes.* Illustrated by Shane W. Evans. Holt, 2003. Ages 10–13. Narrative about an African-American family in poetic verse.

Soto, Gary. *Petty Crimes.* Harcourt, 1998. (**COL**) Ages 10–14.

Staples, Suzanne Fisher. *Haveli: A Young Woman's Courageous Struggle for Freedom in Present-day Pakistan.* Knopf, 1993. Ages 12–16.
———. *Shabanu: Daughter of the Wind.* Knopf, 1989. Ages 12–16.
———. *Shiva's Fire.* Farrar, 2000. Ages 12–16.
———. *Under the Persimmon Tree.* Farrar, 2005. Ages 12–16.

Stratton, Allan. *Chanda's Secrets.* Annick, 2004. Ages 12–18.

Temple, Frances. *Grab Hands and Run.* Orchard, 1993. Ages 12–16.

Whelan, Gloria. *Homeless Bird.* HarperCollins, 2000. Ages 12–16.

Williams-Garcia, Rita. *No Laughter Here.* HarperCollins, 2004. Ages 10–14. Female circumcision.

Woodson, Jacqueline. *I Hadn't Meant to Tell You This.* Delacorte, 1994. Ages 12–15.
———. *Locomotion.* Putnam, 2003. Ages 9–12. Free verse.

Yep, Laurence. *Thief of Hearts.* HarperCollins, 1995. Ages 10–13.

Yumoto, Kazumi. *The Friends.* Translated by Cathy Hirano. Farrar, 1996. Ages 8–12.

Zemser, Amy Bronwen. *Beyond the Mango Tree.* Greenwillow, 1998. Ages 11–15.

Animals

Bauer, Marion Dane. *A Bear Named Trouble.* Clarion, 2005. Ages 8–11.

DiCamillo, Kate. *Because of Winn-Dixie.* Candlewick, 2000. Ages 8–11.

———. *The Tiger Rising.* Candlewick, 2001. Ages 8–11.

Haas, Jessie. *A Blue for Beware.* Illustrated by Joseph A. Smith. Greenwillow, 1995. Ages 8–11.

———. *Jigsaw Pony.* Illustrated by Ying-Hwa Hu. Greenwillow, 2005. Ages 7–10. Transitional book.

Hearne, Betsy. *The Canine Collection: Stories about Dogs and People.* McElderry, 2003. (COL) Ages 10–14.

Hiaasen, Carl. *Hoot.* Knopf, 2003. Ages 10–14.

McKay, Hilary. *Dog Friday.* Simon & Schuster, 1995. Ages 9–11.

Naylor, Phyllis Reynolds. *Shiloh.* Atheneum, 1991. Ages 8–11. A dog story with sequels.

Rylant, Cynthia. *Every Living Thing.* Illustrated by S. D. Schindler. Bradbury, 1985. Ages 11–15.

Savage, Deborah. *Under a Different Sky.* Houghton, 1997. Ages 12–15.

Staples, Suzanne Fisher. *The Green Dog: A Mostly True Story.* Farrar, 2003. Ages 9–12.

Sports

Bloor, Edward. *Tangerine.* Harcourt, 1997. Ages 11–14.

Christopher, Matt. *Undercover Tailback.* Illustrated by Paul Casale. Little, 1992. Ages 8–11.

Deans, Sis. *Racing the Past.* Holt, 2001. Ages 10–13.

Deuker, Carl. *Runner.* Houghton, 2005. Ages 12–18.

Esckilsen, Erik E. *Offsides.* Houghton, 2004. Ages 10–14.

Hughes, Dean. *Team Picture.* Simon & Schuster, 1996. Ages 11–14.

Johnson, Scott. *Safe at Second.* Philomel, 1999. Ages 11–18.

Koertge, Ron. *Shakespeare Bats Cleanup.* Candlewick, 2003. Ages 11–14.

Lynch, Chris. *Shadow Boxer.* HarperCollins, 1993. Ages 14–18.

Lupica, Mike. *Heat.* Philomel, 2006. Ages 11–15.

———. *Travel Team.* Philomel, 2004. Ages 10–13.

Myers, Walter Dean. *Slam!* Scholastic, 1996. Ages 12–18.

Powell, Randy. *Run If You Dare.* Farrar, 2001. Ages 12–16.

Ritter, John H. *The Boy Who Saved Baseball.* Philomel, 2003. Ages 10–13.

———. *Choosing Up Sides.* Philomel, 1998. Ages 10–14.

———. *Under the Baseball Moon.* Philomel, 2006. Ages 11–14.

Roberts, Kristi. *My Thirteenth Season.* Holt, 2005. Ages 10–14.

Spinelli, Jerry. *There's a Girl in My Hammerlock.* Simon & Schuster, 1991. Ages 10–16.

Mysteries

Abrahams, Peter. *Down the Rabbit Hole.* Harper-Collins, 2005. Ages 11–15.

Allison, Jennifer. *Gilda Joyce: Psychic Investigator.* Dutton, 2005. Ages 10–14. Humor.

Alphin, Elaine Marie. *The Perfect Shot.* Carolrhoda, 2005. Ages 12–18. Flashbacks.

Balliett, Blue. *Chasing Vermeer.* Illustrated by Brett Helquist. Scholastic, 2004. Ages 9–14.

———. *The Wright 3.* Illustrated by Brett Helquist. Scholastic, 2006. Ages 9–14.

Broach, Elise. *Shakespeare's Secret.* Holt, 2005. Ages 11–15.

Coman, Carolyn. *The Big House.* Illustrated by Rob Shepperson. Front Street, 2004. Ages 8–12. Humor.

Crew, Gary. *Angel's Gate.* Simon & Schuster, 1995. Ages 11–16.

Curtis, Christopher Paul. *Mr. Chickee's Funny Money.* Random, 2005. Ages 9–13. Humor.

DeFelice, Cynthia. *Death at Devil's Track.* Farrar, 2000. Ages 10–13.

———. *The Missing Manatee.* Farrar, 2005. Ages 10–14.

Fitzgerald, John D. *The Great Brain Is Back.* Dial, 1995. Ages 8–11.

Fleischman, Sid. *Bo & Mzzz Mad.* Greenwillow, 2001. Ages 10–13. Humor.

Hiaasen, Carl. *Flush.* Knopf, 2005. Ages 10–14.

Hobbs, Will. *Ghost Canoe.* Morrow, 1997. Ages 11–14.

Jennings, Richard W. *Mystery in Mt. Mole.* Houghton, 2003. Ages 9–12.

Plum-Ucci, Carol. *The Body of Christopher Creed.* Harcourt, 2000. Ages 13–18.

Sachar, Louis. *Holes.* Farrar, 1998. Ages 10–14.

———. *Small Steps.* Delacorte, 2005. Ages 10–14. Sequel to *Holes.*

Sobol, Donald J. *Encyclopedia Brown and the Case of Pablo's Nose.* Illustrated by Eric Velasquez. Delacorte, 1996. Ages 8–11.

Sorrells, Walter. *Fake ID.* Dutton, 2005. Ages 12–16.

Springer, Nancy. *The Case of the Missing Marquess: An Enola Holmes Mystery.* Philomel, 2005. Ages 10–14.

Van Draanen, Wendelin. *Sammy Keyes and the Hotel Thief.* Knopf, 1998. Another in this series with a female protagonist is *Sammy Keyes and the Sisters of Mercy.* Knopf, 1999. Ages 9–12. Also *Sammy Keyes and the Search for Snake Eyes.* Knopf, 2002. Ages 10–13. Also *Sammy Keyes and the Dead Giveaway.* Knopf, 2005.

Werlin, Nancy. *Black Mirror.* Dial, 2001. Ages 12–18.

———. *Double Helix.* Dial, 2004. Ages 12–18.

———. *The Killer's Cousin.* Delacorte, 1998. Ages 12–18.

Moral Choices

Bauer, Marion Dane. *The Double-Digit Club.* Holiday House, 2004. Ages 9–12.

Curtis, Christopher Paul. *Bucking the Sarge.* Random, 2004. Ages 11–16. Humor.

DeFelice, Cynthia. *Under the Same Sky.* Farrar, 2003. Ages 12–15.

Flake, Sharon. G. *Money Hungry.* Hyperion, 2001. Ages 12–16.

Fleischman, Paul. *Whirligig.* Holt, 1998. Ages 12–16.

Myers, Walter Dean. *Monster.* HarperCollins, 1999. Ages 13–18.

Naylor, Phyllis Reynolds. *Shiloh.* Atheneum, 1991. Ages 8–11.

O'Connor, Barbara. *Taking Care of Moses.* Farrar, 2004. Ages 9–12.

Park, Linda Sue. *Project Mulberry.* Clarion, 2005. Ages 10–13.

Soto, Gary. *Baseball in April and Other Stories.* Harcourt, 1991. Ages 10–18.

Spinelli, Jerry. *Maniac Magee.* HarperCollins, 1990. Ages 9–12.

Woodson, Jacqueline. *Hush.* Putnam, 2002. Ages 11–15.

Yolen, Jane, and Bruce Coville. *Armageddon Summer.* Harcourt, 1998. Ages 11–13. Chapters alternate between boy and girl protagonists.

Romance and Sexuality

Anderson, Laurie Halse. *Speak.* Farrar, 1999. Ages 12–18.

Conford, Ellen. *I Love You, I Hate You, Get Lost.* Scholastic, 1994. (COL) Ages 11–15. Humor.

Deak, Erzsi, and Kristin Embry Litchman, editors. *Period Pieces.* HarperCollins, 2003. (COL) Ages 10–14.

Flake, Sharon. *Who Am I without Him?* Hyperion, 2004. (COL) Ages 11–18.

Fox, Paula. *The Eagle Kite.* Orchard, 1995. Ages 11–16.

Hartinger, Brent. *Geography Club.* HarperTempest, 2003. Ages 12–18.

Howe, James. *Totally Joe.* Atheneum, 2005. Ages 10–14.

Kerr, M. E. *Deliver Us from Evie.* HarperCollins, 1994. Ages 12–18.

Larochelle, David. *Absolutely, Positively Not.* Scholastic, 2005. Ages 12–18. Humor.

Lawrence, Iain. *Ghost Boy.* Delacorte, 2000. Ages 12–18.

Naylor, Phyllis Reynolds. *The Grooming of Alice.* Simon & Schuster, 2000. Ages 11–13.

Nelson, Theresa. *Earthshine.* Watts, 1994. Ages 10–14.

Peters, Julie Anne. *Luna.* Little, Brown, 2004. Ages 13–18.

Sanchez, Alex. *So Hard to Say.* Simon & Schuster, 2004. Ages 11–15.

Sones, Sonya. *What My Mother Doesn't Know.* Simon & Schuster, 2001. Ages 12–16. Free verse.

Tashjian, Janet. *The Gospel According to Larry.* Holt, 2001. Ages 12–16.

Van Draanen, Wendelin. *Flipped.* Knopf, 2001. Ages 10–14.

Wild, Margaret. *One Night.* Knopf, 2004. Ages 12–18. Free verse.

Williams. Lori Aurelia. *When Kambia Elaine Flew in from Neptune.* Simon & Schuster, 2001. Ages 12–18.

Wolff, Virginia Euwer. *Make Lemonade.* Holt, 1993. Ages 12–18.

———. *True Believer.* Atheneum, 2001. Ages 11–16. Free verse.

Woodson, Jacqueline. *From the Notebooks of Melanin Sun.* Scholastic, 1995. Ages 11–16.

———. *The House You Pass on the Way.* Delacorte, 1997. Ages 11–16.

Young, Karen Romano. *The Beetle and Me: A Love Story.* Greenwillow, 1999. Ages 11–16.

Coming of Age

Bedard, Michael. *Stained Glass.* Tundra, 2001. Ages 12–18.

French, Simon. *Where in the World.* Peachtree, 2003. Ages 10–13.

Henkes, Kevin. *Olive's Ocean.* Greenwillow, 2003. Ages 10–13.

Lawrence, Iain. *Ghost Boy.* Delacorte, 2000. Ages 12–18.

Leavitt, Martine. *Tom Finder.* Red Deer Press, 2003. Ages 12–18.

Lynch, Chris. *Slot Machine.* HarperCollins, 1995. Ages 13–16. Humor. Also *Extreme Elvin* (1999) and *Me, Dear Dad & Alcatraz* (2005).

Oates, Joyce Carol. *Small Avalanches and Other Stories.* HarperCollins, 2003. (COL) Ages 14–18.

Olsen, Sylvia. *The Girl with a Baby.* Sono Nis, 2004. Ages 12–18.

Peters, Julie Anne. *Mom and Jo.* Little, Brown, 2006. Ages 12–14.

Rylant, Cynthia. *A Fine White Dust.* Bradbury, 1986. Ages 9–12.

Saldaña, René, Jr. *Finding Our Way.* Wendy Lamb, 2003. (COL) Ages 12–16. Collection of 12 short stories about Latino experiences.

Salisbury, Graham. *Island Boyz: Short Stories.* Wendy Lamb, 2002. (COL) Ages 12–16. Set in Hawaii.

St. Anthony, Jane. *The Summer Sherman Loved Me.* Farrar, 2006. Ages 10–14.

Adventure and Survival

Bauer, Joan. *Backwater.* Putnam, 1999. Ages 12–16.

Coleman, Michael. *Weirdo's War.* Orchard, 1998. Ages 9–13.

Couloumbis, Audrey. *The Misadventures of Maude March, or, Trouble Rides a Fast Horse.* Random, 2005. Ages 10–13. Humor.

Creech, Sharon. *The Wanderer.* HarperCollins, 2000. Ages 11–14.

Ellis, Sarah. *The Several Lives of Orphan Jack.* Illustrated by Bruno St.-Aubin. Groundwood, 2003. Ages 7–11.

Farmer, Nancy. *A Girl Named Disaster.* Orchard, 1996. Ages 11–16.

Fleischman, Sid. *Bo and Mzzz Mad.* Greenwillow, 2001. Ages 10–13.

George, Jean Craighead. *Julie.* HarperCollins, 1994. Ages 11–15.

———. *Julie of the Wolves.* Illustrated by John Schoenherr. Harper, 1972. Ages 11–15.

———. *My Side of the Mountain.* Dutton, 1959. Ages 9–12.

Hobbs, Will. *Crossing the Wire.* HarperCollins, 2006. Ages 10–15.

———. *Jackie's Wild Seattle.* HarperCollins, 2003. Ages 10–15.

———. *The Maze.* Morrow, 1998. Ages 11–16.

———. *Wild Man Island.* HarperCollins, 2002. Ages 11–16.

Jennings, Richard W. *The Great Whale of Kansas.* Houghton, 2001. Ages 10–13.

Key, Watt. *Alabama Moon.* Farrar, 2006. Ages 11–15.

Lee, Tanith. *Piratica: Being a Daring Tale of a Singular Girl's Adventure Upon the High Seas.* Dutton, 2004. Ages 11–14. Presented in three acts.

Mikaelsen, Ben. *Touching Spirit Bear.* HarperCollins, 2001. Ages 11–18.

Myers, Walter Dean. *Scorpions.* Harper, 1988. Ages 10–16.

Paulsen, Gary. *Hatchet.* Bradbury, 1987. Ages 9–12.

———. *The River.* Delacorte, 1991. Ages 10–16.

Philbrick, Rodman. *The Young Man and the Sea.* Scholastic, 2004. Ages 10–14.

Salisbury, Graham. *Lord of the Deep.* Delacorte, 2001. Ages 11–15.

Snicket, Lemony. *The End: Book the Thirteenth.* Illustrated by Brett Helquist. HarperCollins, Ages 10–14. The last of this series of adventure and clever satire.

Taylor, Theodore. *Ice Drift.* Harcourt, 2004. Ages 9–13.

———. *Rogue Wave: And Other Red-Blooded Sea Stories.* Harcourt, 1996. (COL) Ages 10–15.

Related Films, Videos, and DVDs

Because of Winn-Dixie. (2005). Author: Kate DiCamillo (2000). 106 minutes.

Bridge to Terabithia. (1985). Author: Katherine Paterson (1977). 58 minutes.

A Cry in the Wild. (1990). Author Gary Paulsen, *Hatchet* (1987). 82 minutes.

Finding Buck McHenry. (2000). Author: Alfred Slote (1991). 94 minutes.

Harriet the Spy. (1996). Author: Louis Fitzhugh (1964). 102 minutes.

Holes. (2003). Author: Louis Sachar (1998). 117 minutes.

Homeward Bound. (1993). Author: Sheila Burnford, *The Incredible Journey* (1961). 84 minutes.

Hoot. (2006). Author: Carl Hiaasen (2002). 91 minutes.

Iron Will. (1993). Author: John Reynolds Gardiner, *Stone Fox* (1980). 109 minutes.

Lemony Snicket's A Series of Unfortunate Events. (2004). Author: Daniel Handler, *The Bad Beginning* (1999). 107 minutes.

Maniac Magee. (1992). Author: Jerry Spinelli (1990). 30 minutes.

The Mighty. (1998). Author: Rodman Philbrick, *Freak the Mighty* (1993). 100 minutes.

Shiloh. (1997). Also *Shiloh 2.* (1999). Author: Phyllis Reynolds Naylor, *Shiloh* (1991) and *Shiloh Season* (1996). 93 minutes, 96 minutes.

Summer of the Monkeys. (1998). Author: Wilson Rawls (1976). 101 minutes.

Whale Rider. (2002). Author: Witi Ihimaera (2003/1987). 101 minutes.

Where the Red Fern Grows. (2003). Author: Wilson Rawls (1961). 86 minutes.

Sources for Films, Videos, and DVDs

The Video Source Book. Syosset, NY: National Video Clearinghouse, 1979–. Published by Gale Research, Detroit, MI.

An annual reference work that lists media and provides sources for purchase and rental.

Websites of large video distributors:

www.libraryvideo.com
www.knowledgeunlimited.com

chapter 9

Historical Fiction

Ancestors

On the wind-beaten plains
once lived my ancestors.
In the days of peaceful moods,
they wandered and hunted.
In days of need or greed,
they warred and loafed.
Beneath the lazy sun, kind winds above,
they laughed and feasted.
Through the starlit night, under the moon,
they dreamed and loved.
Now, from the wind-beaten plains,
only their dust rises.

—Grey Cohoe

Historical fiction brings history to life by placing appealing child characters in accurately described historical settings. By telling the stories of these characters' everyday lives as well as presenting their triumphs and failures, authors of historical fiction provide young readers with the human side of history, making it more real and more memorable.

Definition and Description

Historical fiction is realistic fiction set in a time remote enough from the present to be considered history. Stories about events that occurred at least one generation (defined as twenty years or more) prior to the date of the original publication have been included in this chapter and categorized as historical fiction.

Although historical fiction stories are imaginary, it is within the realm of possibility that such events could have occurred. In these stories, historical facts blend with imaginary characters and plot. The facts are actual historical events, authentic period settings, and real historical figures. An imaginary story is constructed around these facts. In the *Reference Guide to Historical Fiction for Children and Young Adults,* Adamson (1987) states:

> Historical fiction recreates a particular historical period with or without historical figures as incidental characters. It is generally written about a time period in which the author has not lived or no more recently than one generation before its composition. For example, fiction written in 1987 must be set, at the latest, in 1967, to be considered historical. Fiction written in 1930 but set in 1925 does not fulfill this criterion for legitimate historical fiction. (p. ix)

In the most common form of historical fiction, the main characters of the story are imaginary, but some secondary characters may be actual historical figures. An example of this type of historical fiction is the classic novel *Johnny Tremain* by Esther Forbes. Set in the U.S. Revolutionary War period, this story tells of Johnny, a fictitious character, who is apprenticed to a silversmith. In the course of the story, Samuel Adams, John Hancock, and Paul Revere are introduced as minor characters. Another example, Carolyn Meyer's *Mary, Bloody Mary,* written from Mary's point of view, is set in sixteenth-century England. Mary Tudor, who was briefly Queen of England, interacts with her father, King Henry, Anne Boleyn, and other court figures.

In another form of historical fiction, the past is described complete with the social traditions, customs, morals, and values of the period but with no mention of an actual historical event nor actual historical figures as characters. The physical location is also accurately reconstructed for the readers. An example of this story type is *The Witch of Blackbird Pond* by Elizabeth George Speare. The Puritan way of life in Connecticut in the 1600s is depicted in this story about young Kit from Barbados who becomes involved in a witchcraft trial. Another example of this type of story is Geraldine McCaughrean's *Stop the Train!* in which the Oklahoma Land Rush and homesteading in the 1890s are captured in lively detail.

A third type of historical story is one in which elements of fantasy are found, and therefore the story does *not* qualify as historical fiction. For example, time warps and other supernatural features may be found in Thea Beckman's *Crusade in Jeans* and in Jane Yolen's *The Devil's Arithmetic.* These stories are **historical fantasy** and are included in Chapter 7.

 # Evaluation and Selection of Historical Fiction

Historical fiction must first tell an engaging story, have rounded, complex characters with whom children can identify, and impart a universal theme that is worthy and thought provoking without being didactic. In addition, historical fiction must present historical facts with as much accuracy

Excellent Historical Fiction to Read Aloud

Curtis, Christopher Paul. *Bud, Not Buddy.* Ages 9–13.
Cushman, Karen. *The Loud Silence of Francine Green.* Ages 11–15.
Kadohata, Cynthia. *Kira Kira.* Ages 10–15.
Park, Linda Sue. *A Single Shard.* Ages 9–13.
Peck, Richard. *The River Between Us.* Ages 12–18.
Provensen, Alice. *Klondike Gold.* Ages 7–10.
Ray, Delia. *Ghost Girl: A Blue Ridge Mountain Story.* Ages 10–13.
Roy, Jennifer. *Yellow Star.* Ages 10–15.
Salisbury, Graham. *House of the Red Fish.* Ages 10–15.
Turner, Ann. *Mississippi Mud: Three Prairie Journals.* Illustrated by
    Robert J. Clark. Ages 5–8.
White, Ruth. *Tadpole.* Ages 10–15.
Wolff, Virginia Euwer. *Bat 6.* Ages 10–18.
Woodson, Jacqueline. *Coming on Home Soon.* Illustrated by E. B.
    Lewis. Ages 5–9.

and objectivity as books of history. This means that a setting must be described in sufficient detail as to provide an authentic sense of that time and that place without overwhelming the story. Details such as hair and clothing styles, home architecture and furnishings, foods and food preparation, and modes of transportation must be subtly woven into the story to provide a convincing, authentic period setting. The characters must act within the traditions and norms of their times.

Expressing the language or dialect of the period presents a particular challenge to the author of historical stories. Dialogue that occurs within the text often becomes problematic for the writer. If the speech of the period is greatly different from that of today, then the author faces a decision: Remain true to the language of the time but cause readers difficulties in comprehending, or present the language in today's dialect but lose the flavor and authenticity of the language of the period. In any case, it seems important that the language not jar the reader by its obvious inappropriateness or lose the reader by its extreme difficulty. Most children's authors strive to attain the middle ground—some flavor of a language difference but modified to be understandable to the child reader.

Many educators are convinced of the benefits students gain through integrating history and literature as part of the social studies curriculum. Smith, Monson, and Dobson (1992) found that the students in fifth-grade classrooms in which historical novels were used along with standard instructional materials recalled more historical facts and indicated greater enjoyment in their social studies classes than the students in classrooms that had a similar curriculum without the addition of historical novels.

Many adults today are unaware that the history they learned as children may have been biased or one-sided. Some authors attempt to include more modern interpretations of historical events in historical fiction by setting the record straight or adding a minority presence to the story. However, as was previously mentioned, care must be taken that the characters behave in a historically accurate fashion.

The Scott O'Dell Award, established in 1982 by the author Scott O'Dell, honors what is judged to be the most outstanding work of children's historical fiction published in the previous year. The work must be written by a U.S. citizen and be set in the New World. The Scott O'Dell Award winners found in Appendix A can be a source of outstanding historical fiction for use with students. The National Council of Social Studies publishes a list of the most notable trade books in the field of social studies from the preceding year in the April/May issue of its journal, *Social Education.* This list includes many works of historical fiction, as well as nonfiction works, and is a useful source to locate recent books of this genre.

Early Books and Trends in Historical Fiction

Although historical stories were written for children as early as the 1800s, few titles remain of interest from those early years. The early books placed an emphasis on exciting events and idealized real-life characters—much in the style of heroic legends.

Between World War I and World War II, a few historical stories appeared in which well-developed characters involved in realistic events were portrayed in authentic period settings. Between 1932 and 1943, the first eight books of the Little House series by Laura Ingalls Wilder were published. These stories have continued to grow in popularity, partially as a result of the long-lasting television series based on the books. *Johnny Tremain* by Esther Forbes was awarded the Newbery Medal in 1944 and is considered a children's classic.

The period after World War II saw a flowering of historical fiction for children in both English and American literature. Many outstanding books were published in the fifteen years following the war. Examples are *The Door in the Wall* by Marguerite de Angeli, published in 1949; *Calico Captive* by Elizabeth George Speare, published in 1957; the best-selling Newbery Medal–winning book *The Witch of Blackbird Pond* by Elizabeth George Speare, published in 1958; and *The Cabin Faced West* by Jean Fritz, published in 1958. In 1954, the Laura Ingalls Wilder Award was awarded to (and named for) Laura Ingalls Wilder, an author of historical fiction. This award, the "Hall of Fame" of children's authors and illustrators, honors an author or illustrator whose books, published in the United States, have made a substantial and lasting contribution to children's literature. By 1960, the genre of historical fiction was well established as a fine resource for children's enjoyment and enrichment. The accompanying Milestones feature highlights the development of historical fiction.

Historical fiction continues to flourish today. Some older historical fiction novels have been criticized for portraying some cultural groups in an extremely negative light. For example, two Newbery Medal winners, *Caddie Woodlawn* by Carol Ryrie Brink and *The Matchlock Gun* by Walter D. Edmonds, have been faulted for their negative portrayals of Native Americans. However, minority authors have written a number of excellent works based on the early experiences of their cultural groups in North America; for example, see *Song of the Trees* and its sequels by Mildred Taylor and *Journey to Topaz* and its sequel by Yoshiko Uchida. The establishment in 1982 of the Scott O'Dell Award for Historical Fiction has begun to offer additional recognition for authors of this genre.

Topics in Historical Fiction

Two ways of considering the topics treated in historical fiction novels are by the universal themes presented in the books and by the historical periods in which the books are set. First, some *common themes* that can be found within historical fiction novels for children are suggested with titles of books in which the theme is developed. Next, seven *historical periods* are reviewed in capsule form.

MILESTONES in the Development of Historical Fiction

Date	Event	Significance
1888	*Otto of the Silver Hand* by Howard Pyle	Early recognized work of historical fiction
1929	The Newbery Medal given to *The Trumpeter of Krakow* by Eric Kelly	National recognition for an early work of historical fiction
1932–1943	Publication of the first eight books of *Little House* series by Laura Ingalls Wilder	Classic historical fiction
1944	*Johnny Tremain* by Esther Forbes given the Newbery Medal	Classic historical adventure set during the American Revolution era
1949–1960	Many historical novels published, including *The Witch of Blackbird Pond* by Elizabeth George Speare and *The Lantern Bearers* by Rosemary Sutcliff	Dramatic increase in the quality and quantity of historical novels for children
1954	Establishment of the Laura Ingalls Wilder Award, first awarded to Wilder	Recognition of a historical fiction author for the entire body of her work
1961	Scott O'Dell's *Island of the Blue Dolphins* awarded the Newbery Medal	Landmark book of historical fiction with a strong female protagonist from a minority culture
1971	*Journey to Topaz* by Yoshiko Uchida	Early historical work about and by a minority (Japanese American)
1972	Scott O'Dell awarded the Hans Christian Andersen Award	International recognition of a U.S. author of historical novels
1975	*The Song of the Trees* by Mildred Taylor	First in a series of books about an African-American family's struggle starting in the Depression era
1982	Establishment of the Scott O'Dell Award	Award given for outstanding historical novel set in North America brings recognition to the genre
1989	Elizabeth George Speare awarded the Laura Ingalls Wilder Award	Recognition of an author of historical fiction for her substantial contribution to children's literature

Universal Themes in Historical Fiction

Common themes that extend across time and place in historical stories can be an approach for presenting historical fiction to children. For example, a theme, such as seeking new frontiers, is explored through a small group of books set in different times and places. Some possible themes for development in this manner are listed here with suggestions of books that might be considered for the study of the theme. Other themes may be discovered when you read historical fiction novels and consider the commonalities to be found among them.

Seeking New Frontiers

The Ballad of Lucy Whipple by Karen Cushman. Ages 10–13.
Frozen Summer by Mary Jane Auch. Ages 11–15.
The Barn by Avi. Ages 9–13.
Worth by A. Lafaye. Ages 10–14.
The Legend of Bass Reeves by Gary Paulsen. Ages 10–14.
Crooked River by Shelley Pearsall. Ages 10–13.
Mississippi Mud: Three Prairie Journals by Ann Turner. Illustrated by Robert J. Clark. Ages 10–14.
Double Crossing: A Jewish Immigration Story by Eve Tal. Ages 11–15.
I Have Heard of a Land by Joyce Carol Thomas. Illustrated by Floyd Cooper. Ages 8–12.
Black Storm Comin' by Diane Lee Wilson. Ages 11–16.

Search for Freedom from Persecution

Emil and Karl by Yankev Glatshteyn. Ages 10–15.
Star of Fear, Star of Hope by Jo Hoestlandt. Illustrated by Johanna Kang. Ages 9–12.
Yellow Star by Jennifer Roy. Ages 10–15.
Letters from Rifka by Karen Hesse. Ages 9–12.
Flight to Freedom by Anna Veciana-Suarez. Ages 11–16.
The Traitor by Laurence Yep. Ages 10–14.
The Cats in Krasinski Square by Karen Hesse. Illustrated by Wendy Watson. Ages 9–12.

Effects of War

Bat 6 by Virginia Euwer Wolff. Ages 10–15.
The Purple Heart by Marc Talbert. Ages 10–13.
Soldier Boys by Dean Hughes. Ages 13–18.
Private Peaceful by Michael Morpurgo. Ages 13–18.
Eyes Like Willy's by Juanita Havill. Illustrated by David Johnson. Ages 12–16.
Willow Run by Patricia Reilly Giff. Ages 9–12.
The Butterfly by Patricia Polacco. Ages 9–12.

Family Closeness in Times of Adversity

Fever 1793 by Laurie Halse Anderson. Ages 11–15.
Nory Ryan's Song by Patricia Reilly Giff. Ages 9–13.
Esperanza Rising by Pam Muñoz Ryan. Ages 9–13.
The Well: David's Story by Mildred Taylor. Ages 9–13.
Ghost Girl: A Blue Ridge Mountain Story by Delia Ray. Ages 9–14.
House of the Red Fish by Graham Salisbury. Ages 10–15.
Show Way by Jacqueline Woodson. Illustrated by Hudson Talbott. Ages 8–11.
Going North by Janice Harrington. Illustrated by Jerome Lagarrigue. Ages 7–11.

Periods of History in Fiction

The natural relationship of historical fiction stories to the study of history and geography suggests building whole units of study around periods of both world and U.S. history in which good stories for children are set. The following capsule statements about seven historical periods will give you an idea of how these units might be organized. Historical fiction books for units on other eras can be selected from the lists at the end of chapter, and biographies can be found in the lists

Notable Authors of Historical Fiction

Avi [Wortis], author noted for the Newbery Award–winning historical fiction novel *Crispin: The Cross of Lead* and two Newbery Honor books, including *The True Confessions of Charlotte Doyle*. www.avi-writer.com

Christopher Paul Curtis, African-American author of two historical novels: the Newbery Medal book, *Bud, Not Buddy*, a Depression era novel, and Newbery Honor book, *The Watsons Go to Birmingham—1963*. www.christopherpaulcurtis.com

Karen Cushman, author of two Newbery acclaimed historical novels set in the Middle Ages. *Catherine, Called Birdy; The Midwife's Apprentice*. www.karencushman.com

Karen Hesse, author of Newbery Medal winner, *Out of the Dust*, set in Oklahoma in the 1930s. Also noted for historical novel *Letters from Rifka* and *The Cats in Krasinski Square*.

Kimberly Willis Holt, author of novels about characters with disabilities and set in small towns of the American South. *My Louisiana Sky; When Zachary Beaver Came to Town*. www.kimberlywillisholt.com

Lois Lowry, author of the historical fiction novels, *Number the Stars*, Newbery Medal winner, and *The Silent Boy*. Also noted for works of science fiction, *The Giver*. www.loislowry.com

Linda Sue Park, Newbery Award–winning author whose novels about historical eras in Korea bring understanding about another culture. *A Single Shard; When My Name Was Keoko; The Kite Fighters*. www.lindasuepark.com

Richard Peck, Newbery Award–winning author noted for his young adult novels and his historical novels set in rural Illinois. *A Year Down Yonder; The River Between Us*. www.richardpeck.smartwriters.com

Carolyn Reeder, author of historical novels set in the U.S. Civil War era. *Across the Lines; Shades of Gray; Before the Creeks Ran Red*. www.reederbooks.com

Graham Salisbury, an author who writes historical and realistic novels set in the Hawaiian Islands where he was raised. *Under the Blood-Red Sun;* its sequel, *House of the Red Fish; Eyes of the Emperor*. www.grahamsalisbury.com

Mildred Taylor, author of seven stories of an African-American land-owning family, beginning in the 1930s and set in rural Mississippi. *Roll of Thunder, Hear My Cry*.

Gloria Whelan, winner of the National Book Award for young people's literature for *Homeless Bird*, set in India. Also wrote *Angel on the Square*, set in Russia. www.gloriawhelan.com

Laurence Yep, author of historical fiction about Chinese Americans and their adjustments to life in the United States. *Dragonwings; Spring Pearl*.

at the end of Chapter 10, where you will find books organized by the seven historical periods beginning 3000 B.C.

Beginnings of Civilization up to 3000 B.C.

This period represents prehistoric cultures and civilizations. Early peoples (Java, Neanderthals, Cro-Magnons) and early civilizations in the Middle East and Asia are included. Egyptians, Syrians, and Phoenicians developed civilizations; and Hebrews produced a religious faith, Judaism, that resulted in the Old Testament. The subcontinent of India was the site of Aryan civilizations. Chinese dynasties were responsible for excellent works of art and agricultural systems of irrigation. Good examples of historical novels set in this time period are Peter Dickinson's *A Bone from a Dry Sea* and Betty Levin's *Thorn*.

Civilizations of the Ancient World, 3000 B.C. to A.D. 600

The era of the Greek city-states was followed by a period of Roman rule in western Europe. Christianity was founded in Jerusalem and spread throughout Europe. Ancient Asia was the site of enduring civilizations that bred two remarkable men born about 560 B.C.: the Indian religious leader Buddha and the Chinese philosopher Confucius. Both have had a lasting influence on their civilizations. Sonia Levitin's *Escape from Egypt*, a novel set in this time period, retells the story of Moses leading his people from Egypt to the promised land.

Civilizations of the Medieval World, 600 to 1500

The eastern part of the Roman Empire maintained its stability and preserved the civilization from the capital of Constantinople. This civilization, the Byzantine Empire, created a distinct culture and branch of the Christian Church—the Orthodox Church—which influenced Russia to adopt both the religion and the culture. The rise of the Islamic religion began in the early 600s with Muhammad preaching in Mecca. Following the fall of the Roman Empire, western Europe dissolved into isolated separate regions without strong governments. Many of the responsibilities of government were carried out by the Christian Church. The Church dominated the economic, political, cultural, and educational life of the Middle Ages in western Europe. These feudal societies eventually gave rise to the separate nations of modern Europe. During this era, early African and American civilizations arose independently. The great civilizations of China and Japan continued to flourish throughout these centuries. As examples, K. M. Grant's *Blood Red Horse* and Karen Cushman's *Catherine, Called Birdy* portray medieval life in England.

The Emergence of Modern Nations, 1500 to 1800

The Renaissance, a literary and artistic movement, swept western Europe. Many important developments of this period included the invention of the printing press, a new emphasis on reason, a reformation of the Christian Church, and advances in science. During this same period, central governments throughout Europe increased their power. Spain, and then France, dominated Europe in the 1500s and 1600s. In the 1700s, Russia, Austria, and Prussia rose to power. This was also a time when Europeans explored and settled in Africa, India, and the Americas. The Portuguese and Spanish took the lead in explorations and acquired many foreign colonies. England, the Netherlands, France, and Russia also colonized and influenced East Asia, India, Africa, and the Americas.

Revolutions created new governments and new nations. The American Revolution (1776–1781) created a new nation; the French Revolution in 1789 affected the direction of governments toward democracy in all of Europe. Napoleon built an empire across Europe, resulting in the uniting of European nations to defeat Napoleon. The nations of Latin America also began to gain their independence. China expanded gradually under the Ming and Ch'ing dynasties. Japan prospered under the Tokugawa shogunate. The United States and Canada were the sites of rapid population increases due to immigration; the settlements in North America were predominantly along the eastern coasts. Some westward expansion was beginning in the United States and Canada. For example, a story relating the challenges of settling the Maine frontier in the 1700s is Elizabeth George Speare's *The Sign of the Beaver*.

The Development of Industrial Society, 1800 to 1914

The 1800s were marked by a rapid shift from agricultural societies to industrial societies. Great Britain was an early site for this change. The factory system developed and prospered, while working and living conditions deteriorated for the worker. Two stories about life as a millworker in this period are Katherine Paterson's *Lyddie* and James Lincoln Collier and Christopher Collier's *The Clock*. New technology—railroad trains, steamboats, the telegraph, and telephone—affected transportation and communications. Advances in science and medicine helped to explain the nature of life and improved the quality of life. Education developed into an important institution in western Europe and North America. Europe underwent revolutions that readjusted boundaries and eventually led to the unification of new nations. The colonization of sub-Saharan Africa by European nations expanded rapidly from 1870 to 1890. Most of the region was under control of the various European nations by the end of this period.

The westward movement was fully realized as pioneers settled across the United States and Canada. The building of railroads hastened the establishment of new settlements. Native Americans struggled for survival in the face of these massive population shifts. Black slavery had existed in the American colonies from earliest days, but in the 1800s, slavery became a social and economic issue. Julius Lester's *Day of Tears: A Novel in Dialogue* reconstructs the largest slave auction in American history that took place in Savannah, Georgia, in 1859. The despair and tragedy of slavery through the personal accounts of the slaves and the slave owners are vividly portrayed. Slavery was abolished as a result of the Civil War (1861–1865) and the Union was preserved at the cost of 600,000 lives and a major rift between the North and the South. Carolyn Reeder's *Shades of Gray* portrays a family torn apart by this war.

The United States grew in economic and political strength. An age of imperialism resulted in firm control of large areas of the world by other world powers such as England, France, and Belgium. Great Britain dominated India and parts of Africa and continued its influence over Canada, Australia, and New Zealand, while Japan became a powerful force in east Asia.

World Wars in the Twentieth Century, 1914 to 1945

This era includes World War I (1914–1918) in Europe, in which the United States and Canada joined and fought with the Allies (Great Britain, France, Russia, Greece, and Rumania); the between-wars period that included the Great Depression; Hitler's rise to power in 1933; and World War II (1939–1945) in Europe and Asia, in which Canada and the United States joined forces with England, France, and Russia to battle Germany, Italy, and Japan. In 1917, the Bolshevik Revolution established a Communist government in Russia. In 1931, Great Britain recognized Canada, Australia, New Zealand, and South Africa as completely independent. However, each nation declared its loyalty to the British monarch and continued its cultural ties with Great Britain. The Holocaust during World War II—the persecution and killing of Jewish and other people by the Nazi regime—stands out as one of the most atrocious periods in modern history. In Jennifer Roy's *Yellow Star*, Sylvia, a Jewish girl, and her family struggle to survive in the Lodz ghetto in Poland from 1939 to 1945 during the Nazi occupation. World War II ended shortly after the United States dropped nuclear devices on Hiroshima and Nagasaki, Japan.

Post-World War II Era, 1945 to 1980s

During this era, the United States and western European nations were involved in a struggle for world influence against the Communist nations, particularly the Soviet Union and China. A massive arms buildup, including nuclear weapons, was undertaken by the major nations of both sides. The Korean War (1950–1953) and the Vietnam War (1965–1973) were major conflicts in which the United States fought to contain Communist expansion. The Korean War, combined with the postwar economic recovery of Japan, drew attention to the growing importance of East

Asia in world affairs. A novel for children, *The Purple Heart* by Marc Talbert, describes the Vietnam War era. The Soviet Union launched a series of satellites beginning with *Sputnik I* on October 4, 1957, inaugurating the space age. An explosion of scientific knowledge occurred as a result of increased spending for weapons development and space exploration. The 1950s, 1960s, and 1970s have been described as the Cold War decades because of the increasing hostility between the Soviet Union and the United States, gradually ending with the defeat of the Soviet regime in the early 1990s. In the 1970s, public pressure mounted in the United States to reduce the nation's external military commitments following the Vietnam War.

During the 1960s, a strong Civil Rights Movement, led by Martin Luther King Jr. and other prominent figures of the era, fought for equal treatment of African Americans. The movement led to desegregation of schools, restaurants, transportation, and housing. Another racial struggle occurred in South Africa against the policies of racial separation in the 1970s and 1980s. The end of apartheid was declared in 1990, followed by free elections in 1994. Equal rights for women were also sought during the feminist movement in the 1970s. An example of a book depicting the civil rights struggle is Christopher Paul Curtis's *The Watsons Go to Birmingham—1963*.

Many fine works of historical fiction for children can now be found. Children have an opportunity to live vicariously the lives of people from long ago—people from different cultures and different parts of the world.

Topics for Further Investigation

- Select and read a historical fiction novel, then research the time period and location of its setting. Contrast the actual historical facts with the events in the story. Develop a time line to display both the historical facts and the story events.
- Choose one of the seven periods of history listed in this chapter. Select five recommended works of historical fiction set in this era and read them to develop a plan for sharing these works with students during a unit of study.
- Pick a theme often found in historical fiction novels and suggested in this chapter. Compare and contrast several books from the list of books exemplifying the theme.

 See the companion website at www.ablongman.com/lynchbrown6e for additional suggestions.

References

Adamson, L. G. (1987). *A reference guide to historical fiction for children and young adults.* Westport, CT: Greenwood Press.

Cohoe, G. (1972). Ancestors. In T. Allen (Ed.), *The whispering wind: Poetry by young American Indians.* New York: Doubleday.

Smith, J. A., Monson, J. A., & Dobson, D. (1992). A case study on integrating history and reading instruction through literature. *Social Education, 56,* 370–375.

Recommended Historical Fiction Books

Ages indicated refer to content appropriateness and conceptual and interest levels. Formats other than novels will be coded as follows:

    (PI) Picture book
    (COL) Short story collection

Locales and dates of settings are noted. Historical biographies are arranged by these same eras and placed at the end of Chapter 10.

Beginnings of Civilization up to 3000 B.C.

Brennan, J. H. *Shiva*. Lippincott, 1990. Ages 11–15. Prehistoric Europe, Neanderthal, and Cro-Magnon tribes. Sequels are *Shiva Accused: An Adventure of the Ice Age* and *Shiva's Challenge: An Adventure of the Ice Age.*

Cowley, Marjorie. *Anooka's Answer*. Clarion, 1998. Ages 10–15. Southern France, Upper Paleolithic era.

———. *Dar and the Spear-Thrower*. Clarion, 1994. Ages 10–15. Southeastern France, Cro-Magnon era.

Craig, Ruth. *Malu's Wolf*. Orchard, 1995. Ages 9–13. Stone Age Europe, prehistory, domestication of wolves.

Denzel, Justin. *Boy of the Painted Cave*. Philomel, 1988. Ages 10–14. Prehistory, Stone Age, France and Spain, cave paintings.

———. *Return to the Painted Cave*. Philomel, 1997. Ages 10–14. Prehistory, Stone Age, France and Spain, cave paintings.

Dickinson, Peter. *A Bone from a Dry Sea*. Delacorte, 1993. Ages 11–15. Story of a prehistoric tribe.

———. *Po's Story*. Putnam, 1998. Ages 8–12. Prehistoric clans. (Others in The Kin series include *Suth's Story,* Putnam, 1998; *Mana's Story,* Putnam, 1999; and *Noli's Story,* Putnam, 1999.)

Levin, Betty. *Thorn*. Front Street, 2005. Ages 12–16. Prehistoric times, birth defects.

Osborne, Chester. *The Memory String*. Atheneum, 1984. Ages 8–12. Siberian Peninsula, 25,000 B.C.

Civilizations of the Ancient World, 3000 B.C. to A.D. 600

Hunter, Mollie. *The Stronghold*. Harper, 1974. Ages 9–14. British Isles, 100 B.C.

Lawrence, Caroline. *The Thieves of Ostia: A Roman Mystery*. Millbrook, 2002. Ages 11–14. Roman port city Ostia, A.D. 79.

Levitin, Sonia. *Escape from Egypt*. Little, Brown, 1994. Ages 14–18. Jews, 1200 B.C.

Paton Walsh, Jill. *Children of the Fox*. Farrar, 1978. Ages 10–14. Ancient Persia, 400 B.C.

Sutcliff, Rosemary. *Frontier Wolf*. Dutton, 1981. Ages 10–16. Young Roman army officer in northern England facing invading tribes, before 409 A.D.

———. *The Light Beyond the Forest: The Quest for the Holy Grail*. Dutton, 1980. Ages 12–18. Recreation of the times of King Arthur and his knights, c. 520 A.D.

———. *The Road to Camlann: The Death of King Arthur*. Dutton, 1982. Ages 12–18.

———. *Song for a Dark Queen*. Crowell, 1978. Ages 10–16. British Isles, revolt against the Romans in 62 A.D.

———. *Sun Horse, Moon Horse*. Dutton, 1978. Ages 10–16. British Isles, pre-Roman England, 100 B.C.

Civilizations of the Medieval World, 600 to 1500

Alder, Elizabeth. *The King's Shadow*. Farrar, 1995. Ages 12–16. England, end of Saxon era, pre-1066.

Avi. *Crispin: At the Edge of the World*. Hyperion, 2006. Ages 10–16. England, 1377.

———. *Crispin: The Cross of Lead*. Hyperion, 2002. Ages 12–16. England, fourteenth century.

Branford, Henrietta. *The Fated Sky*. Candlewick, 1999. Ages 12–16. Norway, Iceland, Viking era.

———. *Fire, Bed, and Bone*. Candlewick, 1998. Ages 10–14. Fourteenth-century England.

Cadnum, Michael. *Book of the Lion*. Viking, 2000. Ages 12–16. Twelfth-century England.

———. *Raven of the Waves*. Orchard, 2001. Ages 12–16. England, Norsemen, A.D. 794.

Cushman, Karen. *Catherine, Called Birdy*. Clarion, 1994. Ages 11–15. England, manor life, 1290s.

———. *Matilda Bone*. Clarion, 2000. Ages 11–15. Medieval England, medical practitioner.

———. *The Midwife's Apprentice*. Clarion, 1995. Ages 12–16. England, Middle Ages.

Dorris, Michael. *Morning Girl.* Hyperion, 1992. Ages 9–12. Taino Indians, 1490s.

Grant, K. M. *Blood Red Horse.* Walker, 2005. Ages 12–16. Crusades, 1185–1193 A.D.

Love, D. Anne. *The Puppeteer's Apprentice.* Simon & Schuster, 2003. Ages 9–12. England in the Middle Ages.

McCaughrean, Geraldine. *The Kite Rider: A Novel.* HarperCollins, 2002. Ages 12–16. China, thirteenth century.

Napoli, Donna Jo. *Breath.* Atheneum, 2003. Ages 14–18. Germany, late 1200s.

———. *Daughter of Venice.* Random, 2002. Ages 11–15. Venice, Italy in the sixteenth century.

Park, Linda Sue. *The Kite Fighters.* Clarion, 2000. Ages 8–12. Korea, 1473.

———. *A Single Shard.* Clarion, 2001. Ages 9–13. Korean village in twelfth century.

Sedgwick, Marcus. *The Dark Horse.* Random, 2003. Ages 12–18. Set in ancient Britain, Viking tribes.

Shulevitz, Uri. *The Travels of Benjamin of Tudela: Through Three Continents in the Twelfth Century.* Farrar, 2005. (PI) Ages 9–14. A journey across southern Europe and the Middle East beginning in 1159.

Skurzynski, Gloria. *Spider's Voice.* Simon & Schuster, 1999. Ages 13–18. Medieval lovers Abélard and Héloïse, France, 1100s.

———. *What Happened in Hamelin.* Four Winds, 1979. Ages 10–14. Germany, 1200s.

Temple, Frances. *The Ramsay Scallop.* Orchard, 1994. Ages 12–16. England, 1299.

Tingle, Rebecca. *The Edge on the Sword.* Putnam, 2001. Ages 11–15. Feudal England in the late 800s.

Yolen, Jane, and Robert Harris. *Girl in a Cage.* Putnam, 2002. Ages 11–16. England in 1306.

The Emergence of Modern Nations, 1500 to 1800

Anderson, Laurie Halse. *Fever 1793.* Simon & Schuster, 2000. Ages 11–16. Philadelphia, yellow fever epidemic, freed slaves' role, 1793.

Bowen, Gary. *Stranded at Plimoth Plantation, 1626.* Illustrated by Gary Bowen. HarperCollins, 1994. (PI) Ages 10–13. Jamestown, settler life, 1620s.

Bruchac, Joseph. *The Arrow over the Door.* Dial, 1998. Ages 9–12. Quaker boy and Abenaki Indian boy in 1777.

———. *The Winter People.* Dial, 2002. Ages 11–16. French and Indian War, Abenaki village, 1759.

Dorris, Michael. *Guests.* Hyperion, 1994. Ages 8–12. First Thanksgiving feast, Native American boy.

———. *Sees behind Trees.* Hyperion, 1996. Ages 8–12. Sixteenth century, pre-Colonial America, partially sighted, Native American boy.

Duble, Kathleen Benner. *The Sacrifice.* Simon & Schuster, 2005. Ages 11–15. U.S. colonial era, Salem witch hunts, 1692.

Forbes, Esther. *Johnny Tremain.* Houghton, 1943. Ages 10–13. U.S. Revolutionary War era, 1770s.

Haugaard, Erik Christian. *The Boy and the Samurai.* Houghton, 1991. Ages 10–13. Japan, 1500s.

———. *The Revenge of the Forty-Seven Samurai.* Houghton, 1995. Ages 12–16. Feudal Japan, 1700s.

Hearn, Julie. *The Minister's Daughter.* Atheneum, 2005. Ages 14–18. Christianity, pregnancy, witchcraft, English village, 1645.

Hesse, Karen. *Stowaway.* Simon & Schuster, 2000. Ages 10–15. British sailing ship, Captain Cook's voyage, 1768.

Ketchum, Liza. *Where the Great Hawk Flies.* Clarion, 2005. Ages 10–14. Relationships between white settlers and Peqout Indians, intermarriage, in Vermont, 1782.

Lasky, Kathryn. *Beyond the Burning Time.* Scholastic, 1994. Ages 11–14. U.S. colonial era, Salem witch trials, 1690s.

Lawrence, Iain. *The Wreckers.* Delacorte, 1998. Ages 10–14. Adventures on the high seas; pirates, treasure, mystery in the 1800s. The trilogy includes *The Smugglers* (1999) and *The Buccaneers* (2001).

Lunn, Janet. *The Hollow Tree.* Viking, 2000. Ages 10–14. U.S. Revolutionary War, 1777.

McCully, Emily Arnold. *Beautiful Warrior.* Arthur A. Levine, 1998. (PI) Ages 9–12. Kung fu; Chinese women near the end of the Ming dynasty, 1600s.

Meyer, Carolyn. *Mary, Bloody Mary.* Harcourt, 1999. Ages 11–15. Mary Tudor and the court of her father, Henry VIII of England, 1600s.

McCaughrean, Geraldine. *The Pirate's Son.* Scholastic, 1998. Ages 12–16. Pirates, England to Madagascar, early 1700s.

McCully, Emily Arnold. *The Escape of Oney Judge: Martha Washington's Slave Finds Freedom.* Farrar, 2007. (PI) Ages 9–12. Washington, D.C., late 1800s.

Myers, Laurie. *The Keeping Room.* Walker, 1997. Ages 9–12. U.S. Revolutionary War, South Carolina.

Park, Linda Sue. *The Firekeeper's Son.* Illustrated by Julie Downing. Clarion, 2003. (PI) Ages 8–12.

Rees, Celia. *Pirates!* Bloomsbury, 2003. Ages 12–16. Swashbuckling adventure in 1725.

Rinaldi, Ann. *A Break with Charity: A Story about the Salem Witch Trials.* Harcourt, 1992. Ages 12–16. Salem witch trials, 1692.

———. *The Fifth of March: A Story of the Boston Massacre.* Harcourt, 1993. Ages 11–15. Boston, indentured servant, 1770s.

———. *A Stitch in Time.* Scholastic, 1994. Ages 12–15. Salem, Massachusetts, family saga, 1788–1791.

Rockwell. Anne. *They Called Her Molly Pitcher.* Illustrated by Cynthia Von Buhler. Knopf, 2002. (PI) Ages 8–11. U.S. Revolutionary War, 1778.

Speare, Elizabeth George. *The Sign of the Beaver.* Houghton, 1983. Ages 8–12. Maine frontier, 1700s.

———. *The Witch of Blackbird Pond.* Houghton, 1958. Ages 10–14. U.S. colonial era, 1680s.

Sturtevant, Katherine. *A True and Faithful Narrative.* Farrar, 2006. Ages 11–16. Seventeenth-century London, England.

———. *At the Sign of the Star.* Farrar, 2000. Ages 10–15. Bookseller in London in 1677.

Turner, Ann. *Katie's Trunk.* Illustrated by Ron Himler. Simon & Schuster, 1992. Ages 7–10. U.S. Revolutionary War, Tory supporters.

Van Leeuwen, Jean. *Hannah's Helping Hands.* Phyllis Fogelman, 1999. Ages 7–10. U.S. Revolutionary War, Connecticut, 1779.

The Development of Industrial Society, 1800 to 1914

Aiken, Joan. *The Teeth of the Gale.* Harper, 1988. Ages 12–18. Spain, 1820s.

Anderson, Rachel. *Black Water.* Holt, 1995. Ages 9–12. Late nineteenth-century England, boy with epilepsy.

Armstrong, Jennifer. *Black-Eyed Susan.* Illustrated by Emily Martindale. Crown, 1995. Ages 8–12. Dakota Territory, pioneer life.

Auch, Mary Jane. *Frozen Summer.* Holt, 1998. Ages 11–15. Pioneer family life in western New York, 1816. Others in this family trilogy: *Journey to Nowhere* (1997) and *Road to Home* (2000).

Avi. *The Barn.* Orchard, 1994. Ages 9–13. Farm life in Oregon in the 1850s.

———. *Beyond the Western Sea: The Escape from Home.* Orchard, 1996. Ages 11–14. Ireland, 1851.

———. *Silent Movie.* Illustrated by C. B. Mordan. Atheneum, 2003. (PI) Ages 8–12. Swedish immigrants, New York City, early 1900s.

———. *The True Confessions of Charlotte Doyle.* Orchard, 1990. Ages 8–12. England, United States, 1830s.

Bartoletti, Susan Campbell. *No Man's Land: A Young Man's Story.* Blue Sky, 1999. Ages 11–15. Confederate Army, Georgia Okefenokee Regiment, U.S. Civil War, 1860s.

Battle-Lavert, Gwendolyn. *Papa's Mark.* Illustrated by Colin Bootman. Holiday, 2003. (PI) Ages 6–9. African-American man voting in post–Civil War South.

Belpré, Pura. *Firefly Summer.* Piñata, 1996. Ages 10–13. Puerto Rico, about 1900.

Blackwood, Gary. *Second Sight.* Dutton, 2005. Ages 11–15. Civil War backdrop, 1864.

Boling, Katharine. *January 1905.* Harcourt, 2004. Ages 9–13. Child labor, U.S. mill town, 1905.

Brown, Don. *Kid Blink Beats the World.* Roaring Brook, 2004. (PI) Ages 7–11. Striking against newspaper owners, 1899.

Bunting, Eve. *Train to Somewhere.* Illustrated by Ronald Himler. Clarion, 1996. (PI) Ages 5–8. Orphan train from New York to the Midwest in 1878.

Byars, Betsy. *Keeper of the Doves.* Viking, 2002. Ages 9–13. Kentucky in 1899.

Cadnum, Michael. *Blood Gold.* Viking, 2004. Ages 12–18. Adventure, California Gold Rush, 1849.

Carvell, Marlene. *Sweetgrass Basket.* Dutton, 2005. Ages 12–15. Native Americans at an off-reservation boarding school in the early 1900s.

Clark, Clara Gillow. *Nellie Bishop.* Boyds Mills, 1996. Ages 12–15. Pennsylvania canal town, 1880s.

Collier, James Lincoln, and Christopher Collier. *The Clock.* Delacorte, 1992. Ages 9–12. Connecticut mill life, early 1800s.

———. *With Every Drop of Blood.* Delacorte, 1994. Ages 10–14. Virginia, race relations, slavery, Civil War era.

Conlon-McKenna, Marita. *Fields of Home.* Illustrated by Donald Teskey. Holiday, 1997. Ages 9–12. Ireland, mid-1800s.

———. *Under the Hawthorn Tree.* Illustrated by Donald Teskey. Holiday, 1990. Ages 10–12. Ireland, mid-1800s.

Cushman, Karen. *The Ballad of Lucy Whipple.* Clarion, 1996. Ages 10–13. Massachusetts to California, Gold Rush.

————. *Rodzina.* Clarion, 2003. Ages 9–14. Trip from Chicago to California, orphan train, 1881.

DeFelice, Cynthia. *Bringing Ezra Back.* Farrar, 2006. Ages 9–13. Ohio frontier, 1830s. Sequel to *Weasel.*

————. *Weasel.* Macmillan, 1990. Ages 9–12. Ohio frontier, 1830s.

Donnelly, Jennifer. *A Northern Light.* Harcourt, 2003. Ages 12–16. Mystery and suspense in upstate New York, 1906.

Erdrich, Louise. *The Game of Silence.* HarperCollins, 2005. Ages 10–14. Ojibwes and white settlers, Northern Wisconsin, 1850.

Fleischman, Paul. *Bull Run.* HarperCollins, 1993. Ages 10–16. U.S. Civil War era, 1860s.

Fleischman, Sid. *Bandit's Moon.* Illustrated by Joseph A. Smith. Greenwillow, 1998. Ages 8–12. California Gold Rush era, Mexican bandit Joaquin Murieta.

Giff, Patricia Reilly. *Maggie's Door.* Random, 2003. Ages 9–13. Ireland, potato famine, immigration, 1840s.

————. *Nory Ryan's Song.* Delacorte, 2000. Ages 9–13. Ireland, potato famine, 1845.

————. *Water Street.* Random, 2006. Ages 9–14. Irish American immigrants in Brooklyn, 1876.

Hansen, Joyce. *The Captive.* Scholastic, 1994. Ages 11–14. U.S. slave trade, Civil War era.

Hill, Kirkpatrick. *Minuk: Ashes in the Pathway.* Illustrated by Patrick Faricy. Pleasant, 2002. Ages 10–14. Eskimo village in Alaska, 1890.

Holland, Isabelle. *Behind the Lines.* Scholastic, 1994. Ages 11–16. U.S. Civil War.

Holub, Josef. *An Innocent Soldier.* Translated from the German by Michael Hofmann. Scholastic, 2005. Ages 14–18. Napoleon's Russian campaign, 1812.

Hurst, Carol Otis. *Through the Lock.* Houghton, 2001. Ages 10–13. Farm community, nineteenth-century Connecticut.

Ibbotson, Eva. *Journey to the River Sea.* Dutton, 2002. Ages 11–14. Brazil, 1910.

————. *The Star of Kazan.* Illustrated by Kevin Hawkes. Dutton, 2004. Ages 10–14. Germany and Austria, late 1800s.

Kudlinsky, Kathleen V. *Night Bird: A Story of the Seminole Indians.* Viking, 1993. Ages 8–11. Florida, Seminole Indians, 1850s.

LaFaye, A. *Worth.* Simon & Schuster, 2004. Ages 10–14. Orphan train, Nebraska, late 1800s.

Lester, Julius. *Day of Tears: A Novel in Dialogue.* Hyperion, 2005. Ages 12–18. Largest slave auction in American history; Savannah, Georgia, 1859.

Lowry, Lois. *The Silent Boy.* Houghton, 2003. Ages 9–15. Small New England town during 1908–1911, character with developmental disability, autism.

Lyons, Mary E. *Dear Ellen Bee: A Civil War Scrapbook of Two Union Spies.* Simon & Schuster, 2000. Ages 10–13. Richmond, Virginia, Civil War era.

————. *Letters from a Slave Girl: The Story of Harriet Jacobs.* Scribner's, 1992. Ages 10–16. North Carolina, slavery, early 1800s.

McCaughrean, Geraldine. *Stop the Train!* HarperCollins, 2003. Ages 10–13. Homesteading in Enid, Oklahoma, in 1893.

Myers, Anna. *Assassin.* Walker, 2005. Ages 11–15. Alternating narratives. Assassination of Abraham Lincoln, 1865.

O'Dell, Scott, and Elizabeth Hall. *Thunder Rolling in the Mountains.* Houghton, 1992. Ages 10–14. Native American removal to reservations, 1870s.

Paterson, Katherine. *Bread and Roses, Too.* Clarion, 2006. Ages 10–14. Mill workers' strike, Massachusetts, 1912.

————. *Jip, His Story.* Dutton, 1996. Ages 10–14. Vermont poor farm, 1850s.

————. *Lyddie.* Dutton, 1991. Ages 12–16. Massachusetts, mill life, mid-1800s.

————. *Preacher's Boy.* Clarion. 1999. Ages 10–13. Vermont, turn of the century.

Paulsen, Gary. *The Legend of Bass Reeves.* Random, 2006. Ages 10–14. Escaped slave, lawman, Oklahoma Territory, 1860s.

————. *Nightjohn.* Delacorte, 1993. Ages 11–15. U.S. slavery.

————. *Sarny: A Life Remembered.* Delacorte, 1997. Ages 11–15. New Orleans, freed slaves, 1860s.

————. *Soldier's Heart.* Delacorte, 1998. Ages 10–13. Minnesota, Civil War.

Pearsall, Shelley. *Crooked River.* Knopf, 2005. Ages 10–13. Relations between white pioneers and Indians on the Ohio frontier, 1812.

————. *Trouble Don't Last.* Knopf, 2002. Ages 11–15. Northern Kentucky, slavery, 1859.

Peck, Richard. *Fair Weather.* Dial, 2001. Ages 9–12. Rural Illinois in 1893.

————. *The River Between Us.* Dial, 2003. Ages 12–18. 1861, early Civil War era, Southern Illinois town.

————. *The Teacher's Funeral: A Comedy in Three Parts.* Dial, 2004. Ages 10–14. Rural Indiana, 1904. Humor.

Place, François. *The Old Man Mad about Drawing: A Tale of Hokusai.* Translated from the French by William Rodarmor. Godine, 2003. Ages 10–14. Artist Hokusai, customs of his age, Japan, 1800s.

Polacco, Patricia. *Pink and Say.* Philomel, 1994. (**PI**) Ages 9–12. Race relations, U.S. Civil War, 1860s.

Provensen, Alice. *Klondike Gold.* Simon & Schuster, 2005. (**PI**) Ages 8–11. Canadian Gold Rush in the Yukon Territory, late 1890s.

Reeder, Carolyn. *Across the Lines.* Simon & Schuster, 1997. Ages 8–11. Race relations, 1864–1965.

———. *Before the Creeks Ran Red.* HarperCollins, 2003. Ages 11–15. Beginning of the U.S. Civil War, three linked novellas set in different locations.

———. *Shades of Gray.* Macmillan, 1989. Ages 9–12. U.S. Civil War era, 1860s.

Rinaldi, Ann. *An Acquaintance with Darkness.* Harcourt, 1997. Ages 12–16. Washington, D.C., Lincoln assassination.

———. *In My Father's House.* Scholastic, 1993. Ages 12–16. U.S. Civil War era, 1860s.

———. *Numbering All the Bones.* Hyperion, 2002. Ages 12–15. U.S. Civil War, Andersonville Prison in southwest Georgia, slavery, 1864.

Robinet, Harriette Gillem. *Forty Acres and Maybe a Mule.* Atheneum, 1998. Ages 8–12. Reconstruction era, slave families in South Carolina and Georgia, 1865.

———. *Missing in Haymarket Square.* Atheneum, 2001. Ages 10–15. Working conditions, Chicago, 1886.

Schmidt, Gary. *Lizzie Bright and the Buckminster Boy.* Clarion, 2004. Ages 12–18. Race relations, Christian life, Maine, 1912.

Siegelson, Kim. *Trembling Earth.* Putnam, 2004. Ages 12–18. Survival story, Okefenokee Swamp, Georgia, U.S. Civil War era, 1860s.

Snyder, Zilpha Keatley. *Gib Rides Home.* Delacorte, 1998. Ages 9–12. Taken from an orphanage to work on a farm, early 1900s. Also, *Gib and the Gray Ghost.* Delacorte, 2000.

Stolz, Joelle. *The Shadows of Ghadames.* Translated from the French by Catherine Temerson. Delacorte, 2004. Ages 12–15. Muslim traditions, sex roles, Libya, late 1800s.

Tal, Eve. *Double Crossing: A Jewish Immigration Story.* Cinco Puntos, 2005. Ages 11–15. Emigration from the Ukraine in 1905.

Taylor, Mildred D. *The Land.* Phyllis Fogelman, 2001. Ages 11–15. The South, post–U.S. Civil War, 1870s.

———. *The Well.* Dial, 1995. Ages 9–11. Mississippi, 1910 drought, Logan family.

Thomas, Joyce Carol. *I Have Heard of a Land.* Illustrated by Floyd Cooper. HarperCollins, 1998. (**PI**) Ages 8–12. Homesteading, African-American women, Oklahoma territory, 1800s.

Turner, Ann. *Mississippi Mud: Three Prairie Journals.* Illustrated by Robert J. Clark. HarperCollins, 1997. (**PI**) Ages 10–14. Kentucky to Oregon, pioneers. Free verse.

Whelan, Gloria. *Angel on the Square.* HarperCollins, 2001. Ages 11–15. St. Petersburg, Russia, fall of the Russian Empire, 1913.

Wilson, Diane Lee. *Black Storm Comin'.* Simon & Schuster, 2005. Ages 11–16. Mixed-race family, Missouri to California, Civil War backdrop, 1860.

Winthrop, Elizabeth. *Counting on Grace.* Random, 2006. Ages 10–15. Laboring in a Vermont mill, 1910.

Wisler, G. Clifton. *Jericho's Journey.* Dutton, 1993. Ages 9–13. Tennessee to Texas, pioneer life, 1850s.

Woodson, Jacqueline. *Show Way.* Illustrated by Hudson Talbott. Putnam, 2005. (**PI**) Ages 8–12. African-American women's stories on quilts; slavery through the Civil Rights period.

Yep, Lawrence. *Dragon's Gate.* HarperCollins, 1993. Ages 9–12. Sierra Nevada, transcontinental railroad, 1867.

———. *Dragonwings.* Harper, 1979. Ages 9–12. California, early 1900s.

———. *Spring Pearl.* Pleasant, 2002. Ages 9–14. Opium Wars, Canton, China, 1857.

———. *The Traitor.* Farrar, 2003. Ages 10–14. Chinese and Western coal miners in the Wyoming Territory in 1885.

Yin. *Coolies.* Illustrated by Chris Soentpiet. Philomel, 2001. (**PI**) Ages 8–12. Chinese-Americans, transcontinental railroad, 1860s.

World Wars in the Twentieth Century, 1914 to 1945

Adler, David. *The Babe and I.* Illustrated by David Widener. Harcourt, 1999. (**PI**) Ages 9–13. Depression-era in the Bronx, New York.

Anderson, Rachel. *Paper Faces.* Holt, 1993. Ages 12–16. England, World War II.

Avi. *Who Was That Masked Man, Anyway?* Orchard, 1992. Ages 9–12. United States, World War II.

Baer, Edith. *Walk the Dark Streets.* Farrar, 1998. Ages 13–18. Effects of Hitler's rise to power on a small German town, 1933–1940.

Bat-Ami, Miriam. *Two Suns in the Sky.* Front Street, 1999. Ages 13–16. World War II in New York state, relations among European refugees and U.S. citizens.

Booth, Martin. *War Dog: A Novel.* Margaret K. McElderry, 1997. Ages 10–14. A spy dog sent to France in World War II.

Burandt, Harriet, and Shelley Dale. *Tales from the Homeplace: Adventures of a Texas Farm Girl.* Holt, 1997. Ages 10–14. Texas cotton farm in the Depression, 1930s.

Chang, Margaret, and Raymond Chang. *In the Eye of the War.* Macmillan, 1990. Ages 10–12. China, World War II.

Coerr, Eleanor. *Mieko and the Fifth Treasure.* Putnam, 1993. Ages 9–13. Nagasaki bombardment during World War II, Japan, 1945.

Cormier, Robert. *Frenchtown Summer.* Delacorte, 1999. Monument, Massachusetts, post–World War I. Ages 11–14.

Currier, Katrina Saltonstall. *Kai's Journey to Gold Mountain.* Illustrated by Gabhor Utomo. Angel Island, 2005. Ages 9–13. (PI) Emigrated from China, interned on Angel Island, 1934.

Curtis, Christopher Paul. *Bud, Not Buddy.* Delacorte, 1999. Ages 9–13. Michigan, Depression era.

Doucet, Sharon Arms. *Fiddle Fever.* Clarion, 2000. Ages 9–13. Cajun life in southern Louisiana, World War I.

Dowell, Frances O'Roark. *Dovey Coe.* Atheneum, 2000. Ages 9–13. North Carolina, 1928 murder trial.

Fuqua, Jonathon Scott. *Darby.* Candlewick, 2000. Ages 9–12. Racism, South Carolina, 1926.

Gee, Maurice. *The Fat Man.* Simon & Schuster, 1997. Ages 13–16. Depression, New Zealand, haunting psychological thriller.

Giff, Patricia Reilly. *Lily's Crossing.* Delacorte, 1997. Ages 9–12. United States, World War II.

———. *Willow Run.* Random, 2005. Ages 9–12. Homefront deprivations during World War II.

Glatshteyn, Yankev. *Emil and Karl.* Translated from the Yiddish by Jeffrey Shandler. Roaring Brook, 2006. Ages 10–15. Nazi persecution, pre–World War II Vienna, 1930s.

Greene, Bette. *Summer of My German Soldier.* Dial, 1973. Ages 9–12. United States, World War II.

Hahn, Mary Downing. *Following My Footsteps.* Clarion, 1996. Ages 10–13. North Carolina, physical disability, polio, World War II.

Hall, Donald. *The Farm Summer 1942.* Illustrated by Barry Moser. Dial, 1994. (PI) Ages 7–11. Set in the United States during World War II.

Hartnett, Sonya. *Thursday's Child.* Candlewick, 2002. Ages 12–16. Australia in the Great Depression.

Hautzig, Esther. *The Endless Steppe.* Harper, 1968. Ages 10–14. Russia, Jews, World War II.

Havill, Juanita. *Eyes Like Willy's.* Illustrated by David Johnson. HarperCollins, 2004. Ages 12–16. Austrian and French friends on opposite sides, World War I era.

Hesse, Karen. *The Cats in Krasinski Square.* Illustrated by Wendy Watson. Scholastic, 2004. (PI) Ages 9–12. Nazi occupation of Warsaw, Jewish ghetto, World War II era. Free verse.

———. *Letters from Rifka.* Holt, 1992. Ages 9–12. Russian immigration to the United States, 1919.

———. *Out of the Dust.* Scholastic, 1997. Ages 11–18. Oklahoma, 1930s.

———. *Witness.* Scholastic, 2001. Ages 10–18. Ku Klux Klan, Vermont, 1924. Told in a series of poems in five acts.

Hoestlandt, Jo. *Star of Fear, Star of Hope.* Illustrated by Johanna Kang. Translated by Mark Polizzotti. Walker, 1995. (PI) Ages 9–12. German occupation, persecution of Jews, Northern France, 1942.

Hughes, Dean. *Soldier Boys.* Atheneum, 2001. Ages 13–18. An American and a German in World War II era. Chapters alternate point of view.

Janeczko, Paul B. *Worlds Afire.* Candlewick, 2004. Ages 12–15. Hartford, Connecticut, fire in 1944. Narrative poems.

Kadohata, Cynthia. *Weedflower.* Simon & Schuster, 2006. Ages 10–14. An internment camp in Arizona desert, Japanese American family, World War II era.

Larson, Kirby. *Hattie Big Sky.* Delacorte, 2006. Ages 11–15. Homesteading in Montana, discrimination toward Germans during World War I, 1918.

Lawrence, Iain. *B for Buster.* Delacorte, 2004. Ages 12–18. Canadian Air Force, World War II, deployment to England for raids over Germany, 1943.

———. *Land of the Nutcracker Men.* Delacorte, 2001. Ages 11–15. England and France, World War I.

Levitin, Sonia. *Anne's Promise.* Atheneum, 1993. Ages 10–14. German immigration to United States, World War II era.

Lisle, Janet Taylor. *The Art of Keeping Cool.* Simon & Schuster, 2000. Ages 10–13. United States and Canada, World War II.

Lowry, Lois. *Number the Stars.* Houghton, 1989. Ages 8–12. Denmark, World War II.

Lyon, George Ella. *Borrowed Children.* Watts, 1988. Ages 10–14. Kentucky, Depression era, 1930s.

Maguire, Gregory. *The Good Liar.* Clarion, 1999. Ages 9–12. World War II, occupied France.

Mazer, Norma Fox. *Good Night, Maman.* Harcourt, 1999. Ages 10–14. Holocaust survivors, Jewish refugees in Oswego, New York, World War II era.

Mikaelsen, Ben. *Petey.* Hyperion, 1998. Ages 11–15. Cerebral palsy and its treatment, 1920s.

Mitchell, Margaree King. *Uncle Jed's Barbershop.* Illustrated by James Ransome. Simon & Schuster, 1993. (PI) Ages 7–10. African American, rural south in 1920s.

Morpurgo, Michael. *Private Peaceful.* Scholastic, 2004. Ages 13–18. England and France during World War I era.

Myers, Anna. *Fire in the Hills.* Walker, 1996. Ages 12–16. Rural Oklahoma, World War I, German immigrant family, conscientious objector.

Napoli, Donna Jo. *Stones in Water.* Dutton, 1997. Ages 9–13. Italy, work camps, World War II.

Park, Linda Sue. *When My Name Was Keoko: A Novel of Korea in World War II.* Clarion, 2002. Ages 10–14. Japanese occupation of Korea, 1940s.

Parkinson, Siobhan. *Kathleen: The Celtic Knot.* Pleasant, 2003. Ages 10–14. Ireland, poverty in Dublin, 1937.

Pearson, Kit. *Looking at the Moon.* Viking, 1992. Ages 11–15. Toronto, World War II, 1943.

Peck, Richard. *Here Lies the Librarian.* Dial, 2006. Ages 11–16. Rural Indiana, 1914. Humor.

———. *A Long Way from Chicago.* Dial, 1998. Ages 10–15. Southern Illinois, 1930s. Humor.

———. *A Year Down Yonder.* Dial, 2000. Ages 10–15. Southern Illinois, Depression era, 1937. Humor.

Peck, Robert Newton. *Horse Thief.* HarperCollins, 2002. Ages 13–18. Florida, Depression era, 1930s.

Polacco, Patricia. *The Butterfly.* Philomel, 2000. (PI) Ages 9–12. French Resistance, persecution of Jews, World War II.

Ray, Delia. *Ghost Girl: A Blue Ridge Mountain Story.* Clarion, 2003. Ages 10–13. Depression era 1929–1932, Virginia.

Reuter, Bjarne. *The Boys from St. Petri.* Translated from Danish by Anthea Bell. Dutton, 1994. Ages 12–16. Danish resistance, World War II era.

Richter, Hans Peter. *Friedrich.* Translated from the German by Edite Kroll. Holt, 1970. Ages 10–14. Germany, Jews, World War II.

Roy, Jennifer. *Yellow Star.* Marshall Cavendish, 2006. Ages 10–15. Nazi occupation of the Lodz ghetto, Poland, 1939–1945.

Ryan, Pam Muñoz. *Esperanza Rising.* Scholastic, 2000. Ages 9–13. Mexico and United States, Depression era.

Salisbury, Graham. *Eyes of the Emperor.* Random, 2005. Ages 12–18. Japanese American in World War II, prejudice, training scout dogs.

———. *House of the Red Fish.* Random, 2006. Ages 10–14. Sequel to *Under the Blood-Red Sun.*

———. *Under the Blood-Red Sun.* Delacorte, 1994. Ages 10–14. Japanese residents of Hawaii, racism, World War II era.

Skurzynski, Gloria. *Good-Bye Billy Radish.* Bradbury, 1992. Ages 10–14. Pennsylvania steel mill town, World War I era.

Snyder, Zilpha Keatley. *Cat Running.* Delacorte, 1994. Ages 9–12. California, U.S. Depression, 1933.

Spillebeen, Geert. *Kipling's Choice.* Translated from the Flemish by Terese Edelstein. Houghton, 2005. Ages 12–16. France during World War I, with an epilogue that provides historical context.

Spinelli, Jerry. *Milkweed.* Random, 2003. Ages 11–16. Warsaw, persecution of Jews, 1940s.

Taylor, Mildred. *The Road to Memphis.* Dial, 1990. Ages 12–16. U.S. South, African Americans, 1941.

———. *Roll of Thunder, Hear My Cry.* Dial, 1976. Ages 10–14. U.S. South, African Americans, 1930s.

Taylor, Theodore. *The Bomb.* Harcourt, 1995. Ages 12–16. Hiroshima, 1944–1945.

Uchida, Yoshiko. *Journey to Topaz.* Illustrated by Donald Carrick. Scribner's, 1971. Ages 10–14. United States, internment of Japanese Americans, World War II.

Vos, Ida. *Dancing on the Bridge of Avignon.* Houghton, 1995. Ages 10–16. Nazi occupation of the Netherlands, World War II era.

Wells, Rosemary. *Wingwalker.* Illustrated by Brian Selznick. Hyperion, 2002. Ages 8–11. Oklahoma in the Depression era, 1930s.

Whelan, Gloria. *Burying the Sun.* HarperCollins, 2004. Ages 10–14. World War II, German occupation, Leningrad, 1941.

———. *The Impossible Journey.* HarperCollins, 2003. Ages 10–14. Opposition to Stalin, journey into Siberia, 1934.

Woodson, Jacqueline. *Coming On Home Soon.* Illustrated by E. B. Lewis. Putnam, 2004. (**PI**) Ages 5–9. African-American mother in Chicago for the war effort, World War II.

Yep, Laurence. *Hiroshima: A Novella.* Scholastic, 1995. Ages 9–14. Dropping of the atomic bomb, Japan, 1945.

Post-World War II Era, 1945 to 1980s

Clinton, Catherine. *A Stone in My Hand.* Candlewick, 2002. Ages 11–16. Palestine, 1980s.

Conrad, Pam. *Our House: The Stories of Levittown.* Illustrated by Brian Selznick. Scholastic, 1995. Ages 9–12. Six family stories set on Long Island, each decade from 1940.

Curtis, Christopher Paul. *The Watsons Go to Birmingham—1963.* Delacorte, 1995. Ages 8–12. Flint, Michigan, to Birmingham, Alabama, Civil Rights Movement.

Cushman, Karen. *The Loud Silence of Francine Green.* Clarion, 2006. Ages 10–15. McCarthyism in Los Angeles, 1950s.

Freeman, Suzanne. *The Cuckoo's Child.* Greenwillow, 1996. Ages 10–13. Beirut to Tennessee, 1962.

Going, K. L. *The Liberation of Gabriel King.* Putnam, 2005. Ages 9–12. Facing prejudice, Georgia, 1976.

Grimes, Nikki. *Jazmin's Notebook.* Dial, 1998. Ages 11–16. Harlem, 1960s.

Harrington, Janice. *Going North.* Illustrated by Jerome Lagarrigue. Farrar, 2004. (**PI**) Ages 7–11. African-American family leaves Alabama for jobs, 1964.

Herrera, Juan Felipe. *Downtown Boy.* Scholastic, 2005. Ages 10–14. Free verse. Migrant workers in California, 1958–1959.

Hobbs, Valerie. *Sonny's War.* Farrar, 2002. Ages 12–16. Vietnam War era, California, 1966.

Holt, Kimberly Willis. *Dancing in Cadillac Light.* Putnam, 2001. Ages 11–14. Small town life in Texas, 1968.

———. *My Louisiana Sky.* Holt, 1998. Ages 10–13. Small town in Louisiana in 1957.

———. *When Zachary Beaver Came to Town.* Holt, 1999. Ages 10–14. Small town in Texas in 1971, Vietnam War era.

Houston, Julian. *New Boy.* Houghton, 2005. Ages 13–18. Civil rights struggle, first black student in a Connecticut boarding school, late 1950s.

Jiang, Ji-li. *Red Scarf Girl: A Memoir of the Cultural Revolution.* HarperCollins, 1997. Ages 12–14. China, Mao's Cultural Revolution, 1960s.

Kadohata, Cynthia. *Kira-Kira.* Simon & Schuster, 2004. Ages 11–18. Japanese Americans, small-town Georgia in the late 1950s.

Kim, Helen. *The Long Season of Rain.* Holt, 1996. Ages 12–16. Seoul, Korea in 1960s.

Krisher, Trudy. *Spite Fences.* Delacorte, 1994. Ages 13–16. Georgia, race relations, 1960s.

Lawrence, Iain. *Ghost Boy.* Delacorte, 2000. Ages 13–18. Death of a parent in World War II; joining a circus, late 1940s.

Levine, Ellen. *Catch a Tiger by the Toe.* Viking, 2005. Ages 10–14. McCarthy hearings, Communism, issues of freedom of expression, 1953.

Lyon, George Ella. *Sonny's House of Spies.* Simon & Schuster, 2004. Ages 12–15. Family secrets, homosexual father, Alabama, 1940s and 1950s.

Mah, Adeline Yen. *Chinese Cinderella: The True Story of an Unwanted Daughter.* Delacorte, 1999. Ages 12–18. China, 1940s and 1950s.

Mankell, Henning. *Secrets in the Fire.* Translated from the Swedish by Anne Connie Stuksrud. Annick, 2003. Ages 11–14. Land mines, poverty, Mozambique civil war, southern Africa, 1970s and 1980s.

Martin, Ann M. *Belle Teal.* Scholastic, 2001. Ages 9–12. Rural South, 1962.

———. *A Corner of the Universe.* Scholastic, 2002. Ages 9–13. Small town, 1960.

Nuzum, K. A. *A Small White Scar.* HarperCollins, 2006. Ages 11–14. Colorado rodeo life in the 1940s.

Park, Frances, and Ginger Park. *My Freedom Trip: A Child's Escape from North Korea.* Illustrated by Debra Reid Jenkins. Boyds Mills, 1998. Ages 7–10. Picture book. Crossing the 38th parallel prior to the Korean War.

Talbert, Marc. *The Purple Heart.* HarperCollins, 1992. Ages 10–14. United States, Vietnam War era.

Veciana-Suarez, Ana. *The Flight to Freedom.* Orchard, 2002. Ages 11–16. Cuban immigrant to Miami, 1967.

White, Ruth. *Belle Prater's Boy.* Farrar, 1996. Ages 10–15. Loss of mother; Virginia, 1950s.

———. *Memories of Summer.* Farrar, 2000. Ages 13–18. Life in Virginia and Michigan, 1950s.

———. *The Search for Belle Prater.* Farrar, 2005. Ages 10–15. Sequel to *Belle Prater's Boy.*

———. *Tadpole.* Farrar, 2003. Ages 10–15. Appalachian mountains, 1950s.

Wolff, Virginia Euwer. *Bat 6.* Scholastic, 1998. Ages 10–18. California, 1948, Japanese Americans, post–World War II adjustments.

Related Films, Videos, and DVDs

Civil War Diary. (1991). Author: Irene Hunt. *Across Five Aprils,* (1964). 82 minutes.

The Devil's Arithmetic. (1999). Author: Jane Yolen (1988). 97 minutes.

Lyddie. (1995). Author: Katherine Paterson (1991). 90 minutes.

A Midwife's Tale. (1997). Author: Laurel Ulrich (1990). 88 minutes.

My Louisiana Sky. (2001). Author: Kimberly Willis Holt (1998). 98 minutes.

A Picture of Freedom. (1999). Author: Patricia McKissack (1997). Dear America Series. 30 minutes.

Sarah, Plain and Tall. (1991). Author: Patricia MacLachlan (1985). 98 minutes.

Seabiscuit. (2003). Author: Laura Hildenbrand (2001). 141 minutes.

The Sign of the Beaver. (1996). Author: Elizabeth George Speare (1983). 100 minutes.

Skylark. (1999). Author: Patricia MacLachlan (1994). 98 minutes.

So Far from Home. (1999). Author: Barry Denenberg (1997). Dear America Series. 30 minutes.

Sounder. (2003). Author: William H. Armstrong (1969). 90 minutes.

Standing in the Light. (1999). Author: Mary Pope Osborne (1998). Dear America Series. 30 minutes.

The Whipping Boy. (1990). Author: Sid Fleischman (1986). 38 minutes.

Winter of the Red Snow. (1999). Author: Kristiana Gregory (1996). Dear America Series. 30 minutes.

Sources for Films, Videos, and DVDs

The Video Source Book. Syosset, NY: National Video Clearinghouse, 1979–. Published by Gale Research, Detroit, MI.

An annual reference work that lists media and provides sources for purchase and rental.

Websites of large video distributors:

www.libraryvideo.com

www.knowledgeunlimited.com

chapter 10

Nonfiction: Biography and Informational Books

Questions at Night

Why
Is the sky?

What starts the thunder overhead?
Who makes the crashing noise?
Are the angels falling out of bed?
Are they breaking all their toys?

Why does the sun go down so soon?
Why do the night-clouds crawl
Hungrily up to the new-laid moon
And swallow it, shell and all?

If there's a bear among the stars,
As all the people say,
Won't he jump over those pasture-bars
And drink up the Milky Way?

Does every star that happens to fall
Turn into a firefly?
Can't it ever get back to Heaven at all?
And why
Is the sky?

—Louis Untermeyer

Children are naturally curious. Their interest in the world around them is boundless. Teachers, librarians, and parents want to nourish that curiosity with lively, intelligent answers, provocative questions, and stimulating books that provide answers and a thirst for further knowledge. Today's constantly innovative and improving works of nonfiction are an excellent source of information for children and the adults who guide their learning.

Definition and Description

Nonfiction is usually classified as either biography or informational literature. *Biography* gives factual information about the lives of actual people, including their experiences, influences, accomplishments, and legacies. An *autobiography* is similar in every respect to biography, except that the author tells about his or her own life. *Memoirs,* although related to autobiographies in that they deal with the authors' lives, focus on the authors' revelations of what events in their lives meant to them, not the events themselves (Barrington, 1997). *Informational books* give factual information about, or explain, any aspect of the biological, social, or physical world, including what is known of outer space.

Nonfiction can be further defined in terms of emphasis: The content emphasis of children's nonfiction is documented fact about the natural or social world. Its primary purpose is to inform. In contrast, the content of fictional literature is largely, if not wholly, a product of the imagination, and its purpose is to entertain. Nonfiction writing is often referred to as *expository writing,* or writing that explains, whereas fiction writing is called *narrative writing,* or writing that tells a story.

Some countries now recognize a type of literature that has elements of both fiction and nonfiction and call it *faction.* Faction presents accurate factual information on an entertaining ribbon of fiction. For example, in *My Place in Space* by Robin and Sally Hirst, illustrated by Roland Harvey with Joe Levine, humorous fanciful illustrations along the bottom of the pages tell a fictional story, while facts about the solar system and the universe are presented in the text and in illustrations along the top of the pages. In North America, faction is treated as a part of nonfiction.

Biography

The writing in biographies is more narrative in nature than expository and adheres to the elements of fiction, as discussed in Chapter 3. Reading biographies benefits children in several ways. They find inspiration in stories of the lives and accomplishments of people, many of whom overcame hardships and disabilities in their early years to succeed and make their marks on history. They learn history from the context of the lives of historical figures. Readers also recognize the importance of childhood experiences, since many biographies for children emphasize the early years of subjects' lives.

Evaluation and Selection of Biography

In evaluating biography for use with children, consider the following criteria:

- Subjects of biographies should be interesting to children. The subjects' lives or accomplishments should somehow intersect with young readers' lives and interests.
- The facts should be accurate with no "idealization" of the subject.
- Biographical selections should include diverse subjects (female and male, people of all ethnicities and abilities).

- The depth of coverage should be at an appropriate level for the intended audience.
- The documentation should be unobtrusive.

Through My Eyes by Ruby Bridges fulfills all of these criteria and is particularly appealing to young readers because it is told from the perspective of the author as a 6-year-old.

 ## Types of Biographies

In adult nonfiction, biographies must be completely documented to be acceptable. In biographies for children, more latitude is allowed, and biographers use varying degrees of invention. This invention ranges from choosing what aspect of the subject the biographer wants to emphasize as the theme of the book (e.g., great energy or love of freedom) to actually inventing fictional characters and conversation.

Biographies, then, can be classified by degree of documentation, as discussed next.

Authentic Biography

In *authentic biography,* is also based all factual information is documented through eyewitness accounts, written documents, letters, diaries, and, more recently, audio and videotape recordings. Details in the lives of people who lived long ago, such as conversations, are often difficult to document, however. So, for the sake of art, biographers must use such devices as interior monologue (telling what someone probably thought or said to himself or herself based on known actions), indirect discourse (reporting the gist of what someone said without using quotation marks), attribution (interpretation of known actions to determine probable motives), and inference to make their stories lively and appealing and worth the children's time to read. It is advisable to read and compare several biographies of a subject, if possible, to counteract any bias an author might have. *The Great Little Madison* by Jean Fritz is an example of an authentic biography.

Fictionalized Biography

Fictionalized biography is also based on careful research, but the author creates dramatic episodes from known facts by using imagined conversation. The conversation is, of course, carefully structured around the pertinent facts that are known, but the actual words are invented by the author. An example of this type of biography is *Carry On, Mr. Bowditch* by Jean Lee Latham.

Biographical Fiction

Much artistic license is allowed in *biographical fiction,* including invented dialogue, fictional secondary characters, and some reconstructed action. The known achievements of the biographical subjects are reported accurately, but in other respects these works are as much fiction as fact. Due to a trend toward greater authenticity in children's nonfiction, biographical fiction is relatively rare today. A recent example is *If a Bus Could Talk: The Story of Rosa Parks* by Faith Ringgold.

Biographies can also be classified by coverage of the subject's life. In evaluating the following types of biographies, you will want to look for a balance between the need for adequate coverage and the tolerance that the target child audience has for detail.

- The *complete biography* covers the entire life of the subject from birth to death. An example is *Columbus and the World around Him* by Milton Meltzer.
- The *partial biography* covers only part of the life of the subject. Biographies for very young children will often be of this type, as will, of course, the biographies of living persons. An example is *The Young Hans Christian Andersen* by Karen Hesse, illustrated by Erik Blegvad.
- The *collected biography* includes the life stories of several people in one book, organized into chapters. An example is *Lives of the Writers: Comedies, Tragedies (and What the Neighbors Thought)* by Kathleen Krull, illustrated by Kathryn Hewitt.
- The *biography series* is a multivolume set of books with each book containing one separate biography. For example, the First Biographies series by David A. Adler includes biographies on such subjects as Thomas Jefferson, Martin Luther King Jr., and Jackie Robinson.

Informational Books

As noted in the definition at the beginning of this chapter, informational books differ from biographies and fictional literature in several respects. As the name implies, these books are written to inform or explain. The realm of this literature is the real world and facts about it. The style of writing used in informational books, *expository,* means to explain. The major benefits of this literature for young people are that it satisfies their inborn curiosity to find out about the world and it opens doors to information that can carry them far beyond the confines of schools and textbooks.

Elements of Informational Literature

Understanding the parts, or elements, of informational books and how they work together can help you become more analytical about this kind of literature. This knowledge can also improve your judgment of informational literature.

Structure

Structure has to do with how the author organizes the information to be presented. Most informational literature is structured in one or more of the following ways:

- *Description.* The author gives the characteristics of the topic (e.g., *Spiders* by Gail Gibbons).
- *Sequence.* The author lists items in order, usually chronologically or numerically (e.g., *How to Make a Chemical Volcano and Other Mysterious Experiments* by Alan Kramer).
- *Comparison.* The author juxtaposes two or more entities and lists their similarities and differences (e.g., *Do You Know the Difference?* by Andrea and Michael Bischhoff-Miersch).
- *Cause and Effect.* The author states an action and then shows the effect, or result, of this action (e.g., *Blizzard: The Storm That Changed America* by Jim Murphy).
- *Problem and Solution* (also referred to as *Question and Answer*). The author states a problem and its solution or solutions (e.g., *What Do You Do with a Tail Like This?* by Steve Jenkins and Robin Page).

Some informational books will employ a single text structure; others, particularly longer works, will employ several.

Theme

Theme in informational literature is the main point made in the work. Although an informational book may communicate hundreds of facts about a topic, the theme of the work will answer the question "What's the point?" (Colman, 1999, p. 221). Sometimes the theme will be a cognitive concept, such as the way viruses multiply; in other cases it will be an emotional insight, such as a new or deepened awareness of the social injustices that are a part of the history of the United States (e.g., slavery, child labor), as revealed in Deborah Hopkinson's *Up Before Daybreak: Cotton and People in America*.

Style

Style is how authors and illustrators, with their readers in mind, express themselves in their respective media. Sentence length and complexity, word choice, and formal versus conversational tone are part of the expository style, as are use of technical vocabulary, captions, and graphic elements such as tables, charts, illustrations, photographs, diagrams, maps, and indices. Shelley Tanaka's colorful language and use of large, richly colored photographs, maps, sidebars, and a time line in *Mummies: The Newest, Coolest, and Creepiest from Around the World* demonstrate how style can make informational literature more interesting.

 # Reading Informational Literature

An interesting contradiction concerning informational literature exists in today's schools. Although school and public library records indicate that nonfiction makes up 50 to 85 percent of the circulation of children's libraries, research studies indicate that children in the United States have trouble reading and writing expository texts, partly because of a lack of classroom experience with nonfiction in the early grades. See Table 10.1 for research evidence supporting the reading of nonfiction in the elementary grades.

Studies such as the ones reported in Table 10.1 reveal several critical points about children and reading nonfiction. First, it is only through repeated experience with a specific genre that one learns how to read or write that genre. Second, all children, even primary graders, benefit from learning how to read and enjoy nonfiction, since from middle grades through adulthood, most day-to-day reading demands (textbooks, news reports, instructions, recipes, etc.) are expository. Third, a key factor in comprehending expository text is that readers learn to relate new information found in the text to their own *schemata,* or prior knowledge on the topic stored in their minds.

Particularly in the early grades, teachers and librarians may have to take the lead in introducing nonfiction to their students, since parents and caregivers traditionally select only fiction as read-aloud material. Selecting excellent works of nonfiction for reading aloud and suggesting similar works to parents for at-home reading is a good way to begin. Calling attention to students' prior knowledge on a subject and noting the various text structures while reading will help students learn to read and appreciate this genre. In addition, nonfiction can be included and promoted

Table 10.1   Important Studies on Reading and Nonfiction

Researcher(s)	Subjects	Findings
Mullis, Martin, Gonzalez, & Kennedy (2003)	150,000 fourth-graders from 35 countries	U.S. students scored significantly lower in reading nonfiction than in reading fiction.
Duke (2000)	20 first-grade classrooms, 10 each from very high and very low SES groups	Presence of nonfiction texts and use of nonfiction in class were rare to nonexistent. Consequently, students were unable to read and write informational texts successfully. Findings applied particularly to low-SES students.
Campbell, Kapinus, & Beatty (1995)	National sample of fourth-graders	Students with experience reading magazines and nonfiction had higher average reading proficiencies than those who never read these types of materials.

as options in students' self-choice reading, can be added to classroom library collections (Moss & Hendershot, 2002), and can be used across the curriculum in various ways. See Table 13.1, Literature across the Curriculum, pages 283–284.

Evaluation and Selection of Informational Books

It is important to remember that not every work of nonfiction needs to meet every criterion to be worthy and that no one book can cover a topic completely. By offering children a variety of satisfactory books on the same topic to be read and compared, you more than compensate for the shortcomings of a good-but-not-great book. Selection criteria include the following:

- Children's nonfiction must be written in a clear, direct, easily understandable style. In recent years, a tight, compressed, but conversational, writing style has come to be favored in nonfictional text.
- Facts must be accurate and current. A reliable check is to compare the information with that found in other recently published sources on the topic.
- Captions and labels must be clearly written and informative.
- Informational literature must distinguish between fact, theory, and opinion. When not clearly stated as such, theories or opinions are flagged by carefully placed phrases such as "maybe," "is believed to be," or "perhaps."

Excellent Nonfiction to Read Aloud

Bartoletti, Susan Campbell. *Black Potatoes: The Story of the Great Irish Famine, 1845–1850.* Ages 12–16.

Borden, Louise. *A. Lincoln and Me.* Illustrated by Ted Lewin. Ages 5–8.

Bridges, Ruby, and Margo Lundell. *Through My Eyes.* Ages 9–16. Memoir.

Butterworth, Chris. *Sea Horse: The Shyest Horse in the Sea.* Illustrated by John Lawrence. Ages 4–8.

Chandra, Deborah, and Madeline Comora. *George Washington's Teeth.* Illustrated by Brock Cole. Ages 5–8. Story in verse.

Cowley, Joy. *Chameleon, Chameleon.* Illustrated by Nic Bishop. Ages 4–7.

Fradin, Dennis Brindell. *With a Little Luck: Surprising Stories of Amazing Discovery.* Ages 12–14.

Giblin, James Cross. *The Amazing Life of Benjamin Franklin.* Illustrated by Michael Dooling. Ages 8–11.

Hamilton, Virginia. *Many Thousand Gone: African Americans from Slavery to Freedom.* Illustrated by Leo and Diane Dillon. Ages 10–14. Collected biography.

Hoose, Phillip. *We Were There, Too! Young People in U.S. History.* Ages 10–13. Collected biography.

Sayre, April Pulley. *Stars Beneath Your Bed: The Surprising Story of Dust.* Ages 5–10.

Stanley, Diane. *Leonardo da Vinci.* Ages 9–13.

- *Personification*—attributing human qualities to animals, material objects, or natural forces—should be avoided because the implication is factually inaccurate.
- Works of nonfiction must be attractive to the child. An intriguing cover, impressive illustrations, and balance of text and illustrations make books look interesting to a child.
- Presentation of information should be from known to unknown, general to specific, or simple to more complex to aid conceptual understanding and encourage analytical thinking. Reference aids such as tables of contents, indexes, pronunciation guides, glossaries, maps, charts, and tables make information in books easier to find and retrieve, more comprehensible, and more complete.
- Stereotyping must be avoided. Positive images of cultural diversity should be offered in text and illustrations.
- Format and artistic medium should be appropriate to the content. For example, engineered paper or pop-up illustrations are appropriate when three dimensions are required to give an accurate sense of placement of the parts of a whole, as in human anatomy.
- Depth and complexity of subject treatment must be appropriate for the intended audience. If an explanation must be simplified to the extent that facts must be altered before a child can begin to understand, perhaps the concept or topic should be taken up when the child is older.

Two award programs offer sources of good nonfiction titles. The NCTE's Orbis Pictus Award for Outstanding Nonfiction for Children and the ALA's Robert F. Sibert Informational Book Medal spotlight what are considered to be the best works of nonfiction published in the preceding year.

For a complete listing of the Orbis Pictus and Sibert Award winners, see Appendix A.

Formats of Nonfiction Books

Nonfiction book format has to do with how information is presented on the book page, rather than with the information itself. The most common distinct formats in which informational books for children are currently being produced are as follows:

- *Nonfiction Chapter Book.* This format features a large amount of text that is organized into chapters. Graphics and illustrations are common in the more recent nonfiction chapter books but are still less important than the text. Almost all biographies, with the exception of picture book biographies, appear in this format. Examples include *Blizzard! The Storm That Changed America* by Jim Murphy and *Columbus and the World Around Him* by Milton Meltzer.
- *Nonfiction Picture Book.* This format features large, uncomplicated illustrations and brief text. The illustrations help to convey the information as discussed in Chapter 5. Examples include *What Do You Do with a Tail Like This?* by Steve Jenkins and Robin Page and *Leonardo da Vinci* by Diane Stanley.
- *Science and Social Science Concept Picture Book.* Originally conceived for 4- to 8-year-olds, this type of book presents one or two scientific or social concepts via brief, uncomplicated text accompanied by numerous, large illustrations. It also encourages participation by including an experiment or hands-on activity. These books are now available for older children as well. *Bugs Are Insects* by Anne Rockwell, illustrated by Steve Jenkins, exemplifies the science concept picture book and is part of the well-known "Let's-Read-and-Find-Out" series of books of this kind.
- *Photo Essay.* Presentation of information in the photo essay is equally balanced between text and illustration. Excellent, information-bearing photographs, and crisp, condensed writing style are hallmarks of this nonfictional format. Photo essays are generally written for children in the intermediate grades and up. Examples include *Lincoln: A Photobiography* by Russell Freedman and *Barrio: José's Neighborhood* by George Ancona.
- *Fact Books.* Presentation of information in these books is mainly through lists, charts, and tables. Examples include almanacs, books of world records, and sports trivia and statistics books. For example, see *The Guinness Book of World Records.*

Historical Overview of Nonfiction

The history of children's nonfiction begins in 1657 with the publication of John Amos Comenius's *Orbis Pictus (The World in Pictures).* Not only was this the first children's picture book but it was also a work of nonfiction. This auspicious beginning for nonfiction was cut short, however, by the Puritan Movement. For nearly 200 years the vast majority of books published for and read by children were intended more for moralistic instruction than for information.

Although books of nonfiction continued to be written in the eighteenth and nineteenth centuries, much of the growth and development of this genre occurred in the latter half of the twentieth century.

Rapid development of nonfiction as a genre began in the 1950s and 1960s in response to the launching of *Sputnik,* the first artificial space satellite, by the former Soviet Union. Competing in the race for space exploration and new technology, the U.S. Congress funneled money into science education, and publishers responded with new and improved science trade books. (See Milestones in the Development of Nonfiction for Children.) Particularly noteworthy are the introduction of nonfiction picture books for primary grades and the trend toward more illustrations and less text in nonfiction for all levels.

MILESTONES in the Development of Nonfiction for Children

Date	Book	Significance
1657	*Orbis Pictus* by John Amos Comenius	First known work of nonfiction for children
1683	*New England Primer*	First concept book for American children; reflected didacticism of the Puritan era
1922	*The Story of Mankind* by Hendrik Van Loon	Won the first Newbery Medal; greatly influenced children's books with its lively style and creative approach
1939	*Abraham Lincoln* by Ingri and Edgar Parin d'Aulaire	One of the first picture book biographies for younger children; first biography to win the Caldecott Medal
1940	*Daniel Boone* by James H. Daugherty	First biography to win the Newbery Medal
1948	*The Story of the Negro* by Arna Bontemps	The first important history of the Negro
1952	*Diary of a Young Girl* by Anne Frank	Classic autobiography; helped many to understand the tragedy of the Jewish Holocaust
1960	Let's-Read-and-Find-Out series by Franklyn Branley and Roma Gans	Introduced the science concept picture book for young children
1969	*To Be a Slave* by Julius Lester	African-American nonfiction chosen as Newbery Honor Book
1988	*Lincoln: A Photobiography* by Russell Freedman	First nonfictional photo essay to win a Newbery Medal
1990	First Orbis Pictus Award for Nonfiction (*The Great Little Madison* by Jean Fritz)	Nonfiction as a genre is recognized
2001	First Robert F. Sibert Informational Book Medal (*Sir Walter Ralegh and the Quest for El Dorado* by Marc Aronson)	Nonfiction as a genre is further recognized

As the stature of nonfiction rose and more top-flight authors and illustrators were engaged in its production, the quality of research, writing, and art in these books improved. A lighter, yet factual, tone balanced with high-quality, informative illustrations and graphics emerged as the preferred nonfiction style (Elleman, 1987).

Children's biographies were greatly affected by the more liberal attitudes and relaxed topic restrictions that revolutionized children's fiction in the 1960s. Before this time, certain subjects (ethnic minorities, women, infamous people) and topics (the subjects' personal weaknesses, mistakes, and tragedies) were not often found in children's biographies. It was thought that subjects who were worthy of being commemorated should be placed on a pedestal. By the mid-1960s, this attitude had changed, as Russell Freedman (1988) pointed out in his Newbery Medal acceptance speech: "The hero worship of the past has given way to a more realistic approach, which recognizes the warts and weaknesses that humanize the great" (p. 447).

In 1990, the National Council of Teachers of English established the Orbis Pictus Award for Outstanding Nonfiction for Children. Named in honor of Comenius's book written some 300 years earlier, this award program signaled how far children's nonfiction had come. In 2001, the Robert F. Sibert Informational Book Medal, sponsored by the American Library Association, was established, further documenting the acceptance of nonfiction as an equal player in the field of children's literature. Recent multimedia publication (book and CD versions) of nonfictional books such as David Macaulay's *The Way Things Work* suggests an exciting future for this genre.

 ## Topics of Informational Books

Although nonfiction is confined to just one chapter in this book, it is by far the largest single genre in children's literature in that everything known to humankind is a conceivable topic. Organization of such an enormous variety of topics could, of course, be done in a variety of ways, one of which is the scientific approach used here. The world of information is divided into the biological, the physical, the social, and the applied sciences; the humanities are dealt with separately.

Biological Science

Biological science deals with living organisms and the laws and phenomena that relate to any organism or group of organisms. Topics within this field that interest primary and intermediate graders are dinosaurs, pets, wild animals, ecology, and the environment. *A Dinosaur Named Sue: The Story of the Colossal Fossil: The World's Most Complete T. Rex* by Pat Relf is a good example.

A subtopic of biological science that deserves special attention is human anatomy and sexuality. Young children are naturally interested in their bodies, and as they grow into puberty, they become interested in sex. Experts in the field of sex education suggest that honest, straightforward answers to children's questions about their bodies, bodily functions, sex, and sexual orientation are best. Books on these topics are not necessarily appropriate for use in schools in the elementary grades, but rather for use by parents who want a resource to share with their children.

Notable Authors and Illustrators of Nonfiction

Joanna Cole, author of a variety of informational books for beginning independent readers. Magic School Bus series.

Russell Freedman, author of biographies of famous Americans and of informational books about U.S. history. *Lincoln: A Photobiography; Children of the Wild West.*

Jean Fritz, biographer of political leaders during the U.S. Revolutionary War era. *Can't You Make Them Behave, King George?; And Then What Happened, Paul Revere?*

Gail Gibbons, author/illustrator of numerous informational books for the 5- to 7-year-old that explain how everyday things work or get done. *The Post Office Book; Recycle: A Handbook for Kids.* www.gailgibbons.com

James Cross Giblin, author of informational books about the social implications of cultural developments and inventions. *From Hand to Mouth: Or, How We Invented Knives, Forks, and Spoons and the Tablemanners to Go with Them; When Plague Strikes: The Black Death, Smallpox, AIDS.*

Jan Greenberg and Sandra Jordan, coauthors of several biographies about renowned artists and their works. *Vincent Van Gogh: Portrait of an Artist; Chuck Close, Up Close; Action Jackson.*

David Macaulay, author/illustrator of several books of faction about construction of monumental buildings and informational picture books for older readers. *Cathedral; Building Big.* www.davidmacaulay.com

Jim Murphy, author of informational chapter books about events in United States history. *Across America on an Emigrant Train; The Great Fire.* www.jimmurphybooks.com

Stuart J. Murphy, creator of the MathStart series of informational picture books on the subject of mathematics. www.stuartjmurphy.com

Laurence Pringle, author of many informational books that express concern for the environment. *Vanishing Ozone: Protecting Earth from Ultraviolet Radiation.* www.laurencepringle.com

Seymour Simon, author of over 100 science-related books that often contain practical activities. The Planets series; *The Brain: Our Nervous System.* www.seymoursimon.com

Diane Stanley, author/illustrator of picture book biographies for older readers. *Leonardo da Vinci; Joan of Arc.* www.dianestanley.com

Teachers and librarians should be able to recommend age-appropriate books on these topics, if asked by parents. Robie Harris's book, *It's Not the Stork! A Book about Girls, Boys, Babies, Bodies, Families, and Friends* illustrated by Michael Emberley, is a good example.

Physical Science

Physical science, sometimes referred to as *natural science,* deals primarily with nonliving materials. Rocks, landforms, oceans, the stars, and the atmosphere and its weather and seasons are all likely topics that children could learn about within the fields of geology, geography, oceanography, astronomy, and meteorology that comprise the physical sciences. Not only will children be able to satisfy their curiosity about such topics in this category as volcanoes and earthquakes, but teachers will also find the many books about the planets and our solar system helpful in presenting these topics in class. Examples include *Sand,* written by Ellen J. Prager and illustrated by Nancy Woodman, and *Blizzard! The Storm That Changed America* by Jim Murphy.

Social Science

Social science deals with the institutions and functioning of human society and the interpersonal relationships of individuals as members of society. Through books in this field children can learn about various forms of government, religions, different countries and their cultures, money, and transportation. Most children have a natural interest in books about careers, family relationships, and leisure activities and will appreciate finding answers to their questions without always having to ask an adult. An example is *Kids on Strike* by Susan Bartoletti.

Applied Science

Applied science deals with the practical applications of pure science that people have devised. All machines, for example—from simple levers to supercomputers, from bicycles to space rockets —are part of this field, and many children are naturally interested in finding out how they work. Interest in the applied sciences can be developed in children by pointing out how their lives are affected by these applications. For example, children get sick, and medicine helps to cure them. How? Children get hungry, and food appears. What are the processes by which the food is produced, prepared, packaged, and marketed? Children like toys and buy them in stores. Who designs the toys and how are they manufactured? The answers to questions like these can be found in today's nonfictional literature. For example, see *The Way Things Work* by David Macaulay and *The Longitude Prize* by Joan Dash, illustrated by Dušan Petricic.

A specific type of book within the applied sciences—the *experiment* or *how-to book*— capitalizes on children's natural curiosity and fondness for hands-on activities. Its contents range from directions for conducting various scientific experiments to cookbooks, guides to hobbies, and directions for small construction projects, like clubhouses. For example, see *How to Make a Chemical Volcano and Other Mysterious Experiments* by Alan Kramer.

Humanities

The *humanities* deal with the branches of learning that primarily have a cultural or artistic character. Of greatest interest to children and their teachers are books about the fine arts of drawing, painting, and sculpture; the performing arts of singing, dancing, making instrumental music, and acting; and handicrafts of all sorts. Since many children are artistically creative and often study dance, music, and drawing, they can be led to read about the arts and artists to learn new techniques or to draw inspiration from the experiences of others. Some might read these books to decide whether they are interested in trying to develop their artistic talents. Some books make the arts more accessible or real to children by explaining what to look for in paintings, for example, or by revealing the hard work required of an artist to achieve a spectacular performance or an intriguing work of art. Examples include *What Do Illustrators Do?* by Eileen Christelow and *i see the rhythm* by Toyomi Igus, illustrated by Michele Wood.

Today's nonfictional literature for children is able to meet the needs and interests of young readers in quality, variety, and reader appeal. With these books, children's appetites for learning can be fed while their curiosity for more information is piqued.

Topics for Further Investigation

- Investigate the differences in reading fiction and nonfiction.
- Research findings about U.S. children's ability to read nonfiction.
- Investigate controversial topics in children's nonfiction.
- Explore women and minorities as subjects of children's biography from 1960 to today.
- Select an age-appropriate text set of nonfiction books on a science- or math-related topic under study in a classroom. Booktalk these books to the class, then make the books available for browsing. Note students' responses to these books through observation and interviews.

 See the companion website at www.ablongman.com/lynchbrown6e for further suggestions.

References

Barrington, J. (1997). *Writing the memoir: From truth to art.* Portland, OR: Eighth Mountain Press.

Campbell, J. R., Kapinus, B., & Beatty, A. S. (1995). Interviewing children about their literacy experiences. Data from NAEP's integrated reading performance record at grade 4. Washington, D.C.: U.S. Department of Education.

Colman, P. (1999). Nonfiction is literature, too. *The New Advocate, 12*(3), 215–223.

Duke, N. K. (2000). 3.6 minutes a day: The scarcity of informational texts in first grade. *Reading Research Quarterly, 35*(2), 202–225.

Elleman, Barbara. (1987). Current trends in literature for children. *Library Trends, 35*(3), 413–426.

Freedman, Russell. (1988). Newbery Medal acceptance. *The Horn Book, 64*(4), 444–451.

Jansen, Mogens. (1987). *A little about language, words, and concepts—Or what may happen when children learn to read.* Translated by Lotte Rosbak Juhl. Dragör, Denmark: Landsforeningen af Læsepædagoger.

Moss, B., & Hendershot, J. (2002). Exploring sixth graders' selection of nonfiction trade books. *The Reading Teacher, 56*(1), 6–17.

Mullis, I. V. S., Martin, M. O., Gonzalez, E. J., & Kennedy, A. M. (2003). *PIRLS 2001 international report: IEA's study of reading literacy achievement in primary schools.* Chesnut Hill, MA: Boston College.

Untermeyer, Louis. (1985). Questions at night. In L. Untermeyer (Selector), *Rainbow in the sky.* San Diego: Harcourt.

Recommended Biography Books

Ages refer to approximate reading levels. Biography is organized by historical era as in Chapter 9.

Civilizations of the Ancient World, 3000 B.C. to A.D. 600

Bankston, John. *The Life and Times of Alexander the Great.* Lane, 2004. Ages 11–13.

Demi. *Muhammed.* Simon & Schuster, 2003. (PI) Ages 8–13.

Lasky, Kathryn. *The Librarian Who Measured the Earth.* Illustrated by Kevin Hawkes. Little, Brown, 1994. (PI) Ages 7–10.

Zannos, Susan. *The Life and Times of Socrates.* Lane, 2004. Ages 11–14.

Civilizations of the Medieval World, 600 to 1500

Doak, Robin S. *Galileo: Astronomer and Physicist.* Compass Point Books, 2005. Ages 11–15.

Freedman, Russell. *The Adventures of Marco Polo.* Illustrated by Bagram Ibatoulline. Scholastic, 2006. Ages 12–15.

Krull, Kathleen. *Leonardo da Vinci.* Illustrated by Boris Kulikov. Viking, 2005. Ages 10–14. (Part of the Giants of Science series)

Meltzer, Milton. *Columbus and the World around Him.* Watts. 1990. Ages 12–15.

Poole, Josephine. *Joan of Arc.* Illustrated by Angela Barrett. Knopf, 1998. Ages 7–11.

Shulevitz, Uri. *The Travels of Benjamin of Tudela: Through Three Continents in the Twelfth Century.* Farrar, 2005. (PI) Ages 10–14.

Sís, Peter. *Starry Messenger.* Farrar, 1996. Ages 9–14.

Stanley, Diane. *Joan of Arc.* Morrow, 1998. Ages 11–14.

———. *Leonardo da Vinci.* Morrow, 1996. Ages 9–13.

The Emergence of Modern Nations, 1500 to 1800

Adler, David A. *B. Franklin, Printer.* Holiday, 2001. Ages 9–13.

Anderson, M. T. *Handel, Who Knew What He Liked.* Illustrated by Kevin Hawkes. Candlewick, 2001. (PI) Ages 8–12.

Aronson, Marc. *Sir Walter Ralegh and the Quest for El Dorado.* Clarion, 2000. Ages 12–16.

Fleming, Candace. *Ben Franklin's Almanac: Being a True Account of the Good Gentleman's Life.* Atheneum, 2003. Ages 11–14.

Freedman, Russell. *Confucius: The Golden Rule.* Illustrated by Frédéric Clément. Scholastic, 2002. (PI) Ages 9–14.

Fritz, Jean. *And Then What Happened, Paul Revere?* Illustrated by Tomie dePaola. Coward/McCann, 1973. Ages 8–10.

———. *Can't You Make Them Behave, King George?* Illustrated by Tomie dePaola. Coward/McCann, 1976. Ages 8–10.

———. *The Great Little Madison.* Putnam, 1989. Ages 9–12.

———. *Traitor: The Case of Benedict Arnold.* Putnam, 1981. Ages 9–12.

———. *What's the Big Idea, Ben Franklin?* Illustrated by Margot Tomes. Coward/McCann, 1978. Ages 8–10.

———. *Where Do You Think You're Going, Christopher Columbus?* Illustrated by Margot Tomes. Putnam, 1980. Ages 8–10.

———. *Where Was Patrick Henry on the 29th of May?* Illustrated by Margot Tomes. Coward/McCann, 1975. Ages 8–10.

———. *Why Don't You Get a Horse, Sam Adams?* Illustrated by Trina Schart Hyman. Coward/McCann, 1974. Ages 8–10.

———. *Will You Sign Here, John Hancock?* Illustrated by Trina Schart Hyman. Coward/McCann, 1976. Ages 8–10.

Giblin, James Cross. *The Amazing Life of Benjamin Franklin.* Illustrated by Michael Dooling. Scholastic, 2000. Ages 8–11.

Harness, Cheryl. *The Remarkable Benjamin Franklin.* National Geographic, 2005. (PI) Ages 7–11.

Jurmain, Suzanne Tripp. *George Did It.* Illustrated by Larry Day. Dutton, 2005. (PI) Ages 7–11.

Lasky, Kathryn. *The Man Who Made Time Travel.* Illustrated by Kevin Hawkes. Farrar, 2003. (PI) Ages 8–12.

Lyons, Mary E. *Letters from a Slave Girl: The Story of Harriet Jacobs.* Scribner's, 1992. Ages 10–14.

Marrin, Albert. *George Washington and the Founding of a Nation.* Dutton, 2001. Ages 11–16.

———. *The Sea King: Sir Francis Drake and His Times.* Atheneum, 1995. Ages 11–16.

Meltzer, Milton. *Thomas Jefferson: The Revolutionary Aristocrat.* Watts, 1991. Ages 12–16.

Rosen, Michael. *Shakespeare: His Work and His World.* Candlewick, 2001. Ages 10–14.

Sís, Peter. *Play, Mozart, Play!* Greenwillow, 2006. (PI) Ages 5–8.

Stanley, Diane. *Michelangelo.* HarperCollins, 2000. (PI) Ages 9–14.

———. *Saladin: Noble Prince of Islam.* HarperCollins, 2002. (PI) Ages 9–14.

The Development of Industrial Society, 1800 to 1914

Adler, David A. *America's Champion Swimmer: Gertrude Ederle.* Illustrated by Terry Widener. Harcourt, 2000. Ages 6–10.

Armstrong, Jennifer. *Photo by Brady: A Picture of the Civil War.* Atheneum, 2005. Ages 12–14. (Photoessay)

Blumberg, Rhoda. *The Incredible Journey of Lewis and Clark.* Lothrop, 1987. Ages 9–12.

———. *Shipwrecked! The True Adventures of a Japanese Boy.* HarperCollins, 2001. Ages 10–14.

———. *York's Adventures with Lewis and Clark: An African-American's Part in the Great Expedition.* HarperCollins, 2004. Ages 11–15.

Bolden, Tonya. *Maritcha: A Nineteenth-Century American Girl.* Abrams, 2005. Ages 10–14.

Borden, Louise. *A. Lincoln and Me.* Illustrated by Ted Lewin. Scholastic, 1999. (**PI**) Ages 5–8.

Brown, Don. *Uncommon Traveler: Mary Kingsley in Africa.* Houghton, 2000. Ages 7–10.

Brown, Monica. *My Name Is Gabriela/Me llamo Gabriela: The Life of Gabriela Mistral/La vida de Gabriela Mistral.* Illustrated by John Parra. Luna Rising, 2005. (**PI**) Ages 5–7. (Bilingual English/Spanish)

Burleigh, Robert. *Toulouse-Lautrec: The Moulin Rouge and the City of Light.* Abrams, 2005. (**PI**) Ages 8–14.

Cohn, Amy L., and Suzy Schmidt. *Abraham Lincoln.* Illustrated by David A. Johnson. Scholastic, 2002. (**PI**) Ages 7–11.

Dooling, Michael. *Young Thomas Edison.* Holiday, 2005. (**PI**) Ages 7–11.

Engle, Margarita. *The Poet Slave of Cuba: A Biography of Juan Francisco Manzano.* Illustrated by Sean Qualls. Holt, 2006. (**PI**) Ages 12–14.

Fradin, Dennis B., and Judith B. Fradin. *Ida B. Wells: Mother of the Civil Rights Movement.* Clarion, 2000. Ages 10–15.

Fradin, Judith Bloom, and Dennis Brindell Fradin. *5,000 Miles to Freedom: Ellen and William Craft's Flight from Slavery.* National Geographic, 2006. Ages 12–15.

———. *Jane Addams: Champion of Democracy.* Clarion, 2006. Ages 12–14.

Freedman, Russell. *Indian Chiefs.* Holiday, 1987. Ages 9–12.

———. *The Life and Death of Crazy Horse.* Holiday, 1996. Ages 9–12.

———. *Lincoln: A Photobiography.* Clarion, 1987. Ages 9–12.

———. *The Wright Brothers: How They Invented the Airplane.* Holiday, 1991. Ages 9–12.

Giblin, James. *Good Brother, Bad Brother: The Story of Edwin Booth and John Wilkes Booth.* Clarion, 2005. Ages 11–14.

Greenberg, Jan, and Sandra Jordan. *Vincent Van Gogh: Portrait of an Artist.* Delacorte, 2001. Ages 10–18.

Helfer, Ralph. *The World's Greatest Elephant.* Illustrated by Ted Lewin. Philomel, 2006. (**PI**) Ages 7–12.

Hesse, Karen. *The Young Hans Christian Andersen.* Illustrated by Erik Blegvad. Scholastic, 2005. Ages 7–10.

Hopkinson, Deborah. *Fannie in the Kitchen: The Whole Story from Soup to Nuts of How Fannie Farmer Invented Recipes with Precise Measurements.* Illustrated by Nancy Carpenter. Atheneum, 2001. (**PI**) Ages 6–8.

Johnson, Dolores. *Onward: A Photobiography of African-American Polar Explorer Matthew Henson.* National Geographic, 2005. Ages 11–14.

Jurmain, Suzanne. *The Forbidden Schoolhouse: The True and Dramatic Story of Prudence Crandall and Her Students.* Houghton, 2005. Ages 12–14.

Keating, Frank. *Theodore.* Illustrated by Mike Wimmer. Simon & Schuster, 2006. (**PI**) Ages 7–12.

Kerley, Barbara. *Walt Whitman: Words for America.* Illustrated by Brian Selznick. Scholastic, 2006. (**PI**) Ages 9–12.

Kraft, Betsy H. *Theodore Roosevelt: Champion of the American Spirit.* Clarion, 2003. Ages 10–14.

Krull, Kathleen. *Lives of the Musicians: Good Times, Bad Times (and What the Neighbors Thought).* Harcourt, 1993. Ages 8–10.

———. *Lives of the Writers: Comedies, Tragedies (and What the Neighbors Thought).* Illustrated by Kathryn Hewitt. Harcourt, 1994. Ages 8–10.

Lasky, Kathryn. *Vision of Beauty: The Story of Virginia Breedlove Walker.* Illustrated by Nneka Bennett. Candlewick, 2000. Ages 8–11.

Marrin, Albert. *Sitting Bull and His World.* Dutton, 2000. Ages 11–18.

McClafferty, Carla Killough. *Something Out of Nothing: Marie Curie and Radium.* Farrar, 2006. Ages 12–16.

McCully, Emily Arnold. *Marvelous Mattie: How Margaret E. Knight Became an Inventor.* Farrar, 2006. (**PI**) Ages 5–8.

Nelson, Marilyn. *Fortune's Bones: The Manumission Requiem.* Front Street, 2004. Ages 12–18. (Poems)

Old, Wendie C. *To Fly: The Story of the Wright Brothers.* Illustrated by Robert Andrew Parker. Clarion, 2002. (**PI**) Ages 8–11.

Paulsen, Gary. *The Legend of Bass Reeves.* Random, 2006. Ages 11–14.

Rosen, Michael. *Dickens: His Work and His World.* Illustrated by Robert Ingpen. Candlewick, 2005. Ages 11–14.

Rumford, James. *Sequoyah: The Man Who Gave His People Writing.* Houghton, 2004. (**PI**) Ages 6–10.

Silverman, Erica. *Sholom's Treasure: How Sholom Aleichem Became a Writer.* Illustrated by Mordecai Gerstein. Farrar, 2005. (**PI**) Ages 5–9.

Sís, Peter. *The Tree of Life.* Farrar, 2003. (**PI**) Ages 12–16. (Charles Darwin)

Varmer, Hjørdis. *Hans Christian Andersen: His Fairy Tale Life.* Translated from the Danish by Tiina Nunnally. Illustrated by Lillian Brøgger. Groundwood, 2005. Ages 10–14.

Weatherford, Carole B. *Moses: When Harriet Tubman Led Her People to Freedom.* Illustrated by Kadir Nelson. Jump at the Sun, 2006. (**PI**) Ages 7–11.

White, Linda Arms. *I Could Do That! Esther Morris Gets Women the Vote.* Illustrated by Nancy Carpenter. Farrar, 2005. (**PI**) Ages 7–10.

World Wars of the Twentieth Century, 1914 to 1945

Adler, David A. *Lou Gehrig: The Luckiest Man.* Illustrated by Terry Widener. Harcourt, 1997. Ages 8–11.

Anderson, M. T. *Strange Mr. Satie.* Illustrated by Petra Mathers. Viking, 2003. (**PI**) Ages 8–12.

Barbour, Karen. *Mr. Williams.* Holt, 2005. (**PI**) Ages 5–8.

Bartoletti, Susan C. *Hitler Youth: Growing Up in Hitler's Shadow.* Scholastic, 2005. Ages 11–14.

Bausum, Ana. *Dragon Bones and Dinosaur Eggs: A Photobiography of Explorer Roy Chapman Andrews.* National Geographic, 2000. Ages 9–15.

Britton-Jackson, Livia. *I Have Lived a Thousand Years: Growing Up in the Holocaust.* Simon & Schuster, 1997. Ages 12–16.

Brown, Don. *Mack Made Movies.* Millbrook, 2003. (**PI**) Ages 6–10.

Burleigh, Robert. *Home Run: The Story of Babe Ruth.* Illustrated by Mike Wimmer. Silver Whistle/Harcourt, 1998. (**PI**) Ages 7–11.

Christensen, Bonnie. *Woody Guthrie: Poet of the People.* Knopf, 2001. (**PI**) Ages (**PI**) 6–8.

Cline-Ransome, Lesa. *Satchel Paige.* Illustrated by James Ransome. Simon & Schuster, 2000. (**PI**) Ages 7–10.

Currier, Katrina S. *Kai's Journey to Gold Mountain: An Angel Island Story.* Illustrated by Gabhor Utomo. Angel Island Association, 2004. (**PI**) Ages 9–13.

Denenberg, Barry. *Shadow Life: A Portrait of Anne Frank and Her Family.* Scholastic, 2005. Ages 12–14.

dePaola, Tomie. *26 Fairmount Avenue.* Putnam, 1999. Ages 7–9.

Fleischman, Sid. *Escape! The Story of the Great Houdini.* Greenwillow, 2006. Ages 10–14.

Fleming, Candace. *Our Eleanor: A Scrapbook Look at Eleanor Roosevelt's Remarkable Life.* Atheneum, 2005. Ages 11–14.

Giblin, James C. *Charles A. Lindbergh: A Human Hero.* Clarion, 1997. Ages 9–14.

Grimes, Nikki. *Talkin' about Bessie: The Story of Aviator Elizabeth Coleman.* Illustrated by E. B. Lewis. Scholastic/Orchard, 2002. (**PI**) Ages 8–13.

Krinitz, Esther N., and Bernice Steinhardt. *Memories of Survival.* Hyperion, 2005. Ages 10–12.

Martin, Jacqueline Briggs. *Snowflake Bentley.* Illustrated by Mary Azarian. Houghton, 1998. (**PI**) Ages 6–9.

Maurer, Richard. *The Wright Sister.* Millbrook, 2003. Ages 12–16.

Millman, Isaac. *Hidden Child.* Farrar, 2005. (**PI**) Ages 11–14. (Autobiography)

Nelson, Marilyn. *Carver: A Life in Poems.* Front Street, 2000. Ages 12–16.

Partridge, Elizabeth. *Restless Spirit: The Life and Work of Dorothea Lange.* Viking, 1998. Ages 11–16.

———. *This Land Was Made for You and Me: The Life and Songs of Woody Guthrie.* Viking, 2002. Ages 11–14.

Poole, Josephine. *Anne Frank.* Illustrated by Angela Barrett. Knopf, 2005. (**PI**) Ages 11–13.

Rabinovici, Schoschana. *Thanks to My Mother.* Translated from German by James Skofield. Dial, 1998. Ages 10–14.

Roy, Jennifer. *Yellow Star.* Marshall Cavendish, 2006. Ages 11–15.

Rubin, Susan Goldman, with Ela Weissberger. *The Cat with the Yellow Star: Coming of Age in Terezin.* Holiday, 2006. Ages 9–13.

Russo, Marisabina. *Always Remember Me: How One Family Survived World War II.* Atheneum, 2005. Ages 8–12.

Ryan, Pam Muñoz. *When Marian Sang: The True Recital of Marian Anderson.* Illustrated by Brian Selznick. Scholastic, 2002. (**PI**) Ages 6–10.

van der Rol, Ruud, and Rian Verhoeven. *Anne Frank: Beyond the Diary: A Photographic Remembrance.* Translated by Tony Langham and Plym Peters. Viking, 1993. Ages 10–15.

Wells, Rosemary. *Mary on Horseback: Three Mountain Stories.* Illustrated by Peter McCarty. Dial, 1998. Ages 7–11.

Whiteman, Dorit Bader. *Lonek's Journey: The True Story of a Boy's Escape to Freedom.* Star Bright, 2005. Ages 11–14.

Yoo, Paula. *Sixteen Years in Sixteen Seconds: The Sammy Lee Story.* Illustrated by Dom Lee. Lee & Low, 2005. (**PI**) Ages 6–10.

Post–World War II Era, 1945 to 2000

Adler, David. A. *A Picture Book of Dwight David Eisenhower.* Holiday, 2002. Ages 7–9.

Aldrin, Buzz. *Reaching for the Moon.* Illustrated by Wendell Minor. HarperCollins, 2005. (**PI**) Ages 7–10. (Autobiography)

Bausum, Ann. *Freedom Riders: John Lewis and Jim Zwerg on the Front Lines of the Civil Rights Movement.* National Geographic, 2005. Ages 12–15.

Bernier-Grand, Carmen T. *César: ¡Sí, Se Puede!/ Yes, We Can!* Illustrated by David Diaz. Marshall Cavendish, 2005. (**PI**) Ages 9–12.

Bridges, Ruby, and Margo Lundell. *Through My Eyes.* Scholastic, 1999. Ages 9–16.

Budhos, Marina. *Ask Me No Questions.* Simon & Schuster, 2005. Ages 12–15.

Chin-Lee, Cynthia. *Amelia to Zora: Twenty-Six Women Who Changed the World.* Charlesbridge, 2005. Ages 9–13.

Delano, Marfé F. *Genius: A Photobiography of Albert Einstein.* National Geographic, 2005. Ages 11–14.

Dendy, Leslie, and Mel Boring. *Guinea Pig Scientists: Bold Self-Experimenters of Science and Medicine.* Holt, 2005. (**COL**) Ages 11–14.

Ellis, Deborah. *Our Stories, Our Songs: African Children Talk about AIDS.* Fitzhenry & Whiteside (Canada), 2005. Ages 12–15.

Fradin, Dennis Brindell. *With a Little Luck: Surprising Stories of Amazing Discovery.* Dutton, 2006. (**COL**) Ages 12–14.

Freedman, Russell. *Babe Didrikson Zaharias: The Making of a Champion.* Clarion, 1999. Ages 10–15.

———. *Martha Graham: A Dancer's Life.* Clarion, 1998. Ages 10–16.

———. *The Voice that Challenged a Nation: Marian Anderson and the Struggle for Equal Rights.* Clarion, 2004. Ages 11–14.

Giovanni, Nikki. *Rosa.* Illustrated by Bryan Collier. Holt, 2005. (**PI**) Ages 8–11.

Govenar, Alan B. *Osceola: Memories of a Sharecropper's Daughter.* Illustrated by Shane W. Evans. Jump at the Sun, 2000. Ages 8–12.

Greenberg, Jan, and Sandra Jordan. *Action Jackson.* Illustrated by Robert Andrew Parker. Millbrook, 2002. (**PI**) Ages 7–10.

———. *Chuck Close, Up Close.* DK Ink, 1998. Ages 10–14.

———. *Frank O. Gehry: Outside In.* DK Ink, 2000. Ages 9–14.

———. *Runaway Girl: The Artist Louise Bourgeois.* Abrams, 2003. Ages 12–16.

Howard, Helen. *Living as a Refugee in America: Mohammed's Story.* World Almanac Library, 2005. Ages 12–14. (Part of Children in Crisis series)

McDonough, Yona Zeldis. *Hammerin' Hank: the Life of Hank Greenberg.* Illustrated by Malcah Zeldis. Walker, 2006. (**PI**) Ages 7–12.

Niven, Penelope. *Carl Sandburg: Adventures of a Poet.* Illustrated by Marc Nadel. Harcourt, 2003. (**PI**) Ages 7–11.

Pinkney, Andrea Davis. *Duke Ellington: The Piano Prince and His Orchestra.* Ilustrated by Brian Pinkney. Hyperion, 1998. (**PI**) Ages 8–11.

Rappaport, Doreen. *Martin's Big Words: The Life of Dr. Martin Luther King, Jr.* Illustrated by Bryan Collier. Hyperion, 2001. (**PI**) Ages 8–10.

Rembert, Winfred. *Don't Hold Me Back: My Life and Art.* Cricket, 2003. (**PI**) Ages 9–13. (Autobiography)

Ringgold, Faith. *If a Bus Could Talk: The Story of Rosa Parks.* Simon & Schuster, 1999. Ages 5–9.

Scieszka, Jon, editor. *Guys Write for Guys Read: Boys' Favorite Authors Write about Being Boys.* Viking, 2005. (**COL**) Ages 11–14.

Winter, Jeanette. *My Name Is Georgia: A Portrait.* Harcourt, 1998. (**PI**) Ages 6–10.

Winter, Jonah. *Dizzy.* Illustrated by Sean Qualls. Scholastic, 2006. (**PI**) Ages 8–14.

———. *Roberto Clemente: Pride of the Pittsburgh Pirates.* Illustrated by Raúl Colón. Atheneum, 2005. (**PI**) Ages 7–11.

Recommended Informational Books

Biological Science

Bishop Nic. *Digging for Bird Dinosaurs: An Expedition to Madagascar.* Houghton, 2000. Ages 9–14.

Butler, Dori Hillestad. *My Mom's Having a Baby.* Illustrated by Carol Thompson. Albert Whitman, 2005. (**PI**) Ages 7–9.

Butterworth, Chris. *Sea Horse: The Shyest Horse in the Sea.* Illustrated by John Lawrence. Candlewick, 2006. (**PI**) Ages 4–8.

Cole, Joanna. *The Magic Schoolbus: Inside the Human Body.* Illustrated by Bruce Degen. Scholastic, 1989. Ages 7–9.

Collard, Sneed B. *The Prairie Builders: Reconstructing America's Lost Grasslands.* Houghton, 2005. Ages 10–14.

Cowley, Joy. *Chameleon, Chameleon.* Photographs by Nic Bishop. Scholastic, 2005. (**PI**) Ages 4–7.

———. *Red-Eyed Tree Frog.* Photographs by Nic Bishop. Scholastic, 1999. Ages 6–9.

Deem, James M. *Bodies from the Bog.* Houghton, 1998. Ages 9–14.

Farrell, Jeanette. *Invisible Allies: Microbes That Shape Our Lives.* Farrar, 2005. Ages 12–18. Human dependence on microbes. Also *Invisible Enemies: Stories of Infectious Disease.* Farrar, 2005. Ages 12–14.

Fisher, Aileen. *The Story Goes On.* Illustrated by Mique Moriuchi. Roaring Brook, 2005. (**PI**) Ages 4–7.

Fleischman, John. *Phineas Gage: A Gruesome but True Story about Brain Science.* Houghton, 2002. Ages 12–14.

Gamlin, Linda. *Eyewitness Science: Evolution.* DK Publishing, 2000. Ages 8–12.

Harris, Robie H. *It's Not the Stork! A Book about Girls, Boys, Babies, Bodies, Families, and Friends.* Illustrated by Michael Emberley. Candlewick, 2006. Ages 5–9. (For parents to use with children)

———. *It's Perfectly Normal: A Book about Changing Bodies, Growing Up, Sex, and Sexual Health.* Illustrated by Michael Emberley. Candlewick, 1994. Ages 11–14.

———. *It's So Amazing! A Book about Eggs, Sperm, Birth, Babies and Families.* Illustrated by Michael Emberley. Candlewick, 1999. Ages 7–12.

Hatkoff, Isabella, Craig Hatkoff, and Paula Kahumbu. *Owen & Mzee: The True Story of a Remarkable Friendship.* Photography by Peter Greste. Scholastic, 2006. Ages 5–12. (Photoessay)

Hawcock, David. *The Amazing Pull-Out Pop-Up Body in a Book.* DK Publishing, 1997. Ages 6–12.

Jenkins, Steve. *Almost Gone: The World's Rarest Animals.* HarperCollins, 2006. (**PI**) Ages 5–8.

———. *Life on Earth: The Story of Evolution.* Houghton, 2002. (**PI**) Ages 8–11.

———. *Prehistoric Actual Size.* Houghton, 2005. (**PI**) Ages 5–10.

———, and Robin Page. *Move!* Illustrated by Steve Jenkins. Houghton, 2006. (**PI**) Ages 4–7.

———. *What Do You Do with a Tail Like This?* Houghton, 2003. (**PI**) Ages 4–7.

Kurlansky, Mark. *The Cod's Tale.* Illustrated by S. D. Schindler. Penguin, 2001. (**PI**) Ages 8–12.

Larson, Peter, and Kristin Donnan. *Bones Rock!: Everything You Need to Know to Be a Paleontologist.* Invisible Cities, 2004. Ages 11–14.

Lasky, Kathryn. *The Most Beautiful Roof in the World: Exploring the Rainforest Canopy.* Illustrated by Christopher G. Knight. Harcourt, 1997. Ages 8–10.

Lewin, Ted, and Betsy Lewin. *Gorilla Walk.* Lothrop, 1999. Ages 9–14.

Mannis, Celeste D. *Snapshots: The Wonders of Monterey Bay.* Viking, 2006. Ages 6–10.

Markle, Sandra. *Little Lost Bat.* Illustrated by Alan Marks. Charlesbridge, 2006. (**PI**) Ages 6–10.

Montgomery, Sy. *Search for the Golden Moon Bear: Science and Adventure in the Asian Tropics.* Houghton, 2004. Ages 11–18.

———. *The Tarantula Scientist.* Photography by Nic Bishop. Houghton, 2004. Ages 11–14.

Pericoli, Matteo. *The True Story of Stellina.* Knopf, 2006. (**PI**) Ages 4–9.

Relf, Pat. *A Dinosaur Named Sue: The Story of the Colossal Fossil: The World's Most Complete T. Rex.* Scholastic, 2000. Ages 12–14.

Rockwell, Anne. *Bugs Are Insects.* Illustrated by Steve Jenkins. HarperCollins, 2001. (PI) Ages 3–6.

Romanek, Trudee. *Squirt! The Most Interesting Book You'll Ever Read about Blood.* Illustrated by Rose Cowler. Kids Can, 2006. Ages 9–12.

Sayre, April Pulley. *Stars Beneath Your Bed: The Surprising Story of Dust.* Illustrated by Ann Jonas. Greenwillow, 2005. (PI) Ages 5–10.

Schlosser, Eric, and Charles Wilson. *Chew on This: Everything You Didn't Want to Know about Fast Food.* Houghton, 2006. Ages 12–14.

Simon, Seymour. *The Brain: Our Nervous System.* Morrow, 1997. Ages 9–12.

———. *Guts: Our Digestive System.* HarperCollins, 2005. (PI) Ages 9–14.

Singer, Marilyn. *What Stinks?* Darby Creek, 2006. (PI) Ages 9–12.

Sloan, Christopher. *The Human Story: Our Evolution from Prehistoric Ancestors to Today.* Photography by Kenneth Garrett. Illustrated by Alfons Kennis and Adrie Kennis. National Geographic, 2004. Ages 11–18.

Turner, Pamela S. *Gorilla Doctors: Saving Endangered Great Apes.* Houghton, 2005. Ages 10–14.

Walker, Sally M. *Fossil Fish Found Alive: Discovering the Coelacanth.* Carolrhoda, 2002. Ages 10–13.

Physical Science

Arnosky, Jim. *Wild and Swampy.* HarperCollins, 2000. (PI) Ages 7–10.

Branley, Franklyn M. *Down Comes the Rain.* Illustrated by James G. Hale. HarperCollins, 1997. (PI) Ages 6–8.

———. *The Planets in Our Solar System.* Illustrated by Kevin O'Malley. HarperCollins, 1998. (PI) Ages 6–8.

Cole, Joanna. *The Magic Schoolbus: Inside the Earth.* Illustrated by Bruce Degen. Scholastic, 1987. (PI) Ages 7–9.

———. *The Magic Schoolbus: Lost in the Solar System.* Illustrated by Bruce Degen. Scholastic, (PI) 1990. Ages 7–9.

Gibbons, Gail. *Weather Words and What They Mean.* Holiday, 1990. (PI) Ages 6–8.

Godkin, Celia. *Fire!* Fitzhenry & Whiteside, 2006. (PI) Ages 6–9.

Grace, Catherine. *Forces of Nature: The Awesome Power of Volcanoes, Earthquakes, and Tornadoes.* National Geographic, 2004. Ages 11–14.

Hirst, Robin, and Sally Hirst. *My Place in Space.* Illustrated by Roland Harvey with Joe Levine. Orchard, 1988. (PI) Ages 9–13.

Krupp, E. C. *The Rainbow and You.* Illustrated by R. Krupp. HarperCollins, 2000. Ages 5–7.

Morrison, Taylor. *Wildfire.* Houghton, 2006. Ages 19–14.

Murphy, Jim. *Blizzard!: The Storm That Changed America.* Scholastic, 2000. Ages 10–14.

Prager, Ellen J. *Sand.* Illustrated by Nancy Woodman. National Geographic, 2000. Ages 4–8.

Simon, Seymour. *Jupiter.* Morrow, 1985. Ages 8–10. (Others in The Planets series: *Mars,* 1987; *Saturn,* 1985; *Uranus,* 1987.)

———. *Our Solar System.* Morrow, 1992. Ages 8–11.

———. *The Stars.* Morrow, 1986. Ages 8–10.

———. *Storms.* Morrow, 1989. Ages 8–10.

———. *The Sun.* Morrow, 1986. Ages 8–10.

———. *Volcanoes.* Morrow, 1988. Ages 8–10.

Skurzynski, Gloria. *Waves: The Electromagnetic Universe.* National Geographic, 1996. Ages 8–12.

Tanaka, Shelley. *The Buried City of Pompeii.* Illustrated by Greg Ruhl. Disney, 1997. (PI) Ages 10–13.

Walker, Sally M. *Earthquakes.* Carolrhoda, 1996. Ages 9–12.

———. *Volcanoes: Earth's Inner Fire.* Carolrhoda, 1994. Ages 9–12.

Wick, Walter. *A Drop of Water: A Book of Science and Wonder.* Scholastic, 1997. Ages 8–11.

Zoehfeld, Kathleen, W. *How Mountains Are Made.* Illustrated by James G. Hale. HarperCollins, 1995. Ages 7–9.

Social Science

Adkins, Jan. *What If You Met a Pirate?* Roaring Brook, 2004. (PI) Ages 7–10.

Allen, Thomas B. *George Washington, Spymaster: How the Americans Outspied the British and Won the Revolutionary War.* National Geographic, 2004. Ages 11–14.

Ambrose, Stephen E. *The Good Fight: How World War II Was Won.* Atheneum, 2001. Ages 11–14.

Ancona, George. *Barrio: José's Neighborhood.* Harcourt, 1998. Ages 8–10.

———. *Charro: The Mexican Cowboy.* Harcourt, 1999. Ages 8–10.

Armstrong, Jennifer. *The American Story: 100 True Tales from American History.* Illustrated by Roger Roth. Knopf, 2006. Ages 9–13.

———. *Shipwreck at the Bottom of the World: The Extraordinary True Story of Shackleton and the Endurance.* Crown, 1998. Ages 10–15.

Atkin, S. Beth. *Voices from the Fields: Children of Migrant Farmworkers Tell Their Stories.* Little, Brown, 1993. Ages 8–12.

Bartoletti, Susan Campbell. *Black Potatoes: The Story of the Great Irish Famine, 1845–1850.* Houghton, 2001. Ages 12–16.

———. *Kids on Strike.* Houghton, 1999. Ages 11–16.

Bial, Raymond. *Tenement: Immigrant Life on the Lower East Side.* Houghton, 2002. Ages 9–14.

Blacklock, Dyan. *The Roman Army: The Legendary Soldiers Who Created an Empire.* Illustrated by David Kannett. Walker, 2004. (**PI**) Ages 11–14.

Blumberg, Rhoda. *Full Steam Ahead: The Race to Build a Transcontinental Railroad.* National Geographic, 1996. Ages 9–12.

Blumenthal, Karen. *Let Me Play: The Story of Title IX: The Law That Changed the Future of Girls in America.* Atheneum, 2005. Ages 12–14.

Bober, Natalie S. *Countdown to Independence: A Revolution of Ideas in England and Her American Colonies: 1760–1776.* Atheneum, 2001. Ages 12–16.

Deems, James M. *Bodies from the Ash: Life and Death in Ancient Pompeii.* Houghton, 2005. Ages 10–14.

Ellis, Deborah. *Our Stories, Our Songs: African Children Talk about AIDS.* Fitzhenry & Whiteside, 2005. Ages 12–14.

Fradin, Dennis Brindell. *Let It Begin Here! Lexington and Concord: First Battles of the American Revolution.* Illustrated by Larry Day. Walker, 2005. (**PI**) Ages 6–10.

Frank, Mitch. *Understanding the Holy Land: Answering Questions about the Israeli-Palestinian Conflict.* Viking, 2005. Ages 12–14.

Freedman, Russell. *Children of the Great Depression.* Clarion, 2005. Ages 11–14.

———. *In Defense of Liberty: The Story of America's Bill of Rights.* Holiday, 2003. Ages 10–14.

———. *Freedom Walkers: The Story of the Montgomery Bus Boycott.* Holiday, 2006. Ages 9–13.

———. *Kids at Work: Lewis Hine and the Crusade against Child Labor.* Photos by Lewis Hine. Clarion, 1994. Ages 9–12.

Gaskins, Pearl Fuyo. *What Are You? Voices of Mixed-Race Young People.* Holt, 1999. Ages 13–16.

Gibbons, Gail. *My Baseball Book.* HarperCollins, 2000. (**PI**) Ages 4–8.

———. *The Post Office Book: Mail and How It Moves.* HarperCollins, 1987. (**PI**) Ages 4–8.

———. *Recycle: A Handbook for Kids.* Little, Brown, 1996. (**PI**) Ages 4–8.

Giblin, James Cross. *When Plague Strikes: The Black Death, Smallpox, AIDS.* Illustrated by David Frampton. HarperCollins, 1995. Ages 12–16.

Goodman, Joan Elizabeth. *A Long and Uncertain Journey: The 27,000-Mile Voyage of Vasco da Gama.* Illustrated by Tom McNeely. Mikaya/Firefly, 2001. (**PI**) Ages 11–14.

Graydon, Shari. *In Your Face: The Culture of Beauty and You.* Annick, 2004. Ages 12–14.

Greenfield, Howard. *After the Holocaust.* Greenwillow, 2001. Ages 12–16. (Oral histories)

The Guinness Book of World Records. Guinness Media, Inc. Published annually. Ages 7–13.

Hill, Laban C. *Harlem Stomp!: A Cultural History of the Harlem Renaissance.* Little, Brown, 2004. Ages 11–14.

Hinds, Kathryn. *The City.* Cavendish, 2000. (See others in Life in the Middle Ages series.) Ages 11–14.

Hoose, Phillip. *The Race to Save the Lord God Bird.* Farrar, 2004. Ages 11–14.

———. *We Were There, Too! Young People in U.S. History.* Farrar, 2001. Ages 10–13.

Hopkinson, Deborah. *Shutting Out the Sky: Life in the Tenements of New York 1880–1924.* Scholastic, 2003. Ages 11–14.

———. *Up Before Daybreak: Cotton and People in America.* Scholastic, 2006. Ages 9–14.

Janeczko, Paul B. *Top Secret: A Handbook of Codes, Ciphers, and Secret Writing.* Illustrated by Jenna LaReau. Candlewick, 2004. Ages 9–14.

Jenkins, Steve. *The Top of the World: Climbing Mount Everest.* Houghton, 1999. Ages 9–12.

————. *What Do You Do When Something Wants to Eat You?* Houghton, 1997. (**PI**) Ages 4–8.

Jukes, Mavis. *It's a Girl Thing: How to Stay Healthy, Safe, and in Charge.* Illustrated by Debbie Tilley. Knopf, 1996. Ages 10–14.

Kalman, Maira. *Fireboat: The Heroic Adventures of the John J. Harvey.* Putnam, 2002. (**PI**) Ages 6–8.

Kennedy, Edward M. *My Senator and Me: A Dog's-Eye View of Washington, D.C.* Illustrated by David Small. Scholastic, 2006. Ages 7–12.

Kuklin, Susan. *Families.* Hyperion, 2006. (**PI**) Ages 5–10.

Lauber, Patricia. *Who Came First? New Clues to Prehistoric Americans.* National Geographic, 2003. Ages 10–14.

Macy, Sue. *Swifter, Higher, Stronger: A Photographic History of the Summer Olympics.* National Geographic, 2004. Ages 11–14.

Markle, Sandra. *Rescues!* Lerner, 2006. Ages 9–13.

Marrin, Albert. *Oh, Rats! The Story of Rats and People.* Illustrated by C. B. Mordan. Dutton, 2006. Ages 8–12.

Martin, Bill, Jr., and Michael Sampson. *I Pledge Allegiance: The Pledge of Allegiance.* Illustrated by Chris Raschka. Candlewick, 2002. (**PI**) Ages 6–9.

McWhorter, Diane. *A Dream of Freedom: The Civil Rights Movement from 1954 to 1968.* Scholastic, 2004. Ages 10–14.

Meyer, Don, editor. *The Sibling Slam Book: What It's Really Like to Have a Brother or Sister with Special Needs.* Woodbine, 2005. Ages 12–14.

Morris, Ann. *Families.* HarperCollins, 2000. Ages 4–7. (Photoessay)

Murphy, Jim. *An American Plague: The True and Terrifying Story of the Yellow Fever Epidemic of 1793.* Clarion, 2003. Ages 9–14.

————. *Gone A-Whaling: The Lure of the Sea and the Hunt for the Great Whale.* Clarion, 1998. Ages 11–16.

————. *The Great Fire.* Scholastic, 1995. Ages 10–14.

————. *Inside the Alamo.* Delacorte, 2003. Ages 9–14.

————. *A Young Patriot: The American Revolution as Experienced by One Boy.* Clarion, 1996. Ages 10–13.

Nevius, Carol. *Karate Hour.* Illustrated by Bill Thomson. Marshall Cavendish, 2004. (**PI**) Ages 5–10.

Osborne, Mary Pope. *Pompeii: Lost & Found.* Illustrated by Bonnie Christensen. Knopf, 2006. (**PI**) Ages 7–12.

Patent, Dorothy Henshaw. *The Buffalo and the Indians: A Shared Destiny.* Illustrated by William Muños. Clarion, 2006. Ages 9–14. (Photoessay)

Peters, Stephanie T. *The Battle Against Polio.* Benchmark, 2004. Ages 10–14. (Also in the proposed five-part Epidemic! set: *The 1918 Influenza Pandemic; Smallpox in the New World; The Black Death*)

Philbrick, Nathaniel. *Revenge of the Whale: The True Story of the Whaleship Essex.* Putnam, 2002. Ages 12–14.

Philip, Neil. *The Great Circle: A History of the First Nations.* Clarion, 2006. Ages 11–15.

Priceman, Marjorie. *How to Make an Apple Pie and See the World.* Knopf, 1994. (**PI**) Ages 5–8.

Schanzer, Rosalyn. *George vs. George: The American Revolution as Seen by Both Sides.* National Geographic, 2004. Ages 9–12. (Also biography)

Sloan, Christopher. *Bury the Dead: Tombs, Corpses, Mummies, Skeletons and Rituals.* National Geographic, 2002. Ages 10–14.

St. George, Judith. *The Journey of the One and Only Declaration of Independence.* Illustrated by Will Hillenbrand. Philomel, 2005. (**PI**) Ages 10–13.

Stanley, Jerry. *Children of the Dust Bowl: The True Story of the School at Weedpatch.* Crown, 1992. Ages 9–13.

Tanaka, Shelley. *Mummies: The Newest, Coolest, and Creepiest from Around the World.* Abrams, 2005. Ages 9–13.

Walker, Sally M. *Secrets of a Civil War Submarine: Solving the Mysteries of the H. L. Hunley.* Carolrhoda, 2005. Ages 12–14.

Wilson, Lori Lee. *The Salem Witch Trials.* Lerner, 1997. Ages 11–16.

Wolf, Bernard. *HIV Positive.* Dutton, 1997. Ages 9–12.

Yue, Charlotte, and David Yue. *The Wigwam and the Longhouse.* Houghton, 2000. Ages 9–14.

Applied Science

Ball, Johnny. *Go Figure!: A Totally Cool Book about Numbers.* DK Publishing, 2005. Ages 10–14.

Branley, Franklyn M. *What Makes a Magnet?* Illustrated by True Kelley. HarperCollins, 1996. (**PI**) Ages 5–8.

Carson, Mary Kay. *Exploring the Solar System: A History with 22 Activities.* Chicago Review, 2006. Ages 11–14.

Curlee, Lynn. *Capital.* Atheneum, 2003. (**PI**) Ages 7–11.

———. *Parthenon.* Atheneum, 2004. (**PI**) Ages 11–14.

Dash Joan. *The Longitude Prize.* Illustrated by Dušan Petricic. Farrar, 2000. (**PI**) Ages 6–13.

Fisher, Valorie. *How High Can a Dinosaur Count? And Other Math Mysteries.* Random, 2006. (**PI**) Ages 6–10.

Gardner, Robert, and Barbara G. Conklin, *Chemistry Science Fair Projects Using French Fries, Gumdrops, Soap, and Other Organic Stuff.* Enslow, 2004. Ages 11–14.

Giblin, James Cross. *Secrets of the Sphinx.* Illustrated by Bagram Ibatoulline. Scholastic, 2004. Ages 11–14.

Hakim, Joy. *The Story of Science: Aristotle Leads the Way.* Smithsonian, 2004. Ages 11–14. (Also in The Story of Science series, *Newton at the Center,* 2005)

Jackson, Donna M. *ER Vets: Life in an Animal Emergency Room.* Houghton, 2005. Ages 12–14.

Katzen, Mollie. *Salad People and More Real Recipes.* Tricycle Press, 2005. Ages 5–8.

Leedy, Loreen. *The Great Graph Contest.* Holiday, 2005. (**PI**) Ages 6–8.

Macaulay, David. *Building Big.* Houghton, 2000. (**PI**) Ages 12–16.

———. *Castle.* Houghton, 1977. (**PI**) Ages 10–16.

———. *Cathedral: The Story of Its Construction.* Houghton, 1973. (**PI**) Ages 10–16.

———. *Mosque.* Houghton, 2003. (**PI**) Ages 12–16.

———. *The Way Things Work.* Houghton, 1988. Ages 10–15. [CD-ROM version: Dorling Kindersley, 1995.]

Ross, Val. *The Road to There: Mapmakers and Their Stories.* Tundra, 2003. Ages 12–16.

Rubin, Susan Goldman. *There Goes the Neighborhood: Ten Buildings People Loved to Hate.* Holiday House, 2001. Ages 12–16.

Severance, John. *Skyscrapers: How America Grew Up.* Holiday, 2000. Ages 10–14.

Skurzynski, Gloria. *Are We Alone? Scientists Search for Life in Space.* National Geographic, 2004. Ages 10–14.

Sullivan, George. *Built to Last: Building America's Amazing Bridges, Dams, Tunnels, and Skyscrapers.* Scholastic, 2005. Ages 12–16.

Swett, Sarah. *Kids Weaving: Projects for Kids of All Ages.* Photography by Chris Hartlove. Illustrated by Lena Corwin. Stewart, Tabori & Chang, 2005. Ages 7–13.

Humanities

Aliki. *Ah, Music!* HarperCollins, 2003. (**PI**) Ages 6–9.

———. *William Shakespeare and the Globe.* HarperCollins, 1999. (**PI**) Ages 8–12.

Amendola, Dana. *A Day at the New Amsterdam Theatre.* Photography by Gino Domenico. Disney, 2004. Ages 10–14.

Christelow, Eileen. *What Do Illustrators Do?* Clarion, 1999. Ages 6–10.

Cummings, Pat, compiler-editor. *Talking with Artists,* Vol. 1. Illustrated by various artists. Bradbury, 1992. Ages 8–12. Vol. 2, 1995; Vol. 3, 1999.

Ellabbad, Mohieddin. *The Illustrator's Notebook.* Groundwood, 2006. Ages 11–14. (Arabic culture; also autobiography)

Fritz, Jean. *Leonardo's Horse.* Illustrated by Hudson Talbot. Putnam, 2001. Ages 9–13.

Govenar, Alan. *Extraordinary Ordinary People: Five American Masters of Traditional Arts.* Candlewick, 2006. Ages 12–15.

Hamanaka, Sheila, and Ayano Ohmi. *In Search of the Spirit: The Living National Treasures of Japan.* Morrow, 1999. Ages 10–14.

Igus, Toyomi. *i see the rhythm.* Illustrated by Michele Wood. Children's, 1998. (**PI**) Ages 9–14.

Marcus, Leonard S. *A Caldecott Celebration: Six Artists Share Their Paths to the Caldecott Medal.* Walker, 1998. Ages 8–16.

———. *The Wand in the Word: Conversations with Writers of Fantasy.* Candlewick, 2006. Ages 11–14.

O'Connor, Jane. *The Emperor's Silent Army: Terracotta Warriors of Ancient China.* Viking, 2002. Ages 9–12.

Sayre, Henry. *Cave Paintings to Picasso: The Inside Scoop on 50 Art Masterpieces.* Chronicle, 2004. Ages 11–14.

Stevens, Janet. *From Pictures to Words: A Book about Making a Book.* Holiday, 1995. (**PI**) Ages 5–8.

Thomson, Peggy, and Barbara Moore. *The Nine-Ton Cat: Behind the Scenes at an Art Museum.* Houghton, 1997. Ages 9–14.

Warhola, James. *Uncle Andy's: A Faabbulous Visit with Andy Warhol.* Putnam, 2003. (**PI**) Ages 5–8.

Wolf, Allan. *Immersed in Verse: An Informative, Slightly Irreverent & Totally Tremendous Guide to Living the Poet's Life.* Illustrated by Tuesday Mourning. Lark Books, 2006. Ages 12–14.

Related Films, Videos, and DVDs

Building Big. (2000, mini-series). Author: David Macaulay. 327 minutes.

Castle. (1986). Author: David Macaulay. 60 minutes. Also in the PBS series of hour-long documentaries based on books by Macaulay: *Cathedral* (1986); *Pyramid* (1988); *Roman City* (1994).

The Diary of Ann Frank. (1959). Author: Ann Frank. 171 minutes.

Just a Few Words, Mr. Lincoln. (1999). Author: Jean Fritz. Illustrator: Charles Robinson. 21 minutes.

The Man Who Walked between the Towers. (2005). Author/Illustrator: Mordicai Gerstein. 10 minutes.

Rascal. (1969). Author: Sterling North. 85 minutes.

Snowflake Bentley. (2003). Author: Jacqueline Briggs Martin. Illustrator: Mary Azarian. 16 minutes.

What's the Big Idea, Benjamin Franklin? (1993). Author: Jean Fritz. Illustrator: Margot Tomes. 30 minutes.

Will You Sign Here, John Hancock? (1997). Author: Jean Fritz. Illustrator: Trina Schart Hyman. 30 minutes.

Sources for Films, Videos, and DVDs

The Video Source Book. Syosset, NY: National Video Clearinghouse, 1979–. Published by Gale Research, Detroit, MI.

An annual reference work that lists media and provides sources for purchase and rental.

Websites of large video distributors:

www.libraryvideo.com

http://teacher.scholastic.com/products/westonwoods

chapter 11

Literature for a Diverse Society

Oh, the Places You'll Go
Uh-huh, I've travelled
By car, train, boat, plane
To Kenya, Uganda
France, Italy, Spain.

Still many a country
I plan to explore
Here's how you do it
I've done it before.

Weather won't stop you
Nor cost of the flight
You'll fly the world over
By day and by night.

The means are at hand
You've not far to look
Oh, the places you'll go
When you travel by book.

—Ashley Bryan

This chapter is presented in two parts. The first part, Strategies for Culturally Responsive Instruction, focuses on ways teachers can make their teaching relevant to their students and to the world their students will inhabit. The second part, Multicultural and International Literature, identifies literature that supports culturally responsive instruction.

Section One: Strategies for Culturally Responsive Instruction

A serious mismatch exists in today's schools in the United States. On the one hand, school curricula present predominantly mainstream, Euro-American perspectives. Moreover, the cadre of teachers in this country are predominantly (84.3 percent in 1999–2000) from Euro-American, suburban backgrounds (U.S. Department of Education, 2000c) and have been trained to teach in ways that work best with people like themselves. Most teachers have not had close, sustained relationships with individuals from different ethnic, cultural, and lower socioeconomic backgrounds (Schmidt, 2005). On the other hand, school populations in the United States have become increasingly diverse, as evidenced by the United States Department of Education's prediction that the school-aged minority populations will become the majority populations by 2010 (U.S. Department of Education, 2002b).

The resulting mismatch has contributed to an education system that is not working for many students. The Office of National Assessment for Educational Progress, for instance, since its inception in 1992, has reported a continuing reading achievement gap between whites on the one hand and Native Americans, Latinos, and African Americans on the other. In 2005, the average reading scores for eighth-grade whites was 271 versus 249 for Native Americans, 246 for Latinos, and 243 for African Americans (National Center for Education Statistics, 2005). Other evidence of the problem is the school dropout rates of some minority populations. As reported by the National Center for Education Statistics (U.S. Department of Education, 2002a), the high school dropout rate in 2000 for Latinos was 27.8 percent and 13.1 percent for African Americans as compared to 3.8 percent for Asian Americans and 6.9 percent for whites. Clearly, teachers and school administrators need to become more familiar with the realities of culture and its impact on teaching and learning (Ford & Moore, 2004, p. 34).

To address this problem, some within the field of education are exploring ways to make instruction more culturally responsive. *Culturally responsive instruction* is grounded in making the school experience relevant to all students by (1) reshaping school curricula to encompass the perspectives of all cultures represented in the student body while adhering to standards of achievement and (2) employing teaching strategies that suit the learning styles of all students. The goal is to make connections with students' backgrounds, interests, and experiences so that all students will feel part of the school experience, remain engaged, and experience success in learning (Schmidt, 2005). Next, we address teaching strategies that take into consideration students' cultural differences, particularly as they relate to literacy learning and achievement.

 ## Culturally Responsive Teaching Strategies and Literature

Schmidt (2005) outlines several characteristics of culturally responsive instruction, most of which can be understood as strategies that can be directly related to literature. These strategies and examples of their application follow.

High Expectations

■ *High expectations support students as they develop the literacy appropriate to their ages and abilities.* All students need support in their literacy acquisition, but our focus here is on providing that support to children who have traditionally not received it in full measure—members of certain ethnic minorities and resistant readers, two groups that often overlap. As discussed in Chapter 2, resistant readers often cite irrelevance of teacher-selected reading materials to their lives and instructional practices as reasons for not reading. Important ways teachers can actively support the literacy development of those who reject reading are:

■ *Find reading material for independent reading and reading aloud that is relevant to students' lives.* Believing that all students can achieve is closely connected to becoming acquainted with students personally and finding ways to help them achieve, including being knowledgeable about literature that is culturally relevant to them. For minority students this may be literature about young people whose lives and cultures are similar to their own. For boys this will be reading material appealing to boys. For second-language learners this may be bilingual literature, one of the languages being the student's native tongue, so as to make learning English easier.

■ *Ensure that school and classroom literature collections reflect the cultural diversity of the classrooms, schools, and communities.* In cases where schools and communities are culturally homogeneous, librarians and teachers would nonetheless be wise to select books that reflect the diversity of the greater world their students will live in.

■ *Give students a choice in their reading material.* This may require teachers and librarians to broaden the scope of what they consider appropriate reading material to include less conventional formats such as picture books for older readers, graphic novels, nonfiction such as automotive manuals and cookbooks, magazines, and audiobooks. Giving students a choice in what they read acknowledges them and shows them that their teachers and librarians are interested in them and care that they learn.

■ *Conference with students about their reading* as *often as possible.* These one-on-one discussions give teachers an opportunity to learn about their students' individual reading interests and needs, to supply pinpoint reading instruction as needed, to express their interest in what the students are currently reading, and to suggest other books they might like to read.

■ *Establish routines, many of which can be literature-related.* Routines help stabilize the school day and give students something to look forward to. A simple but important daily routine is greeting each student with a smile and a hello at the classroom door. Beyond this, teachers can start or end the day (or class) with a poem, being sure that the poems reflect the cultures represented in their classes. Collections such as Véronique Tadjo's *Talking Poems: A Selection of Poems from Africa South of the Sahara* would be ideal for sharing with upper elementary and middle-graders. Because the poems originate from sixteen different African nations, a teacher might choose to read a poem from one nation each day and then show on a map the location of the nation. A good follow-up to reading poems aloud is to post copies of the poems on the bulletin board for students to reread later.

Examples of other literature-related routines include (1) having regular times to read aloud to students and to devote to independent reading, (2) having students list in their journals the titles of books read independently, and (3) having students recommend books to other students either during a once-weekly open forum or by listing recommended books on a permanent wall chart for all to see.

Culturally Sensitive Curriculum

■ *Cultural sensitivity-reshaped curriculum—mediated for culturally valued knowledge—connects with the standards-based curriculum as well as individual students' cultural backgrounds.* A reshaped curriculum will be more inclusive than the traditional one. Social studies and history curricula, for example, will include perspectives of those long neglected—Native Americans, African Americans, Asian Americans, to name a few. Science curricula will include important contributions made by minority scientists. Reading and literature curricula will include works by minority or foreign authors. For example, a literature unit could focus on a notable minority author such as Francisco Jiménez, a Mexican American whose works describe the struggles of immigrants and their families who work in the California fields. Generally in these units teachers will choose one of the featured author's works to read aloud and others for students to read in literature circles. Lists of Notable Authors can be found in Chapters 4 through 10 and include some minority authors. In this chapter there are two lists of Notable Authors, Multicultural and International, for consideration of author choices.

The goal of those who write, publish, and promote multicultural and international children's literature is to help people learn about, understand, and, ultimately, accept those different from themselves, thus breaking the cycles of prejudice between peoples of different ethnicities, religions, and language-related cultures. Progress toward this goal in the United States may well begin when young people read or listen to works of multicultural or international literature and realize how *similar* they are to children of different cultures and how *interesting* their differences are. These books help build bridges and erase borders between people of different nationalities and cultures, to use the metaphors of Jella Lepman (1964/2002) and Hazel Rochman (1993).

Teachers and librarians can be instrumental in achieving this worthy goal by integrating multicultural and international literature into their school curricula. Here are some ideas for bringing these books to your students' attention and facilitating their reading or listening.

■ Match or pair similar works (in genre, theme, or topic) of multicultural or international literature with works by mainstream authors and illustrators, saying, "If you liked this (mainstream) book, you would probably like this (multicultural or international) book, too."

■ Use lists of character names, if unusual or numerous, or maps of story settings as story aids, if warranted. These lists or maps can be kept in view as a story is read.

■ Integrate multicultural and international books into instructional or thematic units. In social studies and history units, these books can lend an authentic, "I was there" flavor to the learning experience.

■ Encourage students to search for further information about a culture or country represented in a book. This can be an individual or a whole class effort and can be done as the book is being read or after it is finished. Encourage students to chart the similarities and differences in their cultures and those of the other culture or country.

- Operate from the conviction that international books are for everyone, not just for "gifted" students.
- Post titles of other books written or illustrated by a current favorite multicultural or international author or illustrator.

Active Teaching Methods

- *Active teaching methods will involve students in a variety of reading, writing, listening, speaking, and viewing behaviors throughout the lesson plan.* Throughout this textbook we have encouraged independent reading and reading aloud to students daily, if possible. We have also included lists of literature-related films in each genre chapter to encourage the use of this medium. Furthermore, Chapter 13 is devoted to ways to enhance all students' experiences with literature. To make these activities culturally relevant, teachers and librarians need to select as material for reading or study a balanced selection of literature by and about the ethnic, religious, or language groups represented in their classrooms, schools, and communities. As a start, see the Excellent Multicultural Literature to Read Aloud list and the Excellent International Literature to Read Aloud list in this chapter. In addition, teachers and librarians can booktalk and display culturally diverse books regularly along with mainstream books (see Chapter 13 for a discussion of book-talking) and include culturally relevant books in text sets for classroom study or independent reading. A collection of picture books to booktalk on the subject of families, a common topic investigated in the primary grades, might include

> *Families* by Ann Morris (cross-cultural)
> *I Love Saturdays y Domingos* by Alma Flor Ada, illustrated by Elvivia Savadier (Mexican-American)
> *Mayeros: A Yucatec Maya Family* by George Ancona (Native American)
> *My Mei Mei* by Ed Young (Chinese-American)
> *Quinnie Blue* by Dinah Johnson, illustrated by James Ransome (African-American)
> *Uncle Peter's Amazing Chinese Wedding* by Lenore Look, illustrated by Yumi Heo (Chinese-American)

Instruction in Groups and Pairs

- *Plan instruction around groups and pairs—completing assignments individually, but usually in small groups or pairs with time to share ideas and think critically about the work.* The reason culturally relevant instruction promotes students working in groups and pairs is to decrease anxiety students experience when left on their own. Advantages specific to shared reading activities are that more able students give less able ones insights into how good readers get meaning from a text, various interpretations of the text are shared, and discussions and predictions ensue, all leading to a fuller understanding of what is read.

Response to literature can also be a group effort. Choice, planning, preparation, and presentation of the response can all be done in pairs or small groups. Of course, some methods of response work better than others as group efforts. Responses particularly well-suited to pairs or small groups include rewriting part of the book into a skit or radio play and performing it, drawing a mural based on the book, or creating a jackdaw around the book's setting. *Hot Day on Abbott Avenue* by Karen

English and illustrated by Javaka Steptoe, for example, lends itself to being reinterpreted as a skit with two players and a narrator, because the book itself is about a day in the life of two friends.

Positive Relations with Families and the Community

■ *Positive relations with families and community will demonstrate clear connections with student families and communities in terms of curriculum content and relationships.* Regular contact between school personnel and those most involved with a child's education at the present time—whether parents or members of the child's extended family—keeps lines of communication open and also sends the message that students and their families are valued by the educational establishment. Positive exchanges can be in the form of responses to literature that lead students back to their families or communities. For individuals this may involve interviewing an older family member about their family history after reading a work of historical fiction. Such interviews can be the basis for writing family stories that can be collected into a class anthology. For a whole class it may be involvement in a community civic action project, such as improvement of housing for migrant workers in their community, stemming from their reading of a work of multicultural literature, as in Beth Atkin's *Voices from the Fields: Children of Migrant Farmworkers Tell Their Stories.*

Section Two: Multicultural and International Literature

In Section One we built a case for culturally responsive instruction and for the fact that good literature relevant to students' lives is central to such instruction. In this section we will define and discuss two bodies of literature that support culturally responsive instruction—multicultural and international literature. Multicultural literature and international literature are not separate genres; rather, they occur in all genres.

You will have noted many references to multicultural and international books and authors throughout the previous chapters in discussions of trends and issues, notable author and illustrator lists, and end-of-chapter recommended booklists. In an ideal, culturally integrated world, such inclusion would be sufficient. But the groups and perspectives represented in multicultural literature have, until recently, been totally absent from or misrepresented in books for children and remain underrepresented today. Furthermore, neither multicultural nor international literature is well known or fully recognized by the educational mainstream. Changing demographics in this country and globalization of our society require school curricula and materials that will prepare young people to live in a changing and ever more diverse world.

 ## Multicultural Literature

Definition and Description

Multicultural literature is defined in various ways within the educational community. Some define it broadly as *all* books about people and their individual or group experiences, originating both in this country and in other countries. Some define it more narrowly as literature by and about groups in this country that have been overshadowed and to various degrees disregarded by the dominant, Euro-American culture. This definition includes all racial, ethnic, religious, and language group minorities, those living with physical or mental disabilities, gays and lesbians, and the poor. Examples of multicultural literature used in this section emphasize literature by and about the racial, religious, and language groups in the United States that have created a substantial body of children's literature. This includes literature by and about African Americans; Asian Americans (including people of Chinese, Hmong, Japanese, Korean, and Vietnamese descent); Latinos (including Cuban Americans, Mexican Americans, Puerto Ricans, and others of Spanish descent); religious cultures (including Buddhist, Hindu, Jewish, and Muslim); and Native Americans (a general term referring to the many tribes of American Indians). Examples of books about other marginalized groups may be found throughout the genre chapters, especially in lists of recommended books at the end of each genre chapter.

Benefits of Multicultural Literature for Children

Multicultural literature benefits children in the following ways:

- It addresses contemporary issues of race, religion, poverty, living with exceptionalities, and sexual orientation from the perspective of members of those groups. This perspective helps give young people a more complete understanding of these current issues and of the people who belong to these groups, thus reducing the likelihood of prejudices against those different from themselves. Realistic fiction is particularly appropriate in this regard.
- It adds the perspective of disenfranchised groups to the study of history, thereby giving students a more complete understanding of past events. Historical fiction, biography, and nonfiction history books are excellent sources for these varied perspectives.
- It helps young people realize the social injustices endured by some people in the United States and abroad both now and in the past and it builds a determination to work for a more equitable future.
- It gives young people who are members of marginalized groups the opportunity to develop a better sense of who they are, improve self-esteem, and, consequently, hope for a better future through civic action.

Evaluation and Selection of Multicultural Literature

In addition to the standard requirement for high literary merit, *critical reading* with attention to whether characters are portrayed honestly and respectfully and to whether themes are worthwhile are of utmost importance in evaluating and selecting multicultural literature. The following criteria are part of critical reading and should be considered when evaluating and selecting multicultural books for school and classroom libraries:

- *Authentic depiction of the cultural experience from the perspective of that group.* Either the story is told by someone of the culture or by someone not of the culture who has carefully researched the culture.
- *Accuracy of cultural details in text and illustrations.* This extends to accuracy when describing subgroups *within* a larger group—for example, a specific Native American tribe.

Excellent Multicultural Literature to Read Aloud

Canales, Viola. *The Tequila Worm.* Ages 12–15. (Mexican-American)

Curtis, Christopher Paul. *Mr. Chickee's Funny Money.* Ages 8–12. (African-American)

English, Karen. *Hot Day on Abbott Avenue.* Illustrated by Javaka Steptoe. Ages 5–8. (African-American)

Jaramillo, Ann. *La Línea.* Ages 11–15. (Mexican-American)

Mikaelsen, Ben. *Touching Spirit Bear.* Ages 11–14. (Native American)

Mollel, Tololwa. *My Rows and Piles of Coins.* Illustrated by E. B. Lewis. Ages 5–8. (Set in Africa)

Na, An. *A Step from Heaven.* Front Street, 2001. Ages 13–18. (Korean-American)

Nelson, Kadir. *He's Got the Whole World in His Hands.* Ages 4–8. (African-American)

Nislick, June Levitt. *Zayda Was a Cowboy.* Ages 9–13. (Jewish)

Park, Linda Sue. *Mulberry Project.* Ages 10–14. (Korean-American)

Soto, Gary. *Chato and the Party Animals.* Illustrated by Susan Guevara. Ages 5–8. (Mexican-American)

- *Positive images of minority characters.* Even in books about topics that have no positives, such as slavery, some pivotal characters should be shown as undaunted or hopeful for a better future. This can have a positive influence on young readers' self-esteem.
- *Balance between historic and contemporary views of groups.* Native Americans of today, for example, do not always wear traditional dress and ride horses, so contemporary book images should not depict them so.
- *Adequate representation of any group.* No one book can definitively describe a culture or a cultural experience. The more good books about a culture, the more complete the picture.

Book awards for special content can guide teachers and librarians toward high-quality multicultural books. The best known of these is the Coretta Scott King Award, founded in 1969 and, since 1979, sponsored by the American Library Association. This annual award is given to the African-American author and (since 1974) illustrator whose books published in the preceding year are judged to be the most outstanding inspirational and educational literature for children. The Américas Award, founded in 1993, and the Pura Belpré Award, founded in 1996, by honoring outstanding Latino authors and illustrators of children's books, have done much to encourage the publication of high-quality books for this rapidly growing segment of the population. The first Asian Pacific American Award for Literature, honoring outstanding work of Asian-American authors and illustrators, was given in 2001. Awards such as these encourage the publication of more and better-quality multicultural literature.

In recent years, small presses such as those in the following list have given teachers and librarians a source of multicultural books that are particularly valuable for their distinctly multicultural point of view.

Asian American Curriculum Project. In addition to its own publications, this company distributes Asian-American books from other small and large presses. E-mail: aacpinc@best.com

Children's Book Press. This company publishes folktales and contemporary stories, often bilingual, in picture book format for Native American, Asian-American, and Latino children. Webpage: www.childrensbookpress.org

Piñata Books/Arte Público, University of Houston, 4800 Calhoun, Houston, TX 77204. This alternative press publishes children's books with a Latino perspective. Webpage: www.arte .uh.edu

Just Us Books. This company produces Afrocentric books that enhance the self-esteem of African-American children. Webpage: www.justusbooks.com

Lee & Low Books. This Asian-American–owned company stresses authenticity in its contemporary stories for Asian-American, Latino, and African-American children. Its Latino titles are also offered in Spanish. Webpage: www.leeandlow.com

Pemmican Publications. This Canadian company publishes excellent realistic stories about contemporary Native American children and educational books for the Métis people about Métis history and culture. Webpage: www.pemmican.mb.ca

Evaluating, selecting, and then bringing multicultural literature to your classroom, although essential, are not enough to ensure that your students will actually read the books. Without adult guidance, children tend to choose books about children like themselves (Rudman, 1984), so you must also purposefully expose mainstream children to multicultural books through reading aloud, booktalking, and selecting particular titles for small group reading.

Historical Overview of Multicultural Literature

Members of many microcultures living in the United States were long ignored as subjects for children's books. On the few occasions that representatives of these groups did appear, they did so as crudely stereotyped characters, objects of ridicule, or shadowy secondary characters. Helen Bannerman's *The Story of Little Black Sambo* (1900) and Hugh Lofting's *The Voyages of Dr. Dolittle* (1922) come under this category. Today, books such as these either have been rewritten to eliminate the racism or have disappeared from children's library shelves.

The first harbinger of change came in 1949 when an African-American author, Arna Bontemps, won a Newbery Honor Award for his *Story of the Negro* and became the first member of a minority group to receive this honor. A more sympathetic attitude toward American microcultures, at least in literature, emerged in the 1950s, as evidenced by the positive, yet somewhat patronizing, treatment of multicultural characters in such Newbery Medal winners as *Amos Fortune, Free Man* by Elizabeth Yates (1950) and *. . . And Now Miguel* by Joseph Krumgold (1953).

The Civil Rights Movement of the 1960s focused attention on the social inequities and racial injustices that prevailed in the United States. The spirit of the times resulted in two landmark publications. The first of these was *The Snowy Day* by Ezra Jack Keats (1962), the first Caldecott Medal–winning book to have an African American as the protagonist. The second publication was a powerful article by Nancy Larrick entitled "The All-White World of Children's Books." In this article, which appeared in the September 11, 1965, issue of *Saturday Review,* Larrick reported that in nearly all U.S. children's books the African American either was omitted entirely or was scarcely mentioned (p. 63). American trade book publishers, the education system, and the public library system were called on to fill this void.

MILESTONES in the Development of Multicultural Literature

Date	Event	Significance
1932	*Waterless Mountain* by Laura Armer wins Newbery Medal	One of the few children's books about minorities in the first half of the twentieth century
1946	*The Moved-Outers* by Florence C. Means wins Newbery Honor	A departure from stereotyped depiction of minorities begins
1949	*Story of the Negro* by Arna Bontemps wins Newbery Honor	First minority author to win a Newbery Honor
1950	*Song of the Swallows* by Leo Politi wins Caldecott Medal	First picture book with a Hispanic-American protagonist to win the Caldecott Medal
1963	*The Snowy Day* by Ezra Jack Keats wins Caldecott Medal	First picture book with an African-American protagonist to win the Caldecott Medal
1965	"The All-White World of Children's Books" by Nancy Larrick published in *Saturday Review*	Called the nation's attention to the lack of multicultural literature
1969	Coretta Scott King Award founded	African-American literature and authors begin to be promoted and supported
1975	*M. C. Higgins, the Great* by Virginia Hamilton wins Newbery Medal	First book by a minority author to win the Newbery Medal
1976	*Why Mosquitoes Buzz in People's Ears* illustrated by Leo and Diane Dillon wins Caldecott Medal	First picture book illustrated by an African American to win the Caldecott Medal
1990	*Lon Po Po: A Red-Riding Hood Story from China* translated and illustrated by Ed Young wins Caldecott Medal	First picture book illustrated by a Chinese American to win the Caldecott Medal
1993	Américas Award founded	Encouraged authors and illustrators to publish excellent books portraying Latin America, the Caribbean, and Latinos in the United States
1994	*Grandfather's Journey* written and illustrated by Allen Say wins Caldecott Medal	First picture book illustrated by a Japanese American to win the Caldecott Medal
1996	Pura Belpré Award founded	Latino literature, authors, and illustrators promoted
2001	*The Trip Back Home* by Janet S. Wong, illustrated by Bo Jia, wins first Asian Pacific American Award for Literature	Asian-American literature, authors, and illustrators promoted

In 1969, the Coretta Scott King Award was established to recognize distinguished writing in children's books by African-American authors. Although several books with multicultural protagonists or themes were chosen as Newbery winners in the early 1970s, it was not until 1975 that an author of color, Virginia Hamilton, author of *M. C. Higgins, the Great,* won a Newbery Medal. After 1975, the prevailing opinion among U.S. children's book publishers and professional reviewers seemed to be that members of a group were the ones most able to write authoritatively about their own particular cultures and experiences. Euro-American authors were no longer as likely to win major awards for writing about minorities as they were in the early 1970s.

The late 1990s saw some much-needed development in Latino literature. Bilingual books published in response to the demands of ESOL/ELL (English for speakers of other languages/English language learners) programs and the founding of the Américas Award and the Pura Belpré Awards contributed to this growth.

Although the last several decades have seen positive changes in the status of multicultural literature in the United States, there is still a marked shortage of books of this kind. Multicultural authors and illustrators of children's books are also in short supply. In 2005, for instance, only 75 (2.5 percent) of the approximately 3,000 new children and young adult books reviewed by the Cooperative Children's Book Center were written or illustrated by African Americans (Horning, Lindgren, Rudiger, & Schliesman, 2006), a group that represents 12.3 percent of the U.S. population. A broader indication of this shortage is that in 2005 only 323 (6 percent) of the approximately 5,000 new children's books published in the United States were by or about all people of color (principally African Americans, Asian Americans, Latinos, and Native Americans), even though these groups represent approximately 30 percent of the population (U.S. Census Bureau, 2000).

Types of Multicultural Literature

Before discussing the literature of each microculture, a general caution is in order. Each of these groups contains subgroups that differ remarkably from one another in country of origin, language, race, traditions, and present location. Teachers must be especially conscious of and sensitive to these differences and guard against presenting these groups as completely uniform or of selecting literature that does so. Gross overgeneralization is not only inaccurate but also a form of stereotyping.

African-American Literature

Of all multicultural groups living in the United States, African Americans have produced the largest and most rapidly growing body of children's literature. Every genre is well represented in African-American literature, but none better than poetry. Because it is so personal, poetry portrays a culture well, as is evident in the sensitive yet powerful work of poets Arnold Adoff, Gwendolyn Brooks, Nikki Giovanni, Eloise Greenfield, and Langston Hughes. For example, see *In Daddy's Arms I Am Tall: African Americans Celebrating Fathers* by Javaka Steptoe.

Tapping into their rich oral tradition, African Americans have contributed Anansi the Spider, Brer Rabbit, High John the Conqueror, and John Henry the Steel Drivin' Man to the list of favorite U.S. folklore characters. Even today, authors are bringing folktales to the United States from Africa.

Examples include *Ananse and the Lizard: A West African Tale* by Pat Cummings and *The Girl Who Spun Gold* by Virginia Hamilton, illustrated by Leo and Diane Dillon.

In some cases, African Americans have reclaimed their tales by retelling (without racist elements) stories that were first written down in this country by Euro-American authors, as Julius Lester has done in his retelling of Joel Chandler Harris's *The Tales of Uncle Remus: The Adventures of Brer Rabbit.* More recent memories and family stories have begun to be written by African-American authors as modern folktales. For example, see *Mirandy and Brother Wind* by Patricia McKissack.

African Americans have told the stories of their lives in the United States through both historical and realistic fiction. The stories for older readers often include painfully harsh but accurate accounts of racial oppression, as in James Berry's slavery story *Ajeemah and His Son* or Mildred Taylor's historical fiction saga of the close-knit Logan family (*The Song of the Trees; Roll of Thunder, Hear My Cry; Let the Circle Be Unbroken; The Road to Memphis;* and *The Land*). Teachers can see to it that such stories are balanced, however, with more positive, encouraging contemporary stories such as Jacqueline Woodson's contemporary realistic novel, *Locomotion* and Angela Johnson's *Heaven.*

Recently, African-American faces have begun to appear more frequently in picture books. Although these books tend to address universal topics rather than those dealing specifically with race, they can still be culturally conscious. The works of illustrators Leo and Diane Dillon, Tom Feelings, Jerry Pinkney, Brian Pinkney, E. B. Lewis, and Kadir Nelson deserve special notice. Examples include *He's Got the Whole World in His Hands* by Kadir Nelson and *The Middle Passage: White Ships/Black Cargo* by Tom Feelings.

African-American nonfiction is mainly biography. In the 1960s and 1970s, a large percentage of these biographical subjects were sports heroes, but more recent subjects have come from a broader spectrum of achievement. For example, see *Through My Eyes* by Ruby Bridges and edited by Margo Lundell.

Asian-American Literature

Asian-American children's literature is mainly represented in the United States by stories about Chinese Americans, Japanese Americans, and Korean Americans possibly because these groups have lived as microcultures in this country longer than others, such as Vietnamese Americans. A major theme in much of the fiction and nonfiction for older readers is the oppression that drove the people out of their homelands and the prejudice that they faced as newcomers in this country. A more positive theme is that of learning to appreciate one's cultural heritage while adjusting to life in the United States. A good example is An Na's *A Step from Heaven.*

Traditional stories from Asia retold in English have contributed many interesting folktales and folktale variants to children's libraries. Characters who are generally thought of as European, such as Little Red Riding Hood and Cinderella, have their Asian counterparts. Examples are *Lon Po Po: A Red-Riding Hood Story from China,* translated and illustrated by Ed Young, and *Yeh Shen: A Cinderella Story from China* by Ai-Ling Louie, illustrated by Ed Young.

Asian-American artists have brought the sophisticated style and technical artistry of the Orient to U.S. children's book illustration. Ed Young's use of screenlike panels and exotic, textured paper and Allen Say's precision are especially noteworthy. Examples are *Tea with Milk* by Allen Say and *Monkey King* by Ed Young.

The body of Asian-American children's literature is small. Nonfiction, poetry, and fantasy are almost unrepresented, with the notable exception of Rhoda Blumberg's works of nonfiction, such as *Shipwrecked! The True Adventures of a Japanese Boy*. The recently established Asian Pacific American Award for Literature, as well as small presses, such as Lee & Low Books, will help to improve this situation.

Latino Literature

Few Latino children's books are published in the United States, despite the fact that Latinos represent an estimated 13 percent of the population and are considered the fastest-growing segment of the population (U.S. Census Bureau, 2000). Recent developments hold promise for improvement in the amount and quality of Latino literature. The books that are available are mainly about Puerto Ricans and Mexican Americans; the works of Alma Flor Ada, George Ancona, Lulu Delacre, and Gary Soto are outstanding examples. Good examples are *Chato and the Party Animals* by Gary Soto, illustrated by Susan Guevara, and *The Circuit: Stories from the Life of a Migrant Child* by Francisco Jiménez.

The establishment in 1993 of the Américas Award for a U.S. work that authentically presents the experience of individuals in Latin America or the Caribbean or of Latinos in the United States and, in 1996, of the Pura Belpré Award honoring outstanding Latino children's authors and illustrators will undoubtedly promote the creation of more high-quality Latino literature for children. In addition to the recommended books by and about Latinos at the end of this chapter, another source is the website of the Barahona Center for the Study of Books in Spanish for Children and Adolescents at the University of California San Marcos (www.csusm.edu/csb), which contains lists of books in English about Latinos and books in Spanish.

Native American Literature

Almost from the moment that European explorers landed on this continent some 500 years ago, Native Americans have suffered at the hands of Euro-Americans. Consequently, in books written from the Native American perspective, oppression by the white population is a pervasive theme. Appreciation, celebration, and protection of nature—central tenets of Native American cultures—are other recurrent themes in this body of literature. Examples are *Crazy Horse's Vision* by Joseph Bruchac, illustrated by S. D. Nelson, and *The Birchbark House* by Louise Erdrich.

Although much has been written *about* Native Americans, relatively little has been written *by* members of this microculture. Small press publishers specializing in literature by Native Americans may help to change this situation. Native Americans who are known for their children's books include Cynthia Leitich Smith for her novels, Joseph Bruchac for his retold stories, and Michael Lacapa and Shonto Begay for their illustrations. Examples are *Rain Is Not My Indian Name* by Cynthia Leitich Smith and *The First Strawberries* retold by Joseph Bruchac, illustrated by Anna Vojtech.

Numerous other writers and illustrators have told and retold the folktales and history of Native Americans in picture books, historical fiction, and informational books. Paul Goble is particularly well known for his impressively illustrated retellings of the legends of the Plains Indians, as are Scott O'Dell and Canadian Jan Hudson for their award-winning works of historical fiction featuring young Native American women. The body of nonfictional works about Native Americans is particularly rich, the works of Ann Nolan Clark, Russell Freedman, Milton Meltzer,

Notable Authors and Illustrators of Multicultural Literature

AFRICAN-AMERICAN

Leo and Diane Dillon, illustrators of two Caldecott Medal–winning books. Leo Dillon is the first African American to win a Caldecott Medal. *Why Mosquitoes Buzz in People's Ears; Ashanti to Zulu.*

Angela Johnson, author whose stories about family relationships range from board books to novels for young adults. *Tell Me a Story, Mama; Heaven; The First Part Last.*

Patricia McKissack, author of modern African-American folktales and informational books. *Mirandy and Brother Wind.*

Walter Dean Myers, author of sometimes gritty contemporary realistic fiction about African Americans growing up. *Scorpions; Monster.*

Brian Pinkney, illustrator whose swirling lines and black backgrounds in intricate scratch-board renderings create a sense of intrigue and mystery. *Cendrillon: A Caribbean Cinderella; The Faithful Friend.*

Jerry Pinkney, illustrator whose light-filled watercolors capture the beauty of African Americans. *Goin' Someplace Special.*

Mildred Taylor, author whose award-winning books of historical fiction chronicle the experience of growing up black in southern United States in the 1940s and 1950s. *Roll of Thunder, Hear My Cry; The Land.*

Jacqueline Woodson, author of introspective novels dealing with overcoming adversity and loss. *Miracle's Boys; Hush; Locomotion.* www.jacquelinewoodson.com

ASIAN-AMERICAN

Laurence Yep, author of historical and contemporary realistic fiction about growing up as a Chinese American. *Dragonwings; Traitor: Golden Mountain Chronicles, 1885.*

Ed Young, first Asian-American illustrator to win the Caldecott Award. *Lon Po Po: A Red-Riding Hood Story from China.*

LATINO

Alma Flor Ada, author, reteller, and translator of stories, folktales, nursery rhymes, concept books, and bilingual books for and about children of Mexican heritage. *I Love Saturdays y Domingos; Gathering the Sun: An Alphabet in Spanish and English.* www.almaflorada.com

George Ancona, Mexican-American photographer who writes about and photographs the life and culture of Mexico and Mexican Americans. *Carnaval; Fiesta U.S.A.*

Francisco Jiménez, author of autobiographical stories of his childhood as an illegal Mexican immigrant farm worker in California. *The Circuit: Stories from the Life of a Migrant Child; Breaking Through.* www.scu.edu/fjimenez

Pat Mora, author of picture storybooks, biographies, and poems about the Mexican-American experience. *Tomás and the Library Lady; Confetti: Poems for Children.* www.patmora.com

Gary Soto, author of contemporary stories about the Mexican-American experience. *Taking Sides; Snapshots from the Wedding.* www.garysoto.com

NATIVE AMERICAN

Joseph Bruchac, reteller of Native American folktales and legends and biographer of famous Native Americans. *The First Strawberries; Crazy Horse's Vision.* www.josephbruchac.com

Louise Erdrich, author of works of historical fiction about an Ojibwa tribe living on the coast of Lake Superior in the mid-nineteenth century. *The Birchbark House; The Game of Silence.*

Paul Goble, reteller and illustrator of the folktales and legends of the Native Americans of the Great Plains. *The Girl Who Loved Wild Horses; Storm Maker's Tipi.*

Scott O'Dell, author of several works of award-winning historical fiction featuring strong female Native American heroines. *Island of the Blue Dolphins.* www.scottodell.com

RELIGIOUS CULTURES

Adèle Geras, anthologist of folktales and other stories celebrating the Jewish tradition. *My Grandmother's Stories: A Collection of Jewish Folktales; The Kingfisher Treasury of Jewish Stories.* www.adelegeras.com

Eric Kimmel, reteller of tales, many of which are from the Jewish culture. *Gershon's Monster: A Story for the Jewish New Year.* www.ericakimmel.com

John Bierhorst, Brent Ashabranner, and Alex Bealer being outstanding. Examples include *The Girl Who Loved Wild Horses* by Paul Goble, *Island of the Blue Dolphins* by Scott O'Dell, and *Only the Names Remain: The Cherokees and the Trail of Tears* by Alex Bealer.

Religious Cultures Literature

Because the United States is traditionally a Christian nation, the nonmainstream religious cultures represented in children's books in the United States include Buddhist, Hindu, Jewish, and Muslim. Good, contemporary children's fiction set within the context of a religious culture and written from the perspective of a member of that religion is scarce. An example is Asma Mobin-Uddin's *My Name Is Bilal,* a picture book for older readers illustrated by Barbara Kiwak, which explores the topic of fitting into the U.S. mainstream while remaining true to one's Islamic culture and heritage. Nonfiction and folklore on the subject of religion are more plentiful. Author-illustrator Demi, for example, is known for her picture book biographies and story collections about Buddha and Buddhism and Muhammed and Islam.

The body of Jewish children's literature is by far the largest produced by the nonmainstream religious cultures in this country. The terrible experience of the Jewish Holocaust in Europe during the 1930s and 1940s has had a tremendous influence on Jewish children's literature. The prejudice and cruelty that led to the Holocaust and the nightmare of the death camps themselves are recurring themes in both fiction and nonfiction for older readers. Since many Jewish people immigrated to the United States as the Nazi threat grew in Europe, much Holocaust literature has been written by eyewitnesses or by those whose relatives were victims. Examples are *Thanks to My Mother* by Schoschana Rabinovici and *Smoke and Ashes: The Story of the Holocaust* by Barbara Rogasky.

Illustrated Jewish folktales offer excellent, witty stories and high literary quality. Recent examples include the works of Simms Taback such as *Joseph Had a Little Overcoat* and the collection *Kibitzers and Fools.*

The Jewish community has produced a number of excellent authors and illustrators of children's books. Literary creativity is promoted through two book award programs: the National Jewish Book Awards and the Association of Jewish Libraries' Sydney Taylor Awards for children's and young adult literature.

Bilingual Literature

Bilingual books, which are those having text in two languages, are appearing in the United States with greater frequency each year, particularly English/Spanish books, reflecting the rapid growth of the Latino population in this country. Picture books and shorter chapter books predominate, since longer books in two languages would be bulky and costly and are not generally useful to more advanced readers. These books, if well done, are helpful to children in ESOL/ELL programs and their teachers. Not all bilingual books have artful, or even accurate translations, so careful selection is advisable. The concept book, *Siesta,* written by Ginger Guy and illustrated by René King Moreno, is notable for its integration of the concepts of color and everyday household items in text and illustrations to make the English and Spanish texts easier to understand.

International Literature

Definition and Description

International literature in the United States refers to those books originally written and published in countries other than the United States for children of those other countries and then published in this country. These books can be subdivided into three categories:

- *English Language Books.* Books originally written in English in another country, such as Australia, then published or distributed in the United States. Example: *Let's Get a Pup, Said Kate* by Bob Graham (Australia).
- *Translated Books.* Books written in a language other than English in a country other than the United States, then translated into English and published in this country. Example: *The Friends* by Kazumi Yumoto (Japan).
- *Foreign Language Books.* Books written and published in a country other than the United States in a language other than English then published or distributed in this country in the foreign language. Example: *Le Petit Prince* by Antoine de Saint-Exupéry (France).

Some children's authors and illustrators from the United States write worthy books set in other countries. These books are written and published in the United States primarily for an audience of American children and are a part of the body of U.S. literature. Gloria Whelan, for example, writes works of realistic fiction such as *Homeless Bird,* which is set in India, and historical fiction such as *Angel on the Square,* which is set in early twentieth-century Russia. This U.S. literature can be found in the genre chapters.

Value of International Literature for Children

The value of international children's literature in developing an understanding of and appreciation for other cultures is undeniable. The understanding of people of other countries must be fostered early and allowed to grow throughout life.

- Through this literature, the history, traditions, and people of other countries are brought to life.
- By interpreting events in the everyday lives of their characters and by depicting long-term changes in the characters' lives, authors present a truer and more understandable picture of life in other countries than does the crisis-prone, single-event coverage of television and newspapers.
- Compelling stories build students' interest in the people and places they are reading about and pave the way to a deeper understanding and appreciation of the geographical and historical content encountered in textbooks.
- Literature written by natives of a country or region gives authenticity and an international perspective to classroom materials.
- Many students in the United States speak a foreign language and have a foreign heritage. International literature reflects the cultural and language diversity often found in classrooms today. By reading international books, students can learn to respect the heritage of others and take pride in their own.

■ Through international literature, children are given an opportunity to enjoy the best-loved stories of their peers around the world. This, in turn, can help students to develop a bond of shared experience with children of other nations and can enable them to acquire cultural literacy with a global perspective.

In a study by Monson, Howe, and Greenlee (1989), 200 U.S. children, ages 9 to 11, were asked what they would like to know about their counterparts in other countries. Their responses, categorized into nine questions, then formed the basis for a comparison of eight social studies textbooks and fifteen works of fiction appropriate for the age group about one country, Australia. It was found that both textbooks and trade books gave information about the country. The novels answered more of the children's questions, however, and were richer in detail of daily life and human emotion than the textbooks. The social studies texts gave many facts about the country, while the novels showed the implications of the facts for children's lives and helped the readers "live in" the country for a time.

Evaluation and Selection of International Literature

In addition to the standard requirement for high literary merit, the following criteria apply when evaluating and selecting international literature for library and classroom use:

■ Appeal to young readers and listeners. The saying, "A good book is a good book anywhere" should apply. Are the characters appealing? Will the story or topic interest children?
■ In translated books, a fluent style that retains some flavor of the country of origin. This is accomplished by using a few words or names in the original language. Glossaries of foreign terms, if not overly extensive, are a plus.
■ Tolerance for some stylistic differences, such as more character introspection, less action in text, or illustrations that contain visual symbolism or are surreal. These differences can be overcome with help from teachers and can be a valuable learning experience for students.

The Recommended International Books list at the end of this chapter is a good beginning for international book selection. Other selection aids for international literature include the United States Board on Books for Young People (USBBY) Quarterly Newsletter and the USBBY bibliographies of international children's books.

Historical Overview of International Literature

Much of the children's literature that was available in the United States during the seventeenth, eighteenth, nineteenth, and early twentieth centuries came from Europe. These early children's books are an important part of our cultural heritage, but we seldom think of the fact that they were originally published in other countries and many in other languages. They are so familiar to us in the United States that we consider them our children's classics, and indeed they have become so. The accompanying Milestones feature lists a sampling of international children's classics published from the end of the seventeenth century up to World War II.

With the rapid growth in the U.S. children's book field in the twentieth century, the flow of books from other countries became overshadowed by large numbers of U.S. publications. In addition, during World War II, little cultural exchange occurred across international borders. The

Excellent International Literature to Read Aloud

Boyce, Frank C. *Millions.* Ages 11–14. England.
Carmi, Daniella. *Samir and Yonatan.* Ages 9–12. Israel.
Erikson, Eva. *A Crash Course for Molly.* Ages 5–7. Sweden.
Goscinny, René. *Nicholas.* Illustrated by Jean Jacques Sempé. Ages 9–12. France.
Graham, Bob. *Let's Get a Pup! Said Kate.* Ages 3–8. Australia.
Hathorn, Libby. *Way Home.* Illustrated by Gregory Rogers. Ages 7–12.
    Australia.
McKay, Hilary. *Indigo's Star.* McElderry, 2004. Ages 11–13. England.
Skármeta, Antonio. *The Composition.* Illustrated by Alfonso Ruano.
    Ages 8–12. Venezuela.
Valckx, Catharina. *Lizette's Green Sock.* Ages 3–6. France.
Yumoto, Kazumi. *The Friends.* Ages 10–14. Japan.

end of World War II saw a change in the international mood, and two developments occurred that had far-reaching effects on the children's book field: (1) children's books in translation began to be published in unprecedented numbers (Carus, 1980) and (2) the international children's book field was established. Prominent features of the international children's book field include:

- The International Board on Books for Young People (www.ibby.org), an organization involving people from many nations who are involved in all aspects of the children's book field. The U.S. affiliate organization is the United States Board on Books for Young People (www.usbby.org).
- Book award programs, the most prominent of which is the Hans Christian Andersen Award. (See Appendix A for Hans Christian Andersen Award winners.)
- A biennial IBBY world congress and a biennial USBBY conference. (See each organization's website for information about these conferences.)
- A journal, *Bookbird: Journal of International Children's Literature.*

In 1968, the first Mildred L. Batchelder Award was announced by the American Library Association in honor of a U.S. publisher of the most distinguished translated children's book published in the preceding year. This award is given annually to encourage the translation and publication of international books in the United States. (See Appendix A for the award list.)

The future of international children's literature depends on our success in several arenas. First, we must encourage the development of stronger national literatures from developing nations where most literature remains at the stage of the oral tradition. Second, we must promote more literary exchange with nations whose literature is now growing rapidly to bring more of the world's best literature to our children's attention. Finally, we must support those organizations that can assist in these endeavors.

International Books by World Regions

The international books that are most often available in the United States have been and continue to be books from other English-speaking countries. The largest numbers of them come from Great Britain, Australia, and Canada. Although the books do not require translation, they are often

Early MILESTONES in International Children's Literature

Date	Event	Signficance
1657	*Orbis Pictus* by John Amos Comenius	Earliest nonfiction picture book
1697	*Tales of Mother Goose* by Charles Perrault	Earliest folktales from France
1719	*Robinson Crusoe* by Daniel Defoe	Two early adult adventure books from England,
1726	*Gulliver's Travels* by Jonathan Swift	adopted by children
1812	*Nursery and Household Tales* by Jakob and Wilhelm Grimm	Traditional folktales from Germany
1836	*Fairy Tales* by Hans Christian Andersen	Early modern folktales from Denmark
1846	*Book of Nonsense* by Edward Lear	Early humorous poetry from England
1865	*Alice's Adventures in Wonderland* by Lewis Carroll	Classic English modern fantasy
1880	*Heidi* by Johanna Spyri	Early realistic story from Switzerland
1881	*The Adventures of Pinocchio* by Carlo Collodi	Modern fantasy from Italy
1883	*Treasure Island* by Robert Louis Stevenson	Adventure tale from England by a Scottish author
1885	*A Child's Garden of Verses* by Robert Louis Stevenson	Classic collection of Golden Age poems from England
1894	*The Jungle Book* by Rudyard Kipling	Animal stories set in India by an English author
1901	*The Tale of Peter Rabbit* by Beatrix Potter	Classic English picture book
1906	*The Wonderful Adventures of Nils* by Selma Lagerlöf	A fantasy trip around Sweden
1908	*The Wind in the Willows* by Kenneth Grahame	Animal fantasy from England
1908	*Anne of Green Gables* by Lucy M. Montgomery	Realistic family story from Canada
1926	*Winnie-the-Pooh* by A. A. Milne	Personified toy story from England
1928	*Bambi* by Felix Salten	Personified deer story from Germany
1931	*The Story of Babar* by Jean de Brunhoff	Personified elephant story from France
1945	*Pippi Longstocking* by Astrid Lindgren	Classic fantasy from Sweden

published in the United States with other changes: spelling, characters' names, place names, and, sometimes titles and cover illustrations. The major awards and award winners from English-speaking countries are listed in Appendix A.

Translated books come to the United States from around the world, but the largest numbers come from Western Europe. Today, many books come from Sweden, Norway, Denmark, Switzerland, the Netherlands, Germany, France, and Belgium. A few books come from Italy and Spain. An example from Sweden is *In Ned's Head* by Anders Jacobsson and Sören Olsson.

Most translated children's books from the Middle East are novels for middle-graders or young adults and come to the United States from Israel. Books from or set in other countries in this region—such as *Zlata's Diary: A Child's Life in Wartime Sarajevo* by Zlata Filipovic and *A Hand Full of Stars* by Rafik Schami, set in Syria but published in Germany—are all the more welcome for their rarity.

Translated children's literature from Asia originates mostly in Japan, but books from Korea, China, and Thailand can occasionally be found. Japan has an extremely sophisticated field of book illustrating, and many beautifully illustrated picture books are now making their way into the U.S. market. An example from South Korea is *While We Were Out* by Ho Baek Lee.

African nations, with the exception of the Republic of South Africa, have produced little children's literature that has been exported to the United States. The reasons for this are many, but the most influential one is probably that of economics. Publishing books is expensive, especially in full color; therefore, the publishing industry is not firmly established in developing countries. Books of realistic fiction in which contemporary life in another country is portrayed are rare but worth locating. Beverley Naidoo's *The Other Side of Truth,* for example, is set in Nigeria, then London, and addresses political persecution.

Notable Authors and Illustrators of International Literature

David Almond, British Carnegie Medal–winning author of novels often described as magical realism. *Skellig; Kit's Wilderness.* www.davidalmond.com

Quentin Blake, British illustrator known for his sketchy, humorous, vivacious style, and particularly for his collaboration with the late Roald Dahl. *All Join In; Clown.* www.quentinblake.com

Anthony Browne, British author/illustrator whose stark surrealism reveals modern social ills. *Willy the Wizard; Gorilla.*

Mem Fox, Australian author of picture story-books for beginning readers. *Wilfrid Gordon McDonald Partridge; Where Is the Green Sheep?* www.memfox.com

Bob Graham, Australian author and illustrator of whimsical picture books. *Jethro Byrd, Fairy Child.*

Jean Little, Canadian author of realistic chapter books featuring children with emotional and physical disabilities. *Mama's Going to Buy You a Mockingbird.* www.jeanlittle.com

Beverley Naidoo, South African author and Carnegie Medalist whose novels deal with the effects of political injustice on children. *The Other Side of Truth; No Turning Back.* www.beverleynaidoo.com

Philip Pullman, British creator of *His Dark Materials* fantasies, a trilogy comprised of *The Golden Compass, The Subtle Knife,* and *The Amber Spyglass.* www.philip-pullman.com

Emily Rodda, Australian writer of popular fantasy adventures for intermediate-grade readers. *Rowan of Rin* and its sequels. www.emilyrodda.com

J. K. Rowling, British author of the popular, best-selling series about Harry Potter, a child wizard. *Harry Potter and the Sorcerer's Stone* and its sequels. www.jkrowling.com

Margaret Wild, Australian author of picture books about friendship and its power to heal. *Fox; The Pocket Dogs; The Very Best of Friends.*

Paul Yee, Canadian author who writes about the Chinese Canadian experience. *Tales from the Gold Mountain; Dead Man's Gold and Other Stories.* www.paulyee.ca

There is reason to hope that the current unrest between cultures will not always be the case. Ethnic prejudice and bias are not natural behaviors; they are learned. One of the most intriguing challenges to those who work with children is to combat the ignorance that is at the root of racial, cultural, and religious prejudice and intolerance. Children's literature, particularly the rich multicultural and international selections that are currently available, is a powerful tool in this effort, for it shows that the similarities between all people are much more fundamental than the differences.

Topics for Further Investigation

- Select a minority group whose perspectives have been omitted or inadequately covered in the study of U.S. history. Examples include Native Americans and their forced removal to reservations in the 1800s, Japanese Americans and their internment in prison camps during World War II, and Chinese Americans and their role in the construction of the transcontinental railroad in the 1860s. Read several works of age-appropriate historical fiction or nonfiction about that era written from the perspective of that group. Discuss how including these books in the study of U.S. history is likely to change students' understanding of the particular historical era.
- Research the history of African-American children's literature, noting milestone books and events.
- Select a country or region outside the United States that you will likely have to teach about. Compile an annotated bibliography of ten to twenty children's books, both fiction and nonfiction, that could promote interest in and help young people learn more about the country or region.

 See the companion website at www.ablongman.com/lynchbrown6e for further suggestions.

References

Bryan, A. (1998). Oh, the places you'll go. *Book poems.* New York: The Children's Book Council.

Carus, M. (1980). Translation and internationalism in children's literature. *Children's Literature in Education, 11*(4), 171–179.

Ford, D. Y., & Moore, J. L. (2004). Creating culturally responsive gifted education classrooms: Understanding "culture" is the first step. *Gifted Child Today, 27*(4), 34–39.

Horning, K. T., Lindgren, M. V., Rudiger, H., & Schliesman, M. (2006). *CCBC Choices, 2006.* Madison: University Publications, University of Wisconsin–Madison.

Larrick, N. (1965). The all-white world of children's books. *Saturday Review* (September 11), 63–65, 84–85.

Lepman, J. (2002). *A bridge of children's books.* Dublin, Ireland: The O'Brien Press in association with IBBY Ireland and USBBY. (Originally published in 1964 as *Die Kinderbuchbrüke* by S. Fischer Verlag, Frankfurt am Main, Germany)

Monson, D. L., Howe, K., & Greenlee, A. (1989). Helping children develop cross-cultural understanding with children's books. *Early Child Development and Care, 48*(special issue), 3–8.

National Center for Education Statistics. (2005). *The nation's report card: Reading 2005.* Retrieved from http://nces.ed.gov/nationsreportcard/pdf/main2005.

Rochman, H. (1993). *Against borders.* Chicago: ALA Books.

Rudman, M. (1984). *Children's literature: An issues approach* (2nd ed.). New York: Longman.

Schmidt, P. R. (2005). *Culturally responsive instruction: Promoting literacy in secondary content areas.* Naperville, IL: Learning Point Associates.

U.S. Census Bureau. www.census.gov.

U.S. Department of Education, National Center for Education Statistics. (2002a). *Dropout rates in the United States.* Washington, DC: NCES.

U.S. Department of Education, National Center for Education Statistics. (2002b). *Minority population growth.* Washington, DC: U.S. Department of Education.

U.S. Department of Education, National Center for Education Statistics. (2000c). *School and staffing survey: 1999–2000 public school teacher questionnaire and public charter school teacher questionnaire.* Washington, DC: NCES.

Recommended Multicultural Books

Ages refer to approximate interest levels.
  (**PI**) Picture book
  (**COL**) Short story collection

African-American Literature

Berry, James. *Ajeemah and His Son.* HarperCollins, 1992. Ages 9–12.

Bridges, Ruby and Margo Lundell (ed.). *Through My Eyes.* Scholastic, 1999. Ages 9–15.

Cline-Ransome, Lesa. *Satchel Paige.* Illustrated by James Ransome. Simon & Schuster, 2000. Ages 7–10. (biography)

Curtis, Christopher Paul. *Mr. Chickee's Funny Money.* Wendy Lamb/Random, 2005. Ages 8–12.

English, Karen. *Hot Day on Abbott Avenue.* Illustrated by Javaka Steptoe. Clarion, 2004. (**PI**) Ages 5–8.

Fradin, Dennis Brindell, and Judith Bloom Fradin. *Ida B. Wells: Mother of the Civil Rights Movement.* Clarion, 2000. Ages 10–16. (biography)

Grimes, Nikki. *Bronx Masquerade.* Dial, 2002. Ages 12–18.

———. *Danitra Brown, Class Clown.* Illustrated by E. B. Lewis. HarperCollins, 2005. (**PI**) Ages 7–10.

Hamilton, Virginia. *Many Thousand Gone: African Americans from Slavery to Freedom.* Illustrated by Leo and Diane Dillon. Random, 1992. Ages 10–14.

———. *The People Could Fly: The Picture Book.* Illustrated by Leo and Diane Dillon. Knopf, 2004. (**PI**) Ages 11–15.

Hopkinson, Deborah. *A Band of Angels: A Story Inspired by the Jubilee Singers.* Illustrated by Raúl Colón. Atheneum, 1999. (**PI**) Ages 8–10.

Howard, Elizabeth Fitzgerald. *Virgie Goes to School with Us Boys.* Illustrated by E. B. Lewis. Simon & Schuster, 2000. (**PI**) Ages 6–9.

Hudson, Wade, and Cheryl W. Hudson, compilers. *In Praise of Our Fathers and Our Mothers: A Black Family Treasury of Outstanding Authors and Artists.* Just Us Books, 1997. Ages 9–14. (collected biography)

Johnson, Angela. *The First Part Last.* Simon & Schuster, 2003. Ages 12–16.

———. *Heaven.* Simon & Schuster, 1998. Ages 12–16.

———. *Tell Me a Story, Mama.* Illustrated by David Soman. Scholastic, 1992. (**PI**) Ages 3–7.

Johnson, Dinah. *Quinnie Blue.* Illustrated by James Ransome. Holt, 2000. (**PI**) Ages 6–8.

Johnson, Dolores. *The Children's Book of Kwanzaa: A Guide to Celebrating the Holiday.* Atheneum, 1996. Ages 8–14.

Lester, Julius. *Day of Tears: A Novel in Dialogue.* Hyperion, 2005. Ages 12–14.

———. *From Slave Ship to Freedom Road.* Illustrated by Rod Brown. Dial, 1998. Ages 11–15. (informational)

———. *John Henry.* Illustrated by Jerry Pinkney. Dial, 1994. (**PI**) Ages 7–10.

———. *The Old African.* Illustrated by Jerry Pinkney. Dial, 2005. (**PI**) Ages 9–13.

McGill, Alice. *Molly Bannaky.* Illustrated by Chris K. Soentpiet. Houghton, 1999. (**PI**) Ages 7–11.

McKissack, Patricia. *Goin' Someplace Special.* Illustrated by Jerry Pinkney. Scholastic, 2001. (**PI**) Ages 6–9.

———. *Mirandy and Brother Wind.* Illustrated by Jerry Pinkney. Knopf, 1988. (**PI**) Ages 7–9.

———. *Rebels against Slavery: American Slave Revolts.* Scholastic, 1996. Ages 11–16. (nonfiction chapter book)

McKissack, Patricia, and Fredrick McKissack. *Christmas in the Big House, Christmas in the Quarters.* Illustrated by John Thompson. Scholastic, 1994. Ages 8–11.

McKissack, Patricia C., and Onawumi Jean Moss. *Precious and the Boo Hag.* Illustrated by Kyrsten Brooker. Atheneum, 2005. (**PI**) Ages 5–8.

Mollel, Tololwa M. *My Rows and Piles of Coins.* Illustrated by E. B. Lewis. Clarion, 1999. (**PI**) Ages 4–8.

Mosley, Walter. *47.* Little, Brown, 2005. Ages 12–16.

Myers, Walter Dean. *Glorious Angels: A Celebration of Children.* HarperCollins, 1995. Ages 3–14. (poetry)

———. *Malcolm X: A Fire Burning Brightly.* Illustrated by Leonard Jenkins. HarperCollins, 2000. (**PI**) Ages 7–11. (biography)

———. *Scorpions.* Harper, 1988. Ages 9–12.

Nelson, Kadir. *He's Got the Whole World in His Hands.* Dial, 2005. (**PI**) Ages 4–8.

Nelson, Marilyn. *Carver: A Life in Poems.* Front Street, 2000. Ages 12–15. (biography)

Schroeder, Alan. *Minty: The Story of Young Harriet Tubman.* Illustrated by Jerry Pinkney. Dial, 1996. (**PI**) Ages 7–10.

Taylor, Mildred. *The Land.* Putnam, 2001. Ages 12–16.

———. *Roll of Thunder, Hear My Cry.* Dial, 1976. (See others in the Logan family saga: *The Song of the Trees,* 1975; *Let the Circle Be Unbroken,* 1981; *The Road to Memphis,* 1990) Ages 9–12.

Tillage, Leon W. *Leon's Story.* Illustrated by Susan L. Roth. Farrar, 1997. (**PI**) Ages 9–13. (nonfiction)

Woodson, Jacqueline. *Hush.* Putnam, 2002. Ages 11–14.

———. *Locomotion.* Putnam, 2003. Ages 9–12.

———. *Miracle's Boys.* Putnam, 2000. Ages 10–16.

———. *The Other Side.* Illustrated by E. B. Lewis. Putnam, 2001. (**PI**) Ages 5–8.

———. *Show Way.* Illustrated by Hudson Talbott. Putnam, 2005. (**PI**) Ages 7–12.

Asian-American Literature

Balgassi, Haemi. *Peacebound Trains.* Illustrated by Chris K. Soentpiet. Clarion, 1996. (**PI**) Ages 8–12.

Bercaw, Edna Coe. *Halmoni's Day.* Illustrated by Robert Hunt. Dial, 2000. (**PI**) Ages 5–8.

Brown, Jackie. *Little Cricket.* Hyperion, 2004. Ages 11–14. (Hmong)

Cha, Dia. *Dia's Story Cloth: The Hmong People's Journey to Freedom.* Stitchery by Chue and Nhia Thao Cha. Lee & Low, 1996. (**PI**) Ages 8–11.

Falwell, Cathryn. *Butterflies for Kiri.* Lee & Low, 2003. (**PI**) Ages 5–7.

Gilmore, Rachna. *A Gift for Gita.* Illustrated by Alice Priestley. Tilbury, 2002. (**PI**) Ages 6–9. (See others in the series: *Lights for Gita; Roses for Gita*)

Gower, Catherine. *Long-Long's New Year: A Story about the Chinese Spring Festival.* Illustrated by He Zhihong. Tuttle, 2006 (**PI**) Ages 5–8. (Set in China)

Kadohata, Cynthia. *Kira-Kira.* Atheneum, 2004. Ages 11–14. (Japanese-American)

———. *Weedflower.* Atheneum, 2006. Ages 11–14. (Japanese-American)

Krishnaswami, Uma. *Chachaji's Cup.* Illustrated by Sumeya Sitaraman. Children's Book Press, 2003. (**PI**) Ages 5–9.

Lee, Milly. *Nim and the War Effort.* Illustrated by Yangsook Choi. Farrar, 1997. (**PI**) Ages 7–10.

Levine, Ellen. *A Fence Away from Freedom: Japanese Americans and World War II.* Putnam, 1995. Ages 12–16. (nonfiction)

Look, Lenore. *Henry's First-Moon Birthday.* Illustrated by Yumi Heo. Atheneum, 2001. (**PI**) Ages 4–8.

———. *Uncle Peter's Amazing Chinese Wedding.* Illustrated by Yumi Heo. Atheneum, 2006. (**PI**) Ages 5–8. (Chinese-American)

McKay, Lawrence, Jr. *Journey Home.* Illustrated by Dom and Keunhee Lee. Lee & Low, 1998. (**PI**) Ages 8–12.

Mochizuki, Ken. *Baseball Saved Us.* Illustrated by Dom Lee. Lee and Low, 1993. (**PI**) Ages 7–10.

Na, An. *A Step from Heaven.* Front Street, 2001. Ages 13–18.

Park, Linda Sue. *Mulberry Project.* Clarion, 2005. Ages 10–14. (Korean-American)

Say, Allen. *Grandfather's Journey.* Houghton, 1993. (**PI**) Ages 7–9.

———. *Kamishibai Man.* Houghton, 2005. (**PI**) Ages 6–10. (Japanese-American)

———. *Tea with Milk.* Lorraine/Houghton, 1999. (**PI**) Ages 6–9.

Schmidt, Jeremy, and Ted Wood. *Two Lands, One Heart: An American Boy's Journey to His Mother's Vietnam.* Photography by Ted Wood. Walker, 1995. Ages 7–10. (photoessay)

Shea, Pegi Deitz. *The Whispering Cloth.* Illustrated by Anita Riggio. Stitchery by You Yang. Boyds Mills, 1995. (**PI**) Ages 7–11.

Sheth, Kashmira. *Blue Jasmine.* Hyperion, 2004. Ages 11–14. (Indian-American)

Strom, Yale. *Quilted Landscape: Conversations with Young Immigrants.* Simon & Schuster, 1996. Ages 11–14. (varied cultures)

Uchida, Yoshiko. *Journey to Topaz.* Scribner's, 1971. Ages 9–12. (See sequel: *Journey Home,* Atheneum, 1978.)

Whelan, Gloria. *Chu Ju's House.* HarperCollins, 2004. Ages 12–14. (Chinese)

Wong, Janet S. *Apple Pie 4th of July.* Illustrated by Margaret Chodos-Irvine. Harcourt, 2002. (**PI**) Ages 4–7.

———. *The Trip Back Home.* Illustrated by Bo Jia. Harcourt, 2000. (**PI**) Ages 7–9.

Yee, Paul. *Dead Man's Gold and Other Stories.* Illustrated by Harvey Chan. Groundwood, 2002. (**COL**) Ages 12–14.

Yep, Laurence. *Dragon's Gate.* HarperCollins, 1993. Ages 12–14.

———. *Dragonwings.* Harper, 1975. Ages 9–12.

———. *Sea Glass. Golden Mountain Chronicles, 1970.* HarperCollins, 2002 (1979). Ages 9–12.

———. *The Tiger's Apprentice.* HarperCollins, 2003. Ages 9–14.

———. *Traitor: Golden Mountain Chronicles, 1885.* HarperCollins, 2003. Ages 12–14.

Young, Ed. *Monkey King.* HarperCollins, 2001. (**PI**) Ages 5–8.

———. *My Mei Mei.* Philomel, 2006. (**PI**) Ages 4–7. (Chinese, Chinese-American)

Latino Literature

Ada, Alma Flor. *I Love Saturdays y Domingos.* Illustrated by Elivia Savadier. Atheneum, 2002. (**PI**) Ages 4–8.

Alvarez, Julia. *Before We Were Free.* Knopf, 2002. Ages 11–14.

Ancona, George. *Barrio: José's Neighborhood.* Harcourt, 1998. Ages 6–9. (photoessay)

———. *Carnaval.* Harcourt, 1999. Ages 7–11. (photoessay)

———. *Fiesta U.S.A.* Lodestar, 1995. Ages 8–10. (photoessay)

Canales, Viola. *The Tequila Worm.* Random, 2005. Ages 12–15. (Mexican-American)

Carling, Amelia Lau. *Mama and Papa Have a Store.* Dial, 1998. (**PI**) Ages 6–8. (Spanish, Mayan, and Chinese cultures)

Cofer, Judith O. *An Island Like You.* Orchard, 1995. (**COL**) Ages 12–15.

Freedman, Russell. *In the Days of the Vaqueros: America's First True Cowboys.* Clarion, 2001. Ages 10–14. (nonfiction)

Hanson, Regina. *The Face at the Window.* Illustrated by Linda Saport. Clarion, 1997. (**PI**) Ages 6–9.

Jaramillo, Ann. *La Línea.* Roaring Brook, 2006. Ages 11–15. (Mexican-American)

Jiménez, Francisco. *Breaking Through.* Houghton, 2001. Ages 12–14.

———. *The Circuit: Stories from the Life of a Migrant Child.* Houghton, 1999 (1996). (new ed.) (**COL**) Ages 10–14.

———. *La Mariposa.* Illustrated by Simón Silva. Houghton, 1998. (**PI**) Ages 8–11.

Joseph, Lynn. *The Color of My Words.* HarperCollins, 2000. Ages 10–14.

Kroll, Virginia. *Butterfly Boy.* Illustrated by Gerardo Suzán. Boyds Mills, 1997. (**PI**) Ages 5–8.

Mora, Pat. *Confetti: Poems for Children.* Illustrated by Enrique O. Sanchez. Lee & Low, 1996. Ages 6–9.

———. *A Library for Juana: The World of Sor Juana Ines.* Illustrated by Beatriz Vidal. Knopf, 2002. (**PI**) Ages 7–9. (biography)

———. *Tomás and the Library Lady.* Illustrated by Raul Colón. Knopf, 1997. (**PI**) Ages 6–8. (biography)

Resau, Laura. *What the Moon Saw.* Delacorte, 2006. Ages 11–15. (Mexican-American)

Ryan, Pam Muñoz. *Becoming Naomi León.* Scholastic, 2004. Ages 11–15. (Mexican-American)

Soto, Gary. *Chato and the Party Animals.* Illustrated by Susan Guevara. Putnam, 2000. (**PI**) Ages 5–8.

———. *Chato's Kitchen.* Illustrated by Susan Guevara. Putnam, 1995. (**PI**) Ages 5–8.

———. *Snapshots from the Wedding.* Illustrated by Stephanie Garcia. Putnam, 1997. (**PI**) Ages 5–8.

———. *Taking Sides.* Harcourt, 1991. Ages 10–13.

Veciana-Suarez, Ana. *Flight to Freedom.* Orchard, 2002. Ages 12–14.

Winter, Jonah. *Frida.* Illustrated by Ana Juan. Scholastic, 2002. (**PI**) Ages 6–9. (biography)

Native American Literature

Ancona, George. *Mayeros: A Yucatec Maya Family.* Lothrop, 1997. Ages 7–11. (photoessay)

Bealer, Alex. *Only the Names Remain: The Cherokees and the Trail of Tears.* Little, Brown, 1972. Ages 9–12.

Boyden, Linda. *The Blue Roses.* Illustrated by Amy Córdova. Lee & Low, 2002. (**PI**) Ages 5–8.

Bruchac, Joseph. *Code Talker.* Dial, 2005. Ages 12–15.

———. *Crazy Horse's Vision.* Illustrated by S. D. Nelson. Lee & Low, 2000. (**PI**) Ages 6–10. (biography)

———. *Eagle Song.* Illustrated by Dan Andreasen. Dial, 1997. Ages 9–11.

———. *The First Strawberries.* Illustrated by Anna Vojtech. Dial, 1993. (**PI**) Ages 7–10.

———. *Pushing Up the Sky: Seven Native American Plays for Children.* Illustrated by Teresa Flavin. Dial, 2000. Ages 7–11. (plays)

———. *Wabi: A Hero's Tale.* Dial, 2006. Ages 12–14.

———. *The Winter People.* Dial, 2002. Ages 12–15.

Curry, Jane Louise. *Hold Up the Sky and Other Indian Tales from Texas and the Southern Plains.* Illustrated by James Watts. McElderry, 2003. (**COL**) Ages 8–12.

Erdrich, Louise. *The Birchbark House.* Hyperion, 1999. Ages 8–12. (historical fiction)

———. *The Game of Silence.* Hyperion, 2005. Ages 11–14.

George, Jean Craighead. *Julie.* HarperCollins, 1994. Ages 10–14.

———. *Julie of the Wolves.* Harper, 1972. Ages 9–12.

Goble, Paul. *The Girl Who Loved Wild Horses.* Bradbury, 1978. (**PI**) Ages 6–8.

Hudson, Jan. *Sweetgrass.* Philomel, 1989. Ages 12–15.

Ketchum, Liza. *Where the Great Hawk Flies.* Clarion, 2005. Ages 10–14.

Mikaelsen, Ben. *Touching Spirit Bear.* HarperCollins, 2001. Ages 12–14.

O'Dell, Scott. *Island of the Blue Dolphins.* Houghton, 1960. Ages 9–12.

———. *Sing Down the Moon.* Houghton, 1970. Ages 12–16.

Ross, Gayle. *How Turtle's Back Was Cracked: A Traditional Cherokee Tale.* Illustrated by Murv Jacob. Dial, 1995. (**PI**) Ages 7–9.

Smith, Cynthia Leitich. *Rain Is Not My Indian Name.* HarperCollins, 2001. Ages 10–14.

Religious Cultures Literature

Bunting, Eve. *One Candle.* Illustrated by Wendy Popp. HarperCollins, 2002. (**PI**) Ages 6–9. (Jewish)

———. *One Green Apple.* Illustrated by Ted Lewin. Clarion, 2006. (**PI**) Ages 6–8. (Muslim)

Fagan, Cary, adapter. *The Market Wedding.* Illustrated by Regolo Ricci. Tundra, 2000. (**PI**) Ages 6–8. (Jewish)

Geras, Adèle. *My Grandmother's Stories: A Collection of Jewish Folk Tales.* Illustrated by Anita Lobel. Knopf, 2003 (1990). (**PI**) Ages 8–10. (Jewish)

———. *The Kingfisher Treasury of Jewish Stories.* Illustrated by Jane Cope. Kingfisher, 2003. (**COL**) Ages 5–9. (Jewish)

Hautzig, Esther. *The Endless Steppe: A Girl in Exile.* Crowell, 1968. Ages 9–12. (Jewish)

———. *A Picture of Grandmother.* Illustrated by Beth Peck. Farrar, 2002. Ages 7–10. (Jewish) (transitional)

Hershenhorn, Esther. *Chicken Soup by Heart.* Illustrated by Rosanne Litzinger. Simon & Schuster, 2002. (**PI**) Ages 4–7. (Jewish)

Hesse, Karen. *The Stone Lamp: Eight Stories of Hanukkah through History.* Illustrated by Brian Pinkney. Hyperion, 2003. (**COL**) Ages 9–13. (Jewish)

Hest, Amy. *Love You, Soldier.* Illustrated by Sonja Lamut. Candlewick, 2000 (1991). Ages 8–11. (Jewish) (transitional)

Kimmel, Eric, reteller. *A Cloak for the Moon.* Illustrated by Katya Krenina. Holiday, 2001. Ages 4–8. (Jewish) (modern folktale)

———, reteller. *Gershon's Monster: A Story for the Jewish New Year.* Illustrated by Jon J. Muth. Scholastic, 2000. Ages 6–11. (Jewish) (legend)

———. *Wonders and Miracles: A Passover Companion.* Scholastic, 2004. (**COL**) Ages 11–14. (Jewish)

Krishnaswami, Uma. *Chachaji's Cup.* Illustrated by Soumya Sitaraman. Children's Book Press, 2003. (**PI**) Ages 6–8. (Hindu)

———. *The Closet Ghosts.* Illustrated by Shiraaz Bhabha. Children's Book Press, 2005. (**PI**) Ages 6–8. (Hindu)

Kyuchukov, Hristo. *My Name Was Hussein.* Illustrated by Allan Eitzen. Boyds Mills, 2004. (**PI**) Ages 6–8. (Muslim)

Levine, Karen. *Hana's Suitcase: A True Story.* Second Story Press, 2002. Ages 11–14. (Jewish)

Levitin, Sonia. *Journey to America.* Atheneum, 1970. Ages 12–15. (Jewish) (See sequel: *Silver Days,* 1989.)

Lowry, Lois. *Number the Stars.* Houghton, 1989. Ages 7–9. (Jewish)

Millman, Isaac. *Hidden Child.* Illustrated. Farrar, 2005. Ages 9–14. (Jewish)

Mobin-Uddin, Asma. *My Name Is Bilal.* Illustrated by Barbara Kiwak. Boyds Mills, 2005. (**PI**) Ages 9–12. (Muslim)

Nislick, June Levitt. *Zayda Was a Cowboy.* Jewish Publication Society, 2005. Ages 9–13. (Jewish)

Oberman, Sheldon. *The Wisdom Bird. A Tale of Solomon and Sheba.* Illustrated by Neil Waldman. Boyds Mills, 2000. (**PI**) Ages 5–9. (Jewish)

Rocklin, Joanne. *Strudel Stories.* Delacorte, 1999. Ages 7–12. (Jewish)

Rogasky, Barbara. *Smoke and Ashes: The Story of the Holocaust.* Holiday, 1988; revised and expanded, 2002. Ages 12–15. (Jewish)

Rubin, Susan Goldman. *Fireflies in the Dark: The Story of Friedl Dicker-Brandeis and the Children of Terezin.* Holiday, 2000. (**PI**) Ages 11–14. (Jewish) (biography)

Schmidt, Gary. *Mara's Stories: Glimmers in the Darkness.* Holt, 2001. Ages 11–14. (Jewish) (traditional and modern folktales)

Staples, Suzanne Fisher. *Shiva's Fire.* Farrar, 2000. Ages 12–16. (Hindu)

Vos, Ida. *The Key Is Lost.* Translated by Terese Edelstein. HarperCollins, 2000. Ages 10–13. (Jewish)

Bilingual Literature

Ada, Alma Flor. *Gathering the Sun: An Alphabet in Spanish and English.* English translation by Rosa Zubizarreta. Illustrated by Simón Silva. Lothrop, 1997. Ages 5–9. (poetry) English/Spanish

————. *The Lizard and the Sun/La Lagartija y el Sol.* Illustrated by Felipe Davalos. Doubleday, 1997. (**PI**) Ages 5–7. English/Spanish

Alarcon, Francisco X. *Laughing Tomatoes and Other Spring Poems/ Jitomates Risuenos y otros poemas de primavera.* Illustrated by Christina González. Children's Book Press, 1997. Ages 6–12. (poetry) English/Spanish. (See other titles in this quartet.)

————. *Poems to Dream Together/Poemas para soñar juntos.* Illustrated by Paula Barragán. Lee & Low, 2005. (**COL**) Ages 8–12. English/Spanish

Argueta, Jorge. *A Movie in My Pillow/Una película en mi almohada: Poems.* Illustrated by Elizabeth Gómez. Children's Book Press, 2001. (**PI**) Ages 8–12. (poetry) English/Spanish

Bateson-Hill, Margaret. *Lao-ao of Dragon Mountain.* Illustrated by Francesca Pelizzoli. Paper cuts by Sha-liu Qu. Stewart, Tabori & Chang, 1996. (**PI**) Ages 4–8. English/Chinese

Carlson, Lori, selector. *You're On! Seven Plays in English and Spanish.* Morrow, 1999. Ages 9–15.

Cohn, Diana. *¡Sí, se puede!/Yes, We Can!: Janitor Strike in L. A.* Translated by Sharon Franco. Illustrated by Francisco Delgado. Cinco Puntos, 2002. (**PI**) Ages 6–8. English/Spanish

Corpi, Lucha. *Where Fireflies Dance/Ahi, Donde Bailan las Luciernagas.* Illustrated by Mira Reisberg. Children's Book Press, 1997. (**PI**) Ages 7–12. English/Spanish

Cowcher, Helen. *Tigress.* Translated by Mei-Ling Christine Lee. Millet, 1997. (**PI**) Ages 5–9. English/Vietnamese

Cumpiano, Ina. *Quinito's Neighborhood/El vecindario de Quinito.* Illustrated by José Ramírez. Children's Book Press, 2005. (**PI**) Ages 4–7. English/ Spanish

Despain, Pleasant, reteller. *The Emerald Lizard: Fifteen Latin American Tales to Tell.* Illustrated by Don Bell. Translated by Mario Lamo-Jiménez. August House, 1999. Ages 7–12. English/Spanish

Elya, Susan Middleton. *Bebé Goes Shopping.* Illustrated by Steven Salerno. Harcourt, 2006. (**PI**) Ages 4–7. English/Spanish

Galindo, Mary Sue. *Icy Watermelon/Sandía fría.* Illustrated by Pauline Rodriguez Howard. Arte Público, 2000. (**PI**) Ages 3–8. English/Spanish

Garza, Carmen L., with Harriet Rohmer. *In My Family/ En Mi Familia.* Edited by David Schecter. Translated by Francisco X. Alarcón. Children's Book Press, 1996. (**PI**) Ages 5–12. English/ Spanish

————, as told to Harriet Rohmer. *Magic Windows: Cut-paper Art and Stories/Ventanas Magicas.* Children's Book Press, 1999. (**PI**) Ages 5–12. English/ Spanish

Gomi, Taro. *My Friends/Mis amigos.* Chronicle, 2006. (**PI**) Ages 3–6. English/Spanish

Guy, Ginger Foglesong. *Siesta.* Illustrated by René King Moreno. Greenwillow, 2005. (**PI**) Ages 3–6. (concept book) English/Spanish

Herrera, Juan Felipe. *Grandma and Me at the Flea/Los meros meros remateros.* Illustrated by Anita DeLucio-Brock. Children's Book Press, 2002. (**PI**) Ages 4–8. English/Spanish

Ho, Minfong. *Maples in the Mist: Children's Poems from the Tang Dynasty.* Illustrated by Jean and Mou-sien Tseng. Translated by Minfong Ho. Lothrop, 1996. Ages 8–14. (poetry) English/Chinese

Holt, Daniel D. (Ed.). *Tigers, Frogs, and Rice Cakes: A Book of Korean Proverbs.* Illustrated by Lu Han Stickler. Shen's Books, 1998. (**PI**) Ages 7–10. English/Korean

Jiménez, Francisco. *The Christmas Gift/El regalo de Navidad.* Illustrated by Claire B. Cotts. Houghton, 2000. (**PI**) Ages 6–8. English/Spanish

Kitsao, Jay. *McHeshi Goes to the Market* (see others in the McHeshi series). Illustrated by Wanjiku Mathenge et al. Jacaranda Designs, 1995. (**PI**) Ages 3–5. English/Swahili

Lee, Jeanne. *Song of Mu Lan.* Front Street, 1995. (**PI**) Ages 5–8. English/Chinese

Loya, Olga. *Magic Moments: Tales from Latin America/Momentos mágicos.* Translated by Carmen Lizardo-Rivera. August House, 1998. (**COL**) Ages 10–15. English/Spanish

Luenn, Nancy. *A Gift for Abuelita: Celebrating the Day of the Dead/Un regalo para Abuelita: En celebración del Día de los Muertos.* Illustrated by Robert Chapman. Rising Moon, 1998. (**PI**) Ages 4–8. English/ Spanish

MacDonald, Margaret Read. *The Girl Who Wore Too Much: A Folktale from Thailand.* Thai text by Supaporn Vathanaprida. Illustrated by Yvonne LeBrun Davis. August House, 1998. (**PI**) Ages 4–8. English/Thai

Mado, Michio. *The Magic Pocket.* Illustrated by Mitsumasa Anno. Translated by the Empress Michiko of Japan. McElderry Books, 1998. Ages 3–5. (poetry) English/Japanese

Masurel, Claire. *Un gato y un perro/A Cat and a Dog.* Illustrated by Bob Kolar. Translated by Andrés Antreasyan. Ediciones Norte-Sur, 2003. (**PI**) Ages 4–7. Spanish/English.

Medina, Jane. *The Dream on Blanca's Wall/El sueño pegado en la pared de Blanca.* Illustrated by Robert Casilla. Boyds Mills/Wordsong, 2004. Ages 11–12. English/Spanish

Nye, Naomi Shihab, editor. *The Tree Is Older Than You Are: A Bilingual Gathering of Poems and Stories from Mexico with Paintings by Mexican Artists.* Simon & Schuster, 1995. (**COL**) Ages 8–16. English/Spanish

Pérez, Amada Irma. *My Diary from Here to There/Mi diario de aquí hasta allá.* Illustrated by Maya Christina González. Children's Book Press, 2002. (**PI**) Ages 8–10. English/Spanish

Robles, Anthony. *Lakas and the Makibaka Hotel/Si Lakas at ang Makibaka Hotel.* Translation by Eloisa D. de Jesús. Illustrated by Carl Angel. Children's Book Press, 2006. Ages 7–9. English/ Tagalog

Rodríguez, Luis J. *It Doesn't Have to Be This Way: A Barrio Story/No tiene que ser así: Una historia del barrio.* Illustrated by Daniel Galvez. Children's Book Press, 1999. (**PI**) Ages 10–14. English/Spanish

Stewart, Mark, and Mike Kennedy. *Latino Baseball's Finest Fielders/Los más destacados guantes del béisbol latino.* Translated by Manuel Kalmanovitz. Millbrook, 2002. (**COL**) Ages 9–13. (biographies) English/Spanish. (See companion volume, *Latino Baseball's Hottest Hitters,* 2002.)

Zhang, Sonng Nan, reteller/illustrator. *The Ballad of Mulan/Bai Ca Moc Lau.* Translated by Nguyen Ngoc Ngan. Pan Asian Publications, 1998. (**PI**) Ages 5–7. English/Vietnamese

Recommended International Books

Ages refer to approximate interest levels. Country of original publication is noted.
(**PI**) Picture book
(**COL**) Short story collection

English Language Books

Ahlberg, Janet, and Allan Ahlberg. *Each Peach Pear Plum.* Viking, 1979. Ages 3–6. U.K.
———. *The Jolly Postman.* Little, Brown, 1986. Ages 5–8. U.K.

Alborough, Jez. *Fix-It Duck.* HarperCollins, 2002. (**PI**) Ages 2–5. U.K.

Anderson, Rachel. *Black Water.* Holt, 1995. Ages 10–14. U.K.

Ardagh, Philip. *The Fall of Fergal.* Illustrated by David Roberts. Holt, 2004. Ages 11–12. (Also in the Unlikely Exploits Trilogy: *Heir of Mystery,* 2004, and *The Rise of the House of McNally,* 2005). Humor. U.K.

———. *A House Called Awful End.* Illustrated by David Roberts. Holt, 2002. Ages 9–12. U.K. (Also in the trilogy, *Dreadful Acts,* 2002, and *Terrible Times,* 2003.)

Asare, Meshack. *Sosu's Call.* Kane/Miller, 2002. (**PI**) Ages 6–9. Ghana.

Baker, Jeannie. *The Hidden Forest.* Greenwillow, 2000. (**PI**) Ages 6–10. Australia.

———. *Where the Forest Meets the Sea.* Greenwillow, 1987. (**PI**) Ages 7–12. Australia.

Base, Graeme. *The Water Hole.* Abrams, 2001. (**PI**) Ages 4–8. Australia.

Boyce, Frank C. *Framed.* HarperCollins, 2006. Ages 11–14. Humor. U.K.

———. *Millions.* HarperCollins, 2004. Ages 11–14. Humor. U.K.

Breslin, Theresa. *Whispers in the Graveyard.* Heinemann, 1994. Ages 12–14. U.K.

Briggs, Raymond. *The Man.* Random House, 1995. (**PI**) Ages 9–14. U.K.

Brooks, Martha. *Traveling on into the Light: And Other Stories.* Orchard, 1994. (**COL**) Ages 12–16. Canada.

Browne, Anthony. *Gorilla.* Knopf, 1985. (**PI**) Ages 6–8. U.K.

———. *Willy the Champ.* Knopf, 1986. (**PI**) Ages 4–8. U.K.

———. *Zoo.* Julia McRae, 1992. (**PI**) Ages 6–10. U.K.

Brugman, Alyssa. *Being Bindy.* Delacorte, 2006. Ages 12–15. Australia.

Burgess, Melvin. *Kite.* Farrar, 2000. Ages 12–16. U.K.

Child, Lauren. *I Will Never Not Ever Eat a Tomato.* Candlewick, 2000. (**PI**) Ages 3–8. U.K.

———. *What Planet Are You from, Clarice Bean?* Candlewick, 2002. (**PI**) Ages 6–8. U.K.

Clark, Judith. *Kalpana's Dream.* Front Street, 2005. Ages 12–15. Australia.

Colfer, Eoin. *Artemis Fowl.* Hyperion, 2001. Ages 10–12. Ireland.

Crossley-Holland, Kevin. *The Seeing Stone.* Scholastic, 2001. Ages 10–15. U.K.

Dahl, Roald. *Matilda.* Illustrated by Quentin Blake. Viking, 1988. Ages 9–12. U.K.

Daly, Niki. *The Boy on the Beach.* Simon & Schuster, 1999. (**PI**) Ages 3–7. South Africa.

———. *Jamela's Dress.* Farrar, 1999. (**PI**) Ages 4–7. South Africa.

———. *Once Upon a Time.* Farrar, 2003. (**PI**) Ages 4–8. South Africa.

Dhami, Narinder. *Bindi Babes.* Delacorte, 2004. Ages 11–14. Humor. U.K.

Doyle, Brian. *Mary Ann Alice.* Douglas & McIntyre, 2002. Ages 9–13. Canada.

Doyle, Malachy. *Who Is Jesse Flood?* Bloomsbury, 2002. Ages 11–16. Northern Ireland.

Fine, Anne. *The Jamie and Angus Stories.* Illustrated by Penny Dale. Candlewick, 2002. Ages 7–9. U.K.

Foreman, Michael. *Saving Sinbad.* Kane/Miller, 2002. (**PI**) Ages 4–8. U.K.

French, Jackie. *Hitler's Daughter.* HarperCollins, 2003. Ages 9–12. Australia.

Gavin, Jamila. *Coram Boy.* Farrar, 2001. Ages 11–16. U.K.

Gilmore, Rachna. *A Group of One.* Holt, 2001. Ages 11–15. Canada.

Graham, Bob. *Jethro Byrd, Fairy Child.* Candlewick, 2002. (**PI**) Ages 4–7. Australia.

———. *Let's Get a Pup! Said Kate.* Candlewick, 2003. (**PI**) Ages 3–8. Australia.

———. *Oscar's Half Birthday.* Candlewick, 2005. (**PI**) Ages 3–5. Australia.

Greenwood, Kerry. *A Different Sort of Real: The Diary of Charlotte McKenzie, Melbourne 1918–1919.* Scholastic, 2001. Ages 10–13. Australia.

Hathorn, Libby. *Way Home.* Illustrated by Gregory Rogers. Knopf, 1994. (**PI**) Ages 7–10.

Hendry, Diana. *Harvey Angell.* Aladdin, 2001. Ages 9–12. U.K.

Heneghan, James. *Flood.* Farrar, 2002. Ages 10–14. Canada.

Honey, Elizabeth. *Fiddleback.* Knopf, 2001. Ages 9–12. Australia.

———. *Remote Man.* Knopf, 2002. Ages 11–15. Australia.

Horacek, Petr. *Silly Suzy Goose.* Candlewick, 2006. (**PI**) Ages 4–6. U.K.

Ibbotson, Eva. *Journey to the River Sea.* Illustrated by Kevin Hawkes. Dutton, 2001. Ages 9–12. U.K.

———. *The Secret of Platform 13.* Dutton, 1998. Ages 9–13. U.K.

———. *Star of Kazan.* Dutton, 2004. Ages 11–13. U.K.

———. *Which Witch?* Dutton, 1999. Ages 10–14. U.K.

Ihimaera, Witi. *Whale Rider.* Harcourt, 2003. Ages 12–15. New Zealand.

Johnston, Julie. *In Spite of Killer Bees.* Tundra, 2001. Ages 12–15. Canada.

King-Smith, Dick. *The Nine Lives of Aristotle.* Illustrated by Bob Graham. Candlewick, 2003. Ages 7–9. U.K.

Little, Jean. *Mama's Going to Buy You a Mockingbird.* Viking, 1985. Ages 10–15. Canada.

———. *Willow and Twig.* Viking, 2003. Ages 11–14. Canada.

Loyie, Larry, with Constance Brissenden. *As Long as the Rivers Flow.* Illustrated by Heather D. Holmlund.

Douglas & McIntyre, 2002. (PI) Ages 8–12. Canada.

Lunn, Janet. *Laura Secord: A Story of Courage.* Illustrated by Maxwell Newhouse. Tundra, 2001. Ages 9–12. Canada.

Marsden, John. *Letters from the Inside.* Houghton, 1994. Ages 12–16. Australia.

———. *So Much to Tell You.* Joy Street, 1989. Ages 12–16. Australia.

Matas, Carol. *Sparks Fly Upward.* Clarion, 2002. Ages 9–13. Canada.

McCaughrean, Geraldine. *The Kite Rider.* Harper Collins, 2002. Ages 10–14. U.K.

McKay, Hilary. *Indigo's Star.* McElderry, 2004. Ages 11–13. U.K.

———. *Permanent Rose.* McElderry, 2005. Ages 10–13. U.K.

———. *Saffy's Angel.* McElderry, 2002. Ages 9–12. U.K.

Morpurgo, Michael. *The Wreck of the Zanzibar.* Illustrated by François Place. Viking, 1995. Ages 12–14. U.K.

Murray, Martine. *The Slightly True Story of Cedar B. Hartley (Who Planned to Live an Unusual Life).* Scholastic, 2003. Ages 9–13. Australia.

Naidoo, Beverley. *Chain of Fire.* Lippincott, 1990. Ages 11–18. South Africa.

———. *Journey to Jo'burg.* Lippincott, 1986. Ages 10–13. South Africa.

———. *No Turning Back: A Novel of South Africa.* HarperCollins, 1997. Ages 10–14. South Africa.

———. *The Other Side of Truth.* HarperCollins, 2001. Ages 10–15. South Africa.

———. *Out of Bounds: Seven Stories of Conflict and Hope.* HarperCollins, 2003. Ages 10–14. South Africa.

Nicholson, William. *The Wind Singer.* Hyperion, 2000. Ages 10–13. U.K. First of trilogy, Wind on Fire, that includes *Slaves of the Master* (2001) and *Firesong* (2002).

Norling, Beth. *Little School.* Kane/Miller, 2003. (PI) Ages 3–5. Australia.

Orr, Wendy. *Peeling the Onion.* Holiday, 1997. Ages 11–15. Australia.

Overend, Jenni. *Welcome with Love.* Illustrated by Julie Vivas. Kane/Miller, 2000. Ages 5–8. Australia.

Pratchett, Terry. *The Amazing Maurice and His Educated Rodents.* HarperCollins, 2001. Ages 11–15. U.K.

Pullman, Philip. *Clockwork.* Illustrated by Leonid Gore. Scholastic, 1998. Ages 9–13. U.K.

———. *The Golden Compass.* Knopf, 1996. Ages 12–15. First of His Dark Materials trilogy. Also *The Subtle Knife,* Knopf, 1997, and *The Amber Spyglass,* Knopf, 1999. U.K.

———. *I Was a Rat!* Illustrated by Kevin Hawkes. Knopf, 2000. Ages 8–12. U.K.

Rees, Celia. *Pirates!* Bloomsbury, 2003. Ages 12–15. U.K.

———. *Witch Child.* Candlewick, 2001. Ages 11–15. U.K. The sequel is *Sorceress,* 2002.

Riddle, Toby. *The Singing Hat.* Farrar, 2001. (PI) Ages 5–8.

Rodda, Emily. *The Charm Bracelet.* Illustrated by Raoul Vitale. HarperCollins, 2003. Ages 7–11. Australia.

———. *Rowan of Rin.* Greenwillow, 2001. Ages 8–12. Australia. (Also in this series, *Rowan and the Travelers,* 2001; *Rowan and the Keeper of the Crystal,* 2002; *Rowan and the Zebak,* 2002; and *Rowan and the Ice-Creepers,* 2003.)

Rosoff, Meg. *Meet Wild Boars.* Illustrated by Sophie Blackall. Holt, 2005. (PI) Ages 4–8. U.K.

Rowling J.K. *Harry Potter and the Sorcerer's Stone.* Scholastic, 1998. The first in a series of quest fantasies, including *Harry Potter and the Chamber of Secrets,* 1999; *Harry Potter and the Prisoner of Azkaban,* 1999; *Harry Potter and the Goblet of Fire,* 2000; *Harry Potter and the Order of the Phoenix,* 2003; and *Harry Potter and the Half-Blood Prince,* 2005. Ages 9–13. U.K.

Scrimger, Richard. *The Nose from Jupiter.* Tundra, 1998. Ages 10–13. Canada.

Slade, Arthur. *Dust.* Wendy Lamb, 2003. Ages 11–15. Canada.

Stanley, Elizabeth. *The Deliverance of Dancing Bears.* Kane/Miller, 2002. (PI) Ages 5–9. Australia.

Thompson, Kate. *Wild Blood.* Hyperion, 2000. Ages 11–15. Ireland. Last in the trilogy that began with *Switchers,* 1998, and was followed by *Midnight's Choice,* 1999.

Updale, Eleanor. *Montmorency.* Scholastic, 2004. Ages 12–16. Part of a series. U.K.

Waddell, Martin. *Farmer Duck.* Illustrated by Helen Oxenbury. Candlewick, 1992. (PI) Ages 4–6. U.K.

Wallace, Ian. *Boy of the Deeps.* DK Ink, 1999. (PI) Ages 8–11. (PI) Canada.

———. *The Naked Lady.* Roaring Brook, 2002. (PI) Ages 6–12. Canada.

———. *The True Story of Trapper Jack's Left Big Toe.* Roaring Brook, 2002. (PI) Ages 5–9. Canada.

Walsh, Alice. *Heroes of Isles aux Morts.* Illustrated by Geoff Butler. Tundra, 2001. Ages 4–8. Canada.

Waugh, Sylvia. *Space Race.* Delacorte, 2000. Ages 9–12. U.K.

Wild, Margaret. *Fox.* Illustrated by Ron Brooks. Kane/Miller, 2001. (**PI**) Ages 6–8. Australia.

———. *The Pocket Dogs.* Illustrated by Stephen Michael King. Scholastic, 2001. (**PI**) Ages 3–7. Australia.

———. *The Very Best of Friends.* Illustrated by Julie Vivas. Harcourt, 1990. (**PI**) Ages 4–9. Australia.

Wilson, Budge. *A Fiddle for Angus.* Illustrated by Susan Tooke. Tundra, 2001. (**PI**) Ages 5–9. Canada.

Wilson, Jacqueline. *The Story of Tracy Beaker.* Illustrated by Nick Sharratt. Delacorte, 2001. Ages 9–12. U.K.

Wynne-Jones, Tim. *The Boy in the Burning House.* Farrar, 2001. Ages 12–15. Canada.

Yee, Paul. *Dead Man's Gold and Other Stories.* Illustrated by Harvey Chan. Douglas & McIntyre, 2002. (**COL**) Ages 11–14. Canada.

———. *Tales from Gold Mountain: Stories of the Chinese in the New World.* Macmillan, 1990. (**COL**) Ages 7–12. Canada.

Translated Books

Arcellana, Francisco. *The Mats.* Illustrated by Hermès Allègre. Kane/Miller, 1999. Ages 5–9. Philippines.

Ashbé, Jeanne. *What's Inside.* Kane/Miller, 2000. (**PI**) Ages 2–5. Belgium.

Björk, Christina. *Vendela in Venice.* Illustrated by Inga-Karin Eriksson. Translated from the Swedish by Patricia Crampton. R & S, 1999. Ages 9–12. Sweden.

Bluitgen, Kåre. *A Boot Fell from Heaven.* Illustrated by Chiara Carrer. Kane/Miller, 2003. (**PI**) Ages 5–9. Denmark.

Bredsdorff, Bodil. *The Crow-Girl: The Children of Crow Cove.* Translated from the Danish by Faith Ingwersen. Farrar, 2004. Ages 11–12. Denmark.

Buchholz, Quint. *The Collector of Moments.* Translated from the German by Peter F. Niemeyer. Farrar, 1999. (**PI**) Ages 9–12. Germany.

Carmi, Daniella. *Samir and Yonatan.* Translated from the Hebrew by Yael Lotan. Scholastic, 2000. Ages 9–12. Israel.

Erikson, Eva. *A Crash Course for Molly.* Translated from the Swedish by Elisabeth Dyssegaard. Farrar, 2005. (**PI**) Ages 5–7. Sweden.

Filipovic, Zlata. *Zlata's Diary: A Child's Life in Wartime Sarajevo.* Translated from the French by Fixot et editions Robert Lafont. Penguin, 1994/2006 (revised edition). Ages 12–18. Bosnia.

Fournier le Ray, Anne-Laure. *Grandparents!* Illustrated by Roser Capdevila. Kane/Miller, 2003. (**PI**) Ages 4–7. France.

Frank, Anne. *Anne Frank: The Diary of a Young Girl.* Translated from the Dutch by B. M. Mooyaart. Doubleday, 1967. Ages 13–18 Netherlands.

Friedrich, Joachim. *4½ Friends and the Secret Cave.* Translated from the German by Elizabeth D. Crawford. Hyperion, 2001. Ages 8–11. Germany.

Funke, Cornelia. *The Thief Lord.* Translated by Oliver Latsch. Scholastic, 2002. Ages 10–14. Germany.

Goscinny, René. *Nicholas.* Illustrated by Jean Jacques Sempé. Translated from the French by Anthea Bell. Phaidon, 2005. (**COL**) Ages 9–12. France.

Gündisch, Karin. *How I Became an American.* Translated from the German by James Skofield. Cricket, 2001. Ages 9–12. Germany.

Harel, Nira. *The Key to My Heart.* Illustrated by Yossi Abulafia. Kane/Miller, 2002. (**PI**) Ages 4–7. Israel.

Highet, Alistair. *The Yellow Train.* Based on a story by Fred Bernard. Illustrated by François Roca. Creative, 2000. (**PI**) Ages 4–7. Canada.

Hoestlandt, Jo. *Star of Fear, Star of Hope.* Illustrated by Johanna Kang. Translated from the French by Mark Polizzotti. Walker, 1995. (**PI**) Ages 7–12. France.

Hogeweg, Margriet. *The God of Grandma Forever.* Translated from the Dutch by Nancy Forest-Flier. Front Street, 2001. Ages 9–13. Netherlands.

Holtwijz, Ineke. *Asphalt Angels.* Front Street, 1999. Translated from the Dutch by Wanda Boeke. Ages 12–16. The Netherlands. Story set in Rio de Janeiro.

Jacobsson, Anders, and Sören Olsson. *In Ned's Head.* Translated by Kevin Read. Atheneum, 2001. Ages 9–12. Sweden.

Jung, Reinhard. *Dreaming in Black and White.* Translated from the German by Anthea Bell. Phyllis Fogelman Books, 2003. Ages 10–14. Germany.

Kodama, Tatsuharu. *Shin's Tricycle.* Illustrated by Ando. Translated by Kazuko Hokumen-Jones. Walker, 1995. (**PI**) Ages 10–13. Japan.

Landström, Lena. *Boo and Baa Have Company.* Illustrated by Olof Landström. Translated from the Swedish by Joan Sandin. Farrar, 2006. (**PI**) Ages 4–7. (Part of the Boo and Baa series) Sweden.

Lee, Ho Baek. *While We Were Out.* Kane/Miller, 2003. (**PI**) Ages 3–6. South Korea.

Léonard, Marie. *Tibili, the Little Boy Who Didn't Want to Go to School.* Translated from the French. Illustrated by Andrée Prigent. Kane/Miller, 2001. (**PI**) Set in Africa. Ages 5–8. France.

Liu, Jae Soo. *Yellow Umbrella.* Kane/Miller, 2002. (**PI**) Ages 2–6. (Includes a companion CD with music composed by Sheen Dong Il.) South Korea.

Meyer, Kai. *The Water Mirror.* Translated from the German by Elizabeth D. Crawford. Simon & Schuster, 2005. Ages 10–14. (Set in Venice) Germany.

Moeyaert, Bart. *Bare Hands.* Translated by David Colmer. Front Street, 1998. Ages 10–15. Netherlands.

Morgenstern, Susie. *A Book of Coupons.* Translated from the French by Gil Rosner. Illustrated by Serge Bloch. Viking, 2001. Ages 9–12. France.

Orlev, Uri. *Run, Boy, Run.* Translated by Hillel Halkin. Houghton, 2003. Ages 10–13. Israel.

Popov, Nikolai. *Why?* Translated from the German. North-South, 1996. (**PI**) Ages 7–14. Switzerland.

Pressler, Mirjam. *Halinka.* Translated from the German by Elizabeth D. Crawford. Holt, 1998. Ages 10–15. Germany.

———. *Malka.* Translated from the German by Brian Murdoch. Philomel, 2003. Ages 12–16. Germany.

Sakai, Komako. *Emily's Balloon.* Translated from the Japanese. Chronicle, 2006. (**PI**) Ages 3–5. Japan.

Schami, Rafik. *A Hand Full of Stars.* Translated from the German by Rika Lesser. Dutton, 1990. Ages 12–16.

Skármeta, Antonio. *The Composition.* Illustrated by Alfonso Ruano. Translated from the Spanish by Elisa Amado. Groundwood, 2000. (**PI**) Ages 8–12.

Stark, Ulf. *Can You Whistle, Johanna?: A Boy's Search for a Grandfather.* Illustrated by Anna Hoglund. Translated from the Swedish by Ebba Segerberg. RDR Books, 1999. (**PI**) Ages 6–8. Sweden.

Stolz, Joelle. *The Shadows of Ghadames.* Translated from the French by Catherine Temerson. Delacorte, 2004. Ages 11–14. (Set in Libya) France.

Valckx, Catharina. *Lizette's Green Sock.* Translated from the French. Clarion, 2005. (**PI**) Ages 3–6. France.

Vejjajiva, Jane. *The Happiness of Kati.* Translated from the Thai by Prudence Borthwick. Atheneum, 2006. Ages 10–12. Thailand.

Weninger, Brigitte. *Special Delivery.* Translated by J. Alison James. Illustrated by Alexander Reichstein. North-South, 2000. (**PI**) Ages 3–5. Austria.

Xiong, Kim. *The Little Stone Lion.* Translated from the Chinese. Heryin, 2006. (**PI**) Ages 4–7. China.

Yumoto, Kazumi. *The Friends.* Translated by Cathy Hirano. Farrar, 1996. Ages 10–14. Japan.

Zullo, Germano. *Marta and the Bicycle.* Translated from the French. Illustrated by Albertine. Kane/Miller, 2002. (**PI**) Ages 4–8. Switzerland.

Related Films, Videos, and DVDs

A Hero Ain't Nothin' but a Sandwich. (1991). Author: Alice Childress. 107 minutes. (African American)

Amazing Grace. (1993). Author: Mary Hoffman. 30 minutes. (Originally published in England)

I Love Saturdays y Domingos. (2002). Author: Alma Flor Ada. Illustrated by Elvivia Savadier. 18 minutes. (Bilingual)

Millions. (2005). Author: Frank C. Boyce. 98 minutes. (Originally published in England)

Sources for Films, Videos, and DVDs

The Video Source Book. Syosset, NY: National Video Clearinghouse, 1979–. Published by Gale Research, Detroit, MI.

An annual reference work that lists media and provides sources for purchase and rental.

Websites of large video distributors:

www.libraryvideo.com

http://teacher.scholastic.com/products/westonwoods

part III

Literature in the School

Chapters 12 and 13 focus on curriculum and teaching strategies. Planning for and evaluating a literature curriculum as it pertains to a specific lesson, a unit of instruction, a yearlong classroom plan, and a schoolwide literature program are explained in Chapter 12. The two main approaches to teaching reading—basal reading programs and literature-based reading—are discussed here in terms of strategies for incorporating literature into the teaching of reading. Features such as sample planning webs, evaluation checklists, sample focus books for a yearlong curriculum, and literature-related activities to help preservice teachers in school practicums gain experience with literature provide practical procedural suggestions and advice. Chapter 12 concludes with a discussion of censorship, selection, and First Amendment rights.

Strategies for sharing literature successfully with children and encouraging them to respond in a variety of ways to these literary experiences are presented in Chapter 13. The chapter discusses incorporating literature across the curriculum, teaching reading in the content areas with emphasis on helping students learn to read both fiction and nonfiction, using books as writing models and as sources for creative drama and readers' theatre, using audiobooks and films based on children's books, and selecting literature as the foundation of character education and social justice education.

chapter 12

Planning the Curriculum

My Plan

When I'm a little older
I plan to buy a boat,
And up and down the river
The two of us will float.

I'll have a little cabin
All painted white and red
With shutters for the window
And curtains for the bed.

I'll have a little cookstove
On which to fry my fishes,
And all the Hudson River
In which to wash my dishes.

—Marchette Chute

This chapter deals with long-range planning for literature instruction. Short-range planning is discussed in Chapter 13. First, the literature curriculum is defined, and approaches to organizing such a curriculum are presented. Guidelines for developing the literature curriculum and a discussion of how literature can be integrated into a school's reading program follow. The latter part of the chapter includes sections on evaluating a literature program; implementing a schoolwide literature program; gaining experience with literature as a preservice teacher; and learning about censorship, selection, and First Amendment rights (primarily free speech) as they pertain to literature in the schools.

Defining the Literature Curriculum

Literature is more than a collection of well-written stories and poems. Literature also has its own body of knowledge. A term that is sometimes used to label this treatment of literature is *discipline-based literature instruction.* The object of such a course of study is to teach children the mechanics of literature: the terms used to define it, its components or elements, its genres, and the craft of creating it. The terms and elements of fiction are presented in Chapter 3; the terms and elements of nonfiction are presented in Chapter 10; the genres and their characteristics are presented in Chapters 4 through 11.

Choosing the Approach

Most often, elementary and middle-school teachers organize the literature curriculum either by genre, theme or topic, author or illustrator, literary element or device, or notable books. An alternative is to create a hybrid literature curriculum by including aspects of several of these approaches in the plan.

Genre

By organizing a literature curriculum around literary genres, teachers provide a context for students to learn about the various types of literature and the characteristics of each. In the beginning, the teacher will have to direct students' attention to similarities in books of like genre—for example, the students will learn that works of historical fiction are always set in the past or that characters in folktales are two-dimensional. Soon, however, students will begin to read with more genre awareness and will enjoy finding common elements within and differences between genres.

One advantage of this plan is that students over the school year can be exposed to a wide variety of literature. Knowledge of different genres gives students useful *schemata*—frameworks for understanding born of prior knowledge and experience—for story types. A genre approach can work in all grade levels, given thoughtful selection of titles and delivery of literary concepts. Planning involves choosing the genres to be studied, selecting the representative children's books for each, and determining the order in which the genres will be studied.

Theme or Topic

Teachers who choose to organize a study of literature by theme or topic want their students generally to become aware of the power of literature to explain the human condition. Themes and topics will vary according to ages and circumstances of students. For example, primary-grade children will be interested in themes and topics having to do with school and family life. Those in the middle grades, on the other hand, will be more intrigued by themes and topics dealing with the discovery and use of inner resources to become more independent or even to survive.

Possible themes that a seventh- or eighth-grade class might explore through a year include the following:

Effects of Poverty
Surviving in the Modern World
Alienation and Acceptance by Peers
Coping with Parents and Younger Siblings
Teenagers through History: The Same Old Problems?
Dependence and Independence
The Future World
What Is the Nature of Difference?
Community Involvement and Activism
Walking in Someone Else's Shoes: The Importance of Perspective

Possible themes and topics for a younger group might include these:

Families Come in All Shapes and Sizes
School Now and in the Past
Use Your Wits
The Importance of Having Good Friends
Stories from Other Countries
Old Ones and Young Ones Together
Famous People Were Children, Too

In this approach, each child reads or listens to the book or books chosen by the teacher to accompany each theme. After the reading, students explore the theme through discussion, writing, drama, art, and further reading on the theme or topic.

Themes and topics are chosen by the teacher on the basis of students' needs and interests, current events, and prior successes with previously developed thematic units. The length of time spent on any one theme or topic can vary from a school year to a day, but several weeks' duration is the norm.

Two pitfalls of thematic curriculum models must be avoided:

1. Do not choose a theme or topic just because a few related books are at hand. Remember: The unit theme or topic drives literature selection, not vice versa.
2. Do not choose literature because it relates to the theme or topic but with no regard to its quality or appropriateness for the students. Boring books make boring thematic instructional units.

Author or Illustrator

The goal of a curriculum in literature organized by author or illustrator is to make students more familiar with the works and styles of selected children's book authors and illustrators. An additional goal may be knowledge of the authors' or illustrators' lives insofar as these life experiences influenced the subjects' works. The choice of authors and illustrators will naturally be guided both by students' reading interests and the teacher's desire to introduce students to important authors and illustrators and their works. The number of works chosen to represent an author or illustrator will vary, but even when an author's books are lengthy, more than one work is recommended.

As a class experiences a sampling of the chosen author's or illustrator's work, attention will be focused on trademark stylistic elements such as unusual use of words or color or media, as well as themes, characters, character types, or settings common to these works. Later, information about the person's life can be introduced through reports, audiotaped and videotaped interviews, and even guest appearances by the author or illustrator. Websites, biographies, and biographical reference volumes, such as *Something about the Author* (Gale Research, 2006) and *Children's Literature Review* (Gale Research, 2006), provide information about children's book authors and illustrators.

Success of author and illustrator studies is not necessarily defined by wholesale student approval of the featured artists. Students must be allowed to decide whether they like a person's work or not and should be encouraged to discover why they have these feelings. Wholesale *disapproval* by students of the works of a featured author or illustrator, however, is an important form of *teacher* evaluation that should not be ignored. In such a case, the teacher's choice of author or books to be studied was not appropriate for this purpose and should be reconsidered. Students are evaluated informally through observation of their recognition of featured authors' or illustrators' works and their ability to compare literary and artistic styles of various authors and illustrators.

Literary Element and Device

When teachers say that their teaching of literature is organized by literary element, they are usually referring to the elements of fiction and nonfiction, as presented in Chapters 3 and 10, respectively. Other elements, such as artistic styles, media, and book format, could be addressed as well. A *literary device* is "any literary technique deliberately employed to achieve a special effect" (Baldick, 1990, p. 55). Irony, symbolism, parody, and foreshadowing are examples of devices that add richness to stories.

The goal of a literature curriculum organized by literary elements and devices is to give students a better understanding of the craft of writing so that they can read more perceptively and appreciatively and possibly apply this knowledge to their own writing. Since this approach is analytical and somewhat abstract, it is more appropriate for students in the fourth grade or above.

Careful selection of children's books to accompany the investigation of each literary element or device is crucial to the success of this approach. The featured element must be prominent and must have been used by the author with extraordinary skill. In addition, the story itself must captivate young readers. Note that in this approach, books of various genres can be grouped to demonstrate the same literary element. Note also that picture books are particularly good at presenting literary elements and devices clearly and in relatively simple contexts so that they can be understood more easily. An excellent resource for selecting picture books for this use is Hall's *Using Picture Storybooks to Teach Literary Devices,* Vols. 1 and 2 (1990, 1994).

Students' acquaintance with the literary elements and devices can go far beyond mere definition. Close reading of key passages reveals the author's craft at developing character, establishing mood, authenticating setting, or using such devices as inference, symbolism, or fore-shadowing. Re-creation of these elements and devices in their own art, drama, and writing not only gives students a personal and more complete understanding of these concepts but it also gives teachers a way to evaluate their students' grasp of these concepts.

Notable Book

In the primary grades, teachers will most likely read the notable books aloud to students. Reading aloud by teachers works for intermediate and middle grades as well, but an alternative at these levels is independent reading of the selected books by students. In this approach, the teacher or students read one or more chapters of the selected book each day and then discuss what they have read. Students can compare their understandings of the story with one another, clarify word meanings and any confusing parts of the story, make predictions about where the story is heading, or analyze any of the story's literary elements. Traditionally, these discussions are led by the teacher, but some instructors have found that student-led discussions in small groups, if well managed, are just as effective and have the added advantage of giving students practice in leading serious discussions.

Teachers who organize their literature curriculum by notable books must be careful to remain flexible in book selections from year to year so that the list of notable books reflects students' current interests and reading preferences. A list of notable books that never varies can result in student disinterest and stale teaching.

 # Developing the Literature Curriculum

Planning for a literature curriculum involves two practical considerations: building a classroom library collection and outlining a yearlong literature curriculum.

Building a Classroom Library Collection

Most, if not all, of the responsibility for acquiring a sufficiently large and varied collection of books in your classroom will be yours. With perseverance, it can be done. Most good classroom libraries have a permanent collection as well as a collection that comes from the school or public library and changes regularly. Beginning teachers who are willing to plan ahead with their school and public librarians can borrow enough books for adequate temporary classroom libraries while they build their own collections. Even after a large permanent collection is established, a rotating selection from the school and public library can be coordinated with specific units of study, providing depth and breadth to the unit content and to the students' learning experience.

Careful selection of titles for the classroom library makes the most of limited resources. Children's librarians can provide invaluable advice in selecting titles for a classroom library and should be consulted. If this is not an option, browsing in a well-stocked children's bookstore and consulting publishers' catalogs are alternative ways of finding out what is available. Publishers of children's books issue one or two catalogs annually in which they describe their new publications and list their previous publications that are currently available (the backlist). If your school or public librarian does not have these catalogs, publishers will supply them on request. Some teachers use catalogs to get an overview of what is available before going to a bookstore.

Your own permanent trade book collection can be built inexpensively by using several proven approaches. These include the following:

- Requesting an allocation from your principal or PTO for purchase of books
- Submitting a small grant proposal ($250–$1,000) to your school district or professional organization for purchase of trade books
- Taking advantage of bonus books offered by student paperback book clubs
- Informing students' parents that you are building a collection and would like to have first refusal of any children's books that they plan to discard
- Establishing a "give a book to the classroom" policy for parents who want to celebrate their child's birthday or a holiday at school in some way
- Frequenting garage sales and library book sales, where good books can often be purchased for pennies

Most bookstores offer a 20 percent discount to teachers who use their own money to buy books to add to their classroom collections. An alternative to the bookstore is the book jobber, or wholesale dealer for many publishers. Jobbers offer even greater discounts to teachers, sometimes up to 40 percent, but it is important to remember that most jobbers do not carry small-press publications. Your school librarian probably uses a jobber and can assist you in setting up a staff account with the same firm. Some of the larger firms include Baker & Taylor, Brodart, and Ingram Book Company.

With these methods and sources, classroom collections grow quickly. From the beginning, you will need to devise a coding system for your permanent collection to streamline shelving and record keeping. Many teachers find that color coding their books by genre with colored tape on the spines works well. If at all possible, students should be trained and given the responsibility for color coding, checking in and out, repairing, and reshelving books.

Remember that the whole point of building a classroom library is to promote reading, not to provide a handsome display. Inevitably, if children use their classroom library, books will be lost and damaged. Severe reprimands for losing or damaging a book may work against your ultimate goal.

Outlining a Yearlong Literature Curriculum

Outlining a yearlong literature curriculum helps teachers determine a practical scope of content and logical sequence of presentation and gives them time to gather the necessary resources by the time they are needed. Recommended steps in outlining for a yearlong literature curriculum are reviewed in the following subsections.

Establish Goals

Goals in a literature curriculum are those aims one expects to accomplish by the end of the course of study. Central to this part of the planning process is deciding on the literary concepts to be taught. Since goals largely determine the parameters of the curriculum, they must be established early in the planning process.

Goals for a literature curriculum are established by individual teachers and sometimes by schools or school districts. Goals for a primary-grade teacher who has chosen a mixed genre/author organization to teaching literature would be these, among others.

- Students will enjoy reading a variety of genres of literature.
- Students will be familiar with the characteristics of folktales, modern fantasy, contemporary realistic fiction, and nonfiction and will be able to classify a book as belonging to one of the featured genres when reading it.
- Students will become familiar with several leading authors (or collectors in the case of folktales) of each of the genres and will be able to identify characteristics of the writing of each author.

Determine Literature Units

After goals have been identified and set, the next step in outlining a literature curriculum is to determine the units of study through which the literature content will be delivered. In this way, a tentative schedule can be set in order to foresee needs in terms of time and materials and to coordinate delivery of the units with the school calendar.

Select Focus Books

Early selection of unit titles is important for several reasons. Balance in the overall book selection, for instance, is achieved much more easily in the planning stages. Balance in book selection, as presented in Chapter 3, means that the books selected present a diversity of characters (type, gender, age, ethnicity, place of origin) who have relevance to children's lives, settings (urban, rural, familiar, foreign), and themes. Another advantage of early selection is being able to estimate the time necessary for each unit. Some units will take longer than others, depending on such variables as the extent of content to be covered, the length and difficulty of books to be read, the type and complexity of planned book extension activities, and the ability to locate and obtain the books and related resources such as films and guest speakers. A sample list of units, books, and featured authors for a fifth-grade teacher who is implementing a combined genre/author organization for teaching literature is shown in the accompanying box.

Unit 1: Traditional Literature
(Females in Traditional Literature)

Mythology
Changing Woman and Her Sisters: Stories of Goddesses from Around the World by Katrin Hyman Tchana, reteller, illustrated by Trina Schart Hyman
The Gods and Goddesses of Olympus retold and illustrated by Aliki

Legends and Tall Tales
Cut from the Same Cloth: American Women of Myth, Legend, and Tall Tale retold by Robert D. San Souci, illustrated by Brian Pinkney

Folktales
Cinderella retold by Ruth Sanderson
Walt Disney's Sleeping Beauty by Disney

Read-Aloud
Not One Damsel in Distress: World Folktales for Strong Girls retold by Jane Yolen, illustrated by Susan Guevara

(continued)

Unit 2: Modern Fantasy
(Unusual Characters and Strange Situations)

Finders Keepers by Emily Rodda
The Power of Un by Nancy Etchemendy
Things Not Seen by Andrew Clements

Read-Aloud
Tuck Everlasting by Natalie Babbitt
Featured Author: Natalie Babbitt

Unit 3: Historical Fiction (World War II)
(Life in the United States during World War II)

Lily's Crossing by Patricia Reilly Giff (also sequel, *Willow Run*)
Under the Blood-Red Sun by Graham Salisbury
Weedflower by Cynthia Kadohata

Read-Aloud
Journey to Topaz by Yoshiko Uchida
Featured Author: Yoshiko Uchida

Unit 4: Contemporary Realistic Fiction
(Cultural Diversity)

Crossing Jordan by Adrian Fogelin
The Tequila Worm by Viola Canales
Taking Sides by Gary Soto
Yolanda's Genius by Carol Fenner

Read-Aloud
Locomotion by Jacqueline Woodson
Featured Author: Jacqueline Woodson

Unit 5: Mystery
(Young Sleuths)

Down the Rabbit Hole by Peter Abrahams
Holes by Louis Sachar
Hoot by Carl Hiaasen

Read-Aloud
Sammy Keyes and the Hotel Thief by Wendelin Van Draanen
Featured Author: Wendelin Van Draanen

Unit 6: Science Fiction
(Future Worlds)

The City of Ember by Jeanne Duprau

The Giver by Lois Lowry
The House of the Scorpion by Nancy Farmer

Read-Aloud
The Boy Who Reversed Himself by William Sleator
Featured Author: William Sleator

Developing Literature Units

Thinking through, organizing, and writing down the details of daily lessons and activities in the various units are the final steps in planning for a literature curriculum. Two helpful tools in organizing the details of literature units are webs and lesson plans.

Webs

Webbing is a way of creating a visual overview of a literature unit complete with its focus, related book titles, and activities. Ideas for a web are generated through brainstorming. The main advantage of webbing is that the process clarifies and even suggests ties or associations between concepts, books, and activities. Activities can be drawn from all content areas and all skill areas—writing, reading, listening, thinking, speaking, art, crafts, drama, and music. The web in Figure 12.1 shows ideas for a unit of study on the literary element, character. The web in Figure 12.2 shows ideas for a unit of study on the topic of immigration.

A disadvantage of a web is that it gives no indication of the chronology of events or time allotments. The set of daily or weekly lesson plans that can be developed from a web provides the more linear format preferred by most teachers.

Lesson Plans

Lesson plans are organized by day or week. Specificity will vary according to the needs and experience of the teacher, but each day's or week's lesson plan usually includes the following components:

- *Objectives,* which are short-range aims to be accomplished day by day or week by week. An objective for a teacher conducting a literature unit on the topic of Immigration, as found in Figure 12.2, might be for students to realize that most Americans or their ancestors are immigrants and deserve respect regardless of how recently they have arrived in this country.
- *Procedures and methods,* which tell what the teacher does, in what order and with what materials, what tasks or assignments students will be given, and what the teacher expects of them. Procedures of the teacher conducting the Immigration unit in Figure 12.2 in order to fulfill the objective stated above might be to read aloud Margy Knight's book, *Who Belongs Here: An American Story* (2003), then ask students to share in small groups their own or their families' stories of how they came to this country.
- *Evaluation,* in which teachers must consider how they intend to evaluate their students and themselves in terms of how well the students met the objectives and how well their plans worked. *Student evaluation* can take the form of written examinations, oral questions,

Figure 12.1   Web Demonstrating Investigation of a Literary Element, Grades 2–4

Small Group Reading

Note whether the characters in these stories changed or remained the same. If they changed, how?

Realistic Fiction
Rosy Cole's Worst Ever, Best Yet Tour of New York City by Sheila Greenwald
The Castle in the Attic by Elizabeth Winthrop

Modern Fantasy
Petronella by Jay Williams
Rumpelstiltskin's Daughter by Diane Stanley
Swamp Angel by Anne Isaacs

Traditional Literature
Sleeping Beauty by Trina Schart Hyman
Cinderella by Ruth Sanderson

Read-Aloud

Listen for ways that the author helps you get to know the main character.

Number the Stars by Lois Lowry
Rowan of Rin by Emily Rodda

Independent Reading

Look for protagonists, antagonists, secondary characters, and character foils in these stories.

Hot Fudge Hero by Pat Brisson
Amber Was Brave, Essie Was Smart by Vera B. Williams
A Dog on Barkham Street by Mary Stolz
The Bully of Barkham Street by Mary Stolz
The Gold-Threaded Dress by Carolyn Marsden
Tooter Pepperday by Jerry Spinelli
Ramona Quimby, Age 8 by Beverly Cleary
Ramona and Her Father by Beverly Cleary
Morgy Makes His Move by Maggie Lewis
Finders Keepers by Emily Rodda
Hating Alison Ashley by Robin Klein
A Taste of Blackberries by Doris B. Smith

Characterization

Character Development

Character Types

CHARACTER

Discussion

How are characters in works of realistic fiction different from characters in works of traditional literature?

How would you describe the female characters in the works of traditional folktales you read? How do they compare with the female characters in the modern folktales?

Find a paragraph in a book you read that describes the protagonist. Why is this a good description?

How do you learn about characters in the books you read?

Writing

List the ways that a character in a book you read changed from the beginning to the end of the story.

Select as many adjectives as you can to accurately describe a character in one of the books you read.

With a partner, write interview questions for a story character. Write answers to these questions, as if you were that character. Make sure that your answers are in keeping with the character's personality.

Art

Using descriptions found in the story, draw a portrait of a character you liked.

Draw a scene from the story that, in your opinion, caused the protagonist to change the most.

Drama

Select a scene that shows character development from a story you read with a small group. Adapt this scene for readers' theatre. Make an audio recording of your reading for others in your class to enjoy.

Figure 12.2 Web Demonstrating Use of Literature across the Curriculum, Grades 5–8

Literature Circle Reading
THE IMMIGRANT EXPERIENCE

Facing Prejudice

Journey to Topaz
  by Yoshiko Uchida

Dragon's Gate
  by Laurence Yep

Assimilation of a New Culture

Blue Jasmine
  by Sheth Kashmira

A Step from Heaven
  by An Na (Korea)

Retaining One's Native Culture

*Two Lands, One Heart: An
  American Boy's Journey
  to His Mother's Vietnam*
  by Jeremy Schmidt

Child of the Owl
  by Laurence Yep

Read-Aloud
IMMIGRATION TODAY

*Who Belongs Here?
  An American Story*
  by Margy Knight

*Quilted Landscape:
  Conversations with
  Young Immigrants*
  by Yale Strom

Independent Reading
IMMIGRATION, 1840s–PRESENT

Fiction

Two Suns in the Sky
  by Miriam Bat-Ami (Yugoslavia)

Journey of the Sparrows
  by Fran Buss (El Salvador)

Esperanza Rising by Pam M. Ryan

Letters from Rifka
  by Karen Hesse (Russia)

Journey to America
  by Sonia Levitin (Germany)

Tonight By Sea
  by Frances Temple (Haiti)

Nonfiction

Immigrant Kids by Russell Freedman

*The Circuit: Stories from the Life of a
  Migrant Child* by Francisco Jiménez
  (Mexico)

*If Your Name Was Changed at Ellis
  Island* by Ellen Levine

*Coming to America: The Story of
  Immigration* by Betsy Maestro

Reading

**COMING TO AMERICA:
IMMIGRATION**

Discussion

What are the causes of
prejudice against recent
immigrants?

How do experiences of recent
immigrants compare to those of
the past?

Debate: "Should the U.S. allow
immigrants into the country
today? Why or why not?"

Listening

Invite someone who immigrated to
the U.S. (a parent, grandparent,
friend, someone from your
community) to speak to your class.
How does this person's experience
compare to the experiences of the
protagonists in the books you read?

Writing

Adapt a pivotal scene from
a book you read for a
dramatic presentation.

Interview a recent
immigrant to the U.S.
Describe this person's
experience.

Find out as much as you
can about where your
ancestors came from and
their immigration story. Tell
this story.

From your reading, list all
the reasons people might
wish to immigrate to the
U.S.

**Reading–Writing
Connections**

Read a newspaper or news
magazine article about
immigration. Summarize the
article by answering the five
questions journalists must
answer in their writing: "Who,
What, When, Where, Why."

Then write a newspaper article
based on the work of fiction
you read, being sure to fulfill
the same five requirements of
journalistic writing.

Art

In a small group, design and create a
mural that explains why people
immigrate to the U.S.

Create a poster that expresses your
thoughts about immigration to the U.S.

Design an immigration postage
stamp.

listening to students' comments during whole-class or small group discussions, reading students' journals in which they record their learning, and examining students' written, oral, artistic, and dramatic responses to literature. *Self-evaluation by the teacher* can be in terms of student interest in the lesson, student success in meeting the stated objectives, and the plan's success in predicting time and materials needed and effectiveness of methods and procedures. At regular intervals during the literature unit teachers will want to evaluate their students' progress in meeting the unit and yearlong goals and, if necessary, revise the plans or the goals.

Because literature units are several weeks long, they usually include a culminating activity that gives students an opportunity to reflect on what they have learned, review major points, and sometimes celebrate the focus of the unit in some way. An overall unit evaluation is valuable to teachers, particularly if they intend to use the unit with another group of students. The unit should indicate the method of evaluation. Revisions can make the unit even more successful in succeeding years.

Literature in the Reading Program

Nowhere in the school curriculum is literature more important than in the reading program. In the primary grades literature can be instrumental in helping teach children to read, and in the intermediate and middle grades it can keep young people's interest in reading alive, helping struggling readers strengthen their reading skills and encouraging all students to become lifelong readers. In the following sections the two most common approaches to teaching reading in the United States will be presented while demonstrating literature's role in each.

Basal Reading Program Supplemented by Children's Literature

Just as children bring a variety of learning styles and needs to the task of learning, so do teachers bring a variety of teaching styles and needs to teaching. A single approach to teaching reading cannot suit all teachers or all students. The most common approach to the teaching of reading is the *basal reading approach supplemented by children's literature.*

The basal reading program has been the traditional approach to teaching reading in U.S. elementary schools for decades. According to Durkin (1987), it is "composed of a series of readers said to be written at successively more difficult levels" (p. 417). The core materials include a student reader, a teacher's manual, student workbooks, and tests. The strength of the basal program is that it provides teachers with an organized instructional framework on which to build (Lapp, Flood, & Farnan, 1992). In other words, the teacher using this approach does not develop a reading program by selecting materials and planning the related activities. Basal reading programs offer teachers considerable guidance and help with the decisions and challenges involved in teaching children to read.

The learning theory on which basal reading materials have been based for the last century is that learning complex skills begins with mastering the simplest components of that skill before attempting the next larger components and so on until the whole skill is learned. In terms of learning to read, this means that the letters of the alphabet are learned first, followed by letter–sound patterns, words, and then sentences. Finally, when the components of reading are learned, whole works of literature, such as stories, plays, and poems, are read.

In the 1980s, U.S. publishers of basal readers made an effort to improve the quality of stories written specifically for the basal readers. Multicultural characters began to appear in basal stories with more frequency than in the past. Most important, excerpts from high-quality trade books and some whole, albeit brief, literary works were integrated into basal readers. These changes were incorporated while retaining the skill-based instruction (particularly phonics instruction for beginning readers) that researchers regard as important to well-rounded reading programs (Anderson, Hiebert, Scott, & Wilkinson, 1985).

Even with these changes, basal readers are not designed to be a complete substitute for trade books. Even though some basal stories are good literature, not excerpted or adapted, the brevity of these selections is a problem for intermediate grades. Most students in these grades are capable of reading novel-length chapter books and should be doing so regularly in their school reading program. Students in classes where anthologies and basal readers are used exclusively are denied the all-important self-selection of reading material from a wide variety of books.

Ideally, each teacher should be allowed to choose the approach to teaching reading that best suits his or her philosophy of learning and teaching style. In many school districts across the United States, however, the use of a basal approach to teach reading is mandated. Even more restrictive is mandated Direct Instruction (DI), a lockstep method of teaching reading relying on highly scripted, prescribed teacher plans that must be followed to the letter, accommodating no teacher or student variation. School administrators would be wise to note Ryder, Sekulski, and Silberg's (2003) three-year study of methods of teaching reading that showed that DI has limited applicability, should not be used as the main method of reading instruction, and is not as effective as traditional teaching methods that allow teachers a more flexible approach.

Many teachers, despite mandates, have begun to move away from a slavish, "read-every-page-or-bust" attitude toward these programs. They have found ways to improve their teaching of reading by using their basal programs in innovative ways that eliminate some of the skills exercises of this approach and allow time for literature as well. Some guidelines drawn from the example of these teachers are as follows:

- Use only the best literary selections the basal offers. Substitute good trade literature for the rest.
- Let students read some of the better-written basal selections simply for enjoyment. It is the joy and wonder of reading marvelous tales or interesting information that motivate children to learn to read, not the tests on their comprehension of these stories. Use the time saved from skill, drill, and comprehension questions for silent reading.
- Eliminate the stigma of ability grouping by forming one whole-class, heterogeneous reading group. Use the time saved from planning and conducting three or four different reading lessons to hold individual reading conferences.
- Use basal readers' phonics lessons and drills only when, in the teacher's opinion, an individual student or group of students will benefit from them. (This need is exhibited by students in their individual reading conferences and in their writing.) Children do not learn according to an imposed schedule, but only when they are ready to learn. Use the time saved from ineffective exercises to read aloud from good books or for silent reading from self-choice books.

- Avoid comprehension questions at the end of basal reading lessons that trivialize the stories or demean the students. Use the time saved to allow children to share their personal reactions to the story, to offer literary criticisms of the selection, or to respond to the story in writing, drama, or art.
- Make phonics instruction a regular but brief (10–15 minutes) part of primary-grade reading instruction. Avoid letting phonics instruction become the main attraction of reading. That role should be reserved for good stories.

Basal readers are most effective when used in concert with a wide variety of trade books that reflect students' interests and reading abilities. In this arrangement, the basal reader provides guidance and structure to both teaching and learning, while the trade books provide the variety, opportunity for self-selection, and interest that motivate children to want to read.

Literature-Based Reading

Literature-based reading is an approach to teaching reading through the exclusive use of trade books. The learning theory in which literature-based reading is grounded is that children learn by searching for meaning in the world around them, constantly forming hypotheses, testing them to determine whether they work, and subsequently accepting or rejecting them.

Teachers using the literature-based approach to reading will structure a classroom environment in which children are immersed in good literature. In these classrooms, children hear literature read aloud several times a day, they see good readers reading voluntarily, they discover that good books can entertain them and tell them things they want to know, and they constantly practice reading books that they themselves have chosen because they are interested in the topics. Frequent student–teacher conferences allow teachers to check students' comprehension, discover skills weaknesses, and prescribe remediation.

As in basal reading programs, explicit reading instruction is an important feature of literature-based reading, particularly in the primary grades. Phonics, concepts of print, and vocabulary are taught in literature-based reading, *but within the context of interesting literature.* Unlike basal reading programs, these skills are never taught in isolation, where they have no real meaning, are never the focus of the entire reading period, and are taught only when needed.

As noted in Chapter 1, literature-based reading instruction addresses the components of instruction considered essential to the teaching of reading by the National Reading Panel: phonemic awareness, phonics, and reading comprehension, including fluency and vocabulary instruction. By including daily teacher read-aloud and self-choice independent reading components, this method of teaching reading is more likely to engender some valuable intrinsic behaviors in students that cannot be taught: a positive attitude toward reading, self-motivation to read, and a lifelong reading habit.

Key elements of the literature-based reading classroom include the following:

- Daily reading aloud of good literature by the teacher
- Reading skills taught when needed and then within meaningful contexts, never in isolation
- Quantities of good trade books in the classroom (five or more books per child) selected to match specific interests and approximate reading abilities of the students in the class
- Daily silent reading by students of books that they choose

- Daily opportunities for students to share their reactions to books orally
- Daily opportunities for students to respond to literature in a variety of ways, including writing, drama, and art
- Frequent individual student–teacher reading conferences (See the discussion of individual conferences in Chapter 13.)

Decisions about what to teach, when to teach it, and what materials to use are made by the teacher in the literature-based reading classroom. These decisions and the responsibility for materials selection and acquisition may make literature-based reading more demanding of teachers' professional judgment than other reading instruction methods; however, when it is managed well, this approach has proven to be very effective, not only in teaching students to read but also in creating a positive attitude toward reading. Moreover, the stimulus of new and exciting materials and students' unique personal responses to them can make teaching more exciting and enjoyable.

The absence of a prescribed, lockstep program is one of the greatest strengths of literature-based reading, but it also makes this approach vulnerable to many abuses. The following practices have no place in the literature-based reading classroom:

- Using mediocre literature in the reading program solely on the basis of having it at hand and with no regard to its appeal to students or its suitability to curricular goals
- Regularly using class sets of single trade books with a predetermined reading schedule and fill-in-the-blank worksheets (a practice referred to as the "basalization of literature")
- Reading works of literature by round-robin reading
- Selecting and assigning every title read by students
- Assigning book reports regularly under the guise of book response to check comprehension
- Excluding multicultural and international titles, poetry, and a balance of genres and character types from the classroom selection

There is no one right way to teach literature-based reading. The method cannot be packaged. Your best protection against bogus claims, materials, and practices is to have a complete understanding of the theory behind the practice. *Transitions* and *Invitations* by Routman (1988, 1991); *Literature-Based Reading Programs at Work,* edited by Hancock and Hill (1987); and *How to Teach Reading with Children's Books* by Veatch (1968) are a few of the excellent, practical resources that have stood the test of time.

 ## Evaluating the Literature Program

Ongoing evaluation is part of responsible teaching, since it reveals students' strengths and weaknesses in learning and teachers' strengths and weaknesses in instruction and indicates where intervention or revision is needed. In today's schools, reading and mathematics skills are given the lion's share of attention in standardized evaluation programs, and all too often, no attention is paid to children's growth in literary understanding. This section focuses on how to evaluate a literature program from both students' and teachers' perspectives.

Well-known student assessment methods include traditional paper-and-pencil testing, portfolio assessment, conferencing, and observing. Teachers have found the latter three most informative in assessing how well a literature program is meeting children's needs. Portfolio assessment and conferencing can leave information gaps, however, and do not necessarily assess the teacher's performance or the program itself. We find that observation, when carefully directed, provides a full description of the students' progress, the teacher's strengths and weaknesses, and the literature program. It is also the most efficient method of assessment, since it can be done while one is engaged in other tasks.

Observation and Assessment of Student Learning

Evaluation of students in relation to a literature curriculum will focus mainly on the curriculum's effect on student behaviors rather than on the students' grasp of concepts. Consequently, the evaluation will be accomplished primarily by observing students rather than by testing them. An important principle to remember in planning for evaluation of teaching and learning is that evaluation must parallel the goals and objectives of the instructional plan. To look for conceptual understandings or behaviors in students when those concepts or behaviors have not been taught or encouraged is to invite failure and disappointment.

Experienced teachers often develop checklists to use in observation and assessment of various aspects of their literature programs. Also, generic checklists can be developed by teams of teachers and librarians at each grade level in a school and then may be tailored by individual teachers to fit their own specific plans.

Checklist for Student Involvement with Books

Some of the behaviors that teachers look for in their students' interaction with literature will vary by grade level and the students' development. Other behaviors will show up on checklists for all grade levels. For example, preschool or first-grade teachers would be likely to look for evidence that their students know the terms *author* and *illustrator,* use the terms correctly in their discussions of books, and recognize the work of specific authors and illustrators. Middle-grade teachers, on the other hand, would be more likely to look for evidence that students are choosing and reading novel-length stories independently. Teachers at all grade levels will be looking for evidence that their students are enjoying reading and voluntarily choosing to read. Figure 12.3 gives an idea of what such an evaluation instrument might look like.

Observation and Assessment of Teacher Effectiveness

Regular self-assessment is an important part of a teacher's professional development. The following two checklists were conceived with preservice teachers in mind, mainly for the purposes of self-evaluation and guiding their observation of the classrooms they visit during their school participation experiences.

Checklist for Classroom Environment

The environment of a classroom is determined mainly by what the resident teacher values in learning and teaching. These values, in turn, determine how the classroom is arranged, which

Figure 12.3   Checklist for Student Involvement with Literature

Evaluator: _____   Date: _____

Behavior	*Yes*	*No*	*Comment*
Reading			
Student reads voluntarily and willingly	___	___	_____
Student enjoys reading	___	___	_____
Student reads during silent reading time	___	___	_____
Student reads for entertainment	___	___	_____
Student reads for information	___	___	_____
Student reads a variety of fiction, nonfiction, and poems	___	___	_____
Response to Literature			
Student talks intelligently about books read or heard	___	___	_____
Student shares responses to books with peers	___	___	_____
Student is attentive during read-aloud sessions	___	___	_____
Student is able to discuss a work of fiction in terms of			
character	___	___	_____
plot	___	___	_____
setting	___	___	_____
theme	___	___	_____
style	___	___	_____
Student is able to discuss a work of nonfiction in terms of			
structure	___	___	_____
theme	___	___	_____
style	___	___	_____
Student is able to accept that different people may have different responses to the same story	___	___	_____
Student is able to relate stories to personal experience, where applicable	___	___	_____
Student is able to compare and contrast stories, authors' writing styles, and illustrators' artistic styles	___	___	_____
Selection of Literature			
Student knows how to select appropriate books for independent reading	___	___	_____
Student keeps a log of books read independently	___	___	_____
Student is developing personal preferences in literature	___	___	_____
Student tries new book genres	___	___	_____

Figure 12.4   Checklist for Promoting Literature through Classroom Environment

Evaluator: _____	Date: _____			
Behavior		**Yes**	**No**	**Comment**
Physical Plant				
Desks are arranged to promote student-to-student discussion		___	___	_____
Room arrangement provides quiet areas for reading and thinking		___	___	_____
Reading area is well lighted		___	___	_____
Reading area has comfortable seating		___	___	_____
Reading area has adequate and convenient shelving for books		___	___	_____
Reading area is well organized and orderly		___	___	_____
Student response projects are displayed		___	___	_____
Materials				
Classroom has a trade book library		___	___	_____
Classroom library is adequate in				
scope (variety of genres, both fiction and nonfiction)		___	___	_____
depth (variety of books within a genre)		___	___	_____
quality (light reading for entertainment to excellent quality for study)		___	___	_____
providing for varying reading abilities		___	___	_____
recent books		___	___	_____
multicultural and international books		___	___	_____
poetry collections		___	___	_____
Classroom has a temporary collection		___	___	_____
Temporary collection				
addresses gaps in permanent collection		___	___	_____
is exchanged regularly		___	___	_____
provides for varying student interests		___	___	_____
is coordinated with topics of study		___	___	_____
Classroom library materials are				
easy for students to reach and reshelve		___	___	_____
coded and organized logically		___	___	_____
Scheduling				
Time is provided for self-choice reading every day		___	___	_____
Time is provided for browsing and selection of books regularly		___	___	_____
Time is provided for response to literature		___	___	_____

materials are available, and what sorts of events and activities are regularly scheduled. Figure 12.4 incorporates all of these features.

Checklist for Teaching Activities

Success in making children lovers of books and reading certainly does not depend on generous supplies of equipment or a certain physical layout, although these can facilitate the job. In the end, it is what the teacher does with literature that makes the biggest impression on children. Activities that make the learning experience positive and nonthreatening are generally the most successful with children. This point of view is evident in Figure 12.5.

Figure 12.5   Checklist for Promoting Literature through Teaching Activities

Evaluator: _____	Date: _____		
Behavior	*Yes*	*No*	*Comment*
Making Literature Enjoyable			
Read aloud daily (high-quality literature)	____	____	_____
Select books for read-aloud that			
reflect students' interests	____	____	_____
represent a wide variety of genres	____	____	_____
represent outstanding examples of each genre	____	____	_____
Share poetry orally on a regular basis	____	____	_____
Popular poets	____	____	_____
NCTE Award–winning poets	____	____	_____
Golden Age poets	____	____	_____
Share stories through storytelling	____	____	_____
Motivating Students to Read			
Introduce books regularly through booktalks	____	____	_____
Encourage student response to literature			
by asking open-ended or divergent question	____	____	_____
by encouraging varied responses	____	____	_____
oral response	____	____	_____
written response	____	____	_____
graphic response	____	____	_____
Allow students to choose books for independent reading	____	____	_____

(continued)

Make both fiction and nonfiction options
   for independent reading

Take class to school library weekly or more
   frequently for book browsing or selection

Take class to public library for a field trip

Invite a librarian to your class to booktalk
   and tell stories

Modeling Reading Behaviors

Read during silent reading time

Talk enthusiastically about books read

Show students how to select books

Showing the Relevance of Literature

Include literature that is culturally relevant
   to students

   in read-aloud selections

   in booktalks

   in text sets for group reading

Integrate literature across the curriculum

   health/science

   social studies/history

   language arts/reading

   mathematics

Encouraging Literature Appreciation

Present a yearlong literature curriculum

Reaching beyond the Classroom

Send read-aloud suggestions to parents

Encourage parents to visit library with
   their children

Invite parents and community leaders to be guest
   readers for read-aloud

Evaluation

Record student growth

   in understanding literary concepts

   in choices of books to read

   in attitude toward reading

   in quality of responses (verbal, written, artistic)

Implementing a Schoolwide Curriculum in Literature

Having a schoolwide curriculum in literature benefits teachers and students and is worth pursuing. The main benefit to students is that their teachers' efforts will be coordinated from year to year. Repetition of content and titles will be avoided, and continuity will be improved. The main benefits to teachers are that ideas, expertise, and materials will be shared and planning will be facilitated by knowing what experiences with literature incoming students have had or should have. The task of developing a schoolwide literature curriculum should be shared by a committee that has a representative from each grade level and the library media specialist.

A literature curriculum committee's function is to determine what literature content will be presented at each grade level. A set of trade books appropriate for delivering the literature curriculum at each grade level can also be suggested by the committee, although the ultimate choice of books to be used in a classroom will be the individual teacher's decision. Literature curriculum committees often select and update their schoolwide read-aloud list. Such a list helps to prevent duplication of teachers' read-aloud choices at different grade levels and to assure that students hear a well-balanced selection of books over the years. Having such a list may also convince some teachers to begin a read-aloud program.

School Library Media Center

The well-stocked, efficiently run library media center is the heart of a school, and the knowledgeable media center director has his or her finger on the pulse of each classroom. Ideally, library media specialists and teachers have a shared responsibility for teaching. Teachers tell librarians their resource needs, and librarians help teachers by identifying and locating appropriate resources, keeping teachers updated with the newest literature and suggesting ways to present books to students. For these reasons, the librarian should be encouraged to play a key role in planning and developing a schoolwide curriculum in literature.

Book Clubs

A marketing phenomenon of our times is the publisher-owned book club. These clubs send monthly catalogs to teachers who then distribute them to students, collect and process student book orders, and receive bonus points for each item ordered. Paperback books representing a full range of quality from award-winning books to joke books, posters, and stickers are offered at prices far below bookstore cost. Children and teachers who lack access to well-stocked libraries are especially dependent on these clubs. Another advantage of book clubs is that the selection, ownership, and reading of these books involves parents.

Being knowledgeable about children's literature enables you to help your students select the best book club titles. You can gently redirect children's choices from the "junk" offerings to the better books by going over the catalog with students and giving booktalks about the titles you recommend. Care should be given to verify topic and age appropriateness of any selections with which you are unfamiliar.

Teachers who participate in these clubs often use their bonus points to build their classroom book collections. With this in mind, you may want to subscribe to more than one club to have a wider choice of titles.

Bookfairs

A bookfair is a book sale that is organized by a book vendor, such as a bookstore owner, and held in the school building for one or more days. Books are displayed so that children and their parents can browse and select items for purchase. Bookfairs always call attention to literature and reading and can even be considered a reading motivator. They are especially appropriate in areas where there are no children's bookstores or well-stocked libraries.

Bookfairs send strong messages to children and their parents about a school's stance on reading and about what sorts of reading materials teachers and librarians in the school endorse. Bookfairs in which joke collections, scented stickers, stamps, commercialized series books, coloring books, and posters are prominent send the wrong message to children and their parents about reading. Bookfairs in which a wide variety of good literature is prominent send an entirely different (and more defensible) message about reading. Excellent bookfairs are the result of careful planning and active involvement in selection of books by teachers and school librarians. Book selection should not be left solely to the book vendor.

Parent Involvement

Parental involvement in literature begins with getting support for the school reading program at home. Parents are almost always willing to promote their children's academic efforts at home if they are told how to do it. Many teachers give parents lists of activities that support reading, including brief, carefully worded explanations where necessary. Some typical suggestions include the following:

- Read to your child at night, especially if he or she is a resistant reader. (Lists of good read-alouds can be sent home regularly.)
- Listen to your child read aloud.
- Take your child to the library to select books.
- Give books to your child as gifts. (Lists of good gift book suggestions can be sent home prior to birthdays and holidays.)

Some parents are willing to help in classrooms on a regular basis. Ways in which parents can help teachers include the following:

- Listen to children read orally.
- Read aloud to small groups or individual students.
- Type, assemble, and bind the storybooks that children write.
- Read stories and poems on audiotapes for listening.
- Make book bags for carrying books back and forth from home.

Guest Authors and Illustrators

Professional children's authors and illustrators often visit schools to speak to children about their careers and their books. Teachers are usually instrumental in selecting, inviting, and organizing these visits. Guest authors and illustrators may be chosen on the basis of availability, but more often they are chosen because of the students' interest in their books or the relevance of their work to a topic that students are studying. Such visits are powerful reading motivators.

The standard procedure is to contact the marketing director or editor of the author's or artist's publishing house to determine availability and terms. Since most established children's authors and illustrators charge an honorarium and travel expenses, schools within a system often share the author and the costs. Many state reading associations have developed lists of children's authors and illustrators who live in state. These lists can usually be found in public libraries.

Local Public Library

The community has no more valuable resource than its public library. Each time students, teachers, and parents seek the educational resources they need in their public libraries, the natural link between schools and public libraries is reaffirmed. Public libraries provide many services in addition to loaning books. Consider the impact of the following list of services:

- The interlibrary loan system, which gives patrons access to library holdings throughout the state, region, or nation
- Summertime reading programs for children
- Summertime bookmobile programs
- Special observances, such as National Book Week, Banned Book Week, and Hans Christian Andersen Day, which help to bring important literacy issues to the public's attention
- Story hour for young children
- Audiovisual versions of many books
- Guest appearances of authors and illustrators

Teachers can help to make the public library more effective by making students and their parents aware of the library and its programs and services.

 ## Gaining Experience with Literature in School Practicums

Many elementary and early childhood education programs include multiweek, school-based practicum experiences. These school participation experiences give preservice teachers opportunities to observe teaching and classroom management styles, acquire firsthand experience working with children, and test the theories and ideas presented in their teacher training courses, such as those involving the use of good literature with young people.

An important part of practicum assignments involving literature is the selection of age- and content-appropriate books that will interest young readers. Although testing one's own ability to select appropriate books is important, it is advisable in school-based practicums to ask the classroom teacher to approve books prior to their use with children.

In the accompanying box are sample literature activities that we have found to work in school-based practicums. Observations and lessons learned are even more valuable when shared with other preservice teachers for similarities and differences.

Learning about Children as Readers

1. Interview three children in the classroom, preferably at three different levels of reading ability, to find their exposure to literature, their attitude toward reading, their purposes for reading, and their sources of reading material.

2. Interview a number of students about their reading interests. Based on your findings, suggest to students appropriate titles for independent reading from books available in the school.

3. Conduct a class survey of reading interests. Use the procedure described on pages 26–27. Compile and analyze findings. Suggest titles for independent reading.

Learning How to Help Children Experience Literature

1. Booktalk a set of four or five books appropriate for students in the class. (See Chapter 13, pages 278–279.) Be sure to include one or two works of multicultural literature. (See Chapter 11.) After the booktalk, display the books in the classroom and observe students' interest in reading them.

2. Read aloud one or two picture books and a chapter book. After each read-aloud session allow students to give their reactions. Compare your experiences of reading aloud from the two types of books. Compare students' responses to the two types of books. For example, how much attention do children pay to illustrations in a picture storybook?

3. Select a poem, guide students in arranging it for choral reading, rehearse the students, and present the choral reading to any available audience. (See Chapter 4, pages 71–72.) Note students' response to this activity and to the poem selection.

4. Introduce students to a specific children's book author or illustrator by demonstrating how to give an author or illustrator profile. These profiles are often required of preservice students, but they can be done by young people as well and have merit as reading motivators. *Author and illustrator profiles* generally include interesting facts about the author, perhaps a recent picture, the *one* or *two* most distinguishing characteristics of the author's work (such as favorite topic, themes, style of illustration, or writing style), what the presenter liked about the author's work, and other books the author has written. A one-page handout summarizing this information and including major works by the author will be appreciated by other preservice teachers and the cooperating teacher. Elementary- and middle-grade students presenting author or illustrator profiles can post their summary sheets on the class bulletin board.

    Traditionally, author and illustrator reports are presented orally to the class. Interesting variations include:

    - Presenting the profile in first-person format as the author or illustrator (costumes or props can be used)
    - Presenting the profile as a biographical skit about the author (presentation by a pair of students or a small group)
    - Making a poster or bulletin board display about the author or illustrator
    - Presenting the profile as a pretend interview (one student is the interviewer and one student pretends to be the author)

Learning about Student Response to Literature

1. Select a picture book or a chapter from a novel that involves four to six characters. Read it aloud to a group of students. Lead the children in a creative drama, readers' theatre, or graphic arts response to the book you have shared. (See Chapter 13 for ideas and guidance.) Note students' insights into the work as revealed in their responses.
2. Help students design and construct a literature-related bulletin board. This could range from a mural based on a whole-class read-aloud selection to response to books read independently by students in the class. This display can be mounted in the school hallway for observation by students in other classrooms. Note students' interest in the book(s) featured in the display.

 # Censorship and the First Amendment

The First Amendment to the United States Constitution guarantees to all citizens the right to free speech and freedom of the press, among other rights. Teaching children about their First Amendment rights is important because there are those who would take these rights away through censorship. *Censorship* is "the actual removal, suppression, or restricted circulation of literary, artistic, or educational materials . . . on the grounds that they are morally or otherwise objectionable" (Reichman, 2001). When a person or persons attempt to remove material from the curriculum or library, thereby restricting the access of others, it is called a *challenge*. Most book challenges occur locally, and most fail. When a challenge is successful and materials are removed from the curriculum or library, it is called a *banning* (www.ala.org/ala/oif).

Our position regarding censorship is:

- *Teachers and schools have the right and the obligation to select reading materials suitable for the education of their students. With this right comes the professional responsibility to select good quality literature that furthers stated educational goals while remaining appropriate for the age and maturity level of the respective students.*
- *Parents are within their rights to protect their children from materials or influences they see as potentially damaging to their children. In the instance that a parent believes that material selected by a school or teacher is potentially harmful to his or her child, that parent has the right to bring this to the attention of the school and request that his or her child not be subjected to this material. Parents must indicate the reason for their concern.*
- *The school must take the parent's objection seriously and provide a reasonable substitute for the material of concern. If an alternative procedure is necessary in order to effect the substitution (for example, the student will listen to a different book in the library while the teacher is reading aloud), the alternative provided should respect the student and be sensitive to his or her feelings.*

> ■ *The parent does not have the right to demand that the material in question be withheld from other students. This would interfere with the right and professional duty of the teacher and school to educate the students. Once a student is given a reasonable alternative, the school has fulfilled its obligation and should not interfere with the First Amendment rights of other students.*

As adults, we cherish our right to choose our reading material and use it nearly every day of our lives. Elementary and middle-school social studies and civics textbooks proudly proclaim the freedom of choice that citizens of the United States have in their daily lives. But do we, as parents, teachers, and librarians, actually extend these rights to our children? Specifically,

- Do we allow ourselves to be bullied by outspoken special-interest groups into taking good, but controversial, books off the library shelves, or do we stand by our convictions and book selections?
- Do we self-censor by only selecting books on "safe" topics, or do we select books on the bases of quality and age appropriateness?
- Do we listen to young readers' ideas about the books that they have read, or do we only ask them "comprehension" questions?
- Do we allow children to reject books that they do not like, or do we force them to read what we have chosen for them to read?

In other words, do we actually teach students, by our actions as well as by our words, about their First Amendment rights?

A study by Wollman-Bonilla (1998) of pre- and inservice teachers' ideas about acceptable and unacceptable children's books reveals a tendency toward teacher bias in book selection for children. The researcher found that teachers "commonly objected to texts that reflect gender, ethnic, race, or class experiences that differed from their own" (p. 289). This subtle form of censorship is made worse by the fact that most teachers are unaware of their own biases in text selection (Jipson & Paley, 1991; Luke, Cooke, & Luke, 1986). Wollman-Bonilla makes a strong point in favor of First Amendment rights for children when she concludes, "If we are to know how books actually affect children, we need to hear *children's* voices and understand *their* experiences before, during, and after reading" (p. 293).

Teaching the First Amendment

Teaching students about their First Amendment rights might begin by posting a copy of the First Amendment, having students read it, and then discussing what this amendment means to them and what its loss might mean to them. Lists of children's books that some have declared "objectionable" could be posted. Children who have read the books could discuss why they might have been found objectionable and why banning these books would violate their First Amendment rights. Children's and young adults' fiction about censorship could be read and discussed. Good examples are *The Rebellious Alphabet* by Jorge Diaz, *The Landry News* by Andrew Clements,

The Last Safe Place on Earth by Richard Peck, *The Trials of Molly Sheldon* by Julian Thompson, and *Save Halloween!* by Stephanie Tolan. As teachers and librarians, we should do everything possible to promote the kinds of books that encourage critical thinking, inquiry, and self-expression, while maintaining respect for the views of others.

Dealing with Censorship Attempts

The American Library Association's Office of Intellectual Freedom monitors the challenges made against children's books in the United States. Most adults and children who have read the highly regarded books that often appear on these "most challenged books" lists find the reasons given for the challenges perplexing, if not incredible. For example, the following titles appeared on the ALA's list of Most Frequently Challenged Children's Books for 2002:

The *Harry Potter* series by J. K. Rowling for its focus on wizardry and magic

The *Alice* series by Phyllis Reynolds Naylor for being sexually explicit, using offensive language, and being unsuited to the age group

The *Captain Underpants* series by Dav Pilkey for insensitivity, being unsuited to the age group, and encouraging children to disobey authority

Bridge to Terabithia by Katherine Paterson for offensive language, sexual content, and occult/satanism

Often, individuals challenge books on the basis of a single word or phrase, or on hearsay, and have not read the book at all. Teachers and library media specialists have found that a written procedure is helpful for bringing order and reason into discussions with parents who want to censor school materials. Most procedures call for teachers and librarians to give would-be censors a complaint form and ask them to specify their concerns in writing. There are advantages to such a system: Both teachers and parents are given time to reflect on the issue and to control their emotions; and the would-be censor is given time to read the book in its entirety, if he or she has not done so already. Developing written procedures and complaint forms for dealing with a would-be censor are important tasks for the literature curriculum committee. Figure 12.6 presents a model form produced by the National Council of Teachers of English (NCTE) for reconsideration of a work of literature.

The American Library Association's Office for Intellectual Freedom has several publications about censorship such as Reichman's *Censorship and Selection: Issues and Answers for Schools* (2001) that provide important and helpful information to schools on this topic. (For a catalog of all ALA publications, go to www.ala.org.) People for the American Way, an organization that provides advice and assistance in combatting school censorship, can be contacted at www.pfaw.org.

The National Council of Teachers of English also offers a valuable document about censorship, *The Students' Right to Read* (Committee on the Right to Read, 1982), which explains the nature of censorship, the stand of those opposed to it, and ways to combat it. This document and the *Citizen's Request for Reconsideration of a Work* are available free of charge at www.ncte.org/position/right.html.

Figure 12.6   Citizen's Request for Reconsideration of a Work

Author _____ Paperback _____ Hardcover _____

Title _____

Publisher (if known) _____

Request initiated by _____

Telephone _____

Address _____ City _____ Zip Code _____

Complainant represents:

___ Himself/Herself

___ (Name Organization) _____

___ (Identify other group) _____

1. Have you been able to discuss this work with the teacher or librarian who ordered it or used it? _____ Yes _____ No

2. What do you understand to be the general purpose for using this work?

   a. Provide support for a unit in the curriculum? _____ Yes _____ No

   b. Provide a learning experience for the reader in one kind of literature? _____ Yes _____ No

   c. Other _____

   _____

3. Did the general purpose for the use of the work, as described by the teacher or librarian, seem a suitable one to you? _____ Yes _____ No

   If not, please explain. _____

   _____

4. What do you think is the general purpose of the author in this book? _____

5. In what ways do you think a work of this nature is not suitable for the use the teacher or librarian wishes to carry out? _____

   _____

6. Have you been able to learn what is the students' response to this work? _____ Yes _____ No

7. What response did the students make? _____

   _____

8. Have you been able to learn from your school library what book reviewers or other students of literature have written about this work? _____ Yes _____ No

9. Would you like the teacher or librarian to give you a written summary of what book reviewers and other students have written about this book or film? _____ Yes _____ No

10. Do you have negative reviews of the book? _____ Yes _____ No

11. Where were they published? _____

12. Would you be willing to provide summaries of the reviews you have collected? _____ Yes _____ No

13. What would you like your library/school to do about this work?

    ___ Do not assign/lend it to my child.

    ___ Return it to the staff selection committee/department for reevaluation.

    ___ Other–Please explain

    _____

14. In its place, what work would you recommend that would convey as valuable a picture and perspective of the subject treated? _____

Signature _____ Date _____

Source: Committee on the Right to Read. (1982). *The students' right to read.* Urbana, IL: National Council of Teachers of English.

Topics for Further Investigation

- Using a book such as *Webbing with Literature: Creating Story Maps with Children's Books* (2nd Edition) by Karen D'Angelo Bromley, find out more about planning with literature webs. Develop a literature web around a children's book author or illustrator, a trade book, or a genre of literature. This web may be designed for use in elementary- or middle-school reading or language arts classes or it may extend across the curriculum.
- Check the webpage of the Office of Intellectual Freedom (**www.ala.org/ala/oif**) for a recent list of the most frequently challenged children's books. Read five of these books and analyze them for the reasons the would-be censors found them objectionable. Develop an argument for or against the censorship attempt for each book.
- Develop a two-to-three week literature teaching unit. Include goals, a list of focus books, and a daily schedule with objectives, procedures, activities and assignments, materials, and evaluation tools.

 See the companion website at www.ablongman.com/lynchbrown6e for further suggestions.

References

Abrahams, P. (2005). *Down the rabbit hole.* New York: HarperCollins/Laura Geringer.

Aliki. (1994). *The gods and goddesses of Olympus.* New York: HarperCollins.

Anderson, R. C., Hiebert, E. H., Scott, J. A., & Wilkinson, I. A. (1985). *Becoming a nation of readers: The report of the commission on reading.* Champaign, IL: Center for the Study of Reading.

Babbitt, N. (1975). *Tuck everlasting.* New York: Farrar.

Baldick, C. (1990). *The concise Oxford dictionary of literary terms.* New York: Oxford University Press.

Bat-Ami, M. (2000). *Two suns in the sky.* Chicago: Front Street/Cricket.

Brisson, P. (1997). *Hot fudge hero.* Illustrated by D. K. Blumenthal. New York: Holt.

Bromley, K. D. (1995). *Webbing with literature: Creating story maps with children's books* (2nd ed.). Boston: Allyn & Bacon.

Buss, F. L., & Cubias, D. (1991). *Journey of the sparrows.* New York: Lodestar.

Canales, V. (2005). *The tequila worm.* New York: Random.

Children's literature review: Excerpts from reviews, criticism, and commentary on books for children and young people, vols. 1–115. (1976–2006). Detroit: Thomson Gale.

Chute, M. (1957). My Plan. In H. Ferris (Ed.), *Favorite poems old and new.* New York: Doubleday.

Cleary, B. (1977). *Ramona and her father.* Illustrated by A. Tiegreen. New York: Morrow.

———. (1981). *Ramona Quimby, age 8.* Illustrated by A. Tiegreen. New York: Morrow.

Clements, A. (1999). *The Landry News.* New York: Simon & Schuster.

———. (2002). *Things not seen.* New York: Putnam.

Committee on the Right to Read. (1982). *The students' right to read.* Urbana, IL: National Council of Teachers of English.

Diaz, J. (1993). *The rebellious alphabet.* Illustrated by Ø. S. Jorfald. Translated by G. Fox. New York: Holt.

Disney, W. (1976). *Walt Disney's Sleeping Beauty.* New York: Golden.

Duprau, J. (2003). *The city of Ember.* New York: Random.

Durkin, D. (1987). *Teaching young children to read* (4th ed.). Boston: Allyn & Bacon.

Etchemendy, N. (2000). *The power of un.* Asheville: Front Street.

Farmer, N. (2002). *The house of the scorpion.* New York: Simon & Schuster.

Fenner, C. (1995). *Yolanda's genius.* New York: McElderry.

Fogelin, A. (2000). *Crossing Jordan.* Atlanta: Peachtree.

Freedman, R. (1980). *Immigrant kids.* New York: Dutton.

Giff, P. R. (1997). *Lily's crossing.* New York: Delacorte.

———. (2005). *Willow Run.* New York: Random/Wendy Lamb.

Greenwald, S. (2003). *Rosy Cole's worst ever, best yet tour of New York City.* New York: Holt.

Hall, S. (1990). *Using picture storybooks to teach literary devices: Recommended books for children and young adults.* Phoenix: Oryx.

———. (1994). *Using picture storybooks to teach literary devices: Recommended books for children and young adults* (Vol. 2). Phoenix: Oryx.

Hancock, J., & Hill, S. (1987). *Literature-based reading programs at work.* Portsmouth, NH: Heinemann.

Hesse, K. (1992). *Letters from Rifka.* New York: Holt.

Hiaasen, C. (2003). *Hoot.* New York: Knopf.

Hyman, T. S. (1977/2001). *The sleeping beauty.* New York: Little, Brown.

Isaacs, A. (1994). *Swamp angel.* Illustrated by P. O. Zelinsky. New York: Dutton.

Jiménez, F. (1999). *The circuit: Stories from the life of a migrant child.* Boston: Houghton.

Jipson, J., & Paley, N. (1991) The selective tradition in children's literature: Does it exist in the elementary classroom? *English Education, 23,* 148–159.

Kadohata, C. (2006). *Weedflower.* New York: Atheneum.

Kashmira, S. (2004). *Blue jasmine.* New York: Hyperion.

Klein, R. (1987). *Hating Alison Ashley.* New York: Viking.

Knight, M. B. (1993/2003). *Who belongs here: An American story.* Illustrated by A. S. O'Brien. Gardiner, ME: Tilbury House.

Lapp, D., Flood, J., & Farnan, N. (1992). Basal readers and literature: A tight fit or a mismatch? In K. D. Wood & A. Moss (Eds.), *Exploring literature in the classroom: Content and methods* (pp. 33–57). Norwood, MA: Christopher-Gordon.

Levine, E. (1993). *If your name was changed at Ellis Island.* Illustrated by W. Parmenter. New York: Scholastic.

Levitin, S. (1970). *Journey to America.* New York: Atheneum.

Lewis, M. (1999). *Morgy makes his move.* Boston: Houghton.

Lowry, L. (1993). *The giver.* Boston: Houghton.

———. (1989). *Number the stars.* Boston: Houghton.

Luke, A., Cooke, J., & Luke, C. (1986). The selective tradition in action: Gender bias in student teachers' selections of children's literature. *English Education, 18,* 209–218.

Maestro, B. (1996). *Coming to America: The story of immigration.* Illustrated by S. Ryan. New York: Scholastic.

Marsden, C. (2002). *The gold-threaded dress.* Cambridge, MA: Candlewick.

Na, A. (2001). *A step from heaven.* Asheville, NC: Front Street.

Paterson, K. (1977). *Bridge to Terabithia.* New York: Crowell.

Peck, R. (1995). *The last safe place on earth.* New York: Delacorte.

Reichman, H. (2001). *Censorship and selection: Issues and answers for schools.* Chicago: American Library Association Editions.

Rodda, E. (1991). *Finders keepers.* New York: Greenwillow.

———. (2001). *Rowan of Rin.* New York: Greenwillow.

Routman, R. (1988). *Transitions: From literature to literacy.* Portsmouth: Heinemann.

———. (1991). *Invitations: Changing as teachers and learners K–12.* Portsmouth: Heinemann.

Ryan, P. M. (2000). *Esperanza rising.* New York: Scholastic.

Ryder, R. J., Sekulski, J. L., & Silberg, A. (2003). Results of direct instruction reading program evaluation longitudinal results: First through third grade, 2000–2003. Madison: Wisconsin Department of Public Instruction.

Sachar, L. (1998). *Holes.* New York: Farrar.

Salisbury, G. (1994). *Under the blood-red sun.* New York: Delacorte.

San Souci, R. D. (1993). *Cut from the same cloth: American women of myth, legend, and tall tale.* Illustrated by B. Pinkney. New York: Philomel.

Sanderson, R. (2002). *Cinderella.* New York: Little, Brown.

Schmidt, J., & Wood, T. (1995). *Two lands, one heart: An American boy's journey to his mother's Vietnam.* New York: Walker.

Sleator, W. (1986). *The boy who reversed himself.* New York: Dutton.

Smith, D. B. (1973). *A taste of blackberries.* New York: HarperCollins.

Something about the author: Facts and pictures about authors and illustrators of books for young people, vols. 1–169 (1971–2006). Detroit: Thomson Gale.

Soto, G. (1991). *Taking sides.* New York: Harcourt.

Spinelli, J. (1995). *Tooter Pepperday*. Illustrated by D. Nelson. New York: Random.

Stanley, D. (1997). *Rumpelstiltskin's daughter*. New York: Morrow.

Stolz, M. (1963). *The bully of Barkham Street*. Illustrated by Leonard Shortall. New York: Harper.

———. (1960). *A dog on Barkham Street*. Illustrated by Leonard Shortall. New York: Harper.

Strom, Y. (1996). *Quilted landscape: Conversations with young immigrants*. New York: Simon & Schuster.

Tchana, K. H. (2006). *Changing woman and her sisters: Stories of goddesses from around the world*. Illustrated by Trina Schart Hyman. New York: Holiday.

Temple, F. (1995). *Tonight by sea*. New York: Orchard.

Thompson, J. (1995). *The trials of Molly Sheldon*. New York: Holt.

Tolan, S. (1993). *Save Halloween*. New York: HarperCollins.

Uchida, Y. (1971). *Journey to Topaz*. New York: Scribner's.

Van Draanen, W. (1998). *Sammy Keyes and the hotel thief*. New York: Knopf.

Veatch, J. (1968). *How to teach reading with children's books* (2nd ed.). New York: Richard C. Owen.

Williams, J. (1973/2000). *Petronella*. Illustrated by M. Organ-Kean. North Kingstown, RI: Moon Mountain.

Williams, V. B. (2001). *Amber was brave, Essie was smart: The story of Amber and Essie told here in poems and pictures*. New York: Greenwillow.

Winthrop, E. (1985). *The castle in the attic*. New York: Holiday.

Wollman-Bonilla, J. E. (1998). Outrageous viewpoints: Teachers' criteria for rejecting works of children's literature. *Language Arts, 75*(4), 287–295.

Woodson, J. (2003). *Locomotion*. New York: Putnam.

Yep, L. (1977). *Child of the owl*. New York: Harper.

———. (1993). *Dragon's gate*. New York: HarperCollins.

Yolen, J. (2000). *Not one damsel in distress: World folktales for strong girls*. Illustrated by S. Guevara. New York: Silver Whistle.

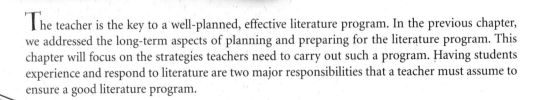

chapter 13

Developing Teaching Strategies

I Meant to Do My Work Today

I meant to do my work today—
But a brown bird sang in the apple tree,
And a butterfly flitted across the field,
And all the leaves were calling me.

And the wind went sighing over the land
Tossing the grasses to and fro,
And a rainbow held out its shining hand—
So what could I do but laugh and go?

—Richard LeGallienne

The teacher is the key to a well-planned, effective literature program. In the previous chapter, we addressed the long-term aspects of planning and preparing for the literature program. This chapter will focus on the strategies teachers need to carry out such a program. Having students experience and respond to literature are two major responsibilities that a teacher must assume to ensure a good literature program.

Experiencing Literature

Many teaching strategies can be used to provide students with opportunities to experience enjoyable, exciting, and thought-provoking literature. Students experience prose, poetry, fiction, and nonfiction (1) by having it read aloud to them by a skillful oral reader; (2) by reading it silently to themselves; (3) through shared reading activities with a parent, librarian, teacher, or peer; (4) through stories told to them; and (5) through other media such as audiobooks and films related to children's books.

Reading Aloud by Teachers

Reading aloud to children by family members and teachers is essential for children's acquisition of reading skills and positive attitudes toward reading. It is the centerpiece of a curriculum in literature. Beginning in their infancy and throughout the elementary- and middle-school years and beyond, children should hear books and poems read aloud. Although some teachers at the intermediate-grade level do not often read aloud, this teaching strategy is just as important in the development of readers at this stage as it is in primary grades.

Some important reasons that teachers read aloud are as follows:

- To develop in students larger and richer vocabularies
- To increase their cognitive abilities, including their abilities to think critically and their abilities to comprehend connected discourse
- To help students understand literary devices and the conventions of story, such as genres, characters, settings, themes, and story components, including the beginning, middle, and end of stories
- To provide a model of expressive, fluent reading by sharing emotional, funny, exciting, and stimulating literature with students
- To build background and interest in subject matter that will soon be taught in an upcoming content-area unit of instruction
- To share with students exciting and stimulating reading material that is beyond their reading ability, but well within their listening ability
- To cause students to love reading and literature

Three distinct aspects of the read-aloud experience need to be examined to make it as effective a teaching strategy as possible. Those aspects are (1) selecting the literature to read, (2) preparing the students for read-aloud time, and (3) reading the book aloud. Each aspect needs to be taken into consideration for a successful read-aloud experience.

Book Selection

No matter which book you choose to read aloud, it is essential that you first read the book to yourself. When you preread a book, you can determine whether you find the story enjoyable and worthy of children's time and whether you believe it is of an appropriate level of difficulty for your students. You also can begin to note ways in which the story lends itself to student response.

Over the course of a school year you will want to read aloud a variety of literature: poems, short stories, picture books, and chapter books of different genres and moods. You will also want to ensure that there is a balance of males and females as main characters in the books and that the main characters come from different backgrounds and settings, including multicultural and international ones.

Lists of Excellent Books to Read Aloud are provided in Chapters 5 through 11. These recommendations are a good place to begin in considering the selection of books for this purpose. You may also want to look at two reference works that suggest books for reading aloud: Judy Freeman's *Books Kids Will Sit Still for, 3: A Read-Aloud Guide* (2006) and Jim Trelease's *The Read-Aloud Handbook* (2006).

The most recognized works in children's literature, though sometimes complex, deserve to be shared with students over the course of their elementary school years. When a book or poem is challenging for students, you need to be prepared to guide the students' understanding. Without this help, many children would never experience and enjoy some of the more difficult but worthy pieces of literature. Conversely, you will want to avoid choosing books for reading aloud that students can and will consume eagerly on their own, reserving those books for students' independent reading.

When first reading aloud to a new class, however, you will want to start with shorter and easier works, known to be popular with students, and gradually build up to longer and more challenging works as you become better acquainted with your students, their interests, and their abilities. For more discussion of students' preferences in literature, refer to Chapters 2 and 4.

Preparation

Once a selection is made, the next step is to prepare the class for read-aloud time. For students to profit from read-aloud experiences, they need to be attentive. You can prepare students for reading aloud by having them remove distractions, such as pencils and other objects, from their immediate vicinity; by having them sit quietly in the designated place for read-aloud time; and by asking them to be ready to listen. If the book has concepts that you believe will baffle your students, you may want to clarify their meaning before beginning to read.

Introduce the book by stating the title, author, and illustrator of the book, even with the smallest children. This will teach children that books are written by real people called authors and that the illustrations are made by people called illustrators. Sometimes you may want to ask the students to predict what they believe the story will be about from looking at the cover and the title; other times you may want to explain briefly why you chose this book to read to them. For example, you may say that you are going to read this book because "it's another story by one of our favorite authors, William Steig" or that "the book will tell us more about what it was like to live on the prairie in the nineteenth century." Some teachers read aloud several picture books by the same author over the course of a week to make students aware of a particular notable author. Book introductions should be kept short. They serve the purpose of preparing students to be attentive to and interested in the story.

Reading Picture Books Aloud Effectively

Consider the following steps:

- Position yourself close to the class so that all students can see the pictures.
- Show the pictures as you read the book. Remember that in a good picture book the text and pictures are carefully integrated to convey the story as a whole. Hearing and seeing picture books should be simultaneous.

- After the introduction, begin reading the book aloud, placing emphasis on the meaning of the story. Think of reading aloud as a type of dramatic performance.
- Your body movements and facial expressions can also be used to enhance the drama of the read-aloud experience. Leaning forward during a scary, suspenseful part of a story and smiling or chuckling during a funny part can convey to the students your involvement in the story.
- Maintain eye contact with your students. Be sure you are aware of their nonverbal responses to this reading experience. Good eye contact with the students helps you observe when a word of explanation may be needed.
- Read the book from beginning to end without interruptions except on an as-needed basis. Some books, such as concept books and interactive books, do call for interruptions in the read-aloud process. This is particularly true for informational books.

Reading Chapter Books Aloud Effectively

Many of the same considerations discussed in reading aloud picture books also hold true with chapter book read-alouds. Of course, chapter books have few, if any, illustrations, so holding the book for students to see the pictures is not necessary. In addition, chapter books are usually read aloud over a relatively long period of time, from a few days to many weeks. Often, teachers find reading novel-length chapter books aloud challenging, and sometimes unsuccessful.

Following are some practices that teachers have used successfully during chapter book read-alouds to help hook the students on the book and to keep them tuned in and involved.

- Keep a chart of the characters—their names, relationships, and roles in the story—as the characters appear. This strategy is especially helpful if the story has a large number of characters. For example, in *The Westing Game* (1978) by Ellen Raskin, the many characters of this mystery must be remembered for the plot to make sense.
- Design and display a map of the story setting to track the events of the story in sequence. In most quest fantasies this visual aid can assist students in following the characters' journey for the quest.
- Develop a time line, somewhat like a horizontal mural, on which the dates are set at intervals above the line and the story events placed below the line at the appropriate date. For historical fiction and biographies, a time line can serve as a mnemonic device for the storyline as well as for the historic events of the era. For this purpose, the dates and historic events would be noted on a third tier of the time line.

Independent Reading by Students

Another way for students to experience good literature is to read it to themselves. Indeed, the ultimate goal of a literature program is to turn students into readers who, of their own free will, read self-selected literature with enjoyment, understanding, and appreciation. To assist students in becoming independent, lifelong readers, teachers in grades K–8 need to set aside time each day for students to read independently in these formative years of reading development. The amount of time for independent reading must be tailored to the reading attention spans of students. Kindergarten and first-grade students may spend only five to ten minutes reading independently, and often a quiet hum occurs as beginning readers say the words aloud as they read. Fourth- and fifth-grade students will often read silently for up to an hour.

Many schools have instituted *sustained silent reading (SSR)* programs on a schoolwide basis in order to promote the reading habit in students. In these SSR programs a certain time each day is set aside for all students, teachers, librarians, coaches, principals, custodians, and office and kitchen staff to take a "reading break." The philosophy behind SSR programs is that students need to see adults who read and who place a high priority on reading. In SSR programs, students read materials of their own choosing and are not usually required to write book reports or give oral reports on these materials.

If your school utilizes a commercial reading incentive program, you may take advantage of the availability of the literature that is provided as part of the program. However, you can use the program flexibly in ways that develop intrinsic motivation for reading, avoid many of the negative competitive aspects of the program, and help students achieve individual goals set by the students and you for their independent reading. Whether or not you are in a school that has an SSR program, you will want to provide your students with independent reading time each day.

Teachers can design their own *reading incentive programs* that avoid these drawbacks and still help students get started as independent readers. In these programs students usually keep a record of their own free-choice silent reading, have opportunities to respond to books in a variety of ways, and work to achieve individual silent reading goals set by the student and teacher together. The rewards, such as a special celebration party, are provided for the whole class for reading, as a group, more total pages or books than were read during the last grading period. Such group rewards avoid the negative consequences of highly competitive programs.

Here are some tips for having successful independent reading periods:

- Have a well-stocked classroom collection of books—poetry books, plays, picture books, novels, and information books. See Chapter 12 for more information on this topic.
- Conduct booktalks regularly so that students become aware of books they may wish to read. These booktalks can be given by teachers and librarians who will often serve as resource persons.
- Display new books attractively in the classroom and show videos of notable authors talking about their books and craft. These techniques are effective in "selling" books to children.
- Schedule the same time each day for independent reading and adhere to it. Allow enough time for students to get well into their books and to achieve some level of satisfaction from the reading.
- Insist on attentiveness to books during this time. With primary-grade students, quiet talking in pairs about books or individual lipreading aloud may be on-task behavior, but children in intermediate grades can read silently and usually prefer to do so.
- Spend the independent reading period engrossed in books, setting yourself as an example of a reader. Be knowledgeable of and interested in the books the students are reading.

Booktalks

A *booktalk* is an oral presentation by a teacher, a librarian, or a student who tells about a book to stimulate the students' interest and motivate them to read it. Booktalks are not book reports, analyses of the author's style, or the old-fashioned book report that discusses characters, setting, theme, and plot (Bodart, 1980). Booktalks have been used effectively for years by librarians who have developed this strategy into an art for the purpose of encouraging students to check out books from the library. Teachers can give booktalks on five to ten books each week from their classroom and school library collections; in this way, they can entice students to read and experience good literature.

Some teachers who give frequent booktalks also advocate having students give booktalks to induce other students to read the suggested books. A regular feature of *Reading Rainbow,* the public television program about children's books, is children giving booktalks. One teacher taped two or three of these *Reading Rainbow* booktalks and showed them in class to help her students learn how to give good booktalks. For more tips on developing and giving booktalks, see www. arrowhead .lib.mn.us/more/rabktalk and www.thebooktalker.com.

The following are our recommendations for giving a good booktalk:

- Read the book before trying to do a booktalk on it.
- Choose books that you have liked, wholly or in part, or that you think your students will enjoy. Sincere enthusiasm for a book is stimulating and infectious.
- Have the book available to show to the students as you give the booktalk. Format aspects— such as cover illustrations, length, size, and shape of the books—which also influence book choices, can be weighed by students only if they can see the book.
- Keep the booktalk brief, generally no more than two or three minutes. Do not tell too much about the book or the students will see no reason to read it. For most books, four to six sentences will suffice.
- Tell the topic and something about the action in the story, but *do not tell the plot.* Feature a scene or character that the story revolves around, but do not discuss the scene that gives away the ending.
- Booktalk a group of books that share the same theme; in this case you will want to talk briefly about each book and how it fits with the others.

The following is an example of a booktalk on *The House of the Scorpion* (2002) by Nancy Farmer:

> If you ever think about what life will be like in the future, 100 years from now, you will enjoy reading *The House of the Scorpion,* a novel about young Matt, who has spent his life locked away in a hut because he is a clone and clones are outcasts hated by human society. As Matt comes of age he discovers that he is the clone of El Patrón, the cruel ruler of Opium, a drug kingdom farmed by "eejits," brain-dead clones. Opium is located between the United States and Aztlán, once called Mexico. In El Patrón's household, Matt finds support from a cook and a bodyguard, and eventually Maria, who begins to care about Matt. When Matt realizes that his life is at risk, he makes a break for freedom and escapes to Aztlán only to face more hardships and adventures. Matt wonders who he is, why he exists, and whether, as a clone, he has free will. *The House of the Scorpion* by Nancy Farmer has received many honors, including winning the National Book Award for young people's literature.

After you have given the booktalk, place the book back on the reading table for students to peruse and to consider for reading. Over time, you should give booktalks on a variety of books at different levels of reading difficulty, on different topics, and with male and female protagonists from many cultures. In this way, you will appeal to the wide range of interests and abilities that exist among students in a classroom.

Storytelling

Storytelling is the oldest medium for sharing literature. Oral literature flourished for thousands of years before writing was invented and books became commonly available. When a teacher tells stories, another delightful means for children to experience literature becomes available to the class. Teachers who tell stories in their classrooms report that their students are appreciative listeners and soon begin telling stories themselves.

By bringing stories to life through personal expression and interpretation, a storyteller establishes a close communication with the audience. A storyteller begins by selecting a good story. Next, she practices it until she is able to tell it with ease and then tells it to different audiences again and again.

Selection of a Story

To find stories for telling, begin with collections of folktales and short stories. Read some of these until you find a few you especially like. Then consider these two points:

- Good stories for telling usually have few characters (from two to five), high conflict, action that builds to a climax, and a quick conclusion that ties together all the threads of the story. Humorous elements are also worth seeking.
- The first stories you tell should take no longer than ten minutes. As you develop your storytelling gifts, you may want to tell longer stories.

A good resource for teachers and students in grade 4 and above who want to tell stories more formally is Pellowski's *The Storytelling Handbook: A Young People's Collection of Unusual Tales and Helpful Hints on How to Tell Them* (1995). Some websites providing stories, storytelling resources, and tips on becoming a good storyteller for you and your students are:

www.storyarts.org
www.storynet.org
www.themoonlitroad.com
www.timsheppard.co.uk/story

Preparation for Telling

Once you have selected a story to tell, outline the story content in terms of the plot. Many storytellers note on 3" × 5" cards the title and source of the tale, the characters' names and story events, and any other information that may be helpful. These cards can then be consulted quickly just before one tells a story. A story file can be a nice resource to keep as more stories are prepared for telling. One storyteller tapes her stories and then uses them to refresh her memory for later retellings.

Practice

Tell the story aloud to yourself again and again. Do not memorize the story, but keep in mind the characters and sequence of main story events. Each time you tell the story, it will change a bit, becoming more and more your own story as you include personal touches. Some storytellers find props useful. They can be simple (a hat, a stick-on mustache, or a stuffed toy) or more elaborate (a mask, a puppet, or a costume).

When puppets are used, a separate puppet is made for each character and is held by the storyteller while the character speaks. Puppets can be purchased or made by the storyteller. Another more elaborate use of props is the feltboard story—a storytelling aid some teachers especially enjoy. Pictures or objects are attached to a feltboard or display board and are moved around during the story. Cumulative stories, especially, lend themselves to feltboard presentations.

Shared Reading

Shared reading is a term we use to describe a number of teaching strategies that attempt to draw on the natural literacy learning that has long occurred in book-loving homes around the world. These various strategies—*shared-book experience, assisted reading,* and *paired reading*—provide children with opportunities to experience good literature as they are learning to read. The strategies have in common a semistructured modification of the parent–child interaction with repeated readings of favorite books as the child gradually acquires an understanding of print and its relationship to our sound system or to the words we speak. A list of pattern books suitable for use in shared reading activities can be found at the end of Chapter 5.

The *shared-book experience* is an adaptation of a natural home-learning strategy used with groups of beginning readers in school settings. Enlarged-text books of 24" × 30" or larger, called *Big Books,* usually well-loved children's picture books, are presented to groups of beginning readers in a sequence proposed by Holdaway in 1982. First, favorite, well-known poems and songs are repeated in unison by the students and the teacher while the teacher points to the text of the Big Book. A review story is then used to teach skills in context. Following this activity, the teacher involves the students in language play, such as alphabet games, rhymes, and songs that use letter names. Then a new story in Big Book format is presented by the teacher. Students participate by repeating the story, line by line, after the teacher. Later, students read independently from a wide selection of favorite books and compose original stories, often modeled after the new story.

Assisted reading (Hoskisson, Sherman, & Smith, 1974) is a one-to-one strategy for use with impaired readers. In assisted reading, the child and the adult sit side by side with a book. The child reads aloud until she or he has difficulty, at which point the adult supplies the word.

Paired reading is guided practice with an adult who reads in a soft voice and invites the child to fill in words when the adult pauses and the child knows the word. Paired reading can also be enjoyed by two children of compatible personalities who read back and forth to one another.

In all of these strategies, well-chosen literature is important; the nature of the experience is companionable, not authoritative; and the child reader must see the text and hear the words simultaneously. Sometimes, the adult places a finger under each word as it is being read to draw the child's attention to the print. Selecting favorite, loved stories is essential because the success of these strategies is contingent on frequent rereadings of the same book.

The primary purpose of these three shared-reading strategies is to provide learning situations in which children can learn to read using books and activities familiar to them in home and preschool settings. The effect of these strategies can also be the promotion of a love of literature.

Literature across the Curriculum

Students may also experience good literature in content-area classes when teachers supplement or replace textbooks with trade books for instruction. *Literature across the curriculum* refers to using works of literature in the content areas of social studies, science, health, and mathematics. Many advantages accrue to teachers who incorporate trade books into their teaching. Students will also gain from this practice.

Students who lack motivation and struggle in reading can benefit from reading attractively illustrated trade books on the topic under study. Selection of trade books of both greater and lesser difficulty can meet the needs of students of different reading levels, unlike textbooks written on a single readability level, usually at a higher level than the grade at which they are used.

Trade books make social studies content more memorable because the stories are presented from a child's point of view. Children see the world through a narrative framework. In learning about their world, stories and narrative are more real to children than informational texts. Children are more likely to understand and remember history if it is presented as a story with characters, settings, and events. Later, they move from an interest in the narrative to an interest in the history itself.

Trade books also permit students to read multiple perspectives on topics, which helps them develop critical thinking. Comparing historical information from various sources is a valued practice that helps students encounter differing perspectives on any particular era of history. Students may start with the textbook, then research the facts from other books, or read a work of fiction and then seek to verify to what extent the facts within the story are accurate. In addition, trade books couch political and social events in terms of the moral events related to them. Children can see how these events affected the lives of real people and can better understand the morality underlying their choices. Unlike textbook authors who must write to please all viewpoints, authors of children's literature are more likely to face controversial issues head-on. For ideas on planning social studies units incorporating trade books, fiction and nonfiction, see the web on immigration, Figure 12.2. Books to use in many subjects can be found in Table 13.1.

Trade books in science and health offer the advantage of presenting different sources as a means to verify facts. Students can compare the facts presented in the textbook with those found in various trade books on the same topic. Global warming, a topic of general discussion in the news, is addressed in science textbooks, and a number of trade books are concerned with this topic. For example, Laurence Pringle's *Global Warning: The Threat of Earth's Changing Climate* (2001) and Alvin Silverstein, Virginia Silverstein, and Laura Silverstein Nunn's *Global Warning* (2002) are two fairly short, well-written informational books, while Marcus Sedgwick's science fiction novel *Floodland* (2001) features a girl who searches for her parents after the sea, as a result of global warming, has risen causing cities to become islands. Another work of science fiction, *The House of the Scorpion* (2002) by Nancy Farmer, can become the basis for investigations into cloning and its ramifications.

Trade books can benefit all subjects. For example, many trade books on health and science present information in interesting ways through graphs, tables, figures, authentic photographs, and other visual presentations, coupled with a lively style of writing in the text. Comparison of information from different sources can be readily provided when students are not limited to a single source for their information. Teachers who draw on materials of various types for their instruction have discovered that literature has the power to educate the mind, while enlightening the spirit.

Content-area reading is the ability to read to acquire, understand, and connect to new content in a particular discipline. When students enter schools with departmentalized organizations, the teaching of reading is often neglected. Content-area teachers feel more responsibility to impart

Table 13.1   Examples of Using Literature across the Curriculum

Subject	Suggested Books
Art	Balliett, Blue. *Chasing Vermeer.* Illustrated by Brett Helquist. Ages 10–14. Detective mystery involving a missing Vermeer painting and lots of puzzles. Greenberg, Jan, and Jordan Sandra, *Chuck Close, Up Close.* Ages 10–14. Picture book biography of the American artist who creates oversized portraits despite paralysis. Greenberg, Jan, and Jordan Sandra, *Vincent Van Gogh: Portrait of an Artist.* Ages 10–14. Biography of the nineteenth-century Dutch painter. Reynolds, Peter H. *The Dot.* Ages 5–9. A girl discovers her artistic talent with the help of her teacher.
Geography	Knight, Margy B., & Melnicove, Mark. *Africa Is Not a Country.* Illustrated by Anne S. O'Brien. Ages 8–11. A look at the 53 diverse countries that make up the African continent. Lasky, Kathryn. *The Librarian Who Measured the Earth.* Illustrated by Kevin Hawkes. Ages 7–11. The life of Eratosthenes of Cyrene, a geographer who estimated the circumference of the Earth in around 200 B.C. Petty, Kate. *The Amazing Pop-Up Geography Book.* Illustrated by Jennie Maizels. Paper engineering by Ruth Wickings. Ages 7–10. Scientific, political, and geographical information about the earth in a pop-up format.
Health	Gantos, Jack. *Joey Pigza Swallowed the Key.* Ages 9–12. Life with attention deficit disorder. Katzen, Mollie. *Salad People and More Real Recipes.* Ages 5–8. Twenty recipes for nutritious, healthy food. Peters, Stephanie T. *The Battle Against Polio.* Ages 10–14. Part of the five-book *Epidemic!* set (other book topics include influenza, smallpox, bubonic plague). Schlosser, Eric, & Wilson, Charles. *Chew on This: Everything You Don't Want to Know about Fast Food.* Ages 12–14. Simon, Seymour. *Guts: Our Digestive System.* Ages 9–14. A well-illustrated book on how the digestive system works, including the components and processes of digestion.
Language Arts, Reading	Agee, Jon. *Palindromania!* Ages 9–14. 170 palindromes humorously illustrated. Hoberman, Mary Ann. *You Read to Me, I'll Read to You: Very Short Fairy Tale to Read Together.* Illustrated by Michael Emberley. Ages 5–7. Eight fairy tales for reading together. Perkins, Lynne Rae. *Criss Cross.* Ages 11–15. A character study featuring different perspectives, poems, prose, haiku, and question-and-answer formats. Wolf, Allan. *Immersed in Verse: An Informative, Slightly Irreverent & Totally Tremendous Guide to Living the Poet's Life.* Illustrated by Tuesday Mourning. Ages 11–14. How-to guide to writing poetry. Wong, Janet S. *You Have to Write.* Illustrated by Teresa Flavin. Ages 8–11. Help for common problems young people have with creative writing.
Mathematics	Ball, Johnny. *Go Figure! A Totally Cool Book about Numbers.* Ages 10–14. Filled with facts, figures, and brainteasers, including geometry, predictability, and logic. Leedy, Loreen. *The Great Graph Contest.* Ages 6–8. Careful explanations of all sorts of graphs are given as animals vie to see who can make the best one.

(continued)

Table 13.1 *(Continued)*

	Wise, Bill. *Whodunit Math Puzzles.* Illustrated by Lucy Corvino. Ages 10–14. Twelve-year-old junior detective uses math to solve a series of 22 short mysteries.
	Wishinsky, Frieda. *What's the Matter with Albert? A Story of Albert Einstein.* Illustrated by Jacques Lamontagne. Ages 9–13. Vignettes in picture book format of Albert Einstein's childhood, told from the viewpoint of a young newspaper reporter interviewing Albert Einstein.
Music	Anderson, M. T. *Handel, Who Knew What He Liked.* Illustrated by Kevin Hawkes. Ages 8–11. Picture book biography of the eighteenth-century German-born English composer, Handel.
	Krull, Kathryn. *Lives of the Musicians: Good Times, Bad Times (and What the Neighbors Thought).* Illustrated by Kathryn Hewitt. Ages 10–14. Snapshot biographies of 16 musical greats from classic to ragtime.
	Nelson, Kadir. *He's Got the Whole World in His Hands.* Ages 4–8. Picture book rendering of the African-American spiritual.
	Ryan, Pam M. *When Marian Sang: The True Recital of Marian Anderson.* Illustrated by Brian Selznick. Ages 6–10. Biography of the twentieth-century African-American singer.
Physical Education	Bloor, Edward. *Tangerine.* Ages 11–14. A legally blind, soccer-playing seventh-grader confronts several issues, including his amoral football-hero brother.
	Morrison, Lillian. *Way to Go! Sports Poems.* Illustrated by Susan Spellman. Ages 9–14. 42 poems.
	Ritter, John. *The Boy Who Saved Baseball.* Ages 10–14. The town's future rides on the outcome of a game between the ragtag local team and an all-star neighboring team.
Science	Collard, Sneed. *The Prairie Builders: Reconstructing America's Lost Grasslands.* Ages 11–14. Present-day recreation of the tallgrass prairie in Iowa.
	Hiaasen, Carl. *Hoot.* Ages 10–14. Ecological mystery involving a proposed development project and endangered miniature owls.
	Lasky, Kathryn. *The Man Who Made Time Travel.* Illustrated by Kevin Hawkes. Ages 10–13. Picture book biography of the eighteenth-century British clockmaker John Harrison who solved the problem of tracking longitude in shipboard navigation.
	McNulty, Faith. *If You Decide to Go to the Moon.* Illustrated by Steven Kellogg. Ages 5–8. Facts about space travel and Earth.
	Montgomery, Sy. *The Tarantula Scientist.* Photographs by Nic Bishop. Ages 9–13. View of the life of a scientist at work in the field. (Part of the Scientists in the Field series)
	Scieszka, Jon. *Science Verse.* Illustrated by Lane Smith. Ages 7–11. Verses short on scientific content but long on humor and parody offer comic relief for science classes.
Social Studies, History	Armstrong, Jennifer. *The American Story: 100 True Tales from American History.* Illustrated by Roger Roth. Ages 9–13.
	Bridges, Ruby, & Lundell, M. *Through My Eyes.* Ages 9–12. Memoir of events in 1960–1961 when the author became the first person to integrate Louisiana schools.
	Jackson, Ellen. *It's Back to School We Go! First Day Stories from around the World.* Illustrated by Jan D. Ellis. Ages 5–8. First-person accounts of children from 11 countries. (Also Geography)
	Lester, Julius. *Day of Tears: A Novel in Dialogue.* Ages 12–15. Fictionalized account of the biggest slave auction in American history (Savannah, Georgia, 1859).
	Myers, Laurie. *Lewis and Clark and Me: A Dog's Tale.* Illustrated by Michael Dooling. Ages 9–13. Seaman, Meriwether Lewis's Newfoundland dog, describes Lewis and Clark's expedition, which he accompanied from St. Louis to the Pacific Ocean.
	Rotner, Shelley, & Kreisler, Ken. *Everybody Works.* Photographs by Shelley Rotner. Ages 5–7. A concept book about different types of work in urban and rural settings.
	Smith, David J. *If the World Were a Village: A Book about the World's People.* Illustrated by Shelagh Armstrong. Ages 8–11. Statistics on the world's population in easy-to-understand terms.

knowledge about the particular subject matter in which they specialize and may ignore the need to assist students in their literacy development. For example, technical vocabulary in a subject needs to be explained, practiced, and developed over time before students "own" it. Most students require substantial exposure to new vocabulary.

In content-area classes students are often assigned textbooks, a type of expository text. Mullis, Martin, Gonzalez, and Kennedy's (2003) report of findings from an international study suggests that children in the United States read expository texts with more difficulty than narrative texts. Teachers can make the reading of textbooks easier if they teach students how such texts are structured and explain other specialized features of them. In Chapter 10, the elements of nonfiction are explained with examples provided. Robb (2003) also provides practical ideas for teaching social studies, science, and mathematics.

Students deserve access to an ample variety of excellent books that they can read and want to read. They are entitled to sufficient time to visit the school media center and time to read as part of their weekly routines. Teachers can support independent reading by assigning some homework time as reading time. Some individual teachers and teams of content teachers have made this request explicit by requiring 100 to 150 minutes a week to be logged onto a form with date, author, book title, number of minutes read, and parent signature. This form is turned in once a week for credit. If teachers in schools with departmentalized organizations agree that spending time reading is important, then the time set aside becomes part of the homework expectations. Teachers help make this type of effort successful by showing and talking about books, by reading aloud books or excerpts from books, by inviting the media specialist to talk about new books, and by sharing their personal enthusiasm for books. Each content-area teacher can focus on books that relate to the current focus of study in class. Trade books can enhance the teaching of other subjects while providing students with rich literary experiences.

Audiobooks

Audiobooks of children's literature are available today on CDs, with older ones available in audio cassettes. Many are read by well-known actors and professional readers. Some audiobooks are expensive, so teachers will want to purchase them through school library media centers or by using other school budgets. Bookclubs sometimes offer audiobooks to teachers with the accumulation of a certain number of points from book purchases by students.

For assistance in selecting excellent-quality audiobooks, the major review journals (listed in Chapter 3) review audiobooks in each journal issue. The following websites are publishers of fairly substantial numbers of audiobooks:

www.randomhouse.com
www.recordedbooks.com
www.scholastic.com

Audiobooks are an excellent teaching tool. Consider some of the following uses:

- Have the students listen to an audiobook in class rather than listen to the teacher read the book aloud. The novelty of the performance—something different from the teacher's reading—may add interest.

- Use audiobooks at a listening center where a group of children can work independently. An experience of this kind may be enhanced when each child has a copy of the book to follow the narration.
- When assigning homework reading to students, offer students who have difficulties in reading the option of listening to the audiobook. They may also choose to follow the narration in a copy of the book. Students who otherwise would be unable to participate in class discussions of the book with their peers will be able to contribute.
- Encourage the formation of listening groups at various times during the day. These groups can meet in the library at lunch time or during other breaks in the day, or after school. For some students, this may be a welcome alternative to the school activities with which they are uncomfortable and can bring children together to form friendships and to learn at the same time.

Films Based on Children's Books

If films are to be a regular feature of your literature class, you will want your students to be active viewers and know how film is similar to and different from text. Both have plots, characters, settings, themes, styles, and points of view. Both are edited and both can have dialogue and narration. Film differs from text in that it has sound (spoken words, music, and sound effects) and photography (its use of color or black and white, angles, close-ups, and panoramas). Additionally, films have actual people or animated characters inhabiting the character roles and actual settings, whereas books ask readers to form their own images of characters and settings.

With this rudimentary background in the elements of cinema, students can be guided to become better "readers" of film and better equipped to discuss or write their personal responses to films based on literature. Films that support or contradict the content of the book may be suitable for classroom use depending on the teacher's intent. Generally, teachers have shown the film based on a book after the book has been read and discussed. The film then provides an opportunity to compare and contrast the book and the film while considering the advantages and limitations of the two media. For some students the movie experience may be motivation to read the book or others in the same series or by the same author.

At the end of Chapters 5 through 11, lists of films related to book categories are provided. Also, since 1991, the American Library Association has awarded on an annual basis the Andrew Carnegie medal for Excellence in Children's Video, awarded to the producer of the video. Teachers will want to select films based on children's books for viewing in school settings that meet the following considerations and criteria:

- Teacher familiarity with and approval of the book on which the film is based
- A preview of the film itself
- Films that are age- and content-appropriate for viewing in a school setting to a child audience, based on the teacher's professional judgment and the film's rating, if there is one

Some sources for films, videos, and DVDs are as follows:

- *The Video Source Book* (Syosset, NY: National Video Clearinghouse), published by Gale Research, Detroit, MI. This annual reference work lists media and provides sources for purchase and rental.

- Two websites of large video distributors are www.libraryvideo.com and www.knowledge unlimited.com.
- The Internet Movie Database (www.imdb.com) is a large film database with production, ratings, and other movie details with links to external reviews.

Bibliotherapy

Bibliotherapy is the use of books by professionally trained therapists in treating emotionally disturbed individuals. Most teachers and librarians are not trained as psychologists, and misguided bibliotherapy may damage students. On the other hand, we know that our students benefit psychologically from reading and talking about powerful stories and the thoughts, feelings, and actions of characters in these stories. Children all face difficult situations at times; discovering that other children have faced similar problems is reassuring. Learning how others have coped successfully with problems gives children confidence that they too will be able to solve problems that may arise later in their lives. Books shared by sensitive and caring teachers and librarians may help students to develop understanding and empathy for others and come to a realization of their own unkind behaviors. Bibliotherapy as a professional treatment should, however, be left to trained therapists.

Character Education

Character education is a process intended to establish core values believed to be important to develop in young people and to build awareness of these values among teachers and parents in order to encourage children to adopt these values. The Josephson Institute of Ethics, in conjunction with a nonsectarian coalition of legislators, corporate officers, and others, has promoted a framework, *Character Counts,* in which six values with related traits are espoused. Although this program is promoted in schools with accompanying materials available for purchase, these same values are often expressed in good literature, which can be the basis for understanding and developing moral reasoning. Stories such as the ones listed below for each of the six values promulgated by *Character Counts* can help children formulate their own concepts of right and wrong.

Trustworthiness
- Bredsdorff, Bodil. *The Crow-Girl: The Children of Crow Cove.* Ages 9–12.
- Park, Linda Sue. *The Firekeeper's Son.* Illustrated by Julie Downing. Ages 8–12.
- D'Amico, Carmela and Steven. *Ella Takes the Cake.* Ages 5–9.

Respect
- DeFelice, Cynthia. *Under the Same Sky.* Ages 12–15.
- Lowry, Lois. *The Silent Boy.* Ages 9–12.
- Lorbiecki, Marybeth. *Jackie's Bat.* Illustrated by Brian Pinkney. Ages 6–9.

Responsibility
- Haas, Jessie. *Jigsaw Pony.* Ages 7–10.
- Johnson, Angela. *The First Part Last.* Ages 12–18.

Fairness
- Lee, Tanith. *Wolf Tower*. Ages 10–13.
- Fuqua, Jonathan Scott. *Darby*. Ages 9–12.
- Spinelli, Eileen. *Three Pebbles and a Song*. Illustrated by S. D. Schindler. Ages 5–8.

Caring
- Polacco, Patricia. *Mr. Lincoln's Way*. Ages 5–9.
- Lowry, Lois. *Messenger*. Ages 11–15.
- Paterson Katherine. *The Same Stuff as Stars*. Ages 10–14.

Citizenship
- Battle-Lavert, Gwendolyn. *Papa's Mark*. Illustrated by Colin Bootman. Ages 6–9.
- Leavitt, Martine. *Tom Finder*. Ages 12–18.

Moralizing and preaching are seldom appreciated by children; literary works for the purpose of character education should meet the same standards for good literature as all other selections. If the moral or lesson overpowers the story, many children will resist the obvious preaching and balk at reading such stories. Children want to read powerful stories that excite them, amuse them, and inspire them.

Social Justice Education

Unfortunately, many individuals and cultural groups in this country have experienced and continue to experience social oppression, discrimination, or loss of civil rights. Some schools have responded to this situation by adapting their curricula to include *social justice education,* the "conscious and reflexive blend of content and process intended to enhance equity across multiple social identity groups, foster critical perspectives, and promote social action" (Carlisle, Jackson, & George, 2006, p. 56). An important component of social justice education is literature that documents the history and contemporary stories of the disenfranchised, presents their perspectives, and allows members of these groups to be heard. Those who read these works are introduced to information not always presented in textbooks and have the opportunity to forge relationships, albeit vicarious, with people and cultural groups they would not otherwise know. Literature for social justice education can be found throughout this book in the Recommended Books at the end of chapters and especially in the Recommended Books in Chapter 11.

Character education and social justice education differ in some ways. Character education emphasizes the values and resulting behaviors for adoption by individual children. Social justice education emphasizes equity across multiple social and cultural groups in our society and the importance of looking at institutional behaviors as well as individual behavior in our democratic society.

Chapter 11 emphasized the importance of culturally responsive teaching strategies. It is important to consider whether the values espoused in character education and social justice programs are consistent with the cultural values of the students you are teaching.

Responding to Literature

When students experience a story by listening to it, by reading it, or by viewing it, they may naturally wish to respond or express their reactions to the experience in some way. In sharing their responses with others, students profit by recapturing the experience through translating it to a new form or medium; they develop a better understanding of what they experienced by organizing and deepening their feelings and thoughts on the experience; they discover that other readers' experiences with the same book may not have been the same as theirs; and they bring closure to the experience. Although it is important to give students opportunities to respond to books, not every book needs or merits a lengthy response. Rosenblatt (1978) reminds us that no two people have the same prior experiences and that it is the transaction that occurs between the text, the reader, and the present context that provokes a particular response. Teachers may generate opportunities for students to share their individual insights to literary experiences in many different ways.

Book Discussions

Whole-class discussion usually accompanies the reading aloud of a book to the class. In these discussions, comprehension is assumed and the discussion centers on the different ways students feel and think about the book, its characters, its events, and its outcome. Thus, to stimulate a good class discussion, a teacher will encourage students to share their individual responses to open-ended questions; the teacher will not seek supposedly right answers in order to check comprehension or recall. In a class discussion, the teacher has the pivotal role as discussion leader. The discussion tends to be a teacher-to-students, students-to-teacher format. And with a large class, only some of the students will have an opportunity to express their viewpoints.

Another format for students to discuss their responses to literature is the *literature circle,* sometimes called a *literature response group.* In literature circles, students share their responses with peers about a book they have read as a group or a book read aloud by the teacher to the whole class. One of the goals of literature response groups is to have all children learn to work with one another and to value the opinions and views of others. The following features are typically found in the literature circle format:

- Groups can be established by the desire to read the same book, by friendship, by heterogeneous assignment by the teacher, or by random assignments.
- Small groups are usually set up with two to six students for optimal functioning. Students who have less skill working in groups often function better in dyads or triads.
- The small-group discussion is a student-to-student form of communication that permits students more control over the discussion and more roles to perform as group members. For example, students may assume the role of leader, recorder, arbiter, listener, or devil's advocate.
- The advantages of small-group discussions are that students are in control, have more opportunities to express their opinions, and can become more actively involved. Unless students have been taught to work together, however, groups do not function well.

■ Small-group discussions with the teacher as a participating member and joint planning by teacher and class before groups begin working can enable the group to set rules, goals, and time lines.

Individual conferences between a teacher and a student are another means of discovering students' responses to literature. Although a teacher may choose to set up conferences daily, occasional conferences in which the student comes prepared to talk about a book she or he has recently finished can be instructive for the teacher and motivating for the student. The conference is focused on what the student thought and felt about the book. Some teachers ask the student to read aloud a favorite part of the story and tell why it was selected. Individual conferences are from five to ten minutes long and usually end with considering the next book the student will read or the response activity the student has planned (Veatch, 1968).

Eliciting a good discussion with substantial student participation is not an easy art. Certain strategies for promoting discussions need to be considered for use in leading class discussions, in guiding literature response groups, and in interacting with students in individual conferences. Whether you, as the teacher, will be leading the discussion or guiding your students in the art of discussion leader, the questions to be posed are very important. The purpose of discussions of fiction, then, is to elicit students' responses to the work—in other words, to find out what the students think about the story and feel about the story.

A question that can be answered by "yes," "no," or a single word or phrase will not lead to an interactive discussion. The question, "Did you like the story?" may result in a simple "yes." "Which part of the story did you like best and what did you like about it?" is likely to elicit a more detailed response. *Divergent* questions have no one right answer but a number of possible answers. They naturally provoke more discussion than **convergent questions,** for which only one answer is correct.

The best ideas for questions to stimulate book discussions flow directly from your response to the particular book and why you want the students to experience the book. Usually, you will have students read works of fiction for the aesthetic experience they will have with it—enjoyment, appreciation, emotional involvement, deeper understanding of life, and so on. In this case, your questions need to permit students to talk about their experiences. *Divergent* questions are best suited to this goal. Your questions will tell your students what you believe is important in reading. If your questions are *convergent* ones about the details of the plot, characters, and setting, then you are telling your students that reading fiction is a type of egg hunt for the particular eggs laid by this author and previously located by you. On the other hand, if you ask *divergent* questions that permit them to explore their individual experiences with a work of fiction, students will soon discover that you really want to understand their feelings and thoughts about books.

The purpose of reading informational books, though perhaps partially aesthetic, is usually efferent; that is, the reader's attention is centered on what should be retained after the actual reading event. Locating specific pieces of information to support an argument and comparing information from two or more sources are examples of reasons for efferent reading of literature. *Convergent* questions in this case would reflect that purpose. The following questions can be adapted to different books and may help you in designing good questions for specific books:

■ What important ideas did you find in this story?
■ How do you think the story should have ended, and why do you think so?

- How would you have acted if you had been (*book character*)?
- What do you think the author's main message (theme) was in this story? Why do you think so?
- Which part of the story did you like best or least? Why?
- Which character did you like best or least? Why?
- Which character do you identify with? Tell why and how you identify with him or her.
- What has happened in your life that you are reminded of by this story (character, situation)?
- What would (*character*) have done if . . . ?

See the companion website at www.ablongman.com/lynchbrown6e for a section on suggestions for genre-specific discussion questions.

Creative Drama

Creative drama is informal drama that lends itself readily to the reenactment of story experiences. In discussing the features of creative drama, McCaslin (1990) urges teachers and librarians to keep the following in mind:

- The drama is based on a piece of literature.
- Dialogue is created by the actors; lines are not written or memorized.
- Improvisation is an essential element.
- Movement on "stage" by actors is an integral part of creative drama.
- Scenery and costumes are not used, although an occasional prop may assist the children's imaginations.
- Drama is a process rather than a product. It is performed not for an audience, but for the benefit of the participants. Several different dramas or different dramatic interpretations of the same piece of literature can occur simultaneously in the classroom.

Creative drama can be used with students at all grade levels, from kindergarten to high school. A single scene from a chapter book may be enacted, or a picture book or short story may be dramatized in its entirety. The most suitable stories to start with are relatively simple, involving two to six characters and high action. Many folktales fit this description and lend themselves to being enacted.

These are steps to follow in guiding creative drama in the classroom:

- Once a story is selected, the students listen to it being read to them or they read it independently.
- Next, they decide whether they like the story enough to want to act it out. If so, they listen to it again or read it, paying particular attention to the characters and the story scenes in sequence.
- The students then list the characters and the scenes on the chalkboard or on chart paper.
- They assign parts to actors. If enough students are interested in dramatizing the same story, you may want to assign two or more casts of actors immediately. In this way, each cast of characters can observe the performances of the others and learn from them.
- Next, each cast uses the list of scenes to review the plot, ensuring that all actors recall the events. Discuss the characters at this time, too, having students describe the actions, talk, and appearance for each.

- Give the cast of characters a few minutes to decide how to handle the performance. Then run through it. The first attempt may be a bit bumpy, but by the second time, it usually goes quite smoothly.
- After completing the drama, the class or the group of students then evaluates its success. McCaslin (1990) suggests these questions:
  1. Did they tell the story?
  2. What did you like about the opening scene?
  3. Did the characters show that they were excited (angry, unhappy, etc.)?
  4. When we play it again, can you think of anything that would improve it?
  5. Was anything important left out? (p. 174)

The Creative Drama and Theatre Education Resource site, www.creativedrama.com, although not current, has many useful ideas for the classroom. A useful resource book, *Making Make-Believe: Fun Props, Costumes, and Creative Play Ideas* (Kohl, 1999), offers many ideas for engaging prekindergarten to fourth grade students in dramatic play. One chapter presents numerous open-ended dramatic activities related to popular children's books.

Because of its improvisational nature and simplicity of costumes and scenery, creative drama appropriately places importance on the learning and experiencing process, not on performance, and it permits drama to become a frequent means of responding to literature in the classroom. Informal performances for the principal, the class next door, and so on, give students additional opportunities for practice and provide them with an opportunity to feel proud of their efforts.

Readers' Theatre

Readers' theatre is the oral presentation of literature by two or more actors, and usually a narrator, reading from a script. Children's literary response is made evident through expressive oral reading and group interpretation. This form of response is especially enjoyable for children who are able to read aloud with some fluency. Features typically associated with readers' theatre include the following:

- The readers and narrator typically remain on the "stage" throughout the production.
- Readers use little movement; instead, they suggest action with simple gestures and facial expressions.
- Chairs or stools are used for readers and narrator to sit on, and performers usually remain seated throughout the performance. Sometimes, certain readers sit with their backs to the audience to suggest that they are not in a particular scene.
- No costumes or stage settings are necessary and, at most, should be suggestive, rather than complete or literal, to permit the imaginations of the audience to have full rein. The use of sound effects may enhance the performance and give the impression of a radio play.

Scripts can be developed for readers' theatre by the teacher or by older students adapting a work of literature enjoyed by the class. Picture books readily lend themselves to adaptation, as do short stories. Some teachers have successfully adapted well-selected scenes from a favorite chapter book for readers' theatre (see Figure 13.1). Alan Armstrong's novel *Whittington* (2005), a New-bery Honor Book, is an animal fantasy that intertwines three plots: the contemporary barnyard, the medieval folktale, and Ben's reading problems, through Whittington's marvelous storytelling.

Figure 13.1   Sample Page of a Script Developed for Readers' Theatre

Whittington (adapted from Chapter 1, pp. 2–5)
by Alan Armstrong
Random House, 2005.

CHARACTERS:
Narrator
Whittington (cat)
The Lady (duck)
Other characters appear later in the story

Narrator:	This scene takes place in the barnyard.
Whittington:	Hello.
The Lady:	Who are you?
Whittington:	Whittington.
The Lady:	Whittington? That's a funny name for a cat. It's more like the name of a town.
Whittington:	Doesn't it mean anything to you?
The Lady:	No.
Whittington:	Then you don't know history. Whittington is a person in history. He's in books. Anyway, what's your name?
The Lady:	They call me Lady because I'm in charge.
Narrator:	Whittington, the cat, explains that he needs a place to live.
The Lady:	You don't have a home?
Whittington:	I did. A boy took me in when I was a kitten Then they sent him away because he read things backwards. They were ashamed. They sent him to a special school out west. He was going to take me along but they said no.
The Lady:	So what do you want from me?
Whittington:	A place in the barn.
Etc.	

The qualities to seek in a promising story are natural-sounding dialogue, strong characterization, drama or humor, and a satisfactory ending. If the original work has extensive dialogue, the script writing is a very easy activity. The script begins with the title of the book being adapted, the name of the author, a list of characters, and usually an opening statement by the narrator. Following the introduction, the dialogue is written into script form, with the narrator scripted for the remaining nondialogue, narrative parts.

Scripts can also be purchased, but finding scripts that are both well written and adapted from the literature you are using in your classroom may prove difficult. A list of recommended plays appears in Chapter 4; some are adaptations of well-known literature and may suit your purpose. If you decide to develop readers' theatre scripts from the literature you are using, remember that developing the first script is the most difficult. Once you have created the first one, you will find out how easy the process is. Intermediate-grade students take readily to script development once they have a model to imitate. Aaron Shepard's RT Page www.aaronshep.com/rt is a website guide to readers' theatre with tips on scripting, staging, and performing. Readers' theatre can become a frequently selected response option of literature response groups.

Figure 13.2   Picture Books Adaptable for Readers' Theatre Scripts

Albert and the Angels by Leslie Norris
Amazing Grace by Mary Hoffman
Buttons by Brock Cole
Chrysanthemum by Kevin Henkes
Duck on a Bike by David Shannon
Frog and Toad Are Friends by Arnold Lobel
The Great Kapok Tree: A Tale of the Amazon Rainforest by Lynne Cherry
Little Brown Bear Won't Go to School by Jane Dyer
Nice Work, Little Wolf! by Hilda Offen
So, What's It Like to Be a Cat? by Karla Kuskin
Three Little Pigs and the Big Bad Wolf by Glen Rounds
The Three Little Wolves and the Big Bad Pig by Eugene Trivizas
Tommy at the Grocery Store by Bill Grossman
Two Old Potatoes and Me by John Coy

Choice of literature to use can include virtually any literary genre—picture storybooks, novels, biographies, long poems, letters, diaries, and journals. See Figures 13.2 and 13.3 for books suitable for script development. Another example, Paul Fleischman's *Bull Run* (1993), a historical novel set during the Civil War, is written as a series of episodes told by different characters at different stages of the war. At the end of the book, the author provides a list of each character's entries for the use of those who wish to produce readers' theatre performances. Variations on readers' theatre can be accomplished through the addition of background music, choral poems, and brief scenes from different stories tied together by a common theme, among other options to enliven this dramatic enactment of literature.

Figure 13.3   Novels Adaptable for Readers' Theatre Scripts

Bud, Not Buddy by Christopher Paul Curtis
Dave at Night by Gail Levine
Ella Enchanted by Gail Levine
Ghost Girl: A Blue Ridge Mountain Story by Delia Ray
The Giver by Lois Lowry
Out of Order by Betty Hicks
Rowan and the Zebak by Emily Rodda
Whittington by Alan Armstrong

Preparation for a readers' theatre presentation gives students a good opportunity to strengthen their oral reading abilities and to try out their expressive skills. The group typically reads through the script once or twice and then works on refining the interpretive aspects of each performer. Decisions need to be made on the arrangement of chairs and speakers for greatest visual effect. Following each presentation, an evaluation is made by the group with the goal of improving future performances.

McCaslin (1990) states that "the simplicity of production and effectiveness of result make it [readers' theatre] singularly desirable in schools with inadequate stage facilities and where rehearsal time is at a premium" (p. 263). For these same reasons, readers' theatre is extremely well suited to classroom reenactments of literary experiences. In readers' theatre, students have the opportunity to translate their experiences with a literary work to a new medium—the medium of drama—with considerable ease and pleasure.

Storytellings and Retellings

Children who hear good stories read aloud by teachers, librarians, and parents often recapture those happy experiences by making the stories their own through retellings. In addition, in their natural play activities during preschool years, children enjoy role-playing and making up their own stories to tell to a playmate, real or imagined. The foundation for children's storytelling comes from the children's language environment—the talk they have heard and the stories that have been read to them. As young students learn to tell and retell stories, they reinforce their concept of story and are provided with opportunities for oral language development and expansion. Children who can tell a story with a beginning, a middle, and an end have the groundwork laid for later writing activities. You will note that storytellings and retellings by children are different in purpose than storytelling by teachers, as discussed in an earlier section of this chapter. Teachers tell stories as one of many ways of sharing literature with their students.

Teachers can foster the telling and retelling of stories by structuring a classroom environment that is conducive to this activity. Setting off an area of the classroom where children can gather for quiet talk and equipping it with some props such as story puppets, feltboards with cut-out story figures, toy story characters (stuffed animals, dolls, plastic and metal figures), wordless books, and children's favorite storybooks can entice children into telling and retelling their favorite stories. Some children take the book shared by the teacher during storytime and page through it, retelling the story from the pictures; others take story puppets and re-create the story or make up an entirely new adventure with the same characters.

Tape recorders also inspire younger students to record and listen to their favorite stories, while older students find a tape recorder an incentive for developing radio shows based on favorite books. Their favorite readers' theatre performances are well suited to radio show productions.

Written Expression

The simplest and most direct way for teachers to elicit written responses to stories is to ask students to write their ideas and feelings about a book listened to or read. *Divergent,* open-ended questions, rather than *convergent* questions, will elicit students' feelings and ideas about a scene, a character, or the story as a whole, and will help students explore their personal involvement with the story. Each student's writing ability must be considered in selecting an appropriate writing activity. Emergent writers may find it possible to write the name of their favorite character and draw a picture of that character; more able writers may be able to write a detailed character description. A notable children's author, Marion Dane Bauer, has published a book useful to young writers, *What's Your Story? A Young Person's Guide to Writing Fiction* (1992). The Purple Crayon, www.underdown.org, offers writing tips to children and adults and includes suggested readings and submission requirements for publication.

Some teachers have found a literature journal—in which students make frequent written responses to books read—a motivating tool for students. Teachers read and comment on the entries periodically, and students gain a sense of pride in their reading accomplishments.

In some cases, reactions to books by one student can be enjoyed by the rest of the class. One teacher clipped blank response sheets with columns for responses (Author, Title, Reaction) inside the front cover of books in the classroom collection. After reading the book, a student enters his or her name and writes views on the book. Other students enjoy reading the book to see whether their reaction will be the same. Some teachers have had students write 4" × 6" notecards about each book as it is read. These cards are kept on file in the library corner so that each new reader can add his or her impressions to the card.

Literary Works as Writing Models

When children read and listen to stories, they accumulate vocabulary, sentence structures, stylistic devices, and story ideas and structures. Well-written stories and poems, such as those in Tables 13.2 and 13.3, serve as models for children in their own writing. When an 8-year-old boy who wrote extremely well-developed, interesting stories was asked how he learned to make up such good stories, he replied, "It's really a secret, but I'll tell you if you won't tell my teacher. I don't really make up the stories. When I was little, my mother read lots of books to me; then in school my teachers read a lot more. So what I do is take a beginning from one of the stories, a middle from another, and the end from another. And then I make up a title." Children who have a rich literary background have a well-stocked storehouse of beginnings, middles, and endings to put to use in their storytelling and writing.

Modeling after different literary forms can be used as a means of response to a literary work. Writing a story modeled after another story can be an enjoyable re-creation of the experience. In modeling, the student adapts a story form or idea into a new creation. Examples include the following:

- Students create another episode using the same characters.
- Students write a different ending to the story read.
- Students take the perspective of another character in the story and recast the story with a shift in point of view. Two examples of a change in point of view can be found in Jon Scieszka's *The True Story of the 3 Little Pigs by A. Wolf* (1989), which gives the Big Bad Wolf's version, and Scieszka's *The Frog Prince Continued* (1991), which tells the shocking truth about "happily ever after."
- Students write a prequel to a story.
- Students take a story set in the past and rewrite it with a modern-day setting. Alternatively, a character from the historical narrative can become a visitor to modern times.

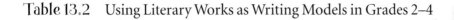

Table 13.2   Using Literary Works as Writing Models in Grades 2–4

Literary Device or Element	Suggested Books
Characterization	*Olivia* by Ian Falconer
	Sheila Rae the Brave by Kevin Henkes
	Farmer Duck by Martin Waddell
	Albert and the Angels by Leslie Norris
	Duck on a Bike by David Shannon
Dialogue	*Albert and the Angels* by Leslie Norris
	Little Brown Bear Won't Go to School by Jane Dyer
	Two Old Potatoes and Me by John Coy
	Owen Foote, Super Spy by Stephanie Greene
Episodic Plot	*Starring Grace* by Mary Hoffman
	Double Fudge by Judy Blume
	When Mules Flew on Magnolia Street by Angela Johnson
Journal Writing	*The Journey* by Sarah Stewart
	Good-Bye for Today: The Diary of a Young Girl at Sea by Peter and Connie Roop
Setting	*The 18 Penny Goose* by Sally M. Walker
	The Snowy Day by Ezra Jack Keats
	Miss Rumphius by Barbara Cooney

Traditional Book Reports

Requiring students to list author, title, date, genre, setting, main characters, and a summary of the plot seldom causes students to delve more deeply into their experiences with literature. Students usually view traditional book reports as tedious busywork. Although teachers assign book reports to get students to read, students often report that they never read the books they report on, but rather read the bookflap, read a page or two at the beginning and end, and write the report.

Recently, some so-called literature response forms or worksheets have been published for use by teachers who adopt literature-based reading approaches. Be cautious in your use of these worksheets. They need to be examined carefully; some of them are little more than disguised book report forms asking for plot, setting, characters, and theme. Such comprehension assessment may be justified occasionally in the reading class, but if your interest is to elicit students' responses to literature, you should stay away from worksheets.

Table 13.3   Using Literary Works as Writing Models in Grades 5–8

Literary Device or Element	Suggested Books
Characterization	*Goose Girl* by Shannon Hale *The Seeing Stone* by Kevin Crossley-Holland
Dialogue	*Ruby Holler* by Sharon Creech *Don't You Know There's a War On?* by Avi
Metaphor	*Uptown* by Bryan Collier *Dovey Coe* by Frances O'Roark Dowell *Green Angel* by Alice Hoffman
Mood	*Dawn* by Uri Shulevitz *Don't Let the Pigeon Drive the Bus* by Mo Willems *The Wolves in the Walls* by Neil Gaiman *Star of Fear, Star of Hope* by Jo Hoestlandt
Journal Writing	*Tibet through the Red Box* by Peter Sís *Catherine, Called Birdy* by Karen Cushman *Stowaway* by Karen Hesse *Witch Child* by Celia Rees *Maata's Journal: A Novel* by Paul Sullivan
Point of View	*Faith and the Electric Dogs* by Patrick Jennings *Lewis and Clark and Me: A Dog's Tale* by Laurie Myers *Flipped* by Wendelin Van Draanen *The Misfits* by James Howe
Flashbacks	*Who Is Jesse Flood?* by Malachy Doyle *Racing the Past* by Sis Deans *Hush* by Jacqueline Woodson *Pictures of Hollis Woods* by Patricia Reilly Giff *A Northern Light* by Jennifer Donnelly

Some alternatives to traditional book reports are listed in Figure 13.4. Some of the suggestions are suited to individuals, others to groups of students.

Pictures and Collages

Students can make pictures and collages—artistic compositions made by pasting onto a background such items as fabric, string, fragments of paper, newspapers, and photographs—to illustrate a favorite story or poem. Having a variety of materials available to choose from in designing

Figure 13.4   Alternatives to Traditional Book Reports

Individual

1. List ten facts learned from this work of nonfiction.
2. Draw a picture of the main character in a major scene from this book. Then write a sentence below the picture that describes the scene.
3. Write a newspaper article summarizing this book. Be sure to include a title and to answer "who, what, when, where, and why."
4. Collect at least eight interesting words or phrases from your book. Tell what each means and why you think it is interesting.
5. Choose one of the main characters from this story. Tell the class the name of the character and five things that happened to him or her in the order that they happened. Use complete sentences.
6. Design and keep a word book in which you record interesting words, phrases, and sentences in each book you read for use in your own writing.
7. Select a character from each of two different stories you have read. Write or tell a story that might result from the interactions between these two characters.
8. Select a character from this story. Write interview questions for this character, based on what happened in the story and on what might have happened to the character after the story ended. Then, with a friend, tape the interview, with your friend being the interviewer and you being the character.
9. Select new vocabulary words from this book. Write each word on one card and the meaning of each word on another card. The cards may be designed to look like a feature symbolizing the story. For example, after reading *Donuthead* (2003) by Sue Stauffacher, design each word card to look like a doughnut and each meaning card to look like a filled doughnut. Then have your classmates try to match them.
10. Find out as much as you can about the topics that the author of this book writes about. Make a poster about this author to get others interested in his or her books. Use the author's website, if he or she has one.
11. Describe the author or book character you would like to meet in person. Explain why you want to meet this person or character.
12. Make a book cover for this book. Include an illustration, the book title, and author's name on the front. Design the illustration so that it is faithful to the story and will interest others in reading the book. On the front inside flap, write a story blurb, making sure not to give the story away. On the back inside flap, put your name and a description of your favorite part of the book. Display the book cover in the classroom reading center.
13. Plan a booktalk for this book. Broadcast your booktalk on the school sound system, or videotape or audiotape it for the school media center or class use.
14. Write a letter to another classmate to recommend this book. Tell why you liked the book, but don't tell the ending! Alternatively, write the letter to your classmates and post it on the bulletin board.
15. Select a favorite author and look up information about the author either online or in the library. Then write a brief biography of the person and list two or three of the author's best-known books. Tell why you believe this author's books will be remembered.

(continued)

Individual (*continued*)

16. Write the story's problem or conflict on 4" × 5" index cards. Tell how the author might have handled the problem differently. Finally, tell how the author did handle the problem.

17. Find objects that were part of this story. Place these objects in a bag. Then booktalk your story, and take out each object to show when appropriate.

18. Write a comparison of the movie and book versions of this story. Tell the similarities and differences and which version you preferred and why.

19. Contribute a card to the class book review file in which you write the title of this book, author, illustrator, and your review of the book. Tell what you liked and didn't like. Finally, give the book a 1-to 5-star rating.

20. Select a character from this work of historical fiction. Divide a page into two columns, and compare your life with the life of that character. Include as many similarities and differences as you can.

21. What was the main problem in this story? State the problem, how the main character dealt with it, and how you would have dealt with it differently.

22. After reading this biography, list the subject's good and not-so-good qualities.

23. Write a letter to the main character of this book giving him or her advice about dealing with future problems.

24. Pretend that you are the main character of this book. Think about how the events in the story changed you. In two paragraphs, describe yourself at the beginning and at the end of this story.

25. Look carefully at the cover illustration of this book. List the ways that you would change the illustration and why. If you wish, draw an improved cover illustration.

26. Go online or ask a librarian to help you find five other books for someone your age about the same topic as this book. Write the topic at the top of a page and list these titles. Display the list for others who might be interested in reading about this topic.

Small Group

1. Have a panel discussion for the class by four to six students who have read this book. Likely topics are why others would enjoy the book, why others would relate to the characters or theme, or what readers would gain from the book.

2. Select a brief, but important, scene from this book. Rewrite the scene as a readers' theatre script, and audiotape the group reading. Place the tape in the classroom listening center as a way to encourage others to read the book.

Whole Class

1. As a class, write news stories, personal ads, want ads, for sale ads, advice columns, editorials, comic strips, and sports stories based on the books you have read. Write the headline and a brief news article about the events leading up to the publication of this newspaper. Collate all contributions into a class newspaper.

2. (For near the end of a school year) Nominate your favorite books read this year. Booktalk any books that are not well known, then vote on the five class favorites. Advertise the winning books to other classes for summer reading.

their re-creations of literature increases students' enthusiasm and creativity. Paints, colored pencils, chalk, crayons, collage materials (cloth, yarn, lace, tissue paper), colored construction paper, and magazines with pictures and printed words for cutting up and shaping into pictures can be kept readily available for use in the classroom. Teachers foster good design by asking students to think about the purpose and desired effects and by pointing out interesting visual elements in other media, especially in picture books. For example, when students observe the different ways in which illustrators frame their pictures, outline figures, and use blank space and perspective for highlighting an object, they often can replicate and adapt these techniques for their own classroom design projects.

Teachers have often overused the activity of "draw a picture of the story" by assigning it too frequently, by not planning the activity adequately, and by permitting students little or no choice of media and project. An activity that is repeated to the point of monotony becomes little more than busywork to students. Remember that it may be unnecessary to have a response activity of any kind after reading a book or that a worthy response to a book would be finding another book by the same author and reading it next.

When more active response seems warranted, however, it is important to plan worthwhile ways for students to express those responses. Providing students with a choice of projects and media and then planning collaboratively with the students on the execution of the project are the roles the teacher needs to assume. Your art specialists and school and public librarians can be of great assistance in helping you plan response activities.

Murals

Murals are made from a long roll of paper mounted horizontally. The entire length of paper is usually divided into sections and often presents a chronology of the story events. Murals may feature a particular theme, such as animals from stories around the world, different kinds of homes the characters live in, personified dolls and toys from a unit on stories with personification, or various ways young story characters have overcome obstacles as they grow and mature. Groups of children decide on the theme or topic, design the segments, and allocate tasks to group members. Sometimes, students work directly on the mounted mural; other times they cut it into sections and work at tables then tape it back together for mounting. This device is well suited for literature response groups whose members collaborate in selecting, planning, and implementing the mural. The product is often dramatic and showy, offering the group members a feeling of real accomplishment.

Roller Movies

This technique produces a simulated movie or filmstrip of a story. The pictures are designed, frame by frame, on a long roll of paper. Once completed, each end of the paper is taped to a dowel rod or broom handle; then the paper is rolled onto the feeder rod so that the beginning frame is viewed first when the paper is unrolled. The ends of each rod are inserted into holes on the sides of a cardboard box so that the paper can be stretched from one roller to the other across the box opening and then rolled to the receiver rod to move the frames along. The box is turned on its side, television style, to face the audience, and the story unfolds as the frames are rolled onto the receiver rod. The group writes a script to go along with each frame. The need for group collaboration makes this an ideal project for literature response groups. Roller movies are useful to help students decide on the major events and their sequence in the story. Then the finished movie lends itself to story retellings.

Dioramas and Displays

A diorama is a three-dimensional display in which objects and figures are placed into a background or setting to create a scene. Dioramas are often made in classrooms by using shoeboxes set on the side, providing a framework on which to construct a setting, such as a floor, ceiling, and three walls of a room. Many materials may be used to make the figures, their background, furniture, and clothes, including modeling clay, collage materials, matchboxes, dried leaves, pine straw, and tiny dolls. Dioramas are especially well suited to individuals and pairs of students who may work alone or cooperatively in selecting and recreating in miniature an important scene from a story.

Displays are three-dimensional re-creations of a setting—a town or a battle scene, for instance—placed on a large flat surface, such as a table or piece of plywood. The use of clay and cardboard for figures, papier-mâché for hills, colored construction paper for lakes and land surfaces, and so on permits students to design impressive displays from story settings. More artistically talented students can be given opportunities to excel in these design activities.

Books and Big Books

Children can make their own stories and poems into books for a more finished presentation of their writing efforts. There are many different ways to make books in the classroom, ranging from the simple process of stapling together students' separate pictures on a topic with an illustrated cover to the more complex task of developing books with hard covers made of cardboard covered in clear or patterned adhesive paper or fabric, and then sewn together and bound for a "real book" look.

Big Books are often modeled after a favorite picture book that the class enjoyed, with the pictures drawn by students and the text printed by the teacher on 24" × 30" heavy paper or posterboard, which is then laminated, bound on metal rings, and hung on an easel. Many schools have laminators for use in these projects. Lamination is also done at many commercial copy and print shops at a moderate cost.

Making books is an activity that is most suited for individuals or pairs of students. However, a collaborative book organized around a theme or pattern can be made by a larger group in which each member contributes a story or poem. In this type of book, a table of contents with the names of each contributor offers recognition of all students while also calling students' attention to this useful part of a book. When students are first learning the steps of making books, considerable guidance from an adult is required. Parent volunteers and teacher aides can be shown how to provide this assistance. The step-by-step processes of making different types of books can be found in these sources:

- Guthrie, Bentley, and Arnsteen's *The Young Author's Do-It-Yourself Book: How to Write, Illustrate, and Produce Your Own Books* (1994) is a 64-page illustrated book for beginning writers with step-by-step instructions on how to write a fiction or nonfiction story, illustrate it, assemble it, and hand bind it.

- Johnson's *Get Writing! Creative Book-Making Projects for Children* (2006) is an extensive collection for student publishing. The projects have easy-to-follow directions with illustrations and are useful for teachers in elementary and middle school.
- Johnson's *Making Books* (2000), a 64-page illustrated book, offers thirty well-planned book projects, including some for every grade level.
- Marshall's *From Idea to Book* (2004) explains the process of making a book from beginning to end and prepares children, ages 5 to 8, for a bookmaking project.
- Stevens's *From Pictures to Words: A Book about Making a Book* (1995) is a picture book about how a book is made for students, ages 5 to 8.
- Stowell's *Step-by-Step Making Books* (1994) is an easy, helpful guide for making books, appropriate for students, ages 8 to 12.

Completed books need to be displayed for admiration and made available for reading by others. A special place in the reading corner can be reserved to exhibit student-made books.

Newspapers and Newsletters

A collaborative endeavor in which students write about the books they have been reading and tell about their book-related projects can result in class newspapers and newsletters. Each issue of the paper can focus on a different topic, such as favorite authors, illustrators, story characters, and poetic forms. In some intermediate-grade classrooms, a different literature response group accepts editing responsibilities for the newsletter each month, selecting the focus, soliciting manuscripts, designing pages, and making editorial decisions. The newsletters are sent home to parents with suggestions of good books to read and new authors to check out. Since computers are generally available in schools, individuals with word processing skills can usually be found, often among the students, to produce interesting newspapers and newsletters.

Time Lines, Maps, Diagrams, and Charts

A type of visual figure that details a period of time covered in a story is a *time line*. The figure is made by drawing a line on a long strip of mural paper, then placing the dates below the line at scaled intervals. The story events are logged in above the line. This graphic aid organizes the events of the story and can permit the students to compare events from a novel of historical fiction or from a biography with actual dates from history.

Time lines can be excellent visual aids when used in conjunction with reading aloud a progressive plot chapter book. The time line is set up with the dates, then the story events are recorded after each day's reading. The time line can also serve as a reminder of what has happened thus far as a review before beginning the next chapter.

Time lines can also be useful when students are reading a variety of material on a single period of history: biographies, historical fiction novels, and photo essays on World War II, for instance. Historical events from different sources can be compared for authenticity by using parallel time lines or by adding more tiers to the same time line. Individual students may develop time lines to follow the events of an entire series of books, such as science fiction novels and quest adventure stories.

Maps are especially suitable for charting the settings in chapter books of many genres. They can be designed by individuals or groups of students and make interesting and helpful visual aids for telling others about books. Some chapter books in which maps are included as part of the book can be used by students as models to imitate for drawing storymaps on other books. Some books with maps that can be used as models are *The Thief Lord* (2002) by Cornelia Funke, *Lewis and Clark and Me: A Dog's Tale* (2002) by Laurie Myers, *The Kite Rider: A Novel* (2001) by Geraldine McCaughrean, and *Stowaway* (2000) by Karen Hesse. Maps are also suitable for laying out the events in picture books and books with a circular journey motif in which the protagonist leaves home, encounters adversity, overcomes it, and returns home.

A *diagram* presents textual material in visual form and can be used to illustrate arrangements and relations within a story. Many information books use diagrams, and students can develop ideas for presenting information through diagrams by perusing these books. Diagrams can also be developed to show relationships found in book series and long works, such as the Arthurian legends. Teachers and students can use diagrams to display the progression of a story, which is especially useful to help students understand unusual plot twists. As an example, Kenneth Oppel's *Airborn* (2004) includes a diagram of an airship, an essential part of the fantasy.

Charts, sometimes referred to as *graphs,* give information in table form to show relationships, summarize information, and present facts in a capsule form. When students use nonfiction books for studying content areas, they can be encouraged to consider visual means for presenting and summarizing the information gained. Loreen Leedy's *The Great Graph Contest* (2005), a picture storybook about a contest to see who can make the best graph, also includes information on different types and uses for graphs and diagrams.

Jackdaws

Jackdaws are collections of artifacts or copies of realia from a particular historical period or event; jackdaws are often available in museums for study of a period of history, and some museums lend them to teachers for use in schools. The term *jackdaw* refers to a common European bird that is related to the crow and known to collect colorful objects for its nest. Educators have borrowed the term to refer to a teaching tool that can be used to connect historical books with the real events of the times depicted through concrete objects (Devitt, 1970). For example, a teacher may put together a jackdaw based on homesteaders in Oklahoma in the 1800s, then use the jackdaw to build background knowledge to introduce the study of the historical fiction novel *Stop the Train!* (2001) by Geraldine McCaughrean.

Jackdaws are made by collecting a wide array of related materials in their original form or in reproductions. Materials that are often collected are regional maps, photographs or models of homes, farms, machines, household furnishings, toys and dolls, kitchen tools, recipes for foods commonly eaten, newspapers and books of the era, clothing, modes of transportation, government of the time (president, congress, political parties, statehood), educational institutions, cultural artifacts such as songs, paintings, and architectural landmarks. After collection the realia are placed in a decorated box with labels and explanations attached, if desired. The jackdaw can be used as an extension activity for a book read in class as well as for building background. Many teachers enlist students in the development of jackdaws and share jackdaws with other teachers who are studying the same historical book.

Bulletin Boards

Designing and making bulletin boards provide groups of students with opportunities to demonstrate their book experiences in innovative ways. Planning bulletin boards and displays requires students to select an interesting and worthy focus or message to call attention to the display and to get the message across effectively. Students will appreciate seeing bulletin boards displaying their own book-related projects more than having sophisticated commercial displays about books.

Giving students choices of books to read and choices in the ways in which they respond to them is an essential component of a good curriculum in literature. This chapter presented a smorgasbord of ideas for having students experience literature and respond to those literary experiences.

Topics for Further Investigation

- Select a picture book or a scene from a novel and rewrite it into a script for readers' theatre as exemplified in this chapter. If possible, try the piece with a group of children. Evaluate your selection based on the children's responses.
- Select and learn a folktale for storytelling. If appropriate, develop props. Tell your story to a group of children and report your reactions to storytelling as a means of sharing literature. Also, report your students' reactions to the story.
- Review research conducted on shared reading, assisted reading, and paired reading with emergent readers and struggling readers.

 See the companion website at www.ablongman.com/lynchbrown6e for additional suggestions.

References

Agee, J. (2002). *Palindromania.* New York: Farrar.

Anderson, M. T. (2001). *Handel, who knew what he liked.* Illustrated by K. Hawkes. Cambridge, MA: Candlewick.

Armstrong, A. (2005). *Whittington.* New York: Random House.

Armstrong, J. (2006). *The American story: 100 true tales from American history.* Illustrated by R. Roth. New York: Knopf.

Avi. (2001). *Don't you know there's a war on?* New York: HarperCollins.

Ball, Johnny. (2005). *Go figure! A totally cool book about numbers.* New York: DK Publishing.

Balliett, B. (2004). *Chasing Vermeer.* Illustrated by Brett Helquist. New York: Scholastic.

Battle-Lavert, G. (2003). *Papa's mark.* Illustrated by C. Bootman. New York: Holiday.

Bauer, M. D. (1992). *What's your story? A young person's guide to writing fiction.* Boston: Houghton.

Bloor, E. (1997). *Tangerine.* San Diego: Harcourt.

Blume, J. (2002). *Double Fudge.* New York: Dutton.

Bodart, J. (1980). *Booktalk!* New York: H. W. Wilson.

Bredsdorff, B. (2004). *The crow-girl: The children of Crow Cove.* Translated from the Danish by F. Ingwersen. New York: Farrar.

Bridges, R., & Lundell, M. (1999). *Through my eyes.* New York: Scholastic.

Carlisle, L. R., Jackson, B. W., & George, A. (2006). Principles of social justice education: The social justice education in schools project. *Equity & Excellence in Education, 39*(1), 55–64.

Cherry, L. (1990). *The great kapok tree: A tale of the Amazon rainforest.* San Diego: Harcourt.

Cole, B. (2000). *Buttons.* New York: Farrar.

Collard, S. B. (2005). *The prairie builders: Reconstructing America's lost grasslands*. New York: Houghton.

Collier, B. (2000). *Uptown*. New York: Holt.

Cooney, B. (1982). *Miss Rumphius*. New York: Viking.

Coy, J. (2002). *Two old potatoes and me*. Illustrated by C. Fisher. New York: Knopf.

Creech, S. (2002). *Ruby Holler*. New York: HarperCollins.

Crossley-Holland, K. (2001). *The seeing stone*. New York: Arthur A. Levine.

Curtis, C. P. (1999). *Bud, not Buddy*. New York: Delacorte.

Cushman, K. (1994). *Catherine, called Birdy*. New York: Clarion.

D'Amico, C., & D'Amico, S. (2005). *Ella takes the cake*. New York: Scholastic.

Deans, S. (2001). *Racing the past*. New York: Holt.

DeFelice, C. (2003). *Under the same sky*. New York: Farrar.

Devitt, M. (Ed.). (1970). *Learning with jackdaws*. London: St. Paul's Press.

Donnelly, J. (2003). *A northern light*. San Diego: Harcourt.

Dowell, F. O. (2000). *Dovey Coe*. New York: Atheneum.

Doyle, M. (2002). *Who is Jesse Flood?* New York: Bloomsbury.

Dyer, J. (2002). *Little Brown Bear won't go to school*. Boston: Little, Brown.

Falconer, I. (2000). *Olivia*. New York: Atheneum.

Farmer, N. (2002). *The house of the scorpion*. New York: Atheneum.

Fleischman, P. (1993). *Bull Run*. New York: Harper-Collins.

Freeman, J. (2006). *Books kids will sit still for, 3: A read-aloud guide*. Portsmouth, NH: Libraries Unlimited.

Funke, C. (2002). *The thief lord*. Translated by O. Latsch. New York: Scholastic.

Fuqua, J. S. (2002). *Darby*. Cambridge, MA: Candlewick.

Gaiman, N. (2003). *The wolves in the walls*. New York: HarperCollins.

Gantos, J. (1998). *Joey Pigza swallowed the key*. New York: Farrar.

Giff, P. R. (2002). *Pictures of Hollis Woods*. New York: Wendy Lamb.

Greenberg, J., & Jordan, S. (1998). *Chuck Close, up close*. New York: DK Ink.

———. (2001). *Vincent Van Gogh: Portrait of an artist*. New York: Delacorte.

Greene, S. (2001). *Owen Foote, super spy*. Illustrated by M. Weston. New York: Clarion.

Grossman, B. (1989). *Tommy at the grocery store*. Illustrated by V. Chess. New York: Harper.

Guthrie, D., Bentley, N., & Arnsteen, K. K. (1994). *The young author's do-it-yourself book: How to write, illustrate, and produce your own books*. Brookfield, CT: Millbrook.

Haas, J. (2005). *Jigsaw Pony*. Illustrated by Y. Wu. New York: HarperCollins.

Hale, S. (2003). *Goose girl*. New York: Bloomsbury.

Henkes, K. (1991). *Chrysanthemum*. New York: Greenwillow.

———. (1987). *Sheila Rae the Brave*. New York: Greenwillow.

Hesse, K. (2000). *Stowaway*. New York: McElderry.

Hiaasen, C. (2002). *Hoot*. New York: Knopf.

Hicks, B. (2005). *Out of order*. New Milford, CT: Roaring Brook.

Hoberman, M. A. (2004). *You read to me, I'll read to you: Very short fairy tales to read together*. Illustrated by M. Emberley. Boston: Little, Brown.

Hoestlandt, J. (1995). *Star of fear, star of hope*. Illustrated by J. Kang. Translated by M. Polizzotti. New York: Walker.

Hoffman, A. (2003). *Green angel*. New York: Scholastic.

Hoffman, M. (1991). *Amazing Grace*. Illustrated by C. Binch. New York: Dial.

———. (2000). *Starring Grace*. Illustrated by C. Binch. New York: Fogelman.

Holdaway, D. (1982). Shared book experience: Teaching reading using favorite books. *Theory into practice, 21*, 293–300.

Hoskisson, K., Sherman, T. M., & Smith, L. L. (1974). Assisted reading and parent involvement. *The Reading Teacher, 27*, 710–714.

Howe, J. (2001). *The misfits*. New York: Atheneum.

Jackson, E. (2003). *It's back to school we go! First day stories from around the world*. Illustrated by J. D. Ellis. Brookfield, CT: Millbrook Press.

Jennings, P. (1996). *Faith and the electric dogs*. New York: Scholastic.

Johnson, A. (2000). *When mules flew on Magnolia Street*. Illustrated by J. Ward. New York: Knopf.

———. (2003). *The first part last*. New York: Simon & Schuster.

Johnson, P. (2000). *Making books*. Markham, Ontario: Pembroke.

———. (2006). *Get writing! Creative book-making projects for children*. Markham, Ontario: Pembroke.

Katzen, M. (2005). *Salad people and more real recipes*. Berkley, CA: Tricycle Press.

Keats, E. J. (1962). *The snowy day.* New York: Viking.

Knight. M. B., & Melnicove, M. (2000). *Africa is not a country.* Illustrated by A. S. O'Brien. Brookfield, CT: Millbrook Press.

Kohl, M. F. (1999). *Making make-believe: Fun props, costumes, and creative play ideas.* Beltsville, MD: Gryphon House.

Krull, K. (1993). *Lives of the musicians: Good times, bad times (and what the neighbors thought).* Illustrated by K. Hewitt. San Diego: Harcourt.

Kuskin, K. (2005). *So, what's it like to be a cat?* Illustrated by B. Lewin. New York: Atheneum.

Lasky, K. (1994). *The librarian who measured the earth.* Illustrated by K. Hawkes. Boston: Joy Street.

———. (2003). *The man who made time travel.* Illustrated by K. Hawkes. New York: Farrar.

Leavitt, M. (2003). *Tom Finder.* Calgary: Red Deer.

Lee, T. (2000). *Wolf tower.* New York: Dutton.

Leedy, L. (2005). *The great graph contest.* New York: Holiday.

LeGallienne R. (1969). I meant to do my work today. In L. Untermeyer (Ed.), *The Golden treasury of poetry.* Illustrated by J. W. Anglund. New York: Golden Press.

Lester, J. (2005). *Day of tears.* New York: Hyperion.

Levine, G. (1999). *Dave at night.* New York: Harper-Collins.

———. (1997). *Ella enchanted.* New York: Harper-Collins.

Lobel, A. (1970). *Frog and Toad are friends.* New York: Harper.

Lorbiecki, M. (2003). *Jackie's bat.* Illustrated by B. Pinkney. New York: Simon & Schuster.

Lowry, L. (1993). *The giver.* New York: Houghton.

———. (1989). *Number the stars.* New York: Houghton.

———. (2003). *The silent boy.* Boston: Houghton.

———. (2004). *Messenger.* Boston: Houghton.

Marshall, P. (2004). *From idea to book.* Minneapolis, MN: Lerner.

McCaslin, N. (1990). *Creative drama in the classroom* (5th ed.). New York: Longman.

McCaughrean, G. (2001). *The kite rider.* New York: HarperCollins.

———. (2001). *Stop the train!* New York: HarperCollins.

McNulty, F. (2005). *If you decide to go to the moon.* Illustrated by S. Kellogg. New York: Scholastic.

Montgomery, S. (2004). *The tarantula scientist.* Photographs by N. Bishop. Boston: Houghton.

Morrison, L. (2001). *Way to go! Sports poems.* Illustrated by S. Spellman. Honesdale, PA: Wordsong/Boyds Mills.

Mullis, I. V. S., Martin, M. O., Gonzalez, E. J., & Kennedy, A. M. (2003). *PIRLS 2001 international report: IEA's study of reading literacy achievement in primary schools.* Chestnut Hill, MA: Boston College.

Myers, L. (2002). *Lewis and Clark and me: A dog's tale.* Illustrated by M. Dooling. New York: Holt.

Nelson, K. (2005). *He's got the whole world in His hands.* New York: Dial.

Norris, L. (2000). *Albert and the angels.* Illustrated by M. Gerstein. New York: Farrar.

Offen, H. (1992). *Nice work, Little Wolf!* New York: Dutton.

Oppel, K. (2004). *Airborn.* New York: EOS.

Park, L. S. (2003). *The fire-keeper's son.* Illustrated by J. Downing. New York: Clarion.

Paterson, K. (2002). *Same stuff as stars.* New York: Clarion.

Pellowski, A. (1995). *The storytelling handbook: A young people's collection of unusual tales and helpful hints on how to tell them.* Illustrated by M. Stoberock. New York: Simon & Schuster.

Perkins, L. R. (2005). *Criss cross.* New York: Greenwillow.

Peters, S. T. (2005). *The battle against polio.* New York: Benchmark.

Petty, K. (2000). *The amazing pop-up geography book.* Illustrated by J. Maizels. New York: Dutton.

Polacco, P. (2001). *Mr. Lincoln's way.* New York: Philomel.

Pringle, L. (2001). *Global warming: The threat of earth's changing climate.* New York: SeaStar.

Raskin, E. (1978). *The westing game.* New York: Dutton.

Ray, D. (2003). *Ghost girl: A Blue Ridge Mountain story.* New York: Clarion.

Rees, C. (2001). *Witch child.* Cambridge, MA: Candlewick.

Reynolds, P. H. (2003). *The dot.* Cambridge, MA: Candlewick.

Ritter, J. H. (2003). *The boy who saved baseball.* New York: Philomel.

Robb, L. (2003). *Teaching reading in social studies, science, and math.* New York: Scholastic.

Rodda, E. (2002). *Rowan and the Zebak.* New York: Greenwillow.

Roop, P., & Roop, C. (2000). *Good-bye for today: The diary of a young girl at sea.* Illustrated by T. B. Allen. New York: Atheneum.

Rosenblatt, L. M. (1978). *The reader, the text, the poem: The transactional theory of the literary work.* Carbondale: Southern Illinois University Press.

Rotner, S., & Kreisler, K. (2003). *Everybody works.* Photographs by S. Rotner. Brookfield, CT: Millbrook Press.

Rounds, G. (1992). *Three little pigs and the big bad wolf.* New York: Holiday.

Ryan, P. M. (2002). *When Marian sang: The true recital of Marian Anderson.* Illustrated by B. Selznick. New York: Scholastic.

Schlosser, E., & Wilson, C. (2006). *Chew on this: Everything you don't want to know about fast food.* Boston: Houghton.

Scieszka, J. (1991). *The frog prince continued.* Illustrated by S. Johnson. New York: Viking.

———. (1989). *The true story of the 3 little pigs by A. Wolf.* Illustrated by L. Smith. New York: Viking.

———. (2004). *Science verse.* Illustrated by L. Smith. New York: Viking.

Sedgwick, M. (2001). *Floodland.* New York: Delacorte.

Shannon, D. (2002). *Duck on a bike.* New York: Blue Sky.

Shulevitz, U. (1974). *Dawn.* New York: Farrar.

Silverstein, A., Silverstein, V., & Nunn, L. S. (2002). *Global warming.* Brookfield, CT: Twenty-First Century.

Simon, S. (2005). *Guts: Our digestive system.* New York: HarperCollins.

Sís, P. (1998). *Tibet through the red box.* New York: Farrar.

Smith, D. J. (2002). *If the world were a village: A book about the world's people.* Illustrated by S. Armstrong. Toronto: Kids Can Press.

Spinelli, E. (2003). *Three pebbles and a song.* New York: Dial.

Stauffacher, S. (2003). *Donuthead.* New York: Knopf.

Stevens, J. (1995). *From pictures to words: A book about making a book.* New York: Holiday.

Stewart, S. (2001). *The journey.* Illustrated by D. Small. New York: Atheneum.

Stowell, C. (1994). *Step-by-step making books.* New York: Kingfisher.

Sullivan, P. (2001). *Maata's journal: A novel.* New York: Atheneum.

Trelease, J. (2006). *The read-aloud handbook.* (6th ed.). New York: Penguin.

Trivizas, E. (1993). *The three little wolves and the big bad pig.* Illustrated by H. Oxenbury. New York: Macmillan.

Van Draanen, W. (2001). *Flipped.* New York: Knopf.

Veatch, J. (1968). *How to teach reading with children's books* (2nd ed). New York: Richard C. Owen.

Waddell, M. (1992). *Farmer Duck.* Illustrated by H. Oxenbury. Cambridge, MA: Candlewick.

Walker, S. M. (1998). *The 18 penny goose.* Illustrated by E. Beier. New York: HarperCollins.

Willems, M. (2003). *Don't let the pigeon drive the bus.* New York: Hyperion.

Wise, B. (2001). *Whodunit math puzzles.* Illustrated by L. Corvino. New York: Sterling.

Wishinsky, F. (2002). *What's the matter with Albert? A story of Albert Einstein.* Illustrated by J. Lamontagne. Toronto: Maple Tree Press.

Wolf, A. (2006). *Immersed in verse: An informative, slightly irreverent & totally tremendous guide to living the poet's life.* Illustrated by T. Mourning. New York: Lark.

Wong, J. S. (2002). *You have to write.* Illustrated by T. Flavin. New York: Simon & Schuster.

Woodson, J. (2002). *Hush.* New York: Putnam.

Children's Book Awards

Some of the following awards were established prior to 1980. For access to the complete lists of winners and honor books for these awards, go to the companion website for this book at www.ablongman.com/lynchbrown6e.

National, General Awards

The United States

Caldecott Medal

This award, established in 1938 and sponsored by the Association for Library Service to Children division of the American Library Association, is given to the illustrator of the most distinguished picture book for children published in the United States during the preceding year. Only U.S. residents or citizens are eligible for this award. For access to the complete list of winners and honor books, go to the companion website for this book at www.ablongman.com/lynchbrown6e.

1980 *Ox-Cart Man* by Donald Hall. Illustrated by Barbara Cooney. Viking (Historical fiction [New England, 1800s], ages 5–8).

HONOR BOOKS:

Ben's Trumpet by Rachel Isadora. Greenwillow (Realism, ages 5–7).

The Treasure by Uri Shulevitz. Farrar (Traditional, ages 6–8).

The Garden of Abdul Gasazi by Chris Van Allsburg. Houghton (Fantasy, ages 6–8).

1981 *Fables* by Arnold Lobel. Harper (Modern folktales, ages 3–6).

HONOR BOOKS:

The Bremen-Town Musicians retold and illustrated by Ilse Plume. Doubleday (Traditional, ages 5–7).

The Grey Lady and the Strawberry Snatcher by Molly Bang. Four Winds (Fantasy/Wordless, ages 6–8).

Mice Twice by Joseph Low. Atheneum (Animal fantasy, ages 3–6).

Truck by Donald Crews. Greenwillow (Concept, ages 3–6).

1982 *Jumanji* by Chris Van Allsburg. Houghton (Fantasy, ages 6–8).

HONOR BOOKS:

A Visit to William Blake's Inn: Poems for Innocent and Experienced Travelers by Nancy Willard. Illustrated by Alice and Martin Provensen. Harcourt (Biography/Poetry, ages 7–10).

Where the Buffaloes Begin by Olaf Baker. Illustrated by Stephen Gammell. Warne (Traditional, ages 7–10).

On Market Street by Arnold Lobel. Illustrated by Anita Lobel. Greenwillow (Alphabet, ages 4–6).

Outside Over There by Maurice Sendak. Harper (Fantasy, ages 7–10).

1983 *Shadow* by Blaise Cendrars. Translated and illustrated by Marcia Brown. Scribner's (Traditional, ages 8–11).

HONOR BOOKS:

When I Was Young in the Mountains by Cynthia Rylant. Illustrated by Diane Goode. Dutton (Realism, ages 7–9).

A Chair for My Mother by Vera B. Williams. Greenwillow (Realism, ages 6–8).

1984 *The Glorious Flight: Across the Channel with Louis Blériot* by Alice and Martin Provensen. Viking (Historical fiction [France, 1909], ages 7–10).

HONOR BOOKS:

Ten, Nine, Eight by Molly Bang. Greenwillow (Counting, ages 3–6).

Little Red Riding Hood by the Brothers Grimm. Retold and illustrated by Trina Schart Hyman. Holiday (Traditional, ages 5–8).

1985 *Saint George and the Dragon* adapted by Margaret Hodges. Illustrated by Trina Schart Hyman. Little, Brown (Traditional, ages 9–12).

HONOR BOOKS:

Hansel and Gretel adapted by Rika Lesser. Illustrated by Paul O. Zelinksy. Dodd (Traditional, ages 6–8).

The Story of Jumping Mouse retold and illustrated by John Steptoe. Lothrop (Traditional, ages 7–10).

Have You Seen My Duckling? by Nancy Tafuri. Greenwillow (Animal fantasy, ages 4–6).

1986 *The Polar Express* by Chris Van Allsburg. Houghton (Fantasy, ages 5–9).

HONOR BOOKS:

The Relatives Came by Cynthia Rylant. Illustrated by Stephen Gammell. Bradbury (Realism, ages 6–9).

King Bidgood's in the Bathtub by Audrey Wood. Illustrated by Don Wood. Harcourt (Fantasy, ages 5–8).

1987 *Hey, Al* by Arthur Yorinks. Illustrated by Richard Egielski. Farrar (Fantasy, ages 7–10).

HONOR BOOKS:

The Village of Round and Square Houses by Ann Grifalconi. Little, Brown (Traditional, ages 7–9).

Alphabatics by Suse MacDonald. Bradbury (Alphabet, ages 4–6).

Rumpelstiltskin by the Brothers Grimm. Retold and illustrated by Paul O. Zelinsky. Dutton (Traditional, ages 6–9).

1988 *Owl Moon* by Jane Yolen. Illustrated by John Schoenherr. Philomel (Realism, ages 5–8).

HONOR BOOK:

Mufaro's Beautiful Daughters retold by John Steptoe. Lothrop (Traditional, ages 6–9).

1989 *Song and Dance Man* by Karen Ackerman. Illustrated by Stephen Gammell. Knopf (Realism, ages 7–10).

HONOR BOOKS:

Free Fall by David Wiesner. Lothrop (Fantasy/Wordless, ages 7–10).

Goldilocks and the Three Bears retold and illustrated by James Marshall. Dial (Modern folktale, ages 5–8).

Mirandy and Brother Wind by Patricia McKissack. Illustrated by Jerry Pinkney. Knopf (Traditional, ages 7–9).

The Boy of the Three-Year Nap by Diane Snyder. Illustrated by Allen Say. Houghton (Traditional, ages 7–10).

1990 *Lon Po Po: A Red-Riding Hood Story from China* translated and illustrated by Ed Young. Philomel (Traditional, ages 5–8).

HONOR BOOKS:

Hershel and the Hanukkah Goblins by Eric Kimmel. Illustrated by Trina Schart Hyman. Holiday (Modern folktale, ages 7–10).

The Talking Eggs adapted by Robert D. San Souci. Illustrated by Jerry Pinkney. Dial (Traditional, ages 6–9).

Bill Peet: An Autobiography by Bill Peet. Houghton (Biography, ages 7–10).

Color Zoo by Lois Ehlert. Lippincott (Concept, ages 3–6).

1991 *Black and White* by David Macaulay. Houghton (Mystery, ages 8–12).

HONOR BOOKS:

Puss in Boots by Charles Perrault. Illustrated by Fred Marcellino. Farrar (Traditional, ages 5–7).

"More, More, More." Said the Baby: 3 Love Stories by Vera Williams. Greenwillow (Realism, ages 3–5).

1992 *Tuesday* by David Wiesner. Clarion (Fantasy/Wordless, ages 7–10).

HONOR BOOK:

Tar Beach by Faith Ringgold. Crown (Multicultural [African-American], ages 6–9).

1993 *Mirette on the High Wire* by Emily Arnold McCully. Putnam (Realism, ages 7–9).

HONOR BOOKS:

Seven Blind Mice by Ed Young. Philomel (Modern folktale, ages 6–10).

The Stinky Cheese Man and Other Fairly Stupid Tales by Jon Scieszka and Lane Smith. Illustrated by Lane Smith. Viking (Modern folktales, ages 7–11).

Working Cotton by Sherley Anne Williams. Illustrated by Carole Byard. Harcourt (Realism [African-American], ages 7–9).

1994 *Grandfather's Journey* by Allen Say. Houghton (Biography, ages 7–9).

HONOR BOOKS:

Peppe the Lamplighter by Elisa Bartone. Illustrated by Ted Lewin. Lothrop (Realism, ages 7–9).

In the Small, Small Pond by Denise Fleming. Holt (Pattern, ages 5–7).

Owen by Kevin Henkes. Greenwillow (Animal fantasy, ages 5–7).

Raven: A Trickster Tale from the Pacific Northwest by Gerald McDermott. Harcourt (Traditional [Native American], ages 7–9).

Yo! Yes? by Chris Raschka. Orchard (Realism/Multicultural, ages 5–7).

1995 *Smoky Night* by Eve Bunting. Illustrated by David Diaz. Harcourt (Realism/Multicultural, ages 6–8).

HONOR BOOKS:

Swamp Angel by Anne Isaacs. Illustrated by Paul O. Zelinsky. Dutton (Modern folktale, ages 6–9).

John Henry by Julius Lester. Illustrated by Jerry Pinkney. Dial (Traditional, ages 6–9).

Time Flies by Eric Rohmann. Crown (Wordless, ages 6–9).

1996 *Officer Buckle and Gloria* by Peggy Rathmann. Putnam (Animal fantasy, ages 5–7).

HONOR BOOKS:

Alphabet City by Stephen T. Johnson. Viking (Concept, ages 7–9).

The Faithful Friend by Robert D. San Souci. Illustrated by Brian Pinkney. Simon & Schuster (Traditional, ages 10–14).

Tops & Bottoms by Janet Stevens. Harcourt (Traditional, ages 6–8).

Zin! Zin! Zin! A Violin by Lloyd Moss. Illustrated by Marjorie Priceman. Simon & Schuster (Concept, ages 5–7).

1997 *Golem* by David Wisniewski. Clarion (Traditional, ages 6–12).

HONOR BOOKS:

Hush! A Thai Lullaby by Minfong Ho. Illustrated by Holly Meade. Orchard (Poetry, ages 2–6).

The Graphic Alphabet by David Pelletier. Orchard (ABC/Art, ages 7–10).

The Paperboy by Dav Pilkey. Orchard (Realism, ages 8–10).

Starry Messenger by Peter Sís. Farrar (Biography, ages 9–14).

1998 *Rapunzel* by Paul O. Zelinsky. Dutton (Traditional, ages 7–10).

HONOR BOOKS:

The Gardener by Sarah Stewart. Illustrated by David Small. Farrar (Realism, ages 7–10).

Harlem by Walter Dean Myers. Illustrated by Christopher Myers. Scholastic (Poetry, ages 10–14).

There Was an Old Lady Who Swallowed a Fly by Simms Taback. Viking (Folk poem/Engineered, ages 5–7).

1999 *Snowflake Bentley* by Jacqueline Briggs Martin. Illustrated by Mary Azarian. Houghton (Biography, ages 8–12).

HONOR BOOKS:

Duke Ellington: The Piano Prince and His Orchestra by Andrea Davis Pinkney. Illustrated by Brian Pinkney. Hyperion (Biography, ages 8–10).

No, David! by David Shannon. Scholastic. (Realism/Pattern, ages 3–5).

Snow by Uri Shulevitz. Farrar (Realism, ages 4–6).

Tibet through the Red Box by Peter Sís. Farrar (Biography/Magic realism, ages 7 and up).

2000 *Joseph Had a Little Overcoat* by Simms Taback. Viking (Traditional/Pattern, ages 4–7).

HONOR BOOKS:

When Sophie Gets Angry—Really, Really Angry by Molly Bang. Scholastic (Realism, ages 4–6).

A Child's Calendar by John Updike. Illustrated by Trina Schart Hyman. Holiday (Poetry, ages 5–9).

The Ugly Duckling adapted and illustrated by Jerry Pinkney. Morrow (Modern folktale, ages 4–7).

Sector 7 by David Weisner. Clarion (Modern fantasy/Wordless, ages 5–9).

2001   *So You Want to Be President?* by Judith St. George. Illustrated by David Small. Philomel (Informational/Biography, ages 7–10).

HONOR BOOKS:

Casey at the Bat: A Ballad of the Republic Sung in the Year 1888 by Ernest L. Thayer. Illustrated by Christopher Bing. Handprint (Poetry, ages 7–12).

Click, Clack, Moo: Cows That Type by Doreen Cronin. Illustrated by Betsy Lewin. Simon & Schuster (Animal fantasy, ages 6–9).

Olivia by Ian Falconer. Atheneum (Animal fantasy, ages 4–8).

2002   *The Three Pigs* by David Wiesner. Clarion/Houghton Mifflin (Traditional, ages 5–7).

HONOR BOOKS:

The Dinosaurs of Waterhouse Hawkins by Barbara Kerley. Illustrated by Brian Selznick. Scholastic (Informational, ages 7–10).

Martin's Big Words: The Life of Dr. Martin Luther King, Jr. by Doreen Rappaport. Illustrated by Bryan Collier. Hyperion (Biography, ages 5–9).

The Stray Dog by Marc Simont. HarperCollins (Realism, ages 4–7).

2003   *My Friend Rabbit* by Eric Rohmann. Roaring Brook/Millbrook (Animal fantasy, ages 4–8).

HONOR BOOKS:

The Spider and the Fly by Mary Howitt. Illustrated by Tony DiTerlizzi. Simon & Schuster (Poetry, ages 6–12).

Hondo and Fabian by Peter McCarty. Holt (Realism, ages 3–6).

Noah's Ark by Jerry Pinkney. SeaStar/North-South (Traditional, ages 6–10).

2004   *The Man Who Walked Between the Towers* by Mordecai Gerstein. Roaring Brook/Millbrook (Realism, ages 5–9).

HONOR BOOKS:

Ella Sarah Gets Dressed by Margaret Chodos-Irvine. Harcourt (Realism, ages 3–5).

What Do You Do With a Tail Like This? by Steve Jenkins and Robin Page. Houghton Mifflin (Informational, ages 4–7).

Don't Let the Pigeon Drive the Bus by Mo Willems. Hyperion (Fantasy, ages 4–7).

2005   *Kitten's First Full Moon* by Kevin Henkes. Greenwillow (Animal fantasy, ages 3–5).

HONOR BOOKS:

The Red Book by Barbara Lehman. Houghton (Fantasy/Wordless, ages 4–9).

Coming on Home Soon by Jacqueline Woodson. Illustrated by E. B. Lewis. Putnam (Historical fiction [Rural U.S., World War II], ages 5–8).

Knuffle Bunny: A Cautionary Tale by Mo Willems. Hyperion (Realism, ages 3–6).

2006   *The Hello, Goodbye Window* by Norton Juster. Illustrated by Chris Raschka. Hyperion (Realism, ages 4–7).

HONOR BOOKS:

Rosa by Nikki Giovanni. Illustrated by Bryan Collier. Holt (Biography, ages 8–11).

Zen Shorts by Jon J. Muth. Scholastic (Traditional/Religious, ages 5–9).

Hot Air: The (Mostly) True Story of the First Hot-Air Balloon Ride by Marjorie Priceman. Atheneum (Historical fiction [1783], ages 4–8).

Song of the Water Boatman and Other Pond Poems by Joyce Sidman. Illustrated by Beckie Prange. Houghton (Poetry, ages 7–12).

2007   *Flotsam* by David Wiesner. Clarion (Fantasy/Wordless, ages 5–9).

HONOR BOOKS:

Gone Wild: An Endangered Animal Alphabet by David McLimans. Walker (ABC/Nonfiction, ages 8–14).

Moses: When Harriet Tubman Led Her People to Freedom by Carole Boston Weatherford. Illustrated by Kadir Nelson. Hyperion/Jump at the Sun (Biography, ages 7–11).

Newbery Medal

This award, established in 1922 and sponsored by the Association for Library Service to Children division of the American Library Association, is given to the author of the most distinguished contribution to children's literature published during the preceding year. Only U.S. citizens or residents are eligible for this award. For access to the complete list of winners and honor books, go to the companion website for this book at www.ablongman.com/lynchbrown6e.

1980   *A Gathering of Days: A New England Girl's Journal, 1830–32* by Joan Blos. Scribner's (Historical fiction [New England, 1830s], ages 11–15).

HONOR BOOK:

The Road from Home: The Story of an Armenian Girl by David Kherdian. Greenwillow (Historical fiction [Turkey, Greece, 1907–24], ages 11–15).

1981   *Jacob Have I Loved* by Katherine Paterson. Crowell (Historical fiction [USA, 1940s], ages 12–16).

HONOR BOOKS:

The Fledgling by Jane Langton. Harper (Modern fantasy, ages 9–11).

A Ring of Endless Light by Madeleine L'Engle. Farrar (Modern fantasy [science fiction], ages 10–12).

1982   *A Visit to William Blake's Inn: Poems for Innocent and Experienced Travelers* by Nancy Willard. Illustrated by Alice and Martin Provensen. Harcourt (Picture book biography/Poetry, ages 7–10).

HONOR BOOKS:

Ramona Quimby, Age 8 by Beverly Cleary. Morrow (Realism, ages 7–9).

Upon the Head of the Goat: A Childhood in Hungary, 1939–1944 by Aranka Siegal. Farrar (Historical fiction, ages 10–13).

1983   *Dicey's Song* by Cynthia Voigt. Atheneum (Realism, ages 9–12).

HONOR BOOKS:

The Blue Sword by Robin McKinley. Greenwillow (Modern fantasy [quest], ages 12–15).

Doctor De Soto by William Steig. Farrar (Picture book/Animal fantasy, ages 5–8).

Graven Images by Paul Fleischman. Harper (Modern fantasy, ages 10–12).

Homesick: My Own Story by Jean Fritz. Putnam (Biography, ages 9–11).

Sweet Whispers, Brother Rush by Virginia Hamilton. Philomel (Modern fantasy/Multicultural [African-American], ages 12–16).

1984   *Dear Mr. Henshaw* by Beverly Cleary. Morrow (Realism, ages 8–10).

HONOR BOOKS:

The Sign of the Beaver by Elizabeth George Speare. Houghton (Historical fiction [Colonial America], ages 9–11).

A Solitary Blue by Cynthia Voigt. Atheneum (Realism, ages 11–13).

Sugaring Time by Kathryn Lasky. Photographs by Christopher Knight. Macmillan (Informational, ages 9–13).

The Wish Giver by Bill Brittain. Harper (Modern fantasy, ages 9–12).

1985   *The Hero and the Crown* by Robin McKinley. Greenwillow (Modern fantasy [quest], ages 12–15).

HONOR BOOKS:

Like Jake and Me by Mavis Jukes. Illustrated by Lloyd Bloom. Knopf (Picture book/Realism, ages 7–9).

The Moves Make the Man by Bruce Brooks. Harper (Realism/Multicultural [African-American], ages 11–15).

One-Eyed Cat by Paula Fox. Bradbury (Realism, ages 9–12).

1986   *Sarah, Plain and Tall* by Patricia MacLachlan. Harper (Historical fiction [U.S. western frontier, 1800s], ages 8–10).

HONOR BOOKS:

Commodore Perry in the Land of the Shogun by Rhoda Blumberg. Lothrop (Informational, ages 9–13).

Dogsong by Gary Paulsen. Bradbury (Realism/Multicultural [Native American], ages 10–13).

1987   *The Whipping Boy* by Sid Fleischman. Greenwillow (Historical fiction [Medieval England], ages 9–11).

HONOR BOOKS:

On My Honor by Marion Dane Bauer. Clarion (Realism, ages 8–11).

Volcano: The Eruption and Healing of Mount St. Helens by Patricia Lauber. Bradbury (Informational, ages 8–13).

A Fine White Dust by Cynthia Rylant. Bradbury (Realism, ages 10–12).

1988   *Lincoln: A Photobiography* by Russell Freedman. Clarion (Biography, ages 8–12).

HONOR BOOKS:

After the Rain by Norma Fox Mazer. Morrow (Realism, ages 12–16).

Hatchet by Gary Paulsen. Bradbury (Realism, ages 9–13).

1989 *Joyful Noise: Poems for Two Voices* by Paul Fleischman. Harper (Poetry, ages 9–14).

HONOR BOOKS:

In the Beginning: Creation Stories from around the World by Virginia Hamilton. Harcourt (Traditional, ages 9–12).

Scorpions by Walter Dean Myers. Harper (Realism/ Multicultural [African-American, Hispanic-American], ages 10–13).

1990 *Number the Stars* by Lois Lowry. Houghton (Historical fiction [Denmark, 1940s], ages 8–10).

HONOR BOOKS:

Afternoon of the Elves by Janet Taylor Lisle. Orchard (Realism, ages 10–13).

Shabanu, Daughter of the Wind by Suzanne Fisher Staples. Knopf (Realism, ages 12–16).

The Winter Room by Gary Paulsen. Orchard (Realism, ages 10–13).

1991 *Maniac Magee* by Jerry Spinelli. Little, Brown (Realism, ages 9–13).

HONOR BOOK:

The True Confessions of Charlotte Doyle by Avi. Orchard (Historical fiction [England, USA, 1830], ages 10–13).

1992 *Shiloh* by Phyllis Reynolds Naylor. Atheneum (Animal realism, ages 8–10).

HONOR BOOKS:

Nothing but the Truth by Avi. Orchard (Realism, ages 10–14).

The Wright Brothers: How They Invented the Airplane by Russell Freedman. Holiday (Informational/Biography, ages 9–12).

1993 *Missing May* by Cynthia Rylant. Orchard (Realism, ages 10–13).

HONOR BOOKS:

The Dark-Thirty: Southern Tales of the Supernatural by Patricia McKissack. Knopf (Modern fantasy/Ghost stories [African-American], ages 8–12).

Somewhere in the Darkness by Walter Dean Myers. Scholastic (Realism [African-American], ages 11–14).

What Hearts by Bruce Brooks. HarperCollins (Realism, ages 11–14).

1994 *The Giver* by Lois Lowry. Houghton (Modern fantasy, ages 10–12).

HONOR BOOKS:

Crazy Lady by Jane Leslie Conly. HarperCollins (Realism, ages 10–12).

Dragon's Gate by Laurence Yep. HarperCollins (Historical fiction [China, USA West, 1860s], ages 12–14).

Eleanor Roosevelt: A Life of Discovery by Russell Freedman. Clarion (Biography, ages 10–14).

1995 *Walk Two Moons* by Sharon Creech. Harper-Collins (Realism [Native American], ages 11–14).

HONOR BOOKS:

Catherine, Called Birdy by Karen Cushman. Clarion (Historical fiction, [England, 1200s] ages 10–14).

The Ear, the Eye, and the Arm by Nancy Farmer. Orchard (Modern fantasy, ages 10–13).

1996 *The Midwife's Apprentice* by Karen Cushman. Clarion (Historical fiction [England, 1200s], ages 10–14).

HONOR BOOKS:

The Great Fire by Jim Murphy. Scholastic (Informational, ages 9–13).

The Watsons Go to Birmingham—1963 by Christopher Paul Curtis. Delacorte (Historical fiction [U.S. South, 1960s; African-American], ages 10–14).

What Jamie Saw by Carolyn Coman. Front Street (Realism, ages 10–14).

Yolanda's Genius by Carol Fenner. McElderry (Realism/Multicultural [African-American], ages 10–14).

1997 *The View from Saturday* by E. L. Konigsburg. Atheneum (Realism, ages 9–12).

HONOR BOOKS:

A Girl Named Disaster by Nancy Farmer. Orchard (Realism/Multicultural [Black African], ages 12–14).

The Moorchild by Eloise McGraw. McElderry/ Simon & Schuster (Modern fantasy, ages 9–12).

The Thief by Megan Whalen Turner. Greenwillow (Modern fantasy, ages 12–16).

Belle Prater's Boy by Ruth White. Farrar (Realism, ages 10–12).

1998 *Out of the Dust* by Karen Hesse. Scholastic (Historical fiction [USA, 1920–1934], ages 13–16).

HONOR BOOKS:

Lily's Crossing by Patricia Reilly Giff. Delacorte (Historical fiction [United States, 1944], ages 9–11).

Ella Enchanted by Gail Carson Levine. Harper-Collins (Modern fantasy, ages 9–12).

Wringer by Jerry Spinelli. HarperCollins (Realism, ages 9–12).

1999 *Holes* by Louis Sachar. Farrar (Realism, ages 10–13).

HONOR BOOK:

A Long Way from Chicago by Richard Peck. Dial (Historical fiction [United States, 1930s], ages 9–12).

2000 *Bud, Not Buddy* by Christopher Paul Curtis. Delacorte (Multicultural [African-American], ages 9–12).

HONOR BOOKS:

Getting Near to Baby by Audrey Couloumbis. Putnam (Realism, ages 10–12).

26 Fairmount Avenue by Tomie dePaola. Putnam (Biography, ages 7–9).

Our Only May Amelia by Jennifer L. Holm. HarperCollins (Historical fiction [United States, 1899], ages 10–14).

2001 *A Year Down Yonder* by Richard Peck. Dial (Historical fiction [United States, 1930s], ages 10–14).

HONOR BOOKS:

Because of Winn Dixie by Kate DiCamillo. Candlewick (Animal realism, ages 8–12).

Hope Was Here by Joan Bauer. Putnam (Realism, ages 12–14).

Joey Pigza Loses Control by Jack Gantos. Farrar (Realism, ages 9–12).

The Wanderer by Sharon Creech. HarperCollins (Realism, ages 12–14).

2002 *A Single Shard* by Linda Sue Park. Clarion/ Houghton (Realism, ages 10–14).

HONOR BOOKS:

Everything on a Waffle by Polly Horvath. Farrar (Realism, ages 12–14).

Carver: A Life In Poems by Marilyn Nelson. Front Street (Poetry/Biography, ages 12–14).

2003 *Crispin: The Cross of Lead* by Avi. Hyperion (Modern fantasy, ages 8–12).

HONOR BOOKS:

The House of the Scorpion by Nancy Farmer. Atheneum (Modern fantasy, ages 11–14).

Pictures of Hollis Woods by Patricia Reilly Giff. Random House (Realism, ages 10–13).

Hoot by Carl Hiaasen. Knopf (Realism, ages 9–12).

A Corner of the Universe by Ann M. Martin. Scholastic (Realism, ages 11–14).

Surviving the Applewhites by Stephanie S. Tolan. HarperCollins (Realism, ages 12–16).

2004 *The Tale of Despereaux: Being the Story of a Mouse, a Princess, Some Soup, and a Spool of Thread* by Kate DiCamillo. Illustrated by Timothy Basil Ering. Candlewick (Modern fantasy, ages 5–8).

HONOR BOOKS:

Olive's Ocean by Kevin Henkes. Greenwillow (Realism, ages 9–12).

An American Plague: The True and Terrifying Story of the Yellow Fever Epidemic of 1793 by Jim Murphy. Clarion (Informational, ages 9–14).

2005 *Kira-Kira* by Cynthia Kadohata. Atheneum (Historical fiction [1950s Georgia], Multicultural [Japanese-American], ages 11–14).

HONOR BOOKS:

Al Capone Does My Shirts by Gennifer Choldenko. Putnam (Realism, Special Challenges [Autism], ages 11–14).

The Voice that Challenged a Nation: Marian Anderson and the Struggle for Equal Rights by Russell Freedman. Clarion (Photo-biography, ages 11–14).

Lizzie Bright and the Buckminster Boy by Gary D. Schmidt. Clarion (Historical fiction [Maine, 1912], ages 13–16).

2006 *Criss Cross* by Lynne Rae Perkins. Greenwillow (Realism, ages 12–15).

HONOR BOOKS:

Whittington by Alan Armstrong. Illustrated by S. D. Schindler. Random (Traditional, Animal fantasy, Special challenges [Dyslexia], ages 9–14).

Hitler Youth: Growing Up in Hitler's Shadow by Susan Campbell Bartoletti. Scholastic (Collected biography, ages 11–15).

Princess Academy by Shannon Hale. Bloomsbury (Modern fantasy, ages 12–14).

Show Way by Jacqueline Woodson. Illustrated by Hudson Talbott. Putnam (Multicultural [African-American], ages 7–12).

2007 *The Higher Power of Lucky* by Susan Patron. Illustrated by Matt Phelan. Simon & Schuster (Realism, ages 9–12).

HONOR BOOKS:

Penny from Heaven by Jennifer L. Holm. Random (Mixed genre: Realism; Autobiography; Historical fiction [1953 Brooklyn], ages 11–14).

Hattie Big Sky by Kirby Larson. Delacorte (Historical fiction [Montana, 1918], ages 12–16).

Rules by Cynthia Lord. Scholastic (Realism: Mental challenges/Autism, ages 9–13).

Boston Globe—Horn Book Awards

These awards, established in 1967 and sponsored by *The Boston Globe* and *The Horn Book Magazine,* are given to an author for outstanding fiction or poetry for children, to an illustrator for outstanding illustration in a children's book, and, since 1976, to an author for outstanding nonfiction for children. For access to the complete list of winners, go to the companion website for this book at www.ablongman.com/lynchbrown6e.

1980 FICTION: *Conrad's War* by Andrew Davies. Crown.

NONFICTION: *Building: The Fight against Gravity* by Mario Salvadori. Atheneum/McElderry.

ILLUSTRATION: *The Garden of Abdul Gasazi* by Chris Van Allsburg. Houghton.

1981 FICTION: *The Leaving* by Lynn Hall. Scribner's.

NONFICTION: *The Weaver's Gift* by Kathryn Lasky. Warne.

ILLUSTRATION: *Outside over There* by Maurice Sendak. Harper.

1982 FICTION: *Playing Beatie Bow* by Ruth Park. Atheneum.

NONFICTION: *Upon the Head of the Goat: A Childhood in Hungary, 1939–1944* by Aranka Siegal. Farrar.

ILLUSTRATION: *A Visit to William Blake's Inn: Poems for Innocent and Experienced Travelers* by Nancy Willard. Illustrated by Alice and Martin Provensen. Harcourt.

1983 FICTION: *Sweet Whispers, Brother Rush* by Virginia Hamilton. Philomel.

NONFICTION: *Behind Barbed Wire: The Imprisonment of Japanese Americans during World War II.* by Daniel S. Davis. Dutton.

ILLUSTRATION: *A Chair for My Mother* by Vera B. Williams. Greenwillow.

1984 FICTION: *A Little Fear* by Patricia Wrightson. McElderry/Atheneum.

NONFICTION: *The Double Life of Pocahontas* by Jean Fritz. Putnam.

ILLUSTRATION: *Jonah and the Great Fish* retold and illustrated by Warwick Hutton. McElderry/Atheneum.

1985 FICTION: *The Moves Make the Man* by Bruce Brooks. Harper.

NONFICTION: *Commodore Perry in the Land of the Shogun* by Rhoda Blumberg. Lothrop.

ILLUSTRATION: *Mama Don't Allow* by Thatcher Hurd. Harper.

1986 FICTION: *In Summer Light* by Zibby Oneal. Viking Kestrel.

NONFICTION: *Auks, Rocks, and the Odd Dinosaur* by Peggy Thomson. Crowell.

ILLUSTRATION: *The Paper Crane* by Molly Bang. Greenwillow.

1987 FICTION: *Rabble Starkey* by Lois Lowry. Houghton.

NONFICTION: *Pilgrims of Plimoth* by Marcia Sewall. Atheneum.

ILLUSTRATION: *Mufaro's Beautiful Daughters* by John Steptoe. Lothrop.

1988 FICTION: *The Friendship* by Mildred Taylor. Dial.

NONFICTION: *Anthony Burns: The Defeat and Triumph of a Fugitive Slave* by Virginia Hamilton. Knopf.

ILLUSTRATION: *The Boy of the Three-Year Nap* by Diane Snyder. Illustrated by Allen Say. Houghton.

1989 FICTION: *The Village by the Sea* by Paula Fox. Orchard.

NONFICTION: *The Way Things Work* by David Macaulay. Houghton.

ILLUSTRATION: *Shy Charles* by Rosemary Wells. Dial.

1990 FICTION: *Maniac Magee* by Jerry Spinelli. Little, Brown.

NONFICTION: *The Great Little Madison* by Jean Fritz. Putnam.

ILLUSTRATION: *Lon Po Po: A Red-Riding Hood Story from China* retold and illustrated by Ed Young. Philomel.

1991 FICTION: *The True Confessions of Charlotte Doyle* by Avi. Orchard.

NONFICTION: *Appalachia: The Voices of Sleeping Birds* by Cynthia Rylant. Illustrated by Barry Moser. Harcourt.

ILLUSTRATION: *The Tale of the Mandarin Ducks* retold by Katherine Paterson. Illustrated by Leo and Diane Dillon. Lodestar.

1992 FICTION: *Missing May* by Cynthia Rylant, Orchard.

NONFICTION: *Talking with Artists* by Pat Cummings. Bradbury.

ILLUSTRATION: *Seven Blind Mice* by Ed Young. Philomel.

1993 FICTION: *Ajeemah and His Son* by James Berry. Harper.

NONFICTION: *Sojourner Truth: Ain't I a Woman?* by Patricia and Fredrick McKissack. Scholastic.

ILLUSTRATION: *The Fortune-Tellers* by Lloyd Alexander. Illustrated by Trina Schart Hyman. Dutton.

1994 FICTION: *Scooter* by Vera B. Williams. Greenwillow.

NONFICTION: *Eleanor Roosevelt: A Life of Discovery* by Russell Freedman. Clarion.

ILLUSTRATION: *Grandfather's Journey* by Allen Say. Houghton.

1995 FICTION: *Some of the Kinder Planets* by Tim Wynne-Jones. Orchard.

NONFICTION: *Abigail Adams: Witness to a Revolution* by Natalie S. Bober. Atheneum.

ILLUSTRATION: *John Henry* retold by Julius Lester. Illustrated by Jerry Pinkney. Dial.

1996 FICTION: *Poppy* by Avi. Illustrated by Brian Floca. Orchard.

NONFICTION: *Orphan Train Rider: One Boy's True Story* by Andrea Warren. Houghton.

ILLUSTRATION: *In the Rain with Baby Duck* by Amy Hest. Illustrated by Jill Barton. Candlewick.

1997 FICTION: *The Friends* by Kazumi Yumoto. Farrar.

NONFICTION: *A Drop of Water: A Book of Science and Wonder* by Walter Wick. Scholastic.

ILLUSTRATION: *The Adventures of Sparrow Boy* by Brian Pinkney. Simon & Schuster.

1998 FICTION: *The Circuit: Stories from the Life of a Migrant Child* by Francisco Jiménez. University of New Mexico Press.

NONFICTION: *Leon's Story* by Leon Walter Tillage. Illustrated by Susan L. Roth. Farrar.

ILLUSTRATION: *And If the Moon Could Talk* by Kate Banks. Illustrated by Georg Hallensleben. Farrar.

1999 FICTION: *Holes* by Louis Sachar. Farrar.

NONFICTION: *The Top of the World: Climbing Mount Everest* by Steve Jenkins. Houghton.

ILLUSTRATION: *Red-Eyed Tree Frog* by Joy Cowley. Illustrated with photographs by Nic Bishop. Scholastic.

2000   FICTION: *The Folk Keeper* by Franny Billingsley. Atheneum.

NONFICTION: *Sir Walter Ralegh and the Quest for El Dorado* by Marc Aronson. Clarion.

ILLUSTRATION: *Henry Hikes to Fitchburg* by D. B. Johnson. Houghton.

2001   FICTION AND POETRY: *Carver: A Life In Poems* by Marilyn Nelson. Front Street.

NONFICTION: *The Longitude Prize* by Joan Dash. Illustrated by Dušan Petricic. Farrar.

ILLUSTRATION: *Cold Feet* by Cynthia DeFelice. Illustrated by Robert Andrew Parker. DK Ink.

2002   FICTION AND POETRY: *Lord of the Deep* by Graham Salisbury. Delacorte.

NONFICTION: *This Land was Made for You and Me: The Life and Songs of Woody Guthrie* by Elizabeth Partridge. Viking.

ILLUSTRATION: *"Let's Get a Pup!" Said Kate* by Bob Graham. Candlewick.

2003   FICTION AND POETRY: *The Jamie and Angus Stories* by Anne Fine. Illustrated by Penny Dale. Candlewick.

NONFICTION: *Fireboat: The Heroic Adventures of the John J. Harvey* by Maira Kalman. Putnam.

ILLUSTRATION: *Big Momma Makes the World* by Phyllis Root. Illustrated by Helen Oxenbury. Candlewick.

2004   FICTION AND POETRY: *The Fire-Eaters* by David Almond. Delacorte.

NONFICTION: *An American Plague: The True and Terrifying Story of the Yellow Fever Epidemic of 1793* by Jim Murphy. Clarion.

ILLUSTRATION: *The Man Who Walked between the Towers* by Mordicai Gerstein. Roaring Brook.

2005   FICTION AND POETRY: *The Schwa Was Here* by Neal Schusterman. Dutton.

NONFICTION: *The Race to Save the Lord God Bird* by Phillip Hoose. Farrar.

ILLUSTRATION: *Traction Man Is Here!* by Mini Grey. Knopf.

2006   FICTION AND POETRY: *The Miraculous Journey of Edward Tulane* by Kate DiCamillo. Illustrated by Bagram Ibatoulline. Candlewick.

NONFICTION: *If You Decide to Go to the Moon* by Faith McNulty. Illustrated by Steven Kellogg. Scholastic.

ILLUSTRATION: *Leaf Man* by Lois Ehlert. Harcourt.

National Book Award for Young People's Literature

This award, sponsored by the National Book Foundation, is presented annually to recognize what is judged to be the outstanding contribution to children's literature, in terms of literary merit, published during the previous year. The award committee considers books of all genres written for children and young adults by U.S. writers. The award, which was added to the U.S. National Book Awards in 1996, carries a $10,000 cash prize.

1996   *Parrot in the Oven: Mi Vida* by Victor Martinez. HarperCollins.

1997   *Dancing on the Edge* by Han Nolan. Harcourt.

1998   *Holes* by Louis Sachar. Farrar.

1999   *When Zachary Beaver Came to Town* by Kimberley Willis Holt. Holt.

2000   *Homeless Bird* by Gloria Whelan. HarperCollins.

2001   *True Believer* by Virginia Euwer Wolff. Atheneum.

2002   *The House of the Scorpion* by Nancy Farmer. Atheneum.

2003   *The Canning Season* by Polly Horvath. Farrar.

2004   *Godless* by Pete Hautman. Simon & Schuster.

2005   *The Penderwicks* by Jeanne Birdsall. Knopf.

2006   *The Astonishing Life of Octavian Nothing, Traitor to the Nation, Vol. 1: The Pox Party* by M. T. Anderson. Candlewick.

Great Britain

Kate Greenaway Medal

This award, established in 1955 and sponsored by the Chartered Institute of Library and Information

Professionals, is given to the illustrator of the most distinguished work in illustration in a children's book first published in the United Kingdom during the preceding year. For access to the complete list of winners, go to the companion website for this book at www.ablongman.com/lynchbrown6e.

1980 *The Haunted House* by Jan Piénkowski. Heinemann.

1981 *Mr. Magnolia* by Quentin Blake. Jonathan Cape.

1982 *The Highwayman* by Alfred Noyes. Illustrated by Charles Keeping. Oxford.

1983 *Long Neck and Thunder Foot.* Kestrel; and *Sleeping Beauty and Other Favorite Fairy Tales.* Gollancz. Both illustrated by Michael Foreman.

1984 *Gorilla* by Anthony Browne. Julia MacRae Books.

1985 *Hiawatha's Childhood* by Errol LeCain. Faber.

1986 *Sir Gawain and the Loathly Lady* by Selina Hastings. Illustrated by Juan Wijngaard. Walker.

1987 *Snow White in New York* by Fiona French. Oxford.

1988 *Crafty Chameleon* by Mwenye Hadithi. Illustrated by Adrienne Kennaway. Hodder & Stoughton.

1989 *Can't You Sleep, Little Bear?* by Martin Waddell. Illustrated by Barbara Firth. Walker.

1990 *War Boy: A Country Childhood* by Michael Foreman. Arcade.

1991 *The Whale's Song* by Dyan Sheldon. Illustrated by Gary Blythe. Dial.

1992 *The Jolly Christmas Postman* by Janet and Allan Ahlberg. Heinemann.

1993 *Zoo* by Anthony Browne. Julia MacRae.

1994 *Black Ships before Troy* retold by Rosemary Sutcliff. Illustrated by Alan Lee. Frances Lincoln.

1995 *Way Home* by Libby Hathorn. Illustrated by Gregory Rogers. Random House.

1996 *The Christmas Miracle of Jonathon Toomey* by Susan Wojciechowski. Illustrated by P. J. Lynch. Walker.

1997 *The Baby Who Wouldn't Go to Bed* by Helen Cooper. Doubleday.

1998 *When Jessie Came Across the Sea* by Amy Hest. Illustrated by P. J. Lynch. Candlewick.

1999 *Pumpkin Soup* by Helen Cooper. Farrar.

2000 *Alice's Adventures in Wonderland* by Lewis Carroll. Illustrated by Helen Oxenbury. Walker.

2001 *I Will Never Not Ever Eat a Tomato* by Lauren Child. Orchard.

2002 *Pirate Diary* by Chris Riddell. Walker.

2003 *Jethro Byrd—Fairy Child* by Bob Graham. Walker.

2004 *Ella's Big Chance* by Shirley Hughes. The Bodley Head.

2005 *Jonathan Swift's "Gulliver"* by Martin Jenkins. Illustrated by Chris Riddell. Walker.

2006 *Wolves* by Emily Gravett. Macmillan.

Carnegie Medal

This award, established in 1936 and sponsored by the Chartered Institute of Library and Information Professionals, is given to the author of the most outstanding children's book first published in English in the United Kingdom during the preceding year. For access to the complete list of winners, go to the companion website for this book at www.ablongman .com/lynchbrown6e.

1980 *Tulku* by Peter Dickinson. Dutton.

1981 *City of Gold* by Peter Dickinson. Gollancz.

1982 *The Scarecrows* by Robert Westall. Chatto and Windus.

1983 *The Haunting* by Margaret Mahy. Dent.

1984 *Handles* by Jan Mark. Kestrel.

1985 *The Changeover* by Margaret Mahy. Dent.

1986 *Storm* by Kevin Crossley-Holland. Heinemann.

1987 *Granny Was a Buffer Girl* by Berlie Doherty. Methuen.

1988 *The Ghost Drum* by Susan Price. Faber.

1989 *Pack of Lies* by Geraldine McCaughrean. Oxford.

1990 *My War with Goggle-Eyes* by Anne Fine. Joy Street.

1991 *Wolf* by Gillian Cross. Oxford.

1992 *Dear Nobody* by Berlie Doherty. Hamish Hamilton.

1993 *Flour Babies* by Anne Fine. Hamish Hamilton.

1994 *Stone Cold* by Robert Swindells. Hamish Hamilton.

1995 *Whispers in the Graveyard* by Theresa Bresling. Methuen.

1996 *Dark Materials: Book 1, Northern Lights* by Philip Pullman. Scholastic.

1997 *Junk* by Melvin Burgess. Andersen.

1998 *River Boy* by Tim Bowler. Oxford.

1999 *Skellig* by David Almond. Delacorte.

2000 *Postcards from No Man's Land* by Aidan Chambers. Bodley Head.

2001 *The Other Side of Truth* by Beverly Naidoo. Puffin/HarperCollins.

2002 *The Amazing Maurice and His Educated Rodents* by Terry Pratchett. Doubleday/HarperCollins.

2003 *Ruby Holler* by Sharon Creech. Bloomsbury/HarperCollins.

2004 *A Gathering Light* by Jennifer Donnelly. Bloomsbury.

2005 *Millions* by Frank Cottrell Boyce. Macmillan.

2006 *Tamar* by Mal Peet. Walker.

Canada

The Governor General's Literary Awards

The Governor General's Literary Awards were inaugurated in 1937, with separate prizes for children's literature (text and illustration) being added in 1987. The Canada Council for the Arts assumed responsibility for funding, administering, and adjudicating the awards in 1959, and added prizes for works written in French. Monetary prizes were introduced in 1951. The current prize to winners in each category—$15,000—dates from 2000. In addition, publishers of the winning books receive $3,000 to assist with promotion.

1987 ILLUSTRATION: *Rainy Day Magic* by Marie-Louise Gay. Stoddart.

TEXT: *Galahad Schwartz and the Cockroach Army* by Morgan Nyberg. Douglas & McIntyre.

1988 ILLUSTRATION: *Amos's Sweater* by Janet Lunn. Illustrated by Kim LeFave. Douglas & McIntyre.

TEXT: *The Third Magic* by Welwyn Wilton Katz. Douglas & McIntyre.

1989 ILLUSTRATION: *The Magic Paintbrush* by Robin Muller. Doubleday Canada.

TEXT: *Bad Boy* by Diana Wieler. Douglas & McIntyre.

1990 ILLUSTRATION: *The Orphan Boy* by Tololwa Mollel. Illustrated by Paul Morin. Oxford.

TEXT: *Redwork* by Michael Bedard. Lester & Orpen Dennys.

1991 ILLUSTRATION: *Doctor Kiss Says Yes* by Teddy Jam. Illustrated by Joanne Fitzgerald. Groundwood.

TEXT: *Pick-Up Sticks* by Sarah Ellis. Groundwood.

1992 ILLUSTRATION: *Waiting for the Whales* by Sheryl McFarlane. Illustrated by Ron Lightburn. Orca.

TEXT: *Hero of Lesser Causes* by Julie Johnson. Lester.

1993 ILLUSTRATION: *Sleep Tight, Mrs. Ming* by Sharon Jennings. Illustrated by Mireille Levert. Annick.

TEXT: *Some of the Kinder Planets* by Tim Wynne-Jones. Groundwood.

1994 ILLUSTRATION: *Josepha: A Prairie Boy's Story* by Jim McGugen. Illustrated by Murray Kimber. Red Deer College Press.

TEXT: *Adam and Eve and Pinch-Me* by Julie Johnson. Lester.

1995 ILLUSTRATION: *The Last Quest of Gilgamesh* by Ludmila Zeman, reteller. Tundra.

TEXT: *The Maestro* by Tim Wynne-Jones. Groundwood.

1996 ILLUSTRATION: *The Rooster's Gift* by Pam Conrad. Illustrated by Eric Beddows. Groundwood.

TEXT: *Ghost Train* by Paul Yee. Groundwood.

1997 ILLUSTRATION: *The Party* by Barbara Reid. Scholastic Canada.

TEXT: *Awake and Dreaming* by Kit Pearson. Viking.

1998 ILLUSTRATION: *A Child's Treasury of Nursery Rhymes* by Kady MacDonald Denton. Kids Can.

TEXT: *The Hollow Tree* by Janet Lunn. Knopf Canada.

1999 ILLUSTRATION: *The Great Poochini* by Gary Clement. Groundwood.

TEXT: *A Screaming Kind of Day* by Rachna Gilmore. Fitzhenry & Whiteside.

2000 ILLUSTRATION: *Yuck, a Love Story* by Don Gillmore. Illustrated by Marie-Louise Gay. Stoddart Kids.

TEXT: *Looking for X* by Deborah Ellis. Groundwood.

2001 ILLUSTRATION: *An Island in the Soup* by Mireille Levert. Groundwood.

TEXT: *Dust* by Arthur Slade. HarperCollins Canada.

2002 ILLUSTRATION: *Alphabeasts* by Wallace Edwards. Kids Can.

TEXT: *True Confessions of a Heartless Girl* by Martha Brooks. Groundwood.

2003 ILLUSTRATION: *The Song within My Heart* by Dave Bouchard. Illustrated by Allen Sapp. Raincoast.

TEXT: *Stitches* by Glen Huser. Groundwood.

2004 ILLUSTRATION: *Jabberwocky* by Lewis Carroll. Illustrated by Stéphane Jorisch. Kids Can.

TEXT: *Airborn* by Kenneth Oppel. Harper-Collins.

2005 ILLUSTRATION: *Imagine a Day* by Sarah L. Thomson. Illustrated by Rob Gonsalves. Atheneum.

TEXT: *The Crazy Man* by Pamela Porter. Groundwood.

2006 ILLUSTRATION: *Ancient Thunder* by Leo Yerxa. Groundwood.

TEXT: *Pirate's Passage* by William Gilkerson. Trumpeter.

Australia

Australian Children's Books of the Year Awards

The Children's Book Council of Australia sponsors five awards for excellence in children's books: the Picture Book of the Year Award (established in 1956); the Book of the Year for Early Childhood Award (established in 2001); the Book of the Year for Younger Readers Award (established in 1982); the Book of the Year for Older Readers Award (established in 1946); and the Eve Pownall Award for Information Books (not listed here). For access to the complete lists of winners, go to the companion website for this book at www.ablongman.com/lynchbrown6e.

Australian Picture Book of the Year Award

(May be for mature readers.)

1980 *One Dragon's Dream* by Peter Pavey. Nelson.

1981 No award

1982 *Sunshine* by Jan Ormerod. Kestrel.

1983 *Who Sank the Boat?* by Pamela Allen. Nelson.

1984 *Bertie and the Bear* by Pamela Allen. Nelson.

1985 No award

Highly commended: *The Inch Boy* by Junko Morimoto. Collins.

1986 *Felix and Alexander* written and illustrated by Terry Denton. Oxford.

1987 *Kojuro and the Bears* adapted by Helen Smith. Illustrated by Junko Morimoto. Collins.

1988 *Crusher Is Coming!* by Bob Graham. Lothian.

1989 *Drac and the Gremlins* by Allan Baillie. Illustrated by Jane Tanner. Viking/Kestrel.

The Eleventh Hour by Graeme Base. Viking/Kestrel.

1990 *The Very Best of Friends* by Margaret Wild. Illustrated by Julie Vivas. Margaret Hamilton.

1991   *Greetings from Sandy Beach* by Bob Graham. Lothian.

1992   *Window* by Jeannie Baker. Julia MacRae.

1993   *Rose Meets Mr Wintergarden* by Bob Graham. Viking/Penguin.

1994   *First Light* by Gary Crew. Illustrated by Peter Gouldthorpe. Lothian.

1995   *The Watertower* by Gary Crew. Illustrated by Steven Woolman. Era.

1996   *The Hunt* by Narelle Oliver. Lothian.

1997   *Not a Nibble* by Elizabeth Honey. Allen & Unwin.

1998   *The Two Bullies* by Junko Morimoto. Translated by Isao Morimoto. Crown.

1999   *The Rabbits* by John Marsden. Illustrated by Shaun Tan. Lothian.

2000   *Jenny Angel* by Margaret Wild. Illustrated by Anne Spudvilas. Penguin.

2001   *Fox* by Margaret Wild. Illustrated by Ron Brooks. Allen & Unwin.

2002   *An Ordinary Day* by Libby Gleeson. Illustrated by Armin Greder. Scholastic.

2003   *In Flanders Fields* by Norman Jorgensen. Illustrated by Brian Harrison-Lever. Sandcastle.

2004   *Cat and Fish* by Joan Grant. Illustrated by Neal Curtis. Lothian.

2005   *Are We There Yet? A Journey around Australia* by Alison Lester. Viking.

2006   *The Short and Incredibly Happy Life of Riley* by Colin Thompson. Illustrated by Amy Lissiat [AKA Colin Thompson]. Lothian.

Australian Book of the Year for Early Childhood Award

2001   *You'll Wake the Baby!* by Catherine Jinks. Illustrated by Andrew McLean. Penguin.

2002   *Let's Get a Pup!* by Bob Graham. Walker/Candlewick.

2003   *A Year on Our Farm* by Penny Matthews. Omnibus/ Scholastic Australia.

2004   *Grandpa and Thomas* by Pamela Allen. Viking.

2005   *Where Is the Green Sheep?* by Mem Fox. Illustrated by Judy Horacek. Viking.

2006   *Annie's Chair* by Deborah Niland. Viking.

Australian Children's Book of the Year for Younger Readers Award

1982   *Rummage* by Cristobel Mattingley. Illustrated by Patricia Mullins. Angus & Robertson.

1983   *Thing* by Robin Klein. Illustrated by Allison Lester. Oxford.

1984   *Bernice Knows Best* by Max Dann. Illustrated by Ann James. Oxford.

1985   *Something Special* by Emily Rodda. Illustrated by Noela Young. Angus & Robertson.

1986   *Arkwright* by Mary Steele. Hyland House.

1987   *Pigs Might Fly* by Emily Rodda. Illustrated by Noela Young. Angus & Robertson.

1988   *My Place* by Nadia Wheatley and Donna Rawlins. Collins Dove.

1989   *The Best-Kept Secret* by Emily Rodda. Angus & Robertson.

1990   *Pigs and Honey* by Jeanie Adams. Omnibus.

1991   *Finders Keepers* by Emily Rodda. Omnibus.

1992   *The Magnificent Nose and Other Marvels* by Anna Fienberg. Illustrated by Kim Gamble. Allen and Unwin.

1993   *The Bamboo Flute* by Garry Disher. Collins/ Angus & Robertson.

1994   *Rowan of Rin* by Emily Rodda. Omnibus.

1995   *Ark in the Park* by Wendy Orr. HarperCollins.

1996   *Swashbuckler* by James Moloney. University of Queensland Press.

1997   *Hannah Plus One* by Libby Gleeson. Illustrated by Ann James. Penguin.

1998   *Someone Like Me* by Elaine Forrestal. Penguin.

1999   *My Girragundji* by Meme McDonald and Boori Pryor. Illustrated by Meme McDonald. Allen & Unwin.

2000   *Hitler's Daughter* by Jackie French. HarperCollins.

2001   *Two Hands Together* by Diana Kidd. Penguin.

2002   *My Dog* by John Heffernan. Illustrated by Andrew McLean. Scholastic Australia.

2003   *Rain May and Captain Daniel* by Catherine Bateson. University of Queensland Press.

2004   *Dragonkeeper* by Carole Wilkinson. Black Dog.

2005   *The Silver Donkey* by Sonya Hartnett. Viking.

2006   *Helicopter Man* by Elizabeth Fensham. Bloomsbury.

*Australian Children's Book of the Year
for Older Readers Award*

(For mature readers)

1980   *Displaced Person* by Lee Harding. Hyland House.

1981   *Playing Beatie Bow* by Ruth Park. Nelson.

1982   *The Valley Between* by Colin Thiele. Rigby.

1983   *Master of the Grove* by Victor Kelleher. Penguin.

1984   *A Little Fear* by Patricia Wrightson. Hutchinson.

1985   *The True Story of Lilli Stubeck* by James Aldridge. Hyland House.

1986   *The Green Wind* by Thurley Fowler. Rigby.

1987   *All We Know* by Simon French. Angus & Robertson.

1988   *So Much to Tell You* by John Marsden. Walter McVitty Books.

1989   *Beyond the Labyrinth* by Gillian Rubinstein. Hyland House.

1990   *Came Back to Show You I Could Fly* by Robin Klein. Viking/Kestrel.

1991   *Strange Objects* by Gary Crew. Heinemann Australia.

1992   *The House Guest* by Eleanor Nilsson. Viking.

1993   *Looking for Alibrandi* by Melina Marchetta. Penguin.

1994   *The Gathering* by Isobelle Carmody. Penguin.

    Angel's Gate by Gary Crew. Heinemann.

1995   *Foxspell* by Gillian Rubinstein. Hyland House.

1996   *Pagan's Vows* by Catherine Jinks. Omnibus.

1997   *A Bridge to Wiseman's Cove* by James Moloney. University of Queensland Press.

1998   *Eye to Eye* by Catherine Jinks. Penguin.

1999   *Deadly, Unna?* by Phillip Gwynne. Penguin.

2000   *48 Shades of Brown* by Nick Earls. Penguin.

2001   *Wolf on the Fold* by Judith Clarke. Allen & Unwin.

2002   *Forest* by Sonya Hartnett. Viking.

2003   *The Messenger* by Markus Zusak. Pan Macmillan Australia.

2004   *Saving Francesca* by Melina Marchetta. Viking.

2005   *The Running Man* by Michael Gerard Bauer. Omnibus.

2006   *The Story of Tom Brennan* by J. C. Burke. Random.

Awards for a Body of Work

Hans Christian Andersen Award

This international award, sponsored by the International Board on Books for Young People, is given every two years to a living author and, since 1966, to a living illustrator whose complete works have made important international contributions to children's literature.

1956   Eleanor Farjeon (Great Britain)

1958   Astrid Lindgren (Sweden)

1960   Erich Kästner (Germany)

1962   Meindert DeJong (USA)

1964   René Guillot (France)

1966   AUTHOR: Tove Jansson (Finland)

ILLUSTRATOR: Alois Carigiet (Switzerland)

1968   AUTHORS: James Krüss (Germany) and José Maria Sanchez-Silva (Spain)

ILLUSTRATOR: Jirí Trnka (Czechoslovakia)

1970   AUTHOR: Gianni Rodari (Italy)

ILLUSTRATOR: Maurice Sendak (USA)

1972   AUTHOR: Scott O'Dell (USA)

ILLUSTRATOR: Ib Spang Olsen (Denmark)

1974   AUTHOR: Maria Gripe (Sweden)

ILLUSTRATOR: Farshid Mesghali (Iran)

1976   AUTHOR: Cecil Bödker (Denmark)

ILLUSTRATOR: Tatjana Mawrina (USSR)

1978   AUTHOR: Paula Fox (USA)

ILLUSTRATOR: Otto S. Svend (Denmark)

1980   AUTHOR: Bohumil Riha (Czechoslovakia)

ILLUSTRATOR: Suekichi Akaba (Japan)

1982   AUTHOR: Lygia Bojunga Nunes (Brazil)

ILLUSTRATOR: Zbigniew Rychlicki (Poland)

1984   AUTHOR: Christine Nöstlinger (Austria)

ILLUSTRATOR: Mitsumasa Anno (Japan)

1986   AUTHOR: Patricia Wrightson (Australia)

ILLUSTRATOR: Robert Ingpen (Australia)

1988   AUTHOR: Annie M. G. Schmidt (Netherlands)

ILLUSTRATOR: Dušan Kállay (Czechoslovakia)

1990   AUTHOR: Tormod Haugen (Norway)

ILLUSTRATOR: Lisbeth Zwerger (Austria)

1992   AUTHOR: Virginia Hamilton (USA)

ILLUSTRATOR: Kveta Pacovská (Czechoslovakia)

1994   AUTHOR: Michio Mado (Japan)

ILLUSTRATOR: Jörg Müller (Switzerland)

1996   AUTHOR: Uri Orlev (Israel)

ILLUSTRATOR: Klaus Ensikat (Germany)

1998   AUTHOR: Katherine Paterson (USA)

ILLUSTRATOR: Tomi Ungerer (France)

2000   AUTHOR: Ana Maria Machado (Brazil)

ILLUSTRATOR: Anthony Browne (United Kingdom)

2002   AUTHOR: Aidan Chambers (United Kingdom)

ILLUSTRATOR: Quentin Blake (United Kingdom)

2004   AUTHOR: Martin Waddell (Ireland)

ILLUSTRATOR: Max Velthuijs (The Netherlands)

2006   AUTHOR: Margaret Mahy (New Zealand)

ILLUSTRATOR: Wolf Erlbruch (Germany)

Laura Ingalls Wilder Award

This award, sponsored by the Association for Library Service to Children of the American Library Association, is given to a U.S. author or illustrator whose body of work has made a lasting contribution to children's literature. Between 1960 and 1980, the Wilder Award was given every five years. From 1980 to 2001, it was given every three years. Beginning in 2001, it has been given every two years.

1954   Laura Ingalls Wilder

1960   Clara Ingram Judson

1965   Ruth Sawyer

1970   E. B. White

1975   Beverly Cleary

1980   Theodore S. Geisel (Dr. Seuss)

1983   Maurice Sendak

1986   Jean Fritz

1989   Elizabeth George Speare

1992   Marcia Brown

1995   Virginia Hamilton

1998   Russell Freedman

2001   Milton Meltzer

2003   Eric Carle

2005   Laurence Yep

NCTE Excellence in Poetry for Children Award

For the list of award winners, see Chapter 4, page 62.

Awards for Specific Genres or Groups

Mildred L. Batchelder Award

This award, established in 1968 and sponsored by the ALA's Association for Library Service to Children, is given to the American publisher of a children's book considered to be the most outstanding of those books originally published in a country other than the United States in a language other than English and subsequently translated and published in the United States during the previous year. For access to the complete list of winners, go to the companion website for this book at www.ablongman.com/lynchbrown6e.

1980   *The Sound of Dragon's Feet* by Alki Zei. Translated from Greek by Edward Fenton. Dutton.

1981   *The Winter When Time Was Frozen* by Els Pelgrom. Translated from Dutch by Raphael and Maryka Rudnik. Morrow.

1982   *The Battle Horse* by Harry Kullman. Translated from Swedish by George Blecher and Lone Thygesen-Blecher. Bradbury.

1983   *Hiroshima No Pika* written and illustrated by Toshi Maruki. Translated from Japanese through Kurita-Bando Literary Agency. Lothrop.

1984   *Ronia, the Robber's Daughter* by Astrid Lindgren. Translated from Swedish by Patricia Crampton. Viking.

1985   *The Island on Bird Street* by Uri Orlev. Translated from Hebrew by Hillel Halkin. Houghton.

1986   *Rose Blanche* by Christophe Gallaz and Roberto Innocenti. Translated from French by Martha Coventry and Richard Graglia. Illustrated by Roberto Innocenti. Creative Education.

1987   *No Hero for the Kaiser* by Rudolf Frank. Translated from German by Patricia Crampton. Illustrated by Klaus Steffens. Lothrop.

1988   *If You Didn't Have Me* by Ulf Nilsson. Translated from Swedish by Lone Thygesen-Blecher and George Blecher. Illustrated by Eva Eriksson. McElderry.

1989   *Crutches* by Peter Härtling. Translated from German by Elizabeth D. Crawford. Lothrop.

1990   *Buster's World* by Bjarne Reuter. Translated from Danish by Anthea Bell. Dutton.

1991   *A Hand Full of Stars* by Rafik Schami. Translated from German by Rika Lesser. Dutton.

HONOR BOOK:

Two Short and One Long by Nina Ring Aamundsen. Translated from Norwegian by the author. Houghton.

1992   *The Man from the Other Side* by Uri Orlev. Translated from Hebrew by Hillel Halkin. Houghton.

1993   No award

1994   *The Apprentice* by Pilar Molina Llorente. Illustrated by Juan Ramón Alonso. Translated from Spanish by Robin Longshaw. Farrar.

1995   *The Boys from St. Petri* by Bjarne Reuter. Translated from Danish by Anthea Bell. Dutton.

1996   *The Lady with the Hat* by Uri Orlev. Translated from Hebrew by Hillel Halkin. Houghton.

1997   *The Friends* by Kazumi Yumoto. Translated from Japanese by Cathy Hirano. Farrar.

1998   *The Robber and Me* by Joseph Holub. Translated from German by Elizabeth D. Crawford. Holt.

1999   *Thanks to My Mother* by Schoschana Rabinovici. Translated from German by James Skofield. Dial.

2000   *The Baboon King* by Anton Quintana. Translated from Dutch by John Nieuwenhuizen. Walker.

2001   *Samir and Yonatan* by Daniella Carmi. Translated from Hebrew by Yael Lotan. Levine/Scholastic.

2002   *How I Became an American* by Karin Gündisch. Translated from German by James Skofield. Cricket.

2003   *The Thief Lord* by Cornelia Funke. Translated from German by Oliver Latsch. Scholastic.

2004   *Run, Boy, Run* by Uri Orlev. Translated from Hebrew by Hillel Halkin. Houghton Mifflin.

2005   *The Shadows of Ghadames* by Joëlle Stolz. Translated from French by Catherine Temerson. Delacorte.

2006   *An Innocent Soldier* by Josef Holub. Translated from German by Michael Hofmann. Arthur A. Levine.

2007   *The Pull of the Ocean* by Jean-Claude Mourlevat. Translated from French by Y. Maudet. Delacorte.

Coretta Scott King Awards

These awards, founded in 1970 to commemorate the late Dr. Martin Luther King Jr. and his wife, Coretta Scott King, for their work in promoting peace and world brotherhood, are given to an African-American author and, since 1974, an African-American illustrator whose children's books, published during the preceding year, made outstanding inspirational and educational contributions to literature for children and young people. The awards are sponsored by the Social Responsibilities Round Table of the American Library Association. For access to the complete list of winners, go to the companion website for this book at www.ablongman.com/lynchbrown6e.

1980   AUTHOR: *The Young Landlords* by Walter Dean Myers. Viking.

ILLUSTRATOR: *Cornrows* by Camille Yarbrough. Illustrated by Carole Bayard. Coward.

1981   AUTHOR: *This Life* by Sidney Poitier. Knopf.

ILLUSTRATOR: *Beat the Story-Drum, Pum-Pum* by Ashley Bryan. Atheneum.

1982   AUTHOR: *Let the Circle Be Unbroken* by Mildred D. Taylor. Dial.

ILLUSTRATOR: *Mother Crocodile: An Uncle Amadou Tale from Senegal* adapted by Rosa Guy. Illustrated by John Steptoe. Delacorte.

1983   AUTHOR: *Sweet Whispers, Brother Rush* by Virginia Hamilton. Philomel.

ILLUSTRATOR: *Black Child* by Peter Magabane. Knopf.

1984   AUTHOR: *Everett Anderson's Good-Bye* by Lucille Clifton. Holt.

ILLUSTRATOR: *My Mama Needs Me* by Mildred Pitts Walter. Illustrated by Pat Cummings. Lothrop.

1985   AUTHOR: *Motown and Didi* by Walter Dean Myers. Viking.

ILLUSTRATOR: No award

1986   AUTHOR: *The People Could Fly: American Black Folktales* by Virginia Hamilton. Knopf.

ILLUSTRATOR: *Patchwork Quilt* by Valerie Flournoy. Illustrated by Jerry Pinkney. Dial.

1987   AUTHOR: *Justin and the Best Biscuits in the World* by Mildred Pitts Walter. Lothrop.

ILLUSTRATOR: *Half Moon and One Whole Star* by Crescent Dragonwagon. Illustrated by Jerry Pinkney. Macmillan.

1988   AUTHOR: *The Friendship* by Mildred D. Taylor. Illustrated by Max Ginsburg. Dial.

ILLUSTRATOR: *Mufaro's Beautiful Daughters: An African Tale* retold and illustrated by John Steptoe. Lothrop.

1989   AUTHOR: *Fallen Angels* by Walter Dean Myers. Scholastic.

ILLUSTRATOR: *Mirandy and Brother Wind* by Patricia McKissack. Illustrated by Jerry Pinkney. Knopf.

1990   AUTHOR: *A Long Hard Journey* by Patricia C. and Fredrick L. McKissack. Walker.

ILLUSTRATOR: *Nathaniel Talking* by Eloise Greenfield. Illustrated by Jan Spivey Gilchrist. Black Butterfly Press.

1991   AUTHOR: *The Road to Memphis* by Mildred D. Taylor. Dial.

ILLUSTRATOR: *Aïda* retold by Leontyne Price. Illustrated by Leo and Diane Dillon. Harcourt.

1992   AUTHOR: *Now Is Your Time! The African-American Struggle for Freedom* by Walter Dean Myers. HarperCollins.

ILLUSTRATOR: *Tar Beach* by Faith Ringgold. Crown.

1993   AUTHOR: *The Dark-Thirty: Southern Tales of the Supernatural* by Patricia McKissack. Knopf.

ILLUSTRATOR: *Origins of Life on Earth: An African Creation Myth* by David A. Anderson. Illustrated by Kathleen Atkins Smith. Sight Productions.

1994   AUTHOR: *Toning the Sweep* by Angela Johnson. Orchard.

ILLUSTRATOR: *Soul Looks Back in Wonder* compiled and illustrated by Tom Feelings. Dial.

1995   AUTHOR: *Christmas in the Big House, Christmas in the Quarters* by Patricia C. McKissack and Fredrick L. McKissack. Illustrated by John Thompson. Scholastic.

ILLUSTRATOR: *The Creation* by James Weldon Johnson. Illustrated by James E. Ransome. Holiday.

1996   AUTHOR: *Her Stories: African American Folktales, Fairy Tales, and True Tales* by Virginia Hamilton. Illustrated by Leo and Diane Dillon. Blue Sky.

ILLUSTRATOR: *The Middle Passage: White Ships Black Cargo* by Tom Feelings. Dial.

1997   AUTHOR: *Slam!* by Walter Dean Myers. Scholastic.

ILLUSTRATOR: *Minty: A Story of Young Harriet Tubman* by Alan Schroeder. Illustrated by Jerry Pinkney. Dial.

1998   AUTHOR: *Forged by Fire* by Sharon M. Draper. Atheneum.

ILLUSTRATOR: *In Daddy's Arms I Am Tall: African Americans Celebrating Fathers* by Javaka Steptoe. Lee & Low.

1999   AUTHOR: *Heaven* by Angela Johnson. Simon & Schuster.

ILLUSTRATOR: *i see the rhythm* by Toyomi Igus. Illustrated by Michele Wood. Children's Book Press.

2000   AUTHOR: *Bud, Not Buddy* by Christopher Paul Curtis. Delacorte.

ILLUSTRATOR: *In the Time of the Drums* retold by Kim L. Siegelson. Illustrated by Brian Pinkney. Hyperion.

2001   AUTHOR: *Miracle's Boys* by Jacqueline Woodson. Putnam.

ILLUSTRATOR: *Uptown* by Bryan Collier. Holt.

2002   AUTHOR: *The Land* by Mildred D. Taylor. Fogelman/Penguin Putnam.

ILLUSTRATOR: *Goin' Someplace Special* by Patricia McKissack. Illustrated by Jerry Pinkney. Atheneum.

2003   AUTHOR: *Bronx Masquerade* by Nikki Grimes. Dial.

ILLUSTRATOR: *Talkin' about Bessie: The Story of Aviator Elizabeth Coleman* by Nikki Grimes. Illustrated by E. B. Lewis. Orchard/Scholastic.

2004   AUTHOR: *The First Part Last* by Angela Johnson. Simon & Schuster.

ILLUSTRATOR: *Beautiful Blackbird* by Ashley Bryan. Atheneum.

2005   AUTHOR: *Remember: The Journey to School Integration* by Toni Morrison. Houghton.

ILLUSTRATOR: *Ellington Was Not a Street* by Ntozake Shange. Illustrated by Kadir A. Nelson. Simon & Schuster.

2006   AUTHOR: *Day of Tears: A Novel in Dialogue* by Julius Lester. Jump At the Sun/Hyperion.

ILLUSTRATOR: *Rosa* by Nikki Giovanni. Illustrated by Bryan Collier. Holt.

2007   AUTHOR: *Copper Sun* by Sharon Draper. Simon & Schuster/Atheneum.

ILLUSTRATOR: *Moses: When Harriet Tubman Led Her People to Freedom* by Carole Boston Weatherford. Illustrated by Kadir A. Nelson. Jump at the Sun/Hyperion.

Gryphon Award for Transitional Books

The Gryphon Award of $1,000 is given annually in recognition of an English language work of fiction or nonfiction for which the primary audience is children in kindergarten through grade 4. The title chosen best exemplifies those qualities that successfully bridge the gap in difficulty between books for reading aloud to children and books for practiced readers of books published in the preceding year. The award, established in 2004, is sponsored by the Center for Children's Books at the Graduate School of Library and Information Science at the University of Illinois in Urbana-Champaign.

2004 *Bow Wow Meow Meow: It's Rhyming Cats and Dogs* by Douglas Florian. Harcourt.

2005 *Little Rat Rides* by Monika Bang-Campbell. Harcourt.

2006 *Stinky Stern Forever* by Michelle Edwards. Harcourt.

Pura Belpré Award

The Pura Belpré Award honors Latino writers and illustrators whose work best portrays, affirms, and celebrates the Latino cultural experience in a work of literature for youth. This biennial award is sponsored by the Association for Library Service to Children and the National Association to Promote Library Service to the Spanish Speaking.

1996 AUTHOR: *An Island Like You: Stories of the Barrio* by Judith Ortiz Cofer. Orchard.

ILLUSTRATOR: *Chato's Kitchen* by Gary Soto. Illustrated by Susan Guevara. Putnam.

1998 AUTHOR: *Parrot in the Oven: Mi Vida* by Victor Martinez. HarperCollins.

ILLUSTRATOR: *Snapshots from the Wedding* by Gary Soto. Illustrated by Stephanie Garcia. Putnam.

2000 AUTHOR: *Under the Royal Palms: A Childhood in Cuba* by Alma Flor Ada. Atheneum.

ILLUSTRATOR: *Magic Windows: Cut-Paper Art and Stories* by Carmen Lomas Garza. Children's Book Press.

2002 AUTHOR: *Esperanza Rising* by Pam Muñoz Ryan. Scholastic.

ILLUSTRATOR: *Chato and the Party Animals* by Gary Soto. Illustrated by Susan Guevara. Putnam.

2004 AUTHOR: *Before We Were Free* by Julia Alvarez. Knopf.

ILLUSTRATOR: *Just a Minute: A Trickster Tale and Counting Book* by Yuyi Morales. Chronicle.

2006 AUTHOR: *The Tequila Worm* by Viola Canales. Random.

ILLUSTRATOR: *Doña Flor: A Tall Tale about a Giant Woman with a Great Big Heart* by Pat Mora. Knopf.

Distinguished Play Award

This award, sponsored by the American Alliance for Theatre and Education, honors the playwright(s) and the publisher of the work voted as the best play for young people published during the past calendar year (January to December). Starting in 1989, two categories were instituted: Category A—Plays primarily for upper and secondary school–age audiences; Category B—Plays primarily for elementary and middle school–age audiences. Beginning in 1998 Category C was established for adaptations.

1983 *My Days as a Youngling, John Jacob Niles: The Early Years,* a musical adapted for the stage and scripted by Nancy Niles Sexton, Vaughn McBride, Martha Harrison Jones; songs by John Niles. Anchorage Press.

1984 *Nightingale* by John Urquhart and Rita Grossberg. Anchorage Press.

1985 *A Play Called Noah's Flood* by Suzan Zeder. Anchorage Press.

1986 *Doors* by Suzan Zeder. Anchorage Press.

1987 *Mother Hicks* by Suzan Zeder. Anchorage Press.

1988 *Babies Having Babies* by Kathryn Montgomery and Jeffrey Auerbach. Baker's Plays.

1989 Category A: *A Separate Peace* by Nancy Pahl Gilsenan. Dramatic Publishing.

Category B: *Becca* by Wendy Kesselman. Anchorage Press.

1990 Category A: *The Man-Child* by Arnold Rabin. Baker's Plays.

Category B: *The Chicago Gypsies* by Virginia Glasgow Koste. Dramatic Publishing.

Category B: *Aalmauria: The Voyage of the Dragonfly* by Max Bush. Anchorage Press.

1991   Category A: *In the Middle of Grand Central Station* by Nancy Pahl Gilsenan. Dramatic Publishing.

Category A: *Jungalbook* by Edward Mast. Anchorage Press.

Category B: *Monkey Magic: Chinese Story Theatre* by Aurand Harris. Anchorage Press.

1992   Category A: *The Secret Garden* by Pamela Sterling. Dramatic Publishing.

Category B: *Amber Waves* by James Still. Samuel French, Inc.

1993   Category A: *This Is Not a Pipe Dream* by Barry Kornhauser. Anchorage Press.

Category B: *The Pinballs* by Aurand Harris. Anchorage Press.

1994   Category A: *Song for the Navigator* by Michael Cowell. Dramatic Publishing.

Category B: *A Woman Called Truth* by Sandra Fenichel Asher. Dramatic Publishing.

1995   Category A: *T-Money & Wolf* by Kevin Willmott and Ric Averill. Dramatic Publishing.

Category A: *Scars and Stripes* by Thomas Cadwaleder Jones. Encore Publishing.

Category B: *Ramona Quimby* by Len Jenkins. Dramatic Publishing.

1996   Category A: *Angel in the Night* by Joanna Halpert Kraus. Dramatic Publishing.

Category B: *The Prince and the Pauper* adapted for the stage by Aurand Harris. Anchorage Press.

1997   Category A: *The Less than Human Club* by Timothy Mason. Smith Kraus, Inc.

Category B: No award

1998   Category A: *Selkie* by Laurie Brooks. Anchorage Press.

Category B: *The Yellow Boat* by David Saar. Anchorage Press.

Category C: *Bambi: A Life in the Woods* by James DeVita. Anchorage Press.

1999   Category A: *North Star* by Gloria Bond Clunie. Dramatic Publishing.

Category B: *Still Life with Iris* by Steve Dietz. Dramatic Publishing.

Category C: *Journey of the Sparrows* by Meryl Friedman. Dramatic Publishing.

2000   Category A: *And Then They Came for Me: Remembering the World of Anne Frank* by James Still. Dramatic Publishing.

Category A: *The Taste of Sunrise* by Suzan Zeder. Anchorage Press.

Category B: *The Wolf Child* by Edward Mast. Anchorage Press.

Category C: No award

2001   Category A: *The Wrestling Season,* by Laurie Brooks. Dramatic Publishing.

Category B: No award

Category C: *Afternoon of the Elves* by Y York. Dramatic Publishing.

2002   Category A: *Belongings* by Daniel Fenton. Dramatic Publishing.

Category B: No award

Category C: *Ezigbo, the Spirit Child* dramatized by Max Bush. Anchorage Press Plays.

Category C: *A Village Fable* by James Still, music by Michael Keck. Dramatic Publishing.

2003   Category A: *Paper Lanterns, Paper Cranes* by Brian Kral. Anchorage Press Plays.

Category B: *Salt and Pepper* by Jose Cruz Gonzalez. Dramatic Publishing.

Category C: *Spot's Birthday Party* adapted for the stage by David Wood, based on the book by Eric Hill. Samuel French.

2004   Category A: *The Music Lesson* by Tammy Ryan. Dramatic Publishing.

Category B: No award

Category C: *Sarah, Plain and Tall* adapted by Joseph Robinette from the book by Patricia MacLachlan. Dramatic Publishing.

2005   Category A: *Eric and Elliot* by Dwayne Hartford. Dramatic Publishing.

Category B: *In the Garden of the Selfish Giant* by Sandra Fenichel Asher. Dramatic Publishing.

Category C: *The Rememberer* by Steven Dietz, based on *As My Sun Now Sets* by Joyce Simmons Cheeka as told to Werdna Phillips Finley. Dramatic Publishing.

2006 Category A: No award

Category B: *The Forgiving Harvest* by Y York. Dramatic Publishing.

Category C: No award

Edgar Allan Poe Award (Mystery)—Best Juvenile Novel Category

This award, established in 1961 and sponsored by the Mystery Writers of America, is given to the author of the best mystery of the year written for young readers. For access to the complete list of winners, go to the companion website for this book at www.ablongman.com/lynchbrown6e.

1980 *The Kidnapping of Christina Lattimore* by Joan Lowery Nixon. Harcourt.

1981 *The Seance* by Joan Lowery Nixon. Harcourt.

1982 *Taking Terri Mueller* by Norma Fox Mazer. Avon.

1983 *The Murder of Hound Dog Bates* by Robbie Branscum. Viking.

1984 *The Callender Papers* by Cynthia Voigt. Atheneum.

1985 *Night Cry* by Phyllis Reynolds Naylor. Atheneum.

1986 *The Sandman's Eyes* by Patricia Windsor. Delacorte.

1987 *The Other Side of Dark* by Joan Lowery Nixon. Delacorte.

1988 *Lucy Forever and Miss Rosetree, Shrinks* by Susan Shreve. Holt.

1989 *Megan's Island* by Willo Davis Roberts. Atheneum.

1990 No award

1991 *Stonewords* by Pam Conrad. Harper.

1992 *Wanted . . . Mud Blossom* by Betsy Byars. Delacorte.

1993 *Coffin on a Case* by Eve Bunting. HarperCollins.

1994 *The Twin in the Tavern* by Barbara Brooks Wallace. Atheneum.

1995 *The Absolutely True Story . . . How I Visited Yellowstone Park with the Terrible Rupes* by Willo Davis Roberts. Atheneum.

1996 *Looking for Jamie Bridger* by Nancy Springer. Dial.

1997 *The Clearing* by Dorothy R. Miller. Atheneum.

1998 *Sparrows in the Scullery* by Barbara Brooks Wallace. Atheneum.

1999 *Sammy Keyes and the Hotel Thief* by Wendelin Van Draanen. Knopf.

2000 *The Night Flyers* by Elizabeth McDavid Jones. Pleasant Company.

2001 *Dovey Coe* by Frances O'Roark Dowell. Simon & Schuster.

2002 *Dangling* by Lillian Eige. Atheneum.

2003 *Harriet Spies Again* by Helen Ericson. Random House/Delacorte.

2004 *Bernie Magruder & the Bats in the Belfry* by Phyllis Reynolds Naylor. Atheneum.

2005 *Chasing Vermeer* by Blue Balliett. Scholastic.

2006 *The Boys of San Joaquin* by D. James Smith. Simon & Schuster.

Scott O'Dell Award for Historical Fiction

This award, donated by the author Scott O'Dell and established in 1984, is given to the author of a distinguished work of historical fiction for children or young adults set in the New World and published in English by a U.S. publisher. The author must be a citizen of the United States.

1984 *The Sign of the Beaver* by Elizabeth George Speare. Houghton.

1985 *The Fighting Ground* by Avi (Wortis). Harper.

1986 *Sarah, Plain and Tall* by Patricia MacLachlan. Harper.

1987 *Streams to the River, River to the Sea: A Novel of Sacagawea* by Scott O'Dell. Houghton.

1988 *Charley Skedaddle* by Patricia Beatty. Morrow.

1989 *The Honorable Prison* by Lyll Becerra de Jenkins. Lodestar.

1990 *Shades of Gray* by Carolyn Reeder. Macmillan.

1991 *A Time of Troubles* by Pieter van Raven. Scribner's.

1992 *Stepping on the Cracks* by Mary Downing Hahn. Clarion.

1993 *Morning Girl* by Michael Dorris. Hyperion.

1994 *Bull Run* by Paul Fleischman. HarperCollins.

1995 *Under the Blood-Red Sun* by Graham Salisbury. Delacorte

1996 *The Bomb* by Theodore Taylor. Harcourt Brace.

1997 *Jip: His Story* by Katherine Paterson. Dutton.

1998 *Out of the Dust* by Karen Hesse. Scholastic.

1999 *Forty Acres and Maybe a Mule* by Harriette Gillem Robinet. Atheneum.

2000 *Two Suns in the Sky* by Miriam Bat-Ami. Front Street/Cricket.

2001 *The Art of Keeping Cool* by Janet Taylor Lisle. Atheneum.

2002 *The Land* by Mildred D. Taylor. Fogelman/Penguin Putnam.

2003 *Trouble Don't Last* by Shelley Pearsall. Knopf.

2004 *The River between Us* by Richard Peck. Dial.

2005 *Worth* by A Lafaye. Simon & Schuster.

2006 *The Game of Silence* by Louise Erdrich. HarperCollins.

2007 *The Green Glass Sea* by Ellen Klages. Viking.

Orbis Pictus Award

This award, established in 1990 and sponsored by NCTE's Committee on Using Nonfiction in the Elementary Language Arts Classroom, is given to an author in recognition of excellence in writing of nonfiction for children published in the United States in the preceding year.

1990 *The Great Little Madison* by Jean Fritz. Putnam.

1991 *Franklin Delano Roosevelt* by Russell Freedman. Clarion.

1992 *Flight: The Journey of Charles Lindbergh* by Robert Burleigh. Illustrated by Mike Wimmer. Philomel.

1993 *Children of the Dustbowl: The True Story of the School at Weedpatch Camp* by Jerry Stanley. Random.

1994 *Across America on an Emigrant Train* by Jim Murphy. Clarion.

1995 *Safari beneath the Sea* by Diane Swanson. Photographs by the Royal British Columbia Museum. Sierra Club.

1996 *The Great Fire* by Jim Murphy. Scholastic.

1997 *Leonardo da Vinci* by Diane Stanley. Morrow.

1998 *An Extraordinary Life: The Story of a Monarch Butterfly* by Laurence Pringle. Illustrated by Bob Marstall. Orchard.

1999 *Shipwreck at the Bottom of the World: The Extraordinary True Story of Schackleton and the Endurance* by Jennifer Armstrong. Crown.

2000 *Through My Eyes* by Ruby Bridges and Margo Lundell. Scholastic.

2001 *Hurry Freedom: African Americans in Gold Rush California* by Jerry Stanley. Crown.

2002 *Black Potatoes: The Story of the Great Irish Famine, 1845–1850.* Susan Campbell Bartoletti. Houghton.

2003 *When Marian Sang* by Pam Muñoz Ryan. Illustrated by Brian Selznick. Scholastic.

2004 *An American Plague: The True and Terrifying Story of the Yellow Fever Epidemic of 1793* by Jim Murphy. Clarion.

2005 *York's Adventures with Lewis and Clark: An African-American's Part in the Great Expedition* by Rhoda Blumberg. HarperCollins.

2006 *Children of the Great Depression* by Russell Freedman. Clarion.

Robert F. Sibert Informational Book Medal

The Robert F. Sibert Informational Book Medal, established by the Association for Library Service to Children division of the American Library Association in 2001, is awarded annually to the author of the most distinguished informational book published during the preceding year.

2001   *Sir Walter Ralegh and the Quest for El Dorado* by Marc Aronson. Clarion.

2002   *Black Potatoes: The Story of the Great Irish Famine, 1845–1850* by Susan Campbell Bartoletti. Houghton.

2003   *The Life and Death of Adolf Hitler* by James Cross Giblin. Clarion.

2004   *An American Plague: The True and Terrifying Story of the Yellow Fever Epidemic of 1793* by Jim Murphy. Clarion.

2005   *The Voice that Challenged a Nation: Marian Anderson and the Struggle for Equal Rights* by Russell Freedman. Clarion.

2006   *Secrets of a Civil War Submarine: Solving the Mysteries of the H. L. Hunley* by Sally M. Walker. Carolrhoda.

2007   *Team Moon: How 400,000 People Landed Apollo 11 on the Moon* by Catherine Thimmesh. Houghton.

Other Notable Book Exhibitions and Awards

New York Times Best Illustrated Children's Books of the Year

Sponsored by *The New York Times,* this list of ten books appears annually in the *Times.* A three-member panel of experts chooses the books.

International Reading Association Children's Book Award

Sponsored by the Institute for Reading Research and administered by the International Reading Association, this international award is given annually to an author for a first or second book that shows unusual promise in the children's book field.

International Board on Books for Young People Honor List

Sponsored by the International Board on Books for Young People (IBBY), this biennial list is composed of three books (one for text, one for illustration, and one for translation) from each IBBY National Section to represent the best in children's literature published in that country in the past two years. The books selected are recommended as suitable for publication worldwide.

State Children's Choice Award Programs

Nearly all states have a children's choice book award program. Usually, a ballot of about twenty-five titles is generated from children's or teachers' nominations. Children from all over the state then vote for their favorite title. For information about your state children's choice award program, contact your state library association.

Professional Resources

Books

Adamson, L. G. (1998). *Literature connections to American history, K–6: Resources to enhance and entice.* Englewood, NJ: Libraries Unlimited.

An annotated bibliography of materials divided by format includes age ranges, descriptive synopses, and awards received. It also includes an excellent subject index and author, illustrator, and title indices.

———. (1999). *American historical fiction: An annotated guide to novels for adults and young adults published since 1985.* Phoenix, AZ: Oryx.

Adamson provides readers with plot summaries of well-written historical fiction.

Bamford, R. A., & Kristo, J. V. (Eds.). (2003). *Making facts come alive: Choosing quality nonfiction literature K–8* (2nd ed.). Norwood, MA: Christopher-Gordon.

This practical guide helps users to find and integrate nonfiction titles across the curriculum.

Bany-Winters, L. (2003). *On stage: Theater games and activities for kids.* Chicago: Chicago Review Press.

An assortment of theater games are divided among improvisations, creating characters, puppetry, costumes, suggestions for monologues, scenes, and plays for grades 1–6.

Barchers, S. I. (2000). *Multicultural folktales: Readers' theatre for elementary students.* Englewood, NJ: Libraries Unlimited, 2000.

Barchers provides practical advice on how to get kids reading and performing stories. The book includes 40 scripts with reading level indicated.

Booth, D. (2005). *Story drama: Creating stories through role-playing, improvising, and reading aloud.* Markham, Ont: Pembroke.

Classroom strategies are provided and explained for learning through drama.

Buss, K., & Karnowski, L. (2000). *Reading and writing literary genres.* Newark, DE: International Reading Association.

Offers readers and writers suggestions on how to understand and model a variety of different genres of literature and their elements.

Children's catalog, The (23rd ed. supplement). (2006). A. Price & J. Yaakov (Eds.). New York: H. W. Wilson.

Part 1 lists books and magazines recommended for preschool children through sixth-graders, as well as useful professional resources. Part 2 helps the user locate entries through one alphabetical, comprehensive key that includes author, title, subject, and analytical listings.

Garcha, R., & Russell, P. Y. (2006). *The world of Islam in literature for youth: A selective bibliography for K–12.* Lanham, MD: Scarecrow.

Sixteen chapters present various aspects of Islam and the Muslim culture with annotated books; video and audio resources and teaching suggestions are included in separate chapters.

Gebel, D. J. (2006). *Crossing boundaries with children's books.* Lanham, MD: Scarecrow.

Includes annotations of nearly 700 international children's books published between 2000 and 2004, as well as selected American books set in countries other than the United States.

Gunning, T. G. (2000). *Best books for building literacy for elementary school children.* Boston: Allyn & Bacon.

Gunning provides explanations of reading levels and useful lists of recommended books by reading levels for beginning and transitional readers.

Hall, S. (1990, 1994, 2002). *Using picture storybooks to teach literary devices: Recommended books for children and young adults* (Vol. 1, 2, & 3). Phoenix, AZ: Oryx Press.

How picture books can be used to teach complex literary devices.

Hill, B. C., Noe, K. L., & Johnson, N. J. (2001). *Literature circles resource guide.* Norwood, MA: Christopher Gordon.

Includes teaching suggestions, forms, and annotated booklists.

Horning, K. T. (1997). *From cover to cover: Evaluating and reviewing children's books.* New York: Harper-Collins.

A handbook on evaluating children's books with recommendations for specific genres.

Leeper, A. (2006). *Poetry in literature for youth.* Lanham, MD: Scarecrow.

Innovative ways to integrate poetry into the K–12 curriculum and annotations of over 900 poetry books are included in this guide.

Lima, C. W., & Lima, J. A. (2006). *A to zoo: Subject access to children's picture books* (7th ed.). Westport, CT: Libraries Unlimited.

This index indicates the subject matter of 14,000 picture books for children with access through author, illustrator, and title, as well as 800 subjects.

Lukenbill, W. B. (2006). *Biography in the lives of youth: culture, society and information.* Englewood, NJ: Libraries Unlimited.

Varied uses of biography, types of biographies, their changes over time, and an extensive bibliography are presented with age appropriateness indicated.

Moss, B. (2003). *Exploring the literature of fact: Children's nonfiction trade books in the elementary classroom.* New York: Guilford.

How to address children's literacy needs using children's nonfiction trade books.

NCTE bibliography series (National Council of Teachers of English):

Adventuring with books: A booklist for pre-K–grade 6 (13th ed.). (2002). Urbana, IL: NCTE.

Kaleidoscope: A multicultural booklist for grades K–8. (4th ed.) (2003). Urbana, IL: NCTE.

Your reading: An annotated booklist for junior high and middle-school students (11th ed.). (2003). Urbana, IL: NCTE.

All of these books include annotated listings of fiction and nonfiction books recommended for children and young people in the grades specified in each title.

Noe, K. L., & Johnson, N. J. (1999). *Getting started with literature circles.* Norwood, MA: Christopher Gordon.

How to establish literature circles and elicit responses to literature from students.

Pellowski, A. (1995). *The storytelling handbook.* New York: Simon & Schuster.

This indispensable guide to the art of storytelling discusses how to tell stories and includes stories from around the world to use for successful storytelling.

Ray, K. W. (1999). *Wondrous words: Writers and writing in the elementary classroom.* Urbana, IL: National Council of Teachers of English.

Ray uses examples of student writing to show how students learn to write from reading such authors as Gary Paulsen and Cynthia Rylant.

Reynolds, M. (2004). *I won't read and you can't make me: Reaching reluctant teen readers.* Portsmouth, NH: Heinemann.

The author shares her many experiences, both as an author and as a teacher, with motivating reluctant young readers. Her techniques and suggestions include questionnaires and forms for guided response and book completion.

Robb, L. (2003). *Teaching reading in social studies, science, and math.* New York: Scholastic.

Provides practical ways to weave comprehension strategies into content-area teaching.

Stan, S. (Ed.). (2002). *The world through children's books.* Lanham, MD: Scarecrow.

A guide to international children's books published in the United States from 1996 to 2000 that includes a selection of children's books written by U.S. authors but set in other countries. An annotated bibliography is included.

Susag, D. M. (1998). *Roots and branches: A resource of Native American literature—Themes, lessons, and bibliographies.* Urbana, IL: National Council of Teachers of English.

Susag examines the historical and literary contexts of Native American literature. Also provides lessons, activities, and detailed, annotated bibliographies.

Tomlinson, C. M. (Ed.). (1998). *Children's books from other countries.* Lanham, MD: Scarecrow.

This complete guide to international children's literature with an annotated bibliography of 724 children's books also provides suggestions on sharing international books with children.

Van Orden, P. (2000). *Selecting books for the elementary school library media center: A complete guide.* New York: Neal-Schuman.

An essential tool for new school libraries and useful for most libraries in balancing collections.

Zipes, J. D. (2000). *Sticks and stones: The troublesome success of children's literature from Slovenly Peter to Harry Potter.* New York: Routledge.

In this series of essays Zipes comments on the field of children's literature and its too frequent homogeneity.

Books about the History of Children's Literature

Bingham, J., & Scholt, G. (1980). *Fifteen centuries of children's literature: An annotated chronology of British and American works in historical context.* Westport, CT: Greenwood.

Davis, D. (1981). *Theatre for young people.* New York: Beaufort.

Gillespie, M. C. (1970). *History and trends: Literature for children.* Dubuque, IA: Brown.

Hunt, P. (1995). *Children's literature: An illustrated history.* Oxford: Oxford University Press.

Hunt, P., & Ray, S. G. (1996). *International companion encyclopedia of children's literature.* London: Routledge.

Marshall, M. R. (1988). *An introduction to the world of children's books: Books about the history of children's literature* (2nd ed.). Aldershot, England: Gower.

McCaslin, N. (1971). *Theatre for children in the United States.* Norman: University of Oklahoma Press.

Murray, G. S. (1998). *American children's literature and the construction of childhood.* New York: Twayne.

Bibliographies: Annual Lists

"CCBC Choices."

An annual spring annotated booklist, published by and for the members of the Friends of the CCBC, Inc. (Cooperative Children's Book Center). For information about CCBC publications and/or membership in the Friends, send a self-addressed stamped envelope to Friends of the CCBC, P.O. Box 5288, Madison, WI 53705-0288.

"Children's Choices."

This yearly list of newly published books, chosen by young readers themselves, appears each October in *The Reading Teacher* as a project of the International Reading Association/Children's Book Council Joint Committee.

"Notable Children's Books."

This annual American Library Association list appears in the March issue of *School Library Journal* and also in the March 15th issue of *Booklist.*

"Notable Children's Books in the Language Arts (K–8)."

This annual list of outstanding trade books for enhancing language awareness among students in grades K–8 appears in each October issue of *Language Arts.*

"Notable Social Studies Trade Books for Young People."

This list appears in the April/May issue of *Social Education* and at www.cbcbooks.org.

"Outstanding Science Trade Books for Students K–12."

This list appears in the March issue of *Science and Children* and at www.cbcbooks.org.

"Teachers' Choices."

This yearly list includes books recommended by teachers. It appears each November in *The Reading Teacher* and at www.reading.org.

"Young Adults' Choices."

The books on this annual list were selected by readers in middle, junior high, and senior high schools. It appears in the November issue of *Journal of Adolescent and Adult Literacy* and at www.reading.org.

Children's Magazines

The following list includes some of the most popular children's magazines available to young people today. It is organized by subject of primary emphasis.

Drama

Plays, the Drama Magazine for Young People. Scripts for plays, skits, puppet shows, and round-the-table readings (a type of readers' theatre). 8–10 scripts per issue. Ages 6–17. 7 issues/year. Order from: www .playsmag.com

Geography

World Newsmap of the Month. Current global issues. Two two-sided, poster-sized maps (world map and focus-country map) per issue. Teacher guide. 9 issues/year. Ages 10–17. Order from: worldnews map.com

Health

Child Life. Articles, fiction, activities with an emphasis on nutrition and safety. Ages 9–11. 6 issues/year. Similar magazines for different age groups by the same publisher include *Turtle* (ages 2–5), *Humpty Dumpty's Magazine* (ages 4–6), *Children's Playmate Magazine* (ages 6–8), *Jack and Jill* (ages 7–10), and *Children's Digest* (ages 10–12). Order from: www.cbhi.org

History

Calliope. Articles, stories, time lines, maps, and authentic photos to generate an interest in world history. Themed issues. Ages 9–14. 9 issues/year. Order from: www.cobblestonepub.com

Cobblestone. Articles about U.S. history. Themed issues. Ages 9–14. 9 issues/year. Order from: www .cobblestonepub.com

Language

Allons-y. Topics of interest to 12- to 18-year-olds in French. Information and cultural details of French-speaking countries. 3 issues/year. Order from: http://teacher.scholastic.com/products/classmags

Das Rad. Topics of interest to 12- to 18-year-olds in German. Information and cultural details of German-speaking countries. 3 issues/year. Order from: http://teacher.scholastic.com/products/ classmags

¿Qué Tal? Topics of interest to 12- to 18-year-olds in Spanish. Information and cultural details of Spanish-speaking countries. 3 issues/year. Order from: http://teacher.scholastic.com/products/classmags

Language Arts

Scholastic Scope. Plays, short stories, reading lists, writing exercises, and skill builders. Ages 12–16. 9 issues/year. Order from: http://teacher.scholastic .com/products/classmags

Storyworks. Focuses on development of grammar, writing, vocabulary, test-taking. Includes read-aloud plays. Ages 8–11. 3 issues/year. Order from: http:// teacher.scholastic.com/products/classmags

Stone Soup: The Magazine by Young Writers and Artists. Stories, poems, book reviews, and art by children 8–13. 6 issues/year. Order from: www.stonesoup.com

Writing! Articles, advice, exercises for writing improvement, interviews with successful authors. Ages 12–16. 7 issues/year. Order from: www.weeklyreader.com

Literature

Cricket. Fiction, nonfiction, book reviews, activities. Features international literature. Ages 9–14. 12 issues/year. Order from: www.cricketmag.com

Lady Bug. Fiction, poems, songs, and games. Ages 3–6. 12 issues/year. Order from: www.cricketmag.com

Spider. Fiction, poems, songs, and games for the beginning reader. Ages 6–9. 12 issues/year. Order from: www.cricketmag.com

Mathematics

DynaMath. Humorously formatted word problems, computation, and test preparation. Ages 8–12. 4 issues/year. Order from: http://teacher.scholastic .com/products/classmags

Scholastic Math Magazine. Math problems, computation, statistics, consumer math, real-life applications, career math, critical reasoning. Ages 12–14. 6 issues/year. Order from: http://teacher.scholastic .com/products/classmags

Nature

National Geographic Kids. Nonfiction articles and nature photography. Promotes geographic awareness. Ages 6–12. 10 issues/year. Order from: www .nationalgeographic.com/ngkids

Ranger Rick. Fiction and nonfiction, photoessays, jokes, riddles, crafts, plays, and poetry promoting the appreciation of nature. Superlative nature photography. Ages 7–12. 12 issues/year. Order from: www .nwf.org

Your Big Backyard. Animal and nature stories and photography for the preschooler. Ages 3–7. 12 issues/year. Order from: www.nwf.org

Recreation

Boys' Life. News, nature, sports, history, fiction, science, comics, Scouting, colorful graphics, and photos. Published by the Boy Scouts of America. Ages 7–18. 12 issues/year. Order from: www.boyslife.org

Electronic Gaming Monthly. Gaming software and hardware previews and reviews. Ages 12–up. 12 issues/year. Order from: www.1UP.com

Highlights. General-interest magazine offering fiction and nonfiction, crafts, poetry, and thinking features. Ages 5–12. 12 issues/year. Order from: www.highlights.com

Junior Baseball Magazine. Articles on baseball skills, sportsmanship, safety, and physical fitness. Ages 10–14. 6 issues/year. Order from: www .juniorbaseball.com

New Moon: The Magazine for Girls and Their Dreams. An international magazine by and about girls. Builds healthy resistance to gender inequities. Ages 8–14. 6 issues/year. Order from: www.newmoon.org

Nick Magazine. Nickelodeon television channel entertainment and humor magazine with television-related celebrity interviews, comics, puzzles, and activities. Ages 7–12. 10 issues/year. Order from: www.nick.com

Sports Illustrated for Kids. Stories about sports and sports celebrities, amateur sports, trivia. Poster included with each issue. Ages 7–10. 12 issues/year. Order from: www.sikids.com

Science

Current Science. News in science, health, and technology; science activities, U.S. national science projects, science mystery photos, and kids in the news. Ages 12–15. 8 issues/year. Order from: www .weeklyreader.com

Odyssey. Articles and illustrations on astronomy, space exploration, and technology. Ages 10–15. 9 issues/ year. Order from: www.cobblestonepub.com

Science World. Articles, experiments, and news to supplement the science curriculum. Ages 12–16. 7 issues/year. Order from: http://teacher.scholastic .com/products/classmags

SuperScience. Science concepts, critical thinking, and reasoning through hands-on activities and experiments. Themed issues. Ages 8–11. 4 issues/ year. Order from: http://teacher.scholastic.com/ products/classmags

Social Studies

Faces. Articles and activities exploring world cultures. Ages 9–14. 9 issues/year. Order from: www .cobblestonepub.com

Junior Scholastic. Features U.S. and world history, current events, world cultures, map skills, and geography. Ages 11–14. 9 issues/year. Order from: http://teacher.scholastic.com/products/classmags

Muse. Nonfiction articles, photoessays, biographies, experiments, cartoons, and jokes. Ages 10–15. 9 issues/ year. Order from: www.cricketmag.com

Skipping Stones: An International Multicultural Magazine. Articles by, about, and for children about world cultures and cooperation. Multilingual. Ages 7–17. 5 issues/year. Order from: www.efn.org/ ~skipping

Transitional Books

These books are generally suitable for ages 6–9.

Bang-Campbell, Monika. *Little Rat Rides.* Harcourt, 2004.

Barrows, Annie. *Ivy and Bean.* Illustrated by Sophie Blackall. Chronicle, 2006. (Part of a series)

Benton, Jim. *Franny K. Stein, Mad Scientist: Lunch Walks Among Us.* Simon & Schuster, 2003.

Brisson, Pat. *Little Sister, Big Sister.* Illustrated by Diana Cain Blumenthal. Holt, 1999.

Cameron, Ann. *Stories Julian Tells.* Illustrated by Ann Strugnell. Knopf, 1989 (1984). (Others in this series: *More Stories Julian Tells; Julian's Glorious Summer; Julian, Dream Doctor; Julian, Secret Agent,* all published by Random House.)

Danziger, Paula. *Amber Brown Is Not a Crayon.* Illustrated by Tony Ross. Putnam, 1994.

Delaney, Michael. *Birdbrain Amos.* Putnam, 2002.

dePaola, Tomie. *26 Fairmount Avenue.* Putnam, 1999.

Doherty, Berlie. *The Famous Adventures of Jack.* Illustrated by Sonja Lamut. Greenwillow, 2001.

Edwards, Michelle. *Stinky Stern Forever.* Harcourt, 2005.

Florian, Douglas. *bow wow meow meow: it's rhyming cats and dogs.* Harcourt, 2003.

Fowler, Susi Gregg. *Albertina, the Animals, and Me.* Illustrated by Jim Fowler. Greenwillow, 2000.

———. *Albertina the Practically Perfect.* Illustrated by Jim Fowler. Greenwillow, 1998.

Graves, Bonnie. *Taking Care of Trouble.* Illustrated by Robin P. Glasser. Dutton, 2002.

Greenwald, Sheila. *Rosy Cole's Worst Ever, Best Yet Tour of New York City.* Holt, 2003.

Grindley, Sally. *Dear Max.* Illustrated by Tony Ross. Simon & Schuster, 2006.

Guiberson, Brenda Z. *Mummy Mysteries: Tales from North America.* Holt, 1998.

Haas, Jessie. *Jigsaw Pony.* Illustrated by Ying-Hwa Hu. Greenwillow, 2005.

———. *Runaway Radish.* Illustrated by Margot Apple. Greenwillow, 2001.

Hest, Amy. *Love You, Soldier.* Illustrated by Sonja Lamut. Candlewick, 2000 (1991).

James, Simon, editor. *Days Like This: A Collection of Small Poems.* Candlewick, 2000.

Jenkins, Emily. *Toys Go Out: Being the Adventures of a Knowledgeable Stingray, a Toughy Little Buffalo, and Someone Called Plastic.* Illustrated by Paul O. Zelinsky. Random, 2006.

Jukes, Mavis. *Blackberries in the Dark.* Illustrated by Thomas B. Allen. Knopf, 1985/2002.

Kerrin, Jessica S. *Martin Bridge: Ready for Takeoff!* Illustrated by Joseph Kelly. Kids Can, 2005. (Part of a series)

King-Smith, Dick. *The Nine Lives of Aristotle.* Illustrated by Bob Graham. Candlewick, 2003.

Lewis, Maggie. *Morgy Makes His Move.* Illustrated by Michael Chesworth. Houghton, 1999.

Levy, Elizabeth. *Big Trouble in Little Twinsville.* Illustrated by Mark Elliot. HarperCollins, 2001.

———. *Night of the Living Gerbil.* Illustrated by Bill Basso. HarperCollins, 2001.

Look, Lenore. *Ruby Lu, Brave and True.* Illustrated by Anne Wilsdorf. Simon & Schuster, 2004.

Marsden, Carolyn. *The Gold-Threaded Dress.* Cambridge, MA: Candlewick, 2002.

Nolan, Lucy. *Down Girl and Sit: Smarter Than Squirrels.* Illustrated by Mike Reed. Marshall Cavendish, 2004.

Pennypacker, Sara. *Clementine.* Illustrated by Marla Frazee. Hyperion, 2006.

Roberts, Ken. *The Thumb in the Box.* Illustrated by Leanne Franson. Groundwood, 2001.

Scieszka, Jon. *Knights of the Kitchen Table.* Illustrated by Lane Smith. Viking, 1991. (Also in *The Time Warp Trio* series: *The Not-So-Jolly Roger.*)

Sobol, Donald J. *Encyclopedia Brown: Boy Detective.* Illustrated by Leonard Shortall. Bantam, 1985 (originally published by Scholastic, 1968). (Others in this series: *Encyclopedia Brown Tracks Them Down; Encyclopedia Brown and the Case of the Midnight Visitor; Encyclopedia Brown Solves Them All.*)

Spinelli, Jerry. *Tooter Pepperday.* Illustrated by Donna Nelson. Random House, 1995.

Index to Children's Books and Authors

Subject Index

Credits and Acknowledgments

Text Credits

Page ii: "A Story is a Doorway" by Richard Peck. Reprinted with permission.

Page 17: "My Book" from *Somebody Catch My Homework* by David L. Harrison (Wordsong, an imprint of Boyds Mills Press, 1993). Reprinted with the permission of Boyd Mills Press, Inc. Text copyright © 1993 by David L. Harrison.

Page 55: "What's a Poem?" from *A Fury of Motion: Poems for Boys* by Charles Ghigna (Wordsong, an imprint of Boyds Mills Press, 2003). Reprinted with the permission of Boyds Mills Press, Inc. Text copyright © 2003 by Charles Ghigna.

Page 59: "Song for a Blue Roadster" from *Poems* by Rachel Field (Macmillan, New York, 1957). Reprinted with the permission of Simon & Schuster Books for Young Readers, an imprint of Simon & Schuster Children's Publishing Division.

Page 59: "Slowly" from *The Wandering Moon and Other Poems* by James Reeves (Puffin Books, 1950). Copyright © 1950 by the Estate of James Reeves.

Page 61: "Speed Adjustments" from *The Monster Den* by John Ciardi. Reprinted with the permission of Boyd Mills Press, Inc.

Page 65: "Giraffes" from *Triptych* by Sy Kahn. Copyright © 1966, Scott, Foresman. Reprinted with the permission of the author.

Pages 65–66: "The Broken Legg'd Man" from *The Things I Want: Poems for Two Children* by John M. Shaw. Copyright © 1967 by the John M. Shaw Collection, Florida State University Library. Reprinted with permission.

Page 68: "Pigeons Masquerade" from *A Pocketful of Poems* by Nikki Grimes. Text copyright © 2001 by Nikki Grimes. Reprinted by permission of Clarion Books, an imprint of Houghton Mifflin Company. All rights reserved.

Page 69: "Autumn Leaves" from *In the Spin of Things: Poetry in Motion* by Rebecca K. Dotlich (Wordsong, an imprint of Boyds Mills Press, 2003). Reprinted with the permission of Boyds Mills Press, Inc. Text copyright © 2003 by Rebecca K. Dotlich.

Page 69: "Concrete Cat" by Dorthi Charles. Reprinted with the permission of the author.

Page 90: "In the Library" by Michael Patrick Hearn. Reprinted with permission.

Page 118: "Listen!" from *The Complete Poems of Walter de la Mare* by Walter de la Mare. Reprinted with permission of the Literary Trustees of Walter de la Mare and the Society of Authors as their representative.

Page 133: "Ladder to the Sky" from *Toes in my Nose and Other Poems* by Sheree Fitch. Copyright © 1987 by Sheree Fitch. Reprinted with the permission of the author.

Page 150: "Listening to Grownups Quarreling" from *The Marriage Wig and Other Poems* by Ruth Whitman. Copyright © 1968 and renewed 1996 by Ruth Whitman. Reprinted by permission of Harcourt, Inc.

Page 168: "Ancestors" by Grey Cohoe, from *Whispering Wind* by Terry Allen. Copyright © 1972 by the Institute of American Indian Arts. Used by permission of Doubleday, a division of Random House, Inc.

Page 187: "Questions at Night" from *Rainbow in the Sky*. Copyright © 1935 by Harcourt Inc. and renewed 1963 by Louis Untermeyer. Reprinted by permission of the publisher.

Page 210: "Oh, the Places You'll Go" from *Book Poems* by Ashley Bryan. Copyright © 1998 Children's Book Council. Reprinted with permission.

Page 243: "My Plan" from *Around and About* by Marchette Chute. Published 1957 by E. P. Dutton. Copyright © renewed 1985 by Marchette Chute. Reprinted by permission of Elizabeth Hauser.

Illustration Credits

Illustration 1: From *Heartland* by Diane Siebert. Text copyright © 1989 by Diane Siebert. Reprinted by permission of HarperCollins Publishers.

Illustration 2: From *Fletcher and the Falling Leaves* by Julia Rawlinson. Reprinted by permission of HarperCollins Publishers.

Illustration 3: From *The Hello, Goodbye Window* by Norton Juster. Copyright © 2005 by Norton Juster. Illustration © 2005 by Chris Raschka. Reprinted by permission of Hyperion Books for Children.

Illustration 4: From *Yo! Yes?* by Chris Raschka. Copyright © 1993 by Christopher Raschka. Reprinted by permission of Scholastic Inc./Orchard Books.

Illustration 5: From *Polar Bear Night* by Lauren Thompson. Illustration copyright © 2004 by Stephen Savage. Reprinted by permission of Scholastic Inc./Scholastic Press.

Illustration 6: From *Changes* by Anthony Browne (1986). Copyright © by Anthony Browne. Reprinted by permission of Alfred A. Knopf, a division of Random House, Inc.

Illustration 7: "Posada," from *Family Pictures/Cuadros de familia* by Carmen L. Garza (1990). Reprinted with the permission of the author.

Illustration 8: From *Chrysanthemum* by Kevin Henkes. Copyright © 1991 by Kevin Henkes. Reprinted by permission of HarperCollins Publishers.

Illustration 9: From *Officer Buckle and Gloria* by Peggy Rathman. Copyright © 1995 by Peggy Rathman. Reprinted by permission of G. P. Putnam's Sons, a division of Penguin Young Readers Group, a member of Penguin Group (USA) Inc., 345 Hudson Street, New York, NY 10014. All rights reserved.

Illustration 10: From *The Subway Mouse* by Barbara Reid, p. 7. Copyright © 2003 by Barbara Reid. All rights reserved. Reprinted by permission of Scholastic Canada Ltd.

Illustration 11: From *Song of the Water Boatman and Other Pond Poems* by Joyce Sidman, illustrated by Beckie Prange. Illustration copyright © 2005 by Beckie Prange. Reprinted by permission of Houghton Mifflin Company. All rights reserved.

Illustration 12: From *A Drop of Water: A Book of Science and Wonder* by Walter Wick. Copyright © 1997 by Walter Wick. Reprinted by permission of Scholastic Inc./Scholastic Press.